# ARAFAT
# The Biography

Andrew Gowers
and
Tony Walker





Virgin

**To Finola and Suzanne**

This revised and updated edition
first published in Great Britain in 1994 by
Virgin Books
an imprint of Virgin Publishing Ltd
332 Ladbroke Grove
London W10 5AH



First published in Great Britain in 1990 as *Behind the Myth: Yasser Arafat* by W. H. Allen.
A revised paperback edition of *Behind the Myth* was published by Corgi in 1991.



A catalogue record for this book is available from the British Library

ISBN 0 86369 7941

Printed and bound in Great Britain by Cox & Wyman Ltd, Reading, Berks

# Contents

PART THREE



PART FOUR



PART FIVE

# Maps

# Preface

The date is 16 June 1989, the scene a spacious seafront villa surrounded by bougainvilleas and chirruping cicadas on the outskirts of Tunis. Behind a tight wall of security and in the company of a motley crew of Palestinian courtiers, we are doing what we have become accustomed to doing in the sleepy Tunisian capital – waiting for Yasser Arafat. And this time, it looks as if our quarry might be within our grasp. After several nights spent pointlessly awaiting the call from Arafat's office, we have been summoned at a few minutes' notice to the residence of the PLO ambassador in Tunis. The Chairman of the Palestine Liberation Organization and President of the State of Palestine has invited us to lunch.

Arafat, as usual, is late and the delay allows us time to survey the other guests. They are nothing if not representative of the multifarious faces of the PLO. Over there is the hulking figure of Mohammed Zaidan, better known as Abul Abbas, leader of a tiny PLO faction that has gained notoriety through a series of crudely executed terrorist attacks on civilian targets, including the hijacking of the *Achille Lauro* cruise liner in the Mediterranean in 1985. On the other side of the room sits Haj Ismail, Arafat's controversial military commander in Lebanon. An assortment of professional PLO politicians, Palestinian diplomats and Arafat acolytes mingles and murmurs in hushed Arabic tones, for all the world like a polite opera crowd anticipating the arrival of the prima donna.

The foreigners are no less of an unlikely collection. Here, hovering on the sidelines, is Jill Morrell, a friend of John McCarthy, the British journalist held hostage by the fundamentalist Hizbollah (Party of God) in Lebanon. She has come to ask Arafat's assistance in securing McCarthy's release. We, for our part, have come to discuss our plans to write a book about the PLO – one of fifty-seven books in many different languages that had been proposed on the subject, as we are told by one of Arafat's spokesmen.

Suddenly there is a roar of cars outside, much slamming of doors, and a small, pudgy figure dressed in neat khaki uniform and matching battle cap strides into the room surrounded by gun-toting bodyguards. Arafat massages the gathering, hugging and kissing PLO comrades and warmly welcoming his foreign guests. 'So you want to write a book about the PLO?' he begins, sitting down, removing his cap and revealing an almost completely bald pate. 'What kind of book? How many pages? You will need an encyclopaedia! No, you will need several encyclopaedias!' Then, to Jill Morrell with a grin: 'I have instructed my military commander to make contact with Hizbollah and find out what it is they want. If it's just a question of money, a few hundred thousand dinars, I'll pay it myself!' Then, triumphantly, back to us: 'You see, this is what happened after we departed from Lebanon, these dirty groups . . . While I was there, I could keep these dirty groups under control! You will put that in your book, yes?'

And so the show goes on – over an informal lunch, featuring traditional Palestinian dishes served with relish by our solicitous host, and over a subsequent cup of sweet honeyed tea in the adjoining lounge. Arafat boasts about his knowledge of the secrets of the Middle East; he receives a report from Lebanon saying Hizbollah has been contacted; he chatters on a portable phone brought to him by one of his aides; he reminisces fleetingly about his early life in Egypt and the Gulf; after carefully donning and adjusting his familiar black-and-white headscarf, he poses for a photo-opportunity with Jill Morrell and her companion. And then, after a few words of encouragement for our project and a promise to meet that night for a proper interview, he is off again, with a screech of tyres and a wail of accompanying police sirens.

That, in brief, is Yasser Arafat: intriguing, theatrical and maddeningly hard to pin down. This book is an attempt to get behind the public mask and to explain how it is that this elusive figure has carved himself an enduring role on the world stage. We hope that our research has yielded a considerable body of material that will be useful to those with a professional interest in the Middle East in general and the Palestinians in particular. We have also tried to be faithful to the historical record, and to cross-check details wherever possible. But the task of producing the definitive academic work on the PLO we leave to others eminently better qualified than ourselves.

This biography is an account, relying heavily on the first-hand testimony of those involved, of Arafat's role in the making of what Palestinians call their 'revolution' – the growth among Palestinians in exile of a national movement with the aim of regaining their lost homeland. It tracks Arafat from his early life as a student leader in Cairo and underground activist in the Gulf, through the crucial events in his more than twenty-year career as leader of the fractious PLO, leading to his recognition of Israel and renunciation of terror in December 1988, his fateful alliance with Iraq's Saddam Hussein in the Gulf crisis of 1990–91 and his historic handshake with Israel's Yitzhak Rabin in September 1993. From the hundreds of hours of interviews we have conducted with the principle protagonists, we have tried to construct an original and accurate account of a far from simple story. But above all, we have tried to paint an accessible portrait of one of the most extraordinary political survivors of the modern world.

Would-be historians of the PLO or biographers of Arafat have all encountered one central difficulty: the enigmatic nature of the man himself. Arafat did indeed assist us in our research, and for this we are indebted to him. But throughout – with us as with other interviewers – he remained evasive about essential details. The PLO leader gives little away about his career or his private self, and such revelations as he does permit himself often turn out to be at variance with the recollections of others. Even the most basic facts, from his birthplace to his political relationships with Middle Eastern leaders, have become the subjects of Arafat's unique brand of myth-making.

Our task has been in part to try to unravel this tangled skein by talking to as many people as possible who have had dealings with Arafat over the last forty or more years. In Cairo, Jerusalem and Gaza, we interviewed members of his family; in Egypt and the Gulf, we tracked down Palestinians who were involved in the national movement during its early years; in Syria and Jordan, we spoke to allies and opponents of the PLO leader; in Tunis, we lost count of the hours we spent with senior Arafat lieutenants; in Israel, Europe and the US, we quizzed officials for whom Arafat had been the enemy. Some of these individuals asked us not to use their names; many others are named in the text and notes; all gave more generously of their time and attention than we could have reasonably expected, and for this we are most grateful.

There are two Palestinians in particular without whom this book would not have been possible. The late Salah Khalaf, Arafat's number two until his assassination in January 1991, and Nabil Shaath, a senior adviser, devoted many painstaking hours to discussing the evolution of the movement from their respective vantage points. For their help, and for the frankness with which they expressed their views, we offer special thanks.

Other Palestinian figures who were unsparing with their time included Farouk Kaddoumi, George Habash, Khaled al-Hassan, Hani al-Hassan, Yasser Abed-Rabbo, Bassel Akel, Munib al-Masri, Gamal Sourani, Jaweed al-Ghussein, Ibrahim Bakr, Fathi Arafat and other relatives including cousin Umm Mohammed, Jamil Hilal, Suleiman Najab, Abdullah Hourani, Abdel Latif Abu Hijleh, Zoheir al-Alami, Mohammed Milhem, Faisal al-Husseini, Sari Nusseibeh, Hanna Seniora, Saeb Erakat, Bashir Barghouti, Mohammed Sobhieh, Ahmed Kora'i, Emad Shakur, Mohammed al-Natour, Rafik al-Natshe, Asad Abdelrahman, Ibrahim Abu Ayyash, Mamdouh Nofal, Ahmed Sidki Dajani, Mohammed Abu Mayzar, Mohammed Said Musa Maragha, Mohammed Hamza, Leila Shaheed, Maghoub Omar, Khaled Fahoum, Sakher Abu Nizar, Abbas Zeki, Bahjat Abu Gharbiyya, Intissar al-Wazir, Ahmed Abdelrahman, Sami Musallam, Bassam Abu Sharif, Ilan Halevy, Yaacoub Diwani, Qais al-Samarai, Abu Ali Moustafa, Abu Daoud Mohammed Awdah, Abdullah Franji, Said Kamal, Afif Safieh, Abdulmajeed Shoman, Selim Zaanoun, Awni Battash, Zakaria Abderrahim, Ahmed Khalidi, Professors Edward Said and Walid Khalidi and the military historian Yezid Sayigh.

On the Israeli side, Generals Aharon Yariv and Avraham Tamir and David Kimche among many others provided special guidance, while Uri Avnery, Uri Milstein, Shlomo Avineri and David Tal were generous with time and counsel. In Egypt, Tahseen Bashir, Esmat Abdel Meguid, Mahmoud Riad, Ahmed Baha el-Dine, Ihsan Bakr, Selim Issa, Sir James Adams and Mohammed Hassanein Heikal were invaluable sources of information and advice; as were in Jordan Taher al-Masri, Marwan Qasem, Zeid Rifai, Jamal Sha'er and Mashour Haditha al-Jazy. In Washington and New York, Cyrus Vance, Richard Murphy, Alfred Atherton, Joe Sisco, Talcott Seelye, John Edwin Mroz, Nicholas Veliotes, Richard Viets, Brian Urquhart, Geoffrey Kemp, Rita Hauser and William Quandt provided many useful insights, and so in Europe did General Vernon Walters, Anders Bjurner and Lakhdar Brahimi. In Tunis, Robert Pelletreau and Stephen Day were always helpful and hospitable.

The book also drew heavily on the efforts of our researchers, Jihan el-Tahri, Shahira Idris and Efrat Shvilly, who put in much hard work on our behalf in Tunis, Cairo and Jerusalem. Suleiman Khalidi offered valuable help in Kuwait, as did Albert Aghazarian, Ziad Abu Amr and Mehdi Abdul-Hadi in Jerusalem and Gaza. A special thank you is in order to our friend and *Financial Times* colleague Lamis Andoni, who conducted several interviews for us and otherwise provided wise counsel.

Naturally, however, the judgements, interpretations and mistakes in the book are entirely our own, and we accept full responsibility for them.

We owe a large debt of gratitude to our editors, Sir Geoffrey Owen and Richard Lambert of the *Financial Times* and Creighton Burns and Michael Smith of *The Age*, for their indulgence towards such a time-consuming project; to our editor at W.H. Allen, Gill Gibbins, for her eagle-eyed attention to the text; to Anthony Geffen and his team at the BBC for the access they gave us to research material and photographs used in their documentary on Arafat; and to our wives, Finola and Suzanne, for their tolerance of our long absences and distracted moods. Thank you, too, to Professor Albert Hourani and to our *Financial Times* colleague Robert Graham for the time they devoted to reviewing the manuscript and for their extremely helpful comments. We owe special thanks to Walter and Randa Helfer in Hamburg for their invaluable help and hospitality. Finally, we would also like to thank our friends Michael and Artemis Anastasi in Tokhni village, Cyprus. It was in Tokhni that the first and revised drafts of the book were written, and it was their hospitality that helped to sustain the project through some of its more difficult moments.

A.G. & T.W.
September 1993

## Dramatis Personae

Mahmoud Abbas (Abu Mazen). Early Fatah member; played a leading role in developing contacts between PLO and left-wing Israelis.

Yasser Abed Rabbo (Abu Bashar). Deputy leader of Democratic Front for the Liberation of Palestine; Arafat adviser.

Bassam Abu Sharif (Abu Omar). Arafat adviser; former member of Popular Front for the Liberation of Palestine.

Yasser Arafat (Abu Ammar). Chairman of the executive committee of the Palestine Liberation Organization; leader of the PLO's largest faction, Fatah; President of the State of Palestine.

Hafez al-Assad. President of Syria, 1971–present.

Sabri al-Banna (Abu Nidal). Fatah renegade and mastermind of numerous terrorist attacks in Europe.

Menachem Begin. Prime Minister of Israel, 1977–83.

Fahd bin Abdel Aziz. King of Saudi Arabia, 1982–present.

Faisal bin Abdel Aziz. King of Saudi Arabia, 1964–75.

Suleiman Franjieh. President of Lebanon, 1970–6.

George Habash (Al Hakim). Veteran leader of the left-wing

Popular Front for the Liberation of Palestine and Arafat's traditional rival in the PLO.

Hani al-Hassan (Abu Tarek). Arafat adviser and special envoy; joined Fatah while studying in Germany.

Khaled al-Hassan (Abu Said). Hani's older brother; early Fatah member; first PLO 'foreign minister' under Arafat and leading moderate.

Nayef Hawatmeh (Abul Nouf). Leader of Marxist Democratic Front for the Liberation of Palestine; a principal PLO ideologue.

Hussein bin Talal. King of Jordan 1953–present; scion of the Hashemite dynasty.

Saddam Hussein. President of Iraq, 1979–present.

Abdel Kader al-Husseini. Leader of Palestinian irregular forces during Israel's War of Independence (1948).

Faisal al-Husseini. Abdel Kader's son; Arafat's chief representative in the Israeli-occupied territories.

Haj Amin al-Husseini. Mufti of Jerusalem and Palestinian leader in the 1940s.

Kamal Jumblatt. Leader of Lebanese National Movement and Arafat's ally; murdered 1977.

Farouk Kaddoumi (Abu Lutf). PLO 'foreign minister'; Fatah hardliner.

Salah Khalaf (Abu Iyad). Fatah founder member and intelligence chief; chief of Black September Organization;

principal Fatah ideologue and No. 2 to Arafat until his death in January 1991.

Ahmed Kora'i (Abu Ala'a). PLO financial czar and linkman in secret negotiations with Israel.

Mohammed Said Musa Maragha (Abu Musa). Among the leaders of the Fatah mutiny against Arafat's leadership, 1983.

Hosni Mubarak. President of Egypt, 1981–present.

Gamal Abdel Nasser. President of Egypt, 1953–70.

Mohammed al-Natour (Abu Tabyib). Chief of Force 17, Arafat's personal security force.

Shimon Peres. Foreign Minister of Israel, 1992–present.

Yitzhak Rabin. Prime Minister of Israel, 1974–77 and 1992–present.

Hassib Sabbagh. Palestinian multi-millionaire and construction magnate; close to Arafat.

Anwar Sadat. President of Egypt, 1970–81.

Ali Hassan Salameh. Arafat's confidant and commander of Force 17 until his death in 1979.

Issam Sartawi. Arafat adviser; leading advocate of contact with Israelis; murdered by Abu Nidal, 1983.

Saad Sayel (Abu Walid). PLO military commander, killed by a Syrian agent in 1983.

Nabil Shaath. Palestinian business consultant and long-serving Arafat adviser.

Yitzhak Shamir. Prime Minister of Israel, 1983–84, 1986–92.

Ariel Sharon. Israeli Defence Minister, 1981–3; master-minded the Lebanon invasion.

Ahmed Shukairy. Chairman of Palestine Liberation Organization, 1964–7.

Khalil-al-Wazir (Abu Jihad). Fatah founder member, military chief and Arafat's No. 2 until his death at hands of Israeli assassination squad, 1988.

Selim Zaanoun (Abul Adeed). Early Fatah member, long-standing friend of Arafat.

Mohammed Zaidan (Abul Abbas). Leader of Palestine Liberation Front and member of PLO executive committee.

# Glossary of Terms

Amal ('Hope'). Pro-Syrian militia unit in Lebanon.

Arab National Movement. Founded by George Habash and others in the 1950s; after the 1967 Arab-Israeli war, transformed itself into the Popular Front for the Liberation of Palestine (q.v.)

Al-Asifa ('The Storm'). The name under which Fatah (q.v.) conducted military operations; now no longer in use.

Baath ('Renaissance'). Pan-Arab political movement that took power in Syria and Iraq in the 1960s.

Black September. The Palestinians' name for their defeat in the Jordanian civil war, September 1970.

Black September Organization. Fatah's terrorist arm, disbanded in 1974.

Camp David Accords. Agreements signed in September 1978 by Israel, Egypt and the US, leading to the Israeli-Egyptian peace treaty.

Central Council. The PLO's 'mini-parliament', mid-way between the executive committee and the Palestine National Council.

Democratic Front for the Liberation of Palestine. Marxist PLO faction, led by Nayef Hawatmeh.

Executive Committee. The PLO 'cabinet', chaired by Arafat.

Fatah ('Conquest'). The Palestine Liberation Movement, the largest faction in the Palestine Liberation Organization (q.v.), founded by Arafat and others in 1958. It is headed by a Politburo, or General Secretariat, under Arafat's leadership, and has its own quasi-democratic institutions of which the largest and most representative is the 1200-member Fatah Congress.

Fedayeen ('Those who sacrifice themselves'). Palestinian guerrillas.

Force 17. Arafat's personal security force.

Haganah. The Jewish regular force in Palestine before the establishment of the state of Israel.

Hizbollah ('Party of God'). Fundamentalist party in Lebanon.

Ikhwan al-Muslimun. The Moslem Brotherhood, a fundamentalist political movement.

Intifada. ('The Shaking'). The Palestinian uprising in the Israeli-occupied territories, December 1987–present.

Irgun. Jewish terrorist group in the 1940s, led by Menachem Begin.

Jihad. Holy war.

Occupied Territories. The West Bank and Gaza Strip, captured by Israel in 1967.

October War (or Yom Kippur War). The 1973 war between Israel and Arab states which led eventually to the peace treaty with Egypt.

Palestine Liberation Front. PLO faction notorious for the hijacking of the cruise liner *Achille Lauro*, 1985.

Palestine Liberation Organization. Body founded by Arab states in 1964 to represent the Palestinians, taken over by Fatah and other guerrilla groups in 1969.

Palestine National Council. The PLO 'parliament'.

Palestine National Fund. The PLO's 'finance ministry', in charge of raising and administering the organization's money.

Palestinian. An Arab who originates from, or whose family originates from, the area formerly known as Palestine, between the Jordan river and the Mediterranean. The Palestinians are estimated to number between five and six million today, of whom around 2.3 million are registered as refugees in Arab countries and the Israeli-occupied territories.

Palestinian National Covenant. The PLO Charter, setting out the Organization's aims and strategy, adapted by the Palestine National Council in July 1968. It calls for the liberation of all Palestine through armed struggle and declares the establishment of Israel 'fundamentally null and void'. Western governments have long urged the PLO to repeal the covenant, and Arafat maintains that it is now outdated.

Palestinian Resistance. Generic term for guerrilla groups.

Popular Front for the Liberation of Palestine. Marxist PLO faction, led by George Habash.

Resolution 242. The 1967 UN Security Council resolution that has been a touchstone for efforts to foster Middle East peace negotiations ever since. The Resolution calls for: '1) withdrawal of Israeli armed forces from territories of recent conflict. 2) termination of all claims or states of belligerency and respect for and acknowledgement of the sovereignty, territorial integrity and political independence of every state in the area and their right to live in peace within secure and recognized boundaries free from threats or acts of force.' Its sole reference to the Palestinians consists of a call for 'a just settlement of the refugee problem'.

Six-Day War. The June 1967 war between Israel and Arab states in which Israel captured the West Bank, the Gaza Strip, the Sinai Peninsula and the Golan Heights.

Stern Gang. Jewish terrorist group in the 1940s, led by Yitzhak Shamir.

Western Sector. Section of Fatah devoted to attacks on Israel, commanded until his death by Khalil al-Wazir.

Zionism. The creed of the Jewish national movement which established the State of Israel in 1948.

# Chronology

November 1947. United Nations General Assembly votes to partition Palestine, then under British rule, into two states, one Jewish, one Arab.

1948. Britain pulls out of Palestine. With Palestinian inhabitants and neighbouring Arab states refusing to implement the partition plan, Jewish leaders establish the State of Israel and defeat the Arabs in the War of Independence. By the end of the fighting, hundreds of thousands of Palestinians have fled.

1950. Jordan, which controls the West Bank of the Jordan river after the 1948 war, formally annexes it, bringing the remaining inhabitants of Palestine under Hashemite control.

1952. Gamal Abdel Nasser comes to power in Egypt; Yasser Arafat is elected president of Palestinian Students' League in Cairo.

1956. Together with Britain and France, Israel attacks Egypt, occupies most of the Sinai Peninsula and the Gaza Strip before withdrawing under US pressure. Palestinian unrest in Gaza on the increase.

July–December 1958. Arafat and other Palestinians agree to establish the Fatah movement in Kuwait.

July 1962. Algeria gains independence from France after an eight-year colonial war. Fatah allowed to establish its first office in Algiers.

January–June 1964. Arab states agree to establish the Palestine Liberation Organization; first session of the Palestine National Council in Jerusalem.

January 1965. Fatah launches armed raids into Israel.

January–May 1966. Arafat arrested and imprisoned twice in Syria.

June 1967. Israel attacks Egypt, Syria and Jordan; captures the West Bank, the Gaza Strip, the Golan Heights and the Sinai Peninsula.

March 1968. Israel attacks Palestinian guerrilla bases in the Jordan Valley, in the Battle of Karameh.

February 1969. Arafat elected chairman of the executive committee of the Palestine Liberation Organization.

September 1970. King Hussein's army moves against PLO guerrillas in Jordan; after fierce fighting, the Palestinians are saved by intervention of Arab states.

July 1971. The last PLO guerrillas are ejected from Jordan and take refuge in Syria and Lebanon.

September 1972. The Black September Organization seizes Israeli athletes at Munich Olympic Games. Nine Israelis die in airport shoot-out.

October 1973. Egypt and Syria launch surprise attack on Israeli forces occupying the Sinai Peninsula and the Golan Heights.

October 1974. Arab leaders, meeting in Rabat, declare the PLO the 'sole legitimate representative' of the Palestinian people.

November 1974. Arafat addresses the United Nations General Assembly in New York.

April 1975. Civil war breaks out in Lebanon, with Palestinian guerrillas fighting alongside Lebanese leftists and Muslims against Maronite Christians.

October 1976. After Syrian intervention in the Lebanese war on the side of the Maronite Christians, Arab leaders agree a ceasefire.

November 1977. Egyptian President Anwar Sadat goes to Jerusalem and in a Knesset address offers peace.

March 1978. Israel invades south Lebanon and attacks PLO guerrillas.

September 1978. Camp David Accords signed by Israel, Egypt and the US.

February 1979. Ayatollah Khomeini returns to Iran at the climax of the Iranian revolution.

March 1979. Egypt and Israel sign peace treaty.

July 1981. 'Katyusha War' between Israel and PLO guerrillas in southern Lebanon.

June 1982. Israel invades Lebanon again in an all-out offensive against the PLO, and its forces reach the outskirts of Beirut.

August 1982. After an 88–day siege, the PLO withdraws its forces and staff from Beirut under a US-brokered agreement, establishes a headquarters in Tunis and scatters its fighters to seven Arab countries.

September 1982. Hundreds of Palestinian refugees massacred by Lebanese Maronite Christian gunmen in Beirut.

June–November 1983. Fatah commanders in Lebanon stage a mutiny against Arafat's leadership; Arafat returns to the Lebanese port of Tripoli, where he is again besieged.

December 1983. After being evacuated from Tripoli, Arafat provokes controversy by visiting Egypt.

February 1985. Arafat, on a visit to Amman, signs a political co-operation accord with King Hussein with the aim of taking part in an international Middle East peace conference.

October 1985. Israeli planes attack PLO headquarters in Tunis. Guerrillas from the Palestine Liberation Front hijack the cruise liner *Achille Lauro* in the Mediterranean.

February 1986. The Arafat-Hussein accord collapses.

December 1987. The Palestinian uprising begins in the Israeli-occupied Gaza Strip and spreads to the West Bank.

April 1988. Khalil al-Wazir slain by Israeli commandos in Tunis.

November 1988. The Palestine National Council declares an independent Palestinian state and implicitly recognizes Israel by accepting UN Security Council Resolution 242.

December 1988. Arafat addresses the UN General Assembly in Geneva, explicitly recognizes Israel and renounces terrorism. The US agrees to open dialogue.

November/December 1989. Mass emigration of Soviet Jews to Israel begins.

May 1990. An Arab League emergency summit convenes in Baghdad at the PLO's behest to debate the Jewish immigration issue.

August 1990. Iraq invades Kuwait. Saddam Hussein links withdrawal from Kuwait with settlement of the Palestine question.

January 1991. Salah Khalaf and two colleagues slain by renegade Palestinian.

January 1991. War breaks out in the Gulf. Allied bombing campaign continues for more than a month.

February 1991. President Bush announces suspension of hostilities and the return to the Middle East of Secretary of State Baker to seek a 'durable' peace.

October 1991. Middle East Peace Conference in Madrid. Israel begins direct talks with its neighbours.

November 1991. Arafat marries Suha Tawil secretly in Tunis.

April 1992. Arafat survives plane crash in Libyan desert. Pilot and co-pilot killed.

June 1992. Yitzhak Rabin's Labour Party wins Israeli election and moves to engage PLO in dialogue.

September 1993. Israel/PLO mutual recognition. Interim self-rule agreement initialled for Gaza and Jericho.

# Prologue

'Shalom, salaam, peace.'

Washington, 13 September 1993. A hush descended on the crowd seated in rows on the White House lawn. Before them three men blinked in the sunshine and eyed one another on a small white stage. The short, pudgy character in military beige and a chequered headdress grinned irrepressibly as he extended his right hand towards the taller, slimmer gentleman with thinning white hair. The latter hesitated, fidgeting awkwardly in his sombre suit. They stood, as if transfixed, for what seemed like an age before the third man, standing between them, gently nudged the second's arm towards the first's.

Thus, with a momentary clasping of hands between two old men in the presence of an American President young enough to be their son, was history made. Yasser Arafat, 64, chairman of the Executive Committee of the Palestine Liberation Organisation and self-styled president of a non-existent state, had reached out to the leader of a country he had once dedicated himself to destroying, proclaiming his desire for peaceful coexistence. Yitzhak Rabin, 71, Prime Minister of the State of Israel, had touched a man he and his predecessors had vowed never to recognise, his voice filled with emotion as he declared: 'Enough of blood and tears. Enough!'

It was an occasion stage-managed for historical effect. The walnut table on which Israel and the PLO signed their ground-breaking agreement on Palestinian autonomy in the West Bank and Gaza Strip had seen service fourteen years before when President Anwar Sadat of Egypt and

Prime Minister Menachem Begin of Israel had signed their own momentous peace treaty. Present in the audience of 3000 were many of the statesmen who had spent years of their lives on the apparently unrewarding search for peace in the Middle East. There was Jimmy Carter, who as President engineered the Camp David Accords. There was Henry Kissinger, pioneer of shuttle diplomacy, erstwhile cold war warrior and bitter foe of Arafat's PLO. And there, near the front, were George Bush and James Baker – the men who had facilitated the Rabin–Arafat handshake by turning the allied victory over Iraq in the Gulf into a new opportunity for peace, and staging the 1991 Madrid conference.

For Yasser Arafat, still beaming constantly like some ageing Cheshire Cat as he worked the crowd and then hurtled off into a frantic round of meetings with politicians, financiers and TV interviewers, it was more than a moment to savour. It was the one he had been awaiting for as long as he could remember. 'I have come bearing an olive branch and a freedom fighter's gun,' he had told the United Nations in New York in 1974. But in the intervening two decades, he had been barred from US shores as a dangerous terrorist and written off repeatedly as an irrelevance: as recently as a month ago, with the PLO apparently crumbling around him, the pundits had been confidently predicting his political demise.

Now, he had staged the biggest comeback in a lifetime full of dramatic escapes. Fêted in fickle Washington as a courageous man of peace, he regaled anyone who would listen with tales of misadventure and expressions of political hope, lobbied furiously for financial aid, and even, in one press conference, compared himself to Jesus Christ.

By midnight, preparing in his Washington hotel suite for the flight back to the Middle East on his borrowed plane, Palestine 1, the euphoria was wearing off. And as Arafat brooded on the immense difficulties that lay ahead in implementing his peace agreement with Israel, another comparison came to mind. 'I don't want to be another Gorbachev,' he said, referring to the Soviet leader who was swept from power by the changes he himself had unleashed: 'I'm no Gorbachev.'[1]

The Washington signing of the Declaration of Principles outlining steps towards Palestinian autonomy in the West Bank and Gaza was, after all, only the possible beginning of the end, and that only on paper. There were no guarantees that it would work on the ground or ultimately fulfil his people's dream of statehood. 'It is on our shoulders that everyone should accept this agreement,' warned the PLO leader, 'but there is little time. This is an experiment that has to succeed. We have no time to waste.'[2]

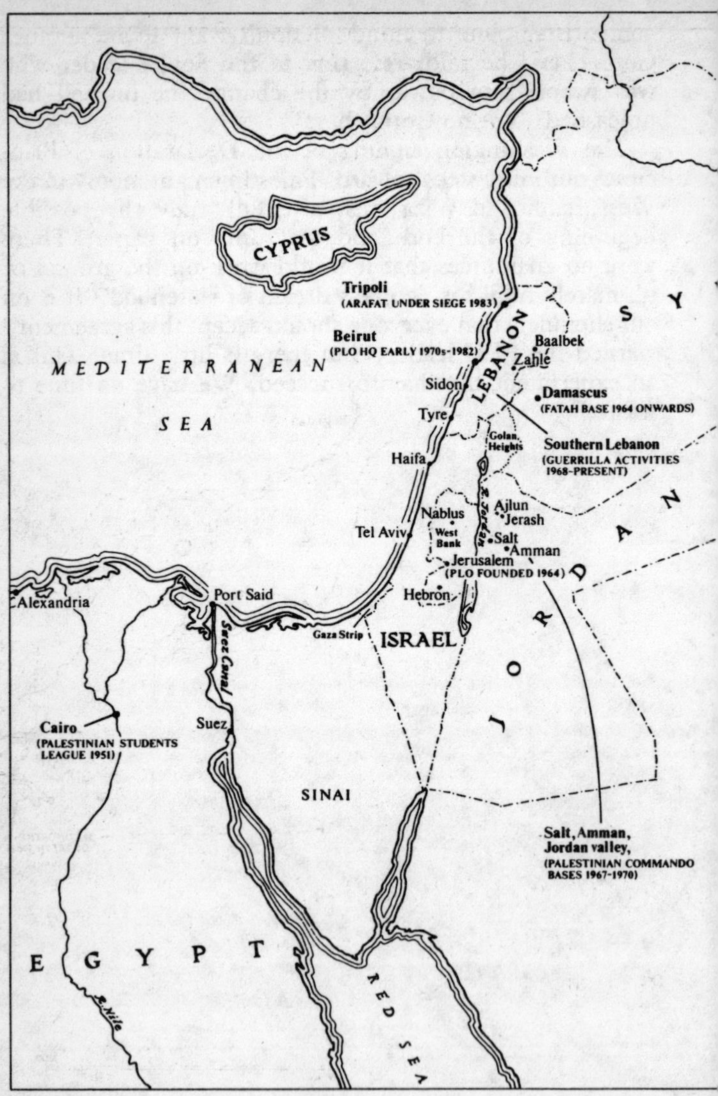
CYPRUS
Tripoli
(ARAFAT UNDER SIEGE 1983)
Beirut
(PLO HQ EARLY 1970s-1982)
MEDITERRANEAN
SEA
LEBANON
SY
Baalbek
Zahlé
Sidon
Damascus
(FATAH BASE 1964 ONWARDS)
Tyre
Golan Heights
Southern Lebanon
(GUERRILLA ACTIVITIES
1968-PRESENT)
Haifa
R. Jordan
Nablus
Ajlun
Jerash
Tel Aviv
West Bank
Salt
Amman
Jerusalem
(PLO FOUNDED 1964)
Alexandria
Port Said
Hebron
JORDAN
Gaza Strip
ISRAEL
Suez Canal
Cairo
(PALESTINIAN STUDENTS
LEAGUE 1951)
Suez
SINAI
Salt, Amman,
Jordan valley,
(PALESTINIAN COMMANDO
BASES 1967-1970)
EGYPT
RED SEA
R. Nile

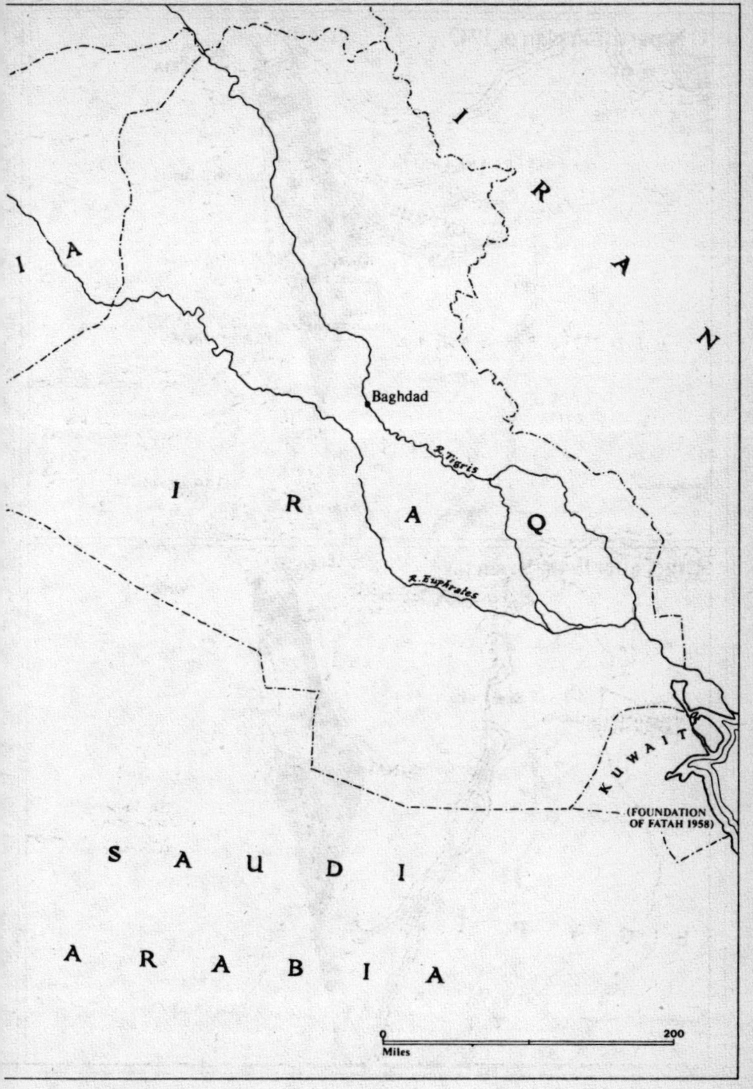

IRAN
IA
Baghdad
R. Tigris
IRAQ
R. Euphrates
KUWAIT
(FOUNDATION OF FATAH 1958)
SAUDI ARABIA
0
200
Miles

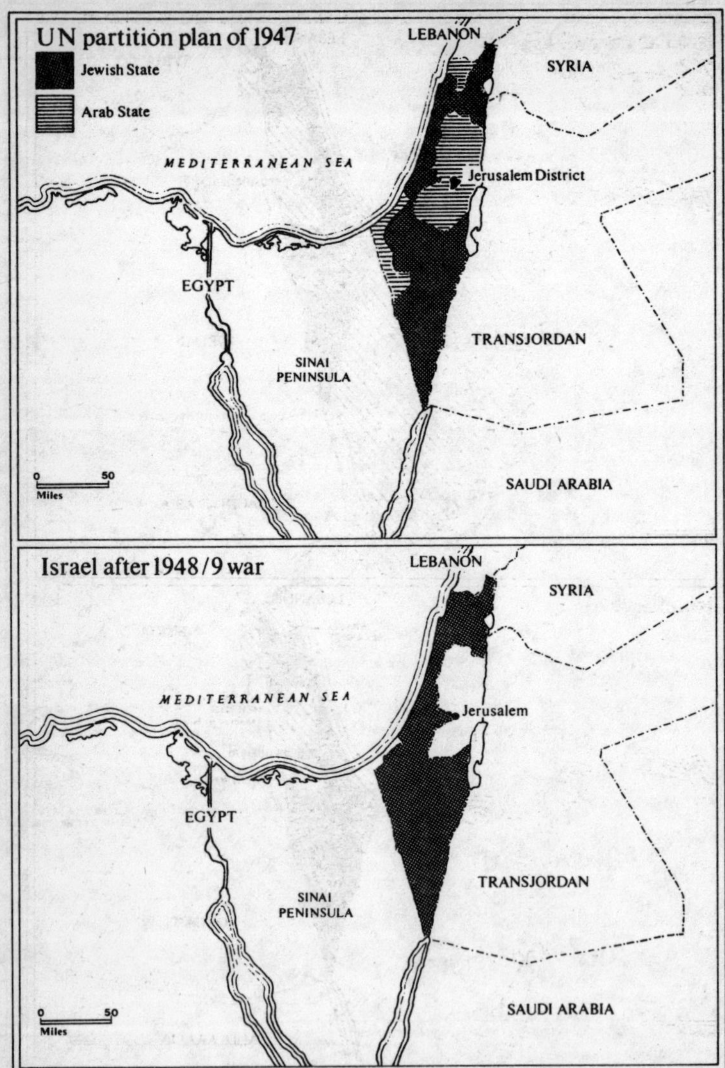
UN partition plan of 1947
Jewish State
Arab State
LEBANON
SYRIA
MEDITERRANEAN SEA
Jerusalem District
EGYPT
TRANSJORDAN
SINAI
PENINSULA
SAUDI ARABIA
0
50
Miles
Israel after 1948/9 war
LEBANON
SYRIA
MEDITERRANEAN SEA
Jerusalem
EGYPT
TRANSJORDAN
SINAI
PENINSULA
SAUDI ARABIA
0
50
Miles

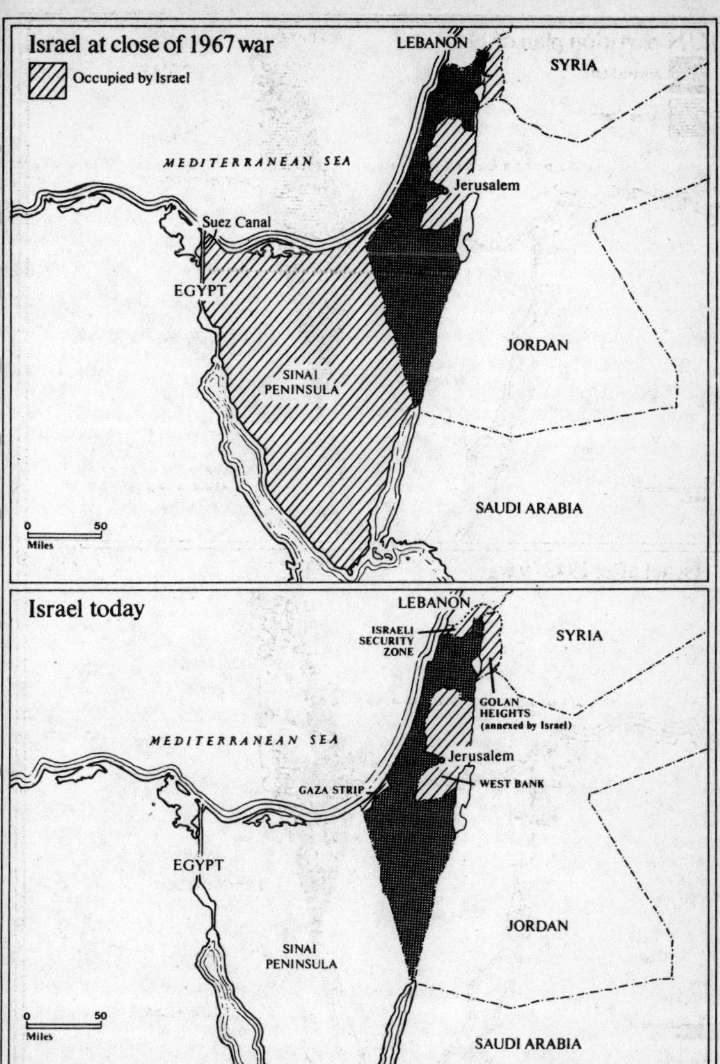
Israel at close of 1967 war
Occupied by Israel
LEBANON
SYRIA
MEDITERRANEAN SEA
Jerusalem
Suez Canal
EGYPT
JORDAN
SINAI
PENINSULA
SAUDI ARABIA
0
50
Miles
Israel today
LEBANON
ISRAELI
SECURITY
ZONE
SYRIA
GOLAN
HEIGHTS
(annexed by Israel)
MEDITERRANEAN SEA
Jerusalem
GAZA STRIP
WEST BANK
EGYPT
JORDAN
SINAI
PENINSULA
0
50
Miles
SAUDI ARABIA

# Part One

# 1
# *Mr Palestine*

'I am a refugee, for I have nothing, for I was banished and dispossessed of my homeland.' Yasser Arafat, interview with *Al-Sayyad*, Beirut, 1969.

The young engineering student with thinning hair and thin features took more than usual care with his appearance. Peering in the mirror in his family's five-room ground-floor apartment at 24 Baron Empain Street in Cairo's respectable suburb of Heliopolis, he noted with approval his clean white shirt, sober tie and the cut of his modish double-breasted suit, with its exaggerated lapels. At the age of 23, the man who would become known to the world as 'Yasser' Arafat was about to take his first tentative steps on to an international stage.

With the inventiveness that had helped secure his election as President of the Palestinian Students' League the previous year, he had dreamed up an idea to engage the attention of Egypt's Prime Minister, Mohammed Naguib – and, more importantly, of the local press. Five years after the Arabs' humiliating defeat in the first of many wars with Israel, he had, together with comrades in the leadership of the League, drawn up a petition written in blood to General Neguib, head of the Revolutionary Command Council, the military junta that ruled Egypt following the 1952 revolution. The thousands of Palestinian students who had gathered in Cairo had a simple plea for the Egyptian leadership: Don't Forget Palestine. The date was 12 January 1953.

The petition in blood produced instant and quite gratifying results. Page eight of *Al-Ahram*, Egypt's daily newspaper, carried a photograph the next day of an earnest-looking Arafat presenting his petition to General Neguib, one of the few Arab commanders to have distinguished himself in the 1948–9 war for Palestine. The Prime Minister's ornate offices in an Ottoman palace near the city's busy Tahrir Square may have witnessed more momentous events, but it can have seen few début appearances that would lead to such a lengthy and melodramatic career: never mind that *Al-Ahram* misspelt Arafat's name at the first attempt, referring to him as 'Mr Farhat'. He was on his way, and had even managed to persuade Egypt's premier to become patron of the Palestinian Students' League, thus guaranteeing its semi-official status.

In reality, Arafat's emergence as leader of a band of embittered and dispossessed students hardly caused a ripple in the Egypt of the early 1950s, much preoccupied, as it was, with its own internal upheavals; but it was no accident that Cairo, turbulent centre of the Arab world, hotbed of revolutionary ideas and ideals, had proved a crucible for the birth of a new Palestinianism. There was no shortage there of willing converts to the cause.

The leaders of the Palestinian revolution-to-be were the sons and daughters of the men and women driven from their homes in Israel's War of Independence. In the great exodus of 1948 and 1949, between 650,000 and 750,000 people out of a total Palestinian population of 1.3 million had been displaced. More than half the Arab inhabitants of what had been the British-ruled territory of Palestine fled, mostly to the West Bank of the Jordan river, but also to Jordan itself, to Lebanon, to Syria, or to the Gaza Strip.[1]

In squalid refugee settlements that gradually became permanent shanty towns, the desire for revenge festered. Haltingly, the new nationalism was born of the memories of Jaffa, of Lydda and of Ramleh, to name just a few of the Arab towns forcibly evacuated as Jewish forces swept aside corrupt, chaotic and, at times, almost non-existent, Arab resistance. Albert Hourani, the Middle East scholar, observed acutely many years later that it was the 'shock of exile' that had created a Palestinian Arab nation.[2]

For Salah Khalaf, later known as Abu Iyad, godfather of the PLO's notorious Black September terrorist group, the date of 13 May 1948 was etched in his memory. As a 14-year-old, Khalaf found himself in a makeshift open boat with dozens of other sobbing residents, fleeing the bombardment of Jaffa, the large Arab coastal town adjacent to Tel Aviv. Families had gathered the few belongings they could carry and rushed towards the sea to escape the shells that were falling thick and fast as the Jewish forces laid siege to Jaffa. Khalaf was 'overwhelmed by the sight of this huge mass of men, women, old people and children, struggling under the weight of suitcases or bundles, making their way painfully down to the wharfs of Jaffa . . . Cries mingled with moaning and sobs, all punctuated by deafening explosions.'[3]

It was an exodus that had few parallels in history, and it was spurred on partly by fears of massacre. On 9 April, the Irgun – a Jewish underground group – had slaughtered as many as 250 inhabitants of Deir Yassin, an Arab village near Jerusalem.[4] Arab radio broadcasts, from Baghdad to Cairo, did their bit to spread word of Deir Yassin to a panic-stricken populace. The Irgun leader, Menachem Begin, Israel's Prime Minister from 1977–83, always denied stories of massacre but later he would say that: 'Out of evil . . . good came. This Arab propaganda spread a legend of terror amongst Arabs and Arab troops, who were seized with panic at the mention of Irgun soldiers. The legend was worth half a dozen battalions to the forces of Israel.'[5]

For a quietly determined 12-year-old named Khalil al-Wazir, 12 July 1948 turned out to be a most fateful day. It was the day on which Prime Minister David Ben-Gurion issued orders to expel the Arabs from the towns of Ramleh and Lydda in what is now the centre of Israel.[6] Wazir, later to emerge as a key figure in the Palestinian underground, joined his mother, brothers and sisters in a pathetic rush by road from the besieged Arab town of Ramleh towards Ramallah. Before long the family found itself in the Gaza Strip – the destination for about one-quarter of the Palestinians dispersed by the fighting of 1948 and 1949, and the breeding ground for violent opposition to the Jewish state.[7]

For George Habash, a good-looking medical student with a volatile temperament, 13 July was a day of truth. The day after Ramleh was emptied of its Arab inhabitants, Lydda succumbed following a fierce bombardment. Habash, later to become founder of one of the PLO's most radical factions, had rushed home from his medical studies in Beirut to work as a hospital orderly. He had witnessed the casualties of war firsthand and had been seized and beaten by soldiers determined to rid the town of its population. It had been a shocking experience. 'From 1948 I was definite about it,' he says. 'When I was expelled and treated in that way, from that time I felt that I had to sacrifice all my life for my just cause.'[8]

And what of Arafat himself? While Khalaf, Wazir and Habash were experiencing the shock of exile, Arafat was completing secondary school in Cairo and did not stray far from the Egyptian capital during the great catastrophe, in spite of his own myth-making about having been, at eighteen, the 'youngest officer' in the Palestine Army of Abdel Kader al-Husseini, the Palestinian hero, who died in the battle of Qastal near Jerusalem on 8 April 1948.[9]

As student friends tell it, Arafat's main activity during the war of 1948 was to act as a go-between in efforts to procure arms for Husseini's ill-equipped Jihad al Muqqadis irregulars as they fought their losing battle. By all accounts, Arafat helped to establish a supply line to Bedu tribesmen in the Western desert who were trafficking in arms left strewn on the Second World War battlefields of Benghazi, Tobruk and El Alamein.

* * *

Mohammed Abdel-Raouf Arafat al-Qudwa al-Husseini was, according to his university record, born in Cairo on 4 August 1929, sixth child of Abdel Raouf al-Qudwa al-Husseini, a stern, bespectacled merchant, and of Zahwa, a member of the prominent Abu Saoud family of Jerusalem. The al-Qudwas had arrived in Cairo from Jerusalem late in 1927 and had settled in a large apartment in the Sakakini district not far from the city centre. They did not attract much attention. Sakakini was one of Cairo's most cosmopolitan areas; Palestinians, Lebanese, Jews, Armenians and Greeks all gravitated to the comfortable residential district with its attractive villas, well-regarded schools and wide, tree-lined streets.

The infant Arafat first saw the light of day in a city very different from today's dusty, traffic-clogged metropolis. Cairo in the 1920s had a population of about one million, housed in an eclectic mixture of the old and decaying, and the modernistic. French architectural influence was strong in the business centre and in some of the grander dwellings on the Nile. The country was in the throes of political ferment. The first of a series of nationalist governments had come to power, demanding complete independence from Britain. Between 1919 and 1936 there were no fewer than twenty governments and eight sets of negotiations in which the Egyptians ceaselessly tried to whittle away British privilege in the face of obstinate resistance. But in spite of this turbulence, war and revolution seemed very far away.

A certain mystery surrounds Abdel-Raouf's departure from Jerusalem, where he had been a moderately successful small trader and before that a policeman in the Ottoman police force, but it seems that he had removed himself and his family to Cairo to pursue an inheritance claim. Arafat himself says that his father fought a long, expensive legal battle to secure title to a large parcel of land in an area that is now dominated by the Ain Shams university in the east of the city.[10] Abdel-Raouf claimed ownership to the land through his Egyptian mother, who was a member of the prominent al-Radwan clan. Years of legal machinations were unsuccessful, however, when laws were arbitrarily changed, after Egypt's 1952 revolution, to restrict transfer of property from one generation to another. It was a crushing disappointment for the elder Arafat who had spent more than two decades fighting the Egyptian courts and bureaucracy.

When Arafat was born his industrious father was already well established in business as a trader in groceries, spices and incense, a well-known figure in Sakakini in the fez he habitually wore. But in 1933, when Arafat was 4, his mother Zahwa, a pleasant-looking, open-faced woman, died suddenly of kidney failure, leaving Abdel-Raouf with seven children on his hands. It was an almost impossible burden, so Arafat and his infant brother, Fathi, were packed off to Jerusalem to stay with their uncle, Selim Abu Saoud, in the large, comfortable family house in the Fakhriyya area of the Old City.

The Abu Saoud house adjoined the 'Wailing Wall', a most sacred site to the Jews. It also lay virtually in the shadow of the Haram al-Sharif, home of Islam's third holiest shrines after Mecca and Medina. The relatively well-to-do Abu Saouds had lived in the area since the middle of the sixteenth century in a collection of fine Mamluk buildings. By chance and at a young age, Arafat found himself in the very front line of the increasing conflict between Arab and Jew. Thus, he saw trouble between Muslims and Jews in the narrow streets of Old Jerusalem during the 1936–9 Arab Revolt; he observed the detention of relatives by the British authorities, whose rule was becoming steadily more oppressive; and he was present during anguished family debates about the future of Palestine.[11]

Despite his youth, he left a strong impression on his relatives. 'He always wanted to be the boss,' recalls his first cousin, the daughter of his father's sister and one of his early playmates in the tangled pathways of the Old City. He also exhibited, in his cousin's words, an early gift for 'showmanship'.[12] He was part of an extended and very traditional Palestinian family. Amira Musa Arafat, his maternal grandmother, was the daughter of Musa Arafat, an important Gazan merchant. Her marriage to an Abu Saoud was referred to with satisfaction in family circles as the 'union of the aristocracy and merchant classes'.[13] While not in the front rank of status-conscious Palestinian society, Arafat was nevertheless well connected, especially on his mother's side. The Abu Saouds were regarded as minor aristocracy.

One story frequently told about his family can be firmly laid to rest. Arafat was not related, as has often been reported, to Haj Amin al-Husseini, the Mufti of Jerusalem and later the exiled leader of the Palestinians. His first cousin in Jerusalem says emphatically that the al-Qudwa (Arafat's father's family) are 'the Husseinis of Gaza. They are nothing to do with the Husseinis of Jerusalem.'[14] Arafat's contacts with the Mufti, who lived in exile in Cairo in the late 1940s, had probably come, she thought, through his uncle, Sheikh Hassan Abu Saoud, who was very close to Haj Amin.[15]

Arafat's sojourn in Jerusalem came to an end in 1937 soon after his father's re-marriage to an Egyptian woman. Summoned home to Cairo, he reluctantly left a city that he would later, with a canny eye for its political significance, claim as his birthplace. The Arafat brothers returned to a country already being buffeted by the storms of the Second World War breaking over Europe, to continue their education at private school in the Abbasiyya district. King Farouk had ascended the throne the previous year, ill-educated and ill-prepared to deal with the internal unrest and strikes that were the order of the day.

Arafat settled into a relatively comfortable middle-class existence with his six brothers and sisters and a disciplinarian father then beginning his second family. He attended Farouk college and earned the nickname 'Yasser', meaning carefree or easygoing. By all accounts, he was a hyperactive child. Inam, his elder sister by about ten years, recalls that even at that relatively young age Arafat showed an almost compulsive need to organize and mobilize others, marshalling children in the street into military formations and marching them up and down with metal plates on their heads, hitting them with a stick if they got out of line.[16]

War in the desert between Rommel and the Allies provided distraction from the looming conflict between Arabs and Jews, but not for long. As Arafat – he had spent the war years in Cairo observing the comings and goings of an odd collection of Allied troops – approached young adulthood in the post-war period, the Palestine question re-emerged with a vengeance.

Shame over the Holocaust had strengthened the hands of those who agreed with the Jewish nationalist, or Zionist, movement in advocating a separate and secure homeland in Palestine for the Jews. The result – adopted amid great controversy by the United Nations in 1947 – was a plan to partition Palestine into two states, one Jewish, one Arab, and existing Arab states, grouped in the Arab League since 1945, proved powerless to prevent what became the Palestinian catastrophe. As a guest in the houses of prominent Palestinians in Cairo and therefore privy to their discussions, Arafat could not but have been affected by the gloom.

The two-stage war for Palestine – first civil resistance and then open warfare – ended in total humiliation for the Arabs. Weak and divided, their armies were no match for the superior organization and firepower of the Zionist military machine. The Palestinians on the ground had been hopelessly hampered by their own internal feuds, and after the war, efforts to build an All-Palestine Government under the leadership of Haj Amin al-Husseini were almost universally regarded as an irrelevant sideshow. The name of Palestine was gradually being erased from the map.

Like many other young Palestinians, Arafat's first inclination in 1949 was to flee the Middle East for a new life elsewhere. He had been appalled by the Palestinian refugee exodus, sickened by the futile Arab response. At nineteen, he applied for admission to a university in Texas. 'I was a very desperate Palestinian, so I decided to leave the whole area like many Palestinians,' he recalls. 'Some of them went to continue their studies in Canada and others in the US and Latin America. So, I decided to continue my studies in the States.'[17]

But Arafat never followed up his application because, in his own words, 'I became completely involved in the atmosphere all around me.'[18] It is not hard to understand why. Cairo in the late 1940s was seething with political activity. A weak and corrupt constitutional government had all but collapsed. The continued presence of British troops on Egyptian soil provoked constant protest and agitation; and the playboy King Farouk, last in a faltering line of discredited rulers, exerted minimal influence over events that were moving inexorably towards revolution. In their Nile-side salons, members of the *ancien régime* were about to be dispossessed of much of their inherited wealth. The rebellious Muslim Brotherhood, the *Ikhwan al-Muslimun*, founded in 1928 by the charismatic Sheikh Hassan al-Banna, was a surging influence in the streets and on the campuses. Attempts by the authorities in 1948 to suppress Muslim militants came too late. Entrenched in the army, the *Ikhwan* had even managed to penetrate the Communist Party. They were the most conspicuous among all Egypt's political groups in championing the cause of Palestine, and had backed that up by committing forces to the battle of 1948, as they had supported the Palestinians in their 1930s revolt against Jewish immigration and British mandatory rule.

Inevitably, Arafat was drawn to the Brotherhood's militant doctrines of anti-imperialism and national revival through Islam. It remains a moot point whether Arafat was actually a member or merely a sympathizer – he insists now that he was never a member[19] – but he drew heavily on *Ikhwan* support in student elections at King Fouad I University (later Cairo University) and subsequently in elections for the Palestinian Students' League. Arafat had entered university in the late summer of 1949 when riots and demonstrations against the despised British were an almost daily occurrence. The rule of law had all but broken down. 'Disorder, destruction, violence and bloodshed, inspired by any and all groups wielding a minimum of power, official or unofficial, were the costly accompaniment of that breakdown,' according to one authoritative account of that period.[20]

The humiliating Arab defeat in Palestine, more than anything, contributed to the ferment in the Arab world in the late 1940s and early 1950s. And nowhere was public sentiment more inflamed than in Egypt itself. 'Public opinion was very deeply humiliated and deeply aroused against the regimes, irrespective of whether they were republics or monarchies,' says Professor Walid Khalidi, the distinguished Palestinian historian. 'Parallel to this was a very interesting intellectual phenomenon of self-criticism that assumed almost masochistic proportions. Our defeat was the result of something very rotten in the state of Denmark, as it were, and this gave rise to radical movements against existing regimes whether in Damascus, in Iraq or in Egypt.' Subsequently, it was the reaction to the Palestinian War, the fall of Palestine, that sealed the fate of the Egyptian monarchy and the Iraqi monarchy, and caused the series of *coups d'état* and revolutions in Syria.[21]

In this highly charged atmosphere, a distracted Arafat began what can only be described as a mediocre university career. His record shows that he completed his preparatory year in the faculty of civil engineering in 1949–50 with a *maqboul* or pass, but he had to repeat two of his subsequent years. Mathematics was certainly not his strong point; he failed the subject in years two and three, and again when he repeated his third year. Zoheir al-Alami, Arafat's best student friend, an early Fatah activist and now a successful engineer in the Gulf, recalls a colleague consumed by politics. 'His only activity was politics,' Alami remembers. 'Very seldom would he come to the School of Engineering.'[22] Unstructured and unfocused through it may have been, Arafat's politicking seems to have begun in earnest in 1949. Faisal al-Husseini, generally acknowledged today to be the most influential PLO figure in Israeli-occupied Jerusalem, recalls Arafat coming to the family house in Heliopolis early in 1949, to help prepare a small poem to be read on Palestinian Martyrs' Day early in April, to commemorate the deaths of, among others, Husseini's father, Abdel Kader.[23]

Other glimpses of Arafat, the budding politician, indicate a precocious desire to organize, canvass and muster support. Husam Abu Shaaban, now a doctor in Kuwait, remembers encountering in 1949 a slim and eager Palestinian outside the Banque Belge et Internationale in Cairo's busy Kasr el Nil Street. He came quickly to the point: 'Are you a Palestinian?' he had asked. When Shaaban answered yes, the young man introduced himself as Yasser Arafat and invited him to discuss Palestine.[24] Shaaban later served on the executive of the Arafat-led Palestinian Students' League.

In the beginning, Arafat did not restrict himself exclusively to Palestinian student politics. An Egyptian contemporary, who recalls Arafat as being 'very thin' and 'rather quiet', said that his election as one of the two representatives of the engineering faculty to the students' union was an error, as those places were strictly reserved for Egyptians.[25] It is possible that Arafat, who to this day speaks with a strong Egyptian accent, had passed himself off as a local.

Throughout 1950 and 1951 agitation against the continued British military presence in the canal zone grew. *Ikhwan* agents stirred anti-imperialist hostility up and down the country, and particularly on university campuses until, responding to overwhelming public pressure, the Egyptian parliament on 16 October 1951 unilaterally abrogated the 1936 Anglo-Egyptian Agreement under which British bases were permitted on Egyptian soil. It was the signal for all-out resistance to the British presence in Egypt.

Egyptians were exultant, one newspaper crowing that 'The helpless and hungry Egyptian horse tied to the British chariot and whipped on by a relentless and cruel driver has been freed.'[26] Whether they wished it or not, the authorities were helpless to prevent the beginning of 'armed struggle' against the British. Thanks to the campaign initiated on university campuses, Arafat was about to get his first rudimentary military training.

Hassan Doh, described by one historian as a 'notorious agent' of the *Ikhwan*, was in charge of military instruction in Egypt's universities as thousands of students flocked to join up. Arafat was merely one among dozens of Palestinians who seized the opportunity to learn about guns and explosives. Doh, a frail and eccentric figure these days, remembers Arafat as one of his best students and one who was particularly adept at climbing the massive dome of the main hall of King Fouad I University. The two used to joke, in fact, that this was good preparation for scaling the dome of the al-Aqsa mosque in Jerusalem. Within a month Arafat became an instructor himself, but Doh does not recall him actually joining students in hostilities against the British in the canal zone in 1951, as Arafat claims.[27]

As the Egyptian revolution got into full swing in the summer of 1951, a young, strongly built Palestinian with an unforgiving nature arrived in Cairo from the Gaza Strip. His name was Salah Khalaf, one of thousands of Gazan students, most of them refugees, who flooded Egyptian universities and other institutes of higher learning in the 1950s and early 1960s, and who were to provide more than a few recruits to the hard core of the PLO.

Embittered by his experiences as a refugee – a constant series of humiliations and hardships – and itching to join the fray, Khalaf was about to begin a relationship with Arafat that spanned more than thirty years. Stormy at times, it was, nevertheless, a partnership that served the interests of the two of them well as they rose through the ranks of the nationalist movement. Khalaf later observed that 'The Cairo years were extremely important in forming our personal relationships and helping us to resolve our differences later on. This is why we never split.'[28]

Neither could later recall the exact date of their first meeting but it was some time late in 1951, and in connection with Palestinian student agitation. The hot-headed Khalaf had been detained for forty-nine days after a demonstration against the Arab League in protest at its decision to cut off funds for needy Palestinian students. The students had 'stormed and ransacked' the office of Ahmed Shukairy, at the time assistant secretary general of the League in charge of Palestinian affairs; he became, in 1964, the controversial first chairman of the PLO. It was by no means the last time Khalaf would see the inside of an Egyptian jail.

Elsewhere in the Arab world, Palestinian students of a new and more militant generation were stirring after the initial shock of exile. In Beirut, George Habash, who graduated in 1951 near the top of his class from the American University Medical School, had begun discussing nationalist ideas with a small group of fellow intellectuals at a waterfront coffee shop. Influenced by Baathism, a pan-Arab version of socialism taking root in Syria and Iraq, and by the revolutionary tide beginning to sweep the Third World, Habash and his associates decided to form a nationalist movement wedded to the idea of reclaiming Palestine in a united Arab struggle.

The decision to form the Arab National Movement, Habash says, was taken with 'six or seven associates' in 1951 before he left to set up medical practice in Amman the following year.[29] Among these associates was Dr Wadi Haddad, who went on to mastermind a bloody rash of Palestinian terrorism in the late 1960s. Habash says that in these formative years, he and Haddad were 'much more than brothers'.[30]

Fashioned in Beirut in the days when it was the playground of the eastern Mediterranean, Habash's pan-Arab ideals were to clash repeatedly over the years with Arafat's own brand of Palestinian nationalism. To this day, Arafat and Habash represent the two broad secular tendencies of Palestinian political activism. They converge on some issues and diverge on the others, but while they have differed bitterly at times there has never been a final rupture between them.

Things went from bad to worse for the foreign presence in Egypt. On Black Saturday, 26 January 1952, in an orgy of burning and looting, 750 buildings in Cairo were damaged or destroyed. An attack on the Turf Club, a popular British watering hole, left ten Britons dead. Outraged, the British Embassy in Cairo accused the Egyptian Government of 'connivance' in the attack in which a 'savage mob under organized leadership broke into the premises . . .'[31]

There is no suggestion that Arafat himself was involved in any of the destruction or killing, but nor is there any question where his sympathies lay. 'I considered this as one movement, one battle and one target,' he says, 'I held the British as the main people responsible for the Palestinian tragedy. Up to now I believe that the main culprits are the British. We were under their mandate and instead of giving us independence we became refugees and stateless. Hence I found it was my duty to participate with the Egyptians against the British troops.'[32]

In Cairo, Black Saturday marked the beginning of the end for the monarchical regime. Within six months, in fact, on the night of 22–3 July, a tall army colonel named Gamal Abdel Nasser seized power in a bloodless coup. Time had run out for King Farouk. In mortal terror, he took refuge in the ornate Ras al-Tin Palace on the Alexandria seafront. Ordered to abdicate on 26 July, Farouk didn't argue. Much relieved to have escaped with his life, he sailed into pampered exile on his private yacht, the *al-Mahrusa* – the same yacht, incidentally, that had transported his grandfather, the profligate Khedive Ismail, into exile in 1879.

Within a few weeks of the Nasser revolution, Arafat and Khalaf, who had by then become firm friends, mounted their own 'coup', taking control of the Palestinian Students' League on a slate they called the 'Student Union'. Arafat's campaign provided an early glimpse of an important political weapon: his skill for consensus-building. His balanced ticket included six independents, one Communist, one Baathist and one member of the *Ikhwan*.[33] The tireless organizer became chairman of the League, and Khalaf, the angry young man of the Palestinian student fraternity, joined him on the nine-member executive committee. Arafat, at this time, was exhibiting another quality that was to stand him in very good stead in later years: an excellent memory for names and faces and the minutiae of Palestinian student life.

While Palestinian mythology has invested much historical importance in the activities of the Students' League under Arafat, in reality the union functioned mostly as a non-ideological self-help body, dealing with the grievances and everyday financial problems of Palestinian students. Money worries were ever-present. Students, who eked out an existence on the miserable stipend they received from the Arab League and from the United Nations Relief and Works Agency (UNWRA), were invariably in financial difficulties, since in most cases their impoverished families were in no position to support them. The League also functioned as a social club. Students would arrange picnics and other get-togethers; early photographs show the young men of the Palestinian movement boating on the Nile, and eating snacks at Cairo Zoo.

As a student politician, Arafat was also learning some of the stagecraft that would become his stock-in-trade in later years. Bashir Barghouti, now an East Jerusalem newspaper editor, who served with him on the student executive in the mid-1950s, remembers emotion-laden and little-varying Arafat speeches in which he would shed tears, as if on cue, after reading the same four-line poem about Palestine. He would also make liberal use of a small selection of Koranic sayings.[34] Repetition continues to be one of Arafat's hallmarks.

Barghouti also recalls an episode in which a distraught Palestinian woman came repeatedly to the union's shabby headquarters to ask for help in securing an entry visa for her daughter, who had been trapped outside Egypt after leaving on a student delegation. The mother encountered Arafat in the student office one day and asked, for the umpteenth time, about progress. Arafat quickly told her that word had just been received that her daughter would be permitted to return. As he was relaying the good news, he reached theatrically into the inside pocket of his coat as if looking for a document to prove it. Finding it was not there, he apologized that he had left it at home. After the woman had departed, an incredulous Barghouti turned to Arafat. There was no such document, and no news on the woman's daughter. Why had he misled her? Arafat replied with a smile: 'We couldn't let her go away disappointed, could we?'[35]

In his years as a student leader, Arafat displayed a gift for publicity, an ability to inflate achievements and to gloss over shortcomings, that played no small part in his subsequent rise to the pinnacle of the Palestinian movement. Jaweed al-Ghussein, a student colleague and now chairman of the Palestine National Fund – the PLO's Finance Ministry – remembers Arafat's elaborate preparations for a visit by a delegation of foreign students to the League's sparsely furnished headquarters at 17 Jawad Hosni Street, near the city's central square. Anxious to create a favourable impression, Arafat had borrowed some smart furniture from the next-door offices of the All-Palestine Government and had paid the doorman downstairs to put through a string of telephone calls purporting to be from fraternal organizations in Czechoslovakia and Romania. The international guests were impressed.[36]

A picture emerges of Arafat in those years as an extraordinarily energetic student leader whose dominance of almost all facets of the League's activities sometimes got on his colleagues' nerves, a pattern of behaviour that continues to this day. He was a compulsive doer, and fellow students would often find that tasks they had been allotted had already been performed by Arafat. Other characteristics that emerged early included a volatile temperament which led him to quick bursts of rage, and chronic unpunctuality.

Arafat had no 'concept of time,' recalled Salah Khalaf. 'He was always late.'[37] Sometimes this worked to his advantage. On other occasions it did not; often he would end up with the worst jobs, such as sweeping up after meetings, since he was invariably the last to arrive. Once, his lack of punctuality actually saved him from arrest. Arriving late on the scene of a demonstration and thus avoiding attention, Arafat told his friends smugly: 'See the advantages of being late.'[38] One characteristic of Arafat that was evident then, as it is now, was his elusiveness. He would simply disappear without explanation. Husam Abu Shaaban recalls that as treasurer of the Students' League in 1953 he urgently needed Arafat's signature on some cheques, but could not locate him in Cairo. Eventually he tracked him down in the Western Desert near El Alamein where he was looking for weapons, discarded during the Second World War, to be sent to the resistance in Gaza.[39]

Arafat's other role was to act as something of an ombudsman-at-large for the Palestinian community in Egypt, and by all accounts he was quite adept at it. Salah Khalaf remembered Arafat in 1953 rushing to the town of Suez at the southern end of the canal to take up the cause of a group of Palestinian pilgrims from Gaza who had been trapped in a dispute over transport to Saudi Arabia. The Governor of Suez was not being all that helpful, but when Arafat produced with a flourish the visiting card of Anwar Sadat, one of the leaders of the 1952 revolution, he changed his tune. 'I have this card from Anwar Sadat, and we want these people to go to Mecca,' Arafat declared. The governor quickly put a detachment of police at his disposal to ensure that the pilgrims would get the next available berths across the Red Sea to Saudi Arabia.[40]

During this time Arafat began to take an increasing interest in developments in Gaza, where his father died in 1953, and where Arafat himself still owns property in a street that bears the family name, al-Qudwa. A frequent visitor to the Gaza Strip after the Egyptian revolution, especially to see one of his sisters, Youssra, living there after her marriage to a high-school teacher, he was not at all disappointed by what he found. Palestinian nationalism was flourishing in the narrow strip of land that would prove so troublesome for its Israeli occupiers. Just forty-five kilometres long and an average of six kilometres wide, it had absorbed a huge number of refugees, trebling its population after the war of 1948. By the mid-1950s, it had become the nursery of the most committed Palestinian nationalists and a focus of resistance activity. It was a place of great significance for the men who went on to lead the PLO.

In those days, Gaza enjoyed a special quasi-independent status under a loose, if corrupt, Egyptian administration. Fortunately for the Palestinian resistance, it was spared the same rigid control that applied in the West Bank after Jordan's King Abdullah annexed it in 1950.

Gamal Sourani, a veteran PLO official and native Gazan, says that unlike refugees elsewhere in the Arab world, Palestinians in Gaza were at liberty to 'shout out loud, I am a Palestinian. Egypt had no ambition to annex Gaza or erase the Palestinian identity,' he recalls. 'Palestinians in

Gaza were the first to organize themselves for the liberation of Palestine.'[41]

Into the liberation struggle plunged Khalil al-Wazir, then in his late teens. In 1954 he became, in a word, a *fedai*, which means literally one who offers up his life. He was one of the earliest students of an Egyptian intelligence officer by the name of Mustapha Hafez, who had been authorized by Nasser to organize an underground resistance movement in Gaza. Under Hafez's direction, Wazir and other young men began cross-border raids into Israel.

'We managed to conduct several operations behind the armistice line at the time,' Wazir wrote in a fragmentary account of his early years. 'We also used to send groups to the Negev desert to plant anti-tank mines and other groups to destroy the water pipes in the [Jewish] settlements.'[42]

Arafat himself was not involved in these activities, nor, it seems, did he actually meet Wazir, who was to become his closest lieutenant, until early in 1955. According to Wazir's own account, their first meeting occurred during Palestinian demonstrations following an Israeli attack on Gaza, in February 1955, in retaliation for guerrilla activities in which Wazir himself had been involved.[43]

It was after this Israeli attack that Palestinian students started talking seriously about armed struggle. 'Then we felt we were helpless, nothing was being done,' recalls Zoheir al-Alami, who was elected to the League's executive in 1955. 'The Egyptians were there in Gaza, but they didn't defend us.'[44] The pot was simmering.

While Palestinian nationalism was stirring in Gaza, Egypt was still far from stable in the face of the restless challenge of the *Ikhwan*. Nasser himself was lucky to survive an assassination attempt in the late afternoon of 26 October 1954. As he addressed a large crowd in Alexandria's main square, pistol shots rang out and a lightbulb above his head shattered. Enraged, Nasser ordered a sweep against his political opponents. Among those caught in the net, according to his own account, was Yasser Arafat.[45] As an associate, if not a member, of the *Ikhwan*, his name was almost certainly recorded in the voluminous files of Nasser's secret police. As Arafat tells it, he was freed after three months on the personal intervention of Kamal el-Din Hussein, one of the original 'Free Officers' who had launched the 1952 revolution.[46] Thirty-five years later, Hussein, a precisely spoken veteran of politics and war, has no recollection of such an encounter. He believes, in fact, that his first meeting with Arafat took place in the northern Lebanese town of Tripoli late in 1983.

For Arafat and his closest colleagues in the League, 1956 was an important year and not only because of the cataclysmic events that briefly raised the spectre of superpower confrontation over the control of the Suez Canal. In August 1956, Arafat and his two fellow executive committee members, Zoheir al-Alami and Salah Khalaf, journeyed to Prague for a meeting of the International Students' Congress. They were to gain full membership for Palestine – a small diplomatic victory, but a victory nevertheless. Short of funds, the three travelled deck cargo from Alexandria to Italy and then by plane to Prague, returning the same way. Faded snapshots show the three of them sitting in deck chairs in the stern of the ferry from Alexandria, earnestly studying documents.

Ever the joker in the pack, Arafat had a surprise for his colleagues when they arrived in Prague. From his luggage, he produced a *keffiyeh*, or head-dress, that would become his political trademark and distinguish him in later years from all his PLO contemporaries. His amused companions had not known that he had planned to dress up for the Prague conference, but after witnessing the attention a *keffiyeh*-clad Arafat attracted to the Palestine delegation, they followed his example at a similar student gathering the following year.[47]

Arafat's first *keffiyeh* was white. For many years, he has worn a carefully starched black-and-white version folded in such a way as to match the dagger-like shape of Palestine. Apart from sensing the *keffiyeh*'s theatrical possibilities, Arafat also wanted to make an historical point, it seems: those engaged in resistance against British troops and the Zionists in Palestine in the 1936–9 revolt had worn the *keffiyeh* as part of their battle-dress.

The Prague mission introduced the aspiring Palestinian leaders to an odd assortment of East Bloc and Third World student activists. These connections would provide them with a network of support in the years ahead, but communication with their fellow student leaders in Prague was not always easy. None of the three Palestinians could speak much English, let alone French or German. On the boat they had each learned a short speech in English about Palestine and would recite it to anyone who would listen. With amusement, Khalaf recalled: that after reciting part of his address to a Norwegian delegate, the woman had interrupted and said: 'By the way, I just met one of your friends who used exactly the same words.'[48]

After the congress, the three received invitations to visit surrounding East Bloc countries. Al-Alami went to Moscow and Khalaf to East Germany. Arafat succumbed to a debilitating virus that laid low many of the student delegates, and was taken to hospital to await his friends' return.[49] But even on his sick bed, Arafat made quite an impact on those around him. Peter Ruehmkorf, a German student activist and now one of his country's better-known poets, has a particularly vivid recollection of his own hospital encounter with the PLO leader-to-be. According to Ruehmkorf, he shared a ward in the Central Hospital with two Indians, two Algerians, one Venezuelan, one Madagascan, one Cuban and one 'Mr Palestine'. When Mr Palestine had recovered sufficiently to engage Ruehmkorf, in the next bed, in conversation, it was to mount an imaginary and full-scale assault on the Jews. 'With extravagant gestures,' Ruehmkorf writes in his autobiography, 'he began to drive the Jews (that was me) into an imaginary sea (to the right of my bed) in the process of which he absent-mindedly turned my bed cover into a map with already occupied towns here, high points still to be captured there, and my dressing gown as the centre of resistance.'[50]

So enthusiastic was Mr Palestine's assault on his imaginary Jewish adversaries that Ruehmkorf, who was afraid of being driven into a make-believe sea himself, put his neighbour in a fraternal arm-lock until Arafat was 'liberated', not by his fellow Third World patients, but by hospital orderlies.[51] For Ruehmkorf, this was not the last word from Arafat. Some time later he received a hand-written note from Cairo expressing 'warm regards to my West German friend', and signed . . . 'Mr Palestine'.[52]

Arafat, Khalaf and al-Alami returned to Nasser's Egypt on the eve of one of the great military and diplomatic dramas of the twentieth century. Sir Anthony Eden, Britain's Prime Minister, appalled by Nasser's abrupt nationalization of the Suez Canal on 26 July, determined to have his revenge. On 29 October, under a secret agreement with France and Britain, Israeli troops crossed into the Sinai. They faced little resistance and within two days had reached the east bank of the Suez Canal. On 5 November, British and French paratroopers parachuted into Port Said at the entrance to the Suez Canal, supported a day later by British troops brought in by sea. Street-to-street fighting over the next few days left 2700 Egyptian civilians and soldiers killed or wounded and some 150 casualties among the British and French. To make matters worse, the canal itself was blocked with sunken vessels.[53]

Qualified as a reserve officer in the Egyptian Army from his university training, Arafat was called up to serve as a bomb disposal expert. He served, he says, in the headquarters of General (later Field Marshal) Abdel Hakim Amer, the commander-in-chief of the Egyptian armed forces.[54] It is not exactly clear what role he played in the hostilities, which in any case turned out to be a short-lived affair.

International pressure forced a ceasefire at midnight on 6 November and Nasser emerged a towering hero in the Arab world. He had defied the might of Britain and France, not to mention Israel. It was a 'victory' that seemed to Arafat and his colleagues to augur well for the Palestinian cause, but as they shortly discovered, nothing could have been further from the truth. In full cry after his triumph over the tri-partite aggression, Nasser cracked down even harder on the *Ikhwan* and anyone else he considered a threat to public order. Student activists who had flirted with the *Ikhwan* were among those kept under close surveillance. The ubiquitous Egyptian secret police had, in any case, long been taking a close interest in Arafat's activities.

His time in the country of his birth was coming to an end. Cairo had ceased to be fertile territory for aspiring revolutionaries whose views did not correspond with Nasser's florid pan-Arabism. 'The atmosphere in Cairo for the Palestinian movement was very difficult,' Arafat recalls. 'The interests of the Egyptians lost touch with the Palestinian movement, and became more involved in Arab Unity and pan-Arabism. After the Suez Canal War, Nasser began to move on the other side.'[55] What Arafat meant was that the Egyptian President had begun to support a Palestinian pan-Arabist tendency that was in opposition to his (Arafat's) own robustly independent views of where the Palestinian movement should be heading. One of the immediate beneficiaries was the Arab National Movement of George Habash. Much to Arafat's chagrin, Habash and his followers began receiving material support from Nasser in the mid-1950s.

Mohammed Abdel-Raouf Arafat al-Qudwa al-Husseini graduated from Cairo University in 1956, seven years after entering the faculty of engineering. His graduation project was a study of local sanitation and his first job as an engineer was with the Egyptian Cement Company, then engaged in a project at Mahallah Kubra, a stiflingly dull industrial town about two hours' drive north of Cairo. It was clear from the start that Arafat's heart was not in his new career. Restlessly, he sought alternatives, establishing a union of Palestinian graduates so that he could continue to have a forum for political activities, taking part in demonstrations in the Gaza Strip after the Suez Canal War, visiting Iraq immediately after the mid-1958 coup in which the monarchy was overthrown.[56] But none of this satisfied his craving for action. Besides, he was under unwelcome pressure from his eldest sister, Inam, to get married to one of his Abu Saoud cousins and settle down.

Bored and unfulfilled, Arafat left the oppressive atmosphere of Egypt soon after his return from Baghdad. Seeking an antidote for the *ennui* that had settled over him since the 1956 Suez crisis – and, just as important, seeking money – he headed for the relative political freedom of Kuwait. In Arafat's words he left for the Gulf state because 'I really wanted to work and I wanted money, to speak frankly, and besides the atmosphere around me in Egypt was not an active one and not healthy.'[57]

# 2

# *Struggle*

> 'Let the imperialists and Zionists know that the people of Palestine are still in the field of battle and shall never be swept away.' Al-Asifa communiqué No. 1, 1 January 1965.

One evening in the second half of 1958, five young Palestinian professionals gathered in a house inhabited by one of their number in Kuwait. Talking into the night, they lamented the loss of Palestine a decade before. They spoke of their disenchantment with the Arab regimes and political parties of the day. And, dropping their voices to a whisper, they talked about organizing themselves for action.

Of the five young men present, two were already firm friends: Yasser Arafat and Khalil al-Wazir. In their earlier meetings in Cairo and Gaza, they had reached two simple conclusions. The Arab states, they reasoned, were not going to recover Palestine by force of arms. The Palestinians would therefore have to take their future into their own hands.[1]

Now, in conditions of great secrecy, Arafat and Wazir had decided to share their thoughts with a few select contemporaries. A revolutionary movement had begun, and it would soon have a name: Fatah.

Kuwait in the late 1950s was not exactly the sort of place where you would expect to find armed revolution being plotted. A sleepy backwater still under a British protectorate, the emirate had been largely sheltered from the political turbulence then sweeping through other parts of the Middle East, but it could not remain immune. As the Gulf states woke up to their oil riches and the need for hospitals, schools and roads, they attracted increasing numbers of young, educated Palestinians in search of work. Arafat and his friends from student days, anxious to earn money in order to pursue their political activities, were no exception. Wazir took a teaching job in Saudi Arabia for six months before landing up in a secondary school in Kuwait. Arafat used his degree to obtain a post as a junior site engineer in the road-building and sewage section of the Kuwaiti Public Works Department.

To the 29-year-old Arafat, arrived from the teeming metropolis of Cairo, Kuwait came as something of a shock. Living and working conditions were spartan to say the least. As one of his Palestinian contemporaries who had arrived earlier in the 1950s recalls: 'There was nothing here when I came. You couldn't say there was an established Palestinian community. There was a sizeable number of Palestinians, and they were sticking together because they were put in houses together. The majority were bachelors or came without their wives. There was no electricity, no glass in the houses, no tiles, no cement. The climate was horrible.'[2]

Arafat found himself living in purpose-built staff quarters with doctors, civil servants and other professionals in Suleibikhat, fifteen miles outside Kuwait city. His office was a prefabricated shed, but the road-building job meant that he was often out in the open, exposed to a searing sun and temperatures of up to 120 degrees Fahrenheit. At first, he did not find the work easy, partly because the chief engineer was British and Arafat's command of English was distinctly shaky.

Kuwait had other attractions, though, which helped to make up for the appalling humidity, the lack of air-conditioning and the rusty-coloured water that trickled out of the taps. For one thing, the political atmosphere was relatively relaxed. Palestinians who had come from countries like Syria sensed the difference immediately: so long as they stayed out of Kuwaiti affairs, they were left to their own devices and enjoyed near-total freedom of expression and assembly. If there were problems, there were Palestinians in positions of influence who could help to sort them out: men such as Talat al-Ghussein, a Palestinian civil servant who later became Kuwait's ambassador to Washington; and Hani al-Kaddoumi, who as director of the Interior Minister's office offered much assistance with visas, sponsorships and introductions to the right people. Above all, there was sufficient money around to give the young Palestinian professionals who had gravitated to the Gulf their first genuine taste of financial independence.

Freedom, money and powerful friends: these three elements turned Kuwait into fertile soil in which the seeds of political activism sown in Cairo began to germinate. There was little else for these bachelors so far from home to do after work in the evenings but talk, and the late-night talk was all about politics and Palestine.

A host of Palestinian groups – by one count, as many as forty in Kuwait alone – sprang up around this time.[3] Most were just informal debating forums with a few members. Some had more serious intentions.

Arafat and Wazir – better known in later years by his *nom de guerre*, Abu Jihad – were in no doubt about what was to be done. They were intent on uniting Palestinians in a violent struggle against Israel. To say this was an ambitious task would be an understatement. Since the 1930s, Palestinian society had been notoriously fractious; indeed, a breakdown of society amid bitter feuding between rival clans had been one reason for the great exodus of Palestinians from their land in 1947–8. In exile the divisions had only widened, exacerbated by the conflicting ideologies – from secular Arab nationalism to militant Islamic fundamentalism – then swirling about the Arab world. Arafat and Wazir, members of a generation that had grown up in exile, were determined to leave all this behind. Their movement, they decided, should embrace all Palestinians, regardless of previous political affiliations. And they began to put across this simple message – liberate Palestine – in a crudely produced magazine that started to appear sporadically in 1958, *Filastinuna: Nida Al Hayat* (Our Palestine: The Call of Life).

*Filastinuna* was essentially the handiwork of Wazir, who had always wanted to be a journalist and indeed displayed a facility for words as well as for organization. Printed at first on a stencil machine, it was filled with lurid sketches, stark photographs and simply written poetry and prose. Anonymous articles – a rare exception being one in the first issue carrying the initials Y.A. – discussed the plight of the Palestinians, expounded their right to return to their homeland, criticized Arab regimes for their failure to act, and called on the Palestinians to unite and take up arms against Israel.

Slogans crowded the magazine's unruly pages: revolutionary violence; popular liberation war. There were pieces drawing attention to the War of Independence then being waged by the Algerians against their French colonial rulers – a struggle whose successful outcome in 1962 would have an enduring impact on the emergent Palestinian leadership. There were also articles dissecting the Zionist movement and its leaders, people like the notorious Jewish underground fighter Menachem Begin. Even at this early stage, Arafat and his associates were trying to learn from their Israeli enemies.

But the magazine was more than just an outlet for rhetoric and rudimentary analysis; its young editors meant it as a channel of communication and organization throughout the Palestinian diaspora. They had, by definition, to be discreet, because they were treading on sensitive political ground. The Arab states, in particular, were most unlikely to approve of their activities. The insecure heirs to Arab rulers who had borne a heavy measure of responsibility for the original displacement of the Palestinians in the 1948 war were now trying to appropriate the Palestinian cause for themselves in an effort to cover their embarrassment. Posing as standard-bearers for the sacred struggle, Arab governments would not brook any rivals – and certainly would not tolerate anything resembling an independent Palestinian organization. Arab countries neighbouring Israel kept the Palestinian refugees to whom they were reluctantly playing host on a tight leash.[4] If the Palestinians were to do something for themselves, they would have to operate underground.

During a visit to Lebanon in 1959, Arafat and Wazir persuaded an influential friend, Tawfik Houri, to seek the authorities' permission to publish *Filastinuna* from Beirut, then the hub of a thriving Arab publishing industry and a centre for political activity of all kinds. From that point, between 5000 and 10,000 copies of the magazine were distributed regularly to Palestinians all over the Middle East and beyond. Every edition carried a Beirut P.O. box number (1684) through which readers could get in touch, creating a network of contacts which proved extremely useful to Arafat and Wazir as they set out to recruit like-minded Palestinians to the cause.[5]

As *Filastinuna* took shape, so did the movement known as Fatah. Arafat and Wazir had already drawn up general guidelines which they now elaborated into a formal political programme and organizational structure, circulated secretly by hand among trusted friends and acquaintances. One of the main issues for debate was what to call the new organization. 'We first agreed that we were neither a party nor an association but a movement with all its dynamic implications,' explained Wazir. 'And the movement was for the liberation of Palestine.'[6] The name Fatah was, according to some accounts, the brainchild of one Adel Abdelkarim, a clever young mathematics teacher who had been present at that first meeting with Arafat and Wazir in 1958 and who thought it up by taking the Arabic words for Palestine Liberation Movement (Harakat Tahrir

Filastin) and reversing their initials. Spelt forwards, the initials meant 'Death' (Hataf); backwards, they spelled the altogether more appropriate word 'Conquest.'[7]

Having laid the foundations, the young activists now faced the task of building up structures that extended beyond Kuwait. According to Salah Khalaf, who had by now joined his friends, this effort began at another discreet meeting in a private house in Kuwait on 10 October 1959. It was a small affair, involving fewer than twenty politically active Palestinians – many of whom had contacted the founders through the all-important P.O. box 1684 – but it marked the real beginning of Fatah as an organization.[8] Members were still engaged in talk rather than in action, but it was clearly understood by all that the eventual goal was to take up arms.

At that stage, their overriding preoccupation was secrecy, a concern inculcated by restrictions on Palestinian activism in other Arab countries and by a desire to insulate the movement from infiltration by Arab intelligence services. It was this which determined the tightly knit cell structure that Fatah began to construct in different locations, the caution its leaders displayed in vetting potential recruits, and the care they took in concealing their movements outside Kuwait.

'At the start we would not talk about our plans to anybody,' said Salah Khalaf. 'We kept our secret so close that the word Fatah would not be mentioned except to a member. Only Fatah members could see our two basic documents, the organizational structure and the political programme.'[9]

Would-be recruits had to be recommended by two or three existing cells and to demonstrate that they had severed all links with Arab political parties. They were then interviewed at length by a member of the inner circle to ensure they could be trusted, and required to take a solemn oath of allegiance which has not changed to this day:

I swear by God the Almighty,
I swear by my honour and my conviction,
I swear that I will be truly devoted to Palestine,
That I will work actively for the liberation of Palestine,
That I will do everything that lies within my capabilities,
That I will not give away Fatah's secrets,
That this is a voluntary oath, and God is my witness.[10]

Members would operate strictly on a 'need-to-know' basis in a cell consisting of only two or three people, often members of the same profession in the same place. They were strictly prohibited from communicating by telephone, and messages from the leadership were delivered in person or via hand-picked emissaries.

All this cloak-and-dagger activity had undoubted theatrical possibilities, which Arafat was quick to exploit. To disguise their identities, Fatah leaders adopted *noms de guerre* based on the Arabic for 'father of', Abu, and often carrying religious or mythical connotations. Arafat chose the name 'Abu Ammar', a reference to the legendary Muslim warrior and close companion to the Prophet Mohammed, Ammar bin (son of) Yasser, a man, incidentally, fabled for his persistence. Wazir became Abu Jihad – *jihad* being the Arabic for holy war.

So insistent were members of the movement on covering their tracks that close relatives often did not know of one another's involvement; legend has it that one married couple only discovered that they both belonged when the wife asked her husband for 50 dinars to give to the cause.

The fact that Fatah's inner circle had known each other for some time was an obvious help. 'One of the reasons for the success of the movement was that it was based on very close friendships,' recalls Hosni Zoaroub, one of the Cairo students recruited by Wazir in 1960. 'This was the secret of its survival.'[11]

Arafat and Wazir were especially close. Apart from the fact that they thought the same way about the need to move from theory to practice, their personalities complemented each other to a striking degree: Arafat impetuous, hot-tempered and hyperactive; Wazir cool-headed, rational and deliberate. Many other early recruits developed an equally strong and durable attachment to the movement: men such as Khaled al-Hassan, a loquacious Palestinian from Haifa, who, as secretary general of the municipal council, was one of Kuwait's most senior civil servants and later became one of Arafat's key political advisers; or Farouk Kaddoumi, a former member of the Baath party who went on to succeed Hassan as 'foreign minister' of the Palestine Liberation Organization.

But there was no doubt, even then, as to who the principal activists were. Arafat, in particular, was already developing a reputation among his peers as a compulsive doer; contemporaries recall him as an intense, single-minded, even obsessive, young man. Inclined neither towards reading books nor towards socializing, awkward in the company of women, he seems to have had no real interests apart from Palestine. And in pursuit of that cause, he and Wazir were without equal for their sheer, dogged perseverance. There was something distinctive and personal about Arafat's monomania; indeed, it contained an echo of his father's costly and single-minded attempts to claim his own inheritance back in the 1940s.

It was now that the freedom and financial autonomy the Palestinians enjoyed in Kuwait proved invaluable. Wazir spent the long school holidays travelling tirelessly, and without telling anyone but his closest friends where he was going, Arafat likewise used his vacations to slip off to other Arab countries to build up useful Palestinian contacts – all filed away in his capacious memory for faces and names. The trips and other expenses were financed entirely from the pockets of Fatah's inner circle, several of whom are said to have devoted half their salaries or more to the cause.

Fatah's need for funds prompted Arafat, within a couple of years of arriving in Kuwait, to supplement his government job with a business career. For him, as for many other expatriates in Kuwait, the oil-fuelled construction boom presented an irresistible opportunity. In 1959, he decided to cash in on the flow of contracts by setting up a private construction venture. By day, he continued to work on the roads; by night, he collaborated with an Egyptian engineer by the name of Abdel Muaz in building up a contracting business specializing in residential property. His government connections enabled him to channel a sizeable quantity of business to Muaz, who managed their joint venture. Palestinian contemporaries report that Arafat personally supervised the construction of six apartment blocks for the sons of a leading Kuwaiti merchant.[12]

With the passage of time, Arafat has taken to exaggerating the scale of his business career and of the wealth it generated. He has told various interviewers that he set up three contracting companies as well as an engineering consultancy; that he owned four cars – two Chevrolets, a Thunderbird and a Volkswagen; and that by the time he eventually left Kuwait he had become a 'small millionaire' with sufficient savings to ensure that he would never have to draw a salary from the Palestinian liberation movement. 'I was very rich . . . I was well on the way to being a millionaire,' he told *Playboy* magazine in 1988.[13] 'I was a contractor. We built roads, highways, bridges. Large construction projects.' To *Time* magazine, the same year, he added; 'Let us say I have enough. Until now I have not taken any money from the PLO or the Fatah organization. I still spend my own money.'[14]

The truth was somewhat different. Palestinian contemporaries agree that he had a penchant for flashy cars and fast driving, but they reckon the sort of sum he stood to make out of his joint venture was in the tens rather than hundreds of thousands of Kuwaiti dinars that he refers to – and in any case Muaz did not hand over any of the money until some time after Arafat left Kuwait. 'He was not very wealthy,' says Khaled al-Hassan, who knew Arafat well from 1960. 'He would have been wealthy if he hadn't joined the revolution.'[15]

There was simply no comparison between Arafat's dabblings and the commercial empires being built up in the Gulf at that time by older Palestinian contractors such as Said Khoury and Hassib Sabbagh – men who became leading business magnates in the Arab world. But this foray into business did give Arafat some experience which would prove very useful in subsequent years. In particular, it taught him the importance of controlling money.

Whatever the state of Arafat's own finances, he and his friends did manage to scrape together enough money to finance a considerable amount of travel for recruitment purposes. The main aim at this stage was to establish a network of influential contacts. Meeting Palestinians around the Gulf and further afield, Arafat and Wazir put the emphasis on quality rather than on quantity. Arafat's principal targets were skilled professionals, especially members of the Palestinian élite who had turned to education as a means of self-advancement – the teachers, doctors, engineers and civil servants who had emerged from the universities of Cairo, Beirut and Damascus and were beginning to dominate the burgeoning bureaucracies of the Arab oil states. Desperate to give their still tiny movement credibility, Arafat and Wazir had few scruples about grossly exaggerating its size and resources, regularly telling potential recruits that they had thousands of fighters and a formidable array of armaments including tanks and helicopters at their disposal. For Arafat, then as throughout his career, the wish was father to the fact.

One important early trip took Arafat down the Gulf to Qatar, another rapidly developing city-state. Qatar, like Kuwait, had enlisted large numbers of Palestinians to staff its schools, oilfields and ministries, and here too they enjoyed unaccustomed personal freedom. 'There had been no censorship since 1956, and we used to hold big rallies under the auspices of the Ministry of Education, which allowed us to address the students about Palestine,' says Rafik al-Natshe, a Palestinian activist who ran the office of the Qatari Education Minister and built up close ties with the emirate's ruling al-Thany family.[16] In parallel with Arafat and his friends in Kuwait, the Palestinians of Qatar had independently begun to organize themselves into secret cells. Several of them were Cairo graduates who remembered Arafat's 'Mr Palestine' exploits and had similar fundamentalist leanings; others knew Wazir from Gaza. During a visit to the emirate in 1961, Arafat persuaded the Qatari group to join forces with Fatah. It was an important step, since the Qatari group had extensive contacts of its own elsewhere in the Gulf and several of the activists involved there later became prominent figures in the Palestinian guerrilla movement. Gradually, during endless smoke-filled meetings in these men's living rooms in Kuwait and Qatar, the plans for revolution were taking shape.

Another significant excursion was to distant Libya, still ruled by a traditional monarchy but in the first throes of its own oil boom. Libya in the early 1960s was home to around 5000 Palestinians. Arafat and Wazir – as ever looking for an influential foothold – sought to recruit the Palestinian deputy director of state security, a man named Abu Nabil, who, as it happened, was a distant relative of Wazir from Gaza. 'They came to me and asked me to join them in Fatah,' he recalls. 'I said I couldn't because I was working for the Libyan security forces, and Palestinian political activity was forbidden under the monarchy. They stayed for three days to try to convince me, and on the fourth day I agreed. They were very keen that I should join because of my contacts with Libyan officials and with the king. Arafat and Abu Jihad were very anxious to get through the king's door.'[17] Their recruitment of Abu Nabil paid handsome dividends in the mid-1960s; as the country's oil revenues rose, wealthy and influential Libyans contributed generously to Fatah's coffers.

There was one other, unexpected area where Fatah's recruitment activities bore quick results: among young Palestinians living in Europe, notably the 3500-strong contingent of Palestinian students in West Germany. From the late 1950s, these radical student activists had begun to organize themselves in the booming German industrial heartland. At the centre was a civil engineering student and former *Ikhwan* firebrand named Hani al-Hassan, whose career had striking parallels with that of Arafat himself.

The younger brother of Khaled al-Hassan, who was already working with Arafat in the Gulf, Hani had been imprisoned in Damascus some years before for his Islamic activities. At the Technical University of Darmstadt, south of Frankfurt, he linked up with like-minded contemporaries to publish a crude magazine by the name of *Al-Awda* (The Return). His group joined forces with the body that Arafat had helped to found some years before, the General Union of Palestinian Students, and at a student congress in Gaza in 1963, Hani al-Hassan's radical views – like Arafat, he called on Palestinians to take the liberation of Palestine into their own hands – brought him to the attention of the Fatah leadership. Several weeks later, Hassan was recruited into the movement by Wazir.

The link thus established between the activists in Kuwait and those in Germany proved a vital source of support for Arafat in the next few years, generating much-needed funds for Fatah's early guerrilla activities and providing numerous trainee commandos. At its peak, the European group had branches in twenty-six German and three Austrian towns, and enlisted Palestinians as far afield as France, Italy, Spain and Sweden. Several of its members later became key Arafat associates, including Hani al-Hassan himself, still a trusted PLO envoy; Abdullah Franji, later the organization's representative in Bonn; and Hail Abdul-Hamid, who, under the name of Abul Houl, is Fatah's security chief. Contacts built up in Europe, notably among revolutionary socialists in

Germany, would also be of vital importance when Fatah turned to international terrorism in the early 1970s.[18]

Such early successes were the exception rather than the rule. In general, recruitment was a slow and painful business, for in its first, clandestine efforts to win broader support among Palestinians, Fatah was swimming against a powerful political tide. Egypt's President Nasser was at the height of his powers and popularity: the hopes of millions had been aroused by his drive to unify the 'Arab nation' and in particular by his country's union with Syria in 1958, which many Palestinians naively saw as a prelude to military action to recover their land. Fatah's narrower view, emphasizing the liberation of Palestine before the mystical goal of Arab unity, struck many contemporaries as heresy. Recalls Khaled al-Hassan: 'It was very difficult for us at the start because Nasser was the great attraction. Most of those who accepted our views were teachers. And every time they went off to other Arab countries for their three-month vacation, we found ourselves having to start all over again on their return.'[19] By 1963, when Fatah – now operating from Wazir's house in the Hawalli district of Kuwait – had contrived to weld together a collection of groups that shared its 'Palestine first' views, the membership still totalled only a few hundred, and the inner circle numbered fewer than twenty.

But in the early 1960s, two events occurred which began to reverse the political tide. First, the Egyptian union with Syria broke up in acrimony only three years after it had begun, swiftly deflating hopes that the Arab regimes were in the process of burying their differences, and Nasser, discreetly putting out word that he had 'no plan to liberate Palestine', initiated instead plans to set up a separate body under his control to represent the Palestinians. Second, in July 1962 the Algerian revolutionaries of the Front de Libération National (FLN) gained independence from France after a bloody, eight-year colonial war. Suddenly, the arguments put forward by Fatah – that guerrilla warfare was the way forward and that Palestinians could and should take it upon themselves to fight the Israelis – began to make more sense.

These developments presented Fatah's leaders with both an opportunity and a challenge. On the one hand, they calculated, the FLN's triumph in Algeria – in a war led both from outside and inside the country by an organization relying principally on its own resources – could serve as a useful model. On the other, Nasser's proposal that the Arab governments set up what was rather vaguely called a 'Palestinian entity' – an idea first put forward at a meeting of Arab League foreign ministers in the picturesque Lebanese town of Chtaura in March 1959 – threatened to fill the same political vacuum that Fatah itself was trying to exploit.

Dimly aware that they were now in a race with the Arab regimes, Arafat and Wazir redoubled their organizing efforts outside Kuwait. In Beirut, Arafat re-established contact with his old friend Zoheir al-Alami, who had arrived back in Lebanon from the US in September 1962 to teach at the American University. Through him, he got to know some of the leading political figures in what was then the cultural capital of the Arab world. Arafat, a dishevelled and preoccupied figure at the time, would show up regularly at Alami's apartment near the Riviera Hotel without so much as a change of clothes. 'In the old days, he never took much care of his appearance,' recalls his friend, who would take Arafat shopping before they embarked on the political round.[20]

Arafat also made a bee-line for Syria. A fiery new leadership had seized power in March 1963 in the latest of many coups and purges, and Arafat sensed that influential figures in the new regime might be persuaded to lend active support. His main target was the military, and he quickly struck gold by making the acquaintance of a Palestinian soldier, Colonel Khaled Hussein, then serving with the

Syrian air force. Hussein was the personal bodyguard of an air force general who had played a key role in the March coup, and who was already developing a reputation for intelligence and ruthlessness in equal measure. The general's name was Hafez al-Assad; this first meeting with Arafat during 1963 marked the beginning of a long and chequered relationship.[21]

But perhaps Arafat's most valuable *entrée* had come in Algeria, while the FLN nationalists were celebrating their 'liberation' from France. He and his friends had long admired the Algerian independence movement, and some Palestinians had actually sought to join the FLN's war, but the link between Fatah and Algeria's revolutionaries had been cemented in Cairo. Arafat's elder brother Gamal had befriended an exiled Algerian freedom fighter named Mohammed Khider and that relationship had yielded an invitation to Yasser Arafat to attend Algeria's independence celebrations, and to Fatah to establish a mission of its own in Algiers.

This was a breakthrough for the Palestinian group, still operating underground and without support from any Arab government. Not only did opening a first office give Fatah the chance to venture cautiously on to the surface of Middle Eastern politics. More than that, Algiers, now becoming a self-styled centre for the world's liberation movements, enabled Arafat and his associates to establish a wide range of new friendships that were to prove vital as they prepared to embark on their 'armed struggle.'[22]

The man chosen to head the new Bureau de la Palestine (after Gamal had made a start but was withdrawn owing to inadequate command of French) was Khalil al-Wazir. In 1963, Wazir became the first Fatah member to leave his job and devote himself to the struggle full time. Together with his teacher wife Intissar, a young baby and a 'family' of office employees, he established himself in penurious circumstances at No. 15 avenue Victor Hugo, Algiers. Living in an attic above the office, he set about increasing the number of Palestinians in Algeria by arranging student scholarships and teaching jobs. He had articles published in Algerian newspapers extolling the virtues of Fatah and armed struggle, much to the puzzlement of the local intelligentsia. And he also worked to consolidate Fatah's ties with the ruling FLN.

The latter was no easy task at first, since the new regime was convulsed by a power struggle between the charismatic post-independence leader, Ahmed Ben Bella, and the military man who eventually ousted him, Colonel Houari Boumedienne. At one point the authorities were being so obstructive that Wazir was ready to quit in defeat. But when Boumedienne took power a period of fruitful cooperation began. Algeria became Fatah's most solid and constant supporter amid the otherwise shifting sands of Arab politics, and to this day, its friendship remains more dependable than any of Arafat's other alliances.[23]

In Algiers, more than 2000 miles from Palestine, Wazir was able in 1964 to establish the first summer training camp for around one hundred fighters, and to arrange instruction in rudimentary guerrilla techniques for a further twenty at the newly opened Cherchel Military Academy. He laid the groundwork for some of Fatah's earliest supplies of arms and funds. Most important of all were the contacts he made with sympathetic foreign governments and liberation movements. Working the diplomatic circuit, Wazir got to know a junior official at the Chinese embassy in Algiers, and managed to obtain an invitation for himself and Arafat to visit Peking as guests of the Chinese Committee for Afro-Asian Solidarity. They arrived on 17 March 1964, travelling on false passports under the respective pseudonyms of Galal Mohammed and Mohammed Rifaat. They met a senior Communist Party official, Liao Cheng-chih, who offered vague expressions of support for the cause, and Wazir went on to North Vietnam, a country then pursuing its own 'liberation struggle'.[24]

Back in Algiers, Wazir and his deputy, Mohammed Abu

Mayzar, had the Palestinians' first and only encounter with that guerrilla icon, Che Guevara. It took place in the summer of 1964 – ironically enough, in the headquarters of the former French governorate, an edifice the Algerian revolutionaries had turned into the Hotel Aletti and were using to host a conference of liberation movements from around the world. 'I remember Guevara with his fatigues, his beret and his cigar,' recalls Abu Mayzar. 'It was the first time he had heard about Palestine. He was astonished that we had not begun our revolution already, but said that if we did begin we would immediately obtain Cuban solidarity.'[25]

Guevara touched a very sensitive nerve, for he obliquely alluded to the central difficulty that had afflicted Fatah since its foundation. For years, as they had put the building blocks of Fatah in place, Arafat and the others had spoken in general terms about launching an 'armed struggle' to wrest Palestine back from the Zionists, but in their preoccupation with organizational tasks, they had been unable to agree on what form the struggle might take, or when it might be mounted; and all they had managed to do thus far was send a few score Palestinians for basic weapons training in Algeria. Arafat himself was impatient to begin, but he was still very much one among equals in the movement. Now their debate was coming to a head as a result of political moves beyond the Palestinians' control.

On 13 January 1964, President Nasser had summoned his fellow Arab leaders to a summit meeting in Cairo. Top of the agenda was a project that was causing immense anger and frustration in the Arab world: Israel's diversion of water from the River Jordan, through its National Water Carrier, to the Negev desert. Nasser feared that Israel's plan would strengthen its capacity to absorb large numbers of new immigrants and in the process erase the Palestinian issue once and for all. But the project had also become an emblem of Arab impotence. Powerless to do more than expostulate, the summit covered its own confusion by agreeing on Nasser's long-nurtured plan for the creation of an institution to represent the Palestinians. The assembled leaders mandated a middle-aged Palestinian lawyer and diplomat named Ahmed Shukairy to explore ways of setting up a representative body for all Palestinians, a body that became known as the Palestine Liberation Organization.

Shukairy, a florid orator, was well known on the diplomatic circuit, having served with the Arab League and represented Saudi Arabia and Syria at the United Nations. In the West, he later gained notoriety for what was taken as a crude threat to throw the Jews into the sea. As he toured the Arab world in the first half of 1964, consulting Palestinians whose views had long been ignored, he was received with tremendous enthusiasm. Palestinians in Kuwait, Syria and elsewhere leapt at his proposal that they take part in elections to a national assembly to be convened in east Jerusalem, then under Jordanian control, and rallied behind the idea of a Palestine Liberation Army to give the new organization military muscle. The assembly itself, held in Jerusalem's Ambassador Hotel at the end of May, was a grand occasion: a gathering of the clans from all parts of the diaspora at a time when Palestinians were subject to strict travel restrictions, it seemed to many of them to herald a new start in the battle to return to Palestine.

'For me personally, going to Jerusalem was something extraordinary. It was full of hope,' recalls Ahmed Sidki al-Dajani, a leading Palestinian intellectual and writer who had founded his own political movement in Libya in 1958.[26] 'It was like the day of resurrection,' agrees Gamal al-Sourani, a veteran activist who is now secretary-general of the PLO. 'People were meeting together for the first time since 1948.'[27]

To the clandestine leadership of Fatah, however, the advent of Shukairy, a standard-bearer of the older generation, was disturbing news. A body like the PLO, dependent on and subservient to the Arab regimes, was not at all what they had in mind. Worse still, Shukairy's army – albeit a puppet force under Arab command – threatened to divert potential recruits from the 'revolutionary' struggle. 'The establishment of a Palestine Liberation Army was fascinating our people. In general, they were very much attracted to the PLO because it was official and endorsed by Nasser,' says Khaled al-Hassan, another veteran activist who played an important role in the debates within Fatah. 'But we were very much afraid that this PLO would be an alternative to the popular movement. We worried that it would be in the fist of the Arab leaders.'[28]

Fatah sent a handful of its militants to that first Palestine National Council in Jerusalem, led by Khalil al-Wazir, the sole publicly identified member of the movement, rather than the then invisible Arafat. Describing themselves as 'independents', they roamed the corridors of the hotel preaching the need for a 'people's war' and telling anyone who would listen that they had a fighting force of 300 to 400 men waiting to be unleashed against Israel through Jordan.[29]

Arafat and his colleagues also sought to open channels to Shukairy himself. In a series of meetings, they proposed that the PLO should give secret support to Fatah in a sabotage campaign against Israel, a relationship similar to that in pre-1948 Palestine between the Jewish Agency's mainstream Haganah forces and irregular terrorist groups such as Menachem Begin's Irgun and Yitzhak Shamir's notorious Stern Gang. Shukairy, who was in any case infuriated by abuse he was receiving from young Palestinian militants, realized that such underhand dealings risked undermining his connections with the Arab regimes. Rejecting the idea, he tried instead to co-opt Fatah members into the PLO. Relations between him and Arafat swiftly soured.

Fatah was thus brought face-to-face with the question of how to seize the initiative. The process of answering it caused fierce controversy. On one side were Arafat, Wazir and a few impetuous supporters who became known as 'the adventurers' or 'the mad ones', arguing that Fatah should embark on military action without further delay. On the other, a group of more cautious colleagues in Kuwait – 'the sane ones' – insisted that the movement should wait until it had adequate supplies of arms, ammunition, manpower and money.[30]

The advocates of caution, led by an articulate Palestinian named Abdullah Danaan, later a professor of linguistics at Kuwait University, certainly had logic on their side. For all its fearsome rhetoric about 'revolutionary violence', Fatah was pitifully short of weapons and funds, it had yet to build significant popular support, it had very few powerful friends and could field only a handful of fighters. The idea that such a force could set out to take on mighty Israel was simply laughable.

Arafat had never been prone to such doubts. In his view, to wait any longer would be to risk being outflanked by Shukairy's 'official' PLO and portrayed as just one more Palestinian talking shop. Now was the time for action, not words. By initiating attacks on Israel – whatever the odds – Fatah's guerrillas would at least be making waves. The fact that something was being done would trigger off a flow of new recruits and arms supplies. Raids on Israel would provoke reprisals that might draw neighbouring Arab states into the fight. Eventually, by a drawn-out process of action and reaction, the movement might succeed in igniting an all-out conflict with the Zionist enemy, with the Palestinians in the vanguard. Such was the theory – if that is not too dignified a word – of 'popular liberation war', although for Arafat, theory and strategy have always been less important than the compulsive need to be active.

Arafat spent more and more of his time during 1964 preparing for action. He travelled to Syria, where such powerful figures as the Maoist military intelligence chief, Ahmed Suwaydani, were expressing support for guerrilla war against Israel – partly as a way of undermining Nasser's Egypt, which was urging restraint – and where Fatah had been allowed the use of two military training camps.[31] He visited Jordan, preparing commandos and arms caches in the West Bank for the forthcoming battle, and sending messengers with mysterious code phrases around the Arab world. In Kuwait, he lobbied his colleagues tirelessly, summoning fellow Fatah leaders from Qatar and Algiers to discuss what was to be done.

He even sought the Almighty's blessing for his plans. Sometime in 1964, in what must rank as one of the more curious encounters in Arafat's long career, he and Khalil al-Wazir called on an elderly Palestinian monk in Beirut to ask advice. His name was Father Ibrahim Iyad and he was then serving as president of one of Lebanon's ecclesiastical courts. Unusual as it was for two practising Sunni Muslims to seek advice from a Catholic priest, it was also shrewd, for Father Iyad had been active in Palestinian politics since the 1930s and was an influential voice among Palestinian Christians. Securing his backing would help Arafat, by now anxious to play down his *Ikhwan* background, to build support within this important segment of Palestinian society. 'They told me about Fatah and the armed struggle,' recalls Father Iyad, a puckish and sharp-witted man. 'I asked them if they were in need of material help. They said: "No. Just your blessing." ' After talking with them for two hours, the priest sent his visitors on their way with the words they wanted to hear, a sentence which Arafat can still quote today: 'Go in God's peace, and I am with you always.'[32]

By 1964, Fatah had become an almost full-time occupation for Arafat. He was away from his road-building job for months at a stretch, and to justify his prolonged absences pleaded sickness, supporting his claim with forged medical certificates provided by a sympathetic Palestinian doctor. Above all, Arafat was driven by a sense of urgency. 'I had already made a pledge to God and myself,' he says, 'that 1964 would see the launching of our armed struggle.'[33]

The problem preventing his private vow from being fulfilled was that his 'sane' opponents were still refusing to sanction military action. Apart from worrying that armed struggle might turn out to be a dismal failure, they hesitated to give the impetuous Arafat too much of a free hand. He was already attracting criticism for dangerous maverick tendencies and for not consulting sufficiently with his colleagues. To win them over, in the autumn of 1964 Arafat offered a compromise: Fatah would start its attacks but under another name – Al-Asifa, meaning The Storm, a title dreamed up one night on a Kuwaiti beach. 'If Al-Asifa succeeded, Fatah would then endorse the armed struggle,' Arafat explains. 'If Al-Asifa did not succeed, then Al-Asifa would take responsibility for the failure, and not Fatah.'[34] To provide additional assurance for the counsellors of caution, military activities would be under the command not of the volatile Arafat but of Mohammed Yousef al-Najjar, a tough Gazan militant then living in Qatar.

Still the argument raged on. As late as December, the 'sane ones' were continuing to set impossible conditions for the commencement of military action, including a demand that a large reserve of cash be set aside to finance the first operations. Against this background, and with time running out for Arafat's pledge, a young Fatah member named Selim Zaanoun was dispatched to Jordan on 26 December to assess whether conditions were now ripe for the armed struggle. After visiting Amman, Nablus and Jerusalem, Zaanoun reported back to Kuwait that it was time to make a start, and the Fatah central committee duly agreed that attacks on Israel should begin.[35]

It was the cue Arafat had been waiting for. He precipitately gave up his job and left Kuwait without so much as handing in his notice to the Ministry of Public Works. His departure from business was equally sudden; when he left, his partner and clients owed him upwards of 20,000 Kuwaiti dinars, a sum he would only recover some years later through the intervention of a senior member of the

Kuwaiti ruling family. As he embarked on his new life as a guerrilla leader, such savings as he did have were sunk into the Palestinian movement. Arafat, the devotee of fast cars, claims that a trusty Volkswagen Beetle was virtually his sole remaining possession.[36]

From then on, life was lived perpetually on the move: between Beirut; a military camp in Damascus, where Fatah established its first base; and the supposedly 'forbidden kingdom' of Jordan, where strict restrictions on Palestinian political activity were in force. For Arafat, it was a great opportunity to develop his stagecraft. Driving himself around at breakneck speed, he vowed never to sleep in the same place for two nights running and for some reason adopted the pseudonym 'Dr Abu Mohammed'. He also liked to use disguise. Selim Zaanoun was astonished, in late December 1964, to discover his Fatah colleague in Jordan disguised as a Pakistani tourist – though apparently Arafat's cover was almost blown by an Egyptian friend he bumped into in Jerusalem.[37]

As the Fatah leaders took stock of their resources that winter, the picture was not exactly encouraging. Their ranks were still deeply divided, with some of those who disapproved of the decision to start fighting now peeling away from the movement. Fatah had a bank account in the Ras Beirut branch of the Palestinian-owned Arab Bank, opened by Zoheir al-Alami with himself and Arafat as co-signatories, but it contained very little money. Indeed, Alami had to finance the first guerrilla operations with an overdraft of between 6000 and 7000 Lebanese pounds.[38] And on the ground, Fatah had a sum total of twenty-six fighters armed with a paltry array of creaking old weapons.[39]

Some of the fighters themselves could scarcely believe that Arafat was planning to launch a military onslaught on Israel on this basis. Preparing for the first actions in December 1964, one of the commando units discovered that five men were supposed to share three firearms, including a hunting rifle and a rusty machine-gun that would disgorge only three bullets in a burst and required persistent thumps to function more than once. One of the guerrillas, a squat, moustachioed man named Abul Ezz, carried what little spare ammunition there was in a handkerchief in his pocket. When he received his orders, Ezz is said to have laughed and asked his masters: 'What does Abu Ammar want, to liberate Palestine with this rusty gun?'[40] Another commando, who had been ordered to go and blow up an Israeli phosphate plant with a hand-made bomb, challenged Arafat with the words: 'Dr Abu Mohammed, you have been talking to us for six months about starting the revolution. Now that we are to start, is it possible that we will start in such a primitive way?' With characteristic bravado, Arafat reassured him: 'When the fuse of this bomb goes off, it will cause an explosion not only in the phosphate factory but in the whole of the Middle East.'[41]

Starting from such meagre origins, the 'Palestinian revolution' was, above all, a revolution of symbols. Fatah lore traces it to New Year's Day, 1965, when a typed statement entitled 'Al-Asifa Communiqué Number One' was dropped into Beirut newspaper offices. It was a piece of bombast that vastly exaggerated the modest dimensions of the first *fedayeen* raids. 'From among our steadfast people, waiting at the borders, our revolutionary vanguard has issued forth, in the belief that armed revolution is our only path to Palestine and freedom,' it grandly proclaimed.[42] There was only one problem. The action this portentous statement was supposed to be announcing, a raid into northern Israel from Lebanon on New Year's Eve, had not taken place. Embarrassingly, the first Fatah *fedayeen* action was a damp squib. The Lebanese authorities had arrested the raiding parties before they set out.

Indeed, most of the Arab states bordering Israel showed no inclination to encourage the *fedayeen*; only a few days into January 1965, Jordanian troops shot a Palestinian guerrilla as he returned from a raid into Israel. It was significant that Fatah's first '*martyr*', Ahmed Musa, died from an Arab bullet.

When Al-Asifa operations did get under way, a few days later, they turned out mostly to be pinprick affairs. Planned in close co-operation with Syrian military intelligence, they were aimed at symbolic targets such as Israel's National Water Carrier – the scheme that had been the subject of so much hand-wringing by the Arab states – and caused few Israeli casualties. The Israeli authorities, who captured their first *fedayeen* prisoner near Jerusalem on 7 January 1965, had little trouble dealing with the small numbers of guerrillas involved. In many cases, the operations were actually carried out by local rustlers and smugglers, a fact which scarcely inclined the Israeli authorities to take the Palestinian insurgency seriously. 'The first terrorist raids were a nuisance, not a strategic threat – not politically, nor militarily,' remarks General Aharon Yariv, at the time Israel's head of military intelligence.[43]

If this was the puny reality of Fatah's early military efforts, its leadership set out in the first few months of 1965 to create a quite different impression. A stream of boastful communiqués started pouring into media organizations in Beirut and Damascus, typed by Khalil al-Wazir in an apartment in west Beirut, copied on a stencil machine and distributed by Arafat in his VW Beetle. Almost invariably they claimed that Al-Asifa units had inflicted heavy casualties on Israeli military patrols or had blown up key parts of the Zionist infrastructure before returning safely to base.

In the Arab world, word of Fatah's attacks set off a variety of conflicting political waves. In terms of money and arms, the decision to launch armed struggle swiftly began to pay dividends, as Arafat had predicted it would. Early in 1965, three Kuwaiti citizens came up with a contribution of between seven and eight thousand Kuwaiti dinars, more than adequate to clear al-Alami's overdraft. Members of the Qatari ruling family also began to stump up secret gifts of money – enough to help the guerrillas buy weapons on the open market to augment their rudimentary arsenal – and of other items, such as Racal communications equipment and a pair of night binoculars. Then came a windfall beyond the leadership's wildest expectations: a donation of 22,000 riyals from a wealthy Saudi. The amount was less important than the identity of the benefactor, none other than Sheikh Ahmed Zaki Yamani, a close confident of King Faisal. The connection was to be of critical importance for Fatah. It was also useful to the Saudis, who approved of the new Palestinian group's *Ikhwan* background and were keen to back any movement likely to be disapproved of by their sparring partner, Egypt. Arafat was already developing an aptitude for manoeuvring amid the perpetual squabbles that divide the Arab world.

In 1965 and 1966, Yamani arranged for members of the leadership to meet the Saudi monarch secretly, and the Saudis began discreetly supplying Fatah with arms, a liaison conducted through an official in their embassy in Ankara who would bring weapons via Syria to Lebanon in his diplomatic car.[44]

Fatah was still not by any stretch of the imagination wealthy or well-equipped; on occasion, Arafat had to borrow money from friends in the Syrian National Guard to finance commando actions. But thanks to Arab financial and military contributions, coupled with collections by those Fatah leaders still in Kuwait and Qatar, the movement was on its way. In 1966, its first official shipment of arms from an Arab government was sent in a transport plane from Algeria, delivered courtesy of Syria's General Hafez al-Assad.

From other Arab countries, however, the reaction to the guerrilla movement's activities was much more circumspect, not to say downright hostile. Since nobody could pinpoint exactly who was behind the mysterious Al-Asifa, everybody leapt to his own self-serving conclusions, conservative Arab states depicting the Palestinian militants as agents of international communism and Ahmed Shukairy's PLO calling them enemies of the Palestinian liberation movement. President Nasser suspected Arafat and his comrades of being a front for the *Ikhwan*. Egyptian intelligence inserted smears in the Cairo and Beirut press, denouncing Fatah as the tool of a grandiose plot by the Western powers and Zionism, aimed at providing Israel with a pretext to attack its Arab neighbours.[45] And Nasser's aides belittled Al-Asifa as 'a group of enthusiastic young Palestinians who think that the operations they undertake inside Palestine will lead to instability within Israel'.[46]

The controversy showed how Fatah's early burst of activity against Israel had set off alarm bells in Arab capitals. The conventional wisdom then was that the Arab states should not act until they were united and ready to defend themselves in a conventional war. Fatah's guerrilla raids risked provoking Israeli reprisals which might drag the Arab front-line states into a fight at a time most emphatically not of their choosing. So it was that Nasser's men put out word that Fatah cross-border attacks should be restrained. Palestinian guerrillas were arrested in the Egyptian-controlled Gaza Strip. Jordan and Lebanon, which had served in spite of official restrictions as the two principal launching pads for Fatah raids into Israel, were only too glad to follow suit. Reports about Al-Asifa's activities were censored, so much so that the oxygen of publicity sustaining Fatah through these early years came mainly from Israeli news reports.

Even within Fatah, opinion was still divided about guerrilla actions. Among the radical students in West Germany who had rallied to the flag in the early 1960s and who were vehement in their rejection of Shukairy's PLO, the fact that the armed struggle had begun provoked a tremendous upsurge of enthusiasm. In Darmstadt and Frankfurt, students made regular collections among Palestinian migrant workers, raising thousands of marks a month. Khalil al-Wazir would travel to Germany to collect the proceeds, using Algerian passports and a variety of pseudonyms and carrying 'official' receipts stamped with the logo of Al-Asifa.[47] But back in Kuwait, unease persisted about the commando activities. Those Fatah leaders, such as Khaled al-Hassan, who had stayed behind in the Gulf, worried that they were losing control of the movement, and their concern was only intensified when Mohammed Yousef al-Najjar, the group's first military commander, handed over to Arafat himself – the leader of the 'mad ones'. Najjar, who had six children, found he had neither the time nor the money to devote to the struggle. The unmarried Arafat, by contrast, had all the time in the world and used it to burnish his credentials as an active guerrilla fighter, as well as to develop his own inimitable leadership style. Arafat's eager participation in raids on Israel brought him much respect, but his autocratic behaviour as leader caused mounting fury among the armchair revolutionaries still working in the Gulf. They tried to rein him in by cutting back the supply of funds for the guerrillas, but to no avail. By early 1966, tensions within the leadership had reached such a pitch that an open split seemed probable. And on 2 May, the Fatah central committee decided to suspend Arafat as military commander on charges that would become familiar in later years. He was accused by his colleagues of dispensing money 'in an irresponsible manner', of 'failing to carry out collective decisions', of taking 'unauthorized trips', and of sending 'false reports, especially in the military field'.[48]

To make matters worse, problems were also looming for the guerrilla movement in Syria, Fatah's front-line base. Behind the scenes in Damascus, a power struggle was unfolding between radicals who believed in promoting all-out guerrilla warfare and a posse of more conventionally minded military men. In 1966, this produced frictions between Arafat and his Syrian sponsors. The more Arafat battled to assert his own leadership of the *fedayeen*, the more the Syrians – who supported and had given army training to a rival guerrilla commander named Ahmed Jibril – worked to bring the Palestinians under tighter control.

There had already been a taste of trouble. Sometime in early 1966, Arafat had been arrested in Syria and accused of having sent a commando unit to blow up the Tapline, the American oil pipeline linking Saudi Arabia with the Mediterranean. Although he was quickly released, the incident only increased friction between the two sides.[49]

On 9 May, just one week after Arafat's suspension as military commander by his Fatah colleagues, tensions with Syria erupted in a violent argument in the house where Arafat was living in the Mazraa district of Damascus. Arafat, it seems, was not present, but the dispute provoked one of the gravest crises between Fatah and the Syrians, and came very close to extinguishing Arafat's own career.

It started as a row between two Palestinians then working with Fatah: a loyal commando by the name of Mohammed Hishme, who had just returned from a raid on Israel in which he had broken his leg, and a Palestinian officer in the Syrian armed forces, Yousef Ourabi, who had been drafted to work with Arafat. As the argument progressed into the evening, Ourabi suggested baldly, according to witnesses, that he, on behalf of Syria, would shortly be taking control of the Palestinian *fedayeen*. Tempers flared, both men pulled out their guns, and both ended up dead.

The circumstances of the killings have still not been adequately explained. Some suggest the two men killed each other; others, including Arafat himself, affirm that a Palestinian officer in the Syrian army who arrived during the argument was responsible. Arafat and many of his colleagues believe to this day that it was a frame-up. As he puts it, 'Fatah was not the aggressor in that incident; it was the target of aggression.'[50]

Whatever the real explanation, the Syrian authorities certainly took advantage of the ensuing confusion to move against the Fatah leadership. As well as arresting those on the scene, they rounded up Arafat (for the second time), Khalil al-Wazir and an aide named Abu Sabri, who had been in a nearby house when the killing occurred, and took them at midnight to military police headquarters. One by one over the next few days, they were taken from the military prison to the Doumeir air base 100 kilometres outside Damascus, and subjected to lengthy and sometimes violent interrogations aimed at ascertaining whether Fatah had had a hand in Ourabi's murder. They were then placed in solitary confinement in the capital's notorious Al-Mezza prison, then as now the home of large numbers of political prisoners.

Arafat was outraged, not least because it seemed that the investigation was being personally overseen by none other than General Hafez al-Assad, then Syria's Defence Minister. From prison, Arafat fired off a powerfully worded letter to the Syrian leadership, alleging that the authorities were trying to abort the Palestinian armed struggle for suspect motives. He then went on hunger strike, and on the thirteenth day collapsed while saying his prayers.[51]

It was not long before word of the prisoners' plight reached other Fatah leaders in Kuwait. More alarming still were the rumours which accompanied the news: that the Syrian regime planned to hang the lot of them, including Arafat.

Deeply dismayed, two of Arafat's friends, Salah Khalaf and Farouk Kaddoumi, hastened to Damascus. Kaddoumi, a former member of the Baath party – the same party that controlled Syria – set about turning his contacts with the regime to good effect, but everywhere he and Khalaf went, they were told the same thing: 'You're talking to the wrong man. The prisoners are with Assad.'

Eventually, their lobbying led them to the office of the Defence Minister himself. It was, according to Khalaf's account, 'a hard and cold meeting'. There were no friendly greetings and Assad did not even invite his visitors to sit down before asking: 'What do you want?' Khalaf, never one to be intimidated, did not bother to disguise his disquiet. 'What is this?' he fired back. 'Is this rumour that you're going to hang them all true, then?'[52]

There was a moment's icy silence before the Defence Minister agreed to discuss the issue. No sooner had they sat down, however, than Assad launched into a fierce attack on Arafat, accusing him *in absentia* of being an agent of Egyptian Intelligence. 'You're fooled that he is a Palestinian,' he said. 'He isn't, he's an Egyptian agent.' Given the state of Egyptian-Syrian relations at the time, it was a fairly devastating charge and one that appeared to rest solely on the Egyptian dialect with which Arafat spoke Arabic. But then, to the two Palestinians' surprise, Assad let the matter drop. 'OK,' he said after another pause, 'you can go to Mezza [the prison] and take them away. But remember one thing: I do not trust Arafat and I never will.'[53]

With that parting shot the case was closed – for the time being. But Arafat's encounter with the Syrian authorities was an ominous taste of things to come. Even then, it was becoming clear that some of Fatah's biggest problems would come not in its confrontation with Israel but in its dealings with Arab regimes intent on trying to hold sway over the Palestinian cause. The impression was reinforced little more than a month after Arafat's release, when he was arrested yet again – this time in southern Lebanon after returning with a group of commandos from a raid on Israel. Throughout two months of interrogation, in which Arafat says he was 'harassed but not tortured', he insisted he was a Syrian army corporal by the name of Mohammed Ali.[54] The Lebanese authorities eventually accepted the story that he and his fellow combatants were members of a Syrian reconnaissance patrol. It was not until after Arafat's release that they learned his true identity.[55] In later years,

Arafat's ability to talk his way out of such scrapes and his frequent resort to bogus identities would become a powerful part of his mystique. The clash with Hafez al-Assad was to have more bitter and enduring consequences. A coldly calculating man with a long memory, Assad was later to become Syria's most powerful President and Arafat's most implacable enemy.

In Arafat's eyes, however, these unpleasant events conveyed another, perversely encouraging message. They showed that despite its modest beginnings and its often ludicrously inflated claims, Fatah had become a factor to be reckoned with in the Middle East equation. Its continuing raids on Israel were being aped by a growing number of other small Palestinian groups, with grandiose names like the Heroes of Return and the Vengeance Youth. What is more, they were provoking Israeli retaliation of increasing magnitude, as Arafat had hoped they would. The Israelis clashed repeatedly with Syrian forces throughout 1966, and on 13 November launched their biggest action to date, an attack on the village of Samu in the Jordanian-ruled West Bank, supposedly a reprisal for guerrilla raids.

Deeply divided among themselves, Arab states responded by outbidding each other with bellicose rhetoric against the enemy. Inexorably, they were being dragged towards war, and the fulminations from Egypt, Syria and Jordan and from the head of the 'official' PLO, Ahmed Shukairy, ignored the fact that they were hopelessly ill-equipped to fight it. At the end of May 1967, on the eve of what was to become known as the Six-Day War, Shukairy was to be found in a suite at Amman's Intercontinental Hotel predicting with typical *braggadocio* that the Arab states would crush Israel if fighting should break out. Of the Israelis he said: 'I don't expect any of them to stay alive.'[56] He did not have long to wait to discover how wrong he was.

# 3
## *Taking Control*

> 'Not only we but the whole world senses that the Palestinian people have risen to champion their own cause by themselves.' President Gamal Abdel Nasser of Egypt, Revolution Day speech, 23 July 1968.

On 9 June 1967, as the dust began to clear after one of the quickest and most decisive military campaigns in history, a small group of Palestinians huddled round a radio set in a military camp just outside Damascus. At the controls was Khalil al-Wazir. The others – fellow members of the full-time Fatah leadership, together with a group of militants who had hastened to Syria from Kuwait when they heard of the outbreak of war – simply listened in stunned silence as Wazir twiddled the dial.

The Arab news blackout that had replaced early, confident trumpetings about the destruction of the Israeli air force had already made it clear that the fighting was not exactly going the Arabs' way. But only now did the Fatah leaders begin to comprehend the scale of the defeat. Here, live on Cairo Radio, was the voice of the great Arab nationalist hero, Nasser himself, speaking of the 'grave setback' he had suffered, admitting his responsibility for serious miscalculations and vowing 'completely and finally' to resign.[1] There, on the enemy channel, were the sounds of Israel's jubilation at the victory that, within the space of a couple of days, had more than doubled the territory under its control and created a sense of invincibility in the Jewish state.[2]

Nobody in that small, gloomy gathering in the Syrian camp had the slightest doubt as to what Israel's walk-over meant for the Palestinians. Ironically, a war that the Arabs had blundered into, telling themselves that they were about to restore Palestinian rights, had enabled Israel to swallow up all that was left of Palestine. The Israelis, having knocked out the entire Egyptian air force on the ground, had snatched the teeming Gaza Strip from Egypt; they were in full control of the West Bank. Worst of all, the holy city of Jerusalem – Palestine's centre of gravity – had fallen to the Jews.

The news meant much, much more than just a military defeat, a loss of Arab territory and a displacement of more Palestinians. It marked a comprehensive overturning of all the hopes that the Palestinians and other Arabs had pinned on their leaders for much of the previous decade. Ever since the mid-1950s, Nasser and his generation had lulled the masses into a belief in inevitable victory once the Arab states pooled their resources in a conventional war against Israel. In the first few months of 1967, the swaggering and bravado had reached a new pitch as Egypt and Syria battled to outbid each other in bellicose devotion to the Palestinian cause. Yet within a matter of hours it was all exposed as a sham. It was a jolt that every politically aware Palestinian can remember vividly to this day.

'Nineteen sixty-seven was the greatest shock of my life,' says Nabil Shaath, a Palestinian business consultant who has become one of Yasser Arafat's top advisers. 'I remember I was in Alexandria attending a management conference when I heard about the war on June the fifth. I immediately went with some colleagues on a train back to Cairo. During the seven-hour journey, we tuned in to my transistor radio and kept listening to the number of planes Israel had lost. By the time we arrived in Cairo, Israel had lost its entire air force. And I believed it all. Until I got to Cairo, I thought I would be given instructions to leave for Palestine. This was the illusion that was perpetuated by

Egyptian propaganda. But as dusk fell, I reached a Cairo that was under curfew. I had never seen it that way. As I walked to my house in Garden City, I felt that things were not going that well.'[3]

For Palestinians who had placed their faith in the Arab regimes, the absurd falsity of Egyptian official communiqués exacerbated what amounted to a wholesale sense of betrayal. But out of their bitterness and despair sprang new feelings of specifically Palestinian nationalism. Although Nasser agreed to stay on in response to popular acclaim, he would never again be revered by the Arabs as he was before the Six-Day War. The 'official' Palestine Liberation Organization of Ahmed Shukairy had been exposed as an impotent sham. If the Arab regimes and their stooges were incapable of defending the Palestinian cause, then perhaps the Palestinians would now really have to do something for themselves.

Fatah's leaders were still smarting from the shock of defeat as they assembled a few days later in the spacious but poorly furnished living room of Khalil al-Wazir's home in a suburb of Damascus. Many of the twenty or so people present – Palestinians from the Gulf and from as far afield as Europe – were meeting for the first time, their task to consider what, if anything, to do next, and in particular whether to relaunch military raids on Israel. By all accounts it was a tearful and acrimonious session, and the target of much of the recrimination was Yasser Arafat himself. Arafat, the compulsive doer, was convinced that the struggle must go on; his more cautious comrades, including his younger brother Fathi, were equally convinced that this was madness.[4] Was it not, after all, Arafat's insistence on launching the 'armed struggle' back in 1964 that had helped to land the Arabs in this mess? Had the spiral of Arab-Israeli tension of which the guerrillas' pinprick raids formed part not done exactly what Arafat's opponents in the leadership had predicted it would: drag the Arab states into a war for which they were singularly ill-prepared?

One by one, the old arguments against precipitate military action that had been endlessly rehearsed during 1964 resurfaced. Leading the attack on this occasion was Mahmoud Mesweida, a Damascus-based Fatah member with leadership ambitions and Syrian support. Mesweida, a man of Islamic fundamentalist sympathies, argued forcefully against restarting guerrilla activity on the grounds that it would risk provoking heavy Israeli retaliation and 'destroying the movement with nothing to show for it.'[5] To the 37-year-old Arafat and his supporters, this was defeatist talk of the most pathetic order. The miserable performance of Arab armies against Israel, he said, merely vindicated what he had been saying all along about the need for the Palestinians to help themselves. The Palestinian revolution must continue in order to revive popular morale. 'The defeat of 1967 is the prelude to a great victory,' predicted Arafat boldly, if rather implausibly, in front of his squabbling comrades.[6]

Once again, the argument was turning into a battle for control of Fatah's military wing, Al-Asifa. Once again, Arafat manoeuvred with a mixture of skill and theatrics – rushing round the room and getting down on his knees – to fight off trouble. The result was a compromise: the cobbling together of a nine-member interim leadership and the postponement of further discussion.

Arafat, however, was not waiting for the debate to play itself out. Concluding that Fatah had no time to lose if it wanted to capitalize on the state of affairs created by the Six-Day War, he had dreamed up a fresh plan of action: to organize resistance among the million Palestinians living in the territories newly occupied by Israel, the West Bank and the Gaza Strip. As his comrades continued to quarrel in Damascus, he hared south into Jordan and from there, evading Israeli frontier controls, crossed the river into the West Bank. Operating alone for much of the time, he set out to construct a network of secret activist cells. He fondly imagined – in line with the teachings of Mao Tse-tung, an Arabic translation of which was now circulating widely among Palestinians – that he could foster a 'people's liberation war' in which his guerrillas, the *fedayeen*, would blend in among Arab residents like fish in the sea.

Many myths surround Arafat's exploits during this period, not least those propagated by the man himself, who still likes to boast of having been on Palestinian soil at this critical moment. He claims that he made regular visits to the territories to 'lead the resistance movement against the occupation'; that he travelled widely throughout the West Bank, Gaza and the towns of Israel itself; and that his life on the run from the Israeli authorities lasted until early 1968.[7]

This is almost certainly an exaggeration. But, as Israeli officials have since acknowledged, security was lax enough in the early days of the occupation to permit Arafat and his deputy, Abu Ali Shaheen, to slip back and forth from Jordan undetected. They set up a clandestine headquarters in the northern village of Kabatiyeh, near Jenin. From there, they recruited potential guerrillas and smuggled them out for training at Fatah camps in Syria, established arms caches and safe houses, and built a network of sympathizers who would provide the revolutionary 'sea'. Arafat's relatives living in Jerusalem say he even had time to say a clandestine prayer in the Al-Aqsa mosque.

One man Arafat did meet at the time was Faisal al-Husseini, son of the Palestinian hero Abdel Kader al-Husseini, who knew Arafat well from Cairo days. Husseini had been a follower of George Habash's left-wing Arab National Movement, had worked for the 'official' PLO after its initial establishment in Jerusalem, and had subsequently received military training at a Syrian officers' academy. But he switched his sympathies to Fatah when he returned to live in the family house outside the Old City of Jerusalem after the 1967 war. 'We exchanged points of view about military and political work,' Husseini says.[8] Arafat agreed to supply weapons to be stored in Husseini's house, and Husseini undertook to begin training guerrillas in the West Bank.[9] Under the ever-watchful gaze of Israeli security, such promises were a tall order. Arafat himself says he recruited many others in the West Bank in 1967, including Fatah's first woman guerrilla commander and a man who would later become PLO ambassador in Romania and Libya.[10]

In most respects, though, Arafat's forays into the territories were failures. The expected armed revolt did not materialize. The inhabitants of the West Bank, a conservative rural society where political activity had been tightly controlled during the previous two decades of Jordanian rule, were simply not ready for it. Local leaders were still looking principally to Jordan to liberate them from Israeli rule, and discouraged collaboration with alien and disruptive revolutionaries. The supply of arms and funds from outside the territories was never more than a trickle.

Not that this deterred the indefatigable Arafat from delivering an enthusiastic report to his comrades in Damascus. Summoned back in late August 1967 for a fresh meeting of the leadership, amid considerable Syrian pressure on Fatah to halt military action, he suggested that the West Bank was a revolutionary tinder-box that merely awaited Fatah's spark. On the strength of his exaggerated account, the decision was taken to defy the Syrians and relaunch 'armed struggle'. The first attack was duly mounted within the occupied territories a few days later.

Arafat sneaked back across the frontier but contrary to the wilfully optimistic presentation he had given his friends, he swiftly found that organizing in the West Bank was an uphill task, not least because the barren terrain was unfriendly to guerrilla activities. Shortly after his return to the territories, Abu Ali Shaheen was arrested in the northern West Bank town of Jenin and held in an Israeli jail. And it was not long before Arafat himself, operating in the same area, was betrayed but made his getaway; amid the many conflicting stories about his escape, his version is that he got out disguised as a married woman carrying a baby. True or not, the close shave gave him another excuse for myth-making, enabling him to boast, as he has done repeatedly ever since, of his uncanny nose for danger.[11]

This was the last time that Arafat set foot in the occupied territories. As time went by and the occupation came to look more and more like a long-term affair, Israel's grip tightened. When Fatah violence started, the authorities – taking advantage of intelligence files left behind by the Jordanians – arrested hundreds of political activists, smashed the embryonic Palestinian cells and dynamited the houses of those suspected of giving them succour. By December 1967, the Israeli Defence Ministry could announce that 60 *fedayeen* had been killed and 300 imprisoned since the June war.[12]

Arafat's underground activities in the West Bank had one unexpected legacy: they gave rise to the affectionate nickname by which he has been known to intimates ever since. To avoid identifying him by name, his contacts in the villages simply referred to the balding but still relatively youthful guerrilla leader as 'Al Khityar' – literally, 'The Old Man'.[13]

Quixotic it may have seemed, but Arafat's determination to persist in efforts to promote an insurrection in the territories did pay dividends. During the summer of 1967 some 400 Palestinian students and workers left their universities and jobs in Germany to join up. They flew first to Algeria, where they stayed in a military encampment and underwent physical training, and then on to the Hama military base in Syria. Recruits received no more than a week's weapons instruction, and seven bullets to practise with, before being despatched on raids into the West Bank. Poorly qualified and ill-equipped, many of them were arrested and some were killed.[14]

Fatah also received the sincerest form of flattery around this time, when a number of Palestinian imitators went into action. Principal among them was the man who was to be

Arafat's life-long rival: George Habash. For much of his political life, Habash had put his faith in Nasser, arguing that any Palestinian action should be co-ordinated with the acknowledged leader of the Arab world. The defeat of 1967 – bitterly described by Habash at the time as the third occasion on which the Arab armies had failed the Palestinians – changed all that. After the war, the doctor turned further leftwards in his political thinking, opted unequivocally for armed struggle, and tried to join forces with Arafat. The meeting, in a Damascus restaurant during the summer of 1967, was their first.

'I think that the first time we saw that they [Fatah] were right was after 1967. Only after that did we feel that the conditions were right for Palestinian armed struggle,' recalls Habash. 'We talked about what happened in June. We agreed that we were facing a new era and that there was no other way but armed struggle . . . At the time we were insistent on starting something together. We knew that in order to have victory there should be unity.'[15]

Yes, said Arafat to himself, but unity under whose leadership? Whatever he may have told Habash that summer, he had no intention of blending anonymously into some kind of cumbersome guerrilla coalition. He wanted to be out in front. Fatah's August decision to relaunch the armed struggle had in effect been a decision to go it alone.

So began a series of parallel races among the Palestinians. Unity talks with other groups collapsed and, later that year, a separate leftist coalition was formed under Habash's leadership: the Popular Front for the Liberation of Palestine. Armed attacks on Israel accelerated, with a profusion of groups under a bewildering variety of names claiming credit in a battle of ludicrously inflated communiqués. Palestinian factions competed for support from rival Arab regimes. And the regimes themselves, fearful of the new Palestinian self-assertion, hastened attempts to harness and control it, either by setting up their own guerrilla clients – as did Syria and Iraq in the form of Al-Saiqa and the Arab Liberation Front respectively – or by building bridges to existing factions.

The war of the communiqués often made the guerrillas look ludicrous. On a number of occasions, Arafat's group made claims that turned out to be pure fiction: when Israeli Defence Minister Moshe Dayan was injured on an archaeological dig, Fatah took responsibility; likewise, it said it had caused an explosion in the garage of former chief of staff Yitzhak Rabin – although Rabin did not have a garage at the time.[16] If this seemed no more than a puerile competition between commando groups to see who could claim to have inflicted the most casualties on the enemy, it had a more serious point: it was also a contest to fill the vacuum that had developed where there should have been a representative body that would make the Palestinians' voice heard. The new generation of activists was determined to give the lie to Israeli propaganda that said, as Prime Minister Golda Meir did of the Palestinians in a 1969 interview with the *Sunday Times*, that 'they did not exist'. Arafat, for his part, had his sights set on assuming the leadership of the resistance movement for himself and for Fatah. It was his good fortune that there were those within the three-year-old 'official' Palestine Liberation Organization who had similar ideas.

After the Six-Day War, it was obvious that the PLO was as discredited in the eyes of the masses as the Arab regimes that had supported its foundation in 1964. Racked by internal divisions, the organization had come to be seen as little more than a platform for the posturings of its chairman, Ahmed Shukairy, who was now seeking to establish militant credentials by announcing a 'revolution' of his own. Most Palestinians rejected Shukairy and the old guard of bureaucrats and politicians he represented, scornfully termed by the *fedayeen* 'the generation of defeat'. Shukairy's blustering statements were beginning to cause great irritation even among his sponsors and during the second half of 1967, other members of the PLO leadership contacted Arafat to see whether he might be capable of stopping the rot.

Principal among these was the PLO's banker, Abdulmajeed Shoman. As deputy chairman of one of the most respected financial institutions in the Middle East, the Arab Bank, Shoman had maintained close ties with the growing network of wealthy businessmen in the Palestinian diaspora, using them to good effect in his role as chairman of the Palestine National Fund, the PLO's financial arm. When the wave of Palestinian nationalism broke after the 1967 defeat, he was in a position of considerable influence.

Shoman, a dignified man with silver hair and a white moustache, relates how he met the guerrilla leaders later in the year and sought to encourage them to co-operate in reinvigorating the PLO: 'We in the Palestine National Fund spotted Arafat after the Six-Day War. He stood out as a fighter who would pursue the fight until we got our land back. We wanted him to co-operate with Shukairy and improve the Organization; we also tried to persuade Habash to work with Shukairy and Arafat. But Arafat and Shukairy never really got on, they were quite different people. Arafat used to reply to us: "Why don't you hand the PLO over to me, I'd do it differently from Shukairy." '[17]

Events were not long in coming that proved Arafat's assertion in spectacular fashion. In December 1967, seven of Shukairy's colleagues on the Executive Committee demanded that he resign. He refused, prompting a tug of war that was only resolved when Shoman cut off the flow of funds to the PLO leadership. Increasingly desperate, Shukairy appealed for support to his old mentor, President Nasser, but Nasser declined to intervene and on Christmas Eve Shukairy retired to write his memoirs in Beirut.[18] It was the second time in less than twenty years that a Palestinian leader had been dismissed into lonely exile. Despite Shukairy's undeniable contribution to the Palestinian movement, he had come to be seen as something of a figure of fun, a man of words rather than of action. The time had come to hand over to a younger, more assertive generation. Shukairy's replacement as PLO Chairman, an ineffectual left-wing lawyer named Yahia Hammouda, was just a caretaker with the job of preparing for the guerrillas' takeover. Arafat's opportunity had arrived.

In the autumn of 1967, guerrillas belonging to Fatah and other factions had begun establishing bases for cross-border raids into Israel in a cluster of Palestinian refugee camps near the Jordan river. Well below sea level, it was a barren place – blazing hot in summer, freezing cold in winter, surrounded by rocky hills. One of these camps, at a place called Karameh, was the scene of a fierce battle between Israeli forces and the *fedayeen* – a real battle which, once embellished in Fatah propaganda, assumed mythic status for the Palestinian movement.

The build-up to Karameh was well and truly under way by the first weeks of 1968. Palestinian guerrillas, now better armed and trained than before and operating with impunity from Jordanian territory, had become a major nuisance for Israel. Transporting their weapons on makeshift rafts made out of tractor tyres, small groups of commandos would slip across the river by night, plant mines, throw grenades and try to slip back. At the end of February 1968, the Israelis claimed that there had been ninety-one incidents so far that year. Although 80 per cent of the attacking guerrillas were killed or captured, their attacks – often aimed indiscriminately at civilians – were doing enough damage to cause the government serious concern.

Israel's military leaders knew that they had not devised an effective response. General Aharon Yariv, then head of military intelligence, recalls that in August 1967 he had warned his colleagues on the Israeli general staff that the guerrillas were going to undertake 'massive infiltration' across the Jordanian border, and proposed that Israel should fence off the entire valley. But the authorities – at that stage surprisingly complacent about the terrorist threat – were slow to act, and the fence was not completed for another two years.[19] In the meantime the Israelis found themselves simply improvising. They frequently shelled the *fedayeen* camps and sometimes became embroiled in artillery duels with Jordanian army units providing covering fire for the guerrillas. These actions, together with occasional bombing strikes from the air, may have settled scores, but the *ad hoc* nature of Israel's retaliation merely served to embolden the guerrillas.

On 18 March 1968, a major showdown with the Palestinians became inevitable when an Israeli school bus ran over a *fedayeen* mine near the Jordanian border. A doctor and a schoolboy were killed and twenty-nine children injured. Israel was stung into action. It resolved to hit the guerrillas, and hit them hard.

Across the river in his Karameh base, Arafat was aware that a large-scale attack was imminent – a senior Jordanian intelligence officer, acting on a tip-off from America's Central Intelligence Agency, had told him as much early in March. On the 18th, Arafat and Salah Khalaf were summoned urgently to Amman by the Jordanian army commander, General Amer Khammash. In a meeting also attended by the head of a 10,000-strong Iraqi army division that had been stationed on Jordanian soil since the 1967 war, Khammash gave the Fatah leaders a stern warning. 'Do you not see the massing of Israeli troops?' he said. 'In the next few hours, they will smash you.'[20]

To enable them to avoid the attack, Khammash said he would for the first time allow the Palestinian guerrillas to leave their riverside camps and take refuge in the nearby hills. But Arafat had a quite different idea. 'Our Arab nation has been escaping and fleeing continuously,' he replied with bravado. 'No, we have to prove to the Israeli enemy that there are people who will not flee. We are going to confront him in the same way that David confronted Goliath.'[21]

It was the height of folly, contrary to all the manuals of guerrilla warfare and all military good sense. But for Arafat, the impending battle was an irresistible opportunity to put the Palestinian resistance on the map.

What followed was one of his boldest pieces of political theatre. Arafat and Khalaf dashed back to Karameh and rallied the troops, shivering in their unheated shacks. Without mentioning the Jordanian warning, they explained the need for the guerrillas to stand their ground, even if all present ran a heavy risk of ending up either dead or in Israeli hands. 'We will make Karameh the second Leningrad,' Arafat proclaimed. Although he offered anyone who disagreed the opportunity to leave, he boasts that no Fatah member did, apart from the sick and lame. But fighters from Habash's Popular Front decided to take themselves off into the surrounding hills and harass Israeli forces from there.[22]

Contrary to the impression projected in subsequent propaganda, Arafat did not leave everything to fate. He had established links with the Jordanian army commander in charge of the area, General Mashour Haditha al-Jazy, who, unlike his superiors back in Amman, sympathized with the guerrillas. Arafat had also discreetly sought to engage the Iraqi army, although in the event this came to nothing.

Battle was joined on 21 March at 5.30 a.m., with Israeli aircraft dropping yellow leaflets urging the terrorists to surrender, and landing paratroopers in the hills behind Karameh. Their task: to encircle the bases and block the guerrillas' escape route to the east before the army swept into Karameh itself. But the paratroopers were astonished to encounter a group of PFLP commandos, who engaged them in hand-to-hand fighting. It was the first of a string of surprises for the Israelis that day. As the main body of Israeli tanks, accompanying a force of several thousand men, lumbered across the border, confusion spread. The paratroopers having failed to 'clean up' the surrounding hills, Israeli ground forces departed from their battle plan, moved east, and ran straight into an unexpected hail of artillery and tank fire from Haditha's Jordanian army division, which had ignored strict orders from Amman to stay out of the fighting. The ensuing duel bogged the Israeli forces down for the rest of the day, distracting them from their main mission of rooting out the guerrilla bases. By the time they were ordered to withdraw, the Israelis had suffered an unanticipated and unacceptable level of casualties: 28 dead, 69 injured and 34 tanks hit. At least one of the tanks remained in the Palestinians' hands together with the charred remains of its driver, and was used by the *fedayeen* to great publicity effect in the next few days.

Not that the guerrillas had escaped unscathed as they battled to stop the Israeli advance. One of the fighters, so the story goes, had wired himself up with explosives and hurled himself at a tank. Seventeen men had dug themselves into trenches along the Jordan river from which they fired rocket-propelled grenades at virtually point-blank range. All but one were killed, but their show of defiance was later immortalized in the name of Arafat's élite security service, Force 17. By the end of the day, 98 of the 400 or so Palestinian fighters at Karameh had been killed, and their base devastated.[23] The survivors were jubilant nonetheless. By the simple act of standing firm against hopeless odds and inflicting casualties on the enemy, they felt they had made an important point. For Arafat (who has always maintained he was present on the battlefield although the Israelis predictably claim he fled east when the fighting commenced) the battle was 'the first victory for our Arab nation after the 1967 war.'[24]

Strictly speaking, it had been the Jordanian army, not the guerrillas, that had done most of the damage and eventually forced the Israelis to withdraw. In the words of General Haditha, 'They [the guerrillas] fought bravely, but they certainly could not have done it alone. If the Jordanian army had stayed out, the *fedayeen* would have been crushed.'[25] That, however, was not the impression that began to reverberate around the Arab world, aided by Fatah's crude but effective propaganda and by the fact that Jordan could not trumpet its own involvement for fear of provoking harsher Israeli reprisals. The battle – bungled by Israel, hushed up by Jordan – was swiftly transformed by the *fedayeen* into a model for Arab steadfastness. Arafat's flair for publicity had pressed Karameh (conveniently enough, the Arabic word for dignity) into service as a potent symbol of Fatah's 'revolution'.

The results were more impressive than he could have dared to hope. In Israel, the battle came as a shock which jolted the military bosses out of their post-1967 complacency. 'After Karameh, we understood that we had on our hands a serious movement,' says General Yariv. 'Although it was a military defeat for them, it was a moral victory.'[26] In the Arab world, Karameh detonated a sudden explosion of support for the *fedayeen*. Palestinian and other Arab volunteers flocked to join the resistance, and Fatah, in particular, was overwhelmed: within 48 hours of the battle it received 5000 applications, many more than it could handle. The columns of Arab newspapers were full of wildly exaggerated tales of Palestinian heroism, and speculation swirled around the role of a shadowy guerrilla leader known only by his *nom de guerre*, Abu Ammar.

Despite its hunger for publicity about its actions, Fatah had long been obsessively secretive about its structure, origins and membership. Journalists' questions concerning the movement received vague and unhelpful replies. Anyone enquiring who was in charge would be referred to a faceless collective leadership. After Karameh, it was clear that this would no longer do. The moment was rapidly approaching when Fatah would have to emerge from underground and present a public face to the world: that of the 38-year-old Yasser Arafat. It is not the smallest irony of

Middle Eastern history that a mishandled Israeli military offensive helped to put him on the road to becoming chairman of the PLO.

The first outsider to identify Arafat in public as Fatah's leader was a journalist on Egypt's *Al-Ahram* newspaper, Ihsan Bakr, who stayed with the guerrillas for a week just after the Battle of Karameh. 'At first, they did not tell me their real names. They all said they were called Abu Maher,' Bakr recalls. 'The one exception was Arafat, who everybody referred to as Abu Ammar, "the father" or "the choice". After two or three meetings with him, I was convinced he was the leader, although when I asked him he said everyone there was leader of the revolution.'[27]

Less than a month later, Arafat was nominated as Fatah's official 'spokesman'. It was typical of the fractious organization that the move was prompted by yet another leadership struggle. Mahmoud Mesweida, Arafat's post-1967 opponent, had started to issue bogus communiqués claiming credit for actions against Israel in the name of Fatah's military wing, Al-Asifa. Word of the problem reached Salah Khalaf, Fatah's intelligence chief, in Damascus in mid-April when all but one of his colleagues in the Fatah leadership were away. To head off trouble, he took it upon himself to issue a statement naming Arafat as the sole person authorized to speak for Fatah, together with a faked declaration from Arafat himself 'accepting' the nomination.[28]

It was scarcely the sort of democratic procedure on which the Palestinian movement prides itself today. Some Fatah members were distinctly uneasy about the appointment, given the reputation Arafat had already developed for acting as a law unto himself. But those who most strongly disapproved drifted away from the movement and the rest deferred to Arafat's age, his pragmatism and above all to his hyperactive character.[29]

Arafat's nomination as front man was a watershed. Suddenly he was strutting on an international stage and the image he had cultivated since the start of the guerrilla struggle was projected to a receptive new audience. Pictured on the front of myriad Arab magazines and newspapers, his chubby face – adorned with the chequered headdress, the wrap-around dark glasses, the five-day stubble and the shabby fatigues – became an emblem of resistance; carefully mythologized versions of his life story were handed out; and as the mystique seeped through to the Western media, he took his theatrics to new lengths, luring camera crews to carefully staged midnight assignations in the hills outside Amman. He could just as easily have met his interlocutors in a downtown hotel, but being filmed with his fighters in a cave helped to inflate the myth. Arafat's appetite for publicity was boundless and he turned the weapon to good effect, making himself available for numerous newspaper interviews with Western reporters, almost invariably talking to them in his idiosyncratic broken English. Before 1968 was out he made the first of several appearances on the cover of *Time* magazine under a headline extolling the *fedayeen* as a powerful new force in the Middle East.

Fatah had already confirmed its status as the largest and most broadly based of the Palestinian guerrilla groups. Now its members began to parade openly with their weapons on the streets of Lebanese and Jordanian towns and to preach the doctrines of 'popular liberation war', *pace* the Algerian revolutionary Frantz Fanon and Mao Tse-tung, in the Palestinian refugee camps. Money was collected through the sale of specially printed stamps around the Arab world. Military and other supplies poured into the guerrilla bases. By the end of 1968, Fatah alone had at least 2000 men under arms, a cadre of officers trained at a military academy in the Chinese city of Nanking and a rapidly growing arsenal of Kalashnikovs, AK47s and other weapons. The Kalashnikov, the 'Klashin', became an object of worship, for which Fatah guerrillas had a special chant:

Klashin makes the blood gush in torrents.
Haifa and Jaffa are calling us.
Commando, go ahead and do not worry:
Open fire and break the silence of the night![30]

Arafat was particularly proud of the measures Fatah was taking to prepare for a long, drawn-out struggle. It set up a special section – known as the Ashbal or 'Cubs' – to train children as young as eight in guerrilla warfare. It also set out to build an array of non-military institutions, responsible for anything from health care (the Palestinian Red Crescent) to vocational training (Samed, Fatah's economic arm). Modelled in part on the organizations that had helped to implant the Jews in Palestine in the 1930s and 1940s, in time they gave the liberation movement many of the characteristics of a Palestinian government in exile.

For their part, Arab governments, faced with an unstoppable surge of public support for the *fedayeen*, had no choice but to lend support. After long years of restricting Palestinian movements, they opened their borders to the resistance, enabling its growing legions of recruits to travel freely on production of a photo-less Fatah identity card. Wealthy countries, such as Libya and Saudi Arabia, vied to contribute to Palestinian coffers. Commando training was dramatically stepped up at bases in Iraq and Syria; one training camp near the Syrian port of Latakia ran six-week courses in guerrilla warfare for 350 recruits at a time.

It was a stunning vindication for Arafat, less than a year after his ambitions had been ridiculed by many of his colleagues. But it was not enough. What he really wanted was something he valued higher than all the money and arms then pouring in: official recognition of Fatah by the Arab regimes. And that meant prising open a door that had consistently remained closed to him, that of President Nasser of Egypt.

A word of support from Nasser could still bestow tremendous prestige, despite his fall from grace in the wake of 1967. Yet the Egyptian President had always viewed Fatah with the deepest suspicion, fuelled by intelligence reports of its leaders' *Ikhwan* connections and ties with Syria. It was only after Nasser's defeat in the Six-Day War and at the urging of his close confidant, the journalist Mohammed Hassanein Heikal, that Nasser began to conclude that Arafat and his hot-headed colleagues might be useful. 'I thought that it was time for us to overcome all these old suspicions because 1967 had changed so much,' recalls Heikal. 'I thought we should give them a chance to prove themselves.'[31]

Nasser, warned by his intelligence people that the Palestinians were plotting to assassinate him, did not readily drop his guard. When he first met Farouk Kaddoumi and Salah Khalaf, he suggested – only half in jest – that a green briefcase Kaddoumi was carrying might be packed with explosives. But after sounding them out thoroughly on Fatah's motives and aims, he agreed in April 1968 to receive Arafat himself. For Nasser, who remained deeply sceptical about what the Palestinian group could achieve, it was a question of expediency. At a time when he was both pursuing a war of attrition with Israel and co-operating with United Nations peace moves, Fatah's continuing armed struggle might serve as a useful, if indirect, signal that the Arab regimes had not given up the fight.

'I would be more than glad if you could represent the Palestinian people and the Palestinian will to resist, politically by your presence and militarily by your actions,' he told Arafat when they met at last in his modest residence, not far from the Fatah leader's family home in the Cairo suburb of Heliopolis.[32] Significantly, he advised Fatah to preserve its independence from Arab regimes, but to co-ordinate with them in the same way that Jewish terrorist groups did with the mainstream Zionist movement before the establishment of Israel – just the sort of relationship Arafat had proposed to Shukairy four years before.[33] Nonetheless, Nasser remained puzzled by the impetuous guerrilla leader. At one point in their conversation, he asked Arafat what time limit he was setting for his revolution. 'Mr President, a revolution has no time limit,' was Arafat's reply.[34]

Thus began a relationship that was to take Fatah into the highest councils of Arab politics within little more than a year. Arafat came to place more trust in Nasser than in any other Arab leader. Apart from offering frequently forthright advice, Nasser promised to – and did – provide Arafat with arms and his men with training. He arranged instruction courses for the Palestinians at Egyptian military bases, covering such matters as intelligence-gathering and sabotage. Just as important, he allowed Fatah to establish its own broadcasting station in Cairo. Known as 'Voice of Fatah', its signature song soon became familiar across the Arab world:

> The Revolution of Fatah exists,
> It exists here, there and everywhere.
> It is a storm, a storm in every house and village.[35]

Nasser also gave Arafat valuable introductions, not least to his super-power ally, the Soviet Union. In July 1968, he allowed the Fatah leader, travelling on a false Egyptian passport bearing the name Muhsin Amin, to tag along with a presidential delegation on a visit to Moscow. Arafat's talks with relatively junior Soviet officials were not all that satisfactory and certainly did not come up to his ambitious expectations. At the time, the Soviets saw Fatah as a band of dangerous 'adventurists' and Arafat was merely allowed the briefest of handshakes with members of the ageing Kremlin leadership before being fobbed off with a modest financial donation.[36] But at least it was a start. Arafat was beginning to learn the tricks of the diplomatic trade. As he had from the outset, he maintained a studied vagueness about his own political views, a fact which not only gave Fatah a broad appeal among Palestinians but also helped it win support from powerful patrons. It was a skill that was to serve him well in later years: the ability to be all things to all men.

To Saudi Arabia's conservative King Faisal, who agreed to deduct a seven per cent 'contribution' to Fatah – a 'liberation tax' – from the salaries of Palestinians working in the kingdom, Arafat was a devout Muslim fighting to recover the holy shrines of Jerusalem. To the Communist Chinese, now stepping up their arms supplies to Fatah, he was an anti-imperialist revolutionary struggling against American hegemony in the Middle East. To 'progressive' and 'reactionary' Arab regimes alike, he cast himself as the keeper of the seals of Arab nationalism: as Fatah put it, the liberation of Palestine was an essential step towards the elusive dream of Arab unity. This last message was one calculated to appeal to the new, more pragmatic generation of Arab leaders coming to power in the wake of the 1967 defeat. For men like Hafez al-Assad in Syria and, later, Anwar Sadat in Egypt – more interested in keeping the peace at home than in going to war abroad in pursuit of some grand Arab design – Fatah had its uses.

Arafat has always taken pride in his ability to play the political chameleon. 'What meaning does the left or the right have in the struggle for the liberation of my homeland?' he said in an interview with the Lebanese newspaper *Al-Sayyad* in January 1969. 'I want that homeland even if the devil is the one to liberate it for me. Am I in a position to reject the participation or assistance of any man? Can I be asked, for example, to refuse the financial aid of Saudi Arabia with the claim that it belongs to the right? After all, it is with the Saudis' money that I buy arms from China.'[37]

Uninterested in ideology Arafat may have been, but other Fatah leaders had by now begun to define some political aims for their movement. Their central idea was spelled out by ex-*Ikhwan* member Salah Khalaf, already Fatah's principal ideologue, at a press conference on the premises of a Beirut newspaper, and it was one which outsiders found highly implausible: a democratic state in the whole of historic Palestine in which 'Arabs and Jews would live together harmoniously as fully equal citizens'.[38]

The dream was drawn from idealized visions of Palestine that had circulated in the 1930s and 1940s and from a slogan adopted by the Arab League back in 1947,[39] but in the Arab world in 1968 it was presented and received as a bold attempt to break with the past. Gone, said Fatah, were the old chauvinistic slogans about revenge and 'throwing the Jews into the sea' that had been the stock in trade of Shukairy's generation of leaders – people who, as one Fatah representative put it, saw only 'the Palestine of the past, that is a Palestine without three million Jews'.[40] Instead, the Palestinians were now proposing to co-operate with those Jews who had been prepared to throw off the shackles of Zionism in building a completely new society. 'In itself this was saying something revolutionary at the time as far as Arabs were concerned: that we were willing to live with the Jews in Palestine,' said Khalaf.[41] Although the proposal initially drew fire both from within Fatah and from other Palestinian Resistance factions, the idea of 'a free and democratic society in Palestine for all Palestinians, including Muslims, Christian and Jews', subsequently became official PLO policy.[42]

Some Arafat associates, such as Nabil Shaath, actually went one step further and sought to interest Israelis in the idea. In 1969 and 1970, with Arafat's blessing, he met and sounded out the Israeli mathematics professor Moshe Makhover and, more importantly, Lova Eliav, secretary-general of the ruling Labour Party who was well known for his doveish views. 'If you stop thinking about revenge and start thinking about one country for all of us, then logically you would want to see how Jews respond to that idea,' Shaath explains.[43] This was indeed something of a change, symbolized also in the teaching of Hebrew in Palestinian refugee camps and the targeting of Palestinian broadcasts in the Jewish language at Israel. In these early meetings are to be found the precursors of many similar contacts – initially secret, then increasingly public – between PLO functionaries and Israeli leftists in the mid- to late 1970s.

There was never any chance that this early initiative would make much impact on the Israeli political mainstream, preoccupied as it was with Palestinian attacks on Jewish civilians. But attempts to signal greater flexibility towards the Jews undoubtedly made for good public relations in the West. In 1968, Fatah, with the aid of its Algerian friends, had been allowed by President de Gaulle to set up its first European mission in Paris. There, the group's representative, Mohammed Abu Mayzar, cultivated contacts with members of the European New Left who had supported the Algerian FLN in its struggle and were beginning to take an interest in the Palestinian cause: academics like Maxime Rodinson and radical chic politicians such as Michel Rocard, later to become Socialist Prime Minister. On 1 January 1969, Abu Mayzar issued a statement in Paris aimed at disseminating the democratic state programme to a wider international audience.[44] De Gaulle's gesture in allowing Fatah to establish a foothold in western Europe is something Arafat has never forgotten. To this day, he wears around his neck a memento the General sent him before he died: La Croix de Lorraine, a symbol of the French Resistance forces De Gaulle commanded. And on the wall of one of the safe houses Arafat inhabits today in Tunis is a framed, and strangely appropriate, wartime quotation from the French leader: 'Nous avons perdu une bataille mais nous n'avons pas perdu la guerre' (We have lost a battle, but we have not lost the war).

Arafat has always been much less interested in airy political theory than in power. Armed with his new battery of Arab support, the Fatah 'spokesman' had embarked on a bid for overall leadership of the Palestinian movement. With

Nasser's assistance, he was to succeed more quickly than anyone could have imagined.

During 1968, serious negotiations began with the aim of reviving the lifeless PLO by bringing in the profusion of guerrilla groups that had sprung up since the previous year. This posed something of a dilemma for Arafat's colleagues, many of whom believed that if Fatah joined the PLO, it would swiftly become bogged down in bureaucracy. Their first inclination had been to try to organize a joint military organization led by Al-Asifa which would serve as an alternative to the PLO. 'The PLO is an organization of offices and cars,' they would tell middle-aged functionaries sent to negotiate with them in the shabby basements of Damascus. 'We don't want offices; we are fighters and our operations must take place only in the occupied territories.'[45]

But if Arafat harboured any reservations about taking over the PLO's existing infrastructure, he swiftly swallowed them. He saw that the Organization, with its diplomatic missions, political institutions and money, could be a useful vehicle. In fact, it might provide the key both to consolidating Fatah's influence and to building up support from the Arab states which, after all, had founded the Organization in the first place.

The important question concerned terms. Some of Arafat's new Arab friends – and several members of the Fatah leadership – advised him that it would be better for Fatah to take over the PLO alone and leave the other, smaller Palestinian factions outside. But here again Arafat had firm views, reflecting the obsession with consensus-building that became his hallmark in later years. Leaving the other groups out, even if it proved possible, might induce strife such as had occurred among Palestinians in the 1930s – a disaster which Arafat has often said he is determined to prevent. Better to gather as many groups as possible within the PLO and turn the Organization into a broad national front along the lines of the motley coalition of political and guerrilla factions that confronted the Americans in Vietnam.

So it was that after much haggling the commando organizations joined the PLO's legislative body, the Palestine National Council, for the first time in July 1968. Reflecting the influence of its militant new members, the Council rewrote the PLO's National Covenant, its statement of beliefs and objectives, with a ringing endorsement of guerrilla war against Israel: 'Armed struggle is the only way to liberate Palestine. Thus it is the overall strategy and not merely a tactical phase.'[46]

Arafat's ascent to the pinnacle of the PLO very nearly did not happen. In early January 1969, he was involved in the most serious of his several car crashes, on the road between Amman and Baghdad. Arafat had always had a *penchant* for fast driving, a predilection he would in later years put down to fear of an Israeli helicopter attack. But on that January morning, seated at the wheel of an ageing black Mercedes, he was in a particular hurry. Bowling along the rainy highway at 130 kilometres an hour, he tried to overtake a truck and found himself headed straight for a car coming in the opposite direction. He slammed on the brakes and skidded under the lorry. 'After a few seconds I heard Arafat moaning and I thought he was dying,' recalls guerrilla commander Abu Daoud, one of Arafat's two passengers. 'He was on the floor of the car, his hand was broken and he was hurt in the chest. He also lost his memory for a few days.'[47]

Less than a month later, Arafat had bounced back sufficiently to make his first appearance at a meeting of the Palestinian 'parliament' in Cairo. On 3 February 1969, a reconvened and restructured PNC, with the *fedayeen* in unchallenged control, duly elected him chairman of the executive committee of the Palestine Liberation Organization. In the presence of President Nasser and in a capital emblazoned with posters of his Fatah movement, Arafat had been hailed as the paramount Palestinian leader. He moved swiftly to assert his dominance, promising to expand military operations until the movement was engaged in a 'fully-fledged war of liberation', rejecting 'all political settlements' and intervening with gusto in the National Council debates.[48]

To those who did not know Arafat well, his behaviour during the meeting seemed peculiar and more than a little annoying. 'He would interrupt everybody; he would shout whenever he thought anybody infringed on his prerogatives; he would stand up and insist on being given the floor,' said his latterday adviser and friend Nabil Shaath. 'At first I thought this was very childish and that if he talked less it would have been better.'[49] It was only later that Shaath and the other participants realized that such shenanigans were all part of the hyperactive Arafat's stock-in-trade.

For the moment, Fatah's triumph seemed almost complete. It had conquered the Palestinian labour union, the writers' and artists' groups, the women's and students' organizations that had grown up in the diaspora. Thanks to Ahmed Shukairy's efforts, it had inherited an organization with a ready-made infrastructure – a 'finance ministry' of sorts, an army under its nominal control, an executive committee for day-to-day decision-making and an irregular parliament. Most important, Arafat had got his hands on an instrument of power that he was to wield with considerable skill: money. In taking over the PLO, he had tied a knot that supposedly bound the Arab regimes to support his new 'autonomous' movement as representative of the Palestinian people. Just how far he had travelled was apparent at a summit meeting in the Moroccan capital, Rabat, in December 1969, when he demanded that Arab leaders contribute the princely sum of 44 million US dollars to the cause. History does not relate how much they actually chipped in then, but Arafat has since succeeded in building the PLO into an organization as rich as a multinational corporation, and every bit as complex.

The honeymoon with the Arab regimes, however, rested on fragile relationships. Even at the moment of success, the divisions within Palestinian ranks were more than obvious: the main leftist group, led by George Habash, refused to recognize Fatah's hegemony and boycotted the National Council in protest at a miserly allocation of seats; and the commanders of the Palestine Liberation Army protested furiously about the guerrilla takeover. Just as significantly, behind the lip service they paid to the PLO, some Arab states were plotting to curb its new-found independence. In Lebanon and more particularly in Jordan, the upsurge of raids into Israel and the resulting Israeli reprisals were already causing ominous political ructions.

Small wonder that when Arafat's election as PLO chairman was announced, the look on his face spoke more of foreboding than of euphoria. Asked by a colleague what was troubling him, he replied with one word: 'Responsibility.'[50]

# 4

# *Blood Feud*

'Leadership is not easy in a jungle of guns.' Yasser Arafat, quoted in the *Los Angeles Times*, 21 June 1981.

One crisp morning in mid-October 1968, tens of thousands of Palestinians, many of them armed, took to the streets of the Jordanian capital, Amman. From their refugee camps and commando bases, they snaked their way along the gravelly hillsides and into the town, chanting slogans against the Jordanian Government and in support of the Palestinian Resistance. They heard speeches from Fatah leaders exalting the guerrilla struggle. They swaggered and fired their rifles in the air.

The occasion was ostensibly one of mourning for a top Fatah leader, Abdel Fattah Hamoud, who had been killed in a car crash near the Syrian border several days earlier. But what started out as a funeral turned into a mass political demonstration, with a grief-stricken Yasser Arafat at its head. It was the first time the *fedayeen* had shown up in force in Amman. For King Hussein bin Talal, Jordan's ruler for fifteen years, it was, to say the least, a disturbing sight.

Ever since their showdown with the Israelis at Karameh the previous March, the Palestinians had been flexing their muscles in Hussein's kingdom. Home to the largest number of Arab refugees from the Arab-Israeli wars of 1948 and 1967, Jordan was also the principal recruiting ground for a proliferation of guerrilla groups, and their main launching pad for attacks on Israel. Hussein, his country and army still shattered by the 1967 defeat, was then in no position to stand in their way. The pro-Western monarch's grip on power had always been somewhat shaky, marred by abortive coups and assassination attempts. But with the *fedayeen* now openly brandishing their Kalashnikovs in Amman and with their raids on Israel attracting inevitable reprisals, Palestinian guerrilla power was beginning to look like a full-scale challenge to his authority. Something would have to be done to bring it under control.

Within days of the October rally, the frictions began to tell. *Fedayeen* leaders complained that Jordanian road-blocks and vehicle searches were hampering them in their armed struggle against Israel; they protested at restrictions on their movements and at attempts by the king's army to control their operations.

Violence was the inevitable result. On 2 November 1968, Palestinians stormed the American embassy in Amman during a demonstration to mark the fifty-first anniversary of the Balfour Declaration – Britain's promise to work for the establishment of a Jewish homeland in Palestine. Security forces dispersed the mob with tear gas and in the ensuing *mêlée* arrested the leader of the small but grandly named guerrilla faction that had organized the riot, the Victory Legions. Next day, followers of the arrested man, a former Syrian army officer named Taher Dablaan, retaliated by ambushing a police car and kidnapping and murdering a group of policemen. When the authorities seized an arms cache in one of Amman's sprawling Palestinian refugee camps, clashes broke out between Dablaan's group and the Jordanian Army, and more than 10,000 people came out on the streets again in a massive anti-government demonstration. Hussein, accusing 'phoney elements' among the commandos of seeking to foment a revolution in Jordan, sent his army in to crush the unrest. Thousands of troops surrounded and shelled the refugee camps for more than three days, while the commandos issued statements accusing Hussein of colluding with Israel in 'a conspiracy to eliminate the resistance'.

Three months before assuming the chairmanship of the PLO, Arafat had thus found himself pitched into a task that was henceforth to take much of his time: damage limitation. With feelings still running high, he toured Amman in the company of a Jordanian police commander, urging Palestinian refugees not to support the renegade Victory Legions. And as the fighting sputtered on, he requested an audience with King Hussein.

It was to be the first of many heated encounters between the two men over the next two years. In some ways they were evenly matched: apart from both being small in stature, they shared a taste for theatrics, a fierce temper and a capacity for deviousness. King Hussein treated Arafat and a group of other Palestinian leaders to a histrionic display of rage in which he pinned responsibility for the disturbances firmly on the resistance leadership and threatened to take action against the guerrillas. Only with great difficulty did they pacify him. The mainstream resistance groups had nothing to do with the kidnapping of the police officers, they assured him, and every interest in maintaining good relations with the Jordanian authorities.[1] The result, on 16 November, was an agreement between the government and the resistance which banned the *fedayeen* from carrying weapons and wearing uniform in the towns and prohibited the shelling of Israeli targets from the East Bank of the Jordan.[2]

It was a victory on points for the regime but although the agreement succeeded in defusing the immediate crisis, the underlying contradictions between the two sides had only been more starkly exposed. For Yasser Arafat, what was to prove a long and brutal lesson in Arab politics and the failings of his own movement had begun.

He and his Fatah comrades had long believed that Jordan, not Syria, was the most natural base for their guerrilla operations. Its long and permeable frontier with Israel; its sympathetic, 60 per cent Palestinian population; its weakened government in the aftermath of the Six-Day

War – all these things led Arafat to conclude that Jordan was 'safe ground' on which to land his 'revolution on a flying carpet'.[3] In time, the *fedayeen* should be able to transform it into a centre of resistance for the Palestinians, as the Vietnamese had Hanoi. Provided that Fatah promised not to interfere in Jordanian politics, there was no reason why the Jordanian authorities should curb the *fedayeen* in their armed struggle against Israel.[4] That, at least, was the theory, and at the outset that is how it worked: deeply unhappy as King Hussein was about the new armed presence on his soil, there was precious little he could do about it. Two days after the Battle of Karameh, a monarch who only a month earlier had threatened to 'act with force and determination' against the guerrillas, had even felt constrained to make his own half-hearted expression of support for them, saying: 'We may well arrive at a stage when we shall all be *fedayeen*.'[5]

Arafat was beginning to feel at home in Jordan. Living with a group of other Fatah leaders in a flat in the Jebel Hussein area of Amman, he spent his time in triumphal tours of his group's guerrilla bases. According to those who were with him, it was a frugal life. Arafat slept little, neither smoked nor drank and – apart from the curious habits of taking honey in his tea and pouring tea over his cornflakes – he had simple tastes, often cooking and eating with his bodyguards. In addition to a rigorous regime of physical exercise, his only diversions consisted of comics, TV cartoons and the occasional game of ping-pong. Although Arafat now tours the world in a private jet rather than Jordan in a pick-up truck, in other respects his routine has changed little; he is nothing if not a creature of habit.

As 1968 progressed, the power of the Palestinian resistance had grown to a point where it began to act as a state within the state. Fatah's military activities had generated enormous enthusiasm among politically active Jordanians as well as the Palestinian refugees. Arafat's followers had managed to penetrate the Jordanian Army, secretly recruiting a number of middle-ranking to senior officers, and they also obtained extensive assistance from the Iraqi army there. For a while, at least, the *fedayeen* had the pleasurable feeling that there were no limits to their freedom of action. As Khalil al-Wazir nostalgically put it a few years later, 'We were mini-states and institutions. Every sector commander considered himself God . . . everyone set up a state for himself and did whatever he pleased.'[6]

But it was an illusion. In emerging so publicly in Jordan, the guerrillas had unleashed forces that would drag them inexorably into conflict with the established order, and ultimately towards their own downfall. One problem was the increasingly fierce Israeli retaliation against Palestinian raids – reprisals that had already turned the fertile Jordan valley into a virtual no-go area. Pushed back from the border, the fighters scattered their bases across an ever-wider area, from the steep and rocky hills of western Jordan to the refugee camps of the capital and the forests of the north. And as Israel adopted a strategy of what it called 'active self-defence', involving air raids and artillery attacks deep inside Jordan, the local population began to suffer.

More problematic still was the behaviour of the *fedayeen*. Placing themselves above the law, they showed scant regard for the sensibilities of ordinary Jordanians or for their government. Already, in 1968, self-styled guerrillas were extorting 'donations' at gunpoint from the residents of Amman. In one clash in May that year, fifteen armed Palestinians tried to break into police headquarters in order to rescue a fellow guerrilla who was under interrogation. The ensuing shoot-out left four policemen wounded and an innocent bystander dead.

Such indiscipline was a symptom of a more basic flaw. In Jordan, guerrilla groups were proliferating like mushrooms. At one point, the government counted fifty-two separate Palestinian factions, some of them numbering only a few members, but all answerable only to themselves or to whichever Arab regime had chosen to sponsor them, all with more or less easy access to money and weapons.[7] The result was that even after Arafat's election as chairman of the PLO in February 1969, his control over the movement – the 'jungle of guns' – was tenuous at best. The multifarious factions, including Arafat's own Fatah, were still in a battle for publicity, members and funds. More to the point, beyond the common aim of fighting Israel, they could not agree among themselves on what strategy to adopt in Jordan.

At one extreme was the pseudo-Marxist Popular Front for the Liberation of Palestine, led by George Habash. He called for a revolution not only against the Jews in Palestine but also against 'reactionary' Arab leaders, principal among whom he counted King Hussein, who was especially close to the US and Britain and, it later emerged, had been on the payroll of the CIA since 1957. At the other, Arafat and his Fatah colleagues sought, at least in principle, to stay out of Jordanian affairs. Trying to take over Jordan, Arafat argued, would bog the movement down in administrative concerns for which it was neither equipped nor disposed, and would quite possibly intensify internal strife. Better for the Palestinians to keep their powder dry for the fight that mattered – the struggle against Israel. 'Under no circumstances will any Arab regime deter us from our goals and push us into side battles,' said a Fatah statement issued in 1968. 'Our bullets will target only the enemy, but at the same time we will not drop our arms under any threats.'[8] Or as Arafat himself put it later that year: 'One enemy at a time is enough.'[9]

The competition between Arafat and his left-wing rivals took on increasingly dramatic forms. In the summer of 1968, just a few months after Karameh had made Arafat the toast of the Arab world, the Popular Front hit on its own arresting way of grabbing the headlines. On 23 July, three

PFLP gunmen seized an Israeli El Al flight en route from Rome to Tel Aviv and diverted it to Algiers, demanding, in exchange for the Israeli passengers and crew, the release of Palestinians held in Israeli jails. Israel issued what was to become a customary disclaimer that it did not negotiate with terrorists, but after more than a month of mediation Algeria released the plane and the last of the passengers and crew. Two days later, Israel freed sixteen convicted Arab infiltrators who had been jailed before the 1967 war. It was the first of a long series of spectacular acts of international terrorism by the PFLP that would have an enduring impact on the public image of the Palestinian Resistance, and play straight into the hands of its enemies.

King Hussein was under mounting pressure to crack down. Especially restive was his loyal Bedu army. As army units skirmished periodically with the *fedayeen*, these troops – and sympathetic officers higher up – found it difficult to understand why the king was hesitating to assert his authority. Nor did they find any respite from their frustrations when off-duty. Back in their home villages and towns, soldiers often found themselves humiliated and stripped of their weapons by Palestinian militiamen anxious to show that they were the real power in the land.

'The army was out of the city, but the soldiers would take holidays and were prevented from coming into town carrying their arms. They were very antagonized,' recalls Zeid al-Rafai, chief of the Jordanian royal court. 'In one incident, the *fedayeen* killed a soldier, beheaded him and played soccer with his head in the area where he used to live. The soldiers would also get reports about their families being attacked. So the army was really antagonized.'[10]

It was clear that Hussein, a moody and suspicious man in constant fear for his throne, was not going to tolerate indefinitely the growth of a Palestinian authority in Jordan rivalling his own. Ever since the establishment of Israel in 1948, his family had claimed what was left of Palestine for itself and he, like his grandfather before him, had long maintained secret contacts with the Israelis to reinforce that claim. The growth of Arafat's nationalist movement could only be a threat to what had become his Number 1 priority – recovery of the territory lost to Israel in the 1967 war – and ultimately to the continuation of Hashemite rule.

Such was the gulf that divided Hussein and Arafat as they manoeuvred uncertainly around each other during 1969. Hussein repeatedly reshuffled his government and his army command as if groping for a way of coming to grips with the complex political equation on his doorstep. Arafat, struggling to hold his movement together and shaken by an unsuccessful attempt to assassinate him by parcel bomb that summer, negotiated hesitantly a *modus vivendi* with the regime. Although the two men were at one in their indecision, theirs was in every other way an uneasy relationship. Pressed by Hussein to impose some discipline on the movement under his nominal command, Arafat instead chose to temporize. Not only was he a hostage to the divisions within the guerrilla factions that made up the PLO; he was also labouring under severe delusions of his own.

Among the Palestinians, power bred arrogance. The *fedayeen* ran their own police force and their own courts. They set up road-blocks at random and careered around the rocky hillsides of Amman in their military vehicles. Palestinian factions took their internecine skirmishing on to the streets. Progressively, the rule of law seemed to be succumbing to the rule of the gun. Stories of petty thuggery and crime circulated. Shopkeepers found themselves strong-armed into contributing to the cause. The leftists, from Habash's Popular Front to a host of radical splinter groups, daubed Maoist slogans round the capital, preached Marx from the mosque loudspeakers, and infiltrated the local labour unions, stirring up unrest. A motley crew from the European New Left, some of whom received military training and went on to found terrorist cells in West Germany, installed itself in the Palestinian refugee camps. 'All power to the resistance' ran the persistent refrain.

Many of Arafat's own followers in Fatah now shared the view that the resistance should be working to take power in Jordan. Abu Daoud, who commanded the 15,000-strong Palestinian militia forces from a base in Amman's Wahdat refugee camp, was one of several Fatah leaders arguing for such a course during 1969. 'Until February 1970, it would have been very easy for us to topple the regime if we had wished to do so,' he says.[11] As Salah Khalaf commented ruefully: 'Our problem was that the regime had only one decision, whereas we always had at least twelve.'[12]

Just turned 40, Arafat was enjoying his first taste of what he took to be real power. He was certainly not about to undermine his position by agreeing to controversial restrictions on his own supporters. He was also inexperienced in statecraft, displaying little understanding of the Jordanian scene. As many PLO leaders are today prepared to admit, he devoted insufficient attention to building links with Jordanian activists who could have warned him of impending danger and might have helped to shelter the *fedayeen* from the fall-out. 'Arafat and his colleagues did not know enough about the facts and intricacies of Jordanian political life. They thought it would be easy for them to become *the* political movement of Jordan,' says Dr Jamal Sha'er, a Jordanian opposition leader. 'Arafat himself had this natural hostility towards established politicians, those who'd already gained respect in the West Bank before 1967 and were already part of the set-up. He considered them in a way competitors. He would listen instead to people from outside, people who came to prominence by riding on his shoulders.'[13]

It was an abiding characteristic, perhaps stemming from Arafat's experience as an underground guerrilla leader: for as long as anyone in the PLO can remember, he has

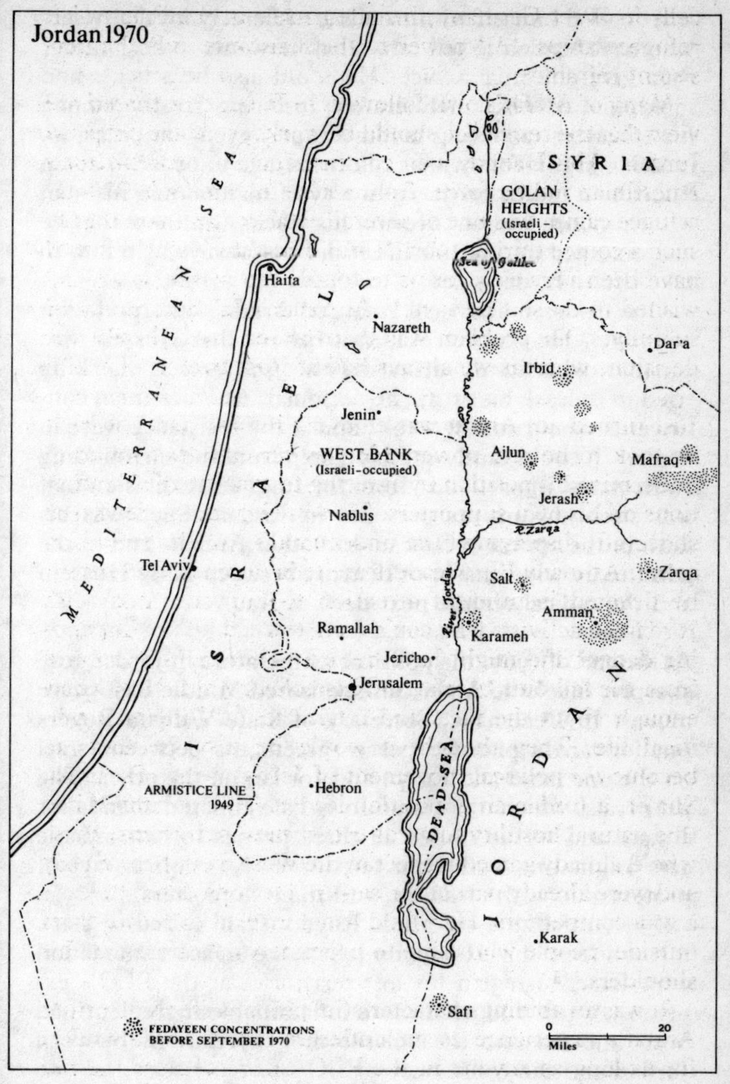

Jordan 1970
MEDITERRANEAN SEA
ISRAEL
SYRIA
GOLAN HEIGHTS
(Israeli - occupied)
Sea of Galilee
Haifa
Nazareth
Dar'a
Irbid
Jenin
WEST BANK
(Israeli-occupied)
Ajlun
Mafraq
Jerash
Nablus
R. Zarqa
Tel Aviv
Zarqa
Salt
River Jordan
Amman
Ramallah
Karameh
Jericho
Jerusalem
JORDAN
DEAD SEA
ARMISTICE LINE
1949
Hebron
Karak
Safi
FEDAYEEN CONCENTRATIONS
BEFORE SEPTEMBER 1970
0
20
Miles

surrounded himself with a coterie of fiercely loyal advisers who have tended to tell him what he wants to hear rather than give objective advice. He could also be a fickle and manipulative boss, deliberately fostering rivalry among his followers, adopting favourites and even, on occasion, creating arguments within his entourage in order to claim kudos as a mediator. It was a way of maintaining his own pre-eminence and of covering his tracks, but now that he had emerged into public life it did not always help him to take the right decisions.

One delusion above all coloured Arafat's interpretation of events. He simply could not believe that Hussein was capable of militarily defeating the *fedayeen*. If the king tried to unleash his army, he reasoned, its Palestinian contingents would surely revolt; and if the resistance were in danger, it could surely count on help from the surrounding Arab states, in particular from the Iraqi army division that was strengthening its presence in Jordan. Such was his faith in the appeal of his cause to other Arabs – and in the admittedly wide chasm of distrust between King Hussein and the radical regime next door in Iraq.

At the end of 1969, the political temperature in Jordan rose sharply, thanks to American-sponsored Middle East peace moves. In December, Secretary of State William Rogers put forward a plan for peace agreements between Israel on the one hand and Egypt and Jordan on the other. The proposals, which did not address Palestinian demands for a state and would oblige all three parties to halt 'hostile acts originating from their territories'[14], set off a wave of protest among the *fedayeen* and their supporters.

For Arafat, the so-called 'Rogers Plan' raised in stark form the fear that Hussein might make an accommodation with Israel to regain his lost territories at the PLO's expense. A new and even more inflammable ingredient had been injected into the volatile mix of relations between Jordan and the resistance.

The explosion began two months later. On 10 February 1970, King Hussein suddenly signalled his intention to restore authority in the kingdom with an eleven-point decree imposing severe restrictions on the *fedayeen*. The use, carrying or stockpiling of firearms and explosives was to be banned; demonstrations, party political activities and pamphleteering would be prohibited; and guerrillas would henceforth have to carry identity cards and license their vehicles.

Infuriated, *fedayeen* leaders denounced the decree as a provocation to civil war. They demanded that the government revoke it, withdraw army units from the cities and give the guerrillas full freedom of action. They staged demonstrations and meted out more 'revolutionary justice' to Jordanian security forces. But Hussein's move had caught the resistance badly off guard. Arafat was out of Jordan, cementing his relations with the Soviet leadership in Moscow, which was now showing increased interest in the PLO as a means of winning friends in the Arab world. And there, inexplicably, he stayed, as the situation in Jordan continued to deteriorate. It was by no means the last occasion in Arafat's career on which he displayed a perverse sense of priorities. Basking in the international spotlight now trained on his movement, he often seemed to prefer dabbling in diplomacy to dealing with crises in his home base.

As the Jordanians moved to enforce the law, fighting broke out between the police force and the *fedayeen*. Scores of people, mainly Palestinians, were killed or wounded in clashes which continued for three days. To step up the pressure, Hussein's forces shut off water and electricity supplies to the Palestinian refugee camps. The resistance, more deeply divided than ever in Arafat's absence, despite belated moves to set up a 'unified command', was in no position to put up a credible fight. In desperation, those PLO leaders still in the country appealed for support to Iraq and Syria, and it was only when both countries duly responded with threatening noises that the Jordanian Government climbed down.

On 14 February, King Hussein suspended his controversial measures, saying the whole affair had been a 'misunderstanding' and that Jordan would remain the home of the Palestinian resistance. On Arafat's return from Moscow a full week later, he met Hussein and signed an agreement formally declaring the crisis closed. Within twenty-four hours, the man who had introduced the anti-*fedayeen* decree in the first place, hard-line Interior Minister Mohammad Rasul al-Kaylani, had resigned.[15]

The *fedayeen* had won the first of a series of tactical victories over King Hussein's regime. Under fire from his supporters for being absent in their hour of need, Arafat sought to restore his position by seeking further concessions from the government, and as negotiations continued throughout the spring, Hussein appeared to be going out of his way to accommodate Arafat's demands. In April, he reshuffled his cabinet yet again and brought in Arafat's old friend from the Battle of Karameh, Mashour Haditha, as army chief of staff. For the resistance, it was a richly symbolic move. Haditha was an active mediator, taking Arafat in his Volkswagen to regular meetings with the king, and pleading with Hussein to avoid a confrontation.[16]

But such triumphs were entirely Pyrrhic, lulling the *fedayeen* into a false sense that they had seized the initiative. Clashes continued between the army and the guerrillas, and it seemed Arafat had neither the capacity nor the inclination to rein in his followers. Although he stepped up his efforts to unify Palestinian ranks under his leadership, he still did not realize how urgent the task had become.

'We in the leadership never concluded that a clash was inevitable,' says Ibrahim Bakr, the tough and sharp-witted lawyer who served under Arafat in 1969 as the PLO's first and last deputy chairman. 'The regime was under internal and Arab constraints not to act against the *fedayeen*. But the leadership interpreted this restraint as weakness. It was under the impression that the regime was not able to defeat them in a military clash. All the time, the Palestinian leadership believed it was in a military and popular position that was stronger than that of the regime. All the time, this was false.'[17]

To this day, Yasser Arafat refuses to admit having miscalculated in Jordan. 'Fatah and myself did not commit mistakes,' he says. 'The mistakes were made by other factions that held Marxist banners inside the mosques.'[18] Yet the fact is that his own group's confusion about its strategy did contribute at least as much to its problems.

'Fatah didn't know what it should do,' says Yasser Abed Rabbo, a guerrilla fighter in Jordan who later became deputy leader of the leftist Democratic Front for the Liberation of Palestine. 'They didn't know whether they should confront the regime or not; they didn't know whether or not they should present local political demands to the king and force him to accept them; they didn't know whether to get involved in local politics or stay out of it. So they did all these things at once, and that was the worst thing because it showed complete hesitation on the Palestinian side. It would have been better to make a wrong choice and stick to it. As it was, we handed the initiative to the regime.'[19]

The tension reached a new peak when fighting broke out on 7 June in the town of Zarqa, site of the Jordanian Army headquarters and of a large Palestinian refugee camp, and rapidly spread to Amman. As troops moved into the capital on 9 June, King Hussein narrowly escaped death when his motorcade came under fire outside the city.[20] Once again, Hussein and Arafat found themselves face-to-face at the negotiating table, but the ceasefire agreement they struck was instantly rejected by radical PLO factions. To turn up the heat, the Marxist Popular Front held sixty-eight Westerners hostage in two downtown hotels for forty-eight hours. King Hussein was pushed to further concessions. On 11 June, he announced the resignation from key army posts of two close relatives, uncle Sharif Nasser bin Jamil and cousin Zeid bin Shaker (whose sister had been killed by Palestinians during that month's fighting). For Hussein this was a humiliation. Not only did the move touch directly on his conduct of affairs of state; it appeared to impugn members of his family, and two men who were popular within the army.

In the ensuing weeks, the king went further in appeasing the Palestinians, allowing their leaders to nominate ministers for a new government that was formed towards the end of June. According to Arafat, he even offered the PLO itself the chance of forming a government. Arafat refused, telling the king: 'We are not hungry for power. It is not my dream to rule any other Arab country but only to reach Jerusalem.'[21]

Even if Arafat's account is true, it seems unlikely that Hussein's offer was genuine, for having effectively suffered two defeats at the hands of the *fedayeen*, the king could not afford to contemplate a further erosion of his power. His resolve was stiffened by the international concern that events in Jordan were provoking. In Israel, a debate was under way within the military establishment about the Palestinian threat to Hussein, and although some voices argued that Israel should stay out of the conflict and let the *fedayeen* take over, the majority took the opposite view: if the Hashemite throne was in serious danger, Israel might have to intervene.[22] Just as ominous for Arafat, Hussein's difficulties were also attracting attention in Washington. The Americans had been worried for some time about the growing strength of the Palestinians – a fact of which senior State Department officials had had firsthand experience earlier in the year, when they had had to cancel a helicopter trip across the Jordan river for fear of being shot down by guerrillas in the valley. In the eyes of Henry Kissinger, President Nixon's National Security Adviser, who counted the 'Little King' as a personal friend, the rise of the *fedayeen*, backed by radical, pro-Soviet regimes in Syria and Iraq, posed almost as much of a threat to American interests as to those of Jordan. Kissinger concluded that the confrontation in Jordan was a superpower trial of strength in the making, and set out during the summer to encourage Hussein to make a decisive move against the *fedayeen*.[23]

Quietly but deliberately, Hussein began to prepare for the worst. He reshuffled senior military officers under his own command and cancelled army leave. To ensure rank and file loyalty, a ferocious propaganda campaign against the *fedayeen* was conducted in the barracks, and special army units disguised as Palestinian guerrillas contributed to the mayhem. Desultory negotiations continued throughout the summer of 1970, but when the time came for Hussein to act, the *fedayeen* had managed, by their own mistakes, to ensure that nobody was eager to come to their aid.

Their biggest blunder was to alienate President Nasser. For more than two years, he had acted as the Palestinians' friend and protector, helping Arafat to take over the chairmanship of the PLO, providing his movement with money and persuading numerous Third World and socialist countries to recognize it. But now he was tired and ill, and looking for at least a breathing space in the cycle of Arab-Israeli violence in which his country had been locked for most of his career. The result was increasing strain in his relationship with the Palestinian leaders, who vehemently opposed all talk of a political settlement.

On 23 July 1970, Nasser unexpectedly accepted a revised American peace plan for the Middle East. The move unleashed a storm of protest among the resistance organizations in Jordan. Even Arafat's Fatah group, hitherto anxious to preserve its ties with Egypt, attacked Nasser by name and threatened in a radio broadcast to 'use bullets to quash any attempt to impose a political solution.'[24] Most insultingly of all, Palestinian demonstrators paraded through the streets of Amman displaying a picture of Nasser attached to a donkey.

Incensed, Nasser closed down PLO broadcasting stations in Cairo and expelled radical Palestinian activists from the country. In Amman, Arafat was swiftly brought to realize that his movement had shot itself in both feet, and he hurried to Cairo in August at the head of a senior PLO delegation, to patch things up. Receiving the Palestinian leaders at his holiday retreat outside Alexandria, Nasser was still in a cold fury. He told them he had been pacing up and down the roof of his house for an hour to get his feelings under control.[25] It was a long and difficult meeting. For seven hours, Nasser sought to explain his position to Arafat and his comrades, and to warn them against trying to topple King Hussein. 'I'm an army officer,' he said. 'Don't give me heroic speeches about resistance. I want to keep Hussein. I'm not asking for your secrets, but I tell you: don't try and do such a thing.'[26]

In late August, Hussein threw down the gauntlet. Returning from a three-day visit to Cairo, he warned the *fedayeen* that he would tolerate no challenge to his 'absolute sovereignty'. It was the cue for intensified street disturbances, more clashes with the army and another attempt on the king's life. Palestinians called for a general strike to protest against Hussein's co-operation with American peace moves, but it was now clear to their enemies in Jordan that few Arab tears would be shed if the resistance were cut down to size. As Jordanian shells rained on PLO headquarters, Arafat appealed to Arab heads of state for immediate intervention. On a visit to Baghdad in early September he was promised the protection of the Iraqi army division stationed in Jordan, and told to 'take any arms you want from our stores'.[27] But from other Arab states, the only response to his appeal was empty sabre-rattling.

Into this highly charged atmosphere, the left wing of the resistance threw a bomb. On 6 September 1970, while their leader George Habash was away in North Korea fraternizing with the Japanese Red Army, members of the Popular Front engaged in an unprecedented frenzy of air piracy. They brought two hijacked planes – a Swissair DC-8 and a TWA Boeing 707 – to a remote desert airstrip known as Dawsons Field, swiftly renamed 'Revolution Airport'. Six days later, after bringing in a hijacked BOAC VC-10 to join the other two and removing the passengers and crews, they blew up all three.

Arafat was furious. Although he had made no conspicuous attempt to stop the two-year wave of PFLP hijackings, he had long told anyone who would listen that he disapproved. Realizing the threat that this latest outrage posed to his already flimsy hold over revolutionary events in Jordan, he had been working to defuse the crisis by laying down guidelines for the release of passengers and planes. Now his authority had been wilfully flouted and all he could do in response was have the Popular Front suspended from the PLO's policy-making Central Committee. It was a case of too little, too late.

Frantic Arab mediators advised the PLO leadership to 'count to ten' and reach an accommodation with Hussein and yet another compromise agreement, imposing restrictions on the resistance, was hammered out in mid-September.[28] But King Hussein was already busy formulating other plans. In a radio broadcast on 16 September, he declared martial law and announced that he was setting up a military government to restore 'order and security'. Within twenty-four hours, bloody fighting had broken out on the hillsides of Amman as the army closed in on the *fedayeen*.

So long in the making, the showdown still caught the Palestinian resistance totally unprepared. It had no battle plan and had not even prepared hiding places for its leaders. Arafat, named PLO commander-in-chief only hours before the fighting started, wavered between calling for the overthrow of the military government and trying frantically to patch things up with King Hussein by telephone. He could not get through. Hussein and his advisers, he was told, were all saying their morning prayers.

But even had he been able to reach the king, it is not clear what he could have said. According to a close adviser of Hussein, the military government had already sent emissaries to Arafat for one last try at salvaging the situation. 'I am sorry,' he is quoted as replying, 'the situation has run out of my hands and all I can do is give the king twenty-four hours to leave the country.'[29]

The conflict of that September – Black September as it came to be known – was bloodier and more protracted than anyone could have possibly imagined. Given the pitifully disorganized state of the resistance, Hussein had anticipated it would all be over within forty-eight hours. But the Palestinians, armed only with Kalashnikovs, hand grenades and a handful of mortars and rocket-propelled grenades, fought with courage and determination, and hundreds of Palestinian and Jordanian army soldiers defected to them. Around the northern town of Irbid, the *fedayeen* managed to establish a 'liberated zone' which they swiftly named the Republic of Palestine. As the army sent tanks into Amman, rounding up any resistance leaders its troops could find and pounding the refugee camps with its artillery, the onslaught began to look like an all-out tribal war. No part of the capital was safe from the relentless shellfire, and dead bodies rotted in the streets as casualties – most of them civilian – climbed into the thousands.

Arafat, in particular, was a marked man. 'It was an attempt to liquidate both the revolution and the PLO,' he says. 'There was a special squad from the Jordanian forces whose sole task was to follow me.'[30] Unlike most of his peers in the Fatah leadership, he evaded capture. Followers, who moved him from house to house to keep him out of harm's way, describe him as active in the front line, co-ordinating the troops by makeshift wireless here, carrying an RPG launcher on his shoulder there.

But the odds against the Palestinians were overwhelming. In response to pleas for help from King Hussein, the United States Sixth Fleet was on the alert in the eastern

Mediterranean and Israel was being encouraged to contemplate intervention by air or land to save his regime. Against such an array of forces, Arafat's supposed Arab friends hesitated to come to his aid. Iraq, which had been warned in the strongest terms by Washington not to mobilize its Jordanian expeditionary force, meekly pulled its troops out of harm's way. The radical leaders of Syria did send a substantial contingent of tanks, painted in Palestinian army colours, into northern Jordan, but they thought better of it and pulled the tanks back when General Hafez al-Assad, the cautious and calculating Defence Minister, failed to provide air cover against a Jordanian counter-attack.

It was not until the sixth day of fighting that Arab efforts to end the fighting got under way. The ailing President Nasser, ordered by his doctors to rest, had been slow to intervene, but on 22 September he convened a summit meeting of Arab leaders at the plush Nile Hilton Hotel to discuss ways of saving the resistance from the destruction that was staring it in the face. They decided to launch a bizarre and dangerous mission: Jaafar Nimeiri, the robust soldier-president of Sudan, was to lead a small delegation to Amman, secure the freedom of the jailed resistance leaders and negotiate a ceasefire.

The events that followed were a cross between thriller and farce. The mediators managed to hammer out an agreement between Hussein and a group of PLO leaders freed from prison, and to take them back to Cairo, but no sooner was the deal broadcast over Radio Amman than Arafat – from his hiding place elsewhere in the capital – rejected it. The resistance would fight 'until the overthrow of the fascist regime in Jordan', he vowed.[31] Given that the *fedayeen* were running low on ammunition and losing ground to the Jordanian offensive, it was a foolhardy stand, but it prompted the Arab leaders to have one more stab at mediation.

Reluctantly, Nimeiri and his fellow envoys returned to Amman in an attempt to find Arafat before the Jordanian

Army did. Speaking from the Egyptian embassy, he made a radio appeal for the PLO leader to meet him. Shortly afterwards Arafat signalled his assent on the PLO's own wireless channel, quaintly named Zamzam 105 after the sacred well in Mecca.

In a hail of shellfire, which the mediators vainly tried to halt by telephoning the king, the two leaders met in a flat in an area of Amman controlled by the resistance. 'You should come with us back to Cairo, because Nasser told us not to return without you,' said Nimeiri.[32] The question was, how was Arafat to escape from a capital where he was in constant danger of being shot? The answer was provided by Sheikh Saad al-Abdullah, crown prince of Kuwait, who was a member of the Arab delegation. 'We're in this together,' he said. 'Either we'll both be killed or we'll both survive.' Whereupon he provided Arafat with a set of Arab robes, and the Palestinian leader was smuggled out of the country disguised as a Kuwaiti official.[33] Escaping in disguise was in danger of becoming a habit.

When he arrived at the Nile Hilton, Arafat, fully armed and on his guard, got straight to work on the assembled Arab heads of state. After a hasty snack, he set about exposing in all its lurid horror King Hussein's 'conspiracy' against the Palestinian revolution.[34] Some of his listeners, at least, turned a willing ear. Colonel Gadaffi, the flamboyant Libyan leader, was all for hanging the 'madman' Hussein in Cairo's central Tahrir Square.[35] There ensued a lengthy debate concerning Hussein's mental health and whether he, too, should be invited to attend.

'What's the use of getting him?' exclaimed Gadaffi. 'He's crazy. He's mad. Isn't his father in an asylum in Istanbul? It's an inheritance in that family. They're all mad.'[36]

This was too much for some of the other leaders present. 'How can you say that about an Arab king?' interjected Saudi Arabia's King Faisal, standing on his dignity. Finally, a weary President Nasser sought to bring the discussion to a close. 'It seems to me that we are all mad,' he said. 'I suggest that we get some doctors to see us and decide who is mad and who is not.'[37]

In due course, Hussein did show up, decked out in military fatigues and carrying a bag he said contained tape recordings that would prove the Palestinians had been plotting to overthrow him. He did not meet the fate Gadaffi intended, but received instead a roasting from his fellow summiteers that must have been almost as uncomfortable. Arafat, for his part, flew into repeated tantrums which almost scuppered the talks.[38]

The upshot, on 27 September, was a frosty handshake between Arafat and Hussein. They signed a fourteen-point agreement providing for a ceasefire, the withdrawal of all forces from Amman and a regrouping of commandos in agreed areas suitable for guerrilla attacks on Israel, and the drawing-up under an Arab committee of another, more durable accord. A civil war that had cost some 3000 lives according to Red Cross estimates – and 20,000 according to Arafat's own inflated guess – seemed, for the moment at least, to be over.[39] One other result of Nasser's peace initiative made news that same night. After spending hours at the airport seeing off his guests, the exhausted President collapsed at home and died of a heart attack. Arafat burst into tears on hearing the news – as well he might. With Nasser's death disappeared the last guarantee that the PLO-Jordanian accords he had expended so much effort in putting together would be implemented. The new Egyptian President, Anwar Sadat, did not have nearly so much clout, nor so much fellow-feeling for the *fedayeen*.

Neither side had the slightest intention of carrying out the agreement to which they had put their names in Cairo. The *fedayeen* – suspecting that he was intent on ejecting them from Jordan altogether rather than allowing them to continue their guerrilla raids – hung on to the sizeable portion of Amman which they still controlled. In secret talks with Israeli Foreign Minister Yigal Allon in October 1970, Hussein promised to do his best to prevent *fedayeen* actions against Israel,[40] and in subsequent meetings between the king's men and the PLO to dot the i's and cross the t's, negotiators found themselves back at square one: the follow-up agreement reached in mid-October merely rehearsed all the old contradictions between the two sides without resolving them.[41]

Bit by bit the Jordanians, under a new hard-line Prime Minister, Wasfi Tal, closed the net on the resistance. First the heat was stepped up on Palestinian bases in the north and west. Then the regime demanded the evacuation of the *fedayeen* from Amman, as provided for under the initial agreement. Finally, all that was left to the resistance was a couple of pockets of forested territory north of the capital, and up there, in the hills around Jerash and Ajlun, a total of around 4000 fighters entrenched themselves in caves and underground excavations. They were tired, isolated from the majority who had taken refuge in Damascus, and desperately demoralized.

Arafat was holed up with his men in the Ajlun area, negotiating fitfully with officials in Amman to preserve some breathing space for the resistance. But as Jordanian troops moved closer to the guerrilla hideaways and began to lay siege to the area in the spring of 1971, he realized that the end was only a matter of time; in April, he prepared to take his leave of a country where only twelve months earlier his movement had been riding so high. From his mountain hideaway, he sent one last urgent appeal for help to Munib al-Masri, a Palestinian friend serving as Minister of Public Works in King Hussein's government. Together with the Saudi ambassador and an officer from the Jordanian army, Masri set off immediately to see what could be done. When they finally found Arafat, he reduced them to tears with his tales of Jordanian atrocities. They decided to take him to see King Hussein and try, yet again, to resolve the problem.

On the journey back towards Amman in the Saudi ambassador's car, Arafat sat between the diplomat and the Jordanian officer, nervously fingering his Kalashnikov. 'At every Jordanian checkpoint, they wanted to shoot him,' says Masri. 'The soldiers were accusing the Palestinians and Arafat of terrible things. I was really scared, but Arafat put on a show of defiance. He would reply by saying: "Soldier, you're talking to the head of the Palestinian revolution. These acts you're talking about didn't happen." And the soldier would quieten down.'[42]

In fact, Arafat had no intention of going back to Amman. Once they had driven down from the hills, he asked instead to be taken to a town on the Syrian border, where he had an urgent task to perform. And there, after despatching the others into the cold night, he slipped away into Syria. 'I don't want to go as a renegade to Amman,' he told Masri before departing. 'I've had reports that my life is in danger. I want to come back as head of state for the PLO.'[43] Arafat would not return to Jordan for another seven years.

The attack on those Palestinians who remained around Ajlun came on 12 July, and it was of a ferocity to rival the fighting of the previous September. The guerrillas were rooted out of their bases; many, including the Fatah commander Abu Ali Iyad, were massacred in cold blood by the king's Bedu soldiers; ninety were so terrified or horrified by what they saw that they were authorized by their commanding officer, Abbas Zeki, to seek refuge across the river in Israel rather than allow themselves to fall into the hands of Jordanian troops. The Israelis willingly took the guerrillas in. 'It was a nice, human gesture,' says General Yariv, the former Israeli military intelligence chief. 'And in the history of relations between Israel and the PLO, human gestures are few and far between.'[44]

Deprived of its main launching pad for attacks against Israel, its ranks decimated by the fighting with Jordan, the Palestinian revolution limped away to lick its wounds in the only other front-line states that would still receive it, Syria and Lebanon. In this second exile, the *fedayeen* were confronted with a series of stark questions about their experience of the past four years. What exactly had gone wrong? How had the resistance movement's internal divisions contributed to the catastrophe? How should they be resolved? Why had the Arab states not done more to assist them? The last question was in a way the most disturbing, for it raised serious doubts about the extent to which the new generation of Arab leaders that had pledged support to Arafat's PLO could deliver. Perhaps men like Assad, by now Syria's President, were less interested in saving the PLO's skin than in preserving their own. Perhaps for them Palestine was a political symbol to be manipulated more than a prize to be won.

Above all, the *fedayeen* leaders asked, where were they to go from here? In the bitterness of defeat, it was not surprising that their thoughts turned to revenge against the regime that had so violently ejected them – and against the world. King Hussein had already been warned what to expect. At a meeting early in 1971, Salah Khalaf had told him: 'If you strike the *fedayeen* in their last hold-outs, I'll follow you to the end of the earth, to my dying breath, to give you the punishment you deserve.' Shaken, the king could only murmur: 'God forbid.'[45]

# 5
# *Black September*

> 'A bomb in the White House, a mine in the Vatican, the death of Mao Tse-tung, an earthquake in Paris; none of these could have produced the far-reaching echo to every man in the world like the operation of Black September in Munich.' Commentary in *Al-Sayyad* newspaper, Beirut, 13 September 1972.

In the early morning of 5 September 1972, a quiet Palestinian checked out of the Eden-Hotel-Wolff, a comfortable, family-style hotel on Arnulfstrasse near the centre of Munich. For anyone anxious to make a quick getaway from the city and its environs, the Eden-Hotel-Wolff was perfectly situated. Opposite was the railway station and right outside the front entrance was an airport bus terminal. If staff had been vigilant they would have noticed that their Middle Eastern guest was in something of a rush to leave behind a city that was just awakening to the news that its attempts to stage a trouble-free Olympic Games had been shattered.

The mysterious Palestinian had registered at the hotel on 25 August with a bogus Iraqi passport in the name of Saad el-Din Wali, a 37-year-old journalist. In a city full of foreign journalists, busy hotel staff had no reason to disbelieve him, although had they monitored his movements carefully they would have seen no evidence of *bona fide* journalistic activity. He spent much of his time in his room in hushed conversation with Arab colleagues. He phoned Beirut, Tripoli and Tunis. 'Wali' was, in fact, one of the chief planners of the Black September Organization and his mission was to oversee preparations for a spectacular assault on the Israeli team headquarters in the Munich Olympic Village.[1]

In the twenty-four hours following his hasty departure, the world was brought face-to-face with Palestinian terror at its most extreme. The code-name Black September, the mainstream PLO's terrorist arm forged from anger and despair after the bloody expulsion of Palestinian guerrilla forces from Jordan in July 1971, was emblazoned across newspaper front pages in dozens of languages. The phrase, 'the Munich massacre', would find a permanent and sinister place in the lexicon of the Palestinian-Israeli struggle. For Western intelligence services and for foreign journalists, the name spawned perturbing questions. What was Black September and, more to the point, who was behind it? It was not long before the world heard an unexpectedly frank accounting from one of the terrorist organization's most senior figures.

On 24 March 1973, just six months after Munich, Abu Daoud Mohammed Awdah, a tall man, his dark hair flecked with grey, was brought before a television camera in Amman. Staring into the camera's baleful eye, Awdah uttered words that cannot but have dismayed his masters in Damascus and in Beirut. Now, in a televised confession he stated there was 'no such thing' as Black September. 'Fatah,' he declared, 'announces its operations under this name so that Fatah would not appear as the direct executor of the operations of the intelligence organ which is run by Abu Youssef [Mohammed Youssef al-Najjar] and Abu Hassan [Ali Hassan Salameh] . . . Abu Iyad [Salah Khalaf],' he added, 'carries out big operations like the Munich operation.'[2]

What the television camera did not show was the extent to which Awdah had been brutally tortured by Hussein's secret police. He had been trussed up like a chicken and could barely walk; to this day, he bears the scars of the rope burns on his legs. Awdah says that he has no recollection of the events leading up to his televised 'confession'. The tape, he claims, was 'doctored'.[3] But at the time his words tended to confirm a widespread assumption: that Fatah was the force behind Black September. Israeli retribution was swift. Within a few weeks three of the PLO's top operatives were slain by Israeli paratroopers; Salah Khalaf himself was lucky to survive.

Khalaf, Fatah's security and intelligence chief, was for a long time the PLO's deadly pragmatist and latterly one of its more moderate voices. But back in July 1971 when the PLO's northern Jordanian bases were smashed by Hussein's Bedu legions, he had been an implacable and angry foe of the Hashemites, of Israel and the West. He was not alone. Demand for revenge pushed PLO leaders of all factions into a bidding war.

'Between 1969 and 1972 we were crazy people,' recalls Yasser Abed Rabbo, a leader of the Marxist Democratic Front, an Arafat confidant and now one of the PLO's leading moderates. 'We wanted to change the whole world. We wanted to fight Israel, the Americans, even the Soviets, because they were not supportive, King Hussein, the Palestinian bourgeoisie – everybody.'[4]

If Arafat had had any doubts about what course to take, the demands for revenge from his own supporters would have been more than enough to convince him. Some Fatah militants were threatening to defect to more extreme factions, such as Habash's Popular Front, and at acrimonious meetings in Damascus in late August and early September 1971 a few select Fatah leaders, including Arafat himself, took the decision to establish a special unit to conduct revenge operations against Hussein's Hashemite regime and other targets. It was a fateful step that would have decidedly mixed consequences for Arafat and his organization but in the atmosphere of anger and shame after Jordan, the demand for vengeance was paramount. 'Our whole purpose was how to tell the world we weren't down and that the world will not enjoy full peace without us,' recalls a close Arafat adviser. 'Up to early 1973 Arafat gave his green light [to major terrorist operations], but details were worked out by others. These were not matters that were debated.'[5] At Arafat's spirited insistence, Fatah leaders also resolved that every effort be made to disguise its links with the terrorist unit. Just as the founders of the guerrilla organization had named their military wing Al-Asifa, to obscure its connection with the parent organization, so they created a new 'front' for terrorist operations. Thus, Black September was born.

As the winter of 1971 approached in the barren hills of the Arqoub region in southern Lebanon, later to be known as Fatahland, preparations were already well under way for a series of stunning terrorist attacks to be carried out in the name of Black September. Recruits came from the embittered ranks of Fatah itself, from Habash's Popular Front, and from splinter factions such as the Syrian-backed Saiqa. Operationally, Fatah and elements of the Popular Front – differences were buried temporarily – came together in the planning and execution of a series of bloody terrorist coups that would in the minds of many in the West associate Arafat and the PLO leadership with violence and mayhem on a grand scale. But it was the Arab world, and Jordan in particular, that bore the initial brunt of the Palestinian desire for vengeance.

On 28 November 1971, at around 1.30 p.m., a solidly built Jordanian, exuding confidence and authority, briskly climbed the steps of the Cairo Sheraton on the banks of the Nile. Tailed by a posse of security guards, Wasfi al-Tal, Prime Minister and strongman of Jordan, was intent on meeting his wife after an early lunch with officials of the Arab League. If he had other thoughts in mind, they may well have concerned his secret discussions with Khaled al-Hassan, the Fatah moderate, on a truce between Jordan and the PLO in the wake of Black September. The two men had been talking about an arrangement that would have allowed Palestinian fighters to continue operating from remote bases in Jordan, but Tal did not live to see these delicate negotiations come to fruition. As he approached the hotel lobby, thronged with tourists and other visitors, he was cut down by a youthful gunman. Coolly, Tal's assassin emptied five shots into the man many Palestinian militants held most responsible for their expulsion from Jordan. In an obscene gesture, and one that underscored the blind hatred behind the attack, the assassin, later identified as Mansur Suleiman Khalifah, was reported to have knelt down and lapped up Tal's blood as it oozed from his wounds on to the hotel steps.

Tal was, in a way, an obvious target. In the lurid Palestinian mythology of the time, he was rumoured personally to have tortured and killed Abu Ali Iyad, the leader of the Fatah militia in Jordan, and then to have ordered that his body be dragged through northern Jordanian villages behind a Centurion tank, though there is not the slightest evidence that this was the case. The four-man terrorist cell responsible for Tal's execution was in fact initially identified as the 'Abu Ali Iyad group'. Little attention was paid at first to the commandos' triumphant cry as they were bundled into a police van outside the Sheraton. 'We are Black September,' they shouted, raising their fingers in an aggressive salute.

Tal's death was greeted with jubilation in the Palestinian diaspora, with dismay among Jordanians and with grim satisfaction by PLO leaders, with one notable exception. Khaled al-Hassan, the moderate who had served since 1969 as PLO 'foreign minister', condemned the slaying, describing it bitterly as 'one of the acts of terrorist, fascist thinking which conflicts with the thinking of the revolution'.[6] But his voice was ignored in an organization bent on revenge, and in any case, Khaled Hassan resigned not many months later.

Although it is inconceivable that Arafat was not aware of the major terrorist operations, this era is not something he is yet prepared to discuss. Indeed, he invariably flies into a rage when questioned on the issue. His deputies, however, have been much more forthcoming. Salah Khalaf, for one, offered a clear rationale for the PLO's resort to terror. In his memoir, he explained with chilling logic that because they were unable to wage classic guerrilla warfare across Israel's borders after they had lost their bases in Jordan in 1971, Fatah's young men 'insisted on carrying out a revolutionary violence of another kind, commonly known elsewhere as "terrorism" '.[7] The slaying of Tal, whom he described as 'one of the butchers of the Palestinian people', was a warning to others in the Arab world who might be tempted to 'sacrifice the rights or interests of the Palestinian people'.[8] At the time, Arafat himself was scarcely less forthright. He told PLO Radio in Cairo that before the year 1971 was out 'four of our revolutionaries had overthrown the traitor Wasfi al-Tal, and our revolutionaries will continue to pursue all traitors in the Arab nation.'[9]

The Tal execution was merely the first of a series of attacks on Jordanian officials, including several plots to do away with Hussein himself. Khalaf made no secret of his own central role as head of the 'underground apparatus' which the PLO leadership established in September 1971 to 'work for the downfall of the [Jordanian] regime'.[10]

A little more than two weeks after Wasfi al-Tal's death, Black September struck again, this time in Europe. On 16 December, a gunman fired thirty to forty rounds from an automatic weapon into a Daimler carrying Zeid al-Rifai, then Jordan's ambassador in London. Rifai, described by Khalaf as 'one of Hussein's minions' and a 'deadly' adviser to the king,[11] was slightly wounded in the hand. Later enmity between Rifai and the Palestinian leadership is not hard to understand in light of this event.

In their fury, the Jordanian authorities wasted no time in associating Arafat's Fatah mainstream faction with Black

September. A broadcast on Amman radio on 17 December charged that the terror front was 'only a mask used by Fatah to hide its treacherous schemes'.[12] But the barrage of words from Amman did nothing to deflect the PLO's hard men from their avowed aim of settling their blood feud with the Hashemites.

Between 1971 and 1973 the PLO made the overthrow of the 'puppet royal regime' of King Hussein its main aim, even it seemed at the expense, at times, of confrontation with Israel. The PLO's Planning Centre in Beirut – the PLO think-tank headed by Arafat's confidant, Nabil Shaath – drew up a blueprint for a Palestinian-Jordanian National Liberation Front with the express purpose of bringing down the Hashemites. The Palestinian 'parliament', the Palestine National Council, in Cairo in April 1972, gave 'legislative' support to these aims when it declared that the 'liberation of Jordan' was as important as removing Israel from Palestine.[13]

Cairo, meanwhile, had witnessed an extraordinary judicial event. On 29 February 1972 after a sham trial a court had released, on bail provided by the PLO, the four defendants who had admitted their role in the assassination of Wasfi al-Tal three months previously. Leftist Arab lawyers vied with each other to represent the 'defendants'. After their release on bail, the four were quietly spirited out of Egypt to Damascus, and never again came to trial. Not only was justice not done, it was seen not to be done.

In a curious postscript to the affair, the Cairo hearing was told that a medical and ballistics report 'found' that the bullets that killed Tal had not been fired from the guns carried by the defendants.[14] This prompted fresh debate as to whether the Black Septembrists were actually responsible or whether a third party, who had escaped detection, might not have been involved. It is entirely possible that the ballistics report was doctored to provide a pretext for acquittal – in the unlikely event that the defendants had really come to trial.

As 1972 dawned, the world's intelligence services were buzzing with talk of Palestinian terrorism. America's CIA was devoting much closer attention to the subject than it had before. So were its European counterparts, and no-one more than the West Germans. Ever since 1970, Germany's intelligence services had known that members of the German Red Army Faction were being trained in terrorist tactics in camps in southern Lebanon and South Yemen. 'We knew perfectly well before Munich that the Middle East conflict would take place on European soil, too,' says one German spymaster. 'After Black September 1970, we were convinced that something was going to explode. Arafat switched his operations to Europe, to hit at soft targets with the assistance of the Red Army Faction.'[15]

But nobody foresaw Munich. Israel's intelligence community had concluded that it would face a continuing surge of Palestinian terrorism, including the danger of spectacular and eye-catching operations, but none of Israel's three intelligence and security services dreamed that the Palestinians would seek to disrupt the Olympic Games, the world's most sacred sporting occasion. 'We thought at the beginning of 1972 that they [the Palestinians] were sort of stymied. We thought they were going for operations that would have a major impact, and it was up to our intelligence to see whether we could forestall them. But we didn't see Munich,' says General Yariv.[16] Perhaps surprisingly, there are those among former heads of Israeli intelligence who believe today that the PLO gained ground from Munich. The organization could not have made a more emphatic or shocking statement about the plight of the Palestinians. Munich, in all its horror, proved in many ways the great divide, the watershed event in the post-1967 Palestinian struggle. Things would not be the same again.

German intelligence documents reveal that the seeds of Munich had begun to germinate in the minds of Black

September commanders in Beirut early in 1972. By mid-year, senior operatives had been despatched to Germany to investigate. They considered several options. One was to kidnap Israeli officials and to hold them hostage against the release of Palestinians in Israeli jails. But it was the attack against the athletes, with its awesome potential to shock, that held most appeal.

On 8 July, as the heat of summer slowed life in Damascus to a crawl, Mohammed Yousef al Najjar, the tough operational head of Black September, held a series of meetings with counterparts from Habash's Popular Front and from the Syrian-backed PLO faction, Saiqa. The terrorist bosses decided, in principle, to proceed. In early August, the two leaders of the chosen Black September commando unit arrived in Munich to 'acclimatize' themselves, followed in succeeding weeks by the rest of the eight-member team.[17] None flew to the Federal Republic. They came by a variety of land routes from Rome and from Belgrade. None of them was to carry guns or explosives across national frontiers either. That detail had been taken care of. Syrian diplomats would act as arms couriers.

The stage was set for the invasion of the Olympic Village at 4.30 a.m. on 5 September by the eight commandos who had no trouble at all breaching the surprisingly flimsy security. Swiftly, the Palestinians, well briefed about the village layout, entered the Israeli team headquarters. Two team members were killed and nine others were kidnapped in the process. A day of high drama that was to end in tragedy had begun. The world watched transfixed as the television cameras beamed pictures live from the Olympic Village. Throughout a long day of almost unbearable tension one image above all others, that of the hooded gunman on the balcony of the team headquarters, was to be repeated over and over again until it came to represent, in the minds of a generation, Palestinian terrorism at its bloodiest. In jittery negotiations, the guerrillas pressed for the release of dozens of Arab prisoners held in Israel.

The Israeli cabinet, meeting in emergency session with Prime Minister Golda Meir in the chair, was adamant that there could be no question of dealing with the terrorists, let alone meeting their conditions. But as night fell the increasingly desperate German authorities had decided that a rescue attempt would have to be made. The PLO commandos, who had demanded that they be flown to Cairo together with their hostages, were taken by helicopter to the Fuerstenfeldbrueck military airport on the outskirts of Munich. They had been duped into believing they would be allowed to board a Lufthansa plane for the Egyptian capital, where negotiations would continue. But the Germans had absolutely no intention of letting them leave the ground with the Israeli athletes still captive. Nor, needless to say, did the Israeli government, which had despatched General Zvi Zamir, the gaunt, balding chief of its feared overseas spyforce, Mossad, to keep an eye on things.

Zamir later told colleagues that he had a 'hollow feeling' as he took the lift to the darkened control tower at Fuerstenfeldbrueck that evening.[18] He was not convinced that German plans to attack the PLO gunmen with sniper fire offered the best chance of freeing the Israeli hostages, but nor did he feel he was in a position to criticize the German tactics. He was reduced to asking questions about the numbers of snipers that would be employed and where they might be deployed.

Zamir's sense of impending disaster deepened as the leaders of the terrorist commando left their helicopters just before 11 p.m. to inspect the Lufthansa Boeing, sitting some distance away on the tarmac. In a fury, the gunmen realized they had been tricked. The plane was cold and empty. There was no crew on board. It was not going anywhere, and certainly not to a safe haven in Cairo. Nervously, they moved back towards the helicopters, but before they could reach them they were cut down by snipers' bullets. In the control tower, the Germans and

Israelis watched, appalled. The Arab gunmen traded shots with German police and fired on their hostages. A grenade was thrown into one of the helicopters, blowing it to pieces; the other caught fire. In the end fifteen people died and a number were wounded. All nine hostages were killed, five of the eight gunmen and one policeman.

In Damascus and Beirut, PLO leaders congratulated themselves on the Munich operation; in their terms it had been a qualified success. But they must also have realized that there would be penalties. Munich would mark the beginning of a vicious underground war as Israel sought vengeance against Black September's leaders. The question then, as now, was whether the price to the Palestinians in terms of howls of international outrage and the certainty of reprisals was worth paying. Black September chief Salah Khalaf had little doubt that the operation had attained at least some of its objectives. In his memoir, he wrote that 'world opinion was forced to take note of the Palestinian drama, and the Palestinian people imposed their presence on an international gathering that had sought to exclude them.'[19]

Arafat and the PLO leadership did not have to wait long for the first Israeli downpayment in its efforts to balance the ledger for Munich. On 8 September, two squadrons of Israeli jets blasted Arab guerrilla targets in Lebanon and Syria. The PLO also came under heavy international fire. George Bush, the US representative at the UN, spoke for the West in condemning the 'senseless and unprovoked terrorist attack in Munich'.[20]

Arafat, for his part, was careful not to comment directly on the Munich episode. The PLO, in an official statement on 14 September, disavowed responsibility, declaring that the 'wave of propaganda' in the Western press was aimed at 'spreading world hatred against the Arabs in general'.[21] As condemnation of the PLO ricocheted around the world, it was left to Mahmoud Darwish, Arafat's favourite poet, to seek to justify what many saw as the unjustifiable:

The one who has turned me into a refugee has made a
bomb of me.
I know that I will die.
I know that I'm venturing into a lost battle today
because it is the battle for a future.
I know that Palestine on the map is far away from me.

I know that you have forgotten its name and that you
use a new term for it.
I know all that.
That is why I carry it to your streets, your homes and
your bedrooms.
Palestine is not a land, gentlemen of the jury.
Palestine has become bodies that move, that move to the
streets of the world,
Singing the song of death because the new Christ has
given up his cross . . .
and gone out of Palestine.[22]

Germany, humiliated and deeply angered over the massacre, took immediate action against Palestinian activists who had made the Federal Republic their European stronghold, summarily expelling 100 student and worker militants, and setting up a special anti-terrorist squad. But, unhappily for the Germans that was by no means the end of the story. On 29 October, two Black Septembrists seized a Lufthansa flight over Turkey and demanded the release of the three surviving Munich gunmen. Germany, fearing another disaster, gave in. The three Munich survivors were flown to Libya to a hero's welcome, and later to Lebanon. Incensed at what it regarded as a show of weakness by the Germans, Israel charged that 'every capitulation encourages the terrorists to continue their criminal acts'.[23]

Within weeks of the Munich massacre, Israeli intelligence had established to its satisfaction who was responsible. It had no doubt it was Fatah. It was also certain that the man operationally in charge had been

Ali Hassan Salameh, young, charismatic, a favourite of Arafat and head of Force 17, the chairman's personal security detachment.

The conclusions Israeli intelligence drew when it began to reassess the threat posed by the PLO were not comforting. Since the Battle of Karameh in March 1968, and the later rash of plane hijackings and terrorism, Fatah and other guerrilla factions had been regarded as a nuisance, but one that could be dealt with militarily. After Munich that all changed, as the realization dawned that the Palestinian leadership was much more sophisticated politically than it had been given credit for. 'They think in strategic terms much better than we do,' is General Yariv's perhaps surprising assessment nearly two decades later. 'They analyse our strategy. They do not always draw the right conclusions, but they understand that the aim of any military operation is political, and that the success of such operations should be measured in political terms.'[24]

Veterans of the Zionists' underground War of Independence in the 1940s, many of them now occupying high positions in the Israeli government, began to see parallels between their own earlier struggle and that of Arafat and the Palestinians. But none of this softened attitudes in Israel after Munich. Golda Meir, who has been likened by one of her close associates at the time to a 'fiercely protective mother shielding her children from some sort of ogre', was determined that the war be carried to those deemed by Israeli intelligence to have been behind the Munich massacre, wherever they could be hunted down. One of her first acts after Munich was to appoint General Yariv, the cool, dapper and cerebral outgoing chief of military intelligence, as her special assistant in combating terrorism. His task was to help co-ordinate the activities of the three intelligence and security services – Mossad, Shin Bet and military intelligence – as the underground war with the PLO reached a peak in the spring of 1973.

'The policy was to go for the leaders, and also to create

circumstances under which it would make it very difficult for them to operate. It was not an easy decision to make, but at the time we believed we had no other choice,' General Yariv recalls. 'There were debates and discussion at the time that maybe there were other defensive ways, and we also understood that it was risky. What we could do, they could do as well.'[25]

Between September 1972 and July 1973, the capitals of Europe witnessed a string of reprisals and counter-reprisals. Arafat estimates that more than sixty of his people were killed or maimed in the ten-month shadow war. Israeli casualties were significantly less, but substantial nevertheless.

Much has been written about the formation of a special Mossad 'Wrath of God squad' to carry out assassinations, but according to an Israeli official intimately involved in planning and directing the underground war, 'no special unit was established that was not there before. What was there was good enough,' he says grimly.[26]

Israeli gunmen and explosives experts struck repeatedly and lethally in actions reminiscent of a gangland war. Their targets ranged across the spectrum of Palestinians in Europe. On 16 October 1972, just a little more than a month after the carnage at Munich, Wael Zuwaiter, a Palestinian writer, was gunned down in Rome as he was returning late one evening to his modest apartment; on 8 December, Mahmoud Hamshari, the PLO's Paris representative, was blown up in his apartment; on 6 April 1973, Bassel Kubeissy, a professor at the University of Baghdad and a PLO supporter, was shot in a Paris street.

Hamshari did not die immediately but more than a month later in hospital. A PLO intelligence officer, sent to Paris to investigate his death, believes to this day that he was killed in hospital. 'Forty days after he was admitted, and after he was making good progress in his recovery, he suffered from an obscure fever and within forty-eight hours he was dead. I'm convinced it was a medical assassination,' he says. Asked whether Hamshari was involved in Munich, the official says cryptically, 'All of us were involved.'[27] These killings, however, seemed like a minor tremor compared to a cataclysmic event that took place less than a week after Kubeissy's death, well away from the European theatre, and much closer to the sliver of land at the heart of the dispute between Arabs and Jews.

Beirut on 10 April 1973 was calm. Its residents, seemingly oblivious to the fact that their country was sliding towards civil war, were enjoying a pleasant eastern Mediterranean spring, the illusion of wellbeing, and the good life. The PLO high command, housed in comfortable apartments in the fashionable Ras Beirut area near the waterfront, was no exception. After its expulsion from Jordan, the guerrilla movement had regrouped surprisingly quickly; within a relatively short time its cadres were engaged, like soldier ants, in building another state within the state.

That April day, Black September chief Salah Khalaf broke his cardinal rule of not appearing in public except when absolutely necessary. He enjoyed a leisurely lunch at a fish restaurant on the waterfront with three of his closest friends in the leadership: Mohammed Yousef al-Najjar, the Black September operations chief; Kamal Adwan, in charge of operations in the occupied territories; and Kamal Nasir, the PLO spokesman. It was their last meal together. By early next morning, three of the four were dead, killed in a hail of bullets by Israeli sea-borne commandos who attacked their apartment building in Verdun Street. The fourth – Khalaf himself – was a prime target but he was saved by a stroke of luck. Ironically, as the attack began, he was in a nearby building, debriefing the three survivors of Munich. Arafat was also in the area.

Quickly on the scene after the attack, Khalaf went straight to the apartment of his best friend, the writer and poet Kamal Nasir. 'The sight that greeted me filled me with horror,' he recalled in his memoir. 'Through a mist of smoke from a rocket the Israelis had fired a few seconds before their assault, I saw my friend's body laid out in the form of a cross, the area around his mouth riddled with at least fifteen bullets.' The symbolism was stark. As well as being the PLO's spokesman, Nasir had been a Christian.[28]

In any terms, the slayings were a devastating blow for the PLO. Najjar, the former school-teacher who had become a powerful PLO orator, and Adwan, the tough, no-nonsense engineer, were key figures in the second tier of Fatah leaders. Their elimination left a gaping hole in the PLO hierarchy. In addition, the Israelis had carried away from Adwan's apartment top-secret archives that helped identify a number of PLO underground cells in the occupied territories. 'It was a catastrophe, and many men were forced to leave Palestine due to those documents,' says a top PLO intelligence official.[29]

Arafat, who two weeks earlier had warned his colleagues about security lapses, now adopted much stricter safety precautions himself. His Force 17 bodyguard, under Ali Hassan Salameh, was given additional resources and he himself became an even more elusive figure, moving from one safe house to another, rarely spending two consecutive days in the same place. He also turned his wrath against the United States, accusing it of complicity in the Israeli attack. Echoing an Algerian radio broadcast calling on Arabs to attack US embassies everywhere, Arafat charged on 13 April 1973 that the Central Intelligence Agency had been behind the Israeli attack. On the same day, the US State Department warned against the anti-American campaign and said such charges could harm the long-range interests of the Palestinian people.[30]

The Israeli assault on the apartment in Verdun Street was not quite the last shot in the underground war's most bloody phase. In Europe, the tit-for-tat conflict continued in fits and starts and on 21 July, it reached the little Norwegian town of Lillehammer. Relentlessly criss-crossing Europe in their efforts to hit Ali Hassan Salameh, Mossad assassins shot the wrong man. Ahmed Bouchiki, a Moroccan waiter, was gunned down as he was strolling home from the cinema late in the evening with his pregnant Norwegian wife. Israeli embarrassment was compounded when six members of the Mossad 'support team' – the two assassins had escaped – were rounded up and put on trial, ensuring maximum publicity for the affair.

Lillehammer marked the end of the all-out underground war in Europe. Mossad scaled down its activities. General Zamir retired. There was relief on both sides, a sentiment fully shared by Europe's counter-terrorism services. 'The Europeans were not at all happy having their countries as a playground for the Arab-Israeli war,' says an Israeli intelligence official who helped direct the hostilities. 'Lillehammer brought about a halt in operations, and that was OK with us.'[31]

Arafat and his senior colleagues had, in any case, been carefully reviewing their options since early 1973, concluding that resort to international terrorism brought only diminishing returns. What had jolted Arafat and the leadership into an acrimonious debate about the benefits of this bloody phase in the organization's history was the furore surrounding an event that remains perhaps the PLO's most controversial terrorist escapade and dogs the Organization's top leadership to this day.

At 7 p.m. sharp on 1 March 1973, a four-wheel drive vehicle with four gunmen on board had crashed through the gates of the Saudi embassy compound in Khartoum, the torpid capital of Sudan. Within seconds the gunmen, firing indiscriminately, had forced their way into the embassy building where a farewell party for G. Curtis Moore, the departing US *chargé d'affaires*, was in progress. The cream of the Khartoum diplomatic corps was present, including the incoming US ambassador, Cleo A. Noel. The gunmen seized Noel and Moore, along with Sheikh Abdullah al-Malhouk, the ambassador of Saudi Arabia, his wife, and the *chargés d'affaires* of Jordan and Belgium.

Inexplicably, Black September – in the persons of an eight-man commando unit bristling with weapons and headed by Selim Rizak, the deputy chief of the PLO office in Khartoum – had assaulted the premises of the wealthiest Arab state and one that had been the earliest and most consistent financier of Arafat's mainstream Fatah faction. The guerrillas issued a chilling ultimatum. They would kill their hostages within twenty-four hours if their demands were not met. Some of their requests were bizarre, to say the least. They included the release of the notorious Abu Daoud and other Fatah members imprisoned in Jordan; the freeing of Sirhan Sirhan, the convicted assassin of Robert F. Kennedy; all Arab women detained in Israel; and members of the Baader-Meinhof urban guerrilla group in West Germany 'because they supported the Palestinian cause'.[32]

Angrily, the US, Jordan and West Germany rejected the hostage-takers' demands, while behind the scenes Sudan and Egypt sought to defuse the crisis. Egypt even offered to send a plane to pick up the eight gunmen and their hostages to bring them back to Cairo for further negotiations. But all these efforts were in vain.

Just before 8 p.m. on Friday, 2 March, as the 24-hour deadline approached, Ambassador Cleo A. Noel made what was to prove the last of several telephone calls to the American embassy in Khartoum. Under the guns of his captors, Noel, who had suffered an ankle wound in the initial attack, enquired about the planned arrival of a senior American official who was expected to take charge of negotiations. When he was told that it would be later that evening, Noel replied tersely: 'That will be too late.'[33]

Soon after 9 p.m., forty equally spaced shots were clearly audible over the sound of a howling dust storm. Noel, Moore and Guy Eid, the Belgian *chargé d'affaires*, had been put up against a wall in the embassy basement and machine-gunned to death in a particularly cold-blooded and brutal slaying. A short time later, the leader of the commandos, Selim Rizak, informed the Sudanese Foreign Ministry by telephone that his gunmen had executed three of their captives.

Incensed, Sudan's ruler, Jaafar Nimeiri, who at some risk to himself had rescued Arafat when he was being hunted down in Jordan in 1970, accused Fatah of a 'criminal rash act devoid of revolutionary spirit and bravery'.[34] Saudi Arabia's King Faisal kept his counsel, but Arafat and his colleagues in Beirut can have been in no doubt about the depths of his displeasure.

The affair continues to haunt Arafat and other top leaders of the PLO but the key question has long since ceased to be whether or not Fatah was behind the Black September assault. Debate now centres on whether Arafat himself communicated directly on the radio link established between the PLO's Beirut communications centre and the Khartoum gunmen.

Israel still claims that it has a tape-recording of Arafat's voice uttering the code-word Nahr el-Bared, which means 'the cold river' in Arabic, to check whether the execution had been carried out. (Nahr el-Bared was a guerrilla training camp in Lebanon attacked by Israeli jets in late February 1973.) Israel has not yet produced the tape and neither has the US: an attempt by a group of Congressmen in 1986 to pressure the Justice Department into bringing an indictment against Arafat for murder on the basis of the alleged tape-recording was deflected by the administration.[35]

A senior US military intelligence official, familiar with details of the Khartoum affair, doubts that a recording of Arafat's voice actually giving instructions to the Khartoum gunmen exists: 'Now, if the Israelis have such a recording why haven't they brought it forward?' he asks. 'There's no reason why they should hold it back, after all. Or why don't they fake it? The answer is that there is a question of credibility here. They didn't fake it or leak it even through cut-outs because they know that there are people around – I think from one of the allied services in Beirut – who do know exactly what happened, and who would call their bluff. This is such a central issue that they dare not be exposed over it.'[36]

The US certainly has recordings of the radio traffic that passed between Khartoum and Beirut in the tense hours after a radio link was established between the gunmen and the Black September headquarters. Both the US embassy in Khartoum and the US mission in Beirut monitored every squeak that came out of each location. In fact, in a confidential cable dispatched within days of the slayings, the US embassy in Khartoum reported that it was 'notable that terrorists were apparently under external control from Beirut and did not murder Ambassador Noel and Moore nor surrender to GoS [Government of Sudan] until receiving specific code-word instructions.'[37]

While Arafat has steadfastly and angrily refused to discuss Khartoum, his late deputy, Salah Khalaf, had been more forthcoming. In his memoir he stated bluntly that the guerrillas' target was 'the American *chargé d'affaires* [G. Curtis Moore], who had been stationed in Amman prior to the 1970 war and bore a heavy responsibility for its preparation'.[38]

Whatever the extent of Arafat's involvement, he took the threats that the Khartoum affair posed to his moderate Arab support extremely seriously. On 18 March, two weeks after the slayings, he despatched the first of several high-level missions to the Sudan. It was led by Mohammed Abu Mayzar, later head of Fatah's foreign relations department, in an attempt to end the damaging rift with Nimeiri, whose rage over the whole business continued undiminished. Several other senior Fatah officials also visited Khartoum, including Ali Hassan Salameh, the PLO's young rising star. Salameh was told by Nimeiri's senior adviser that Sudan's President had a very simple message for the terrorist front: that if it continued to threaten Sudan, he would 'give them a whole year of Black Septembers'. Salameh had replied melodramatically; 'If any man threatens the Sudanese government, I will cut his tongue out.'[39]

Khartoum may have been, as has been claimed, a dying sputter of Black September but the episode certainly served as a dire warning to Arafat and his colleagues of the high cost of guerrilla actions that embarrassed friendly Arab states. It also – and not for the first time – brought suspicion of direct, personal involvement in terror activities uncomfortably close to Arafat himself. Not surprisingly, the *débâcle* prompted a searching re-think of the PLO's strategy. Arafat, who had never publicly evinced as much enthusiasm for the use of the terror weapon outside Israel and the occupied territories as some of his colleagues, resolved to calm the more extreme elements in his own Fatah mainstream. By early 1974, he was telling journalists that 'We must struggle for the liberation of our fatherland, but within the occupied territories, not outside them.'[40]

To their chagrin, however, Fatah leaders would find that turning off the terror tap would prove infinitely more difficult than they imagined. They were to be reminded bitterly of this in the months and years ahead as the Fatah renegade, Sabri al-Banna, better known by his *nom de guerre*, Abu Nidal, continued the work of Black September by various other names after splitting openly with Arafat in 1973. Khartoum amply demonstrated to the Organization the danger of being consumed by the monster it had helped to create.

# Part Two

# 6
# *Lost Illusions*

> 'This is the insidious theme they are harping on: you have had enough fighting, enough battles. The only solution of the Palestine problem is to establish a Palestinian state in the West Bank and Gaza Strip. This is the most dangerous proposal that could be made.' Yasser Arafat, commenting on a meeting with West Bank leaders, after Black September 1970.

At ten o'clock on a quiet November evening in 1973, a large official-looking car pulled up in a leafy street of the Moroccan capital, Rabat. Two men, one burly and broad-shouldered, the other dapper and slight, climbed out and made their way towards an elegant villa set back from the road. To a casual observer, they might just have been members of Morocco's privileged classes pursuing the normal social round. But these were no ordinary visitors, and their business at the house of a senior Moroccan military officer was far from a routine social call, as would have been apparent to anyone noticing the numbers of Moroccan troops surrounding the area in the darkness. The burly man was an American named General Vernon Walters, who happened to be deputy director of the US Central Intelligence Agency. The other, bereft of his usual entourage, was King Hassan II, absolute monarch of Morocco and a long-standing contact of Walters. More intriguing still, the intelligence man was about to be introduced to two representatives of an organization which had murdered his friend Cleo

Noel, the new American ambassador in Khartoum, only nine months before.

Walters' improbable mission was to open a high-level and top-secret channel of communication between the Nixon Administration and the Palestine Liberation Organization, and to deliver a stern warning. 'I must tell you quite clearly that this killing of Americans has got to stop – or else it will come to a situation where torrents of blood will flow, and not all of it will be American,' this bear of a man told the Palestinians in his low growl as they sat alone at a round table for two and a half hours that night.[1]

Walters' blunt message astonished his listeners: Khaled al-Hassan, the veteran Fatah official, and his colleague, Majed Abu Sharar, had not expected to hear such a direct threat from an American official. The Rabat meeting raised other, rather more tantalizing questions for the PLO. For in addition to delivering his chillingly vague hint of reprisals, Walters had also been authorized by Secretary of State Henry Kissinger to sound out the Palestinians on their political thinking, and to assess whether a dialogue might be set in train between the US and the PLO. What was the Organization's approach to a negotiated settlement of the Arab-Israeli conflict? Was it simply out to cause trouble for Arab states then contemplating negotiations, or might it be prepared to set out a realizable political objective of its own? Under what conditions, if any, would it consider recognition of Israel? And what was its real attitude to America's ally, the Hashemite Kingdom of Jordan? After aiming so much vitriol and violence at King Hussein and his followers in the three years since Black September, could the Palestinians conceive of ultimately co-existing with him?

These were the questions round which Walters and Khaled al-Hassan circled warily on 3 November and in another almost as clandestine encounter in a government guesthouse in the Moroccan royal city of Fez on 7 March the following year.[2] It is no surprise that the results of both meetings were inconclusive. Such questions had caused the greatest difficulties for the Palestinian movement from the moment Arafat had emerged at its head in Jordan nearly six years before, and had in any case become the subject of a fierce debate among the factions of the PLO itself at exactly the time when Walters asked them.

The issues had begun to come into focus as the Palestinian movement surveyed the catastrophe that had befallen it in Jordan in 1970–1. It had been a protracted and painful encounter with reality, nowhere more so than within Fatah, the inner core of the PLO. In the process, many of the assumptions underlying resistance activity had been exposed for what they were: illusions.

It was in the early 1970s that Arafat and his colleagues began to realize that their dreamy notion of a shared Palestinian state with the Jews had a fundamental flaw: it was founded on a quite elementary misconception about Israel. PLO leaders, like many Arabs at the time, tended to assume that the Jewish state was weak and divided and that confronted with a Palestinian offer of co-existence after the elimination of Israel, significant numbers of Jews would jump ship and join the struggle. Nothing, of course, could have been further from the truth. PLO officials can recall only one Israeli Jew ever joining the guerrilla war against Israel, and he was captured by the authorities and jailed.[3] Far from suggesting to the Zionists that the only solution was to emigrate, *fedayeen* attacks – coupled with the continuing flood of hostile rhetoric from the rest of the Arab world – caused them to close ranks against the Palestinians and all their works.

For Israelis of most political hues, it had after all long been convenient to pretend that the Palestinian problem did not exist; that the Arab inhabitants of what had been Palestine had fled at the behest of neighbouring states in 1948 and should subsequently have been blending in with the people of the Arab world. The idea of abolishing Israel and becoming a minority in an Arab-dominated bi-national state, as the Palestinian 'terrorists' proposed, was simply too bizarre to contemplate.

Innate Israeli suspicion had only been fuelled by the PLO's studied vagueness about the implications of the proposal. Arafat and his fellow leaders never even tried to spell out in concrete terms how it might be implemented. Unable to accept the Jews as a people in their own right rather than just as practitioners of the Jewish faith, they deliberately fudged the question of which Jews might be allowed to stay in the new utopia or what rights they might enjoy there. The result was to suggest to many Israelis that the whole idea was merely a new variation on the old theme of mass extermination or, at the very least, eviction. Yehoshafat Harkabi, a leading Israeli Arabist who once headed the country's military intelligence and who now believes that Israel should talk to the PLO, set the tone at the time by writing of 'the impossibility of destroying Israel as a state without destroying a considerable part of her inhabitants'.[4]

Asked today whether in the late 1960s he had had a specific vision of how the democratic state might be achieved, Arafat takes refuge in generalities and in an oft-repeated reference to a fringe group in Israel that disputes the legitimacy of the Jewish state: 'Anyone who sees the Berlin Wall collapsing concludes that nothing is eternal and that eventually the people's will prevails. Until now you have some Israeli groups which refuse to call themselves Israelis like the Naturai Carta, and they told me on many occasions that they would like to have ministers in the future state of Palestine. I encourage this very much.'[5] As Khaled al-Hassan, then as now one of the more pragmatic of Fatah's leaders, observes: 'We were very politically naive at the time. Arafat's political thinking was completely undeveloped then and for several years afterwards.'[6]

What baffled and at times exasperated the outside world was the Palestinians' refusal to set a more attainable interim goal, to divide their struggle up into realizable stages. After the Six-Day War, President Nasser, among other Arab leaders, had floated the idea of establishing a Palestinian state in just a part of Palestine as a first step. But within the PLO itself, still wedded to total liberation, such ideas took a long time to provoke anything other than violent rejection. When a few intellectuals and traditional Palestinian leaders in the occupied territories began late in 1967 to promote a plan for a Palestinian 'mini-state' in the West Bank and Gaza, the notion was dismissed by Arafat and his colleagues in their Jordanian fastnesses as treason. They had devoted little or no attention to building mass political support in the territories, and had no desire to see locals challenging their own claims to represent the Palestinian people. In Fatah radio broadcasts and sometimes through the mail, advocates of the proposal were branded as 'collaborators' with Israel and threatened with dire retribution. In December 1967, the *fedayeen* attempted a bazooka attack on the house of Dr Hamdi al-Taji al-Faruqi, who had published pamphlets presenting the case for a Palestinian state.[7] When the idea surfaced again in October 1970, the PLO decided to establish a 'revolutionary tribunal' to judge 'anyone acting in the name of the Palestinian people outside the framework of the revolution'. Arafat bluntly told West Bank leaders: 'If anybody raises his head and demands an abortive state, we shall behead him.'[8] The West Bankers who had risked their necks with the mini-state proposal prudently piped down; they were simply ahead of their time.

It took a calamity on the scale of that which had unfolded in Jordan from September 1970 to suggest that time might not, after all, be on the side of the Palestinian Resistance, and that a fundamental rethink was required. Ironically, the same conditions which had prompted the PLO's lurch into international terrorism also produced the beginnings of a political approach that eventually won Arafat a ticket to the podium of the United Nations. As they licked their wounds in Damascus in 1971, and even as the terrorist Black September Organization moved into action, Fatah's leaders had begun to talk among themselves about a drastic change of tack. According to Salah Khalaf, they had been heavily influenced in their furtive deliberations by the brutal treatment that the Palestinians had received at the hands of King Hussein's Bedu soldiers.

'The one memory that will always stay with me was the incident when scores of *fedayeen* fled from Jordanian troops and asked for asylum in Israel. It was the most difficult thing I have ever faced,' he said. 'We realized at that point that our problem was not just with Israel but also with the Arabs – and to an extent Israel was not as bad as the Arabs. That's when we realized that we'd have to devise a political strategy for setting up a state on any part of liberated Palestinian soil. We didn't make it public, but there was a private decision of that kind among Fatah leaders quite early on.'[9]

Between this discreet coming to terms with reality and public presentation of the idea lay a long and laborious road. Not the least of the Fatah leadership's difficulties was the fact that a 'policy of stages', in which the Palestinians would settle for less than the whole cake to start with, ran counter to everything it had been saying. Only the previous year, Arafat himself had responded to a similar suggestion from West Bank notables by proclaiming: 'In the name of the Palestinian revolution I hereby declare that we shall oppose the establishment of this state to the last member of the Palestinian people, for if ever such a state is established it will spell the end of the whole Palestinian cause.'[10]

There, in essence, was the central dilemma, of which Arafat and his colleagues were all too frequently reminded by hard-line opponents of a phased approach: if they were to settle for a mini-state as a first step towards the liberation of all Palestine, there was a distinct possibility that it would also be the last step. And if so, the refugees that filled the ranks and leadership of the PLO would in effect be abandoning the central aim of their fight: to return to their homes in the land now called Israel. Squaring that particular circle in a way likely to prove palatable to the movement as a whole was to occupy thousands of hours of feverish argument over the next few years.

The problem, on this occasion as on so many others before and since, was that the Palestinians were not in a position to dictate the terms of the debate. Weakened by division and defeat, they were also being buffeted by a host of external pressures. For one thing, the PLO's arch-enemy, King Hussein, was advancing designs of his own on the occupied territories with a proposal, announced on 15 March 1972, to establish a United Arab Kingdom under Jordanian rule after an eventual Israeli withdrawal from the West Bank and Gaza. For another, Israel was proceeding apace with efforts to demonstrate that the Palestinians in the territories had settled down under occupation by staging municipal elections there the same spring. To the PLO leadership, newly ensconced that year in a cluster of offices near the Beirut waterfront, it all looked suspiciously like another 'Israeli-Jordanian plot' against the Palestinians, and one it was powerless to thwart. Despite orders from Arafat for a boycott, and PLO assassination attempts against participants, the polls went ahead as planned and strengthened Jordan's influence at the expense of the PLO.[11] To complicate matters further, Egypt, under its volatile new President, Anwar Sadat, was looking for ways of breaking out of the no-war-no-peace stalemate in which the Arab world had been locked since the 1967 war, and pressing the Palestinians to come up with a more realistic approach. In a speech to the Palestine National Council on 28 September 1972 – just over three weeks after the attack on the Munich Olympics – Sadat urged the guerrilla organization to break with the past and form a government in exile.

It was a suggestion that filled his audience with dismay. Not only would any attempt to form such a government be guaranteed to spark off a fresh bout of squabbling about leadership responsibilities; it would also require the Palestinians to define their territorial aims, to seek diplomatic recognition – and to distance themselves from terrorist acts.[12]

As Arafat himself had put it in 1970: 'We are not acting to set up just any form of government. We have always said that we are a national liberation movement with the goal of liberation and return and we are not anxious for a new showcase which would be a burden on our national liberation struggle. And a Palestinian government to us means greater "officialization" and complications.'[13]

In Arafat's ears, Sadat's proposal rang another alarm bell with a more historic timbre. For he remembered a previous occasion on which Palestinians had formed a government in exile: the Government of All Palestine sponsored by the Arab League exactly twenty-four years before. Set up in Gaza after the defeat of the Arab armies by a newly independent Israel in 1948, it had been doomed to irrelevance and had swiftly disappeared from the map. If there was one fear that haunted and still haunts Arafat above all others, it is the fear of being marginalized in similar fashion.

Yet that was precisely the danger staring the PLO in the face in 1972, despite the spectacular international publicity generated by Palestinian terrorist outrages. As Salah Khalaf observed that summer, the resistance was threatened with 'total collapse'.[14] Watching Jordan gearing up to reclaim the West Bank and Sadat's Egypt setting a new and unpredictable agenda in the Arab-Israeli conflict, Arafat and his movement knew they risked being left on the sidelines in the admittedly comfortable refuge of Beirut unless they found something new to say. Their quest was brought dramatically into focus by the sudden outbreak, just twelve months later, of another Arab-Israeli war.

The first open sign that something was astir within the

Palestinian movement had been prompted by Israel's audacious raid on Beirut and assassination of three of the top PLO leaders there in April 1973. Spontaneously and on an unprecedented scale, protests erupted throughout the West Bank in a mirror image of the demonstration that accompanied the funeral of the murdered men in Lebanon. Palestinian newspapers were filled with death notices and attacks on Israel's leaders, and to give the protests added form, Palestinian flags – red, black, green and white symbols of allegiance to the PLO – began to appear on the streets of Israeli-ruled towns and villages.[15]

More noteworthy still was the political message that the West Bankers and Gazans began to convey to Beirut and to the international community. Quietly at first, then more openly, representatives of Palestinians from the territories were telling the leadership, preoccupied as it was at the time with consolidating its new haven in Lebanon, that they had their own distinctive views concerning the Arab-Israeli conflict that the PLO would do well to take into account. Gradually, beneath the deceptively tranquil surface of the West Bank and the Gaza Strip, a new Palestinian movement was emerging with a vigorous rebuttal of Israel's claims to have pacified the territories.

Unlike many of their exiled brethren, the Palestinians under occupation harboured no illusions about Israel. Many of them had taken jobs in Jewish-owned factories or construction sites; their daily experience taught them that the vision of Israel crumbling to make way for a Palestinian state was a mirage. Some sort of accommodation would eventually have to be found.

In the summer of 1973, more than one hundred prominent figures from all corners of the West Bank political spectrum addressed two memoranda to the United Nations, condemning the Israeli occupation and demanding 'the right to self-determination and to sovereignty on their own land for the inhabitants of the West Bank and Gaza Strip'.[16] The message for the guerrilla bosses in Beirut was clear: priority should be given to ending the occupation and establishing a mini-state.

This wave of self-assertion on the part of a populace that the PLO had long criticized for its apparent quiescence under occupation was intriguing, and to Arafat himself – ever anxious to guard against alternatives to his leadership – not a little unsettling. Something would have to be done to bring the new forces in the territories under PLO influence, and the PLO itself would have to show it was listening. 'It is the duty of all of us together to increase our cohesion and strengthen the strong links that exist between us,' Arafat said in an uneasy message to the Palestinians under occupation at the end of that year. 'We are with you in a single trench.'[17]

To strengthen the relationship between Palestinians inside and the PLO outside, Arafat acquiesced in a move by local activists, led by West Bank communists, to organize themselves along new lines. The so-called Palestinian National Front, established in August 1973, provided the Palestinians under occupation with a novel framework in which to express their defiance of Israel. Significantly, it also gave them an opportunity for concerted lobbying of the exiled leadership in Beirut on behalf of a more feasible approach to the recovery of Palestine.

Within the resistance, the first public airing for such 'treasonous' propositions[18] came not from Arafat or his friends in Fatah's inner circle, who had been nervously keeping their thoughts on the subject to themselves for the previous two years, but from an altogether more unlikely quarter: a left-wing group of intellectuals and fighters known as the Popular Democratic Front for the Liberation of Palestine. Its leader, a dour young Marxist from Jordan, Nayef Hawatmeh, was already carving out a reputation as one of the more intelligent and realistic Palestinian leaders and was to become a pioneer of Palestinian contacts with Israeli leftist groups, as well as instigator of some of the bloodiest PLO terror attacks on Israel during the 1970s.

In the first half of August 1973, he and his comrades set out a new proposal designed to take account of the heavy odds then stacked against the Palestinian movement. Achieving the liberation of all pre-1948 Palestine, they concluded in a clinically worded understatement, was 'not realistic in terms of the present balance of forces'. The Palestinians should therefore concentrate on 'the art of the possible', meaning the more modest aim of forcing Israeli withdrawal from the territories occupied in 1967 and the establishment of what was called a 'national authority' in the West Bank and Gaza.

To the bulk of the guerrilla movement – dominated as it was in Lebanon by refugees from what was now northern Israel, people who had no interest in setting up a 'mini-state' in the West Bank – this was still heresy of the deepest dye. Other leftist and Arab nationalist factions immediately condemned Hawatmeh for voicing unpalatable truths and PDFLP leaders were threatened with assassination. Even within Fatah, a large majority of rank and file members came out against the idea. 'There were differences in Fatah, but Arafat and Khalaf sided with us,' recalls the austere Hawatmeh, still one of the PLO's foremost intellectuals, in his group's spartan offices in Damascus. 'We went through a hard ideological and political struggle in all the different Palestinian organizations.'[19]

In mid-August 1973, with the controversy over Hawatmeh's statement just beginning to rage, Salah Khalaf and Farouk Kaddoumi were invited to call on Egypt's President Sadat at his out-of-town retreat of Borj al-Arab, near the Mediterranean. What they heard, when he received them breezily on the veranda of his residence, had the effect of an electric shock. 'He said there will be a war soon, in the coming months – definitely before the end of 1973,' recalled Khalaf. 'He called it the "spark" and said it would be waged jointly with Syria. And he asked us to prepare our armies so we could join in the fighting and participate in the settlement that would follow.'[20]

Generalized sabre-rattling on the part of the idiosyncratic Egyptian President was nothing new by this point. He had been sporadically sounding the trumpets of war for many months, to the extent that few were any longer prepared to give much credence to his threats. But here he was, promising to set a date for hostilities within a matter of weeks. Khalaf and Kaddoumi were so excited by the prospect of the major Arab power launching an offensive against Israel that they scarcely heard Sadat spell out the limit of his aims: simply to break the deadlock in the Arab-Israeli conflict and then proceed to a peace conference. They hastened back to Beirut, where Arafat, too, could hardly believe his ears. He heard Sadat's promise for himself on 9 September, when the President set it out in more detail before an enlarged delegation of Fatah leaders in his residence in Cairo.

Fresh from a Non-Aligned Summit Conference during which the PLO had received unprecedented diplomatic recognition and Arafat had rubbed shoulders for the first time with scores of Third World statesmen, the Palestinians were sworn to secrecy and told of Sadat's war and post-war plans. Promising to inform Arafat of the date of hostilities at the appropriate time, Sadat said he aimed to convene a peace conference involving the two superpowers and the regional parties, including Israel and the PLO. How, he asked, would the movement reply to an invitation to attend? It was a question to which Arafat and his colleagues were in no position to respond immediately; PLO decision-making bodies would have to be consulted first. But it also crystallized in acute form all the political dilemmas over which the Palestinians had been privately agonizing for the previous year or more.

Still, most of the leadership had difficulty in believing that Sadat was serious. Back in Beirut, Arafat told a few hand-picked followers: 'I have a very strange message from this crazy Sadat. I'm not sure if it's true or not, but I feel that he was not deceiving me. What reason has he got to deceive me?'[21] But when he told members of the PLO Central Committee in vague terms of an impending war for which the Palestinians should prepare, he met with derision. 'Everybody considered it a joke,' said one participant. 'We started to make bets that this would not happen for another ten years.'[22]

They did not have to wait long to find out just how wrong they were. When Khalaf belatedly complied on 4 October with an urgent summons to Cairo, he found war preparations already at an advanced stage. It was not until the very eve of the offensive that Arafat himself got the news, via a hand-carried message from Cairo purporting, under a pre-arranged code, to contain Khalaf's resignation from the movement.[23] For all Sadat's careful efforts to involve the Palestinians – preparations he was later to regret, blaming Salah Khalaf for prematurely leaking news of his plans – the October War seemed to have caught much of the PLO leadership unawares.[24] When Egyptian tanks surged across the Suez Canal on the Israeli holy day of Yom Kippur, the Palestinians found themselves well away from centre stage.

It was not that the resistance was not involved in the war: units of the Palestine Liberation Army fought alongside the Egyptians at the canal and behind Israeli lines in the Golan Heights, and PLO guerrillas sought valiantly to open another front in the north by mounting commando raids across the Lebanese-Israeli border. But their activities were little noticed in the midst of what for a while at least seemed to be another full-blown Arab-Israeli war. With Israel caught off guard and under severe pressure, the superpowers coming close to confrontation, Henry Kissinger making frantic efforts to broker a ceasefire, and the Arab states embargoing oil deliveries to the West – amid all this drama, the Palestinians, whose cause was ostensibly at the centre of the trouble, were strangely forgotten.

With a sinking feeling, the PLO leadership gradually

realized what it all amounted to. By the end of the first day's fighting, it was already dawning on Khalaf and Kaddoumi, who had been invited to join Sadat in the makeshift operations headquarters in his living room, that this was no all-out onslaught on Israel but a more limited endeavour designed to compensate for the defeat of 1967, to pave the way for Arab economic pressure on the US, and to force the door open towards a negotiated settlement. Sadat was playing things just as he had said he would, if only they had listened. Far from pressing ahead to liberate the Sinai Peninsula, his tanks went a few kilometres beyond the canal and stopped, leaving a substantial portion of the Egyptian Army exposed to an Israeli counter-thrust. After three weeks of fierce fighting, Egypt and the other Arab states involved accepted a UN call for a ceasefire and the immediate start of negotiations aimed at establishing 'a just and durable peace in the Middle East'. Implementation of the plan was delayed by Israel's encirclement of the Egyptian Third Army on the west bank of the canal, a diversion that brought the threat of Soviet intervention and a US nuclear alert. But by the end of October the war was, to all intents, over.

For Sadat, it was a performance respectable enough to erase the six-year-old stain of his predecessor's defeat and to justify a dignified move towards peace negotiations. For the Palestinians, the benefits seemed more equivocal. To their advantage was the fact that the war had created a momentary impression of solidarity in the Arab world and had unsheathed the Arab oil weapon. In the prospect of concerted economic as well as political pressure on Israel and the West, Arafat and his PLO comrades saw a potential new source of power.

It was this feeling of increased strength that enabled the leadership, in the face of fierce internal opposition, to take a preliminary step towards abandoning international terrorism. At a meeting in Damascus in February 1974, Arafat and other Fatah leaders decided in principle to draw a line under this desperate and still controversial phase. Salah Khalaf put it as follows: 'The desperation waned because of the change in the situation. The leadership could assert its control.'[25] The Palestinians certainly did not cease terror attacks, but after 1974 the PLO mainstream focused its fire on Israel and the occupied territories. From then on, major acts of violence against innocent civilians outside the Middle East were largely the province of factions other than Fatah and of renegades from the movement like Sabri al-Banna – Abu Nidal.

Sadat's pursuit of a negotiated solution emphasized the deep dilemmas facing the PLO leadership. Would they, as Sadat again asked Khalaf and Kaddoumi on 26 October, now be prepared to participate in the proposed Geneva peace conference? The Palestinians could only prevaricate, pointing out that the basis on which it was likely to be held – UN Security Council Resolution 242 of 1967 – had always been vehemently rejected by their Organization on the grounds that it treated the Palestinians merely as refugees rather than as a people with national rights. But they did promise to put the idea to PLO policy-making bodies in Beirut without delay.[26]

The question was whether to accept the still hypothetical invitation to Geneva and work for establishment of a state in the West Bank and Gaza, or whether to say no and run the risk of leaving the field open to King Hussein, who was showing keen interest in using the proposed peace conference to restore his rule over the occupied territories. There was no shortage of external 'advice'. Apart from the pressure exerted by Sadat, there was the position of the Soviet Union, now firmly backing Arafat but demanding a more realistic political strategy in return, to take into account. Even Fatah's old friends in Algeria were cautioning its leaders to formulate a clear and 'responsible' approach.[27]

The ever-impatient Arafat would not wait for the internal debates to play themselves out before drawing his own conclusions. Showing the streak of individualism which has always provoked intense criticism within the movement – and kept him one jump ahead of his peers – he began to send out discreet signals suggesting that he was ready to play the diplomatic game. As far as Arafat was concerned, at least in his public statements, the October War had been a turning point for the Palestinians, creating opportunities that had to be exploited to the full. 'We have paved the way for it, and taken part in it, and it is still going on for us,' he said in an interview in 1974. 'We must therefore attend to the consequences of this war . . . we must take advantage of them and avoid their negative aspects.'[28] What he meant was that he intended to insert the PLO into the peace negotiations in prospect between Israel and the Arabs, and communicate with the country that had cast itself as principal mediator, the United States.

Even before the war, Arafat had seen encouraging signs. In June 1973, during a visit to the US by President Brezhnev, the two countries had issued a joint statement that referred for the first time to 'the legitimate interests of the Palestinian people'.[29] Arafat took it as a signal that superpower détente was inducing Washington to take more account of Moscow's views on the Middle East, and wanted to know more. That summer he asked a close associate to approach the US ambassador to Iran, Richard Helms, and to propose PLO talks with Washington, based on two premises: that 'Israel is here to stay' and – more controversially – that Jordan should be the home for a putative Palestinian state.[30] It was the first of several messages the PLO leader sent over the next few months to the Nixon Administration through such intermediaries as Morocco's King Hassan.

On 10 October, just four days into the Arab-Israeli war, came another. According to Henry Kissinger, reading Arafat's communications with a mixture of interest and scepticism, its terse message was that the PLO chairman was 'ninety-nine per cent sure that the Israelis will rout the Egyptians and Syrians in the next few days. The United States therefore should not intervene or provide any more aid to Israel until after hostilities. The United States should seek a ceasefire soonest without preconditions.'[31] If the Americans did not resupply Israel while the conflict continued, the PLO would undertake no hostile actions against US personnel and installations. And, Arafat implied, while reserving the right to settle scores with King Hussein, the Palestinians would be willing to participate in eventual peace talks with Israel.

Kissinger did not reply immediately but Arafat's messages evidently set him thinking. On 25 October, the Secretary of State signalled back through Morocco that he was prepared to send a representative to meet PLO officials. So it was that the admirably discreet General Vernon Walters found himself travelling incognito to Rabat little more than a week later. 'This was to be a very special channel, a private channel from the Secretary of State through a trusted emissary,' says Alfred (Roy) Atherton, a genial diplomat who was one of Kissinger's top Middle East aides.'[32]

Walters, who attended the meeting alone, unarmed and in a state of some trepidation, insists that he had been briefed to deliver his blood-curdling warning on terrorism and little else. 'It was all very impressive and dramatic,' he says. 'King Hassan introduced us and then left, saying: "We all believe in one God, and may He show you the way to stop the killing." '[33] Kissinger, in his memoirs, lays emphasis on the political discussions and indicates that the Palestinians, not the American, did most of the talking. He stresses, however, that the PLO officials were told in no uncertain terms that the US would not support any Palestinian manoeuvre aimed at overthrowing King Hussein – a fact, he says, which effectively aborted the talks after the further meeting in March 1974.[34]

The truth, it seems, is somewhat more intriguing, for

Kissinger – despite his innate antipathy to the PLO – appears to have come closer to opening a negotiating channel with the PLO in the months after the October War than he now cares to admit. According to a senior diplomat who later served as US ambassador to Beirut and was then in the State Department itself, the Secretary told colleagues at the time that the US would open a dialogue in a matter of weeks. 'The 1973 war had opened up possibilities that had not existed before, and it had become clear that the PLO could not be ignored if we were to solve this problem,' observes this former official. 'Kissinger had become aware of this through his contacts with Arab states. And he was frustrated at having to talk to the PLO through intermediaries.'[35]

For Arafat, such American soundings were an extremely hopeful portent. Already encouraged by his burgeoning alliance with the Soviet Union, he interpreted them as a sign that the views of the superpowers were converging to the point where they would be able to impose a solution in the Middle East. 'In January 1974, he thought that it was going to be possible to have a state before the end of the year,' says Nabil Shaath. 'He was that sure and that anxious.'[36]

But it was not to be. Opposition on the part of the Israeli Government to any hint of contacts with an organization it saw – and still sees – as a threat to its very existence, strangled the American initiative in its cradle. Bowing to the inevitable, Kissinger, with his skilful step-by-step diplomacy, gradually prised apart the coalition of Arab states that had fought the October War – a process in which he was actively assisted by Sadat's pressing desire for progress towards a settlement. Arafat and his colleagues, who had not after all been invited to the Geneva peace conference that opened and then swiftly adjourned on 21 December 1973, were left out in the cold.

Arafat's failure to get through to Washington was a bitter disappointment and the abortive talks in Morocco marked the beginning of what was to become one of his abiding obsessions: a desire to obtain American support. Like many other Arab leaders, Arafat had become convinced that the US president had the power to 'deliver' Israeli concessions at the negotiating table, if only he could be persuaded to exercise it. The overriding need, therefore, was to persuade the Palestinian movement to accept a more plausible political strategy.

The battle within the resistance on this issue came to a climax in a series of meetings at the American University of Beirut in late 1973 and early 1974. One by one, PLO ideologues trooped to the leafy campus to present their often tortuous arguments before rowdy Palestinian audiences. From the left, Nayef Hawatmeh argued for his 'national authority' proposal with a rigorous presentation of the limited options facing the movement. For Fatah, with Arafat, as always, floating above the debate and not showing his hand, Salah Khalaf entered the lists, making an impassioned plea for 'new and original decisions' to capitalize on the Arab strength asserted in the October War. 'The question we must ask ourselves,' he said, 'is whether, by our refusal to accept anything less than the full liberation of all Palestine, we are prepared to abandon a portion of our patrimony to a third party.'[37] The Zionists, after all, had obtained their state of Israel in the late 1940s by accepting only a portion of the land they claimed. The Palestinians, by consistently saying no, had ended up with nothing.[38]

What none of the speakers advocated was something that most of them knew in their hearts was the real issue: recognition of Israel. It was a question that the Palestinian movement as a whole – Arafat included – was simply not ready to face. The PLO factions who favoured the national authority idea told themselves that having established control over part of Palestine they could use it as a base for continuing the fight against the 'Zionist entity'. How the Israelis might be persuaded voluntarily to evacuate territory under their control in these circumstances was a conundrum that nobody could explain.

It took Arafat's old rival, George Habash, the Arab nationalist and arch opponent of any accommodation with Israel, to remind everyone of the reality. To Habash, it was obvious that under the prevailing balance of power, Israel would extract a heavy price for withdrawing from the occupied territories, including Arab recognition, demilitarized zones, international guarantees and all the other unacceptable paraphernalia of peace-making. 'An Israeli withdrawal from the West Bank is only possible in the event of there being established there a reactionary force that is ready to surrender,' he proclaimed. 'Will Israel withdraw from the West Bank and just say goodbye? No, this is impossible.'[39]

Nevertheless, that was the contradictory strategy the Palestinians adopted at a meeting of the Palestine National Council in Cairo in the first week of June 1974. Refusing to recognize or to make peace with Israel and insisting on the ultimate aim of establishing a democratic state in all of Palestine, they called for the establishment of a 'people's national, independent and fighting authority on every part of Palestinian land that is liberated.'[40] Known subsequently as the PLO's 'transitional programme', it did not long succeed in papering over the cracks. Only weeks after agreeing to the statement, George Habash began publicly to dissociate himself from Arafat's diplomatic manoeuvrings and by the end of September, Habash's Marxists had pulled out of day-to-day involvement in the PLO and formed a 'Front for the Rejection of Capitulationist Solutions', thus opening a damaging split. Nor did the supposed pragmatism of the PLO's statement impress the leaders of Israel, who – still in a state of shock after the October War – instantly focused on the continuing call for the Jewish state's destruction rather than on the suggestion that the Palestinians might be prepared to settle for something less. 'It was clear,' says Shlomo Avineri, then director of

Israel's Foreign Ministry, 'that this was all tactics – that stage one, the establishment of a mini-state, was purely aimed at better enabling them to achieve stage two.'[41]

For the PLO mainstream, however, the June statement, with all its elisions and ambiguities, was in its way an historic document, marking a major step into the real world of Middle East power politics. Above all, it was the first concrete recognition of the gap that existed between the Palestinians' dream and the more practical goals they would ultimately have to accept if they were to get anything at all. The compromise had a host of other consequences for the Palestinian movement, not all of which could have been foreseen. It fostered Arab and international recognition of the PLO as representative of the Palestinian people. It paved the way for clandestine contact between Palestinian representatives and sympathetic Israelis. And it launched Arafat himself into a never-ending round of whistle-stop diplomacy. Within five short months of this decision, and just two years after many outside observers had been inclined to write his movement off, the PLO leader was attracting a blaze of international publicity in a new and unfamiliar guise.

# 7
# *Guerrilla-Diplomat*

> 'Today I have come bearing an olive branch and a freedom fighter's gun. Do not let the olive branch fall from my hand. I repeat: do not let the olive branch fall from my hand.' Yasser Arafat, addressing the United Nations General Assembly, 13 November 1974.

As the scheduled flight from Paris touched down at New York's John F. Kennedy airport, the bespectacled Palestinian professor nervously surveyed his fellow passengers. Could any of them be aware of the sensitive mission on which he was embarked? Could any of them conceivably be out to stop it?

It was early September 1974, and Nabil Shaath was headed for the soulless office complex on the bank of the East River that serves as headquarters of the United Nations. Just a couple of days earlier, he had been asked to go to Manhattan and help prepare for Yasser Arafat's dramatic début on the world stage. He had travelled via Tunis, where he had picked up a Tunisian diplomatic passport – a 'flag of convenience' for the trip to New York – and had changed planes in Paris. Now, with his Egyptian wife at his side, Shaath pondered the risks: the task had already been rejected by several more senior and conspicuous PLO figures than he for fear of Arab assassination squads, or even of violent opposition from within their own ranks.[1] What is more, this was the heart of 'enemy territory'; a city where Arafat was reviled as leader of a murderous terrorist organization and where

Israel's fierce opposition to any form of recognition for the PLO would be powerfully echoed by the local Jewish community.

Yet the Palestinians, too, had influential friends. The Arab states, flushed with partial victory in the fourth Arab-Israeli war and awakened to the power they wielded in the world oil market, now commanded unprecedented attention among members of the world body. Thanks in part to tireless lobbying, cajoling and threatening by Arafat and his followers, that new muscle was being flexed in support of the Palestinian cause. The result was that for the first time since 1952 the General Assembly had set aside time for a special debate on the question of Palestine, and on 14 October 1974 an overwhelming majority of members – no fewer than 115 countries, most of them in the Third World – had voted in favour of inviting the PLO itself to join the discussion as 'representative of the Palestinian people'.

It was a stunning illustration of the way the tables had been turned against Israel and towards the Arabs in the wake of the Yom Kippur War. In all previous petitions to the UN, the maximum number of votes the Palestinians had been able to muster was eighty-two. Now, with the Soviet Union and its allies firmly supporting the Palestinians and even the oil-deficit countries of Western Europe voting for the motion or at most abstaining, only the US, Bolivia and the Dominican Republic joined Israel in voting against. In vain did Israel's ambassador, Yosef Tekoah, circulate official documents detailing 'one hundred PLO crimes' or fulminate that the UN was overturning its own principles in order to welcome 'those who have turned the premeditated murder of innocent women, children and men into a profession'. In vain did the chief US delegate warn that a 'dangerous precedent' was being set.[2] By asking Yasser Arafat to become the first non-governmental representative to address the General Assembly, the UN allowed what even the move's bitterest opponents concede was 'one of the great propaganda coups of the twentieth century'.[3]

For Arafat, the invitation was the most important fruit of a diplomatic offensive that he had been discreetly preparing for over a year. Armed with the PLO's June 1974 decision to pursue the struggle against Israel in stages, he had set out to obtain wider international recognition and to win the Palestinians a say in the peace moves that appeared to be gathering momentum. It was a new role for Arafat, and one that required a new repertoire of cunning, dexterity and manipulative skills. Never mind that his movement's strategy as stated that summer was still riddled with ambiguities: the loopholes merely created greater room for manoeuvre. As translated by the PLO leader to his new international audience, the call for a 'fighting, independent national authority' on liberated land became implicit acceptance of a mini-state after an Israeli withdrawal.[4] The rejection of 'recognition, peace or secure borders' did not mean that the PLO was completely ruling out the idea of joining negotiations, merely that it was waiting for an invitation to the Geneva conference before deciding how to respond.[5]

Arafat's creative reinterpretation of agreed PLO policy swiftly landed him in trouble with his peers, notably the arch-rejectionist George Habash, who accused Arafat – correctly as it turned out – of engaging in secret contacts through Palestinian intermediaries with the embodiment of Western imperialism, the United States. But such squalls must have seemed a small price to pay for the plaudits Arafat was winning with equal rapidity in the outside world. His more reasonable-sounding pronouncements were music to the ears of Egypt's President Sadat. Just as significant, they delighted Arafat's friends in the Soviet Union. Invited to Moscow in July 1974 by the Kremlin's poker-faced Foreign Minister, Andrei Gromyko, the Palestinian leader had been rewarded with official recognition and a promise of Soviet anti-aircraft and anti-tank guns.[6]

The Soviet relationship was one to which Arafat the tactician, as ever subordinating ideology to *realpolitik*, attached the highest importance, and not just because it enhanced his personal prestige. Soviet support was a vital counterweight to the machinations of Henry Kissinger, who had set aside the search for a comprehensive settlement to the Middle East conflict and was then sparing no effort to lure the Arab states singly into peace talks that excluded the PLO. In the words of the capitalist-minded Nabil Shaath, who had many arguments with his boss at the time about this new cosiness with the Communists, 'The chairman definitely felt that he had to secure the alliance with the Soviets for his own protection.'[7]

Before striking out from Beirut for a bigger political stage, Arafat still had to deal with a crucial problem much closer to home. As he was only too uncomfortably aware, it was among the Arab rulers who posed as the Palestinians' friends and protectors that he could be least sure of his position. At the earliest opportunity and in the clearest possible terms, the Arab states had to be forced to make a formal pledge of support to the movement. Extracting such a commitment would mean a showdown, and above all a settling of scores with King Hussein of Jordan, still pushing his claim to speak on behalf of the Palestinians. The struggle came to a head at a gathering of Arab heads of state in the Moroccan capital, Rabat, towards the end of October 1974.

In the middle of that month, King Hassan, Morocco's autocratic head of state, had received an alarming report from his intelligence services that they had uncovered a plot by Palestinian militants for the assassination of several Arab leaders – Hussein of Jordan, King Faisal of Saudi Arabia, President Sadat of Egypt, President Nimeiri of Sudan and himself – at the forthcoming summit. More disturbing still, although fourteen commandos had been captured, thanks to smart work by Moroccan security, no weapons had been seized, which meant that Palestinians might still be on the loose and in a position to execute the plan.

The operation bore all the trademarks of the notorious Black September Organization. Summoning Arafat for an immediate explanation, King Hassan blamed Black September's 'spiritual leader', Salah Khalaf, for the plot. Arafat disavowed all knowledge, but was able to identify two of the commandos. Khalaf insisted that the Fatah leadership had nothing to do with the affair. If so, his subsequent account of the operation, which, he surmises, was aimed only at King Hussein and not the other leaders, betrays surprisingly detailed knowledge of its preparation and planning. A few weeks later, he assumed 'full responsibility' for the plot in a speech at the Arab University of Beirut in defence of the imprisoned commandos.[8]

Albeit unsuccessful, the planned attack evidently served its purpose as far as the PLO leadership was concerned. Behind their verbal expressions of support, the autocrats who ruled the Arab world had long been wary of the PLO – of its potential to create trouble, of its subversive appeal to Arab public opinion, of its disturbingly 'democratic' style. But the suggestion, as they gathered for the summit with customary genteel pomp, that a real gun was pointing at their heads served to concentrate minds wonderfully, creating what Khalaf described as 'a climate of terror'.[9]

A few days before the full meeting of heads of state, Arab foreign ministers gathered in Rabat to contemplate the issues, central among them how the Palestinians were to be represented in the Middle East peace moves then under way. In essence it amounted to a choice between two men who had been bitterly at odds for more than four years: King Hussein of Jordan and Yasser Arafat. The former, a majority of whose subjects were of Palestinian origin, was looking for a green light to involve himself in American-brokered efforts to restore the West Bank from Israeli to Jordanian rule. The latter, anxious to secure his status as unchallenged spokesman for the Palestinian people, was equally keen on thwarting any such Jordanian involvement.

It was a choice that had caused the Arab states the greatest of difficulty in the past and one that they had always fudged, not least during the savage Jordanian-Palestinian civil war of 1970. Even at their previous summit in Algiers in November 1973, when all but one of them agreed in principle that the PLO was 'sole legitimate representative' of the Palestinians, they respected the dissenting voice – that of King Hussein himself – by keeping their decision secret. In the intervening months, President Sadat had attempted again to engineer an accommodation that would allow representation to be shared, thereby drawing a barrage of criticism from the PLO. The fact that the argument was almost entirely hypothetical, given Israel's adamant refusal to withdraw its forces from the West Bank, did not lessen its intensity. As ever in the Arab world, form seemed as important as substance. At stake was not only the self-esteem of two protocol-obsessed leaders but also the future shape of the kingdom of Jordan and the prospects for a peaceful settlement on Israel's eastern frontier. Now, with Henry Kissinger pressing ahead in his mediation between Hussein and the new Israeli Prime Minister, Yitzhak Rabin, the choice would wait no longer.

Neither the Jordanians nor the Palestinians were in a mood to compromise. In the Jordanian corner, Prime Minister Zeid al-Rifai, who three years earlier had narrowly escaped a Black September bullet, 'left no stone unturned to prevent recognition of the PLO', according to the account of one of those present.[10] Claiming that the PLO was undermining a solution which Jordan was on the point of achieving, he resorted to 'pleading and threats, attacks and counterattacks'.[11] For the Palestinians, Farouk Kaddoumi, who had been appointed as PLO 'foreign minister' two years before, responded in kind. Urged on by Arafat, who aimed a rich torrent of abuse down the telephone at the

Arab leaders, he thumped the table, threatened to inflict public embarrassment on the others by walking out, and ensured that his henchmen in the conference committees did not shift one inch in their insistence on PLO demands. 'In fact I talked too much,' recalls Kaddoumi with evident satisfaction. 'I heavily attacked the Jordanians and told them to take their hands off the Palestinian cause.'[12] By the next day, thanks also to the lone support of Egypt's Foreign Minister, Kaddoumi's blunderbuss tactics had paid off. The Arab foreign ministers adopted the PLO's proposals without discussion and transmitted them to the summit.

When the Arab leaders gathered, fretting in their robes, expensive lounge suits and military uniforms, Hussein turned in a masterful performance. In a speech stretching over thirty large pages and lasting two hours, he surveyed the history of his kingdom's involvement in the Palestinian issue, testified eloquently about its right to the West Bank, and pointed out truthfully that he offered the only real chance for restoring it to Arab rule, given Israel's refusal to have any truck with the PLO. But it was all to no avail. After his speech, a long and stony silence descended on the ornate conference hall, broken first by a blunt put-down from the Arab leader who had given Arafat's group its first tangible support, Algeria's President Boumedienne. 'Algeria does not recognize anybody to speak for the Palestinians except the PLO,' he said.[13] As other rulers demonstrated their support for Arafat, Hussein had no choice but angrily to concede defeat and agree to a statement effectively barring him from speaking for the Palestinians.

'It was really a joke,' says Mahmoud Riad, the Egyptian who was serving at the time as Secretary-General of the Arab League. 'The decision was taken without any real study and it became a competition between the Egyptians and the Syrians to see which of them supported the Palestinian cause more than the other.'[14]

Be that as it may, on 28 October 1974, the Arab world unanimously hailed the PLO as 'sole legitimate representative' of the Palestinian people and gave Arafat's movement what purported to be a right of veto over Arab moves towards a settlement with Israel.[15] The high point of the PLO leader's political fortunes to date, it constituted a laying-on of hands by a bloc of countries now seen by the outside world as a formidable power in its own right.

'Today is the turning point in the history of the Palestinian people and Arab nation,' Arafat proclaimed exuberantly in the conference's closing session. 'I vow to continue the struggle until we meet together in Jerusalem with the same smiling faces we see here tonight. Victory is close at hand.'[16] It was vintage Arafat hyperbole and as usual bore little relation to the real balance of forces. But the Rabat summit decision did have a number of positive consequences for him. It gave a large boost to his standing among the Arabs under Israeli occupation in the West Bank and the Gaza Strip, who showed their support for him in a wave of demonstrations. Almost exactly ten years after Arafat's comrades had set out to attack Israel with a couple of rusty guns, Arab leaders were forced to treat him as an equal. Just as important, it paved the way for an increase in official Arab contributions to his Organization's coffers, with a promise from the assembled Arab leaders of 50 million US dollars a year for the PLO. Arafat was already well on his way to being head of the richest liberation movement the world had ever seen.

From now on, Arafat was virtually guaranteed an attentive hearing abroad; indeed, just one week earlier, France had become the first Western country to open high-level contact with the PLO leader by sending its Foreign Minister, Jean Sauvagnargues, to meet him in Beirut. Now the PLO leader could seek to insert himself into continuing peace moves or at least to thwart any such moves that might be taking place without him. As he put it in early November 1974: 'Before the Rabat summit we were only a figure in an equation. Now we are at the peak of events.'[17]

Not the smallest source of gratification to Arafat was the evident dismay the PLO's dramatic gains caused among other diplomatic players on the Middle East stage. For Henry Kissinger in particular, now Secretary of State to a newly installed President Ford, the Rabat decision doomed the whole effort to promote a peaceful settlement involving Israel and Jordan, as well as Egypt, by depriving the only Arab party to which the Israelis would talk about the future of the West Bank of the right to negotiate. Government officials in Jerusalem concluded that negotiations were 'at an impasse',[18] Israeli newspapers began warning – like Arafat himself – of another war, and Prime Minister Rabin commented dourly: 'There is no-one to talk to about peace on the eastern borders. We will not negotiate with the terrorist organizations.'[19] As Zeid al-Rifai, then Jordanian Prime Minister, recalls: 'We were confident that the Rabat resolution was going to delay any meaningful peace process concerning the West Bank for many years to come, and we turned out to be right.'[20]

Arafat had played very shrewdly on the insecurities of the assembled Arab leaders. At a time when some of them, principally President Sadat, were contemplating painful compromises with Israel, none could afford to be seen by domestic public opinion to be short-selling the hallowed Palestinian cause, and Arafat had forced them to translate their devotion to the cause into unqualified support for his Organization. It was a conjuring trick of which he was to make frequent use in later efforts to keep the Arab world on what he saw as the straight and narrow.

Disturbed the Americans may have been by the Rabat resolution, but there was little they could do to prevent Arafat going on to reap the full propaganda advantage of his new status in his visit to the United Nations General Assembly in New York just over a fortnight later.

Denying him entry – as the vocal pro-Israeli lobby did not hesitate to demand and as a subsequent Secretary of State did fourteen years later – was not an option. The administration did bow to Jewish pressure by confining Arafat's visa to a 25-mile radius of the UN building, thus depriving him of the chance to give a lecture at a prestigious university in New England and to appear on a Washington talk show. But to go further, as the State Department saw it then, would not only have violated the agreement regulating relations between the United Nations and the federal government; it would also have constituted a dangerous provocation at a time when America was under continuing pressure from a newly powerful Arab world to pay serious attention to Arafat. To underline the point, the Arab leaders had agreed to send President Suleiman Franjieh of Lebanon – a man not normally noted for his sympathy for the Palestinians but who had buried his differences with the PLO for the occasion – to speak on their behalf in support of Arafat during the General Assembly debate.

Thus on 13 November 1974, the US authorities found themselves playing reluctant hosts and protectors to a man who had vowed to destroy two of Washington's closest allies in the Middle East and whom they strongly suspected of involvement in terrorist acts against American citizens. Not since Fidel Castro and Nikita Krushchev had visited UN headquarters together in 1960 had New York seen a security operation like it. Against a background of threats from extremist Jewish groups that they would not let the PLO leader out of the city alive, and plans for a massive anti-Arafat demonstration on the day of his appearance, thousands of police and secret service men were mobilized. Over a period of four days, New York's mayor Abraham Beame afterwards revealed, his administration had spent some 750,000 dollars to protect Arafat and his entourage, and all this for a visit that lasted less than twenty-four hours. In a city already outraged by the decision to invite the PLO leader, news of the cost went down like a lead balloon.

Arafat, nevertheless, left nothing to chance. His own elite security squad comprised Force 17 commander Ali Hassan Salameh and ten tough commando leaders from southern Lebanon. In the run-up to the trip, his movements were shrouded in more than usual mystery. Courtesy of the Egyptian Government, one aircraft was at his disposal in Cairo; another had been chartered in Damascus; and then, suddenly, just before he was due to depart for New York, he hared off to Algiers to hold a hasty meeting with Swedish Prime Minister Olof Palme. In the end it was a plane specially chartered for him at the eleventh hour by the Algerians that took him to New York. The purpose of all the evasion was simple: to confuse anybody who might have harboured thoughts of shooting Arafat down before he had even left the Middle East.[21]

Precautions were no less tight in mid-town Manhattan. The refined Waldorf Astoria Hotel, where Arafat, using his adviser Nabil Shaath as food-taster, was to partake of lunch after giving his speech, had been turned into a fortress. Over at UN headquarters, a large swathe of territory along the East River was encircled by police, off-limits to visitors and other unauthorized persons from twenty-four hours before Arafat's arrival. And when they landed at 5 a.m. in a remote corner of Kennedy airport, Arafat and his 'favoured son' Salameh were whisked to the UN premises not in the usual noisy motorcade, but in a US military helicopter with a State Department security officer and a secret service agent on board. At dawn, as the chopper hovered awkwardly just above the UN gardens, its curious array of passengers jumped clear on to the grass and Arafat, now in the hands of UN security, was spirited secretly up to a fifth-floor infirmary, where he grabbed a few hours' rest before emerging into the glare of the arc lights. With tens of thousands of protesters in the streets outside chanting 'Arafat go home', he remarked wryly to his aides that it was with this purpose in mind that he had come to New York in the first place.[22]

Every aspect of the PLO chairman's performance that day was stage-managed for maximum effect, with a result poised somewhere between historic occasion and slapstick comedy. His speech had been the subject of hours of haggling, drafting and redrafting by committees of officials and experts in the PLO's shabby Beirut offices. At the last minute, his aides arranged to delay its delivery by two hours so as to deny the Israelis the opportunity for a full reply in time for newspaper deadlines in Europe and the Middle East. Even Arafat's appearance had subtly changed: he had been persuaded to shave off the familiar stubble as part of his bid for new respectability, leaving only a thin moustache.

To round out the picture and complete the Israelis' outrage, the PLO leader's friends in the UN had arranged for him to be treated with all the trappings of a government leader. Just twenty minutes before Arafat was due to be escorted into the packed UN chamber, an aide to Secretary-General Kurt Waldheim spotted a high-backed white leather chair sitting on the podium. Innocent as it looked, the UN officials were horrified, for it was the chair specially reserved for visiting heads of state and it had been placed there unbeknown to the secretariat by the General Assembly president, Algerian foreign minister Abdel Aziz Bouteflika. The symbolism – in this debating forum where symbols often seem of all-consuming importance – was rich. A number of delegations now threatened to join Israel in boycotting the session. Waldheim's officials, unable to remove the chair without compounding the embarrassment, plunged into what one of them describes as 'the most terrible negotiation' in order to persuade Arafat not to sit in it.[23] Eventually he agreed to stand alongside, but not for a moment did he forget the significance of the issue once he had entered the auditorium. As the General Assembly gave him a standing ovation in his drab fatigues, bone-coloured jacket, dark glasses and ever-present head-dress, the more observant people in the hall noticed him stretch out his hand and gently lean on the white leather chair.

'The whole thing had a slight Marx Brothers element to it,' recalls Brian Urquhart, a senior UN official later to have many dealings with the PLO leader. 'I say this with great kindness, but it was sort of like everything that Arafat does, with a certain element of farce and a great deal of rushing about.'[24]

Once positioned at the UN lectern, however, Arafat adopted a solemn tone in keeping with what he sensed was an unparalleled opportunity to bring the grievances of the Palestinians to the world's attention. Had not the UN overseen the very origins of his people's problem by endorsing the right of the Zionists to set up a state on part of Palestine? As Israel's world stature grew, had the UN not relegated Palestinian status to that of refugees – issuing limp calls affirming their 'right of return' but otherwise treating them as people to be compensated, cared for and resettled rather than a distinct people deserving of a homeland? And yet, as a growing number of developing countries were granted independence by imperial powers, had not the UN enshrined the right of peoples to self-determination as a cornerstone of its Charter?

Arafat saw his speech that day as a chance to redress the record. It was a great *pot-pourri*, with ingredients mainly calculated to appeal to the Third World majority then packing the institutions of the UN. Arafat equated the 'Jewish invasion of Palestine' and the actions of the Israeli state with colonialism and apartheid in a simplistic manner that would be understood by the newly liberated nations of Africa, Asia and Latin America. Surveying the history of Palestine and describing himself with some licence as 'a son of Jerusalem', he sought to compare the Palestinian cause with various anti-colonial liberation struggles and even with America's war of independence. 'I am a rebel and freedom is my cause,' he proclaimed.[25]

Less immediately obvious to Arafat's audience was what kind of vision of the future he was offering. It was not that he failed to adopt conciliatory language: there was plenty of soothing rhetoric about peace, about the olive branch accompanying the freedom fighter's gun and about political struggle as a complement to armed struggle. There was Arafat's by now customary attempt to reach out to anti-Zionist Jews and a word of greeting for a 'Jewish revolutionary' then incarcerated in an Israeli jail. But for Israel itself, there was only a torrent of accusations – of racism, terrorism and oppression – and a robust denial of Jewish nationhood. As for the Palestinians' ultimate goal, the PLO leader carefully avoided specifics, reverting to the 'dream' which he had first propounded in public more than six years earlier.

'Why therefore should I not dream and hope?' he asked in a passage consciously reminiscent of the words of the American civil rights leader, Martin Luther King. 'For is not revolution the making real of dreams and hopes? So let us work together that my dream may be fulfilled, that I may return with my people out of exile, there in Palestine to live . . . in one democratic State where Christian, Jew and Muslim live in justice, equality, fraternity and progress.'[26]

If there was any hint here of the compromise that the PLO had debated and adopted the previous June – calling for a 'national authority' in the occupied territories – it was buried deep between the lines, much to the private relief of the Israelis, who had feared that a more specific proposal might put them under real pressure in the UN, and much to the general confusion of Western delegations. 'The speech was long and complex, and nobody could really understand what it meant,' recalls one diplomat who was serving in Britain's UN mission at the time. 'It took our Middle East experts two days to work it out. It just went to underline Arafat's imperfect understanding of the international arena.'[27]

In truth, Arafat and his associates had already concluded back in Beirut that the General Assembly debate was not the place to put forward specific peace proposals. Not only would such a move have strained the Organization's fragile unity to breaking point; they also felt it would, in a curious way, have seemed irrelevant. 'This was supposed to be an historical speech,' says Nabil Shaath, who had a hand in drafting it, along with a cast of characters including Khalil al-Wazir, the Palestinian poet Mahmoud Darwish and a lawyer, Salah Dabbagh. 'It was the first opportunity we ever got to present the case of the Palestinian people to the world on record. Arafat was convinced it was not the moment to talk about a compromise.'[28]

In any case, the search for Arafat's real meaning was swiftly overtaken by a media furore concerning allegations that he had appeared before the UN with a gun on his hip. As he clasped his hands above his head in a triumphal acknowledgement of the General Assembly's tumultuous applause, a holster was spotted poking out beneath his jacket. The fact that the PLO leader was subsequently attested to have been persuaded to leave his trusty Beretta backstage did little to quell the row. Ironically, the fuss surrounding the incident probably did Arafat no harm at all. It was all part of the act; ever conscious of the significance of symbols, he knew that his supporters still wanted to see the gun at least as much as the hypothetical olive branch.

The next day brought bemused and in some cases thunderous reactions to Arafat's UN speech in the American press, particularly to his comparison of himself with such US icons as George Washington, Abraham Lincoln and Woodrow Wilson. It was, opined the *New York Times*, 'a distasteful, hypocritical performance', featuring 'tendentious characterizations of Zionism, highly selective accounts of twentieth-century history', and an 'unimaginative rehash of vaguely Marxist revolutionary ideology'. It was now up to the General Assembly to 'puncture the self-delusions of this shadowy organization'.[29]

Among the Third World delegates, however, the response was something else entirely. After the PLO leader had spoken, in what Israel's chief delegate colourfully described as a 'homage to bloodshed and bestiality',[30] the representatives of a host of African, Asian, socialist and, of course, Arab countries lined up to praise his 'noble', 'inspiring' and 'moving' sentiments; his political realism; his broad-minded tolerance and moderation.[31] At a reception organized by Egypt, Arafat was lionized by senior members of the New York diplomatic corps, with the notable exceptions of its Israeli and American members, and courted by no less a social lioness than Mrs Imelda Marcos, wife of the Filipino dictator and faded beauty queen, who, apparently thinking that to be photographed with Arafat might help defuse growing Muslim opposition at home, arranged a breakfast assignation for the following morning.

The tryst was not to be. In the dead of night, less than a day after arriving in New York, Arafat was on the move again, this time southwards to the safer haven of communist Cuba, leaving his 'foreign minister', Farouk Kaddoumi, to garner the fruits of that day's work. As Kaddoumi discovered, ducking and weaving in a heavy bullet-proof jacket between the UN building and the Waldorf Hotel, the fruits were substantial.[32] Of eighty-one speakers in a subsequent debate lasting nine days, no fewer than sixty-one spoke out against Israel. To cap it all, on 22 November the General Assembly voted overwhelmingly to adopt two resolutions endorsing self-determination for the Palestinians and granting the PLO observer status in UN institutions.

This was a breakthrough of major proportions. In one leap, the PLO was admitted to the UN as if it were the government of an existing state – a position identical to that enjoyed by North and South Korea, Switzerland and the Vatican, and still not achieved by any other non-governmental organization. From now on, the UN would remain a major focus of Palestinian political activity. The PLO used the built-in majority it could command in the

General Assembly to push through a seemingly endless series of motions supporting its views, including some that caused the world body no end of problems with its American hosts, such as the controversial 1975 resolution stating that 'Zionism is racism'. It also set out to conquer, and in the process politicize, many of the specialized United Nations agencies. Over the next year, Palestinian delegations participated in international conferences on subjects as diverse as human rights, health, population problems, food and civil aviation. Late in 1975 the PLO was invited for the first time to participate in a debate in the UN's highest decision-making body, the Security Council.

The fact that these were entirely 'paper victories' – and of dubious relevance to the Palestine question – was beside the point. For Arafat, they served as an important sign that the Palestinian voice was being heard in the world. As the PLO leader now puts it, recalling the 1974 trip that remains his one and only visit to American shores: 'In the UN I felt the return of the soul to the Palestinian body, which the world had been trying to kill.'[33]

The PLO had certainly come a long way from the early, clandestine days of 'armed struggle' in the mid-1960s and from the friendless desperation of the early 1970s. Now, headquartered in a growing sprawl of offices in Beirut, it was developing many of the appurtenances of a government bureaucracy, complete with an army of sorts, a finance ministry and departments to deal with Palestinian internal and external affairs. It built hospitals and schools for Palestinian refugees and paid pensions to the families of Palestinian 'martyrs'. By 1975 it had some form of diplomatic representation in at least forty countries, and a procession of foreign dignitaries lined up to call on the chairman himself as if he were already in charge of a state. All this was a costly business. But then, thanks in large part to Arafat's skills at drumming up millions of dollars in 'conscience money' from the wealthy Arab oil states, principally Saudi Arabia, and at attracting contributions from the Palestinian diaspora, the PLO and its component factions were already by far the richest irredentist movement the world had ever seen.

After his UN appearance, Arafat was plunged into an ever more frenetic diplomatic whirl, hopping between Arab capitals in private jets placed at his disposal by his wealthy sponsors. In a manner he was to make all his own in subsequent years, he took to making fanciful statements as to what sort of settlement the Palestinians would be prepared to accept, like a trader offering an opening bid in some kind of political bazaar. On one occasion, he pronounced himself ready to raise the Palestinian flag, just in the West Bank town of Jericho as a start: on another, he told the Egyptian foreign minister, Ismail Fahmy, that all he wanted at this stage was 'a piece of land wide enough to raise the Palestinian flag, even if it was not more than five kilometres wide'.[34] Strictly speaking, such statements did not contravene the letter of the PLO's June 1974 policy declaration but they stretched its meaning almost beyond recognition and provoked harsh criticism from his internal opponents – people who, Arafat still insists, 'misunderstood, or did not want to understand'.[35]

In the diplomatic arena, however, Arafat's rubbery approach proved a priceless asset, not least in wooing the countries of Western Europe, an increasingly important priority as the 1970s unfolded. It is a quality for which other PLO leaders still profess a sneaking admiration. As the conservative Fatah politician Khaled al-Hassan puts it: 'Abu Ammar never acted without a decision to support him. But he is one of those people who, if asked to manoeuvre in a circle of one mile's radius, will manoeuvre in a circle of ten miles' radius.'[36]

Easily the most controversial, and perhaps the most important, aspect of Arafat's manoeuvring in the mid-1970s was one of which the world was only dimly aware at the time. It involved a series of secret contacts between Arafat associates and left-wing Israelis who professed sympathy for the Palestinian cause, and constituted the first tangible sign that the PLO leader might really be beginning to grope towards some sort of accommodation with the Jewish state. In those early days, it was also a course of action fraught with peril and one that would later cost the lives of two of Arafat's most prominent foreign envoys.

The idea that Palestinians should talk to Israelis was not in itself either new or particularly heretical. As far back as 1969, Nabil Shaath had sought to sound out a number of Israeli and other Jews on the democratic state idea he was then championing. At about the same time, one of the PLO's Marxist factions, the Popular Democratic Front for the Liberation of Palestine, under Nayef Hawatmeh, had sent out feelers to extremist fringe groups in Israel. But these latter contacts, involving left-wing Jews who were deeply opposed to the existence of Israel, were well outside the political mainstream and as such did not provoke much serious attention from a Palestinian movement still focusing its resources on the military struggle against what was seen as a monolithic enemy.

Not until the October War forced the Palestinians to think about political options did the concept of initiating talks develop a head of steam. After 1973, articles began to appear in the Palestinian periodical *Shu'un Filastiniya* about the Israeli left, pointing out that not all Israelis were irrevocably committed to trampling on Palestinian rights. And in March 1974, Hawatmeh took the remarkable step of giving an interview to an American journalist for publication in Israel's top-selling newspaper, *Yediot Ahronot*, in which he called for a dialogue between 'progressive forces' among Israelis and Palestinians.[37] The effect of this initiative in Israel itself was obliterated less than two months later when Hawatmeh's group attacked and seized a school in the northern Israeli village of Maalot. The raid, in which twenty-five people – all but four of them schoolchildren – died, was one of the bloodiest single acts of Palestinian terror against Israel and had a devastating effect on public opinion. But within the Palestinian movement as a whole, in the words of Ilan Halevy, a Jewish Marxist who had left Israel in 1976 to join the PLO: 'Gradually, the idea that there was at least some tiny minority of Israelis with whom you could talk was becoming current.'[38]

Although they refrained from saying so in public, it was a conclusion that Arafat and a small group of colleagues had already privately reached. Meeting in Beirut in late November or early December 1973, the Fatah central committee decided to set up a special team to 'keep in touch with events in Israel'.[39] Its chairmen were to be Arafat's deputy, Khalil al-Wazir, and another long-serving Fatah leader, Mahmoud Abbas, who had written a doctoral thesis on Zionism at the University of Moscow and was 'a pioneer of the idea that you have to study your enemy'.[40] The new team included two men who were to play a crucial role in pursuing contacts with the Israelis: Said Hammami and Issam Sartawi. The former, a bright young guerrilla turned diplomat, was the PLO's man in London. The latter, a headstrong American-educated heart surgeon, had led his own guerrilla faction in the late 1960s but was now a member of Arafat's Fatah group charged with special missions by the PLO chairman.

Hammami, posted to London in 1972, had already caused a stir among diplomats and journalists with his original views on the Palestinian problem. In late 1973, his name appeared on two remarkable articles in *The Times* calling for the establishment of a Palestinian state in the West Bank and Gaza as a means of 'drawing out the poison at the heart of Arab-Israeli enmity' and urging Israeli Jews and Palestinian Arabs to 'recognize one another as peoples'.[41] The articles, while not publicly endorsed by Arafat, were trial balloons for views the PLO leader was keen to convey to the West. In Israel, they attracted the immediate attention of a man who had long been looking for potential interlocutors among the Palestinians: the grey-bearded peace campaigner and maverick parliamentarian, Uri Avnery. Avnery, who himself had fought in a Jewish underground terrorist group before the creation of Israel, lost no time in contacting Hammami through intermediaries. The result, in January 1975, was the first of many secret meetings between this unlikely pair and the beginning of what later became a semi-public dialogue between like-minded Israelis and senior PLO officials acting on the specific instructions of Yasser Arafat.[42]

Avnery, who in June 1975 formed a group known as the Israeli Council for Israel-Palestine Peace, started from a simple premiss: if the Palestinians were to get anywhere in their struggle for statehood, they needed to work to reduce the deep hostility to their organization in Israeli public opinion. In meetings with Issam Sartawi and others throughout 1976, he and his colleagues sought to persuade the PLO to make gestures and declarations that, while not compromising Palestinian rights, would look and sound conciliatory in Israel. It was a question, as Avnery puts it now, of 'trying to break down the psychological inhibitions . . . on both sides'.[43]

As it turned out, the inhibitions were simply too immense. Israel's Prime Minister, Yitzhak Rabin, who received periodic reports of the meetings, was unyielding in his refusal to contemplate even indirect communication with the 'terrorist' PLO, and the persistence of Palestinian raids on Israel merely caused a further closing of Jewish ranks. On the Palestinian side, the idea of negotiating with the 'enemy' was for the most part still way ahead of its time. Conciliatory statements from one official would be swiftly disavowed by others, not least by Farouk Kaddoumi, who used his position as PLO 'foreign minister' to pour buckets of cold water on Sartawi's efforts. Arafat was left in the middle, as ever appearing to temporize between extremes and laying himself open to accusations of double-talk from his foes.

The move had in fact been based on an illusion about Israeli politics. 'Sartawi didn't realize how isolated the people he was dealing with in Israel had become,' says Ilan Halevy, now PLO representative to the Socialist International. 'He thought he'd seized a piece of the establishment and that this was a prelude to a major change in Israel. Fourteen years later this change has not taken place.'[44] Although Arafat deserves credit for seeking to open channels to Israelis, the exercise said as much about his personal leadership style as it did about real prospects for Palestinian-Israeli peace at the time. In any case, Israel had already erected a formidable obstacle to the PLO's involvement in American-brokered Middle East peace moves by persuading the US to abstain from talking to the PLO until it had recognized the Jewish state.

Even as the 'dialogue' continued, events closer to home created a formidable distraction for Arafat and his comrades. For in the country that the PLO had now turned into its main base, Lebanon, the Organization was becoming dragged into another Arab conflict with effects almost as devastating as those of the Jordanian civil war five years earlier.

# 8

# *The Lebanese Quagmire*

> 'I cannot imagine what the connection is between the fighting of Palestinians in the highest mountains of Lebanon and the liberation of Palestine.' President Hafez al-Assad of Syria, Radio Damascus, 20 July 1976.

It was a warm June morning on the wooded slopes above Beirut, but as they drove up the winding road to Baabda, Yasser Arafat and Salah Khalaf experienced a sense of chill. Summoned to call at the hillside palace of Lebanese President Suleiman Franjieh, neither anticipated an easy encounter. For more than two months, Lebanon had been sinking steadily deeper into civil war, and a stormy exchange with the President five weeks earlier had left Arafat in no doubt as to whom Franjieh was inclined to blame.

Even so, the reception awaiting them caught the Palestinians unprepared. Ushered into the presence not only of the Maronite Christian President, a white-haired mountain clan leader with a fearsome reputation, but also of the Saudi and Egyptian ambassadors and a bevy of Muslim army officers, they were treated to a torrent of accusations and demands. 'Your behaviour is intolerable for the Lebanese population,' thundered the grim-faced, chain-smoking President. 'I am asking you today – indeed, I am insisting – in the presence of two Arab ambassadors friendly to your cause, to confine yourselves to the limits of your camps and sectors.'[1] Arafat, accused of dishonesty in his claims about the activities of his Lebanese opponents and – more woundingly – of lacking the courage to discipline his own troops, was reduced to impotent rage. 'I won't tolerate being talked to like that,' he shot back, raising his foot and pointing insultingly to its sole: 'This shoe has seen a lot of courage, Your Excellency. It went into the occupied territories immediately after the defeat in 1967 and walked on the hills of the West Bank.'[2]

After a fierce four-hour exchange which resolved little, Franjieh paradoxically insisted that his visitors stay for a most convivial three-hour lunch. To those not directly involved, it might just have been one of those set-piece encounters, replete with posturing, threats and sudden reconciliation, for which Lebanese politics had long been famous. But to the antagonists, it was in deadly earnest. This meeting, on 23 June 1975, was Arafat's last with the Lebanese President. It provided the starkest possible illustration of the speed with which things had deteriorated for the Palestinians since their diplomatic triumphs of the previous year, when Franjieh had led a nineteen-member Arab delegation to the United Nations and delivered a fulsome speech in support of Arafat's quest for international recognition. Now, here he was, lending his full backing to Lebanese factions who were arming themselves to fight the Palestinians, and paying little heed to Arafat's arguments in self-defence.

Gone were the words of Lebanese solidarity with the Palestinian cause that had wafted down from the UN podium in November 1974; vanished were Franjieh's claims for Lebanon as 'that land of tolerance' and 'a human synthesis of peace and brotherhood'.[3] In their place was a reality that had been hidden beneath the febrile surface of Lebanese society for many years and now erupted in all its ugliness: a spectacle of sectarian prejudice and suspicion, of government enfeebled by division and corruption, and of violence on an appalling scale. Within a matter of months, it ensnared the Palestinians in another full-scale armed confrontation with their Arab brethren. Thanks to the machinations of their foes and in no small measure to their own mistakes, it was a fight for survival every bit as serious as the conflict which had led to the PLO's expulsion from Jordan in 1970–1. It also proved a diversion which distracted them for years from the struggle to liberate Palestine.

Ain Rummaneh was a largely Christian district that had sprung up amid the orange groves south-east of Beirut in the 1950s. On 13 April 1975, as the Maronite Christian patriarch Pierre Gemayel attended the consecration of a new church in a street bearing his name, shots were fired at his entourage from a passing car, killing four men, including a bodyguard and two members of Gemayel's Phalange militia. Precisely who was responsible for the incident was unclear, but members of the Phalange evidently leapt to their own conclusions. Later that same morning in the same suburb, a bus carrying a group of Palestinians back to their nearby refugee camp was ambushed by Christian gunmen and all twenty-eight passengers were shot dead in cold blood.

Within twenty-four hours of the Ain Rummaneh massacre, as if on cue, mortar and machine-gun battles between Phalangist militiamen and Palestinian commandos erupted all over Beirut, setting a pattern in three days that would become tediously familiar in the following eighteen months. Lebanese Christian forces in the east of the city traded artillery fire with Palestinians in their refugee camps; armed gangs rampaged through the Christian quarters of town, looting shops and homes and blowing up cars; gunmen of various sectarian stripes, and of none, committed all manner of senseless crimes; and political leaders poured fuel on the flames with a plethora of provocative declarations. By the time the Arab League had hastily arranged a ceasefire on 16 April, it was already clear that the truce would be broken almost as soon as agreed.

For Yasser Arafat, who from his headquarters in the tumbledown Fakhani district of west Beirut had urged

Arab leaders to intervene on the first day of the fighting, the outbreak of civil war in Lebanon spelled disaster. Its continuation might destroy everything he had worked for since the PLO's expulsion from Jordan four years earlier: the military infrastructure painstakingly constructed in the south for armed raids into Israel; the base for autonomous political and diplomatic action he had managed to establish in Beirut; and the support Arafat had sought to generate for his movement among important segments of the Lebanese political establishment. In effect, the PLO saw Lebanon as its 'last refuge', the only country on the front line with Israel where its presence in force was permitted. All this was now under serious threat. Small wonder that Arafat himself, as ever sensing the work of unseen forces against him, described it all at the outset as 'a conspiracy to disrupt Lebanese-Palestinian relations'.[4]

In truth, he must have known that the root of the trouble went much, much deeper than that. It stretched right back to the foundation both of the Lebanese Republic and of the Palestinian national movement, tapping deep-seated fears and insecurities on both sides. Even without the Palestinians as a focus, the conflict between Lebanon's minority Maronite Christian community and its Muslim and Druze sects over the division of the country's political spoils had a momentum all its own. But undoubtedly it was the Palestinians who were the catalyst for civil war, and it was controversy over the PLO's armed presence that became its principal driving force. In the wake of Israel's War of Independence in 1948, Lebanon had become home to some 180,000 refugees from the towns and villages of what had been northern Palestine, and by the 1960s – thanks to natural increase and further waves of immigration – Palestinians represented around 10 per cent of Lebanon's resident population. Not all of them remained in temporary accommodation by any means, but the ramshackle refugee camps that sprang up along the country's southern coast and in the outer suburbs of

Beirut were an ever-present reminder of the dispossessed. A source of cheap labour for Lebanon's burgeoning industries, the Palestinians of the camps had been kept on a tight rein by the authorities for two decades. Just as the country's much-feared military security service, the Deuxième Bureau, stamped on political activism, so the army sought to suppress early cross-border raids by the underground Fatah movement for fear of Israeli reprisals – as Arafat well knew, remembering the death by torture of a jailed Palestinian guerrilla in 1965 and his own spell in a Lebanese prison the following year.

Towards the end of the 1960s, however, when Arafat had taken the helm of a newly awakened national movement, the Palestinians of Lebanon began to emerge as a force in their own right, and their stirrings had an inevitable ripple effect in a country where divisions along sectarian, social and political lines were in any case becoming increasingly exposed.

Inexorably, as in Jordan at about the same time, the authorities were forced by a wave of public (especially Muslim) support for the Palestinians to loosen their control. Armed *fedayeen* appeared in the streets of Beirut, as they had in Amman. Resistance groups implanted themselves among the refugees and turned their settlements into armed camps. An upsurge of cross-border attacks brought heavy Israeli retaliation. As the Lebanese Army attempted to halt guerrilla activity in the south, it became embroiled in repeated skirmishes with PLO commandos. Among the Maronite Christians, who held the main levers of power under an unwritten agreement dating back to Lebanon's independence from France in 1943, the new military presence in their midst caused an atmosphere of rising alarm.

By October 1969 the situation was rapidly getting out of hand. The Lebanese Army was in no position to implement orders to restrain the *fedayeen*. Bloody clashes between the two both created friction within the government and attracted disapproving attention from the Palestinians' friend and protector, President Nasser, whose foreign minister invited Arafat and the Lebanese army commander, General Emile Boustany, to Cairo to try to work out some sort of *modus vivendi*. The result, on 3 November, was the signing of the so-called Cairo Agreement, which aimed to regulate relations between the Palestinians and Lebanese 'on the bases of confidence, frankness and co-operation'.[5] From now on, in theory, the PLO would confine its military activities to specified areas in the south-east of the country, co-ordinate them with the Lebanese Army, and promise not to interfere in Lebanese affairs. In return, the army would 'facilitate' the passage of commandos to border areas.[6]

In practice, the agreement was shot full of holes. For one thing, it was most unlikely that the Palestinian guerrillas would confine themselves to south-eastern Lebanon when their main recruiting grounds were in the refugee camps of Beirut and the south-west. For another, there was no mechanism to ensure the smooth working of the accord. As Walid Khalidi, a Palestinian professor who mediated between Arafat and the Lebanese Government in the 1970s and was frequently confronted with breaches of the accord, puts it: 'There were so many loopholes in it that it really is difficult to see how it could have been implemented without the most elaborate monitoring system. The idea of confining the military presence of the Palestinians to just a corner of Lebanon at a time when there were hundreds of thousands of refugees along the coast was simply not practical.'[7]

To Arafat, then preoccupied by the worsening crisis in Jordan, this was all beside the point. The important thing for him was that, for the first time, an Arab government had formally recognized the Organization's right to pursue armed struggle from its sovereign territory and had entrusted security in the Palestinian refugee camps to the PLO itself rather than to the hated Lebanese security service. Pocketing these enormous gains, he did not make any strenuous effort to enforce the reciprocal limits on PLO activity. Instead, using the Cairo Agreement as one foundation stone and the Lebanese Government's inherent weakness as the other, he set out to build a state within a state that was to put the Palestinian movement on a collision course with Lebanese Christian hardliners. 'There was no real co-ordination between us and the Lebanese authorities,' comments a senior Palestinian military commander. 'Their aim in the agreement was to control us rather than to co-ordinate, so friction was inevitable.'[8]

Nevertheless, by the early 1970s Lebanon had become the only country where the *fedayeen* could operate in relative freedom. It was the Arab world's closest approximation to a parliamentary democracy and the government, unlike those of Jordan and Syria, was too divided between supporters and opponents of the resistance to call the shots. In Syria, where between 3000 and 4000 *fedayeen* had fled from King Hussein's vengeful legions in 1970 and 1971, the Palestinians had swiftly found themselves subject to onerous restrictions. Hafez al-Assad, the country's new President, had long before developed a deep suspicion of Arafat and had come to think of himself rather than Arafat or Hussein as the rightful guardian of the Palestinian cause, frequently telling visitors that Palestine was historically part of southern Syria. He forbade armed operations against Israel without his army's permission, impeded PLO troop movements with road-blocks, banned *fedayeen* from carrying weapons in public and subjected Palestinians to all manner of petty harassment. Such measures may have made sense from the standpoint of Syrian stability, but to a liberation movement that was still struggling to assert itself, and to a Palestinian leader for whom independence of action was always the most jealously guarded priority, they amounted to an intolerable interference. 'Assad wanted to freeze the operations of the Palestinian movement in Syria, so we went to Lebanon to escape the freezer,' observes Sakher Abu Nizar, an Arafat aide who took charge of Fatah's organization in Lebanon from 1973.[9] Assad, needless to say, had another motive for wanting the Palestinians to enhance their presence in Lebanon rather than on his territory, seeing it as a covert way of increasing his influence in the country on his western borders – as a way, in the words of one senior PLO official, of 'controlling both Lebanon and the Palestinians'.[10]

Thus, with Assad's encouragement, Palestinian fighters began a major infiltration into the barren and hilly Arqoub region of south-eastern Lebanon. Defying attempts by the Lebanese Army to halt their progress, and efforts by local Fatah commanders to resist an invasion of what they regarded as their personal fief, the ill-disciplined and fractious PLO forces gradually built up new bases and amassed an array of heavy weaponry in the coastal refugee camps and in the eastern town of Baalbeck. It was only a matter of time before they became a significant military force in the capital itself, further infuriating the hardcore Maronite Christians, who saw in the PLO presence a shameful violation of Lebanese sovereignty and feared that Lebanon was in danger of becoming a substitute Palestinian homeland.

Already it was all too obvious that the rule of law in Lebanon was crumbling. Unchecked by an efficient security service – one of the first acts of President Franjieh's government after his election in 1970 having been to disband the old Deuxième Bureau – parts of the country, and especially of the capital, slid towards anarchy as armed Palestinian and Lebanese gangs took matters into their own hands. Leftist factions of the PLO, using Beirut as their new revolutionary platform, did not hesitate to confront the authorities. Smuggling and other rackets were on the increase; bank robberies multiplied; and a series of mysterious bomb explosions in Beirut suggested that Arab intelligence services, aided and abetted by the various Palestinian factions in their pay, were using Lebanon as never before for their own nefarious purposes. Although the President himself bore no small measure of responsibility for the atmosphere of growing disorder through his toleration, indeed encouragement, of corruption on a massive scale, it was more often than not the Palestinians who got the blame for Lebanon's manifest ills. What is more, they were now openly allying themselves with Lebanese radicals dedicated to the overthrow of the existing order.

The turning point came in April 1973, after the daring night-time raid on Beirut and assassination of three PLO leaders by Israeli commandos. News of the Israelis' penetration to the very heart of the city provoked an immediate political outcry, with Muslim leaders voicing strong suspicions of collusion by elements in the Lebanese security forces. Saeb Salam, the Sunni Muslim Prime Minister and a friend of Arafat, resigned when President Franjieh refused his demand for the army commander's dismissal, and Palestinians and Lebanese leftists organized mammoth anti-government demonstrations in downtown Beirut.

Within days of the Israeli attack, a series of skirmishes took place between Lebanese security forces and Palestinian commandos, culminating in the arrest of several Lebanese and Palestinian extremists and the kidnapping in return of three Lebanese soldiers by Palestinian leftists. This was the last straw. On 2 May, the army took up positions round Palestinian refugee camps in Beirut's southern suburbs, and when commandos in two of them, Sabra and Shatila, were falsely reported to have shelled the nearby international airport, the Lebanese airforce bombarded the camps. 'Franjieh was absolutely shaking with anger,' recalls Walid Khalidi, who was with the President when the reports of Palestinian shelling reached the Baabda palace above Beirut. 'The airport was not being shelled, but he insisted that it was. And he said, "I have ordered the air force to bomb your camps. The raid is going to take place in five minutes, and you're going to come out on to the terrace and witness it." And lo and behold, while we were arguing, two air force planes appeared in the skies of Beirut and divebombed the outskirts of Sabra and Shatila.'[11]

It took two and a half weeks of frantic Arab mediation for the clashes to be brought to a halt. A substantial legacy of bitterness remained on all sides. President Franjieh could not forgive the Palestinians for challenging his authority. Christian hardliners spearheaded by the Phalange, a militaristic Maronite movement modelled by its leader, Pierre Gemayel, on the fascist youth organizations that had sprung up in other Mediterranean countries in the 1930s, became more vocal in their calls for an end to the presence of the Palestinians on Lebanese soil. Belatedly, Arafat and his fellow PLO leaders, now bereft of powerful friends in the disintegrating government, began to realize they had a serious problem on their hands in a country where they had thought they could operate with impunity.

In effect, the battle lines had been drawn and, as Salah Khalaf later observed, had it not been for the temporary distraction of the October War in 1973, Lebanon would probably have slid all the way to full-scale civil strife a good deal sooner than it did.[12] The respite that followed the war and accompanied Arafat's first foray into the international diplomatic arena was thus an illusion. During the lull, the PLO's Lebanese opponents were feverishly preparing for a conflict they knew would not be long postponed. The hardcore Maronites in particular, convinced that since the government was too weak to act they would have to do the job themselves, scoured Arab and European countries for arms that would enable them to match the formidable arsenal already amassed by the Palestinians and their Lebanese allies.

For Palestinians in general and Yasser Arafat in particular, the situation evoked ominous memories of their recent experience in Jordan. Well aware of the importance of preserving his movement's new refuge, the PLO leader had in fact worked hard to maintain good relations with the most important players in Lebanese politics, including the principal Maronite chieftains. Although the militias of Palestinian extremist groups had been involved willy-nilly in clashes with the Lebanese Army, Arafat had earnestly striven to keep mainstream PLO forces out of the trouble that was brewing in the heart of the country: he had concentrated them in the south and kept their guns pointing towards Israel. But just as in Jordan before September 1970, Israel's fierce retaliatory bombing raids had triggered off a chain reaction among the Lebanese, causing thousands of Shia Muslims from the southern border country to flee to the relative safety of Beirut. Arafat, again unable to control flagrant misbehaviour by rank and file Palestinians, found himself embroiled in another interminable round of mediation and conciliation, this time involving the Phalange.

It was a precarious balancing act, with the spectre of Black September ever present. For if Arafat had learned one lesson above all from Jordan, it was that simply keeping lines of communication to all the relevant parties open was not enough. Something more was required, something the Palestinians had not had among the Jordanians: a dependable and powerful political ally. It so happened that such a figure was readily to hand, in the form of a charismatic Lebanese politician named Kamal Jumblatt.

Jumblatt, leader of a rapidly growing umbrella organization of leftist and Muslim groups known as the Lebanese National Movement, is universally acknowledged to have been an extraordinary man. Lanky and dishevelled, with a high piping voice and a dreamy look in his eyes, he was part feudal lord, part socialist visionary, part vaultingly ambitious politician. As the scion of an ancient clan inhabiting the Chouf Mountains of central Lebanon, he was a landed aristocrat and principal chieftain of what ordinary Muslims regard as an obscure and heretical religious sect, the Druze. At his family seat, a picturesque palace surrounded by cypress trees in the village of Mukhtara, he

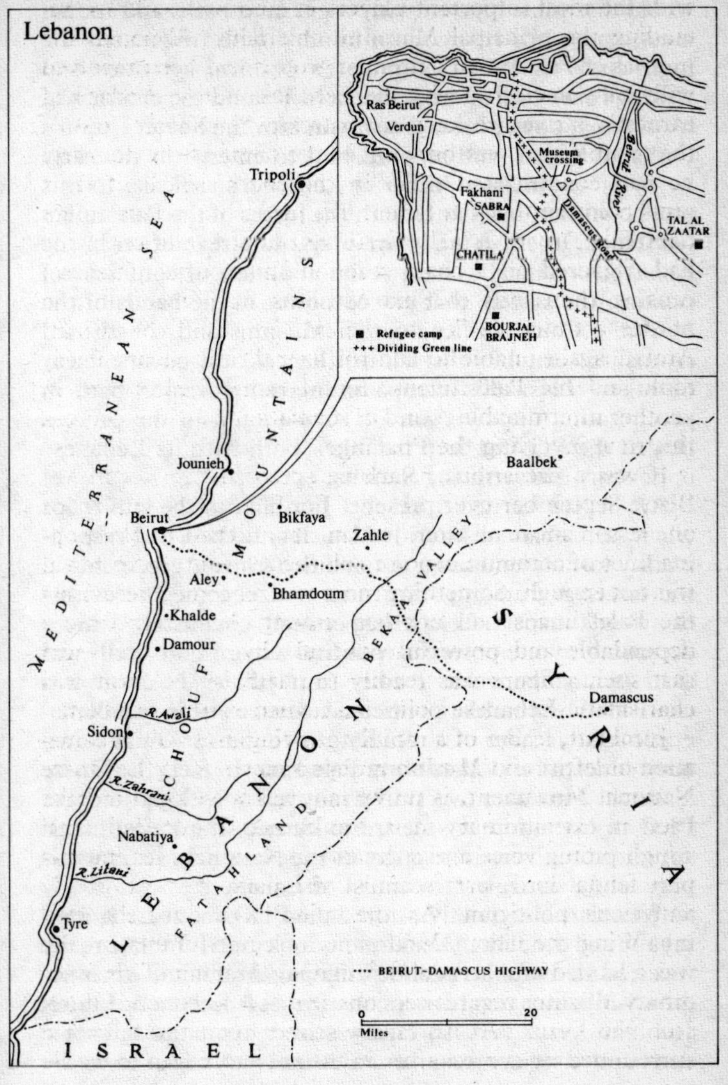
Lebanon
Ras Beirut
Verdun
Museum crossing
Beirut River
Fakhani
SABRA
Damascus Road
TAL AL ZAATAR
CHATILA
BOURJAL BRAJNEH
Refugee camp
+++ Dividing Green line
Tripoli
MEDITERRANEAN SEA
MOUNTAINS
Jounieh
Baalbek
Beirut
Bikfaya
Zahle
Aley
Bhamdoum
Khalde
Damour
BEKAA VALLEY
SYRIA
Damascus
R. Awali
Sidon
CHOUF
R. Zahrani
LEBANON
Nabatiya
FATAHLAND
R. Litani
Tyre
BEIRUT-DAMASCUS HIGHWAY
0
20
Miles
ISRAEL

would discipline himself with yoga, mud baths and Indian mysticism while his modern-minded wife frequented the night-clubs of Beirut. Jumblatt's political activities and writings gave him an influence well beyond the confines of his original power base. They won him the Soviet Union's Order of Lenin, and allowed him to emerge in the early 1970s as uncontested leader of Lebanon's radicals. In this role he set out, in alliance with the forces of the Palestinian resistance, to effect what amounted to a revolution in the Lebanese political system – the abolition of confessional politics, the system that placed power in the hands of the Maronite Christians and Sunni Muslims and constituted an insurmountable obstacle to the political advancement of other sects. His campaign played a major part in precipitating the civil war of 1975–6, and in the process landed the PLO in deep trouble – both with its Lebanese opponents and with the Syrians.

Arafat had learned to respect Jumblatt in the late 1960s when, as Lebanese Interior Minister, he had had responsibility for implementing the doomed Cairo Agreement; in the ensuing years, the two men had become the closest of friends. Apart from the personal chemistry, which, according to one observer who knew them both well, was akin to that between 'Romeo and Juliet',[13] Arafat was captivated by Jumblatt's political ideas, a vision of a democratic secular state that was not dissimilar to Arafat's own hazy conception of the future Palestine. In fact, the Druze leader had his own overriding motive for seeking to enlist PLO co-operation: his desire to harness the Palestinians' superior firepower in support of the National Movement's impending struggle for control of Lebanon.

'Jumblatt had quietly tutored the PLO about Lebanon,' says Walid Khalidi. 'Arafat is no fool, but Jumblatt really invested an awful lot of time in giving Arafat and his inner group of lieutenants his version of what is Lebanon. I think Jumblatt very, very shrewdly seized upon the talk of a democratic secular state [in Palestine] and began to weave a scenario which ideologically appealed to Arafat.'[14]

Profiting from the hard lessons he had learned from Jordan and forgetting all the brave talk of non-interference in Arab countries' affairs, Arafat thus deliberately set out to strengthen the link with Jumblatt and thereby insert the PLO into the fabric of Lebanese society, to a point where the fortunes of the Palestinians and the Lebanese National Movement became inextricably tied together. He also built up links with an increasingly influential Shia Muslim leader, Imam Musa Sadr, offering military training to his supporters and even suggesting a name – Amal, meaning 'Hope' – for his newly founded militia. Amal's slogan – 'arms are the ornament of men' – was also borrowed from the Palestinian movement. Sakher Abu Nizar has a neat way of describing the process. 'We tried,' he says, 'to make sure that it was not a case of Palestinians interfering in Lebanese affairs but of our Lebanese allies interfering in their own affairs.'[15]

It was a dangerous illusion. The Lebanese National Movement was a motley crew, composed of mafioso-style thugs as much as of political idealists. In company with such characters, the Palestinians fooled themselves into thinking that they could put down roots in Lebanon. And Beirut, after all, was comfortable. Careering around the streets in their pick-up trucks bristling with weapons, the guerrillas tended to forget that they were there on sufferance. Arafat, for his part, felt he was becoming a power in the land, a patron in a country where patronage reigned supreme, and a political leader with whom the Lebanese chieftains would have to do business.

Beguiled by his new status, he paid little attention to the corruption and indiscipline that were spreading through his entourage. As in many of the newly rich Arab states, the sudden influx of money brought trouble, turning the PLO into a bloated and in parts rotten bureaucracy. Officials, eyeing the prospect of wealth beyond the imaginings of an ordinary Palestinian refugee, freely siphoned off funds for their own use or dabbled in dubious business deals – and as a rule the higher up they were, the more they made. A notable exception was Arafat himself, who has never been charged with taking from PLO coffers or profiting from his position, but even he did little to discourage the *malaise*, dispensing money to his local clients and tolerating great laxity among his subordinates. As many PLO cadres admit ruefully today, it was all a far cry from the youthful idealism of the early guerrilla struggle.

Arafat even had time during this period to indulge in romantic dalliance. Colleagues recall that he was a frequent caller at a fashionable salon near the Beirut waterfront belonging to a well-endowed and well-connected Palestinian widow, Nada Yashrouti. Nada's late husband, the wealthy contractor Khaled Yashrouti, had been active in the PLO until he was crushed to death by a falling piece of masonry on a building site in 1970. Nada herself maintained family tradition, serving on occasion as an intermediary between Arafat and President Franjieh. So close did she and the PLO leader become that he is said to have asked for her hand in marriage. Nada, so the story goes, gently rebuffed him, saying: 'I love you as a leader, not as an ordinary man.'[16] Arafat, whose personal life has been the subject of all manner of speculation over the years, hardly ever speaks about it, except to say that he is 'married to the revolution'. Asked pointed questions on the subject, he tends to reply that 'the movement is my woman, my family, my life'. But his relationship with Nada Yashrouti set a pattern for a series of close friendships with women in later years – with his Syrian secretary Umm Nasser for one, and his Egyptian biographer Rashida Mahran for another. Like Nada, they were both amply built mother figures.

The distraction did not, on this occasion, last long. Nada Yashrouti was murdered outside her apartment by an unidentified assailant in May 1973. And as the fateful spring of 1975 approached, events in Lebanon and the wider Middle East were themselves distracting enough.

There were, for a start, distinct signs that the coalition of Arab states that had united to fight the October War with Israel and to back the PLO's quest for recognition was coming apart at the seams. Syria's President Assad was making a concerted effort to improve his relations with the Palestinians' enemy, King Hussein. Worse still, Egypt's President Sadat was inching his way, under the guileful auspices of Henry Kissinger, towards a new disengagement agreement with Israel – an accord that, as Arafat saw it, would be bound to entail further concessions at the Palestinians' expense and to fracture an already fragile Arab consensus. Developments back in Beirut were no less threatening, with Phalange leader Pierre Gemayel making a string of inflammatory speeches accusing the Palestinians of abusing Lebanese hospitality, and calling for a referendum on their continued presence in the country. Noting with alarm the support that Lebanon's Maronite Christians appeared to be receiving from important Arab countries, the Palestinian leadership once again concluded that it was the victim of 'a veritable international conspiracy'.[17]

The uncomfortable truth was that little more than a year after the October War, the mainstream Arab leaders were tiring of the excesses of the radical PLO factions and too immersed in domestic preoccupations to bother unduly about the fate of the Palestinians. To countries like Egypt, bent on making peace with Israel and solving its own formidable economic problems, or even Saudi Arabia, grappling with a cornucopia of riches after the quadrupling of oil prices, the PLO's travails in Lebanon had become little more than an irritating sideshow. Arafat's own propaganda had begun to backfire: just as he had argued that the liberation of Palestine had to come before Arab unity, so Arab leaders with states to look after had decided that their domestic affairs were more pressing than some grand Arab design.

Such dismal realities go some way towards explaining why Arafat behaved as he did when war broke out with the retaliatory massacre of a busload of Palestinians that mid-April Sunday morning in 1975. Sensing his political isolation in the Arab world and the utter hostility of the opposing camp, he mistakenly placed all his bets on his alliance with Kamal Jumblatt. His organization's leftist factions – and quite a number of guerrillas from his own Fatah group – were already fighting side by side with Jumblatt's men in any case, and Jumblatt himself went all out for escalation. On 26 April, the Lebanese National Movement responded to the Phalange's apparent involvement in the Ain Rummaneh massacre by demanding the party's removal from the government. When Arafat endorsed the statement, the die was cast: in political if not yet in openly declared military terms, the PLO had taken sides in the Lebanese civil war.

Arafat's decision to support a campaign by one Lebanese party against another had serious consequences for the Palestinians, and caused immediate qualms among some of his closest associates. Walid Khalidi, for one, was horrified. Battling to preserve lines of communication across Lebanon's sectarian divide, he had recently taken the trouble to introduce Arafat and Salah Khalaf to the hard-line leader of the influential Maronite monastic order, a burly monk named Boulos Naaman. The new move, as Khalidi told Arafat during a shouting match in his living room, threatened to undo all this work and reinforce the deepest paranoias on the Christian side. 'I remember literally screaming at him in my own house,' he says. 'I was really very angry because it just didn't make sense for him to say that. I told him that we as Palestinians had no business calling for the ostracism of the Phalangists, and that it would drive them all the way into the hands of the Israelis.'[18]

These were prophetic words: as far as the PLO's relations with the Maronites were concerned, the damage was done. As President Suleiman Franjieh told Arafat and an embarrassed Salah Khalaf during their stormy meeting at his palace on 23 June: 'That was a major mistake on your part. The Phalange represents a significant segment of the Christian population. Your decision will have no other effect than to spread its influence.'[19] Once again, opportunism – a grasping for short-term advantage – seemed to have clouded Arafat's political judgement.

In the next few months, as fighting intensified, ceasefires collapsed and Arab and European negotiators fruitlessly came and went, Arafat redoubled his efforts to mediate between the warring factions and to pretend, despite significant involvement of Palestinian fighters on the Muslim side, that the PLO, and more especially Fatah, had no part in the war. But the conflict between Christian east Beirut and a predominantly Muslim west had developed its own momentum. The Maronite Christians provoked a fresh upsurge of fury among their opponents by starting to talk openly about the partition of Lebanon into separate sectarian enclaves. The Lebanese Muslims and Druze and the Palestinians resolutely opposed Maronite demands that the army be called in to restore order, a move which Arafat, as ever seeking to represent the broadest spectrum of Palestinian opinion, feared would lead to the liquidation of the PLO's extremist factions. The Palestinian leadership's sense of isolation grew sharply in September 1975, when President Sadat signed his second Sinai disengagement agreement with Israel, unilaterally promising in the teeth of PLO and Syrian opposition to resolve the Middle East conflict by peaceful rather than by military means.

Arafat's problems were compounded by the fact that the PLO and even Fatah itself were split, just as they had been in Jordan. Fatah leaders insisted that the conflict was a conspiracy aimed at dividing Lebanon and distracting the Palestinians from their fight against Israel. But they were opposed by a substantial body of opinion among the leftist groups and within Fatah, some of whose most senior military commanders argued with exceedingly dubious logic that the road to liberating Palestine led through the Lebanese Christian port of Jounieh, and that what was at stake was a 'class struggle' between poor oppressed Muslims and rich privileged Maronites.[20]

The confrontation that would tip the balance between these two schools of thought, and dramatically escalate the war, was not long in coming. On 4 January 1976, Maronite militiamen closed in on and laid siege to two Palestinian refugee camps in east Beirut, Tal al-Zaatar and Jisr al-Basha, from where Palestinian leftist forces controlled roads into the city. To the PLO leadership, which demanded the immediate lifting of the blockade and threatened to break it by force if necessary, the move was an intolerable provocation. And when, on 14 January, Maronite forces besieged and overran the Dbayeh refugee camp on a hilltop north of the capital, butchering many of its Palestinian Christian inhabitants, Arafat and his colleagues concluded that the time for action had arrived. Abandoning all pretence that this was not the PLO's war, they and their Lebanese radical allies vowed to respond with all the force at their disposal.

The chosen location for PLO reprisals was Damour, a small Christian town near the coast south of Beirut. Sitting amid a rolling countryside of mulberry fields and silk factories, Damour occupied a strategic position on the coastal highway linking Beirut with the pro-Palestinian south. It was also the stronghold of a Maronite leader, Camille Chamoun, who was a particular target of Palestinian hatred. From mid-January 1976, columns of Fatah fighters from the southern port city of Sidon converged on Damour under the command of a former Jordanian artillery officer, Mohammed Said Musa Maragha: under his *nom de guerre*, Abu Musa, he would gain notoriety seven years later as one of the leaders of a bloody mutiny against Arafat's leadership. Known to colleagues as a tough, even brutal man, Abu Musa was also one of the principal spokesmen for the leftist view that the Palestinians were engaged in a class struggle against the Maronites. After shelling Damour for forty-eight hours, the combined Palestinian and Lebanese Muslim forces broke through into the town on 20 January. As church bells rang out in east Beirut to signal Christian alarm, an orgy of looting, destruction and murder was unleashed on those inhabitants who had not already fled. Damour was reduced to a ghost town. As a senior Fatah intelligence officer puts it: 'I always say that the artillery men are the most dangerous because they do not pinpoint their target, they just cover a whole area with fire. And when they attacked Damour, they considered it a bourgeois area to be taken and looted.'[21]

The drama that unfolded in the ensuing months caught all the combatants in a tangled web of distrust and deception, whose strands were almost entirely of their own weaving. Above all, it is the story of a battle over Lebanon's future between two ruthless and ambitious leaders, Kamal Jumblatt and Hafez al-Assad of Syria, and of the vacillations of a third man torn between the two, Yasser Arafat.

Under heavy pressure from the Palestinian rank and file, Arafat and his fellow Fatah leaders had crossed the Rubicon. A conflict they had previously insisted was a purely Lebanese affair had become an all-out confrontation between Palestinian and Maronite Lebanese forces, and a full-time distraction from the PLO's supposed purpose, the struggle against Israel. It was a fight, moreover, in which Lebanon's powerful eastern neighbour, Syria, was taking an increasingly close interest thanks to the urgent appeals for help which Arafat had addressed to President Assad.[22]

The Syrian leader's main preoccupation was to maintain the balance in Lebanon – to prevent the Maronite Christians from crushing their opponents but equally to keep the Lebanese radicals and Palestinians from overturning the existing order. On 19 January, he had fired a warning shot in support of the resistance by despatching units of the Palestine Liberation Army under Syrian command across the border into Lebanon's Bekaa Valley. A day later he sent his Foreign Minister, Abdel Halim Khaddam, to Beirut at the head of a high-powered mediating team. It swiftly produced what President Franjieh announced on the 22nd as an 'agreement between all the parties towards an overall solution of the Lebanese crisis'.[23] The Syrians promised to co-operate with the Palestinians and the Lebanese in imposing and enforcing an effective ceasefire. The fighting died away, and as the Syrian and Lebanese governments got to work on drafting a programme of political reform, it began to seem as if the civil war might be over.

Nothing, of course, could have been further from the truth. The suspicions ran too deep on all sides for the truce to be any more than a temporary respite, in addition to which both the PLO and Kamal Jumblatt's Lebanese National Movement were now involved in machinations that would lead to a new and even more serious confrontation, this time directly involving the Syrian Army.

Jumblatt was deeply wary of Syrian motives in spite of the arms Assad had provided for his movement over the years and the help he had afforded in January. He was also contemptuous of the political reforms the Syrian President was trying to impose on Lebanon – piecemeal changes which would give the Muslims more power but would leave intact the system that barred anyone other than a Maronite Christian from becoming President. Hence, as Assad stepped up his attempts to arbitrate, Jumblatt caused mounting anger in Damascus by ungratefully digging in his heels against the Syrian plan.

In February and March 1976, Lebanon's armed forces began to show serious signs of disintegration as a breakaway group of Muslim soldiers, calling itself the Lebanese Arab Army, gathered recruits and took control of military barracks in the eastern Bekaa Valley. Then on 11 March, the Muslim commander of the Beirut garrison, a flamboyant officer named Brigadier Aziz Ahdab, seized the capital's radio and television stations, proclaimed himself provisional military governor, and demanded the resignation of President Franjieh within twenty-four hours.

Both moves bore clear traces of PLO involvement, notwithstanding subsequent denials by the leadership. Khalil al-Wazir was keen to improve his firepower with weapons seized from the Lebanese Army, and co-operated with dissident officers to hasten its break-up; and Fatah had undeniably provided the coup-making brigadier with a military escort. But the Palestinians and their Lebanese radical allies were playing with fire, for their activities amounted to an intolerable affront not only to the authority of Franjieh, who vowed that 'the only way I'll leave the presidency is in a coffin', but also to that of Assad himself.[24] Arafat and his intelligence chief Salah Khalaf were duly summoned to Damascus to explain themselves.

The meeting, on 16 March, was long even by Assad's windy standards, lasting a full twelve hours. The Syrian President was in a foul temper, calling Arafat and Khalaf 'men who betrayed his confidence while pretending to be his friends'.[25] When Assad was informed by telephone during the discussions that Jumblatt had made a declaration denouncing Syrian meddling in Lebanese affairs, he flew into a deeper rage and it was only with the greatest difficulty that the Palestinians finally persuaded Assad to make one more attempt to patch things up by receiving Jumblatt in Damascus. Far from reconciling the two men, their meeting eleven days later – against the background of a fresh upsurge of fighting between combined Palestinian and Lebanese radical forces and those of the Maronite Christian right – merely set the seal on their estrangement, prompting Assad to suspend arms deliveries to the Lebanese National Movement.

It had become a personal quarrel of a bitterness unusual even by the standards of the Arab world, based on a curious and unstable chemistry between Assad and Jumblatt, both of whom came from minority sects. Jumblatt, the Druze aristocrat who could not be President of Lebanon, deeply resented the advancement achieved by Assad, the poor farmer's son from Syria's northern Alawi Mountains. And Assad, the Arab leader out to aggrandize his power by securing a major influence in Lebanon, could not forgive Jumblatt – 'that dealer in revolutions and progressivism' as he called him – for spoiling his designs.

Their feud placed Yasser Arafat on the horns of a most awkward dilemma, for he was now under intense pressure to choose between the two. To alienate Assad, president of the country that had given Fatah its first military bases and the wherewithal to launch its armed struggle, would be foolhardy in the extreme. Yet to do as Assad seemed to be demanding and distance the Palestinian movement from Jumblatt, the man who more than any other served as guarantor of the PLO's freedom of action in Lebanon, could have equally serious consequences. 'In short,' said Khalaf, 'the Palestinian resistance was torn between the need to maintain its good relations with its Syrian ally and the moral obligation to stand by the Lebanese left.'[26]

Unable to decide, Arafat took the course of which he was past master: he temporized. At another meeting with Assad on 16 April, he agreed to a seven-point ceasefire plan which he subsequently persuaded a reluctant Jumblatt to swallow. But when the Lebanese parliament gathered on 8 May to replace Franjieh with a new president at Syria's behest, Palestinian units signalled their displeasure by bombarding the assembly building with shells. In a move which further incensed the Syrian leader, Arafat mended his fences with Sadat of Egypt, who then eagerly despatched units of the Palestine Liberation Army to Lebanon. All the while the fighting sputtered on, with the combined Palestinian-Lebanese forces making perceptible gains at the expense of the Maronites. By the end of April 1976, Jumblatt was able to boast that his National Movement controlled 82 per cent of Lebanese territory.[27]

With the repeated and humiliating collapse of his mediation efforts, Assad was rapidly approaching the end of his tether. He had been willing to support the Palestinians and the Lebanese radicals up to a point as a way of bolstering his influence in Lebanon, but he most emphatically did not want to see the overthrow of the existing Maronite-dominated order. So at the end of May he took one of the most contentious decisions of his controversial career: he sent his army into Lebanon to fight alongside Maronite Christian forces and crush the combined Palestinian-Lebanese offensive. By the end of the first week of June, around 12,000 Syrian troops, accompanied by tanks, were advancing into the country in three separate thrusts.

For the PLO and Jumblatt's radicals, this was a challenge of an altogether more serious order than they had faced hitherto. They swiftly formed a unified military command to confront the invaders, put up fierce resistance in the mountains of central Lebanon and in the outskirts of its three main coastal towns, and retaliated by overrunning the Beirut bases and offices of the Syrian-controlled PLO faction, al-Saiqa.

But from the outset, the Palestinian-Lebanese alliance was caught on the wrong foot by the superior Syrian force. Arafat himself was out of the country on a singularly ill-timed diplomatic round. Unable to return because of the fighting, he sent frantic appeals for Arab intervention from the Algerian, Libyan and Egyptian capitals, but although Arab foreign ministers responded to his pleas by persuading the Syrians to accept a ceasefire on 9 June, the resulting stalemate was merely the prelude to an onslaught more ferocious than any that had gone before.

In the eyes of the PLO's leaders, the 'international conspiracy' of which they had been warning for well over a year was proved. If any further proof were needed they had only to point to the evident approval with which Syria's move into Lebanon had been greeted in the United States and even in Israel, which assented to the invasion under a US-mediated 'red line' agreement. The fact that the instrument for carrying out the plot was a supposedly 'progressive' Arab regime, Syria, merely compounded the PLO's bitterness.

In effect, the choice which Arafat had been unwilling to make, between his tactical alliance with Assad and his strategic friendship with Kamal Jumblatt, had been made for him, and his falling out with Syria had serious and lasting consequences. In his relations with the implacable Syrian President, Arafat had passed a point from which there could be any wholehearted return, temporary reconciliations notwithstanding. One chilling conversation he had with Assad during their arguments in 1976 stuck in his mind. 'You do not represent Palestine any more than we do,' the Syrian President told him. 'There is neither a Palestinian people, nor a Palestinian entity, there is only Syria, and you are an inseparable part of the Syrian people and Palestine is an inseparable part of Syria.'[28] Not even the Israeli leader, Golda Meir, who once observed there was no such thing as a Palestinian people, had put it quite so bluntly.

Even with the benefit of fifteen years' hindsight, the leaders of the PLO do not accept that they made a serious strategic error by so openly taking sides in Lebanon's civil war. 'The situation in Lebanon was complex before we even arrived,' said Salah Khalaf, who argued at the time that the PLO had a 'moral obligation' to support Kamal Jumblatt. 'The fact that the area we were in was predominantly Muslim meant that we had to co-ordinate particularly with the Muslim side. We tried to co-operate with the other factions, but we failed.'[29] Many outsiders, though, including Palestinian sympathizers who urged Arafat to observe greater impartiality, are convinced that the Palestinian movement attached its fortunes far too closely to those of one man, to a point where it became a virtual hostage to Kamal Jumblatt's ambitions. 'Jumblatt was one of the very few people who have been able to hijack Palestinian decision-making,' observes a Palestinian businessman who was close to Arafat in Lebanon. 'This was really not constructive.'[30]

Late in June 1976 the Maronite militias seized their moment to fight back. The site was a cluster of Palestinian and Lebanese Shia Muslim settlements in east Beirut; the name of one of them, the refugee camp of Tal al-Zaatar, was to earn a place of enduring notoriety in Palestinian lore. Tal al-Zaatar, a miserable shanty town constructed out of breeze blocks and corrugated iron, had been blockaded since January, its exit roads cut off by hostile gunmen and its inhabitants unable to secure adequate provisions. The PLO leadership had made repeated attempts to lift the siege, whether by military or other means; indeed, at one point Khalil al-Wazir, who was in charge during Arafat's prolonged foreign travels, opened negotiations with the powerful Maronite clergy to buy the land on which the camp was built for four million US dollars. It was a gesture typical of the wheeling-dealing world of Lebanese politics, but it was to no avail.

On 22 June, several hundred Christian militiamen launched a full-scale attack on Tal al-Zaatar as well as the smaller camp of Jisr al-Basha and the nearby Muslim quarter of Nabaa. As mortars and rockets rained down, Tal al-Zaatar's inhabitants took refuge in underground sewage tunnels, and the Syrian Army cut off supply lines to the camp from the mountains behind Beirut. Within six days, Jisr al-Basha had fallen amid angry accusations of Syrian complicity from Arafat, watching impotently from a succession of Arab capitals, but the other settlements managed to hold out.

Wazir was desperate. To break the siege by force would entail redeploying PLO troops from the Lebanese mountains where they were entrenched with those of Kamal Jumblatt's National Movement. The trouble was that Jumblatt had his own priorities, insisting that the Palestinian forces should concentrate on holding their lines in the mountains. In the absence of Arafat, who might have been able to prevail on his friend but who did not return to Beirut until 5 July, nothing the leadership on the spot could say would persuade Jumblatt to change his mind. In the moment of the PLO's greatest need, the nature of its relationship with its principal Lebanese ally was laid bare. Beyond the genuine personal warmth and political sympathy between Arafat and Jumblatt, it was a marriage of convenience in which the demands and ambitions of the Lebanese partner took precedence.[31]

Without reinforcements, the collapse of Tal al-Zaatar was inevitable. On 6 August the Muslim quarter of Nabaa fell to the Maronite militiamen, and on the 12th, after an artillery bombardment that had stretched over fifty-two consecutive days, Tal al-Zaatar itself surrendered under an evacuation agreement hammered out by the Arab League. The camp's 30,000 inhabitants had been brought to the brink of famine, and forced to risk their lives in drawing water from their one polluted well. Even in surrender, there was no end to the suffering. As unarmed refugees began to make their way out of the camp, Maronite gunmen opened fire. Others pushed into the constricted alleyways of the camp, indiscriminately shooting Palestinians – women, babies and the elderly as well as men of fighting age. In all, during the siege and its bloody aftermath, an estimated 3000 – most of them civilians – were killed, with at least as many wounded.

This was a catastrophe on a scale unprecedented even in the battered annals of the Palestinian movement. The day after the massacre, Arafat urgently asked Arab leaders to convene a summit meeting with a view to halting carnage evidently abetted by the 'progressive', Arab nationalist, Syrian Army. Their replies, which arrived in a desultory trickle over the next couple of weeks, were distinctly non-committal.

For the Syrians, the PLO's state of shock created an opening, and they lost little time in pressing home their advantage, mounting an all-out offensive in late September to dislodge the Palestinian and Lebanese opposition forces from their strategic mountain strongholds. Realizing how heavily the odds were stacked against it, the PLO leadership discreetly disengaged itself from a still defiant Jumblatt and withdrew. It was only when the Syrians renewed their attack in mid-October against Palestinian and Lebanese forces dug in at the picturesque summer resort of Bhamdoun above Beirut that Arafat succeeded in obtaining a concrete response to his appeals for Arab help. On 14 October, he got through by telephone to Crown Prince Fahd of Saudi Arabia and explained the Palestinians' plight. 'I will settle the problem,' said Fahd. 'Give me a few hours.'[32]

Arafat and Khalaf took refuge with the Saudi ambassador in Beirut. Within two days, six of the Arab world's most influential men – the rulers of Kuwait, Egypt and Saudi Arabia as well as those directly involved in the conflict – assembled in the desert city of Riyadh to close this bloody chapter of the Lebanese civil war. As the 'mini-summit' convened, President Assad brought eighteen months of bitter fighting to an end by proclaiming a ceasefire, and at a subsequent enlarged meeting in Cairo, the leaders of the Arab world in effect endorsed the establishment of a new order in Lebanon, one dividing the country into separate spheres of influence and giving Syria's military presence – in the thin disguise of an Arab Deterrent Force – a predominant role.

Arafat, rescued once again at the eleventh hour by his wary Arab sponsors, had been temporarily cut down to size. In humiliating recognition of the fact, he had to leave Lebanon in a helicopter provided by Syria and fly to the Saudi capital from a Syrian airport. The toll the conflict had taken on the PLO was enormous, with some 5000 Palestinians killed out of a total of 30,000 and the movement's internal divisions as sharply accentuated as ever. To make matters worse, a few short months later the PLO's main Lebanese ally was dead. On 16 March 1977, Kamal Jumblatt was assassinated in his car near a Syrian roadblock in the vicinity of his ancestral home. Nobody was in any doubt whom to blame.

But all was by no means lost for Arafat in the autumn of 1976. For he, too, had effectively been granted his own Lebanese fiefdom under the compromise agreed at Riyadh: a sizeable swathe of territory between the southern Litani river and Beirut itself. The PLO chairman now tried his hand at another new role, as president of something approaching a real state within the state. Like the sheriff of some latter-day Dodge City, he set out from his offices in west Beirut's dowdy Fakhani district to impose the PLO's rule on the wayward Lebanese, and in the process to win credit in the outside world as a leader of substance.

The PLO's presence in Lebanon was steadily becoming an end in itself, to be defended at all costs. It was a power base that allowed Arafat a measure of independence in facing the machinations of Arab regimes and the undying hostility of Israel. It also appeared to offer him new opportunities to break through the indifference of the Western country he most wanted to talk to: the United States.

# 9

# *Knocking on Washington's Door*

'The US holds the key to Israel.' Yasser Arafat in interview with *Time* magazine, 11 November 1974.

Cyrus Vance could tell something was wrong the moment his limousine drew up at the marbled airport in the western hills of Saudi Arabia. Where optimism had radiated the day before, gloom now clouded the hawk-like features of the Saudi Foreign Minister who had come to bid the American Secretary of State a formal farewell. As a dejected Prince Saud al-Faisal took him off to the VIP lounge for a final round of talks, Vance braced himself for bad news. 'Arafat has been in touch,' he was told, once they had stepped out of the blistering August heat. 'He said he just didn't have the votes to carry the day. The opportunity has gone.'[1]

In his less demonstrative way, the American diplomat shared the prince's frustration. Twenty-four hours earlier, on 7 August 1977, the two men had thought they were close to achieving a breakthrough in Middle East diplomacy. During a flying visit to the Saudi royal family's summer residence in the hill town of Taif, Arafat had promised to persuade his colleagues to recognize Israel's right to exist, a move which might pave the way for full-scale Arab-Israeli negotiations and produce a major triumph for the administration of President Jimmy Carter in its first year. The PLO chairman's failure to do so the previous night in Damascus had put the US, Saudi Arabia and everybody else with an interest in involving the Palestinians in Middle East peace moves back where they started.

Vance left for Israel, the next stop on his second Middle East tour in six months, with a heavy heart. He had gone as far as he could to entice the PLO into breaking down the barrier that prevented it from communicating directly with Washington, and in the process as good as guaranteed himself a hostile reception from the hardline leadership in Jerusalem. Yet he had nothing to show for his pains.[2]

For Yasser Arafat, 850 miles away in Damascus, it was a disappointment of a kind that had become depressingly familiar. Desperately anxious for American recognition, he had been sending conciliatory messages to Washington through Saudi, Syrian and Egyptian intermediaries ever since President Carter's inauguration at the beginning of the year. Now his comrades had blocked his manoeuvres. The concession being demanded of the PLO in return for a dialogue with the US – acceptance of a key UN resolution affirming the right of all states in the region to exist in peace – was simply too much to swallow. A unique political opportunity was slipping away.

The pity of it was that 1977 had begun on such an unusually hopeful note. Rescued by the Saudis from disaster in Lebanon, the Palestinians had picked themselves up with remarkable speed, redeploying their forces in the south of the country to resume the fight against Israel. Arafat, the perpetual survivor, bounced back faster than anyone could have imagined. In one of those intensely public and almost equally cosmetic reconciliations for which Arab politics are notorious, he swiftly made his peace with President Assad of Syria. Only months after the two leaders had called openly for each other's removal, they were pictured together, beaming, all over the government-controlled newspapers in Damascus.[3]

Now, freed for a time from the perpetual task of damage limitation, the PLO leader threw himself into a frenetic new round of diplomacy and debate. With the inauguration of President Carter, the Arab states were preparing themselves for another US mediation effort in the Middle East, and the PLO was beginning to think again about its political objectives.

In mid-March, the organization's legislature, the Palestine National Council, convened for an important session in Cairo, and not before time. The Council had last met nearly three years before, and its subsequent inactivity had become a symbol of the Palestinian movement's disarray. As delegates gathered, they rehearsed all that had changed in the intervening years. The Palestinians within the Israeli-occupied territories were becoming steadily more assertive. The people of the West Bank and Gaza had voted overwhelmingly for pro-PLO mayors in municipal elections staged by Israel in 1976 and now they were demanding that the exiled leadership take account of their views about the need for a political settlement. The PLO itself had been sobered by its experience in Lebanon, but far from eroding Arafat's control of the organization, the Lebanese civil war had strengthened his position at the expense of his leftist opponents. George Habash's Popular Front, which had been in the vanguard of events that dragged the Palestinians into the conflict, emerged from it divided, demoralized and unable to put up effective resistance to Arafat's political moves.

As a result, the Cairo PNC meeting took several steps that would have been inconceivable when participants last gathered there in June 1974. It called explicitly for the establishment of an 'independent national state' on 'national soil'[4] – thereby spelling out a goal that had hitherto been shrouded in obfuscation, that of a Palestinian mini-state in the West Bank and Gaza. It signalled the PLO's desire to participate in international peace negotiations on acceptable terms. Even more controversially, it debated the secret contracts that had existed over the previous year between Arafat associates and leftist Israelis. The man at the centre of these talks, Issam Sartawi, initially came under fierce attack, but after he had been warmly defended by Arafat himself, the assembled Palestinian worthies gave him a rousing burst of applause.

The meeting's closing statement was a delicately poised victory for those PLO leaders who were keen to insert the Palestinian movement into the peace moves that seemed, in early 1977, to be gathering momentum. For Yasser Arafat, once again taking a mile where his colleagues had given a few inches, it was a cue to embark on a political course as full of promise as it was fraught with difficulty: that of reaching out to the United States and its promising new President, Jimmy Carter.

Arafat had long been obsessed with America, and almost equally bewildered by it. There was nothing he wanted more than to make his views heard where it really mattered, in the country on which Israel counted for support. The question was, how?

The PLO had tried terrorism, in the form of the kidnapping and murder of the American ambassador in Khartoum. As well as making crude threats, Arafat had tried sending political messages to President Nixon's National Security Adviser, Henry Kissinger. He had even tried using the rostrum of the United Nations to appeal to American public opinion. 'What, I ask you plainly, is the crime of the people of Palestine against the American people?' he had said plaintively during his November 1974 speech to the UN General Assembly. 'Why do you fight us so?'[5]

But it was all to no avail. Arafat's communications with Kissinger – a man he was later to describe with distaste as 'the mercury of American politics' – had merely elicited a threat from General Walters in reply.[6] The 'terrorist' label had stuck: America's deeply ingrained support for Israel translated into equally deep-seated hostility to the PLO and all its works. Fumbling efforts to break down this barrier preoccupied Arafat for much of his career and caused him no end of trouble with his Palestinian critics.

Arafat's desire to ingratiate himself with Washington manifested itself in sometimes peculiar ways. One of them was intelligence co-operation in Lebanon, where the PLO leader authorized his personal security chief and close confidant, Ali Hassan Salameh, to open a channel of communication to the American Central Intelligence Agency. Some time in the early 1970s, Salameh, a dashing figure with an appetite for fast cars and pretty women, was contacted through intermediaries by a Beirut CIA agent named Robert Ames. They made an unlikely pair: Ames, a bulky giant of a man, his eyes hidden behind dark aviator glasses, consorting with the dapper Salameh. When word leaked later of their relationship, it proved highly controversial. However, Salameh's links with the infamous Black September terrorist organization and with attacks on Americans did not prevent him from providing the CIA with a regular flow of information. 'Salameh was our principal contact and he kept us well informed concerning the plans of militia groups hostile to the US,' recalls Talcott Seelye, a senior American diplomat sent to Beirut as a special emissary of President Ford in 1976. 'As a result of this intelligence, the embassy was often able to take evasive action, such as changing the ambassador's travel plans.'[7]

The relationship had been cemented at a meeting between Salameh and a CIA officer at New York's Waldorf Astoria hotel during Arafat's November 1974 visit to the UN and it grew in importance during the Lebanese civil war, as the PLO consolidated its control over the coastal area of west Beirut in which the American embassy and many other Western missions were located. Salameh shared a wide range of intelligence with the CIA, principally about the situation in Lebanon, and even provided the Americans with written reports. On one occasion, he tipped them off about an alleged threat to the life of US envoy Dean Brown – a gesture of goodwill for which Washington would six years later repay Arafat in person by warning him of a Syrian assassination plot. According to former American officials, Salameh arranged at least one top-secret meeting between Robert Ames and Arafat himself.

At the height of the Lebanon war, an event occurred that brought this unusual security co-operation into the open. On 16 June 1976, US Ambassador Francis Meloy set out across Beirut with his economic counsellor to call on President-elect Elias Sarkis. On Museum Road near the Green Line dividing the capital, a dangerous spot at the best of times, gunmen stopped their convoy and kidnapped the two diplomats and their chauffeur. Desperately casting round for assistance, embassy officials turned to the PLO, but it was too late. Several hours later, Fatah intelligence officers found the bullet-riddled bodies of the ambassador and the two others on a beach-side rubbish dump in west Beirut. 'You should have contacted us before,' observed a Palestinian security man dryly down the telephone. 'Had we known about this soon enough, we could have prevented the murders.'[8]

Over the next eight days, Fatah intelligence chief Salah Khalaf mounted a full-scale inquiry into the assassinations. His men recovered the ambassador's limousine from a warehouse in west Beirut and ascertained that the killing had been the work of a little-known extremist group, possibly in the pay of Iraq.[9] US officials were impressed. 'I don't have any reason to doubt what they told us,' says a former American ambassador in Beirut. 'They did a pretty thorough job.'[10]

From that point on, the PLO became the main protector of US and other Western diplomats in Beirut. As Abdel Latif Abu Hijleh (Abu Jaafar), the amiable director of the PLO's political department who was the Palestinian link man with the Americans, recalls it: 'After the assassination, two American officials came to see me. They said a new ambassador was being appointed, and if anything were to happen to him public opinion in the US would be shocked. We know you control the whole area, they said, so you are the people who can do something for the ambassador's security.'[11] While fighting intensified in Beirut, Palestinians provided pick-up trucks bristling with guns as escorts for American officials; and when the Americans decided shortly afterwards to evacuate all but essential personnel by sea, it was Ali Hassan Salameh's men who oversaw the security arrangements. The PLO's co-operation was publicly acknowledged by President Ford and earned Arafat an official letter of thanks from Henry Kissinger, albeit one not mentioning the organization or its leader by name.[12]

As for Salameh himself, his liaison with the Americans had fatal consequences. Less than three years after these events, the Israeli secret service, Mossad, killed him in a car bomb explosion in Beirut. He had been a top Israeli target since his activities in the Black September terrorist group in the early 1970s, but Mossad jealousy at his link with the CIA may well have been a powerful secondary motive for getting rid of him.[13]

The pattern set in 1976 became an important fact of diplomatic life in Lebanon for the next six years. The PLO now exercised virtual sovereign authority over west Beirut and was universally acknowledged as the main security force in the capital's Muslim areas, putting guards outside Western embassies and warning them of trouble. But for the Americans, Arafat's people reserved special treatment. Most mornings, the US ambassador's office would relay his schedule to the PLO by telephone, and most days it was the PLO that would provide a convoy to accompany him round the city or, on occasion, to the Palestinians' heartland in southern Lebanon. The organization even furnished the US embassy with fuel oil free of charge when it had difficulty obtaining supplies.[14]

In going out of his way to help the Americans, Arafat was hardly practising philanthropy, but it was perhaps naive to imagine that such activities would serve to whittle away the obstacles preventing a political dialogue between the US and the PLO. In September 1975, as part of the price for Israel's signature on a disengagement accord with Egypt, Henry Kissinger as US Secretary of State had made a supposedly secret pledge not to negotiate with the PLO unless the latter could meet stiff political conditions, including recognition of Israel's right to exist. The Israeli Government knew full well in demanding this promise that they were terms that the Palestinians were most unlikely to be able to fulfil; the effect was thus to slam the door to US talks in Arafat's face.

No matter what clever ruses he dreamed up to try to circumvent the ban, Arafat's difficulties in communicating with Washington only increased with the passage of time. It was not that the US was not interested: indeed, a steady procession of curious senators and congressmen trekked to Beirut in the mid-1970s to inspect Arafat like some outlandish museum-piece, and the PLO leader obliged them by making suitably peaceable noises. But when it came to dealing with the administration, he was blocked by the Kissinger pledge and by the underlying pressure brought to bear in Congress by the formidable pro-Israeli lobby. Arafat was also hampered by a more basic problem: ignorance. Neither he nor any of his leadership colleagues had ever understood how the American political system worked. As a result, they fondly imagined that countering Israeli influence in Washington was purely a matter of making suitable private contacts, rather than trying to present an argued case in public. They thought that once they had co-opted the right people, the US would begin to see the light and put pressure on Israel. 'The prevailing notion,' says Edward Said, a Palestinian-American professor in New York who has known and sought to advise Arafat for many years, 'is that America is a slightly larger version of Iraq or Lebanon. It's just a question of paying the right people, or making the right contacts. All the PLO officials without any exception whatsoever who have any interest in the US, starting from Arafat himself and working on down the list, know nothing about it. And that includes the smartest of them.'[15]

The problems this misapprehension could cause were underlined by a bizarre episode in 1976. In October that year, at the height of the American presidential election campaign, Arafat despatched his pro-American adviser Isaam Sartawi on a discreet mission to Washington with a view to opening an office there. It did not remain discreet for long. Travelling on a Tunisian diplomatic passport and arriving with the full knowledge of the authorities, Sartawi swiftly found his presence the subject of a major political outcry. When he refused a State Department request to leave the country, Henry Kissinger forced the Tunisian Government to pull him out by threatening to cut off American food shipments.[16]

It was against this unpromising background that the newly installed Carter Administration turned its attention to the Middle East in early 1977. For Arafat, the advent of Jimmy Carter had seemed a moderately hopeful development, if only because it meant the exit from the scene of Kissinger, a man the PLO leader held personally responsible for many of the afflictions that had befallen him since the late 1960s, not least the crushing defeat in Jordan of Black September 1970. But Arafat certainly had no idea that Carter was planning a radical break with the Middle East policies of his predecessors, Nixon and Ford. As the PLO's laconic 'foreign minister', Farouk Kaddoumi, put it in late February when asked about American efforts to convene a peace conference: 'We believe that the United States is going through the motions, not really taking action. We do not expect anything from this operation, because it is an American manoeuvre.'[17]

Only a few days later, in the midst of the Palestine National Council's deliberations on a new political programme in Cairo, Arafat received word of an intriguing presidential statement which prompted him to think again.

On 16 March 1977, in the unlikely setting of a small town meeting in Massachusetts, Jimmy Carter spontaneously set out his views on the Middle East problem. Dealing with the Palestinian issue was a key requirement for resolving the conflict, he said, going on to voice the hope of inviting all the parties to a reconvened Geneva conference towards the end of the year. 'There has to be a homeland provided for the Palestinian refugees who have suffered for many, many years,' he proclaimed.[18]

Arafat did not know what to make of Carter's apparently off-the-cuff statement, but if it truly reflected the thinking of the US President, something approaching a Copernican revolution in America's attitude to the Palestinians appeared to be under way. No senior US official, still less a president, had ever referred publicly to a Palestinian homeland before, always preferring to treat the problem purely as one of refugees to be handled within the framework of existing Middle Eastern states. Now here was Carter braving the wrath of Israel to associate himself with an aim that seemed tantalizingly close to that of the Palestinians themselves. As Arafat remarked in his astonishment, 'If this is true, he has touched the core of the problem without which there can be no settlement.'[19] Sending out cautiously positive signals in response, he resolved to try once more to find an opening to Washington.

Carter had realized that he was unlikely to succeed in his ambition of engineering a comprehensive Arab-Israeli peace negotiation without involving the PLO. So, as he and Secretary of State Cyrus Vance embarked on a lengthy round of meetings with Arab and Israeli leaders in Washington and the Middle East, they gradually came to focus on the need to bring Yasser Arafat into the picture. Perhaps the PLO leader could be pressed by the Egyptian, Saudi and Syrian Governments, which were all expressing interest in progress towards peace, to say the magic words that would open the way to direct contact between his organization and Washington.[20] The problem, on this as on many later occasions, lay in the tough terms Kissinger had attached to a US-PLO dialogue: in particular, the requirement that the Palestinians accept the UN's Resolution 242 of 1967, long the subject of almost ritual denunciation by the PLO. To the Palestinians it offered nothing beyond a brief reference to 'just settlement of the refugee problem' and ignored their central demand for the right to determine their own future. It was a bitter pill which Carter was to have thc greatest difficulty in sugaring to the PLO's taste.

Arafat was intrigued by the American overtures but more than a touch wary of the demand by which they were accompanied. In June he responded via Saudi Arabia's Crown Prince Fahd, explaining that the Palestinians were ready to accept Israel but needed their own state in return. Back came the persistent reply: first signal your clear acceptance of the UN resolution, then we will be prepared to do business. It was a case of Catch-242, and rapidly degenerated into a tortuous game of semantics as the two sides groped for a form of words which would enable the Palestinians to meet America's terms without compromising their principles. Summer turned to autumn and it became clear that the exercise was doomed.

During Vance's Middle East tour in August, the Saudis sulkily admitted defeat in their mediation effort, blaming Arafat for his failure to deliver the goods. The arguments in Beirut and Damascus intensified, with the PLO leader becoming so agitated during one meeting that he broke a glass table with his fist.[21] By early September 1977, when Carter had one last stab at getting through to the PLO, Arafat was behaving like a man under siege. Carter's personal emissary, a Quaker friend of his wife's named Landrum Bolling, was treated in a series of talks in Beirut between 9 and 11 September to a lengthy litany of complaints: about contradictory messages Arafat had received from his two principal Arab intermediaries, Egypt and Saudi Arabia; about the 'blackmail' Arafat was under from other Arab states, chiefly Syria, not to accept the US terms; and about the convoluted politics of his own organization.[22]

In this atmosphere of recrimination and paralysis, America's attempt to foster a dialogue with the PLO shuddered to a halt. Responsibility for the failure was not all on one side. Carter had scarcely eased the Palestinians' suspicions when he had made what appeared to be contradictory statements, vacillated in the face of Israeli pressure and tightened the restrictions on dealing with the PLO to cover all official contacts.[23] Nor had the PLO's supposed Arab friends helped, when they relayed distorted versions of what the Americans and the Palestinians were trying to say; indeed, Carter was to make the revealing observation two years later that he had 'never met an Arab leader who in private professed the desire for an independent Palestinian state'.[24]

The ultimate problem, however, lay within the Palestinian leadership. Caught between such a host of conflicting pressures, Arafat was in no position to compromise. He, as much as any of his colleagues, feared to concede what the Palestinians saw as one of their very few bargaining cards before they had even got to the negotiating table, and so end up with nothing. Like the merchant's son he was, he also clung to the mistaken idea that he could somehow haggle with the legalistic Americans to improve the terms, whereas in reality there was nothing to bargain about. It was a classic clash of cultures. Conscious of his weakness, he finally told Bolling that he could only move if Carter would do something equally implausible: guarantee the Palestinians a state.

The president's men concluded that the PLO had fluffed a major political opportunity. 'It's too bad, because I think it would have made a big difference if we had been able to cross that bridge at that particular time,' says Vance.[25]

Arafat later called his experience of dealing with the Carter administration 'a very bad lesson' and claimed that the US had let him down.[26] But in his more reflective moments he is prepared to admit that 'We might have lost an opportunity during the Carter days.'[27] Certainly, nothing of the kind has presented itself since.

Arafat subsequently made repeated efforts to throw himself at the US – to an extent that prompted some of his colleagues to compare him jokingly to an importunate woman. He sent messages through a host of third countries asking Washington to recognize the PLO and used a bewildering number of competing Palestinian intermediaries to try to make contact with the American Administration, from academics such as Edward Said and Walid Khalidi to the wealthy Palestinian contractor Hassib Sabbagh, who had good contacts in Washington through his business activities. More often than not, it was a recipe for confusion.

On occasion, Arafat would tell his favoured intermediaries – the Saudis, say, whose oil wealth meant that they commanded considerable attention in Washington – that he was about to come up with a statement that would meet American conditions. But he was invariably promising more than he could deliver, and the result was frustration all round. In any case, the Americans never listened as attentively as they did in 1977 – at least, that is, not until 1988.

'We had messages coming to us from all over the world,' recalls one long-serving State Department official. 'For example Arafat would plant a message on a visit to Indonesia, and sure enough, along would come a cable from the Indonesian Government saying: Why don't you understand the PLO? Don't you realize that if you don't support the moderates, the moderates will collapse? It became sort of like a ritual incantation. But Arafat's problem was that he couldn't deliver.'[28]

Little did Arafat know, as his leadership colleagues continued their obscure and often stormy deliberations through September and October 1977, that events were in the making that would reduce the whole debate to irrelevance. Within a matter of weeks, the PLO would be confronted with a political setback as devastating as any it had encountered before.

The signs on the surface of Middle Eastern politics were ominous enough. In Egypt, President Anwar Sadat appeared increasingly impatient to move towards peace negotiations with or without his stalling Arab brethren. And in Israel, a general election in May had brought a hardline new government to power under a man who had been the stuff of Palestinian legend since the 1940s: the former Jewish terrorist leader, Menachem Begin.

# 10

## *On the Defensive*

'If you put a cat in a corner, it will defend itself.' Yasser Arafat, in interview with *Time* magazine, 9 April 1979.

On 8 November 1977, Yasser Arafat received an urgent summons to Cairo, where Vice-President Hosni Mubarak relayed to him two requests from his boss, Anwar Sadat. First, Arafat was to travel to Tripoli to mediate in a dispute between Sadat and Libya's maverick leader Colonel Gadaffi. Then, he was cordially invited to attend a session of the Egyptian parliament to hear an important speech by Sadat.

Travelling to Libya and back in a military plane laid on by the Egyptians, Arafat, who had never been invited to the People's Assembly before, wondered what Sadat could be up to. His curiosity mounted when he returned to Cairo to discover that the parliamentary session had been specially delayed to await his arrival, and that Sadat took several opportunities during his speech to shower praises on the 'dear and wonderful' PLO leader's head.[1] Even by his own mercurial standards, the Egyptian President was in an excited mood as he regaled the assembled deputies and dignitaries with a catalogue of his untiring efforts to achieve a Middle East settlement, but the address seemed to contain little to justify the headline billing Sadat had given it.

Then, departing from his prepared text, the President dropped his bombshell. 'I am willing to go to Geneva, nay, to the end of the world,' he proclaimed. 'In fact I know that Israel will be astounded when I say that I am ready to go to their very home, to the Knesset, to debate with them.'[2]

What seemed to be an impromptu remark left Arafat puzzled, but he found no clue to Sadat's intentions in the faces of the President's deputy or of his prime minister. Witnesses say that when Sadat had finished speaking, the PLO leader even joined in the polite applause, a happenstance that rankled deeply with Arafat's critics within the PLO. The more Arafat thought about Sadat's words, though, the more incredulous he became. After the speech, he lost no time in collaring Ismail Fahmy, Sadat's Foreign Minister. 'What is the meaning of this?' he asked. 'Is Sadat saying this intentionally in my presence? Have you invited me to come to Cairo in order to hear such a thing?'[3] Attempting to smooth things over, Fahmy assured him that the President's statement should not be interpreted literally. When Sadat breezed into the delegates' lounge, he explained that he had made 'a slip of the tongue' and agreed that all mention of it should be excised from the government-controlled media.[4]

By now Arafat was seething. If Sadat really did intend to go to Israel the consequences did not bear thinking about, and it seemed implausible that he would raise so serious an idea purely as a rhetorical flourish. Worse, by flagging it in the PLO leader's presence, the Egyptian President had created the false impression that Arafat had approved.

In an attempt to cool him down, Vice-President Mubarak took Arafat to his modest villa in Heliopolis, but to no avail. Within a further thirty minutes, the PLO leader was off to the nearby airport. 'A long time will pass before I come again to Egypt,' he sullenly told his aides as he boarded the plane to Damascus en route for Lebanon. It was a prophetic statement. Arafat would not revisit the city of his birth for six long years.[5]

Back in Beirut, Arafat feverishly aired his suspicions to his colleagues. Still they could not quite believe that Sadat had meant what he said. Surely the Egyptian leader could not be seriously contemplating such a drastic step, one that would cut him loose from the rest of the Arab world overnight, scupper all hope of a comprehensive Arab-Israeli negotiation and, worst of all, signal his abandonment of the Palestinian cause in pursuit of a separate peace. Perhaps Sadat had been carried away with his own oratory, or was simply playing to the gallery of Western opinion.

The PLO leaders were clutching at straws. On 16 November 1977 Sadat headed for Damascus in a vain attempt to persuade President Assad not to oppose his planned trip to Jerusalem, and three days later the Palestinians found themselves sitting transfixed in front of their TV sets as the Egyptian presidential Boeing landed at Tel Aviv airport and Sadat strode down the steps to shake the hands of the enemy. Watching impotently from the offices of his organization's political department in Beirut, Arafat shed tears of grief and fury.[6] Worse was to come next day, when Sadat travelled to Jerusalem to deliver his historic address to Israel's parliament, the Knesset. It was bad enough for the Palestinians to witness the leader of the most powerful Arab country visiting what they regarded as their occupied capital; and to see the Egyptian President consorting with the hardline Israeli Prime Minister, Menachem Begin. But when the PLO leaders heard Sadat's Knesset speech, their feeling of betrayal was complete. Although it was packed with fulsome references to the Palestinians' desire for a homeland, there was no mention of the PLO itself.

Much as Sadat attempted to reassure the Palestinians in subsequent weeks that he still had their interests at heart, they knew that an irrevocable rupture had occurred, and one that would only worsen as a result of Sadat's refusal to countenance criticism from others. Although Arafat himself had authorized a dalliance with left-wing Israelis, nobody in the PLO would ever have dreamed of contemplating as direct an approach to the enemy as this. What Sadat had done amounted, in Palestinian eyes, to abject surrender, and one that risked casting the PLO adrift. No longer could Arafat rely on an Egyptian safety net in his delicate balancing act between the Arab regimes. No longer, with the Arab world rapidly polarizing into mutually hostile factions, could there be any pretence of solidarity in defence of the Palestinian cause. From now on, the PLO was on its own, or at best thrown on the not-so-tender mercies of the one frontline state with which it still (just) maintained a working relationship: Syria.

Arafat says today that Sadat's dramatic initiative provoked in him 'strange and mixed feelings', not least because the Egyptian President was able to visit Jerusalem at a time when the world still refused to recognize Israel's annexation of the city as its capital. 'I knew that the Palestinian people were bound to pay dearly for the visit,' he adds.[7] On a more practical level, however, Sadat's move also left him in a serious quandary over relations with a country for which he had always maintained a special affection. To mount, as many of his closest colleagues now demanded, a 'frontal and sustained attack' against the Egyptian leader and any states that supported him would be to risk leaving the PLO dangerously isolated, especially since the peace move enjoyed full American support.

Yet opinion in the movement was so strong that he had no choice but to comply. Three days after Sadat had stood in the Knesset, Arafat was in Damascus issuing a joint call with President Assad for the 'treasonous' Egyptian leader's overthrow. Then, on 2 December, he led a high-powered PLO delegation to a hastily convened summit meeting of leaders hostile to Sadat in the Libyan capital, Tripoli.

By all accounts, it was a stormy affair. The PLO leader flew into a rage and sped off towards the airport when a capricious Colonel Gadaffi accused him of complicity with Egypt. With the Palestinians squabbling publicly among themselves and the other leaders at each other's throats, it was only with the greatest difficulty that a common front was patched together to present to the rest of the Arab world.[8] Full of sound and fury, the meeting signified typically little and certainly did not prevent Arafat from maintaining secret channels of communication to Sadat throughout the ensuing Arab boycott of Egypt. But the hardening of attitudes reflected in the formation of this so-called 'Steadfastness and Confrontation Front' by Syria, Algeria, Libya and South Yemen did stifle any suggestion that the Palestinians might give Sadat's initiative a chance. Angered by the Tripoli meeting's accusations of 'high treason', Sadat immediately severed all relations with the participants. Not surprisingly, when Sadat tried to convene a conference of Israeli, Egyptian and Palestinian officials in December at the Mena House Hotel next to the Pyramids, the PLO refused to attend. It was a fateful decision, for it shut the organization out of any involvement in Sadat's peacemaking. Had Arafat agreed to send someone to Cairo, he might at least have scored some propaganda points by provoking an Israeli walkout. As it was, the Palestinian flag was pulled down outside the hotel before the talks even began.

On 15 December 1977 the US President who had seemed so full of promise earlier in the year formally placed the Palestinians out in the cold, declaring that 'by its completely negative attitude, the PLO has excluded itself from any immediate prospect of participating in the peace negotiations'. Or as his National Security Adviser Zbigniew Brzezinski put it in an oft-quoted interview with *Paris-Match*: 'Bye Bye PLO.'[9]

The valediction infuriated Arafat and, like so many others pronounced on his movement over the years, proved to be wide of the mark, but as the implications of Sadat's move sank in over the next few months, there was no mistaking the steady build-up of pressure on the PLO. The loss of Egypt as an ally was a devastating blow, which, in addition to removing Sadat once and for all from the Arab-Israeli military equation, left the Palestinians perilously exposed in their 'last refuge' of Lebanon.

★

After the civil war of 1975–6, the PLO had lost no time in re-establishing roots in its Lebanese stronghold in the south of the country. Its guerrillas also maintained a considerable presence in the capital and the central Chouf mountains. Taking advantage of an influx of heavy arms seized from the Lebanese Army during the conflict, Arafat had stepped up efforts to reshape his troops into something approximating to a regular defensive army. Specialist divisions were set up and a rank structure established. Gradually, the PLO patched together a lumbering armoury, including sixty obsolete Soviet-built T-34 tanks and an array of firepower from howitzers to anti-aircraft guns and rocket launchers.[10]

The PLO bureaucracy and its increasingly important economic arm, Samed, were also still growing, to a point where Arafat found running them an almost full-time job in itself. From a body founded by Fatah in Jordan eight years earlier to provide work for the families of guerrillas killed in action, Samed had ballooned into one of Lebanon's major industrial employers. In a network of thirty-six factories along the Lebanese coast and in the capital, it produced a wide range of goods from shoes and clothes to furniture and processed food. Under its director, an ultra-discreet former banker by the name of Ahmed Kora'i (Abu Ala'a), Samed had also built up a significant network of international activities and investments, including a commodity trading venture and farms and industries both in other Arab countries and in Africa.[11] But ultimate control, in this as in other departments, still rested with Arafat – by now effectively chairman, managing director, treasurer, company secretary and personnel manager of PLO Inc., a complex multinational organization in which no staff appointment would take place outside his purview. He insisted on ploughing his way through vast amounts of paperwork, sitting up into the small hours with a trunk full of documents and a red pen. Small wonder that he frequently showed signs of becoming swamped by detail and concentrating on short-term tactics at the expense of long-term strategy.

Nowhere was his dominance more apparent, then as now, than in his vice-like grip on PLO finances. Arafat personally oversaw the allocation of money from the budget of the Palestine National Fund, the PLO 'finance ministry', and from his own Fatah treasure chest, a juggling act that required, on occasion, some fairly creative accounting since the PNF was regularly in deficit and depended on annual transfers from Arafat's Fatah fund to make up the shortfall. As to the Fatah fund itself, he jealously guarded its secrets – so jealously that such information was generally withheld from even his most senior colleagues. In his control of the purse strings Arafat showed much of the canniness of the small trader but he also wasted a great deal of money in the dispensation of patronage: to corrupt individuals inside and outside the PLO, to organizations of dubious value, and to impoverished Third World states whose claim to PLO assistance was flimsily based on a single UN vote. Frugal in his personal habits, Arafat liked nevertheless to be seen dispensing largesse in the style of a traditional Arab potentate.

Arafat's management of PLO money had one other almost incalculable advantage as far as his own leadership of the Palestinian national movement is concerned. It put him closely in touch with a class of multi-millionaire Palestinian merchants, traders and builders who became – and remain – one of the pillars on which his authority rested. Arafat took to referring to these mega-rich Palestinians, such as Hassib Sabbagh, the Athens-based construction magnate, as 'my compradours'. It was both a term of endearment – Arafat did not grasp the odious Chinese connotation – and a recognition that in his efforts to reach out to the broadest cross-section of the Palestinian community and to sometimes antagonistic Arab regimes, he needed the services of well-heeled and obliging go-betweens.

For all Arafat's undoubted skill at hustling donations from wealthy rulers in the Gulf – especially from Saudi Arabia, which had effectively been Fatah's paymaster since the mid-1960s and remained by far the biggest donor – it was not always plain sailing; indeed, there was a moment in the late 1970s when an Arafat jest nearly caused the lifeline to be severed.

Sharing a public platform with Muammar Gadaffi, whose dislike of the Saudi ruling family is legendary, Arafat responded to a question from the idiosyncratic Libyan leader about the flow of funds from the Saudis by pulling his pockets out of his trousers to show they were empty. King Khaled and Crown Prince Fahd were livid when they heard about the incident, for Arafat's gesture seemed to suggest that the Saudis were 'withholding' money from the PLO. Arafat was summoned into the presence of the Saudi king and presented with receipts and accounts showing that the money had indeed been paid. After the normal exchange of pleasantries, King Khaled came straight to the point: 'Here are the accounts of the money we set aside for you. You see, we're up to date, so why did you say we're not paying?' To which Arafat replied: 'Your Majesty, not a word passed my lips.' It was then that Khaled flicked on the television showing a video of Arafat and Gadaffi engaging in their little pantomime. Arafat was covered in confusion, and buried his face in the king's robes, apologizing profusely. 'I am sorry,' he pleaded, 'but you have to understand the pressures I'm under.'[12]

By the late 1970s, the organization's elaborate Lebanese infrastructure had created a curious and seductive air of permanence, and keeping it ticking over had come to seem almost an end in itself. But as events were to show, the PLO's presence in Lebanon still rested on the shakiest of foundations. In the first place, Arafat could not ignore a military force that was considerably more powerful than his own: the Syrian Army, which would not hesitate to rein in the Palestinians in the event of trouble. Nor had the Lebanese exactly subsided into a tranquil state. Following the assassination of Kamal Jumblatt the previous year, the Palestinians' Lebanese allies were leaderless and divided, and their old foes in the Maronite Christian community were more intent than ever on pursuing their struggle against a Palestinian movement that looked as though it was in Lebanon to stay.

Most disturbing of all were the threatening gestures emanating from Israel under the militant leadership of Menachem Begin. Arafat held the new Israeli Prime Minister, whose Irgun terrorist group had been responsible for the notorious Deir Yassin massacre during Israel's War of Independence, in a special kind of awe, aware that Begin's ascent to power had radically changed the rules of the game. The Likud-led Government was unlike anything that had gone before, both in its determination to hang on to the occupied Arab territories of the West Bank and Gaza and in its fierce opposition to a Palestinian state. As to the PLO, Begin's election platform had been unequivocal: it was 'no national liberation organization but an organization of assassins' which Israel would 'strive to eliminate'.[13]

No longer having to worry about an Egyptian military threat, the Israelis could now pay much closer attention to Palestinian activities beyond their northern frontier and provide considerable assistance to the Lebanese Maronite Christians. It was only a matter of time before the PLO leadership, desperately looking for a way of asserting itself in the face of Sadat's new 'conspiracy', would provide Israel with an opportunity to strike directly.

In the small hours of 11 March 1978, a group of eleven Fatah commandos, led by a young woman, landed on a beach some fifteen miles south of the Israeli port of Haifa and on the main coastal highway to Tel Aviv hijacked a bus with sixty-three passengers aboard. Careering through police roadblocks with Israeli security forces in hot pursuit, the bus ended up in a bloody shoot-out in a northern suburb of Tel Aviv. By the time the firing stopped, 34 Israelis and 9 guerrillas were dead and a total of 84 were wounded.[14]

The response was not long delayed. During the night of 14 March, after a fierce artillery bombardment, an Israeli armoured force eventually comprising up to 28,000 men lumbered across the border and launched a frontal attack against PLO bases in southern Lebanon. As other units landed on the coast and the Israeli airforce bombed Palestinian camps as far north as Beirut itself, Israeli spokesmen explained that their aim was to 'liquidate terrorist bases along the border' and to establish a so-called 'security belt' to prevent Palestinian infiltration. By the time the Israelis ordered a ceasefire one week later, at least 200 PLO fighters and 500 Palestinian and Lebanese civilians had been killed for the loss of 20-odd Israeli soldiers; scores of Lebanese villages had been destroyed; and hundreds of thousands of refugees had started pouring northwards to the capital. A new phase in Lebanon's steady disintegration was underway.[15]

For Yasser Arafat, despite his confident declarations about the bravery with which PLO fighters had resisted, this first Israeli invasion of Lebanon served to underline how isolated the Palestinians were. Just as during the Israeli attack on Karameh almost exactly a decade earlier, his forces had been far outnumbered and outgunned, but this time no help was forthcoming from a friendly Arab army and no plaudits were heard for Palestinian bravery against insurmountable odds. The Syrians, although the dominant force in Lebanon, kept well out of the way. Sadat, now preoccupied with the next move towards peace with Israel, limited his response to an even-handed condemnation both of the invasion and of the guerrilla raid that had precipitated it. It was only when the UN Security Council called on 19 March for an immediate Israeli withdrawal and the establishment of an international peacekeeping force that serious pressure began to build for an end to the fighting. That was a sign of the times.

Israel's newly aggressive stance was having one mildly positive side-effect in Arafat's eyes: in combination with the continuing occupation of territories captured in 1967, it was helping to turn a significant portion of world opinion against the Jewish state.

Such observations were small consolation to Arafat, however, as he contemplated his immediate prospects. In effect, the PLO had been suddenly pitched into a long battle for its existence in Lebanon against a foe more formidable than any it had faced before. Realizing the implacable nature of the Israeli threat, Arafat looked for protection. He found it, of all places, in the hastily despatched 'blue berets' of the UN peace-keeping force, known as UNIFIL (United Nations Interim Force in Lebanon). On 28 March in his west Beirut offices, Arafat met UNIFIL commander Emmanuel Erskine, and informed him that the PLO would agree to halt hostilities in the area adjoining the border while Israeli forces withdrew.

This was a major departure. For the first time, Arafat was committing himself to a ceasefire to which Israel was also a party. In the process, while swearing blind that the PLO would resist any attempt to limit its freedom of action in southern Lebanon, he was also casting himself in an unfamiliar role: that of Palestinian policeman with a mandate to rein in the unruly forces under his command. Thus in April 1978, when a group of dissident Fatah officers challenged his decision to accept the ceasefire, he moved with unusual decisiveness, using force to crush the mutiny. On 19 April, 123 of those involved, apparently recruited by the militia commander Abu Daoud, were arrested. Ninety of them were subsequently kicked out of Lebanon, and two of the main participants were shifted to pen-pushing jobs in Beirut.[16] It was a marked contrast to the normal indiscipline of PLO forces; clearly, when he wanted to, Arafat could assert control.

As Arafat saw it, a measure of continuing disaffection in the ranks was a small price to pay for the international prestige he could reap from co-operating with UNIFIL. Beleaguered in Beirut, he desperately needed new friends, and he wasted no opportunity to try to impress the UN officials who were now dealing with him on a regular basis. One such occasion presented itself that spring, during a visit to southern Lebanon by UN Secretary-General Kurt Waldheim. Travelling to the port city of Tyre, Waldheim and his entourage ran into a fearsome demonstration by militant Palestinians brandishing unexploded Israeli bombs. They were lucky to escape with their lives. Some days later, Waldheim's senior aide Brian Urquhart met Arafat and heard his version of the story. 'What on earth were you doing with the Secretary-General trying to go to Tyre?' the PLO leader asked. 'This has put ten years on my life. The rejectionists had sent five people to kill Mr Waldheim, in order to discredit me, and I had to send my security men to arrest them. They only caught four.'[17]

But Arafat's manoeuvrings could not disguise the fact that the PLO had by mid-1978 become locked into a defensive posture on all fronts. In Lebanon, its ability to conduct cross-border raids was severely constrained, for although the Israelis had gradually pulled their forces back, they retained control of a strip of territory along the frontier and installed a friendly local militia there to keep up the fight against the Palestinians. Never terribly convincing, the 'armed struggle' now seemed more aimless than ever. Arafat's efforts to introduce a conventional-style army merely sowed confusion in the ranks and the guerrillas drifted, reacting to events, with their often arrogant and unruly behaviour seen by ordinary Lebanese in territory under the PLO's sway as an increasingly tiresome burden.

Arafat fared no better in his relations with Arab regimes. Sadat had failed to achieve the psychological breakthrough he had hoped for in Israel but was pressing on regardless with efforts to make peace. The Arab world, still reeling from the shock of the Egyptian President's trip to Jerusalem, was in deepening disarray. As ever, within the Palestinian movement itself, the PLO leader was confronted with smouldering, sometimes violent disputes. A stream of conciliatory statements by Arafat to Western newspapers concerning coexistence between a Palestinian state and Israel continued to provoke great unhappiness within the rank and file. From outside the mainstream, an assassination campaign waged with Iraqi support by the breakaway terrorist group of Sabri al-Banna (Abu Nidal) claimed the lives of several PLO diplomats, including the organization's representatives in London and Paris, Said Hammami and Ezzeldin Kalak, two men who had worked hard to transmit Arafat's overtures to the West.

Against this background, Arafat made one last effort to convince President Sadat of the error of his ways. In June 1978 he wrote to Sadat pleading with him not to rush into a separate peace with Israel. 'Your position as leader is still strong,' he wrote. 'Don't forget Jerusalem. Don't forget our people who have sacrificed their lives. You *can* insist on stronger guarantees.'[18]

That letter was Arafat's last direct communication with the Egyptian leader. Three months later, Sadat ensconced himself with Jimmy Carter and Menachem Begin at the US President's Maryland retreat of Camp David. They emerged on 17 September, after twelve days of talks, with a set of agreements committing Egypt and Israel to negotiating a peace treaty and calling for the establishment of what was called a 'self-governing authority' to administer Palestinian affairs in the Israeli-occupied West Bank and Gaza Strip. It was the last straw. The Palestinians had no doubt as to what the plan for self-rule really meant: a perpetuation of Israeli sovereignty in the territories where the PLO was demanding a state of its own. Arafat himself had dismissed the proposal when it was put forward by Begin as 'less than a Bantustan'.[19]

Burying their differences, the faction leaders united in denunciation of the Camp David Accords and set out to scupper them by fair means or foul. Arafat, momentarily forgetting his efforts to climb into bed with the United States, began speaking vaguely about striking at American interests in the Middle East. And at the end of September the Israelis foiled an attempt by his Fatah group to mount a seaborne rocket attack on the southern resort of Eilat, which, had it succeeded, would undoubtedly have caused heavy casualties.[20]

In the wider Arab world, too, the Egyptian-Israeli accords caused at least a temporary closing of ranks which resulted, on 2 November, in a summit meeting hosted by Iraq. The Baghdad conference, which urged Sadat anew not to make formal peace with Israel while agreeing to punish him with economic and other sanctions if he did, provided Arafat with some reassurance. It showed that no other Arab leader – not even King Hussein of Jordan, who was under heavy pressure from the US to go along with Sadat – was likely to climb aboard the Camp David bandwagon. And it gave the PLO a hefty financial windfall in the form of a pledge from the wealthy Gulf states of 250 million US dollars a year for the next ten years.[21]

In reality, however, such decisions did little to fill the gaping hole Sadat had left in Arab ranks. Refusing even to hear the summit's appeal, the Egyptian President went ahead and signed his peace treaty with Israel in March 1979. The rupture was final.

As if he did not already have enough to worry about, the PLO leader shortly received a shattering personal blow. On 22 January 1979 in Beirut, a remote-controlled bomb detonated by an Israeli woman agent killed the man he regarded as his 'favourite son': Ali Hassan Salameh. Arafat heard the news in Damascus, where a stormy session of the Palestine National Council had just broken up in acrimony after heavy-handed Syrian and Iraqi efforts to bring the PLO under their control.[22] When he joined the pall-bearers a few days later at an emotional funeral attended by tens of thousands of Palestinians, Arafat's spirits were at a low ebb. He poured out his feelings in a tide of vituperation against the United States, which he blamed directly for Salameh's death. 'It's not fair,' he complained to his advisers. 'The Americans must have known about it. The Israelis don't do anything without the CIA.'[23]

Arafat would not, however, stay down for long. As Salamah's coffin was laid to rest, events far away were already moving rapidly to a climax that would give the PLO leader a quite unexpected lift.

On the evening of 31 January 1979 Arafat stood on the balcony of his residence in west Beirut and triumphantly fired his Beretta pistol in the air. It was the first time anyone close to him could remember Arafat using his personal weapon, and he fired not in anger but as part of a crackling chorus of jubilation all over the Muslim side of the city. That day, an elderly Iranian clergyman by the name of Ruhollah Khomeini had set foot on his country's soil after an exile of fourteen years, to be greeted in Tehran by tumultuous and triumphant demonstrations. The Iranian revolution had arrived.

The fall of Shah Mohammed Reza Pahlavi, King of Kings, and the rise of Ayatollah Khomeini's Islamic Republic sent shock waves through Western and Arab capitals alike. But to the PLO leadership, the installation of a militant new government in Tehran seemed to offer fresh hope: a bastion of Western influence and a staunch friend of Israel had been toppled by a leader who identified himself strongly with the Palestinian cause. More to the point, Khomeini's movement had already developed close ties with the PLO.

The Palestinians' relationship with Iran's Islamic revolutionaries dated back to the mid-1970s, when a close aide to Fatah intelligence chief Salah Khalaf had befriended an Iranian exile, Mohammed Salah al-Husseini, who had joined the Palestinian movement in Lebanon. Through

Husseini, the Fatah official had been introduced to Ayatollah Khomeini, living at the time in the Iraqi city of Najaf, and a regular traffic of messages between the Iranian holy man and the PLO leadership began. In time, through these contacts and through his acquaintance with the Lebanese Shi'ite leader Musa Sadr, Arafat got to know many of the future leaders of the Islamic Republic.[24]

His motives went well beyond the Palestinians' customary reasons for maintaining good relations with other liberation movements. As a Fatah intelligence official explains: 'The Shah was an imperial embodiment of everything we loathed, in his close relationship with Israel, in his suppression of democracy and the hatred he inspired among his people, and in his hostility to Arab nationalism.'[25] By contrast, the Ayatollah's heady brew of politics and religion intrigued the Palestinians, who agreed to provide Khomeini supporters with military training in their camps in southern Lebanon and Syria. Under the auspices of Khalil al-Wazir, hundreds of Iranian militants were schooled in the black arts of terrorism from 1976, devoting special attention to techniques the PLO had developed for maintaining links between the territories under Israeli occupation and the leadership outside.

By late 1978, the Iranians and the Palestinians were still on a political honeymoon in which both sides temporarily forgot the deep cultural and ideological chasm that divided them. When Khomeini had been expelled from Iraq in the autumn of that year, Arafat had even offered him a refuge in southern Lebanon, although the Ayatollah chose in the event to settle in Paris, where he had ready access to Western media. The relationship was at its height when the Ayatollah returned in triumph to Tehran. Arafat, in a delicious moment of revenge on the Carter Administration official who had tried to write him off little more than a year earlier, was moved to crow: 'Bye Bye USA.'[26]

'Arafat considered Khomeini's victory a victory for the Palestinian revolution – not because it was religious but simply because a revolution that was pro-Palestinian had come to power,' recalls one of those involved in building the alliance.[27] As a wave of euphoria swept the Palestinian refugee camps in Lebanon, posters appeared in the streets of Beirut bearing a large portrait of Ayatollah Khomeini and the slogan: 'Today Iran! Tomorrow Palestine!'[28] Nor did Iran's new leaders disappoint Arafat during their early days in power, swiftly rewarding the PLO for its support by allowing it to set up its first Tehran headquarters in no less a building than the former Prime Minister's office. On 17 February 1979, Arafat became the first foreign leader to visit the Iranian capital after the revolution.

The trip was not without its anxious moments. As Arafat's plane approached Tehran, the Iranians sent up a squad of American-made Phantom jets to escort him into the airport, causing him to conclude for a few frightened seconds that the Israelis had come to get him. But in general the reception accorded him on the ground was ecstatic. At a Tehran press conference a buoyant Arafat proclaimed: 'I told His Eminence Ayatollah Khomeini that I really saw the walls of Jerusalem when I heard about the Iranian revolution.'[29]

No less impressive were the practical results. The Iranians turned the former Israeli trade mission over to the PLO as an embassy. In return, the PLO obliged the Islamic Republic by despatching a 76-man military delegation. The officers stayed in the country for about a month, advising the Iranians on the establishment of a body that was to become a lynchpin of the new order: a separate armed force, known as the Revolutionary Guards, to keep watch over the regular army. The Palestinians also helped the Islamic Republic to set up a new intelligence service to replace the Shah's hated secret police force, Savak. That was a task which raised qualms among some of the PLO officials involved, who noted that the Iranian revolutionaries were resorting to the same methods with which they themselves had been oppressed by the Shah.[30]

The alliance with Iran showed Arafat at his most mercurial, involving him as it did in an increasingly complex series of political contortions as he tried to balance his new-found friendship with the fiercely anti-Western mullahs in Tehran with a continuing effort to secure Western recognition. Once again, the PLO leader was trying to have it several ways. To Iranian sensibilities, Arafat sought to present himself as a militant pursuing an Islamic *jihad*, or holy war, against Israel. But in Western capitals, where he was now involved in a fresh diplomatic offensive to bolster his political standing, he stressed his desire for peace in an independent Palestinian state. And in the Middle East, he deftly used his alliance with Iran to put the fear of God into any Arab leaders who might still be hankering after a political settlement excluding the PLO.

Through it all, Arafat was trying to convey a double message: that the treaty signed by Egypt and Israel in March 1979 would not bring peace to the region and could endanger Western interests there; and that the Palestinians would resist Israeli attempts to impose a strictly limited form of self-rule in the West Bank and Gaza with every means at their disposal. In an interview with *Time* magazine in April, he called for an Arab 'boycott' of the United States, adding: 'One year ago, you were thinking that no power could shake your emperor, the Shah of Iran. Where is he now?'[31]

For a while at least, these contradictory manoeuvres appeared to pay off. Over the next year or so, Arafat succeeded in opening new doors in a western Europe that was increasingly disenchanted with Israel and newly re-awakened to the Middle East's economic power by the sharp rise in oil prices that had followed the Iranian revolution. Austrian Chancellor Bruno Kreisky, long a friend of the PLO leader, invited him for an official visit in July 1979, followed by the Spanish Government in September. There were even renewed efforts to institute a dialogue between the PLO and Washington. They got nowhere but in the process cost America's ambassador to the United Nations, Andy Young, his job. And in June 1980, only weeks after Arafat's Fatah movement had issued a ringing call for 'the liquidation of the Zionist entity economically, politically, militarily, culturally and ideologically',[32] the European Community took a big step in the PLO's direction. At a meeting in Venice, EC leaders agreed that the organization should be 'associated' with Middle East peace negotiations.

It was the sort of wheeling and dealing at which Arafat was a past master, but it could not last. Less than a year after the Iranian revolution, the contradictions began to tell and the alliance with Ayatollah Khomeini, on which the PLO leader had pinned his hopes, started to come unstuck.

In truth, the Palestinian resistance and the Iranian revolution had seemed strange bedfellows from the outset – an avowedly secular movement led by conservatively oriented Sunni Muslims in cahoots with a group of radical Shi'ite clerics. The differences between them over strategy were just as fundamental: while Arafat indicated he was striving as a first step for the relatively modest goal of a mini-state in Palestine, Khomeini imagined that his revolution would turn the entire region into one big Islamic theocracy. But predictably it was the PLO chairman's continuing efforts to ingratiate himself with the US – the 'Great Satan' in Iranian parlance – that brought tensions between them to a head.

In early November 1979, Arafat received a most unusual message. Initially conveyed to him by a friend in New York, Edward Said, it came from US Secretary of State Cyrus Vance, and its import could be summed up in one word: Help! A few days before, amid massive anti-American demonstrations, a group of revolutionary Iranian youths had seized the US embassy in Tehran and taken fifty-two diplomats and other staff hostage.

As President Carter desperately cast around for ways to defuse the crisis, his subordinate Vance took the decision to trespass on Washington's ban on dealing with the PLO. The organization, after all, had excellent relations with the Iranian leadership, where America had none. If anyone could get a message through to the mullahs in Tehran, it was Yasser Arafat.[33]

He leapt at the chance. Achieving the release of the hostages would be an enormous propaganda coup, and one that might bring a breakthrough in his persistent attempts to institute a dialogue with the US. Dreaming of the publicity that would greet a PLO-mediated solution and making promises he was not sure he could fulfil, Arafat sent two of his senior aides, his special envoy Hani al-Hassan and military commander Saad Sayel, to try to persuade the Iranians to hand the American diplomats over. They were rudely disappointed. When they met Khomeini's powerful henchman Ali Akbar Hashemi-Rafsanjani, they were greeted with angry incomprehension.

'The Iranians were infuriated by this interference in their internal affairs,' recalls one of those involved in the initiative. 'They said this is a dirty game being played by the Great Satan, and you are supposed to be angels; you have no business with this. They completely refused to give the Palestinians a mediating role. They simply couldn't understand why we wanted to win over the US administration. In fact they thought it was a privilege to be confronting the US.'[34]

Disconcerted by the ferocity of Rafsanjani's response, Sayel and Hassan tried another ploy to convince the Iranians to release just the black and female hostages as a first step. 'We knew that the Iranian leadership used to talk frequently about the oppression of US blacks. So we made up a story to the effect that the blacks were part of an organization that was working against US policy and for the Palestinian cause. We even produced fake witnesses to back up our arguments.'[35]

The result was that on 19 and 20 November, a group of thirteen American hostages – five women and eight blacks – was released. It was enough to earn Arafat an official thank you letter from Vance but well short of the coup he had envisaged. Still, there was a lot more to play for; indeed, the stakes were rising as the 1980 US presidential election approached, a contest in which a man who had shown sympathy for the Palestinians risked being defeated if the hostages were not freed. 'It was clear that Jimmy Carter was willing to sell his mother for another term in office, and that if the hostage affair was not resolved he would lose,' says an Arafat adviser who held dozens of meetings about the embassy crisis with America's ambassador to Beirut, John Gunther Dean, in 1979 and 1980.[36]

More obsessed than ever by the hope of significant political rewards, Arafat resolved to keep trying. At a lunch with Iranian foreign minister Sadeq Ghotbzadeh in west Beirut, he and his officials renewed the argument. 'You Iranians need a get-out, you've taken uncompromising positions,' said one of the Palestinians present. 'These are innocent civilians who have nothing to do with US policy. If you won't deal with the US, just hand the hostages over to us and Arafat will hand them over to the United Nations Secretary-General.'[37] According to Palestinian accounts of the meeting, Ghotbzadeh expressed interest but when he got back to Iran and presented the idea to Ayatollah Khomeini, the proposal ran into a brick wall.[38]

In the end, Arafat's mediation effort did little to advance his cause and a certain amount to retard it, since he was later accused by critics within his own organization of having provided detailed intelligence on the Iranian armed forces to the CIA. Largely unsung in the United States, his effort also took a terrible toll on the PLO's relations with its new-found Iranian allies. Khomeini never forgave the Palestinian leader for seeking to meddle in what he regarded as Iran's heroic confrontation with the Great

Satan and thunderously denied that the PLO had had anything to do with the release of the thirteen black and female hostages. From that point on, he took to referring to Arafat contemptuously as 'Al-Qazam' – The Dwarf.[39]

Nor did the other benefits from the relationship come up to the PLO's expectations. In the early, honeymoon days of the revolution, the Iranians had given the Palestinians extravagant promises of practical assistance in Lebanon, offering to send thousands of volunteers to help them combat Israel and even to provide them with surface-to-surface missiles to deter another Israeli invasion.[40] Few of the fighters came through to Lebanon, and the missiles simply did not materialize. The alliance which Arafat had briefly thought would rescue his movement from isolation and exposure turned out to be built on sand. Little more than a year after the Islamic revolution, the euphoria it had engendered within the PLO was rapidly evaporating, giving way to the more customary muddle and lethargy. And as 1980 progressed, fear of Ayatollah Khomeini was causing renewed disarray in Arab ranks. A new war was looming – this time not against Israel but against a dangerous new adversary to the east.

On 22 September 1980, thousands of Iraqi troops poured across the Iranian border and Iraqi aircraft bombed targets deep inside Iranian territory. The invasion followed months of steadily mounting tensions between the two countries and Arafat knew that it also spelled great danger for the PLO. With two allies (for Iran could still just about be counted as such) now embroiled in mortal combat and resisting all mediation efforts including his own, he was once again going to have to make another choice, a choice made no easier by the fact that another state on which the Palestinians depended, Syria, had sided with Iran against Iraq.

Once again the Palestinians risked being caught in a tightening squeeze between squabbling Arabs on the one hand and an increasingly hard-line Israel on the other, the latter sparing no effort to suppress pro-PLO sentiment in the occupied territories. Haring back and forth between Beirut and Damascus, Arafat did not even attempt to gloss over his movement's isolation. 'Where are the Arab weapons, the Arab masses, the Arab funds, the Arab oil weapon?' he plaintively asked a meeting of the Palestine National Council in the Syrian capital in April 1981.[41]

The funds were continuing to flow, but for the rest the answer was clear enough: resources were being squandered in conflict, and the Arab leader on whom Arafat had again come to depend more than any other – Syria's Assad – barely attempted to disguise his contempt for him. Damascus was Arafat's window on the world but his dealings with the government there remained a source of enormous frustration. 'Because he never flew from Beirut for security reasons, Arafat was perpetually travelling up and down the Beirut to Damascus highway,' says one of his advisers. 'He must have met Assad scores of times in this period. Yet at no point did Assad ever share his plans with us or co-ordinate policy in any way.'[42]

Predictably, as had been the case in 1975 and again in 1978, it was in the PLO's base in Lebanon that its problems came home to roost. The initial signs of trouble involved Syria rather than the PLO. In late April 1981, tension in Lebanon rose sharply when Israel shot down two Syrian helicopters and the Syrians responded by stationing several batteries of SAM-6 anti-aircraft missiles in the country's eastern Bekaa Valley. When Israel threatened to eliminate them by force, a military showdown looked more than likely. Ronald Reagan, newly installed in the White House, despatched veteran troubleshooter Philip Habib to defuse the crisis.

Well aware of the threat a new flare-up in Lebanon would pose to the PLO, Arafat spent much of May that year jetting around the Gulf and North Africa seeking to energize his distracted Arab brethren. The resistance had been especially exposed to Israeli fire since the previous year, when Syria – wary of becoming involved in a dust-up in Lebanon – had suddenly withdrawn its forces from the coastal areas south of Beirut where Palestinians were concentrated. As Israel compensated for the restraint it was showing over the Syrian missiles by stepping up its attacks on Palestinian positions, the urge grew within the PLO to respond in kind. On 10 July 1981, when the Israeli air force conducted another of its periodic pre-emptive raids in southern Lebanon, the urge became irresistible. The PLO retaliated by shelling a northern Israeli settlement.

The ensuing two-week confrontation became known as the 'War of the Katyushas', after the Soviet-manufactured rockets the PLO had installed in its Lebanese bases. The Palestinians rained rockets and artillery shells down on the towns and villages of Galilee, sending thousands of Israelis fleeing southwards to safety. Israel's air force bombed the ramshackle Fakhani district of west Beirut where the PLO had its headquarters, leaving 300 dead and 700 wounded. Philip Habib urgently turned his attention to trying to engineer a ceasefire.

It was not something they had exactly planned in advance, but Arafat and his colleagues watched the unfolding escalation from their Beirut operations room in a state of some excitement. To be sure, their forces were taking heavy casualties as a result of the Israeli pounding, but more important in their eyes was the impact their own rocket bombardment was having in Israel itself. Momentarily, they seemed to have put the Jewish state under more pressure than in all the long years of their ineffectual 'armed struggle'. Most significant of all, a senior US emissary was now struggling – through intermediaries, since he was barred from talking directly to Arafat's people – to arrange what would in effect be a ceasefire between Israel and its arch-enemy, the PLO.

The ceasefire demand, passed to Arafat by the UNIFIL commander, General William Callaghan, prompted an anguished debate among the assembled PLO leaders. Some favoured immediate acceptance with a view to regrouping and opening fire again later; others, including Arafat, argued for a slight delay to put further pressure on Israel, then firm compliance.[43] The latter view won the day, and on 24 July Philip Habib announced in Jerusalem that 'as of 1330 local time, all hostile military actions between Lebanese and Israeli territories in either direction will cease.'[44]

In accepting the ceasefire, Arafat had performed a conjuring trick at which he had become quite adept over the years, turning the Palestinians' pathetically limited military resources to political advantage. But the agreement also changed the ground rules of the conflict between Israel and the Palestinians, for what Habib had hammered out was a thinly disguised understanding between the PLO and a government that had vowed never to negotiate with it. It was an oblique and reluctant form of recognition, and a concession that the Israelis from that point on were determined to annul. 'There is a dialogue through this confrontation. What does this mean?' asked Arafat mischievously in an American TV interview two days after the agreement was concluded.[45]

For Arafat, who knew as well as anyone that the ceasefire was a fragile affair, the unwritten agreement represented both a threat and a potential opportunity. Anxious to preserve the PLO's base in Lebanon at all costs and to project the image of a leader who could honour his side of a bargain, he again kept his troops on a tight rein to prevent ceasefire violations. At the same time, he told himself, the truce might provide the PLO with a useful political opening, either as a prelude to broader negotiations or as a stepping-stone towards the cherished goal of American recognition. It was time for a fresh flurry of diplomatic activity.

That summer, Arafat played a prominent, though unpublicized, role in drafting an eight-point peace plan announced by Crown Prince Fahd of Saudi Arabia. Calling for the establishment of an independent Palestinian state and affirming that 'all states in the region should be able to live in peace',[46] the plan once again split the PLO leadership and provoked ferocious arguments among the Arab states. It was shelved when a hostile President Assad of Syria, more suspicious than ever of Arafat's manoeuvrings and resentful at not having been consulted, boycotted an Arab summit meeting at Fez in November 1981. What only a handful of people knew, as the Arab bickering continued, was that Arafat was also engaged in another, altogether more discreet diplomatic exercise.

In Beirut on 4 August 1981, Arafat met a young American of his acquaintance named John Edwin Mroz, and asked him to pass a message to the Reagan Administration. It contained a seven-point peace proposal similar to the Fahd plan and suggested talks on 'a possible framework for a US-PLO agreement'.[47] Mroz, a genial, plump 32-year-old, had got to know the PLO leader while researching a book on Middle Eastern security issues. He had excellent connections in the US Administration, and in the influential Jewish community; and at the State Department, where he had already been in touch with officials before travelling to Beirut, he found he was pushing a half-open door. After consultations involving both President Reagan and his Secretary of State, Alexander Haig, Mroz was authorized to pursue discussions with the PLO chairman. The goal: to meet America's terms for a dialogue by recognizing Israel's right to exist and renouncing terror.[48]

It is not exactly clear why Reagan agreed to such a move. He had always expressed visceral hostility to PLO 'terrorists' – and indeed, he later tried to deny all knowledge of the Mroz dialogue.[49] But in authorizing this unusual dalliance, the US President probably had wider strategic considerations in mind, not least the desire to prevent a renewed flare-up of violence in Lebanon, which could easily disrupt Egyptian-Israeli peace moves. Whatever the explanation, it resulted in a protracted series of talks that appeared to come tantalizingly close to a breakthrough.

Over the next nine months, Mroz spent no fewer than 400 hours in 50 separate meetings with Arafat. They met in a bewildering variety of locations, including once in a hospital ward where Arafat had just had an operation for the removal of kidney stones. They discussed the whole panoply of Arab politics and the pressures on the PLO. They exchanged texts phrased in obscure diplomatic jargon in search of a form of words acceptable to Washington for the initiation of a formal dialogue. And the Reagan Administration, using the laborious machinery of the Saudi government as a 'back channel' to confirm the messages it was hearing through Mroz, made a number of gestures to reassure Arafat that it was acting in good faith. On one occasion, the CIA, which was in regular touch with Mroz during the dialogue, may well have saved Arafat's life by tipping him off about a Syrian plot to ambush his motorcade.

The problem, as ever, lay in the words Arafat was being asked to pronounce in order to qualify for a dialogue. Just as in 1977, he hesitated to make the concession of recognizing Israel. In any case, he was unsure what to make of the renewed American approach. 'He had his moments when he took it very seriously, and he had his moments when it was just another trial balloon,' says Mroz. 'You could really see the way the organization was being buffeted by external Arab forces. He would constantly tell me: yes, but when the time is right.'[50]

It was the old, familiar balancing act, only on this occasion the forces the PLO leader was balancing looked more menacing than ever. Embarrassingly dependent on Damascus, he was in no position to make peace moves of which the Syrian President disapproved. And if he needed any reminder of the dangers of going it alone in negotiations he had only to look to Cairo where, in October 1981,

President Anwar Sadat had been assassinated by Islamic extremists in retribution for his peace treaty with Israel. 'What am I to do, end up like Sadat?' became Arafat's regular refrain when pressed to make concessions.[51]

Most disturbing of all was the atmosphere in Israel, where the notorious hard-liner Ariel Sharon was now Defence Minister and making intensive new efforts to suppress Palestinian nationalism in the occupied West Bank and Gaza. Unmistakably, the drums of war were again beginning to beat. By May 1982, when John Mroz returned to Beirut for one more try, Arafat was still interested in pursuing the dialogue but his attention frequently wandered to the sabre-rattling from the south. 'Let them come to Beirut if they want to fight us. We are ready,' he proclaimed to the young American.[52] But the bravado was wafer-thin.

Arafat and Mroz fixed a date for another meeting in mid-June, at which the PLO leader promised he would give his response. But for reasons that remain unclear, Mroz was ordered by Alexander Haig not to return to Beirut. Within less than a month, the Israeli invasion of Lebanon had begun. Not the smallest cause of Arafat's subsequent fury was the feeling that he had been the victim of an elaborate American double-cross.[53]

# Part Three

# 11

## *Invasion*

'Lebanon is easy to eat, but almost impossible to digest.'
Bashir Gemayel, ABC News interview, 27 June 1982.

Yasser Arafat was surprisingly calm. Like a man who has long since prepared himself for the worst, he quietly sifted the dramatic news flooding in to his luxury suite in the imposing guest palace in Riyadh, the desert capital of Saudi Arabia. As he riffled through the telex traffic that included secret PLO communications and news agency flashes, his mind was quickly weighing up the latest drama to befall the Palestinians. After a moment's contemplation, he turned to his aides and declared: 'This is not a limited war as the Israelis say, but the all-out war I have been predicting for some time.'[1]

The date was 6 June 1982. That very morning, Israel had launched a massive offensive across its northern boundary into Lebanon. As Arafat studied the latest news from the battlefield, Israeli troops were driving north in a *blitzkrieg* that would bring them in a very short time within sight of Beirut itself. He made an instant decision. He would go straight back to Beirut, cutting short his participation in a Gulf war mediating mission – a mission that had brought him, improbably, to the Saudi capital, just as the winds of Israel's advanced war preparations were gusting northwards towards his Beirut headquarters.

Racing to get home before the Israelis thrust towards the main road connecting the Lebanese capital with Damascus, thus endangering his one relatively secure route into Beirut,

Arafat did not contemplate for one second breaking his cardinal rule: he would not fly direct into Beirut airport. The risk of an Israeli interception over Lebanon's unguarded skies was simply too great. He would, as he normally did, fly to Damascus and then travel the rest of the way by car through the mountains to Beirut.

Arafat left Riyadh at 5 p.m. on 6 June for the 850-mile flight north to Damascus. As he boarded his Gulfstream jet, supplied courtesy of the Saudis, he knew he was a prime target of the Israeli invasion but he could not have realized then that Israel would go as far as it did in its efforts to eliminate both him and the top leadership of the PLO. Arriving in Damascus in the early evening, Arafat wasted no time leaving for Beirut. His bullet-proof limousine and escort were awaiting him at the airport.

As his convoy careered along the Beirut-Damascus highway, a road he had traversed hundreds of times before, but rarely with such urgency, Arafat was briefed on the latest developments. The news was bad. PLO resistance in the south had crumbled and Israel's advance towards Beirut showed no sign of slowing. On the contrary, all the indications even at that early stage were that the Israelis were determined to push much further north than they had ever come before. For Arafat, the news signalled the beginning of the most testing phase of his thirteen-year leadership of the guerrilla organization. It was also a time when he would come face-to-face, in a battle of nerves and bombs, with the PLO's nemesis.

General Ariel Sharon, the paunchy, bellicose Israeli Defence Minister had by the summer of 1982 effectively taken command of Israel's foreign policy. Begin proved a willing accomplice until he realized the costs, but by then it was too late. The United States, in the person of General Alexander Haig, would also be duped in its fumbling efforts to manage a crisis to which it had made no small contribution in the first place. When General

Sharon requested an appointment with Alexander Haig in the second half of May 1982, the Secretary of State's professional advisers shuddered. They knew only too well what was on Sharon's mind and they understood much better than their volatile boss the dangers of what was being proposed.

In often tense and angry discussions with Haig since his appointment as Defence Minister in the second Begin government, in July 1981, Sharon had made no secret of his ambitions. His impossibly grand design envisaged a quiescent and collaborative population in the occupied territories, a Lebanon totally liberated of the PLO and, ultimately, the fulfilment of an oft-stated dream: that Jordan should become Palestine. Jordan would be the repository of Palestinian aspirations and the Palestinian people, thus relieving pressure on an Israel whose territorial ambitions now stretched well beyond its pre-1967 war frontiers. He did not try to hide his almost obsessive desire that the US 'understand' the need for what was described repeatedly as a 'limited operation' against the PLO to relieve the pressure on Israel's northern settlements; never mind that the pressure had already been considerably lessened by the US-brokered ceasefire agreement of the previous year.

Even in his early talks with Haig, Sharon was looking beyond the PLO's ouster to a crucial US role in the remaking of Lebanon and indeed of a big slice of the Middle East. In a two-and-a-half hour discussion on 25 May in Haig's austere suite of offices on the seventh floor of the State Department, Sharon asked, in effect, for the 'green light' to smash the PLO. In the words of one of Haig's advisers, Sharon received a 'qualified red light',[2] but not before there had been a lively discussion about what might constitute a pretext for an Israeli invasion. 'How many Jews,' Sharon had asked acidly, 'have to be killed for it to be clear provocation? One Jew? Two Jews? Five? Six? . . . To us it's obvious.'[3] Haig, whether by design or through an oversight, simply failed to spell out in unambiguous language the US objections to Sharon's proposals.

The subtleties of Haig's 'qualified red light' hardly matched either the circumstances in Israel at the time or the personalities in power. Haig's own appreciation of Middle East complexities was rated by State Department colleagues as weak and, perhaps even more fatally, they believed his own presidential ambitions conflicted with his role as Secretary of State. 'I respected the man,' concluded Nicholas Veliotes, Assistant Secretary of State responsible for Middle East affairs, 'but I believe that his presidential ambitions ran away with him and literally destroyed his judgement.'[4]

The Israelis apparently came away from the meeting believing that the Secretary of State had accepted their arguments for action. Haig's limp warnings against Israel becoming embroiled in something that was beyond its ability to control, allied with advice that if action was taken it should be swift, was music to the ears of Sharon and his colleagues. General Avraham Tamir, who served as Israel's National Security Adviser, says that Sharon was satisfied that Haig 'understood' his arguments for military action in Lebanon, and this is what he reported to the cabinet in Jerusalem.[5]

Throughout the early months of 1982, Arafat himself was acutely aware of the dangers of an impending storm from the south. At meeting after meeting in his headquarters in the shabby Fakhani district of west Beirut, he talked of a planned Israeli attack that would link up with the Christian Lebanese Forces militia in the north in an 'accordion' movement. His men would be trapped in the middle of this pincer exercise. Repeatedly, he warned colleagues: 'Sharon is planning to come all the way to Beirut.'[6]

Arafat's own mood during this period swung wildly between unwarranted bravado and jittery concern. Brian Urquhart, the veteran UN official who got to know him well in the Lebanon years, recalls a strange conversation in Beirut in February 1982, in which he was asked to convey messages both to the Americans and to Begin. In his message to the latter there was more than a hint of pleading. 'Tell Begin,' Arafat had said, 'that I don't like war any more than you do. You have to understand that when I propose a Palestinian entity in the West Bank and Gaza Strip it may not seem much to you, but it's tremendously important on our side, because it's a great concession.'[7] Arafat also had a message of a curiously personal nature for Begin. 'I just want Mr Begin to know that I have learned so much from him. I have followed his historical career very closely, and he has taught me many things.'[8] He concluded by asking Urquhart to point out that his successors would not be so accommodating. There would be much less chance of a peace settlement if he were to be removed from the scene. Begin's response to this bizarre communication on the eve of battle was a bemused: 'Oh, really.'[9]

Marwan Qasem, Jordan's urbane Foreign Minister, dispatched by King Hussein in the spring of 1982 to warn Arafat of an imminent Israeli invasion, found the PLO leader in a very different mood. 'The Israelis are going to hit you once and for all, so be careful. Don't give them a pretext,' warned Qasem. Arafat's response was defiant: 'I am very much aware of Israel's preparations for battle, but I want to assure the king that if the Israelis attempt any such suicidal action we will be ready for them . . . I will turn night into daytime in northern Palestine with my long-range artillery.'[10] Both men knew these were idle threats; the PLO's heavy artillery deployed in southern Lebanon consisted of just two 130mm guns.

Curiously, as the long, hot summer approached in the eastern Mediterranean, the Palestinians, like so many rabbits frozen into immobility by a car's headlights, were slow to respond to multiplying signals that the Israelis were indeed mobilizing for war. Even given the massive differences in firepower between the two sides, Palestinian preparations were puny. Yezid Sayigh, the Palestinian military historian, says that while Arafat himself showed an 'impressive degree of foresight' – he ordered the stockpiling of food and ammunition in Beirut and insisted that additional fortifications be dug – local commanders, especially those in the south, let him down. 'It wasn't enough for him to go and visit them, and brief them. The implementation needed to be overseen,' says Sayigh.[11]

Not for the first time, Arafat found himself in a minority in warning about the dangers of apocalypse. His alarums were supported by his trusted lieutenant, Khalil al-Wazir, and to a lesser degree by Brigadier Saad Sayel, the military commander of the PLO forces, but other members of the leadership took the threat less seriously. After all, wasn't there an American-sponsored ceasefire agreement in place? And even if the Israelis did invade Lebanon, as they had in the so-called Litani operation of 1978, would they dare to trespass so far north that it would bring them into collision with Syrian forces who would almost certainly be obliged to engage them?

By the end of May 1982, Arafat's military advisers were convinced that an Israeli thrust into Lebanon was imminent but they still doubted that Israel would advance on Beirut, and this was the substance of the daily estimates that were presented to Arafat by PLO intelligence. 'The question which I failed to answer, and I made a mistake, was: will they come to Beirut or not? I believed that they would not dare to make war with Syria, and Syria would not allow it to reach that point without clashing with them. What happened was exactly that,' says a senior Arafat adviser ruefully.[12]

Arafat had his own reasons for believing, too, that the US would do more to restrain the Israelis, in particular his lengthy and secret negotiations on mutual recognition with the American emissary, John Edwin Mroz. He should have known better. Arafat and his senior colleagues might also have paid closer attention to developments in east Beirut where, by early in 1982, Israel and the Maronites were in the process of cementing an unholy alliance that would end in tears for both of them, and the United States as well.

In the winter of 1981–2, with Israel's invasion plans taking shape, Sharon secured permission from Begin for a highly delicate mission. He would travel by darkened helicopter at nightfall from Tel Aviv north over the sea to the Christian port of Jounieh in east Beirut where he would meet a young man on whom the Israelis had pinned quite unreasonable hopes. The meeting on Lebanese soil between Sharon and Bashir Gemayel, the tough Christian Lebanese militia commander, would be an event of no small significance.

When the helicopter landed on the darkened beach not far from the headland dominated by the twinkling lights of the Casino du Liban, Bashir Gemayel stepped swiftly forward to greet his bulky visitor, kissing him on both cheeks in traditional Arab style. Sharon's dreams of a strategic partnership between Jews and Christians in a hostile Islamic sea must have seemed, in his gargantuan conceit, almost tangible to him then.

Sharon left his Christian hosts in no doubt in discussion over dinner at Gemayel's palatial Bikfaiya home in the hills behind Beirut that it was only a matter of time before Israel responded to their pleas for help, but he warned them that there were limits to what the Israelis could do. Israel's army would not enter Beirut, nor would it seek to expel the Syrians. But what he did offer the Christians was a partnership in re-making Lebanon to their mutual advantage.

Flying back to Tel Aviv the following night, Sharon peered silent and thoughtful from the helicopter at the lights of Sidon and Tyre, and the estuaries of the Rivers Awali, Zaharani and Litani. He was studying the landmarks-to-be of Israel's drive north in the first furious days of its invasion of Lebanon less than six months later.

Within hours of Sharon's arrival in east Beirut as an honoured guest of the Gemayels, Arafat had been informed: in Lebanon, there are few secrets that remain secrets for very long. The visit was correctly seen by the PLO leaders as one more emphatic sign of the burgeoning military and political co-operation between Israel and the Phalangists, but not yet taken as conclusive proof that an audacious operation was imminent against the PLO's very nerve centre in Beirut. In any case, Arafat and his colleagues had other seemingly more pressing concerns in an Arab world that had been further weakened and divided by the onset of the Gulf war in September, 1980. The PLO lacked a strong Arab sponsor. Syria was openly hostile. Egypt, engaged in final delicate negotiations on Israel's withdrawal from the Sinai, was firmly out of the picture. Iraq was consumed by its war with Iran. The Gulf states, panicked by the nasty conflict to their north, were in no position to offer more than their usual jittery financial support. The Soviet Union, then in the last days of the Brezhnev era, appeared increasingly uninterested in the plight of the Palestinians.

The world at large was also distracted. In early 1982, Alexander Haig had unsuccessfully sought to stave off the war between Britain and Argentina over the Falkland Islands in the south Atlantic. In Poland, martial law had been declared in response to the agitation of the Solidarity trades union movement under Lech Walesa. And the US now had a president whose knowledge of the Middle East did not extend far beyond the Jewish jokes he had learned on the beefsteak and burgundy circuit. Indeed, in the early months of the Reagan Administration Philip Habib, the special US Middle East envoy, was obliged to give mini-lectures on the region to a president whose first reaction when the word Palestinian was mentioned was to equate it with 'terrorist'.[13]

The man General Sharon chose to execute the first part of his great plan was an obscure right-wing professor of

Arabic literature named Menachem Milson. On 1 November 1981, Milson had been appointed to head a new civil administration in the territories. It was hardly an inspired choice. Milson had first come to notice after the landslide victory of PLO-supported candidates in the 1976 municipal elections, with his arguments that the Arafatists had triumphed through bribery and intimidation. The trend could be countered, he argued, by cultivating a pliable, indigenous leadership. Needless to say, Milson's views were readily seized on by Sharon, receptive as he was to any plan that might put the PLO in its place. When, in early 1982, Israel ousted the pro-PLO mayors of three large Arab towns to help make way for the new order, violence erupted in the territories, leaving twenty-one Palestinians dead and scores wounded. Soldiers had fired on stone-throwing youths, and armed Jewish settlers had joined in as well.

Milson's appointment was merely one indication, however, of the new 'smash the PLO' mood of a xenophobic Israeli government. Another ominous sign, as far as Arafat was concerned, was Begin's announcement on 14 December that Israel was annexing the Golan Heights, captured from Syria in the 1967 war. What worried the PLO most was not so much Syria's almost mute reaction – the PLO leadership knew that Syria was in no position to engage Israel by itself – but the lessons to be drawn from Begin's disdain for international censure and limp-wristed US disapproval. The annexation of the Golan was regarded by Arafat as another indication that here was a government prepared to go nearly all the way in pursuit of its aims. But even this event, and others such as the Sharon visit to east Beirut in January, did not dispel the aura of complacency that had settled over many in the PLO leadership in their comfortable west Beirut redoubt.

Not only was the possibility of an Israeli advance to the gates of Beirut discounted, PLO officials explain today, but the leadership had become so inured to the almost daily threats of an imminent invasion that it tended to regard each new signal as further blustering and posturing. The Lebanese and Israeli press were full of reports of troop preparations and the bellicose statements of an Israel preparing for war. General Rafael Eitan, Israel's chief-of-staff and one of its more voluble hawks, left no doubt that he was itching for a fight when he told an Israeli newspaper in mid-May that 'since I have built an excellent military machine worth billions of dollars, I must make use of it.'[14]

By late spring, Israel had sharply increased its flights over Palestinian positions and PLO intelligence in Israel had reported growing troop concentrations in the north. 'For Arafat and those around him,' says one of his advisers, 'we were nearly sure that they would attack, but to what extent, we did not settle the question'.[15]

One curious episode in March had alerted some of the PLO high command that Israel might be planning something much bigger than earlier assessments indicated. An Israeli commando unit had come ashore near Damour, about fifteen kilometres south of Beirut, ambushed a PLO military vehicle and killed the four officers inside. Brigadier Sayel, the PLO military commander, went to the site personally to investigate and concluded that the Israeli incursion had been a reconnaissance mission, and that Israel might be planning to land near Damour, or even further north at Khaldeh. Still, he doubted that Sharon's legions would advance on Beirut itself.

Sharon, on his return to Israel after his January talks with the Gemayels, had initiated an intense period of military preparation, ordering the re-drafting of original war plans significantly to enlarge the proposed military operation. He wanted a much more detailed outline of possible political and military co-operation with the Christians. He was also much preoccupied with Israel's final withdrawal from the Sinai which took place on 26 April amid bitter opposition from right-wing settler groups.

When Israel's Defence Minister presented his expanded battle plan, re-named Operation Pines, to the cabinet on

16 May he was rebuffed, in spite of Begin's support, and told to scale down the operation that would have taken him to the gates of Beirut. He was authorized instead to advance a maximum of forty-five kilometres into Lebanon, to destroy PLO bases in southern Lebanon, and to put Israel's northern settlements beyond the range of PLO artillery.

Sharon certainly did not regard this set-back as the last word as he prepared to set off for Washington and his crucial 25 May meeting with Haig. Begin and Sharon were, by the end of May, so much ensnared in their plans for war that there would be no turning back.

Throughout May, Arafat was, as usual, constantly on the move. Ahmed Sidki al-Dajani, the Palestinian intellectual and PLO executive committee member, remembers accompanying him to India, Pakistan, Kuwait, Qatar and Saudi Arabia before returning with him to Beirut for a crucial meeting of the Executive Committee on Tuesday, 1 June.

The PLO 'cabinet' concentrated its attention almost exclusively on Israel's war preparations. Much of the talk focused, not surprisingly given the PLO's vastly inferior firepower, on what diplomatic initiatives might be taken to deal with an Israeli invasion. Farouk Kaddoumi, the PLO 'Foreign Minister', would go to the United Nations accompanied by Dajani. Arafat would continue with his mission to Saudi Arabia in efforts to mediate in the Gulf war which had taken a decided turn for the worse for the Arabs following Iran's re-capture of Khorramshahr on 24 May. If Arafat's colleagues were surprised that their 'commander-in-chief' should decide to leave Beirut at that critical moment, they did not remark on it at the time. Arafat's quicksilver movements had long since become a fact of life for those close to him. And in any case, a visit to Riyadh now might enable him to line up Saudi support for the PLO in its impending ordeal.

Ariel Sharon, meanwhile, travelled in early June to friendly Romania with a small party of aides, including General Avraham Tamir, his national security adviser. The countdown to war was well and truly under way when, on 3 June 1982, the trigger was pulled. Shlomo Argov, Israel's ambassador to the Court of St James, had been critically wounded in an assassination attempt. Sabri al-Banna (Abu Nidal), the Fatah renegade, had struck again although on behalf of whom it remains unclear to this day. Was Iraq, for example, behind the attack? Wasn't Banna then operating from the Iraqi capital, Baghdad? The Iraqis would not have been at all unhappy to see Syria, Iran's ally and to some extent the PLO's, sucked into conflict with Israel in Lebanon. The conspiracy theorists had a field day.

For Tamir and Sharon the question of whether or not it was a conspiracy to bring down the wrath of Israel on Syria and the PLO was irrelevant. They both knew on that fateful day, 3 June, that this was the pretext to attack that Israel had been waiting for. 'It was only a question of when the government was going to give the green light,' says Tamir cynically. 'If it had not been Argov, then something else would have come along.'[16] Rafael Eitan, the tough-talking army commander, put Israel's attitude on the Argov shooting more bluntly when the argument was raised that Arafat and the mainstream PLO could not be held responsible for the actions of one of its renegades. 'Abu Nidal, Abu Shmidal,' he had replied. 'We have to strike at the PLO.'[17]

By the time Sharon returned hurriedly to Israel from Romania, the Israeli air force had already swept into action to avenge the Argov shooting, striking at targets in southern Lebanon and on the outskirts of Beirut, killing more than 60 people and wounding 200 more. For the PLO leadership it was, to say the least, provocative. Ever since the previous summer, when the 'War of the Katyushas' across Israel's northern border had been ended by a US-mediated ceasefire, PLO guns had been more or less silent. Now they could stay quiet no longer. On the same day as the Israeli air force struck, PLO units retaliated with rocket and artillery attacks on northern Israel and the enclave in southern Lebanon controlled by Israel's puppet, Major Saad Haddad.[18] Sharon and Begin had found their *casus belli*.

Israel's cabinet met on the night of 5 June at the prime minister's residence in the leafy Jerusalem suburb of Rehavia, and approved the invasion forthwith after listening to a presentation from Sharon. Essentially, he went over the details of the limited invasion plan approved at the cabinet meeting on 16 May. The cabinet decision was as brief as it was imprecise. Sharon was not exactly given *carte blanche* in Lebanon, but he would have no trouble stretching the meaning of the four-point decision to fit his own designs.

At 11 a.m. on 6 June, less than twelve hours after Cabinet adjourned, Israeli forces poured across Lebanon's southern boundary, supported by air and naval units which blasted targets further north. Some 40,000 Israeli troops in hundreds of tanks and armoured personnel carriers crossed the border and raced north in three directions: along the coast towards Tyre; in the centre towards Nabatiyeh; and in the east towards Hasbaiya. At the same time, naval units landed near the coastal city of Sidon, site of the PLO's southern command.[19] By daybreak next day, the Israeli juggernaut had achieved most of its ostensible, limited war aims: it was on the way to putting Israel's northern settlements beyond rocket and artillery fire from Palestinian strongholds in southern Lebanon; it had thrown the Palestinian military leadership in the south into almost total disarray; and at that early stage it had avoided direct clashes with the Syrians. It was not quite a rout for the PLO resistance in and around what had become known as 'Fatahland', but it was close to it.

International efforts to restrain the Israeli war machine were ineffectual, and the US – the only power that might have stood a faint chance of doing so – seemed confused. The State Department had issued repeated calls for restraint, and on 5 June, Haig had announced that special envoy Philip Habib would return forthwith to the Middle East to restore the July 1981 ceasefire. But President Reagan, in Versailles for a summit of Western leaders, seemed at odds with his advisers: to the surprise of his fellow heads of government he appeared to justify the invasion when he said it stemmed from the constant bombardment of northern Israel from southern Lebanon. Evidently, he was not aware that the front had been quiet for the best part of a year. Against this background, calls for an immediate ceasefire – whether from the Group of Seven leaders or from the UN Security Council – were not going to deflect Begin and Sharon from their war aims.

On the second day, the dominoes continued to fall. Beaufort Castle, the great Crusader landmark with its commanding views towards Galilee, fell; pockets of resistance in Tyre were pacified; Nabatiyeh and Hasbaiya were seized; the noose around Sidon was tightened; and the Syrians found themselves under increasing pressure to enter the conflict as Israeli troops brushed aside flimsy resistance in the central Chouf Mountains and raced on towards the Beirut-Damascus highway. But on the morning of the third day it was clear that Begin's talk of a 45-kilometre thrust into Lebanon, followed by a quick withdrawal – an aim he repeated on the floor of the Knesset that very day and in repeated messages to the Americans – was a grand deception. Sharon had been given his head, and there would be no stopping him. As General Tamir observes in his memoir: 'What was unfolding on the ground was not the brief limited action which the cabinet had considered at its Saturday night meeting, but Operation Pines, the far more ambitious plan which was meant not only to solve Israel's immediate security problem but also to change the basic situation in Lebanon.'[20]

Under heavy aerial bombardment in Beirut, Arafat and his colleagues prepared to make their last stand. Like their southern commanders, they had been shocked and dismayed by the speed and ferocity of the Israeli advance. Haj Ismail, the military chief in charge of 2000–3000 guerrillas in the south, and later accused by some inside the PLO of cowardice, had been caught outside Sidon when it was encircled by Israeli forces. Palestinian fighters notionally under his command had been reduced to a rabble. The Israeli advance in the south swept on more or less unimpeded, although sporadic resistance continued in the large Ein el-Hilweh camp near Sidon until the middle of June. 'The senior command levels turned out to be very poor,' observes Yezid Sayigh. 'Despite all the warnings they were taken very much by surprise, and the level of contingency planning was very poor.'[21]

Holed up in their Beirut bunkers, Arafat and his colleagues scarcely had time to debate the organization's military failures, but it was clear to all that the organization had fallen into an elementary trap. It had sought to build a conventional armed presence in southern Lebanon complete with larger artillery pieces and the odd tank, when there was never any possibility that it would be in a position to match Israel. PLO fighters, better suited for guerrilla warfare, were caught trying to fight a static engagement for which they were completely unsuited. The error was due in no small part to Arafat's oft-stated ambition to build a conventional army, complete with naval and air force units.

By the third day of the invasion, Sharon was already getting on with the hitherto less conspicuous elements of his grand design. With Israeli forces moving towards Beirut on several fronts, albeit more slowly, he summoned Bashir Gemayel to Israel's northern military headquarters. It was a difficult encounter. Sharon, the strategic mastermind impatient for quick results, briefed Gemayel on his plans to cut the Beirut-Damascus highway, and to link up with the Christian forces. Imperiously, Gemayel was told that he should ready his men to push into west Beirut. Without delay, he was to prepare for the formation of a new government committed to re-establishing Lebanon's independence and sovereignty . . . under Israel's tutelage.

Gemayel, with dreams of reuniting Muslims and Christians under his rule, baulked at what he was being asked to do. What had seemed feasible, even desirable, at the candlelit dinner with Sharon at his Bidfaiya home in January, now seemed like a very bad idea indeed. Did he, Bashir Gemayel, wish to emerge from the fires of the Lebanon engagement, branded an Israeli puppet? Even the cocky Gemayel knew that the chances of surviving such a stain on his reputation were almost nil. So he stalled. It was at that precise moment that Sharon's plan to create a new order in Lebanon, based on Maronite compliance, was shown for what it was: at best, a calculated gamble, at worst a reckless game in which there would be no winners. But having committed 60,000 to 70,000 men to the battle and having vowed to rid Lebanon of the 'malevolent criminal terrorists', as Begin incessantly called the PLO, there was no turning back.

On 9 June, Israeli jets blasted Syrian SAM missile batteries in the Bekaa valley in eastern Lebanon, the same day downing twenty-nine Syrian MIG jets in a series of one-sided air battles. By the end of the first week, Israeli forces were occupying Damour, they had pushed to within a few miles of the Damascus-Beirut highway and they had destroyed a total of seventy-nine planes, or one quarter of the Syrian air force. On 11 June, Israel declared a unilateral ceasefire which did not apply, in Sharon's words, to the 'terrorists of the PLO'. Battered and bruised and with no real desire to fight, the Syrians meekly accepted the ceasefire provided it was 'founded on a total Israeli withdrawal from Lebanon'.[22] These were empty words. Damascus was in no position to set conditions.

The Palestinians were now completely on their own to

fight what has been described by Walid Khalidi, the veteran Palestinian historian, as the second Israeli-Palestinian war. 'In fact,' Khalidi observes, 'it has been said that Israel fought us in 1948, and forgot about us until 1982, and then in 1982 they decided to go at us again.'[23] Not since Abdel Kader Husseini had led his Palestinian irregulars into an unequal struggle with the Palmach and the Haganah, the forerunners of the modern Israeli Army, had the two sides so formally confronted each other. Only, on this second occasion the disparity in firepower, the ability of one side, with a huge modern arsenal at its disposal, to rain death and destruction on the other on a vast scale, was infinitely greater than on the first.

In their Beirut bomb shelters – at one point the PLO leadership was operating from an underground car-park ten floors below street level – Arafat and his colleagues prepared for the siege of Beirut and hoped for a political miracle that would deliver them intact from the storm they were sure was about to engulf them.

On the night of 11 June, and with criticism mounting in Israel itself over the failure of the Christians to enter the war against the PLO 'terrorists', Sharon made a second journey to Jounieh. The atmosphere on this occasion was much less cordial. He had gone to assess on the ground what the Christians might be intending to do to capitalize on the opportunities that had been created for them. The answer was: not very much. Sharon, whose expectations of the Christians had always been wildly unrealistic, came to the dispiriting and belated conclusion that Bashir Gemayel and his commanders were 'not going to be an active ally in the continuing war against the terrorists'.[24]

The next day Israel declared a ceasefire, but like ten others that were to come and go before fighting finally came to a halt two months later, this one had no practical effect. These 'rolling ceasefires' were to be a feature of the war that continued throughout the hot summer months, as Israel endeavoured by all the means at its disposal, short of advancing into the crumbling heart of west Beirut itself, to winkle the Palestinians out of their guerrilla strongholds.

When, on 13 June, Ariel Sharon, in full battle-dress, rode triumphantly, like a latter-day Tamerlane, on top of an armoured personnel carrier into Baabda, the hillside seat of the Lebanese presidency, the PLO's fortunes and morale were at their nadir. Panicky thoughts in the leadership were turning to securing the best terms for evacuation. The Syrians, perhaps the only force that could conceivably have come to Arafat's aid, had been decisively knocked out of the fight. Other Arab governments were sitting by, helpless and in many cases uninterested. Appeals to the UN yielded nothing beyond pious ceasefire resolutions that were totally ignored by Israel.

Worse still was the PLO's position among the Lebanese themselves. In those bleak mid-June days, the PLO had few friends anywhere, and least of all among the Lebanese, many of whom were thoroughly fed up with the years of turbulence that had accompanied the Palestinian guerrilla presence in Lebanon. The arrogant, sometimes criminal, behaviour of local PLO commanders and their troops, especially in the south, had alienated a swathe of the population, as had the conspicuous high-living of some senior PLO cadres.

The result, as the Israelis arrived at the gates of Beirut and kept up a relentless bombardment of the city, was mounting pressure on Arafat and his colleagues to withdraw. The message was clear enough on 14 June when Lebanese President Elias Sarkis formed the grandly named Council of National Salvation. It was, in fact, a thinly disguised vehicle to pressure Arafat into removing himself, his headquarters and his fighters from Beirut: and the sooner the better. The question was: how was he to negotiate his way out, and on what terms?

If not downright hostile, the American position was hardly comforting. The US had done little enough to stop the invasion in the first place. Soon after it began, Haig declared that the US would not deny Israel the 'right of legitimate self-defence'.[25] Haig's attitude was certainly no help to Philip Habib who shuttled ineffectually between Beirut, Damascus and Jerusalem in an effort to secure the PLO's withdrawal on less than humiliating terms, even as a highly ambivalent US policy undermined his credibility as a broker.

The mediation effort was further complicated by logistical difficulties. Communications with the outside were problematic and, on occasion, extremely hazardous. 'Arafat and the others were under the most intense pressure and would call me frequently from their bunkers,' recalls London-based Palestinian businessman and Arafat adviser Bassel Akel. 'But the trouble was that every time one of them called, the Israelis would trace the call and target that particular bunker.'[26]

For the first few weeks of the war, confusion reigned in the PLO. Reports of handwringing in the leadership over a possible withdrawal were threatening to sap the morale of fighters in the field. The sheer physical danger was hardly conducive to open and rational debate, and in the absence of hard information about the leadership's plans, rumours ran riot.

Even the few outsiders who wanted to help were kept in the dark. Saudi Arabia's King Fahd – a man who had rescued Arafat from adversity on more than one occasion – spent hours trying to phone the PLO leader to find out what was going on. If the Palestinians were to negotiate their way out of Beirut, his assistance would be vital. Yet nobody could tell him anything. When he finally got hold of a wealthy Palestinian friend at his home in Europe, he exploded: 'I'm desperately frustrated. Nobody will tell me what's going on and I can't get through to the leadership. I need you to ask them under what conditions they'd be prepared to leave Beirut.'[27] Contact was finally made by a Palestinian businessman in Athens, Hassib Sabbagh, using the Greek government's private communications system.

The PLO was itself divided on how to respond to Fahd's question. One school, identified with Hani al-Hassan, the close Arafat aide, wanted to negotiate forthwith the best terms for withdrawal. Hassan desired three things in return: a political gain as a *quid pro quo* for withdrawal, in other words some form of US recognition of a PLO role in any putative peace process; an acknowledgement of the PLO's 'moral victory' resulting from prolonged resistance; and the retention of a PLO political and military presence in Lebanon as one element in a formula to protect Palestinian civilians in Lebanon.[28]

The opposing group, whose most prominent member was Salah Khalaf, wanted to 'hang tough' for as long as possible, in the hope that Israel and the US would tire of attempts to 'negotiate' the PLO infrastructure out of Lebanon. Khalaf and his supporters were determined to give no sign in the first weeks of the war that they accepted the inevitability of PLO withdrawal with the serious effect that would have on the morale of fighters in the field. 'Negotiations,' Khalaf would later observe drily, 'were a tactic for some in the leadership, and a strategy for others'.[29]

Arafat himself, predictably enough, wavered between these two approaches – privately signalling his readiness to depart under the right conditions while publicly maintaining a façade of defiance. On 17 June and with the PLO in desperate straits, he made his strongest public statement of the war. In a message to the 'Arab, Lebanese and Palestinian masses . . . and to all the fighters in the field' he railed against Arab timidity and cowardice, and vowed that the forthcoming battle of Beirut would be 'the Stalingrad of the Arabs'.[30]

But even as Arafat authorized those brave words he knew that time was running out for the PLO's political and military presence in Beirut. He could temporize and delay, tactics which he had honed to near perfection over the years. He would clutch at straws, such as Haig's resignation as American Secretary of State on 25 June, in the hope of stronger US intervention to stop the war. But it would all be in vain until the brutal spectacle of Israel's punishing bombing raids on Beirut in August forced Reagan's hand.

By early July, Arafat had in any case been obliged, under intense pressure from his Sunni Muslim Lebanese allies, to agree in principle to a PLO withdrawal. The PLO leader knew full well when he was summoned on 3 July to the grand white-washed mansion of the former Lebanese Prime Minister, the septuagenerian Saeb Salam, that he was in for a difficult time. Lebanon's elders, members of the Council of National Salvation, made it all too painfully clear that they believed the PLO had outstayed its welcome in Beirut. Whatever their own feelings about the Arab-Israeli dispute, whatever personal friendships they might have with PLO leaders, they could not stand by any longer and see their capital and their country destroyed. The battle, in their view, was over. The PLO had lost, and now it was time for it to go.

Accompanied by Hani al-Hassan, a weary Arafat faced men whom he had known as friends since he had established his headquarters in Beirut in the early 1970. Among all surviving Lebanese leaders, Saeb Salam was perhaps closest to the Palestinians. Arafat counted him not only as a friend, but also as a committed supporter. Now, as discussion droned on throughout a long, steamy July afternoon in the Muslim fasting month of Ramadan, the PLO leader was brought face-to-face with an unpleasant reality. Even Salam, who had resigned as premier in protest at the failure of the Lebanese army to come to the aid of the Palestinians in the raid on Beirut in 1973 in which three top PLO officials were killed, was telling him to go. Arafat knew in his heart of hearts that Lebanon's tribal elders had every reason to tell him to leave, but this did not make it any easier for him to agree to their demands.

As the afternoon wore on, discussion became more

heated with Arafat insisting that there was no way that he and his fighters could leave Beirut in undignified flight. Neither he nor his men could be seen simply to abandon their strongholds under Israeli pressure. They would rather fight to the death and to hell with the consequences for everybody. Warming to his theme, the PLO leader summoned up the ghost of Yousef al-Azmah, the Syrian hero, who had, in spite of impossible odds, defied the French in the battle of Maysaloun near Damascus in 1920. 'I reminded them,' Arafat recalls today, 'of when Yousef al-Azmah went out to fight the French; he knew he would lose, yet he went out to defend Damascus, so that it would not be said that an Arab city was subjected to an invasion, and no-one defended it.'[31] But even as he regaled his Lebanese listeners with stories of heroic Arab exploits, even as he filibustered through that long afternoon, Arafat understood very well that his time was almost up. Late in the day, after conferring with colleagues, the PLO leader returned to Salem's residence with a handwritten note. Addressed to 'our brother Shafik al-Wazzan', it stated simply and briefly that the Palestinian command had taken a decision to leave Lebanon. Arafat would withdraw, but the timing and conditions for withdrawal were left deliberately vague. Even at that late stage, Arafat and his colleagues were hoping for a change in the situation on the ground: in other words, for a miracle.

In agreeing in principle to go, Arafat calculated that he had bought himself time – and indeed, the pressure did ease somewhat in the ensuing weeks. Through most of July, negotiations continued on terms for an evacuation and for the formation of a multi-national force to oversee the exodus of fighters and headquarters staff. US envoy Habib conferred endlessly with Lebanese politicians and Arab diplomats in Beirut – though he never spoke to the PLO itself; direct American contact with the organization over political matters was still taboo. In Washington, officials began turning their attention to the practicalities, such as arranging the charter of ships to take the Palestinians away. It was a curious business, not without its farcical moments. The Americans discovered that some PLO officials were as anxious about taking their prized possessions with them as they were about escaping in one piece. 'We got these messages from the PLO containing lists of BMWs and Mercedes's that they wanted to get on to the ships,' recalls one White House official who was involved in the evacuation effort. 'They were very concerned to get their fleets of cars on as well as their families. We fell about laughing.'[32]

Arafat, for his part, began to look almost as if he was enjoying himself. He emerged often to talk to the international press, which had grown steadily more hostile towards Israel over civilian casualties in Beirut. He gave an interview to Uri Avnery, the Israeli journalist and peace campaigner, that caused almost as much controversy in PLO ranks as it did in Israel itself. Even in the depths of one of his worst predicaments, Arafat still managed to display flashes of grim humour. When David Hirst of the *Guardian* asked him in an interview published on 4 July whether he had taken refuge in the Soviet embassy as Israel was claiming, he had replied: 'What about to sleep with me tonight? I invite you. I have a spare room, in my new residence. This is a big insult to me. I will die in my headquarters.'[33]

All the while, the clutching at straws continued as Arafat tried to improve the terms of the PLO's eventual departure. He was briefly buoyed by French and Egyptian diplomatic efforts aimed at securing a political gain for the PLO, namely recognition of its role in an international peace effort as the price for its withdrawal. He pinned hope on an Arab League intervention with Reagan. But in the end, the Franco-Egyptian initiative came to nothing, and the Arab League move made no difference. During a visit to Washington, the Saudi and Syrian Foreign Ministers, Prince Saud al-Faisal and Abdel Halim Khaddam, meekly acquiesced in the plan being proposed by US negotiator

Habib for the PLO's removal. Within a few short weeks, Israeli pressure would be such that the Habib plan would come to seem the only way out.

In Israel an angry and bitter debate simmered and boiled over. Begin and Sharon came under increasing political pressure to justify their decision to go to war at such terrible cost to the civilian population in Lebanon, and to what end? 'I don't believe all this rubbish about smashing the PLO infrastructure,' observed the noted and by no means doveish Israeli historian, Yehoshua Porat. 'It is based not on arms caches or on supply dumps, but in the refugee camps. As long as there is no political solution, the human and ideological foundation for its existence will remain.'[34] Yaakov Guterman, tormented by the death of his son in Lebanon, excoriated the leadership for its vainglorious designs. 'Cynically and shamelessly you make a declaration about "Peace for Galilee", after not one shot has been fired from the northern border for a whole year,' he wrote in the daily *Haaretz*. ' . . . How many years and generations were needed for the terrorists to murder and to wound as many soldiers . . . as your own war did in one week?'[35]

Sharon's dreams of a quick victory, of Israeli troops being welcomed in a 'liberated' Beirut as the saviours of a new, free Lebanon, had evaporated almost as soon as his legions had arrived at the gates of the city in late June. The swift and intoxicating Israeli advance had become a static siege, a nagging war of attrition in which Israeli casualties mounted by the day. Sharon was in political difficulties, and he knew it. As the days turned into weeks through July, he railed at the Americans; he ranted at his Israeli critics; and he chafed at the lack of action on the battlefield. For the hyperactive Sharon, the slow machinations of American diplomacy, seeking not only to move the PLO out of Beirut, but also to prepare the ground for a comprehensive peace in Lebanon, were almost intolerable. Something had to give.

From 18 July, Begin and Sharon argued bitterly with their cabinet colleagues, some of whom in Sharon's words wanted to 'leave the wagon',[36] about the need for the toughest possible action to break the impasse. On 1 August, Begin and Sharon won the day in cabinet, after heated debate, by proposing a simple stratagem. They would agree to a ceasefire, but if there was one violation, they would launch massive air strikes against PLO positions. As everyone in the cabinet knew, this was simply a pretext for attack. The cabinet had hardly finished meeting when the Israeli High Command deemed that there had been a violation of the ceasefire. Without delay, Israeli forces attacked from the south and in a fifteen-hour battle took the airport, bringing them perilously close to the PLO refugee camps of Bourj el-Brajneh, Sabra and Shatila, and to the heavily bombed Fakhani area, site of the PLO's headquarters. It was then that Sharon decided to go for the kill.

On 4 August, Israel's Defence Minister ordered the most concerted attacks thus far on PLO strongholds from land, sea and air. The target was Arafat himself, and his senior colleagues. These next few days were ones of maximum personal danger for the PLO leader as he was ferried from one heavily fortified bunker to the next. One of Arafat's senior intelligence aides says that in this period the headquarters staff moved the PLO command centre 'every forty-eight hours . . . We had not one but several alternatives,' he recalls, 'with six telex machines, two international lines and a wireless station. We must have moved as many as ten times between mid-July and mid-August when the bombing stopped.'[37]

With help from agents on the ground and from intercepts of Arafat wireless and telephone communications, Israel was able to pinpoint his whereabouts with uncanny accuracy . . . or so it seemed to the PLO leader. Several bunkers were located in basements in the Hamra district in the business centre of west Beirut. No sooner had he moved to a new fortified location than Israeli jets would zero in on his hideout. It was a deadly game of cat and mouse, and it was being fought with multi-million dollar machines and the most advanced electronic targeting equipment available in any arsenal in the world. Sharon used his pilots as flying assassination squads in relentless and furious pursuit of his quarry.

On 6 August, Israel came awfully close to nailing its man when its pilots, alerted by an agent with an electronic homing device, literally flattened a seven-storey apartment building near Lebanon's Central Bank with a new-fangled 'vacuum bomb', killing or wounding some 200 of those inside. Arafat, who had been using part of the building as his operations room, had left hurriedly moments before. Those were desperate times for a fatigued and disoriented PLO leader. According to one of his close associates: 'He was constantly on the move. Some nights he used to sleep on the beach where it was safer from the bombardments, or in open-air car parks. He could never feel completely secure.'[38] They were nerve-racking times as well for the commanders of a special unit numbering about 150 Force 17 commandos from Arafat's personal bodyguard, who had been given a very special mission at the onset of the invasion: to make whatever sacrifices were necessary to save Arafat, the symbol of the revolution.

Very early in the conflict, says Colonel Mohammed al-Natour, the Force 17 commander, it was decided that the criterion that would be used to judge the success or failure of the Palestinian resistance was whether Arafat himself survived. For al-Natour the task of keeping Arafat alive proved a nightmare under almost daily bombardment from the air, from the land and from the sea. 'Unlike other leaders, Abu Ammar [Arafat] never stayed in one place, but was always moving from one place to another,' Natour recalls. 'It was only fate that protected him.'[39]

The ferocious air, land and sea attacks continued until 12 August when, after eleven consecutive hours of air raids on built-up areas in which Palestinian guerrillas and their leaders had taken refuge, President Reagan finally said: enough. The cumulative effects of growing protests around the world and, more pointedly, the horrible pictures of death and destruction that were appearing on the nightly US television network news, prompted an angry and decisive phone call from the US President to Begin. Reagan expressed 'outrage' over the Israeli actions.[40] He demanded that the bombing stop immediately; otherwise, he warned, he would end US attempts to negotiate the PLO's withdrawal from Beirut.

In an exchange with Begin that must go down in history as one of the sharpest ever to pass between a US president and an Israeli leader, Reagan said grimly: 'Menachem, this is a holocaust.' There was a long and deathly pause, before the Polish-born Begin replied frostily: 'Mr President, I'm aware of what a holocaust is.'[41] Six hours later the bombing stopped.

An uneasy calm settled over the smoking ruins of Beirut as Philip Habib began work on the final details of the PLO's withdrawal. For Habib, the task of trying to unravel the mess in Lebanon had proved a dispiriting exercise. Caught between an Israel determined with all force at its disposal to smash the PLO, and Arafat and his men who were fighting for survival, Habib had often been a helpless spectator, his task as a negotiator complicated by his inability to talk directly to the PLO. That task was left to his go-between, Saeb Salam.

One week after Israel ceased its aerial bombardment, Habib's formal 22-point plan for the evacuation of the PLO from Lebanon was presented to the Lebanese Government and to Israel. PLO fighters would be scattered to the four corners of the Arab world. Arafat himself and his headquarters staff would be re-located in Tunis, 2000 kilometres from the land they called Palestine. The PLO leader had emphatically rejected an offer to go to Damascus. The last thing he wanted was to be, in any way, beholden to Hafez al-Assad.

Like most of his colleagues during the long siege of Beirut, Arafat had been shocked and disgusted by the lack of Arab support. Beyond pious words, not one Arab state had come to the aid of the PLO. In an Eid al-Fitr message on 20 July, marking the end of Ramadan, the PLO leader had invoked the words of Saladin, the Muslim warrior who had expelled the Crusaders from the Holy Land in the twelfth century, in an effort to remind his brother Arab rulers of their obligations. 'I do not need your prayers, but I need your swords,' he declared. ' . . . What then is the explanation for this . . . indifference?'[42] His words were greeted with an almost deafening silence.

As he watched the first of his fighters depart from Beirut port on 21 August, amid highly emotional scenes, Arafat had mixed feelings. The long and bloody siege of Beirut that had lasted from 25 June was over, but once again he knew that another and perhaps even more difficult struggle was beginning. The organization had survived: the leadership, through some miracle, had escaped intact: but for the second time in ten years it was being banished to uncertain exile.

By 30 August when Arafat, taking emotional leave of Lebanese notables including Prime Minister Shafik al-Wazzan and Saeb Salam and proclaiming that he was going 'from one exile to another', joined one of the last shiploads of evacuees on board the Greek vessel *Atlantis*, most of the 10,876 Palestinian guerrillas who were to depart Beirut under the Habib plan had gone, along with 2700 Syrians of the Arab Deterrent Force who had been trapped by the Israeli advance. The PLO fighters left behind a casualty toll that was one of the highest of all Arab-Israeli wars. Some 19,000 people had been killed, according to Lebanese official figures, between the first Israeli bombing raid on 4 June and 31 August. Another 30,000 had been wounded. About half the casualties were civilians. Israel's own death toll was near 400 by the end of the year.[43] The cost of Sharon's grand plan to smash the PLO and create a new Lebanon had been high by any standards, even allowing for the possibility of greatly exaggerated official Lebanese casualty figures.

For the PLO, losing Lebanon was a devastating blow. For more than ten years, despite the travails of civil war, the country had served as a more or less autonomous base for the Palestinians; the only place where they could organize, operate and generate political support with a measure of freedom. Now, the impressive Lebanese infrastructure the PLO had built was shattered, many of its factories destroyed and valuable documents carried off or burned by the Israelis. With its fighters scattered around the Arab world, efforts to continue to pursue 'armed struggle' against Israel would be even more difficult; and with Arafat's headquarters shifting to the distant backwater of Tunis, it was going to be hard work keeping world attention on the cause.

As Arafat looked back towards the shore from the deck of the *Atlantis* for what was to be his last close-up view of Beirut, he was haunted by a fear about the fate of the Palestinians he was leaving behind. Was there a danger of a repeat of the awful massacre of Tal al-Zaatar, the refugee camp overrun by Christian militiamen in 1976? Would Palestinian residents of the camps of Sabra, Shatila and Bourj el-Brajneh be safe in the absence of a PLO armed presence? How could he be sure that US security guarantees would be a sufficient safeguard? There were no satisfactory answers to any of these questions, although Arafat would draw some comfort from the presence of a multi-national force from the US, France and Italy.

Arafat's choice of Athens as his first port of call was a pointed rebuff to his fellow Arabs. He would not go to Damascus, home of arch-foe, Assad; he would not go to Amman where differences with Hussein persisted; he would not go to the Gulf where governments' lukewarm support during the siege had been almost more shocking than the failure of others to provide material help; he would not go to Cairo which had been reduced, because of its separate peace with Israel, to diplomatic posturing; he would not go to Baghdad where President Saddam Hussein was continuing to give shelter to Abu Nidal, whose assassins had provided Israel with the pretext to attack in the first place; and he certainly would not go to Tripoli where Gadaffi had, maniacally, urged the PLO to commit collective 'suicide' in Beirut, rather than agree to evacuate the city.

One week before Arafat left Beirut, on 23 August, the 34-year-old Bashir Gemayel had been elected President of Lebanon. The streetfighter had become a warlord and now a national-leader-in-waiting, with pretensions to rule over all of Lebanon. In an Israel still consumed by recriminations over the war, Gemayel's election raised flickering hopes that a Judaeo-Christian axis might yet be established between Jerusalem and east Beirut. On 12 September, Ariel Sharon travelled to Bikfaiya for what would be his 'last supper' with Gemayel. Talk late into the night touched on the difficulty of resolving Lebanon's internal problems . . . and on the negotiation of a peace treaty. The two agreed to another meeting on 15 September, at which Foreign Minister Yitzhak Shamir would be present. But the meeting would never take place.

On 14 September Bashir Gemayel, President-elect of Lebanon, was blown up in the local headquarters of his right-wing Phalange party in east Beirut by a massive bomb presumed to have been planted by a Syrian agent. His corpse was barely recognizable when it was dragged from the rubble. Assad had spoken, and any further designs that Israel might have had on the re-making of Lebanon vaporized on the spot. David Kimche, director-general of the Israeli Foreign Ministry and one of the architects of Israel's ill-fated policy in Lebanon, was to say, with characteristic understatement: 'The killing of Bashir was a tremendous blow for Israel.'[44] Gemayel's assassination, apart from putting paid to lingering Israeli ambitions in Lebanon, also unleashed a sequence of tragic events that would reverberate around the world and add two words indelibly to the history books: Sabra and Shatila.

Following Gemayel's death, Israeli troops moved into west Beirut, and into the area of Fakhani where Arafat's headquarters were located. The PLO leader, visiting Rome for an audience with the Pope, feared the worst when he was told the news by his staff on 15 September. Turning to Afif Safieh, the PLO's leading catholic layman, Arafat said with deep anxiety in his voice: 'They have entered my office.'[45] A chill settled over the room as the PLO leader anxiously assessed the dangers posed by the Israeli intervention. A day later he demanded that troops of the multi-national force, who had completed their withdrawal from Beirut on 13 September, be returned forthwith. But his call came too late – much too late.

Between early evening on 16 September and the morning of 18 September, blood-crazed Christian militiamen avenging the death of Bashir Gemayel had entered the Sabra and Shatila refugee camps, and had killed and killed repeatedly and indiscriminately . . . men, women and children. Some of the victims were mutilated beyond recognition. Phalangist butchers had been given permission by the Israelis, who were in control of the area, to enter the run-down shanty towns, their task ostensibly to pursue Palestinian fighters who Sharon alleged were still hiding in the camps. For more than thirty-six hours, and while Israeli troops ringed the camps, the carnage went on. At the end of it hundreds were dead. The Palestinians say that 1500 died. The Lebanese Red Cross reported 328 dead and 911 missing. An Israeli commission set up to investigate found that between 700 and 800 had died.[46] Crude attempts had been made to 'hide' some of the dead by bulldozing their remains into mass graves.

When details of the massacre emerged on 18 September, the first international reaction was one of disbelief that turned quickly to horror and then to anger. Nowhere was the reaction more vociferous than in Israel itself. Typical was a despatch from Zeev Schiff, the military correspondent of *Haaretz*, who reported on 20 September that: 'A war crime has been committed in the refugee camps of Beirut. The Phalangists executed hundreds or more women, children and old people. What happened was exactly what used to happen in the pogroms against the Jews.'[47]

Speaking for thousands of Israelis, Abba Eban, the former Foreign Minister, observed that 'a hideous pogrom has been perpetuated with fearful death and torment of innocent people in a place where the Israeli government asserted its responsibility for the maintenance of order and the "avoidance of bloodshed" '.[48] Menachem Begin, on the other hand, feigned astonishment at all the fuss. '*Goyim* are killing *goyim*, and the world is trying to hang the Jews for the crime,' he complained to fellow cabinet ministers in what must go down as one of his least sensitive observations.

For Arafat, stricken with grief and guilt and faced with his demonstrable weakness and isolation, it was one of his bleakest moments. In near despair he retired to the Hotel Salwa, his temporary headquarters on the waterfront at Hammam Shatt, twenty kilometres south-east of Tunis. Inconsolable, he went through a process, according to his adviser, Nabil Shaath, who was with him throughout this period, of 'blaming himself, of blaming the Arabs, and the Americans. He felt betrayed.'[49]

# 12
## *The War of Independence*

'Mr Arafat, you are *persona non grata.*' A Syrian lieutenant-colonel, informing Arafat of his expulsion from Syria, quoted in the *New York Times*, 27 June 1983.

For Brigadier Saad Sayel, better known to his troops as Abu Walid, 27 September 1982 was to be a routine day visiting PLO bases in Lebanon's rich, cannabis-growing Bekaa Valley. The dour, US-trained veteran PLO military chief was traversing a familiar route between the Bekaa's two biggest towns, Zahle and Baalbek, when a fusillade of automatic rifle fire shattered the calm. Sayel's car was riddled with bullets and he was grievously wounded in the femoral artery of his upper thigh. He bled to death in front of distraught comrades.

On the pilgrimage to Mecca, Yasser Arafat was shocked and dismayed when he received the news. For him and for Khalil al-Wazir, who was with him, the death of their comrade-in-arms was a particularly sharp personal blow. The three had pledged, during the darkest days of the Israeli siege of Beirut, that if they survived they would make the pilgrimage together.[1] But in the uneasy aftermath of the PLO's ejection from Beirut, Sayel had stayed behind to be with the 8000 or so PLO fighters still based in the Bekaa.

Most ominously, an internal PLO inquiry established that Sayel was gunned down close to a Syrian checkpoint, and that the gunmen had been allowed to escape unchallenged. For the sake of appearances, an official

Syrian-Fatah commission of inquiry put a different complexion on events. Sayel was killed, it found, by members of the Lebanese Sh'ite militia, Amal, operating autonomously. But few in the PLO, least of all Arafat himself, believed this. The pro-Syrian Amal would not have dared to misbehave in Syrian-controlled territory.[2] The conclusion was inescapable: Sayel's death had been a political assassination and, like that of Bashir Gemayel, one instigated by the Syrians.

Arafat's stage-managed departure from Beirut on 30 August 1982 in a blaze of international publicity had been observed from Damascus by a man with hatred in his heart. Hafez al-Assad had had a wretched Lebanon war. Vilified, unfairly in his view, by PLO commanders for having agreed to a premature ceasefire just five days after the outbreak of the war, he had found himself, in September 1982, close to the lowest point of his twelve-year rule. His air force had suffered a tremendous blow for the second time in ten years. He had felt powerless to relieve a Syrian garrison cooped up in Beirut during the siege. Perhaps most galling of all, he felt he had been duped by the Americans into believing that Israel had had no intention of advancing further than forty-five kilometres into Lebanon, hence his hasty decision to agree to a ceasefire. The man he blamed for many of his troubles was Yasser Arafat, who had pointedly thumbed his nose at Syria and the other Arabs on his expulsion from Beirut and sailed off to a hero's welcome in Athens.

Despite his pressing need for allies, Arafat felt justified in holding aloof from Syria. Bitterly, he complained that at the height of the Israeli bombardments Assad had refused even to acknowledge his phone calls. Syria's premature agreement to a ceasefire had been bad enough, but its failure to lift one finger to help the PLO during the worst of the Israeli attacks on Beirut doubled the blow. According to Nabil Shaath, Arafat is convinced that 'Assad is out to destroy the PLO and keep it only as a small addendum to

.. Mohammed Abdel-Raouf al-Qudwa al-Husseini – Yasser Arafat – before entering college.

2. Abdel Raouf al-Qudwa al-Husseini, Yasser Arafat's father.

3. Arafat with fellow members of the Palestinian Students' League in Cairo, c. 1953

**4.** *Left to right:* **Arafat, Salah Khalaf and Zoheir al-Alami en route to Europe for a meeting of the International Students' Congress, August 1956.**

**5.** *Left to right:* **Arafat, unidentified, Salah Khalaf and Zoheir al-Alami at the congress in Prague.**

**6. Arafat in Kuwait, late 1950s or early 1960s.**

**7. The first published picture of Arafat as the leader of Fatah, 1968.**

**8. Arafat, as PLO leader, 1969.**

**9. The paymaster: Arafat and Saudi Arabia's King Faisal.**

**10. Resolving the Black September crisis:** *left to right:* **Arafat, Jaafar Nimeiri of Sudan, Anwar Sadat of Egypt, Muammar Gaddafi of Libya.**

**11. Muslim brothers:** *left to right:* **Ayatollah Ruhollah Khomeini, Iran's erstwhile spiritual leader; Arafat; Ahmed Khomeini.**

9

10

11

**12. George Habash, leader of the Popular Front for the Liberation of Palestine.**

**13. Victory rally:** *left to right:* **Salah Khalaf, Arafat, Khalil al-Wazir.**

**14. Arafat the guerrilla leader, pictured in 1968.**

**15. Arafat the politician.**

**16-18. The many faces of Yasser Arafat.**

15
16
17
18

**19. The historic handshake between Arafat and Israeli Prime Minister Yitzhak Rabin as President Clinton looks on, 13 September 1993. (Associated Press/Ron Edmonds)**

his intelligence organization, and that he is so ruthless that he would not spare any tactic to achieve that purpose . . . Arafat's feelings about Assad are a matter of great grief and anger. He feels that he has done his best to create good relations, but that he has been repeatedly betrayed.'[3]

It was in the immediate aftermath of the war in Lebanon, and at his moment of greatest apparent weakness, that Assad had proved especially dangerous. The 14 September assassination of Bashir Gemayel had been a classically Levantine response to Israeli and US designs in Lebanon; Saad Sayel's death on 27 September was another sign of Syria's determination to fight back. Assad may have been down, but he was certainly not out. The form that fight was to take was a full-scale Syrian-backed insurrection in Fatah ranks.

Trouble had been brewing for Arafat well before he sailed off to Athens, but the long days of the siege, and the almost constant threat of annihilation, had quietened internal criticism of his leadership. It began again with recriminations about poor preparation for the Israeli invasion and lax terms for withdrawal. His obsession with peace strategems had diverted the guerrilla movement from its core task of confronting Israel. The PLO's disastrous showing in southern Lebanon in the first days of the Israeli invasion was partly attributable to the poor leadership of Arafat-appointed cronies in key military posts. Arafat was blamed for Sabra and Shatila. In the festering mood of discontent that followed the exodus from Beirut, the list of complaints was almost endless, and they were made not simply by embittered Fatah dissidents of the pro-Soviet left. Some of Arafat's closest colleagues, including Salah Khalaf, flirted briefly with the opposing faction.

An early sign of the internal troubles came on 9 September at the Arab League summit in Fez when Nimr Saleh, a neo-Marxist member of the Fatah Central Committee and the man who would become the dissidents' political commissar, voiced strong opposition to a peace plan adopted by the Arab heads of state. Saleh took his stand, knowing full well that the Fahd plan, named after Saudi Arabia's Crown Prince Fahd, who had proposed it the previous year, had been drawn up in close consultation, almost co-authorship, with Arafat himself – through the offices of their longstanding go-between, the Palestinian businessman and former Arab diplomat, Bassel Akel.

To Arafat's intense annoyance, Saleh and his hard-line colleagues angrily rejected an innocuous-sounding clause in the agreement that called for 'the drawing up by the Security Council of guarantees for peace for all the states of the region, including the independent Palestinian state' – not-so-concealed code language for the implied recognition of Israel and the acceptance of a Palestinian mini-state in the West Bank and Gaza Strip.[4] For the Fatah rejectionists, this formal Arab abandonment of the 'all of Palestine or nothing' stand was anathema; never mind that their Syrian sponsors had themselves endorsed it. Saleh's greatest sin, in Arafat's eyes, was that he had begun to 'consort with the enemy' by holding frequent unauthorized meetings with Assad. Arafat subsequently suspended Saleh from the Fatah Central Committee, a weak response to what amounted to an open challenge to the PLO leader's authority.

Upon his arrival, exhausted, in Athens, Arafat had received an interesting pair of visitors in his large suite in the Grande Bretagne Hotel. Marwan Qasem, Jordan's Foreign Minister, and Ahmed Lawzi, the Speaker of the Jordanian parliament, had been despatched by King Hussein with a message of support for Arafat and, more to the point, an offer of partnership in a new peace initiative.

The opportunistic Hussein had wasted no time in making his pitch for Arafat's co-operation. It came pointedly on 1 September, the very day that President Reagan unveiled his first (and last) serious Middle East peace initiative, calling for a 'fresh start' in efforts to bring about full autonomy for the Palestinians in the West Bank and Gaza Strip. Reagan had proposed a 'freeze' on Israeli settlement activity in the territories and – most important from Hussein's perspective – had emphasized that in the 'firm view of the United States . . . self-government by the Palestinians of the West Bank and Gaza in association with Jordan offers the best chances for a durable, just and lasting peace'.[5] It was a firm re-endorsement of that staple of US Middle East policy, the Jordanian option. As it turned out, Israeli opposition ensured that the 'Reagan autonomy plan', as it was called, had a shelf life of about five minutes.[6] Begin totally rejected it, still furious over what he regarded as Reagan's intemperate reference to the holocaust at the height of Israel's bombardment of Beirut in August.

After relaying personal greetings from Hussein, Qasem came quickly to the point: 'You are out of Beirut, and we congratulate you on your safety,' he declared. 'This has been a most difficult experience for you. You have depended on many forces you thought would come to your aid and didn't . . . Now, whatever you decide, your decision has to be free from fear, intimidation and old loyalties because you have been let down. Today, what you say ought to represent fully Palestinian interests, whether it coincides with our policy or it conflicts with it.'[7]

Arafat's reply was evasive. He could not give a definitive reply since he had 'just come from the battlefield',[8] but once he had consulted his colleagues he might have a clearer response, both to the Reagan initiative and to Hussein's proposals for a new peace partnership.

Without delay, the king formally invited Arafat to visit Amman where, not many years before, Palestinian and Jordanian had fought in the streets. Now, the two sides were to discuss, as Hussein told the BBC on 13 September, the formation of a federal union on the two banks of the River Jordan and the formulation of a joint Palestinian-Jordanian diplomatic approach.[9] As Hussein saw it, a

Palestinian West Bank 'mini-state' would be joined in a mutually beneficial confederation with the Hashemite kingdom on the East Bank as an interim, and perhaps even permanent, solution to an age-old problem. If this improbable dream could be realized it would serve to answer the incessant harping of the Israeli right on the theme that Jordan, with its preponderance of people of Palestinian origin, was Palestine. What the king was seeking, in effect, was Arafat's blessing to speak on behalf of the Palestinians in American-sponsored negotiations on the future of the Israeli-occupied territories. Loyalties in Jordan were inevitably divided between the Hashemite throne and Palestinian aspirations, imperfectly symbolized by Arafat himself, and the melancholy Hussein had become increasingly concerned over the years about Israeli attempts to use this to de-stabilize his fragile kingdom.

When Arafat arrived in Amman in October the Reagan plan was already dead in the water but this did not prevent the two old protagonists conducting an elaborate and not always harmonious six-month *pas de deux* in the hope that something could be salvaged. Hussein spent days and weeks trying to cajole Arafat into endorsing the Reagan plan and, more particularly, Resolution 242 calling for Israel's withdrawal from territories occupied in the 1967 war, and for all states in the region to 'live in peace within secure and recognized boundaries free from threats or acts of force'.[10] Hussein, like his American allies, had long regarded acceptance of 242 as the essential centrepiece of any Middle East initiative, and his difficulties in persuading Arafat to endorse it sorely tested his patience. In the early months of 1983, Hussein frequently expressed extreme frustration in private over his attempts to pin down the elusive Arafat. A senior Western official who was privy to his thoughts at the time recalls that the king was 'scathing' about the PLO leader. 'The man's a liar,' he would exclaim in a cold fury. 'He can't be trusted, he's a shadow leader. How can he claim to speak for the Palestinian people?'[11] Hussein eventually persuaded Arafat to agree to a watered-down peace formula based on the Reagan plan and the Fez Arab League summit resolutions of the previous September, but this was as far as their joint 1983 initiative went.

In early April, after a gruelling eight-hour session with Hussein, Arafat travelled from Amman to Kuwait to try to sell the initiative to the PLO Executive Committee, and to the Central Committee of his own Fatah faction. Acceptance of the formula would, he said, open up the possibility of a US-PLO dialogue – naively regarded by the PLO leader over the years as almost an end in itself – and would serve to increase pressure on Israel. He got nowhere. The brethren in Kuwait were in no mood to sanction a peace initiative under which the PLO would have to play second fiddle to Jordan. They were incensed by its fuzziness as to whether a Palestinian sovereign state would be established before or after confederation with Jordan, or even whether it would be established at all. Even qualified endorsement of the Reagan plan was enough to send some of Arafat's hardline colleagues into paroxysms of opposition.

Arafat, who had undertaken to hasten back to Amman bearing the consent of his colleagues, did not return to tell Hussein the bad news. He sent an emissary with suggested amendments instead. A furious Hussein rejected these out of hand and in a statement that reflected the intense pique felt in the palace, the Jordanian cabinet announced on 10 April the abandonment of the joint initiative, and of participation in the Reagan plan. Richard Viets, the US ambassador in Amman at the time, remembers being summoned to meet Hussein at the Prime Minister's office on the very day of the cabinet announcement. 'I have never seen him so angry,' he recalls, 'both at the PLO and at the US which by then had put so much distance between itself and the Reagan initiative.'[12]

* * *

In the weeks and months after his expulsion from Beirut, Arafat had continued to behave in many ways much as before the Israeli invasion. He travelled widely, consulted Arab heads of state, tried quixotically to mediate in the endless and often highly personal disputes that swirl about the Arab world, received Israeli peace campaigners of dubious relevance at his Tunis headquarters, and generally endeavoured to create the illusion that for the PLO it was business as usual. But even as the PLO leader dabbled and temporized, and dreamed up new strategems to keep his name in the headlines, the ground was shifting beneath his feet. He appeared not to notice, or even to care, about ominous noises from some of his erstwhile Fatah colleagues who had, against his wishes, based themselves in Damascus and were now passing their days and nights plotting his downfall. A chilly meeting of the PLO's Central Council came and went in late November without Arafat seeking to force a showdown, but his failure to act was merely storing up trouble. As so often, his tendency to prevaricate made things worse.

The dissident leadership had by then coalesced around four men: Nimr Saleh and Ahmed Kadri, a fellow Fatah Central Committee member, and Colonels Mohammed Said Musa Maragha and Khaled al-Amleh. Of the four, Said Musa, or Abu Musa as he was better known to his colleagues, emerged as the spokesman. A hardened professional soldier who trained in the Jordanian Army, he had joined the Palestinian resistance at the height of its conflict with Hussein in 1970. He had fought bravely and had been rewarded with the post of military commander of southern Lebanon when the PLO expanded its bases there after its expulsion from Jordan. A longstanding member of Fatah's 'leftist' tendency, Musa had made no secret of his opposition to the PLO leader's diplomatic machinations. His career was in something of an eclipse when the Lebanon war broke out. In 1977, after a bitter row with Arafat over the PLO's response to Sadat's announcement that he planned to visit Jerusalem, Said Musa was relieved of his command and spent a year in limbo in Beirut before being given a 'desk job' in the operations division.

A pugnacious, square-jawed man with greying hair, Said Musa says today that the 'challenge to Arafat was there since 1974'. This was when, in the view of the hard-liners, the PLO began formally edging away from its commitment to the all out destruction of Israel and towards a political settlement: towards, in fact, the acceptance of a 'mini-state' in part of Palestine. 'We reject,' he says emphatically, seated in his spruce suite of offices in a Damascus suburb, 'all the policies that have been adopted since 1974 because they contradict all the aims and basis of our struggle.'[13]

On 27 January 1983 Musa had delivered much the same message, but with infinitely more venom, on behalf of the dissidents at a highly charged meeting in Aden of Fatah's Revolutionary Council – the organization's consultative body. According to one of those present, it was an 'ugly, bitter meeting' that acted as only a temporary safety valve for dissident frustrations.[14] Speaking from a text drafted by his co-conspirators in Damascus, Musa had railed against 'capitulationist' policies under Arafat. He expressed violent opposition to the PLO's diplomatic strategy. He demanded a return to armed struggle as the 'sole road to liberation' in Lebanon, the Israeli-occupied Golan Heights and in the West Bank. Fresh efforts should be made to overthrow the Hashemite regime to enable guerrilla raids on Israel to be conducted from Jordanian territory. An underground war should be declared on American interests in the Middle East, and so on.[15]

Arafat and Fatah leaders listened to Musa in stunned silence. The Aden meeting failed totally in its aim of quieting the voices of dissent. Equally inconclusive was a subsequent meeting of the Palestine National Council, in Algiers in mid-February. The gathering of 350 Palestinian delegates glossed over contentious issues as much as possible, so as not to exacerbate the PLO's internal divisions, and ended up mouthing platitudes. Cynics dubbed it the *lam* PNC – a combination of the Arabic words 'no' (*la*) and 'yes' (*nam*). In a close debate on the Reagan plan, Arafat uttered words that could almost be regarded as his signature tune. 'It's true that we are being offered nothing of value, but we can't afford to say no to everything,' he declared. 'We can't say yes to everything either. So we have to learn to say "Yes, but," and "No, but" . . .'[16] Nimr Saleh was not privy to these observations. The leading dissident had been dropped from the Fatah slate for the PNC session.

One man who took strong exception to the failure of the Algiers meeting to address substantial issues was Issam Sartawi, Arafat's peace envoy. Denied the right to speak, a disillusioned Sartawi left Algiers observing that, with the PLO's representative body sliding into irrelevance, it might be better to hold its next session in Fiji. But Sartawi, a deeply controversial figure within the PLO because of his daring diplomatic manoeuvres, did not have long to live. On 10 April, the same day that Jordan formally ended its joint initiative with the PLO, he was gunned down by assassins sent by Abu Nidal while attending a meeting of the Socialist International in the Portuguese coastal resort of Albufeira. Among those who were present and who paid tribute was Shimon Peres, the Israeli Labour leader. In Sanaa, the barren high altitude capital of North Yemen, a tearful Arafat condemned the killers, describing them as Israeli 'hirelings'. It was not the first time the PLO had hinted at Mossad penetration of Abu Nidal's gang but on this occasion, the allusion seemed off-beam. The PLO leader was only too painfully aware that Sabri al-Banna (alias Abu Nidal) had, late in 1982, moved back into Syria's orbit, quietly switching his headquarters from Baghdad to Damascus, and it was from there that the statement claiming responsibility for Sartawi's killing had been issued on behalf of Abu Nidal's Fatah Revolutionary Council. Chillingly, it described the heart surgeon and peace campaigner as 'the enemy of our people'.[17]

As Arafat pursued his restless peregrinations the Lebanese time-bomb continued to tick. Amid a flurry of diplomatic activity and violence prompted by US and Israeli efforts to construct a new Lebanon from the ashes of the old, the world barely noticed a series of political tremors deep in the Syrian-controlled Bekaa Valley. Early in May 1983, a group of Fatah officers led by the arch dissident, Colonel Said Musa, commandeered the headquarters of the PLO's Yarmouk Brigade at Hammara in the Bekaa near the Syrian border. The Fatah mutiny had begun. Its immediate trigger had been Arafat's ill-advised appointment towards the end of April of fifty-one loyalist officers, several of whom had been accused of cowardice during the Israeli invasion, to command posts in central and northern Lebanon, where thousands of PLO troops had re-grouped after the withdrawal from Beirut. Mamdouh Nofal, a PLO military commander and Democratic Front stalwart in Lebanon, recalls travelling through Syrian lines early in the mutiny to plead with Said Musa to abandon his vendetta. 'Fatah needs you, and if you depend on Arab regimes you will lose,' Nofal had implored. 'If you pursue this you will end up as just a small group in Damascus under Syrian domination. So I suggest you stop, and I will try and talk it over with Arafat.'[18] But Said Musa, intoxicated with the possibility of taking control of the Fatah military, was determined to carry the fight to the Arafat loyalists in the Bekaa Valley. Several days later, Nofal again approached him. 'Stop,' he pleaded, 'or your sons will read in a few years time that you are a traitor.' Defiantly, Said Musa replied: 'You've turned me into a traitor now.'[19]

By now thoroughly alarmed by the events in the Bekaa, Arafat had hastened there on 13 May, four days after the mutineers had made their move. From the PLO offices in

Damascus, he shuttled back and forth three times in four days and made a series of concessions to the rebels. He agreed to reinstate rebel officers, purge those who had been negligent during the Lebanon invasion and restore Nimr Saleh to the Fatah Central Committee.'[20] He met Assad – their first meeting since Arafat's expulsion from Lebanon – in a half-hearted and ultimately fruitless attempt to iron out their differences; he also felt obliged to echo some of the hard-line rhetoric of his opponents, declaring in Damascus on 15 May: 'An effective war is the only way to re-draw the map of the Middle East. The way out of this present deadlock is to take a decision to wage war to change the balance of power.'[21] He even tried, in time-honoured fashion, to buy the dissidents off. On one of his visits to the Bekaa he asked Mamdouh Nofal how much Said Musa wanted to keep quiet. 'We'll pay him whatever he wants for a whole year, and then see if we can negotiate,' he said.[22]

But to no avail. Musa and the other rebels were not after money but power, and they were being ruthlessly used by a third party with motives of its own: Syria. As Nofal puts it: 'Abu Musa's aim was to usurp the revolution by depending on Syria. He was not the sort of man who could lead the PLO, and the Syrians knew that very well. They wanted to destroy the revolution.'[23]

In early June, open warfare broke out in the Bekaa. Fatah blood was spilled, and it would continue to flow for the rest of the year. Breaking off a visit to Romania, Arafat rushed to Algeria and then to Saudi Arabia in a desperate effort to enlist wider Arab support against Syrian and Libyan backing for the mutineers. The fact that his leadership was being challenged by such an array of forces was bad enough. Worse still was the ammunition they were using: all-out criticism of the way he had run the PLO. Said Musa, in an interview with the Arab weekly, *Al-Kifah al-Arabi*, accused Arafat of turning the Palestinian revolution into a 'bureaucracy so rotten that it is worse than the bureaucracy in any underdeveloped country,' adding cruelly: 'Naturally, this institution was not capable of fighting. So when the war [in Lebanon] broke out, the leadership ran away, leaving the rank and file to pay the price.'[24]

On 2 June, Arafat bitterly attacked Libya for its support of the Fatah rebels, but he still stopped short of openly condemning Syria in the hope of preventing any further deterioration in his badly strained relations with Assad. It was not as if he did not have cause for complaint. Damascus was by then making little attempt to hide its backing for the rebels: Syrian troops obstructed and detained Fatah commanders, and several times joined in attacks with heavy weapons on loyalist positions in the Bekaa. 'Arab intervention is no longer limited to material support,' Arafat declared angrily, 'but has been translated into action as well.'[25]

On the evening of 23 June, Intissar al-Wazir, wife of Khalil al-Wazir, telephoned Arafat in Damascus to request an urgent meeting. Once at Arafat's office, she told him she had been informed by a Syrian intelligence source that gunmen were planning to ambush his convoy as it returned later that day to Tripoli in northern Lebanon by way of the Syrian town of Homs. 'He laughed and said he didn't care,' she recalls. 'He really didn't believe me, but he said, "Just repeat your story." So I did, and he said, "OK, I promise I won't go." '[26]

Arafat's luck was in again. The convoy, including his bullet-proof limousine with its darkened windows but no Arafat, was ambushed outside Damascus. In the shoot-out, one of his bodyguards was killed and nine others were injured by machine-gun and rocket-propelled grenade fire. At dawn after a sleepless night, a furious Arafat bitterly condemned the Syrian plot to eliminate him, for the first time explicitly charging that Syria was behind the Fatah rebellion.

When Intissar al-Wazir woke to the news that Arafat's convoy had been attacked, she hurried back to his office and to her relief found him alive and closeted with PLO faction chiefs. Seeing her at the door, Arafat rushed over and took her hand. 'Repeat now what you told me last night,' he said grimly.[27] By then, Arafat had already heard from the Syrians, and what he had heard was not to his liking. At 8 a.m., he had received a curt written ultimatum, signed by General Hikmat Shehabi, Syria's chief of staff, giving him six hours in which to leave the country.[28] The expulsion order amounted to a virtual declaration of war. Arafat, leader of the Palestinians, was being kicked out of an Arab capital for the second time in less than a year. But his peremptory expulsion order was nothing compared with the humiliation offered at Damascus airport as he awaited a flight out of the country. Standing with a group of tearful staff, the PLO leader was approached by a relatively junior officer who sputtered insolently in his face: 'Mr Arafat, you are *persona non grata*.'[29] Arafat was then bundled on to a regular Tunis Air flight to Tunis. On arrival there he declared bitterly that his expulsion 'was part of a Syrian-Libyan plot against the Palestinian revolution'.[30]

On the Syrian side, too, the bitterness was out in the open. Damascus charged that Arafat had been expelled because of his 'continuous slandering . . . against Syria, its sacrifices and its positions of principle'.[31] But Arafat's sin was more than his having spoken out of turn. In Assad's view, Arafat had crossed a red line into the forbidden domain of Syrian politics. He had sought to enlist the support of Rifaat al-Assad, the Syrian leader's younger brother, in his struggle to contain the Fatah rebellion.

The high-spirited Rifaat had long been close to mainstream PLO figures and was rumoured to have been involved in joint business ventures with some of them. Sympathizing with Arafat's predicament, he had offered his assistance and had threatened publicly to 'break the neck' of one of the leading rebels.[32]

Khaled Fahoum, the veteran PLO official who has long been close to the Syrians, recalls attending an elaborate wedding at Damascus's social hub, the Sheraton Hotel, on the night before Arafat's expulsion. Many of Syria's top people were present, including chief of staff Shehabi, who signed Arafat's expulsion order. All the talk was of the exchanges between Arafat and the young Assad. Shehabi and his colleagues had little time for the ambitious Rifaat in any case, but they were incensed by the spectacle of him consorting with Arafat under their very noses. The president's own anger almost certainly matched, if not exceeded, that of his senior commanders and it was against this background that Arafat received his marching orders.

Arafat had entered one of his bleakest periods as PLO leader. He had lost the initiative in Lebanon where 10,000 of his best fighters were at the centre of a bitter and bloody test of wills with Fatah mutineers supported by other Damascus-based dissident Palestinians. He had worn out his welcome, one way or the other, in the capitals of all the front-line states that share a common border with Israel. Like a cyclist who has to keep peddling to stay upright, an immobile Arafat was in danger of toppling over, obliged to sit impotently in Tunis while his colleagues in Fatah sought to resolve his differences with the rebels. And in the depths of his anger and despair he could not forget, indeed would not forget, that none of his so-called colleagues from rival Damascus-based factions, such as the Popular Front of George Habash and the Democratic Front of Nayef Hawatmeh, had come to his defence when he was humiliatingly expelled from Syria.

In his darker moments, Arafat wondered if, after all these years, he might not be on the brink of defeat in his long and bitter struggle to retain freedom of manoeuvre for the Palestinian movement. He was haunted by memories of the fate that had befallen his two predecessors – Haj Amin al-Husseini and Ahmed Shukairy – both of whom had died in lonely exile, and he chafed at the prospect that he might become, in the words of Nabil Shaath, the 'third Palestinian leader to go into oblivion far away from the leadership and decision-making of his people'.[33]

By now Syria and Libya were by no means alone in efforts to undermine his leadership. Saudi Arabia had, by the summer of 1983, begun surreptitiously canvassing alternatives. Abdullah Hourani, a member of the PLO Executive Committee, recalls that the Saudis approached a number of PLO leaders at about this time, whispering: 'Why do you insist on Arafat? If you drop him, maybe you could patch things up with Syria?'[34] Possible alternatives mentioned were Farouk Kaddoumi, the PLO 'Foreign Minister'; Khaled al-Hassan, the veteran Fatah official; Khaled Fahoum, the speaker of the Palestine National Council; Mahmoud Abbas (Abu Mazen), another Fatah stalwart; and Ahmed Sidki Dajani, the Cairo-based PLO independent. Throughout a long, hot, aimless summer Arafat was trapped in what came to seem like institutionalized exile in Tunis. At the Hotel Salwa on the waterfront, he dined almost daily with his bored troops. Several of his senior associates began worrying that he was losing his prestige: that rather than acting as leader of the revolution he was becoming 'one of the boys'. About this time Arafat took up horse-riding and was pictured in the *Observer*, looking faintly ridiculous, mounted on a horse.

If there was any consolation for Arafat it lay in the strong backing he received from the occupied territories. On 26 June, just two days after his expulsion from Damascus, Sheikh Saad al-Din al-Alami, head of the higher Islamic Council, declared melodramatically at a public rally in Jerusalem's al-Aqsa mosque that: 'It is the duty of every Muslim to assassinate the Syrian president for the crimes that he committed against the Palestinian people.'[35] Spurred on, Arafat came to the conclusion that he had no other choice but to return to Lebanon to rally his troops and to confront the rebels. The only question was when. He would have to await the critical psychological moment.

Late in June, at a seminar in Tunis attended by leading Palestinian intellectuals and businessmen, Arafat was finally persuaded that an audacious step was required. Discussion focused on the idea of declaring an independent Palestinian state in the West Bank and Gaza, and of forming a provisional government-in-exile to replace the PLO.[36] In the midst of all this theorizing, Arafat felt distinctly uncomfortable. What relevance, he asked himself, did discussion of these controversial ideas have to the immediate problems he was facing? Very little, he concluded. What was worse, he saw himself increasingly as a pawn in a game over which he had lost control. He was especially aggrieved that some of his closest allies among wealthy and powerful Palestinians in the diaspora, the 'compradours' as he called them, were dealing as intermediaries with his bitter foes in Damascus. Besides, enforced inactivity was fraying his nerves.

If Arafat was to break out of this pattern, timing was all. One false move and he would be finished. Syria and the Fatah rebels, not to mention Israel, were waiting to pounce. Ironically, it was the Israelis who unwittingly provided the cue for his dramatic reappearance on the Arab stage.

On 28 August, after months of rising tension, open warfare broke out on the streets of Beirut between the Christian-dominated Lebanese Army and the Internal Security Forces on one side, and local leftists and their Syrian-backed Shi'ite Amal militia allies on the other. Amal gunmen clashed with units of the Lebanese Army near the Bourj al-Brajneh quarter in the city's sprawling southern suburbs. Fighting quickly spread to west Beirut. For the next forty-eight hours the anti-government militia forces held sway in the rubble-strewn streets of the predominantly Muslim half of the capital.

For Arafat, the spirited resistance on the streets of Beirut was a sign that his time was drawing near. But before he made his move, he was momentarily distracted by a melodramatic announcement from Jerusalem. On 29 August, the 69-year-old Menachem Begin told startled cabinet colleagues that 'I cannot go on any longer.' Two weeks later, the ex-Prime Minister went into dispirited seclusion in his small Jerusalem apartment at No. 1 Zemach Street, from where, as Arafat has since observed, he could look down on Deir Yassin, scene of the massacre of Arab villagers by Begin's Irgun terrorists many years before.[37] The Lebanon misadventure, with its daily toll of Israeli casualties, had simply become too much for the increasingly reclusive and guilt-ridden Begin, burdened by depression following the death of his wife late in 1982. His withdrawal was a promising omen for Arafat. Bruised and battered as he was, he had at least outlasted the Israeli leader who had set out to destroy him. But he had little time to savour the moment.

In early September, the opportunity arrived for Arafat loyalists, holed up in Lebanon, to seize the initiative. At midnight on 3 September, just a day or so after the fighting had died down in Beirut, the last Israeli units quietly withdrew from their positions in the mountains overlooking Beirut to a new defensive line along the Awali river, well to the south. The fragile power balance in the Chouf Mountains had been dramatically altered. Lebanon was in for another of its all too frequent convulsions, and into the vacuum created by the Israeli withdrawal stormed the fighters of the youthful and eccentric Druze warlord, Walid Jumblatt, son of Kamal. They were supported by Arafat loyalists and by units of the Fatah mutineers. In the free-for-all that followed, the Christian Lebanese Forces militia and Christian-dominated Lebanese regular army units were driven back from most of their positions in the commanding heights above Beirut – in spite of aerial support from the Israelis and shelling from US warships standing offshore. By mid-September, the attackers were on the perimeter of the heavily guarded Christian stronghold of Souq al-Gharb above the presidential palace at Baabda. Indeed, some of the PLO commanders believed the advance might carry them back into Beirut itself, from where they had been so brutally evicted twelve months before.[38]

Fatah loyalists, and Popular and Democratic Front fighters of what was now dubbed the 'loyal opposition' to Arafat, had seized the opportunity of the Chouf War to break the Syrian shackles that had restrained them in the Bekaa. Alarmed at the possibility that they might establish an autonomous base for themselves, Syria took abrupt action on 15 September, instructing the Druze command to insist on the withdrawal of Palestinian guerrillas from the siege of Souq al-Gharb. This had two effects: it took some of the steam out of the assault on the key Christian stronghold and obliged the Palestinians to fall back towards Syrian lines in the Bekaa. But unbeknown to the Syrians – or indeed to the Israelis – the elusive Arafat was already making his move.

Houdini-like, the PLO leader re-emerged in the northern Lebanese city of Tripoli on 16 September. His timing was near-perfect, and he wasted no time in signalling his presence to the outside world. Going straight to the besieged Baddawi and Nahr al-Bared refugee camps, he declared defiantly for the benefit of his opponents in Damascus that the PLO 'is a towering revolution that no-one can contain or control . . . '[39] Within days, Arafat's plan, worked out during long days of idleness in Tunis, exhibited signs of achieving its goal: to force Damascus and its rebel Fatah clients to show their hand.

In the last week of September, under concerted Syrian pressure, Fatah loyalist fighters withdrew north from the Bekaa towards Tripoli where Arafat was preparing to fight what many believed would be his last battle. Throughout October, the Syrian-backed Fatah rebels tightened their siege, moving closer to the Baddawi and Nahr al-Bared camps and to Tripoli itself. Offshore, Israeli gunboats ceaselessly patrolled, preventing arms and reinforcements reaching Arafat's beleaguered garrison. It was not the smallest of the ironies that Fatah rebels, themselves committed to the destruction of the Jewish state, were making common cause with the Israeli navy.

As October gave way to November, Arafat found himself besieged for the second time in a little more than a year, this time by the Syrians, dissident Palestinians, Lebanese militia and the Israelis. The enemy camp even contained a contingent of Chadian soldiers reportedly despatched by Libya's Colonel Gadaffi under the mistaken impression they were attacking Tel Aviv. In the face of this bizarre assortment of foes, Arafat's sole local ally was an Islamic fundamentalist party with little more than words to offer in support. Under criticism from his own supporters – the veteran Khaled al-Hassan, for one, wondered why it had been necessary for him to go to Tripoli in the first place 'without a collective decision' – Arafat felt he had no choice. His aim was to confront his enemies and to bring into the open the dimensions of the Syrian involvement in the mutiny. Fighting for his political survival, he had decided to make Tripoli his last stand, if necessary. 'In Tripoli we forced the plotters to expose all of their cards,' he says. 'We disproved the claims that the problem was merely an internal Palestinian conflict.'[40]

As the bitter conflict continued into November, with Palestinian ranged against Palestinian, Arafat and his supporters were relentlessly pushed back, first from the Nahr al-Bared camp, and then from al-Baddawi. Before hastily withdrawing from the latter, Arafat bitterly accused Damascus of seeking to turn the PLO into a Syrian 'puppet'. 'They want to end the PLO, to end the independent Palestinian decision,' he said. 'They want to create an alternative PLO that will be a puppet in their hands. But I tell them, I will only bow to God and to the will of my people. I will fight and die here with my people but I will never compromise on my people's dignity, independence or rights.'[41]

Arafat charged that the Syrians had massed up to 25,000 men, 170 tanks and 180 artillery pieces around the refugee camps. Such was the carnage in and around Tripoli in those November days that hospitals ran out of morgue space and a doctor at the Islamic hospital said only the severely wounded were being treated. 'We are saturated and I don't know how we can cope,' he said. 'No medicines. No blood. No electricity. No fuel for generators. And no staff.'[42] These were truly desperate moments with the PLO leader and 4000 of his best fighters cooped up under heavy shellfire in an area scarcely larger than one square mile. He was faced, it seemed, with the choice between a humiliating surrender and a complete rout of his beleaguered forces.

But again fate or, as some would have it, Arafat's phenomenal luck came into play. When his forces were expelled from their last military stronghold in the al-Baddawi camp on 17 November the alarm bells at last began to ring in a hitherto complacent Arab world. Nowhere was the unease greater than in Saudi Arabia, where the hereditary rulers were filled with horror at the thought of a completely destabilized and vengeful Palestinian movement. Crown Prince Abdullah bin Abdel Aziz, on a visit to Kuwait on 21 November, denounced the rebellion as a 'military coup against Arafat's legitimate leadership'.[43] It was a considered intervention and one that produced quick results.

Having decided that 'enough was enough', the Saudis wasted no time in exerting pressure on Syria to cease its onslaught against Arafat's last crumbling redoubt in Lebanon. Prince Saud al-Faisal, the Saudi Foreign Minister, was despatched to Damascus to negotiate terms for Arafat's orderly withdrawal from Tripoli, but strangely absent from all the discussions was the old fox himself, Hafez al-Assad. Complaining of chest pains and exhaustion, Syria's leader had been secretly admitted to hospital on 12 November at the very height of the onslaught against

Arafat's strongholds. A punishing daily schedule of long hours of work and little exercise had taken its toll. His doctors prescribed a complete rest. Assad's confinement to a sickbed at this critical moment was by no means the least fortuitous development in Arafat's precarious career.

After four days of discussion, on 25 November the Saudi-Syrian agreement on the Fatah loyalist withdrawal from Tripoli was announced. Arafat was to be completely banished from Lebanon but, to balance that, Syria had failed to supplant him as the leader of the revolution. The joint agreement was immediately accepted. With his back to the wall, Arafat had no other choice and neither did the Fatah mutineers. Said Musa and his men did what they were told by 'big brother' in Damascus. On the eve of the truce, Arafat pulled off something of a propaganda coup with the announcement that six Israeli prisoners-of-war with the beleaguered Fatah forces in Tripoli had been exchanged for 4500 Palestinian and Lebanese prisoners held by Israel. The event projected Arafat's smiling face on to the front pages of the world's press within days of the leader writers having penned another batch of political obituaries: 'Already crippled by Israel, Yasser Arafat has been finished off by Syria,' commented the *New York Times*. ' . . . Such is the bizarre ending of a movement that, for all its daring, never found a political vision.'[44]

Negotiations on Arafat's evacuation from Tripoli dragged on for three weeks amid moments of high drama and low farce with the PLO leader, as ever, seeking to make the best of yet another historic setback. Not least of Arafat's concerns was the threat posed by the Israelis to plans for an orderly evacuation of PLO fighters under the United Nations flag, thus guaranteeing their safe conduct. Ariel Sharon, for one, said that Arafat 'should not be allowed to leave Tripoli alive'.[45] Israeli gunboats also kept up the pressure, blasting PLO guerrilla bases around Tripoli in the first weeks of December, further delaying his departure. All this tended to play into Arafat's hands in any case, since he was in no hurry to relinquish his last toehold in Lebanon. The Israelis, for their part, made no secret of their determination to prevent Arafat claiming any kudos at all for having defied all attempts by his many opponents to get rid of him. Israel certainly did not wish to see a repeat of the PLO leader's 'triumphal' departure from Beirut the year before. 'We do not want Arafat to leave like a hero. If he leaves, it should be like a dog with his tail between his legs,' said one Israeli official.[46]

Eventually, on 20 December a convoy of five Greek ships flying the UN flag entered the harbour in Tripoli to ferry the Fatah loyalists to camps scattered about the Arab world. But the way for Arafat's evacuation was not cleared until the US had urged Israel to stop its attacks on PLO positions. Arafat's second exodus from Lebanon was less dramatic than the first but in a way more poignant. He was leaving his last base in Lebanon. His movement was badly fractured. In front of him lay, at best, a deeply uncertain future and at worst, political oblivion. As he arrived at the quayside in a white Range Rover, he tried to put the best face on things. 'The struggle is not over,' he declared. 'We will continue until we reach Jerusalem, the capital of our Palestinian state.'[47] In the demonstrable weakness and disarray into which the PLO had fallen, it was hardly a credible call to arms.

As his vessel, the *Odysseus Elytis*, prepared to set sail under French naval escort, Arafat appeared on the upper deck to be greeted with the thunderous and by now, in moments of adversity, ritual discharge of automatic rifles by PLO and Lebanese fighters. Arafat's aides said he was bound for Tunis but it was very soon apparent that this was a ruse. Arafat, the conjurer, had another card up his sleeve.

# 13
## *Climbing Back*

> 'We should realize that this is not the time to strive for the resolution of the Palestinian issue, but rather to concentrate on its preservation, lest it become extinct.'
> Nabil Shaath, *Al-Siyassa*, 15 April 1985.

As Yasser Arafat sailed away from Lebanon, he proclaimed defiantly that he was heading 'from one outpost of struggle to another outpost of struggle'.[1] In fact, he was bound for the land of his birth. Forty-eight hours before he set sail from Tripoli, Arafat had quietly informed Sadat's successor as Egyptian President, Hosni Mubarak, that he would welcome the opportunity for a meeting provided by his passage through the Suez Canal. Aware of the likely furious opposition to his plan – Egypt had been ostracized by the Arab world for more than six years since Sadat's visit to Israel – he did not even share his secret with Khalil al-Wazir, his most trusted lieutenant, who had battled with him in Tripoli to the end. 'I went to Cairo,' he says today, 'to convey a message to the world . . . that if they thought that they were able to get rid of us, they were very wrong . . . in addition I felt there was a need for a big step which would overturn the table, and by going to Egypt I overturned the table.'[2]

That Arafat was willing to risk further fragmenting his movement at this time was a measure of his almost desperate need for new friends and supporters. It was also an indication of the importance he had always attached to Egypt as the Arab world's leading power. Was it not an Egyptian President, Nasser, who had made it possible for him to take over the PLO in the first place? Had Nasser not, as his final act, rescued the movement from destruction in the Jordanian civil war? Had his successor, Sadat, not helped Arafat towards recognition as representative of the Palestinians? Now it was time to make a fresh start. If, by 'overturning the table', he risked further enraging his critics then so be it. Things could hardly get worse.

Arafat was met, when his vessel docked at Port Said, by Mohammed Sobhieh, a long-time loyalist and Cairo resident who was Secretary General of the Palestine National Council. It was hardly a red-carpet reception but Arafat's pulse quickened, nevertheless, at coming back to Egypt after a frustrating six-year absence. 'He was very tired, and full of pain,' recalls Sobhieh. 'But he was also looking forward to renewing personal contacts with the Egyptian leadership.'[3]

As Arafat sailed down the Suez Canal to Ismailia to a formal welcome, he was briefed by Sobhieh and by Nabil Shaath, both of whom had liaised closely with Egyptian officials throughout the Tripoli affair. Appalled by the Syrian-backed onslaught against the organization's leadership, Egypt would do what it could to assist the PLO mainstream to get back on its feet.

In Ismailia, Arafat was greeted by a bevy of top Egyptian officials before being flown by military helicopter the hundred or so kilometres to President Mubarak's administrative headquarters in Heliopolis. It was in every sense a homecoming, for Arafat flew over the street where he had lived and where his family still owns an apartment. Rendered homeless twice in the previous fifteen months by Israeli and Arab antagonists, he could barely contain his elation.

The return to Cairo had been carefully calculated. Arafat, the conciliator, had never been one to allow any estrangement to become final. Indeed, his desire to keep lines open to the widest range of contacts had given rise to wry jokes among his colleagues. In one of them, Arafat is on the *haj*, the Muslim pilgrimage to Mecca. Arriving in the valley of Mina for the ritual stoning of the images of the devil, he does not throw his full allotment of seven stones. Asked why, he replies: 'I don't think we should close the door to anybody.'[4]

In this vein, even at the height of the public acrimony between the PLO and Egypt over Sadat's peace treaty with Israel, Arafat had maintained secret contacts through trusted aides like Mohammed Sobhieh. When Sadat was assassinated, he had discreetly telephoned the new president to congratulate him on his succession. Mubarak, for his part, had shown support for the PLO since the Israeli invasion of Lebanon and during the encirclement of Beirut had angered the Israelis by collaborating with France in a diplomatic initiative calling for PLO participation in peace talks. Now he might reap some reward in the Arab world by extending a welcome to Arafat. Simultaneously, he might quieten criticism within Egypt that the government was not doing enough for the Palestinians.

No sooner had Arafat's helicopter come to rest in the grounds of Kubbeh Palace – where a succession of rulers held court before the overthrow of the monarchy in 1952 – than the chunky figure of the Egyptian president stepped forward to greet him. As the television cameras zeroed in, Mubarak clasped Arafat in a bearhug before taking him off for two hours of private talks in his study. There were no illusions on either side about the problems the visit would cause. Ahmed Abdel Rahman, Arafat's spokesman, observed in casual conversation with senior Egyptian officials that the meeting would cause 'big problems' in the PLO. 'You think you will have problems,' shot back one of the Egyptians. 'It is we who will have problems with Israel.'[5] The Israelis, anxiously observing this dalliance between their newfound 'friends' in Cairo and their

No. 1 enemy, duly obliged by condemning the Mubarak-Arafat talks as a 'severe blow to the peace process in the Middle East'.[6]

The meeting had, however, served the two leaders' purposes tolerably well. For Arafat, it was a public relations coup of major proportions. He emerged from the talks to declare theatrically that he had invited the Egyptian president to join him in prayer at the al-Aqsa mosque in Jerusalem, although he did not elaborate on how or when he planned to achieve this implausible feat. Mubarak simply told reporters that the Arafat visit showed that 'Egypt has been vindicated', and 'It was right all along.'[7]

Within the Palestinian movement, such blunt words only served to inflame Arafat's critics. As he was whisked back to the *Odysseus Elytis*, a storm of protest broke. From Damascus, a host of factions issued furious statements condemning Arafat's 'treasonous' behaviour and calling for his removal. Even Arafat's closest friends had found his latest manoeuvre inexplicable. It reduced Khalil al-Wazir to near-impotent rage. One of the least demonstrative of Palestinian leaders, Wazir fell back on what had become a familiar rebuke at moments of extreme frustration with his old friend: 'How could you do this to us, brother?'[8]

To men like Wazir, Arafat seemed to be cutting himself adrift. He had not deigned to consult them before his Egyptian stopover, and he stayed out of touch as his ship continued its voyage down the Red Sea. Even the ship seemed to have lost its way, for its captain was having great difficulty in locating Arafat's destination: the North Yemeni port of Hodeida. Instead of making straight for the eastern shore of the Red Sea, the Greek vessel – running low on water and with its air conditioning turned off – sailed mistakenly westward towards Port Sudan. Confusion reigned for a few hours. The *Odysseus* seemed a fitting symbol for the state of the PLO itself – wandering aimless and demoralized after the 'war of independence', with a captain whose navigational skills were now open to serious question.

But whatever his colleagues thought, Arafat had not lost his bearings. On board ship, he even permitted himself a wry smile at the unfolding row over his Cairo trip. Even in his latest and least promising voyage into exile, he was not being denied the oxygen of publicity. More to the point, his visit to Cairo had drawn strong support from an increasingly important constituency: Palestinian leaders in the Israeli-occupied West Bank and Gaza Strip. Throughout Arafat's travails, they were the one group who had stood by him constantly. They were also becoming a force to be reckoned with in their own right. It was time for the PLO leader to harness their influence in rebuilding his shattered organization and his own prestige.

Briefing a reporter on board the *Odysseus*, Arafat declared that the organization would now focus its attention much more on the West Bank and Gaza Strip and mused vaguely about renewing his joint peace efforts with King Hussein of Jordan.[9]

In Sanaa, capital of North Yemen, Arafat paused briefly to rally his dispirited troops, then headed back to Tunis and an icy reception from Senior Fatah colleagues. He was neither surprised nor unduly concerned. The only way for the PLO to break out of its dangerous isolation, Arafat believed, was to take risks. Meeting in Tunis in the first week of 1984, the ten-member Fatah Central Committee meekly declared that Arafat's Cairo visit had been a breach of the principle of collective leadership, and sought to limit his freedom of manoeuvre. It was a weak response to a move that had, after all, left official PLO policy concerning Egypt in tatters; and deep down Arafat's colleagues knew that he was no more likely to heed their strictures now than on the many occasions in the past when they had tried and failed to rein him in.

The most important decision taken that week dealt with a quite different subject: Jordan. Arafat and King Hussein had not been speaking since the acrimonious breakdown of their negotiations the previous year. Now the Central Committee gave the PLO leader the mandate he wanted to resume contacts with his old sparring partner. Admittedly, it laid down important conditions, rejecting the Reagan plan of 1 September 1982, which called for an autonomous Palestinian homeland in confederation with Jordan, and insisting that any agreement with Jordan must provide, without qualification, for the establishment of an independent Palestinian state in the occupied territories. But such caveats were of little moment to Arafat. What mattered was that the top leadership of Fatah had given him the go-ahead to rebuild the troubled marriage between Jordan and the Palestinians, essential if he was to stand any chance of reviving his demoralized movement and involving it in Middle East peace moves. The pro-Western Hussein was Arafat's ticket to respectability and even, perhaps, to recognition by the United States.

Sensing that another opportunity had presented itself for him to court Arafat, King Hussein on 16 January reconvened his parliament after a ten-year suspension and in a speech to the opening session called on the PLO to agree on a 'practical formula'[10] for Middle East peace negotiations, leaving no doubt as to what he thought that formula should be. In the gossip-prone Jordanian capital, a fresh appearance by Arafat began to seem an inevitability.

But before mending the breach with Jordan, Arafat's most pressing task was to revive the demoralized PLO. Shaken to its very foundations by the 'war of independence', the splintered organization could hardly have been in worse shape to confront its many challenges. Arafat also knew that an exceptional effort was required to shore up his own position as leader. To this end he had begun working from the day of his removal from Tripoli on convening a meeting of the Palestinian 'parliament', the

Palestine National Council. But it was to take him most of the year to drag his squabbling and depleted ranks to Amman for such a gathering.

That January, the dogged Khalil al-Wazir persuaded Arafat to sanction an all-out effort to unify PLO ranks in the face of concerted Syrian and Libyan attempts to create an alternative leadership. Always intensely sceptical of Arafat's high-wire diplomacy, Wazir argued that unless the organization put its house in order it would be in no position to address the challenges of the day. Somehow the lie had to be given to Syria's argument that Arafat had forsaken the Palestinian consensus. Logically, that would entail trying to achieve a reconciliation at least with the two main Damascus-based splinters – the Popular and Democratic Fronts for the Liberation of Palestine.

Given the depth of animosity to be overcome, the reconciliation effort, in which both Algeria and South Yemen acted as mediators, moved with surprising speed. Early in July, Arafat was able to announce, in a message marking the end of Ramadan, that he was back on speaking terms with George Habash and Nayef Hawatmeh of the Popular and Democratic Fronts.[11] The reconciliation did not mean, however, that all was sweetness and light in the Palestinian movement – Fatah rebels wanted no part of the process and nor, of course, did their Syrian and Libyan masters.

The fragile consensus was enshrined in a set of agreements, announced on 13 July and named the Aden-Algiers Accords. These laid down detailed ground rules for the future conduct of the PLO's component factions and contained numerous clauses aimed at ensuring that Arafat would henceforth toe the party line on such vexed issues as relations with Egypt and Jordan.[12] That, at least, was the theory. In practice, not many months would pass before Arafat was bending and stretching the agreement to an extent which rendered it almost meaningless.

The Aden-Algiers agreements were significant in another respect: in their sharp focus on the occupied territories.

Article 1 dealt at length with the need to pour maximum resources into confronting the Israeli occupation, urging 'every kind of support to the struggle of our people in the occupied territories against Israeli occupation, its repressive terroristic measures, and escalating attempts to expropriate the land, to build settlements and expel the population in preparation for annexing the occupied territories'.[13] During the years in Jordan and Lebanon, the leadership had paid insufficient attention to the problems of the Palestinians under occupation. Distracted by delusions of power and involvement in two civil wars, Arafat and his fellow faction leaders had only sporadically worked on building grassroots support and stiffening resistance to Israeli rule in the territories, but when the PLO had come under increasing pressure in Lebanon and the armed struggle looked ever more forlorn and aimless, the occupied territories had begun to seem the most promising battleground.

None of the PLO factions had been more successful on this front than Arafat's Fatah. As the largest grouping in the organization it had much greater resources to devote to the territories than the others, and also had a determined organizer, in the person of Khalil al-Wazir. After 1981, Wazir, commander of the so-called Western Sector of PLO operations that specifically includes the West Bank and the Gaza Strip, had devoted more and more of his time to the occupied territories. His mission was, in his words, to create a 'parallel authority [to the Israelis] reaching from the kindergarten to the grave'.[14]

With Arafat's approval, he had maintained a vast network of contacts. He had built a detailed personal archive of thousands of individuals throughout the West Bank and Gaza and kept in touch with Palestinian prisoners inside Israeli jails, even devising ways to establish communications between the prisons themselves. After the PLO's expulsion from Lebanon in 1982, he had quietly rented a house in Amman, from where he was in virtual daily contact with his agents across the Jordan river. With his guidance, Fatah had penetrated many of the institutions that had formed in Palestinian society under Israeli rule: it dominated the student organizations, the unions, the press and the women's groups.

Arafat had long viewed Israel's policy of establishing Jewish settlements in the territories as a dire threat, understanding very well that the Israeli right was intent on creating a colonial *fait accompli*, in open defiance of the Americans, with a view to establishing permanent control. Hadn't the publication in the spring of 1984 of an authoritative Israel study of the territories confirmed the worst fears of the Tunis leadership? Funded by liberal American institutions, the report had reached the gloomy conclusion that Israeli settlement activity had passed the point of no-return, and that Israel's 'creeping annexation' of the territories was becoming irreversible.[15]

In the months after his expulsion from Tripoli, Arafat was once again in perpetual motion. Life in Tunis was too dull for him to want to be there for more than a few days at a time, and likewise he refused to become bogged down in the tedious process of Palestinian reconciliation. That was left to his lieutenants, while Arafat dabbled in international diplomacy. By mid-year, he had helped Egypt return to the Islamic Conference Organization, the umbrella grouping for Islamic countries worldwide. He had quixotically offered to mediate again in the Gulf war, then at its fiercest, although he had long since ceased to be a welcome guest in Iran. But the appearance of frenetic activity was deceptive. In reality, Arafat was simply marking time, waiting for the moment to relaunch his peace duet with King Hussein, and anxiously watching developments in Israel where early opinion polls indicated that elections to be held in July would be won by the Labour Party led by Shimon Peres.

The PLO leader was in no doubt that the poll would have a crucial bearing on chances for peace negotiations which he badly wanted to join. A Labour victory under the relatively conciliatory Peres promised progress; a win by Likud under the hard-line Yitzhak Shamir would spell deadlock. Neither occurred. After weeks of unseemly haggling over the formation of a coalition government following a deadlocked election, Peres and Shamir uneasily joined forces in the oddly named 'Government of National Unity'. It was hardly the most propitious development for two Arab leaders intent on another burst of peace-making. By the autumn of 1984 Arafat and Hussein, for better or worse, were set on a new tryst, to be followed by an uneasy wedding, and ultimately by a messy divorce.

For Arafat, a nagging question remained: how was he to bring his movement along with him to the altar? What he needed was a meeting of the PLO 'parliament'. What he seemed to lack was a venue for the proposed session, and a quorum of delegates. Plenty of people were set on preventing a conference that might serve to shore up Arafat's battered leadership and none was more determined than his old foe, President Hafez al-Assad of Syria. If he could not unseat Arafat by fomenting violent insurrection in his own ranks, then he had other cards to play. In September 1984, Assad took the unusual step of leaving his Damascus stronghold and flying to Algeria to implore President Chadli Benjedid not to host Arafat's proposed parliamentary session. Benjedid acquiesced.

From that point on, the Arab world indulged in overheated speculation about the venue for the PLO meeting. Arafat's ability to convene the PNC with the necessary quorum of two-thirds of the body's 384 members – without the attendance of the Damascus-based groups – was rapidly coming to be seen as a gauge of his leadership. Jokingly, Arafat began to tell anyone who would listen that he would hold the session 'on board a ship' in the Mediterranean if all else failed. That would not be necessary, as Arafat was fully aware. He had long since decided where he wanted to hold the PNC: in the Jordanian capital, Amman.

Presiding over a public meeting in Amman would give him access to a potential daily television audience of more than two million Palestinians in the occupied territories and in Israel itself. Such an event would have an electrifying effect in what had become his most prized constituency. By seeking to deny him other venues for the meeting, Arafat's enemies were merely playing into his hands.

So the stage was set for Arafat, the consummate actor, to play one of his crowning roles, ably supported by that other noted Arab thespian, Hussein bin Talal. Broadcasting from Aden on 12 November, the Voice of Palestine radio station proclaimed: 'The leadership has defined with courage, clarity and finality, that 22 November will be the final date for the convocation of the PNC, and that Amman will be the capital in which the PNC's 17th session will be held.'[16] It sounded like a fairground announcement.

On the evening of 22 November, in a sports complex on the rocky hills of Amman, King Hussein officially opened the first large-scale PLO gathering to be held in the Jordanian capital in fourteen years. An extraordinary spectacle greeted the select few journalists and diplomats who witnessed the opening session. Seated in the audience were more than a few ageing revolutionaries whose bloodcurdling threats against King Hussein's life following Black September of 1970 had seemed to preclude any prospect of reconciliation. And yet here they were, back in Amman, listening attentively to a man many of them, including Arafat himself, had dubbed the 'butcher'. Here was Salah Khalaf, the enigmatic godfather of the Black September terrorist organization, who had, by his own admission, sought more than once to do away with Hussein. Here, patrolling the perimeter of the sports complex to protect the delegates, were Hussein's tough Bedu legionnaires who, not many years before, had been shooting PLO guerrillas on sight in the streets of Amman.

Speaking with force and resonance for thirty minutes but never once raising his voice, Hussein called on the

PLO to abandon 'stagnation'. More pointedly, he urged the Palestinians to embrace Security Council resolution 242 'as a basis for a just and peaceful settlement'.[17] The king could not be accused of failing to address the most difficult issue head-on.

For Hussein, acceptance of Resolution 242, with its implied recognition of Israel's right to exist behind pre-1967 war boundaries, was, and is, the *sine qua non* for solving the Arab-Israeli conflict. But for many among his audience, the Resolution's rightful place was in the chamber of conspiracies against Palestinian rights; along with the Balfour Declaration, the Sykes-Picot Agreement, the UN Partition Plan of 1947 and the Camp David Accords. Not that the content of Hussein's speech seemed to matter much at the time. It only came to seem important when the euphoria of the occasion had worn off and the serious talking began.

Arafat had his own role to play, and he played it for all it was worth: to his immediate audience in Amman; to his enemies in Damascus; and, most important, to the people in the next important theatre of PLO operations – the West Bank and the Gaza Strip. 'We are only some kilometres away from our Palestine,' he declared with emotion[18] – all too well aware that while this might be literally true, the PLO was light years away from sitting down at the same table and negotiating with Israel and further still from reclaiming one inch of territory. As so often in the past, illusions were almost more important than substance.

Never mind: Arafat had his own very specific aims. He wanted to prepare for a new peace initiative whose immediate aim was to secure American recognition of Palestinian rights and a clear acknowledgement of the PLO's status as the spokesman of the Palestinians. He wanted to bolster his working relationship with Hussein and Jordan, partly as a cover for the PLO's burgeoning links with the neighbouring occupied territories. Above all, he wanted to shore up his own position as leader in the face of continuing demands from Damascus, and of rumbling criticism of his autocratic leadership style from within the ranks. He chose a characteristically melodramatic means of doing so.

Following some harsh words at a late session about his refusal to consult colleagues, he theatrically tendered his resignation. It was not the first time Arafat had threatened to quit in order to get his way, but he added an additional note of drama to the occasion by inviting his colleagues to 'change this donkey'[19] – a highly pejorative term for Arabs, who regard a donkey as an exceptionally lowly and stupid creature. It was about as close as Arafat would come to apparently serious self-criticism. To increase the drama, he left his resignation on the table throughout the night and into the next day. When the session resumed, Arafat sat quietly in the third row of the audience, fiddling distractedly with his black and white chequered head-dress. He would not be moved, or so he pretended. Selim Zaanoun, an old student friend and deputy speaker of the PNC, was obliged to abandon the session's formal agenda to implore him to withdraw his resignation. 'You do not own yourself,' Zaanoun declared, his voice quivering with emotion. 'You belong to the Palestinian people.'[20]

At that moment a group of elderly refugee camp leaders in traditional Arab garb appeared, like pallbearers at a funeral. They half-carried and half-dragged an unresisting Arafat to the speaker's rostrum. Milking the occasion, he said he would consider withdrawing his resignation, but only because the 'conspiracy' mounted by Syria and the Fatah mutineers was directed not only against himself but against the whole PLO. 'You are the only people who can ask me to stay or leave,' he declared. 'Not this or that Arab regime.'[21] He spoke bitterly of threats from enemies abroad. Hadn't they all heard the bombs that had exploded in Amman in the past few days? Wasn't there a Libyan Sukhoi bomber standing by in Syrian-controlled eastern Lebanon awaiting to attack the conference centre itself?

Standing before his brethren in his familiar khaki uniform, the pudgy Arafat came to the nub of the issue. 'You, the members of the Palestine National Council who represent the legitimacy of the Palestinian people,' he declared, 'you are the ones who can decide: you can say Abu Ammar go, or Abu Ammar stay.'[22]

It was, of course, the cue for a swelling chorus of 'Abu Ammar stay, Abu Ammar stay'. Humbly, Arafat bowed to their blandishments. 'I have no house,' he said. 'I am a soldier of the revolution. I am the last to disobey orders.'[23] The observation brought wry smiles to the faces of some of his senior colleagues who had conspicuously failed over many years to curb Arafat's maverick tendencies, but the gambit had worked. Ever the showman, Arafat had stage-managed his own re-acclamation as leader of the Palestinians: an imperfect symbol, but the only one they had.

In Damascus, the show of support for Arafat caused extreme irritation. Syria's attempts to block the parliamentary session had failed, and so, too, had its half-baked efforts to mount a rival television show to the one being beamed daily via Jordan Television to the Palestinians in the territories. Particularly infuriating was the fact that many of the 250,000 or so Palestinians living in Syria itself spent their days glued to Jordanian broadcasts. If the 1984 PNC, boycotted by all the Damascus-based groups, was one more *coup de théâtre* in the long internal struggle over Arafat's stewardship of the Palestinian movement, its most visible external manifestation was the 'battle of the airwaves', and the winner was not in doubt. In the manipulation of this sort of occasion Arafat has few equals.

While Syria wheeled forward a shadowy bunch of mutineers to denounce a 'traitorous Arafat', the PLO's mainstream leadership was appearing in Palestinian living rooms all over the region, seen to be engaged, for the most part, in constructive and open debate. Typical of reaction in the territories was this simple observation from a young man in Dheisheh refugee camp outside Jerusalem: 'I touched this [Palestinian] democracy through television,' he told reporters.[24] A correspondent for the Israeli daily, *Haaretz*, observed that: 'For the first time people could watch the PLO in action for themselves. Not only could they watch the PNC in Amman on Jordanian television, but at the same time they could tune in and see the anti-Arafat PLO people speaking in Damascus on Syrian television. Arafat's popularity benefited enormously from this comparison. People could see the PNC with the moderate debates and the speeches and then watch this lunatic fringe in Damascus and see how all they wanted to do was hold Arafat back.'[25] In predictable counterpoint, Israel's Foreign Minister Yitzhak Shamir sourly observed that the performance had brought closer the 'voice of the PLO terrorist organization'.[26]

Arafat himself ended the week's deliberations on a defiant note. Speaking at a final, triumphal press conference before flying off to Saudi Arabia to brief King Fahd on the results of the meeting, he sharply criticized Syria and the Palestinian mutineers. 'We are determined,' he declared, 'that this fascism will not drive us from our democratic ideals. We will preserve our ideals in this jungle of guns.'[27]

Before the year was out, Arafat and his lieutenants were to be reminded yet again that the 'jungle of guns' still had the power to disrupt and intimidate. On 29 December, Fahd Kawasmeh, the deported former mayor of Hebron in the West Bank, and one of the new members of the PLO's Executive Committee, was gunned down in Amman. Khalil al-Wazir immediately charged that the killing had been directed from Damascus. It was a quick and bloody riposte from Arafat's enemies, which punctured the euphoria that had accompanied his theatrical 're-election'.

But the Amman meeting had served its purpose nonetheless. As Arafat saw it, the way was now clear for a joint peace initiative with King Hussein that might bring him closer to his cherished goal: a direct and open dialogue with the United States. Their efforts to agree on a new peace formula took on particular urgency, as King Fahd was due to visit Washington in the second week of February 1985. Both Arafat and Hussein had resolved – naively, as it turned out – that the Saudi monarch was the man to present their peace proposal to the Americans.

Fahd was well aware of the PLO-Jordanian efforts to agree on a new peace initiative. He had been kept separately informed by both sides of stuttering attempts to draft an agreement. He was also intensely sceptical about the likelihood of the two coming up with a form of words that would satisfy the Palestinian consensus, the Jordanians and the Americans. He was proved right, but not before Hussein and Arafat, on the very day he was due to have his fireside chat with Reagan, took a clumsy stab at drafting a formula acceptable to all.

# 14
# *The Odd Couple*

> 'After two long attempts, I and the government of the Kingdom of Jordan hereby announce that we are unable to co-ordinate politically with the PLO leadership until such a time as their word becomes their bond, characterized by commitment, credibility and constancy.' King Hussein, address to the nation, 19 February 1986.

It was mid-morning on a sunny winter's day. Yasser Arafat, in his bullet-proof limousine, swept through the heavily guarded entrance to al-Nadwa palace and King Hussein's Bedu guards, in their red chequered *keffiyehs*, saluted smartly as the cavalcade roared up the pine-clad hill overlooking the old city of Amman.

It was a route Arafat had traversed more times than he cared to remember in his long, fractious relationship with the moody Jordanian monarch. Many of his visits to the palace had simply been courtesy calls but this occasion, he had no doubt, would be strictly business. Hussein expected agreement on a new peace initiative to flow from their deliberations that day. Arafat, too, was anxious to reach an understanding. It was 11 February 1985, a date that would go down as one of the most controversial in PLO history.

Hussein greeted Arafat cordially in the embrace Arab etiquette demanded. The two men exchanged pleasantries before adjourning with their advisers for a round of discussions. Talk continued at a good-humoured lunch in which Hussein and Arafat, flanked by their aides, sat facing one another. Underlying all the civilities was a sense of urgency. It was the day of King Fahd's visit to Washington. Both men were possessed of the need to come up with something he could pass on to Reagan and after more than two months of talks, they knew they were little closer to their goal than when they started.

Debate had focused on the same old troublesome issue: Resolution 242 and an independent Palestinian state. The Jordanians, seeking to placate American demands, would seek acceptance of 242 and the PLO would resist. The Palestinians, insisting on their key demands, would try to include the words 'independent state' and 'self-determination', and Jordan would refuse. As described by Taher al-Masri, then Jordan's Foreign Minister, it was an elaborate and uneasy word game involving a host of competing interests. 'We were always trying to find the right formulation of words to satisfy the PLO and make the draft palatable to the US,' he recalls. 'The PLO was worried how the Syrians, the Soviets and their opponents in the organization would react to such a draft.'[1] The two sides also haggled about the terms of a confederation between the kingdom of Jordan and a theoretical Palestinian government in the West Bank and Gaza. Round in circles they went, watched with obsessive interest in the salons of Amman.

The jockeying between Hussein and Arafat continued that February day over a three-course lunch, but during a gap in the conversation, Hussein reached for a menu and scribbled down some points in Arabic. He handed the menu across the table to Arafat who, reading it quickly, declared: 'This is excellent.' Thus, at the eleventh hour they agreed on a compromise formula that would seek to be all things to all men. They need not have bothered. When King Fahd called on President Reagan in Washington later in the day, he did not even mention the agreement. As the Saudis subsequently explained, much to the consternation of the Palestinians and the Jordanians, Fahd was 'not going to embarrass himself again with a US President' with a document signed by Arafat alone and not endorsed by the Executive Committee of the PLO. He had been let down by the PLO leader before.[2]

In Amman, public confusion reigned about what Hussein and Arafat had actually agreed and it continued for several days, the time it took to translate the king's Arabic scrawl on the lunch menu into a publishable document. When Arafat's colleagues were apprised of the details, they were horrified. To their dismay, there was no specific reference to 'an independent Palestinian state' either within or outside a Palestinian-Jordanian confederation. Instead, the issue was obscured in a tangle of verbiage.

Hussein's skills as a legal draftsman certainly did not match his ability as an orator. The key section of the five-point accord – Article 2 – was a piece of gobbledegook that really did read as though it had been scribbled on the back of a menu: 'Palestinians will exercise their inalienable right of self-determination when Jordanians and Palestinians will be able to do so within the context of the formation of the proposed confederated Arab states of Jordan and Palestine.'[3] In agreeing to this, as on so many occasions in the past, the equivocating Arafat had sought to reinterpret PLO policy to suit his own ends.

After several stormy sessions with his colleagues in Tunis, who had all along been opposed to the exercise, an exasperated Arafat despatched Salah Khalaf and Mahmoud Abbas (Abu Mazen), a senior Fatah cadre, back to Amman in March to discuss amendments with the king. A secret codicil was agreed that would make a clear distinction between 'two states of Jordan and Palestine' within a wider *dawlati*, or confederation.

Within the PLO, however, opposition to the Amman accord only grew as its terms became more widely known. Scarcely was the ink dry on the document than Abdel Latif Abu Hijleh, better known by his *nom de guerre*, Abu Jaafar, the veteran director of the PLO's Political Department, or

'Foreign Ministry', was sending messages to PLO diplomatic missions advising them to work against it. A furious Arafat carpeted him in a tense five-hour discussion. 'I don't blame you officially; you have the right to speak out against the accord within the PLO, but I do blame you for expressing this view outside.'[4]

More damaging still, contradictory public interpretations were already circulating in Tunis and Amman about what the accord actually meant. Taher Hikmat, Jordan's Information Minister, stated baldly on 23 February that the PLO had accepted Resolution 242. The PLO Executive Committee had, in fact, that very week repeated its longstanding opposition to the UN resolution.

The inauspicious birth of their joint initiative did not deter Hussein and Arafat from seeking to market it far and wide. Arafat led a delegation to China. Hussein visited Washington in an attempt to interest the Americans, whose reaction had been, to say the least, luke-warm. Taher al-Masri toured the Arab world as part of a joint delegation with PLO officials in an effort to garner support.

But the Arab world had very quickly formed its own negative judgement about the Hussein-Arafat stratagem, and Masri could hardly stir a flicker of interest. Typical was the reception in Algeria, where the government listened politely but gave neither publicity nor encouragement to his mission. Nor was the PLO leadership 100 per cent engaged in the effort. In Algeria, Masri was surprised and not a little irritated by the unexplained absence of the senior PLO military commander, Khalil al-Wazir. His links with the Algerians were very close and he had been expected to attend. Masri's queries as to his whereabouts met vague replies from PLO officials. It would soon become clear what had diverted him.

Deprived of their land bases in Lebanon, Wazir and the PLO leadership were still anxious to keep up their attacks on Israel. In the circumstances, they concluded they had no choice but to give more attention to seaborne operations. So it was that at the end of the second week of April 1985, Wazir gave a final briefing to Fatah naval units aboard the *Atavarius*, a PLO-owned vessel at a naval base outside Algiers – at the very moment when Masri was in Algiers fruitlessly trying to sell the Amman accord.

What was planned was one of the PLO's most audacious missions. The commandos, who had received extensive training in Algiers, were to attack the General Staff Headquarters of the Israeli Army in Tel Aviv, one of the most heavily guarded installations in all of Israel, to take hostages and demand the release of Fatah prisoners in Israeli jails.

The PLO's top leadership had its own special reasons for wanting a spectacular success. It was hoping to lay to rest once and for all the heavy criticism it was under from inside Fatah and from radical splinters who were accusing it of meekly abandoning armed struggle. But dreams of a major coup to silence the critics were in vain.

On the night of 20–21 April, the *Atavarius* was blasted out of the water after an exchange of gunfire with an Israeli naval vessel. Of the twenty-eight on board, only eight survived and were taken prisoner after an Israeli ship-to-ship missile literally tore the *Atavarius* apart. Wazir later told the Saudi daily *Al-Sharq al-Awsat*, that the mission had countered the impression that the PLO was going soft. '. . . In fact political activity does not preclude continuation of military actions,' he declared.[5] Little did either Wazir or Arafat realize it at the time, but the failed *Atavarius* mission would mark the beginning of one of the bloodiest terrorist years on record in and around the Mediterranean – a year that would also witness an event which would bring great discredit to the PLO in the court of American opinion.

Even before the blood was spilled, the Amman accord was heading for the rocks. During April, Arafat had received the unwelcome news from Jordan that Hussein had replaced his prime minister with a man whose history reeked of antagonism towards the PLO. Perhaps assuming that his joint initiative with Arafat was doomed, Hussein brought back his childhood friend, Zeid al-Rifai. The ostensible reason for replacing the traditionalist Ahmed Obeidat was that he had shown little enthusiasm for the Amman accord and that this was affecting US support. A more plausible explanation was to be found in the *realpolitik* of King Hussein himself. In the deadly game of musical chairs that passes for diplomacy in the Arab world, he had decided to improve his shaky relations with his northern neighbour, Syria. Rifai, who had long-standing Syrian connections, was the man for the job. If the Jordanian reconciliation with Damascus was at the expense of Arafat's PLO, then so be it.

Assad was as set as ever on undermining Arafat, and opposition to the Amman accord among radical Palestinian groups provided him with additional ammunition. In late March, Damascus had acted as midwife to the formation of a new Palestinian body, grouping six of the factions under its umbrella in a new anti-Arafat Palestine National Salvation Front. The inclusion of George Habash's Popular Front, which had remained, for the most part, on the sidelines during the Fatah mutiny of 1983, gave the new group a veneer of credibility.

But Syria's relations with even its most obedient Palestinian clients came under tremendous strain in late May and early June when what became known as the 'Camps War' in Lebanon erupted. In a sickening spectacle, the Syrian-backed Shi'ite Amal militia, aided by Shi'ite units of the Lebanese Army, laid siege to the squalid Palestinian refugee camps of Sabra and Shatila, and Bourj el-Brajneh. Less than three years after the massacres of Sabra and Shatila, the inhabitants of these ill-fated shanty settlements again came under assault, only this time the assailants were using heavy weapons and tanks.

The immediate target of the attack was Arafat's fighters who had slipped back into Lebanon after their expulsion at the hands of the Israelis in 1982. But for Assad, it was another opportunity to get at Arafat himself. Hundreds, including women and children, died in the bloody siege.

Arafat's bitterness towards Assad knew no bounds. 'The plot . . . has been aimed at the Palestinian existence in Lebanon,' he told the Kuwaiti daily *Al-Qabas* early in June. 'To control the Palestinian gun, they must expel Palestinians from Beirut and southern Lebanon.'[6] In the long run, far from serving Syria's interests, the attacks unified Palestinian ranks.

Dreadful as the scenes in Beirut were, the Arab world paid little attention. Arab leaders had other preoccupations. Hussein, for one, was still absorbed in his attempts to engage a reluctant US administration in a renewed peace drive, but he got little encouragement. Earlier in May, Secretary of State George Shultz had toured the Middle East in an effort to find 'safe' non-PLO Palestinians to join a Jordanian team in negotiations with Israel. But it was a fruitless process that came more and more to resemble a child's game of pinning the tail on the donkey.

In Peking, Arafat used one of his well-worn metaphors to decry Shultz's insipid diplomacy. 'They are still trying to hide the sun with their finger,' he declared, 'neglecting realities and facts in the area.'[7]

Hussein's Washington visit did produce a minor flurry when he declared at a press conference in the White House Rose Garden on 29 May that the PLO had agreed that the peace talks be conducted under the 'umbrella' of an international conference and on the basis of 'pertinent UN resolutions, including Security Council Resolutions 242 and 338'.[8] In US diplomat-speak, Hussein's intervention became known as the 'Rose Garden' statement, as if the location added fresh fragrance to tired words. In Tunis, Arafat's colleagues were more than a little surprised that Hussein had presumed to make such a bald statement on their behalf, indicating PLO acceptance of 242 and 338; but for the moment, and uncharacteristically, they kept their counsel.

American diplomacy was briefly energized after the Hussein visit, and so, too, was Israeli Labour leader Shimon Peres in his desire to initiate a process that would help to reduce Israel's post-1982 isolation in international forums. But by the autumn, and in the absence of a strong American push, it was clear there was very little of substance behind all the diplomatic toing and froing. Commitment was simply lacking at the top.

Typical of the stop-start US approach to Middle East diplomacy throughout 1985 was the visit to the region in mid-September of Richard Murphy, the State Department's top Middle East official, to conduct exploratory discussions with a joint Jordanian-Palestinian delegation as a step towards direct talks between Jordan and Israel. Shultz's man received a cold shoulder in Middle East capitals for his 'direct talks' proposal – not that he as an experienced Arabist should have been surprised – and so he abandoned his plans to meet representative Palestinians from the territories who were standing by in Amman. Another opportunity was lost.

Arafat and Hussein had, in any case, long since got the message that there was very little Arab support for their joint initiative. An emergency Arab summit in Casablanca in the autumn, boycotted by Syria and Libya among others, had pointedly not endorsed the Amman accord.

Into these unpromising waters waded Margaret Thatcher, Britain's redoubtable Prime Minister. On a visit to Jordan in the third week of September 1985, she told Hussein grandly that she would do her best to use her special relationship with Ronald Reagan to push the reluctant Americans into a more active role. She also offered to facilitate a meeting in London between PLO Palestinians – provided they were not known to have terrorist blood on their hands – and Geoffrey Howe, the British Foreign Secretary. The aim was to encourage PLO 'moderation' and as a *quid pro quo* to give credibility to Arafat's demands for a seat at the negotiating table. What was required, she declared, was that the PLO representatives sign an agreement implicitly recognizing Israel and renouncing terror. In the self-congratulatory atmosphere of Amman and in light of Thatcher's burgeoning friendship with Hussein, it must have seemed so simple.

Prime Minister Zeid al-Rifai and the British ambassador in Amman, a former Thatcher aide named John Coles, were instructed to draw up an acceptable form of words. The choice of Rifai for this delicate task, with his history of antipathy to the Arafat PLO, was not the most judicious step, as subsequent events would show, but even before Thatcher returned to London – and to congratulatory British press notices concerning her bold, new Middle East initiative – an event occurred that put all the pious talk about the quest for peace firmly in perspective.

Khalil al-Wazir and his Western Sector commanders, together with those of Force 17, Arafat's praetorian guard, had become increasingly agitated as the months passed in 1985 over Israel's repeated successes in interdicting PLO seaborne traffic in the eastern Mediterranean. The failure of the *Atavarius* mission in April was one example, but there were others that had affected both Western Sector missions planned for Israel itself and efforts by the two interlocking organizations to ferry men and weapons into Lebanon. This latter task had been made infinitely more urgent by the savage militia onslaught against Palestinian refugee camps in Beirut and in southern Lebanon: the need to bolster guerrilla strongholds in Lebanon was now paramount.

Fatah's dismal relations with Syria, which controlled the only feasible land route into Lebanon, made it absolutely essential to maintain a sea link. In this, the island of Cyprus, less than half a day's sailing from the Lebanese coast, was a vital way-station. It was also a place where the eyes and ears of myriad intelligence services – Western, East Bloc, Arab and Israeli – ceaselessly monitored comings and goings by air and by sea. Long a murky crossroads, Cyprus, in the last week of September, witnessed a cold-blooded slaying with fateful consequences.

On 25 September, Yom Kippur, the Jewish Day of Atonement, three gunmen of Arafat's Force 17 – two Arabs and a blond Briton – stormed an Israeli yacht lying at anchor in the crowded marina at Larnaca, a seedy resort town on Cyprus's south coast. The gunmen shot a woman passenger and subsequently two men on board. The PLO claimed that they were Israeli agents spying on ship movements in the Mediterranean, but Israel angrily denied the charge, and threatened vengeance.

Ahmed Abdel Rahman, the PLO's official spokesman, was shaving when the phone rang just before 10 a.m. on 1 October in his comfortable villa near the Tunis seashore. It was Arafat on the phone, calling from one of his safe houses elsewhere in the city. He was in a talkative mood. Abdel Rahman felt slightly irritated at the interruption. The two men had parted not many hours before after dining late at the elegant seafront residence of Hakem Belawi, the PLO's ambassador in Tunis. Now, Arafat wanted to review his day's schedule which included a discreet eleven o'clock meeting with London-based Arab opposition figures. All in all it promised to be a fairly leisurely day for the PLO leader in and around the Tunisian capital. But just as the two men were concluding their phone conversation they heard, simultaneously, a series of huge explosions from the direction of the PLO headquarters at Hammam Shatt, twenty kilometres south-east of the city on the Gulf of Tunis. They slammed down the phones and raced for their cars.

When Arafat arrived at what was left of his administrative headquarters he was confronted with an appalling sight. Three buildings used by the PLO, including his own offices, had been reduced to rubble by a clutch of attacking aircraft with the Star of David insignia on their tails. Dozens of people, including Palestinians and Tunisians – the final toll was seventy-three dead – had been killed and injured.[9]

Even in Tunis, 2000 kilometres from Tel Aviv as the crow flies, Arafat and his men were not safe from the long arm of Israeli retribution. And the attack could not have come at a worse moment, for relations between the Palestinians and their Tunisian hosts were at that point going through one of their periodic rough patches.

In Washington, Ronald Reagan insensitively praised Israeli 'intelligence capabilities', a remark that scarcely dampened PLO accusations of US complicity in what had manifestly been an attempt to kill Arafat himself. President Mubarak of Egypt, who had just returned to Cairo from Washington, described the bombing as a 'horrible criminal operation'[10] that aimed a major blow at peace efforts. The Security Council condemned the raid 14–0 with one abstention: the US.

It emerged later that at least six F-15 fighter bombers had streaked across the Mediterranean, fuelling in mid-air twice on the way, to drop their deadly payloads on the PLO headquarters. 'Israel,' a shaken Arafat declared as he peered into one of the craters left by a bomb, 'has bombed the peace process.'[11] Never one to miss an opportunity for myth-making, Arafat, who had slipped back into Tunis from Morocco the night before the bombing, put the word out that he was only saved from death because he was away from his headquarters 'jogging' when the raid had occurred. The PLO leader survived – and so did the oft-repeated legend about his 'nose for danger'.

Angry protests over the Israeli raid swirled about the Arab world for several days, only to submerge beneath acres of bad press about the PLO. The world was about to witness one of the messiest and most senseless acts in the long and bloody history of the Palestinian struggle. On 1 October, the same day the Israelis bombed Tunis, an Italian cruise liner, the 23,629-ton *Achille Lauro*, sailed from Genoa on a leisurely voyage around the Mediterranean. Among planned ports of call were Alexandria and the Israeli port city of Ashdod. Many different nationalities had joined the cruise, including a party of American Jews. Also on board were four desperate young men of the Palestine Liberation Front splinter group associated closely with Arafat's Fatah. Their suicide mission, as it later emerged, was to steal ashore in Ashdod in the dead of night and blow up oil storage tanks. They had also been instructed to seize hostages to be traded for the release of Palestinians in Israeli jails. But in the time between the sailing of the *Achille Lauro* from Alexandria and its arrival off Port Said at the entrance to the Suez Canal, something went hideously wrong.

While the *Achille Lauro* was off the coast of Egypt on 7 October, the four PLF gunmen rushed into the dining room, discharging their weapons. They then stormed the bridge and ordered Captain Gerardo de Rosa to sail north towards Syria. The episode was scarcely believable. Four young men, barely out of their teens, were holding hostage 427 passengers and 80 crew on board a large cruise liner steaming the Mediterranean. The world was transfixed. This was piracy on a grand scale. In Tunis, PLO leaders watched in amazement, and in growing dismay, as the seajacking unfolded amid rumours that at least one of the passengers had been killed.

Within a few hours of the story breaking, Mohammed Zaidan, better known as Abul Abbas, the Palestine Liberation Front leader and PLO Executive Committee member, was despatched to Egypt to sort out the mess. Zaidan, a big, raw-boned, tousle-headed Palestinian in his late thirties, wasted no time in summoning his men back from the brink of further disaster, instructing them to return forthwith to the waters off Port Said while negotiations continued on their safe passage out of Egypt. International opinion was outraged. Egypt was outraged. Arafat himself, who was in Senegal in West Africa, was under heavy pressure to intervene. On 8 October, he met the ambassadors of Egypt, France and Italy in Dakar. Ahmed Abdel Rahman, Arafat's spokesman, recalls that in a sometimes fraught and confused four-way discussion conducted in French, Italian, Arabic and English, the PLO leader agreed, as a way of defusing the crisis, to accept responsibility for the hijackers, and to 'discipline' them. At that moment, Rahman insists, neither he nor Arafat was aware that one of the passengers had been killed.[12] It was a situation Arafat had confronted many times before in his long stewardship of the fractious Palestinian movement, and he handled it little differently from other such terror episodes, denying advance knowledge and equally refusing to condemn.

When the *Achille Lauro* anchored off Port Said on 9 October, and American officials were able to go on board, the awful truth emerged. Leon Klinghoffer, a 69-year-old American Jew confined to a wheelchair, had been shot in cold blood and thrown overboard off the Syrian coast. So outraged was Nicholas Veliotes, the American ambassador, when he discovered what had happened that in a ship-to-shore conversation with his colleagues, he demanded that the hijackers, who had been spirited away, be brought to justice. 'You tell the foreign ministry that we demand they prosecute those sons of bitches,' he shouted down the phone.[13]

Coldly infuriated by what it regarded as a gross impertinence by a serving ambassador, Egypt had made arrangements to get the four hijackers and Zaidan himself out of the country as quickly as possible. The last thing the Cairo Government needed or wanted at a time when it was seeking to re-establish its Arab credentials was to come under pressure to put on trial a bunch of Palestinian desperadoes. But there were unaccountable delays. One story had it that Tunis was slow in giving clearance for an EgyptAir plane carrying the hijackers to land; another said that they had been refused passage through Jordan on their way to sanctuary in Iraq. Whatever the reason, the delays enabled the US to put in train an audacious and diplomatically risky plan that would cause dismay in Cairo and jubilation in the White House.

When the EgyptAir Boeing 737 eventually took off late on 9 October from the Al-Maza military airbase outside Cairo, pilot and crew were glad to be airborne. After a long and frustrating day standing by, they did not anticipate any problems on their three-hour flight across the Mediterranean, but President Reagan had other ideas. In what must rank as one of the more bizarre actions ever authorized by an American president, he ordered that a civilian plane belonging to a friendly country be forced down and those inside it detained. F-14 fighters from the USS *Saratoga* of the US Mediterranean Sixth Fleet were scrambled aloft. Guided by US Hawkeye radar aircraft, they made contact with the hapless EgyptAir Boeing as it cruised westward in the darkness, south of Crete.

Swooping round the passenger aircraft with their searchlights blazing, the US fighters forced the EgyptAir captain to land at Sigonella airbase in Sicily, and there the four hijackers and Zaidan were taken into custody by the Italian *carabinieri*. At the White House, Reagan could scarcely contain his glee. Like a boy who had just scored a hit in a computer game, the President of the United States declared: 'They can run, but they can't hide.'[14]

Some of the American euphoria dissipated in the cold light of day when Washington realized the extent to which its unorthodox action had angered and humiliated its main Arab ally – a furious President Mubarak accused the US of 'air piracy'.[15] And the Americans, who had begun attempts to extradite Zaidan, failed to get their man. To Washington's consternation, the Italians allowed him to slip quietly away to Yugoslavia.

A few days after the *Achille Lauro* affair came a further setback for Arafat's battered peace strategy, as if a sort of Palestinian Murphy's Law had taken over, and what could go wrong would. Two members of the PLO's 'cabinet', the Executive Committee, had arrived in London over the weekend of 12–13 October for the much-heralded meeting with Geoffrey Howe. But when Mohammed Milhem, the deported former mayor of the West Bank town of Halhoul, was shown the statement he was expected to sign, he hit the roof. It did not take Milhem, a fluent English speaker, more than a few seconds to realize that if he lent his name to the London document all hell would break loose in the PLO. He had no doubt that his own life would be in danger. Frantically, he attempted to get in touch with Arafat who was then on a visit to the Sudan. Not the least of his problems was securing a line to the Sudanese capital, whose decrepit phone system is among the most cantankerous in the whole of Africa.

Eventually, Milhem tracked Arafat down and was told bluntly that in no circumstances was he to sign the 'London declaration'. Inexplicably, this was the first time Arafat had been told of its details and he was no less astonished than Milhem when he learned of the declaration's contents; for not only did it include specific reference to Resolution 242; it also omitted any mention of an independent Palestinian state.

Together with his colleague, Bishop Elias Khouri, and Jordan's Foreign Minister, Taher al-Masri, Milhem met Stephen Egerton, a senior Foreign Office official, at the Dorchester on Sunday. Milhem sought radical changes, but Egerton insisted there could be no alteration in the wording. 'The statement stands, or there will be no statement,' he declared.[16]

That was by no means the end of the matter. King Hussein, fuming as he watched developments from his private residence outside London, made clear his grave displeasure with the PLO in several television interviews. He felt personal responsibility for the London fiasco. He had embarrassed his friend, Mrs Thatcher. Worse, his own personal undertakings had been shown to have been worthless. Coming as it did within days of the *Achille Lauro* affair, the episode was almost the last straw. 'At the end of the day Arafat didn't deliver, and that,' according to Taher al-Masri, 'was the beginning of the severing of relations between them.'[17]

There was, however, another explanation for the London fiasco and one that did not reflect at all favourably on the king's chief minister. Zeid al-Rifai, the draftsman of the contentious document, had, for reasons that remain unclear, merely shown it to the apolitical Bishop Khouri. He had not tested it on other more senior PLO officials in Amman such as Arafat's deputy, Khalil al-Wazir. By keeping its contents from those closest to Arafat, Rifai had virtually guaranteed that misunderstanding would result. His role hardly improved prospects for future co-operation between Arafat and the palace.

Smouldering over his difficulties with Arafat, Hussein was in any case engaged in new alliances. In mid-October, almost literally on the rebound from his troubled affair with Arafat, he travelled to Paris for secret talks with the Israeli Premier, Shimon Peres, one of many clandestine meetings between the two men over the years. The talks produced quick results: later that month, Peres presented the UN General Assembly with an offer of a peace partnership with Jordan. The result was a flurry of Israeli-Jordanian contacts, in which the two sides came close to establishing a 'condominium of interests' in the occupied territories.

On 10 November, the Jordanian press published an extraordinary letter from the king to his prime minister. Even by Hussein's own melodramatic standards, it was a curious document. In it he admitted Jordan's grievous errors in dealing with Syria – not least the assistance it had provided to the underground *Ikhwan* in its violent struggle to overthrow President Assad's regime. Hussein's *mea culpa* was the price of reconciliation with Damascus. The king, sensing that his initiative with Arafat was all but dead, had decided to cut his losses. He had also concluded that if there was to be any prospect of a Middle East peace process, Syria could not continue to be ignored. For Arafat, who had taken refuge in Baghdad after the Tunis bombing, Hussein's declaration was an ominous development. With the Jordanian monarch reaching out to Assad, the PLO leader was reminded once again of the fickleness of Arab friends.

To make matters worse, Arafat was in trouble in Egypt over the *Achille Lauro* affair. Angry as Cairo had been with Washington, it was also furious with the PLO leadership for not exercising stricter discipline over its people. The last thing cash-starved Egypt needed was any episode that might cut the flow of tourists or aid money. At the end of the first week of November, the Egyptians forced Arafat to read out a statement, in the presence of President Mubarak, in which he denounced and condemned terrorist attacks against 'unarmed civilians in any place'.[18] It was a largely meaningless statement, since it had long been PLO policy to eschew armed operations outside Israel and the occupied territories, but at least it provided the Egyptians with a piece of paper to wave at Washington.

As autumn gave way to winter, Hussein and Arafat continued to make a pretence of co-operating, but there was precious little goodwill remaining between them. The king sought repeatedly to secure Arafat's unqualified acceptance of Resolution 242 but, to his growing chagrin, the PLO leader did not say 'yes', and he did not say 'no'. Matters came to a head in late January when the two men agreed to make one last try to arrive at a satisfactory peace formula. Leading West Bank Palestinians, Palestinian intellectuals from the diaspora, and Arafat aides all descended on Amman for several days of intensive talks. For good measure, a senior American State Department official, the gravelly voiced Wat Cluverius, was on hand to help. Hopes rose and fell, but it gradually became clear that not even the most inventive formulas would clear the hurdle of the PLO's refusal to accept outright Resolution 242, although several came very close.

It was all too late. Moodily watching these machinations from his palace, Hussein was already planning one of his flights of oratory on the troubled state of Jordanian-PLO relations. His sour mood was not helped by intelligence reports he was receiving about Arafat's private conversations in Amman. The Jordanians had become increasingly bemused over Arafat's often contradictory impulses that swayed between acceptance and non-acceptance of 242. 'We wondered then,' observes one of the king's closest aides, 'whether Mr Arafat might not be in need of a psychiatrist.'[19]

Matters came to a head on 29 January at a tense meeting verging on bitterness, held in the prime minister's office and chaired by Hussein himself. Arafat informed the king that he could not accept 242 unless the Americans agreed in writing to recognize Palestinian rights to self-determination. With a poker face, Hussein replied: 'They cannot do more, and we cannot ask for more.'[20] Arafat then said that he would need to consult the Palestinian leadership and left the king alone with his senior advisers. An exasperated Hussein turned to his courtiers, and said: '*Khalast*. That's it.'[21] Arafat remained in Amman for another week, seeking to mend fences and to offer fresh formulas, but it was all in vain.

In his anger and disappointment, Hussein instructed his adviser Adnan Abu Odeh to draft a lengthy speech detailing why his joint initiative with Arafat had failed. For the record, he wanted to review the various twists and turns in his two failed peace efforts with the PLO leader. It was as if he were trying to purge himself of an unpleasant memory.

On 19 February, Hussein appeared on television and spoke with barely concealed bitterness for three hours about his troubled relations with the PLO. He had penned the last *angst*-ridden words himself, and in them he came very close to calling Arafat a liar. 'After two long attempts, I and the government of the Hashemite Kingdom of Jordan hereby announce that we are unable to continue to co-ordinate politically with the PLO leadership until such time as their word becomes their bond, characterized by commitment, credibility and constancy,' he intoned solemnly.[22]

In the weeks after his address, Hussein continued his offensive against the PLO leadership. In private, he railed against Arafat's duplicity. In public, he began a blatant campaign to encourage the growth of an alternative pro-Jordanian leadership in the Israeli-occupied territories. He abandoned all restraint, it seemed, in his bitter criticism of Arafat and his colleagues in Tunis. At the end of February he told the editor of the conservative Kuwaiti daily, *Al-Siyassa*, that the PLO had 'lost credibility and the Palestinians inside and outside the occupied territories will have to choose another leadership, or reconsider their political representation'.[23]

Not since the bleak days of the Jordanian civil war had relations reached quite such a low, and they would not improve for many months as the king and his prime minister, Zeid al-Rifai, sought by all means to whittle away Arafat's position inside and outside the territories. But before their campaign got off the ground an event occurred that should have persuaded them of their folly.

In early March, Zafir al-Masri, the recently appointed mayor of the West Bank town of Nablus, had been shot in broad daylight as he walked to work, by a member of George Habash's Damascus-based Popular Front. Masri's sin, in the view of the PLO radicals, was his willingness to serve under the Israeli Civil Administration in the territories. In other words, they thought he was a stooge of both the Israelis and the Jordanians. They were wrong; he was in fact a popular man, a member of one of Nablus's leading families, and a known supporter of Fatah. Hussein's calls for a new PLO leadership inside and outside the territories had almost certainly hastened his death. Predictably, Fatah cadres turned Masri's funeral into a mass demonstration of support for Yasser Arafat and the PLO, and a mass denunciation of Hussein and all his works, a message that Hussein and his prime minister ignored to their cost.

Arafat had reacted with restraint to the king's 19 February diatribe. Even after Hussein had performed the last rites on the Amman accord, the PLO leader still insisted, rather lamely, that he was bound by it. But the pretence could not last. Hussein was now committed to a political and diplomatic war with the PLO. Once set on a course of action, the stubborn king was not easily deflected.

Goaded on by Rifai, he plunged deeper into confrontation. He sanctioned a crackdown on pro-PLO journalists in Amman; gave support to feeble attempts to promote Atallah Atallah, a discredited former senior PLO official, as an alternative to Arafat; he initiated a West Bank economic development plan in a thinly disguised and unsuccessful attempt to 'buy' support in the territories. He also ordered the closure of some twenty-five PLO offices, including the headquarters of the Palestine National Fund, and the expulsion of dozens of PLO officials, among them Khalil al-Wazir.

By May, the atmosphere in the kingdom was truly dreadful. A chorus of internal criticism over lack of democratic freedoms culminated that month in riots at Yarmouk University in the north, in which several students were killed. The world's press concluded that something was rotten in the state of the Hashemites. In mid-July, Hussein, always extremely sensitive about his international image, summoned select foreign correspondents to lunch in the garden of Al-Nadwa Palace in an attempt to answer some of the criticism, and also to explain in more detail why he had felt obliged to close down the PLO offices. Surrounded in his garden by top aides, including the cigar-smoking Zeid al-Rifai, Hussein patiently answered questions for more than an hour. The PLO, he charged, had interfered in Jordan's internal affairs by funding an opposition candidate in a parliamentary by-election. It had also been involved in stirring up students at Yarmouk. But there was little real conviction in his criticism. He even allowed himself a humorous reference to his nemesis, Yasser Arafat. Asked whether he thought that he and Arafat would ever make up, he replied with a chuckle: 'Stranger things have happened.'[24]

For the moment, however, there was nothing for Arafat and his senior lieutenants to do but to turn their attention back to putting the rickety PLO house in order. Khalil al-Wazir told the Lebanese weekly *Al-Ousbou al-Arabi* that the PLO had formed 'reconciliation committees', and that it was being helped to resolve its internal differences through Algerian and Soviet mediation.[25]

Arafat was back in the Arab political bazaar, clinging to the hope that time would act as a healer. Precedent certainly suggested that it would. As Khaled al-Hassan, one of the PLO's greatest cynics, observed in a radio interview in late 1984: 'I do not believe Arab history has ever known a final estrangement. Our Arab history is full of agreements and differences. When we differ and then grow tired of differing, we agree. When we grow tired of agreeing, we differ, and so on. After every agreement or difference we pass through a time that changes things . . . this is the Arab nature.'[26]

On 20 April 1987, Arafat convened the eighteenth session of the Palestinian 'parliament', the Palestine National Council, in a marbled conference centre some thirty kilometres west of Algiers on the Mediterranean coast. It was a time for 'agreeing', after a fashion. Once again, Arafat was able to elicit a ringing endorsement of his leadership and, since this was the purpose of the exercise, to appear shakily in harmony with some of his erstwhile foes. George Habash's Popular Front returned to the fold, as did Nayef Hawatmeh's Democratic Front. The price Arafat paid for this façade of togetherness was to bury the Amman accord once and for all. It was hardly a high price. Arafat's equivocation and Hussein's impatience had long since rendered it null and void.

The hardly memorable Algiers PNC produced one jarring moment when Egypt reacted angrily to criticism of its peace treaty with Israel. Arafat had fought to prevent any such criticism, but was forced to give way in the end. Infuriated, Mubarak ordered the closure of all PLO offices in Egypt, except those functioning as diplomatic premises.

Momentarily out in the cold with yet another Arab regime, Arafat had re-unified his battered PLO at a very small personal cost. He had also, to his immense satisfaction, further isolated the Fatah mutineers in Damascus. Sourly, Syria tried to prevent Popular and Democratic Front delegates travelling to Algiers, but its efforts to disrupt the gathering lacked conviction. Paradoxically, Arafat had reasons to be grateful to the Syrians. The vicious attacks on Palestinian refugee camps in Lebanon by the Syrian-backed Shi'ite militia since 1985 – and a siege that had continued off and on for nearly two years – had acted as a catalyst for unity. As one delegate in Algiers put it: 'The blood from our martyrs has healed our divisions.'[27]

Once again, Middle Eastern politics had reverted to a familiar holding pattern. If Arafat was to preserve the new-found unity of his Organization, he would have to play it safe. Now was not the time for adventurous diplomacy. And in any case the opportunities were simply not there.

In Israel, the two main blocs – Labour and Likud – continued to work in opposite directions and to cancel each other out. Labour leader Shimon Peres pursued his secret dalliance with King Hussein. In the same month that the Palestinians gathered in Algiers, the two men held another of their clandestine meetings – this time in Britain – and signed what became known as the 'London document', calling for an international peace conference as a cover for direct negotiations between Israel and its Arab enemies, including a joint Jordanian-Palestinian delegation.[28] The dour Likud leader, Yitzhak Shamir, determined to hang on to the occupied territories in perpetuity, described his coalition partner's plan as a 'perverse and criminal idea' that must be 'wiped off' the cabinet table.[29]

Not the least of Arafat's worries were Hussein's continuing efforts to confine him to the sidelines. Nowhere was this campaign more evident than at a summit meeting of Arab leaders that convened in Amman in November 1987. It was an occasion on which Arafat was reduced to near foot-stamping rage over what he believed were deliberate slights administered to him by Hussein and his aides.

Already, before the meeting – called to unify Arab ranks against the perceived Iranian threat to Iraq in the Gulf war – there were warning signs. Pointedly, one of Hussein's closest advisers was telling PLO supporters in Amman in the run-up to the summit that 'We are going to give your friend [Arafat] a hard time.'[30] So it proved.

When Arafat flew in, Hussein, who had greeted all the other visiting kings, emirs and presidents in person, was not at the airport to meet him. Instead, he sent Zeid al-Rifai, the PLO's enemy No. 1 in the Jordanian Government, and the man who had masterminded efforts to undermine Arafat's position in the territories. It was a calculated insult and an enraged Arafat boycotted a Hussein-hosted banquet in protest. Ever protocol-conscious, the leader-without-a-state smouldered and sulked through the summit deliberations, his mood not improved by the fact that the Palestinian issue was virtually ignored. Arab leaders were much more preoccupied about events in the Gulf.

Arafat spent much of his time in his Regency Hotel suite railing against the perfidy of Hussein and Syria's Hafez al-Assad. His staff, accustomed to Arafat's volcanic moods, could scarcely remember a time when he was more irascible. He believed, quite rightly, that Hussein and Assad were attempting to cut his movement down to size. The issue came to a head when Jordan and Syria, entrusted, along with the PLO, with responsibility for drafting the resolution on the Palestine question, sought to exclude specific reference to the PLO's participation in a proposed international conference. Eventually, after much delay and not a little acrimony, the resolution was reworded to take account of PLO objections. The words 'including the Palestine Liberation Organization, on an equal footing' were added to the communiqué.[31] But that was not the end of the story.

Arafat's sour mood did not improve as he watched, on television in his hotel suite, Hussein's performance at his post-summit press conference. Asked at one point whether the PLO would be invited to participate in an international peace conference, the actor-king gave an unctuous smile and said: 'Hopefully'.[32] The implication was clear: the king couldn't care less about the PLO. This was bad enough, but Arafat was rendered almost speechless with rage when he discovered that the English version of the summit's final communiqué omitted the one standard phrase that represented what he saw as the most tangible symbol of his achievements in all his years as PLO leader. Whether by design or accident – it is not clear to this day which – the English text did not include the words 'sole, legitimate representative of the Palestinian people', when referring to the PLO. Arafat naturally assumed the worst. Hussein, he believed, had cunningly engineered the omission; the king had often enough made clear his displeasure at the decision of Arab leaders thirteen years earlier at the Rabat summit to block his own ambitions by vesting Arafat's PLO with sole responsibility for the Palestinians.

For a man accustomed to a position at centre stage, it was a bitter experience indeed, but one that would soon fade. Jordan's attempts, wilful or otherwise, to downgrade the PLO in full view of a large and politically aware Palestinian television audience in the West Bank and Gaza backfired. As the king bade his summit guests farewell, resentment was bubbling in the squalid shanty settlements of the occupied territories, one of the main factors being the perceived efforts on the part of Hussein and Assad to belittle the role of the Palestine Liberation Organization. The king would have reason to regret his point-scoring at Arafat's expense.

# Part Four

# 15
# *Intifada*

With stones in their hands
they defy the world
and come to us like good tidings.
They burst with anger and love, and they fall.
Nizar Kabbani, 'Children Bearing Rocks',
December 1987.

When Shlomo Sakal, a 45-year-old Israeli merchant, was stabbed in the neck in Gaza's seedy Palestine Square on 6 December 1987, it barely rated a mention in the international press. Sporadic violence between Arab and Jew was hardly big news. Sakal's death was just another grim statistic in a ceaseless battle. But within a very short time, it proved to be much more than that, unleashing a series of events that would re-ignite the conflict on a grander scale.

Two days after Sakal's death, in an apparently unrelated incident, an Israeli truck cannoned into a line of oncoming vehicles near the Erez security checkpoint at the northern entrance to the Gaza Strip. Four Palestinian workers died and seven were injured in the accident, which looked to many of the dozen of horrified Palestinian witnesses like a reckless and deliberate act. It did not help that three of those who died were from the Jabaliya refugee camp, whose 50,000 residents were among the most militant in the whole of the festering Gaza Strip. Rumours spread like wildfire that the Israeli driver was avenging the stabbing of Sakal.

Outraged, 10,000 of Jabaliya's inhabitants turned the funerals of those killed in the accident into a huge demonstration against Israeli military rule. They thronged the narrow streets of the squalid shanty town, chanting nationalist slogans and waving the green, red, white and black Palestinian flag. Late into the night they poured out their anger in demands for vengeance. The stage was set for what was to become known as the *intifada*, or literally, 'shaking'. The West, from days of repetition, was about to add an Arabic word to its vocabulary.

Just after 8 a.m on 9 December, an Israeli army patrol entered the Jabaliya camp on a routine mission, but the reception it got was anything but routine. Still agitated from the night before, Jabaliya youths pelted the soldiers in their jeep with stones. The Israelis gave chase on foot, setting a pattern that was to become all too familiar in the weeks and months ahead. When they returned to their vehicle they found it surrounded by an angry mob. Suddenly, out of nowhere, two flaming petrol bombs were thrown. In the panic that ensued the soldiers opened fire on the crowd and a 15-year-old youth named Hatem Sissi died almost instantly of a bullet wound in the heart. The *intifada* had claimed the first of many hundreds of victims. By next day, much of the Gaza Strip was in turmoil. Trouble broke out in Khan Younis, another large refugee camp. Black smoke from burning tyres hung in the air. Rioting youths, their faces masked by *keffiyehs*, set up rudimentary roadblocks, using rocks and anything else they could lay their hands on. Agitation continued in Jabaliya. Thousands demonstrated outside Shifa Hospital in Gaza as the casualties began to mount. Disturbances, like a bushfire in a high wind, spread to West Bank camps near Jerusalem and Nablus, and many other centres besides. A spontaneous rebellion had begun. Palestinian anger and resentment were boiling over and no-one, least of all the PLO leadership in distant Tunis and Baghdad, could be sure where it would lead.

As Arafat studied the first intelligence and wire service reports coming in from the 'battlefront', he was as unsure as his colleagues what it all meant. Was this the start of something big or was it simply another tremor, albeit a bigger one than normal? He consulted Khalil al-Wazir, the godfather of resistance in the territories. Was this planned? 'No, it was not,' Wazir told him, although he couldn't help adding that the PLO's underground organization was in much better shape to sustain a rebellion than it had ever been before.[1]

Arafat, who as a child in Jerusalem had witnessed some of the ferment in Palestine in the first '*intifada*' against British rule and Jewish immigration in 1936, understood the challenges better than most of his colleagues. Almost his first concern was whether the leadership outside could maintain control in the event of a full-scale uprising. Hadn't the national leadership in exile under Haj Amin al-Husseini failed in this regard in the late 1930s? Hadn't local commanders behaved like warlords, taking matters into their own hands and dissipating the energies of the rebellion in senseless acts of violence? Hadn't Arabs killed Arabs in their scores as the uprising turned in upon itself? Hadn't the divisions of the 1930s sapped the resolve of the nationalist movement for more than a generation? Hadn't the failures of the 1930s contributed to the catastrophe of 1948? All this and more went through Arafat's mind as he contemplated the implications of the rioting. Yet he also sensed that here was something different, more profound: that even if it had wanted to, the outside leadership could not turn off the tap. Arafat was, in any case, in a mood for risk-taking. What had he to lose?

He was still smouldering after the indignities he had suffered at the hands of King Hussein at the Amman summit in November and had watched with dismay Hussein's reconciliation with President Hafez al-Assad of Syria. He had sensed with alarm that fellow Arab rulers were once again growing bored with the Palestinian issue in light of their many other problems, and the Soviets, whom he had always counted on for steadfast support, were making friendly gestures towards Israel. Most frustrating of all for the hyperactive leader of a scattered people, he had lost the thread in his efforts to advance their cause politically. Arafat in the early winter of 1987–8 was, in short, at something of a dead end. Might not the violence of 9–10 December offer a way out? The moment must be seized.

On the night of 10 December, PLO Radio, broadcasting from Baghdad, carried the staccato voice of Yasser Arafat exhorting his people to step up the 'uprising'.[2] His use of that all-embracing word, 'uprising', was significant at that early stage: although he could not possibly have appreciated all the implications then, Arafat had given his imprimatur to a full-scale revolt against Israeli rule. He had found a new cause and he would exploit it for all it was worth, pretending that the PLO had initiated the uprising and was in full command of events.

But like all his veteran colleagues in Tunis, Arafat was privately just as perplexed as they were about the chemistry that had produced the mass revolt. How had it spread so quickly throughout the territories? What primal force was driving the rebellion? They all remembered other, similar events in the past that had fizzled out after a few days. Hardened politicians all, they reserved judgement. In a characteristically sober assessment, Salah Khalaf said that 'Nobody had been calculating on such an *intifada*, with its force and power. The one who was most in touch with the occupied territories was Abu Jihad [Khalil al-Wazir], but even he didn't expect it to be like that . . . When the *intifada* broke out, we were at first afraid – we remembered that the 1936 uprising lasted only six months. At the start we didn't estimate the *intifada* would last beyond six months.'[3]

The PLO was not alone in its cautious assessment.

Yitzhak Rabin, Israel's Defence Minister, who left for the United States on 10 December, said publicly that the trouble would be over in a few days. This was also the gist of a telephone conversation Rabin had with Shimon Peres, the Labour leader and Foreign Minister, who was visiting Brazil at the time. 'Don't worry, Shimon,' Rabin said in his guttural, almost metronomic voice, 'the army will assert control very quickly.'[4] Peres and his advisers were not so sure. Avraham Tamir, the feisty director-general of Israel's Foreign Ministry, told Peres that 'This was the beginning of something big.'[5]

As the days of violence turned into weeks, Israeli reaction ranged from bloodthirsty demands for a tougher crackdown – General Sharon told anyone who would listen that he would finish the *intifada* in days – to handwringing among the Israeli doves. General Amram Mitzna, the officer in charge of Israeli forces in the territories, said he and his men found their task so distasteful that 'I don't feel so well when I wake up in the morning.'[6]

Throughout December and January, amid insistent TV images of *keffiyeh*-clad youths battling helmeted Israeli soldiers in rock-strewn streets, Rabin and his military commanders desperately sought a formula to put down the uprising. Curfews, mass arrests, deportations and the use of live ammunition, accompanied by melodramatic threats to apply the 'iron fist', made little impact. The days of rage continued. Rabin's odious 'might, power and beatings' policy, announced on 19 January, brought cries of shame even from some of Israel's most committed US supporters; the then liberal *Jerusalem Post* decried the minister's 'jarringly brutal language'.

Arafat and the Tunis leadership debated how to hitch themselves firmly to the spontaneous uprising, while Israelis and Palestinians alike sifted through possible reasons for the astonishing eruption. No-one on either side could claim to have predicted it, with the possible exception of Dr Meron Benvenisti, a social scientist, former deputy mayor of Jerusalem and Israel's own prophet of doom: in a 1987 study of the occupied territories, Benvenisti had noted a growing incidence of violence and frustration there.[7] In fact, the build-up of tension in the territories throughout the last months of 1987 was so marked that in mid-October, Premier Yitzhak Shamir was obliged to assure Israel Army Radio that the situation was under control. Clearly, it was not.

But had the legions of wise men in rarefied Jerusalem been taking more careful note, they might have been alerted by the troubles in the Gaza Strip that October. Agents of the Israeli Shin Bet security apparatus engaged in a shoot-out with a group of heavily armed Palestinians after a high-speed car chase through the streets of Gaza City, four Palestinians and one Shin Bet agent dying in the gangland-style exchanges. At least two of the dead Palestinians had been members of the militant Islamic Jihad (Holy War) Organization, growing stronger by the day in Gaza's shanty towns and in the old quarter of Gaza City itself. The strengthening Islamic trend reflected developments elsewhere in the Arab world. Festering, overcrowded and impoverished Gaza was a perfect breeding ground for the spread of a new, more militant Islam.

When violent protests erupted in Gaza on 11 October after the burial of several of those killed, Israeli troops used live ammunition against the demonstrators, wounding more than a dozen. Within a few weeks Israel suffered an even ruder shock when the security of its northern border was breached by a lone Palestinian hang-glider, whose daring escapade would be later used to inspire youths in the territories in their 'war of stones' with the Israelis. The incident occurred on 26 November, when a Palestinian guerrilla of the Damascus-based Popular Front for the Liberation of Palestine-General Command (PFLP-GC) crossed into Israel and carried out one of the bloodiest terrorist attacks in nearly a decade. Armed with an AK47 rifle, pistol and grenades, he killed six soldiers and wounded seven in an attack on the Gibor army camp near Kiryat Shemona in the far north of Israel on the border with Lebanon.

An anguished Dan Shomron, the Israeli Army chief of staff, asked the question that most Israelis wanted answered. 'How did it happen' he said on Army Radio, 'that one terrorist killed six soldiers and wounded seven others? We cannot live with an event like this.'[8] The Arab world, by contrast, reacted jubilantly. Israel's stern image of invincibility had been dented. Syria Radio caught the general Arab mood when it declared that 'This operation represents a new important phase in promoting resistance against occupation . . . this proves that Arab resistance is capable of directing the strongest blows at the time and place of its choosing.'[9]

By New Year 1988, when it had become clear that the *intifada* was much more than a passing violent spasm, the first cooler assessments were being made about its causes. Quite simply, the 1.7 million residents of Gaza and the West Bank, fed up with twenty years of increasingly tiresome occupation and with the perceived indifference of the Arab world, had taken matters into their own hands.

To many Arab intellectuals, however, the troubles signified something deeper: an outburst of frustration and disgust on the part of Arabs with their rulers and politicians. None put it better than Nizar Kabbani, the well-known Syrian poet, in his verse praising the 'Children Bearing Rocks'. For the PLO leadership in Tunis, removed by more than distance from the activists in the territories, the message was there:

Like mussels we sit in cafes
one hunts for a business venture
one for another billion
and a fourth wife
and breasts polished by civilization

One stalks London for a lofty mansion
one traffics in arms
one seeks revenge in nightclubs
one plots for a throne, a private army,
and a princedom.

Ah, generation of betrayal
of surrogate indecent men,
generation of leftovers,
we'll be swept away –
never mind the slow pace of history –
by children bearing rocks.[10]

As the storm in the territories showed no sign of abating in the first months of 1988, the occupant of a cell in Ramleh prison in central Israel pondered what it all meant. Like Arafat and the PLO leadership on the outside, he agonized over ways in which the disturbances might be harnessed to produce political gains for the Palestinians. Faisal al-Husseini, son of Abdel Kader al-Husseini, the Arab hero slain in the 1948 war, had been arrested by the Israelis on 12 September 1987. After being held for a month in the Russian compound in Jerusalem, the grim way-station for many Palestinian activists bound for Israeli jails, he had been sent to Ramleh.

At first Husseini, widely acknowledged to be Arafat's chief lieutenant in the territories, disbelieved the accounts he read in the newspapers of the mass outpouring of Palestinian anger. How could this be? he asked himself. A lifelong activist, he had, in 1984, established a local think-tank, the Arab Studies Society, and was forever devising new methods of confronting Israeli rule in the territories. Not in his wildest dreams had he expected Palestinians to rise up in this way. He remained intensely sceptical until his family, on a visit in late 1987, described in detail what was happening.[11] Later he spent time in solitary confinement, starved of news, but drawing some satisfaction from the thought that the *intifada* was fulfilling some of the ideas he had been tossing around in secret with his close confidants. 'It was clear to us that passive resistance would not be accepted by Palestinians,' he says, 'so we settled on a policy of aggressive non-violence.'[12]

As the *intifada* took on the dimensions of a mass popular uprising, Arafat and the Tunis leadership found it a struggle to stay abreast of events. The PLO's co-ordinating committee for the territories, established after the April 1987 Palestine National Council in Algiers, met repeatedly in Tunis and Baghdad in late 1987 and early 1988. According to Suleiman Najab, a veteran communist and member of the committee, the 'aim was to give the *intifada* full support without giving specific instructions; we considered that those on the battlefield knew better what specific steps to take'.[13] This tentative approach reflected continuing deep uncertainties in Tunis and growing concern that the young activists in the territories might be establishing a rival leadership. This was one of Arafat's recurring nightmares. It was not something he could or would tolerate.

Nothing caused quite as much soul-searching in Tunis as the autonomous decision early in 1988 by those steering the uprising to form a unified leadership, grouping the main PLO factions. Nervously, Tunis gave its approval. 'Within the PLO a lot of people at the top were uncomfortable about this,' says Qais al-Samarai, a high-ranking member of the Damascus-based Marxist Democratic Front, better known by his *nom de guerre*, Abu Leyla. 'They saw it as some kind of rival body. But swiftly it made itself felt and influential. Sooner, rather than later, it assumed the full task of running the daily tactical process of the mass movement.'[14]

Not all would be plain sailing, however, for the Unified National Leadership, whose main components were Fatah, the Popular and Democratic Fronts, and the Communists. The Fatah-dominated secularists were repeatedly reminded of the growing strength of the Islamic groups who would often go their own way, calling independent strike days and bitterly taking issue on occasion with the PLO's political strategy. The emergence in mid-year of the militant Hamas, a word that means zeal and is also an acronym for the Movement of the Islamic Resistance, was widely seen as a challenge to the mainstream.

Watching from the outside. Arafat did not always agree with his own people inside – he was against their decision early in 1988 to force the resignation of Arab municipal councils, for example – but was obliged to go along with them. PLO leaders worried that economic pressures would abort the uprising. Khaled al-Hassan, one of Arafat's senior lieutenants, told the Lebanese newspaper *Al-Sayyad* early in January that the riots could not attain the dimensions of a civil revolt because of the economic difficulties that would ensue.[15]

But Hassan and the other sceptics within the exiled Palestinian leadership were about as wrong as they could be. It soon became clear that the people of the territories were more determined to show their opposition to Israeli rule, more prepared to make sacrifices, than ever before. In short, the stone-throwers and their underground leadership had hit on the most effective form of protest in more than twenty years of Israeli occupation. If the Palestinians under occupation had taken matters into their own hands, they were also demanding action from the PLO outside. What was needed was a political initiative to match the practical sacrifices being made on the ground, already generating waves of international sympathy.

Arafat was quicker than most to draw the logical conclusion. In an interview with Jonathan Randal of the *Washington Post* in early January, he dropped some tantalizing hints of where his thoughts were leading. The PLO, he said, should form a government in exile: code phrase for a respectable body that could take responsibility for the people under occupation. 'No doubt,' he added, such a move would be accompanied by 'a major new political platform'. As he ducked and weaved in response to the interviewer's questions, he did not rule out formal recognition of Israel within its pre-1967 borders.[16] His remarks prompted heated debate among the inner circle of PLO leaders in faraway Tunis. 'There were some people who thought from an early stage that this was not just a few demonstrations for a few days, but that it was a new stage,' recalls Yasser Abed Rabbo, a Democratic Front leader, who is now one of Arafat's key advisers. 'We reached the conclusion early on that this movement could be pushed to become a mass uprising, and that it would lead to a new move towards a settlement of the Palestinian question. There were arguments and discussions in a very narrow circle at the top. Some people said making a political statement might draw attention away from the *intifada* itself. Many people were hesitant, they were not confident there was a need for a political step. Others said: on the contrary, this will arm the uprising with a political weapon.'[17]

The question was: how? To come up with a fresh initiative, Arafat would have to reopen all the tired old controversies that had dogged the Palestinian movement since the early 1970s, and above all, he would have to persuade the PLO to come up with a clear statement of its willingness to coexist with Israel in a Palestinian 'mini-state' in the West Bank and Gaza. It was far from clear that he could prevail now where he had failed so many times in the past. At the end of January 1988, with Arafat's encouragement, Abed Rabbo brought up again the hoary idea of a provisional government. The result was a storm of controversy, both within Arafat's own Fatah group and from the movement's more recalcitrant factions. 'The response was completely negative – even from people who, six months later, were demanding the formation of a provisional government,' Abed Rabbo says.[18]

But the matter did not rest there. Arafat, in time-honoured fashion, had sent up an initial trial balloon, and although he had not stated his own position in public, he was awaiting the moment to push the debate forward.

Like their colleagues outside, traditional leaders inside the territories – the so-called Palestinian notables – were also desperately searching for a formula that would give political form and substance to the demands of the street activists. On 14 January, the group had convened at East Jerusalem's National Palace Hotel, hoping to find a means of harnessing the agitation and to lay down principles for a dialogue with Israel. They issued a fourteen-point document. 'Real peace cannot be achieved except through the recognition of Palestinian national rights, including the rights of self-determination and the establishment of an independent Palestinian state on Palestinian national soil,' it warned. 'Should these rights not be recognized, then the continuation of Israeli occupation will lead to further violence and bloodshed, and the further deepening of hatred.'[19]

The appeal fell on deaf ears in an Israel consumed throughout 1988 by preparations for elections in November, and by internal and external pressure to combat the uprising at all costs. Israel was not finding the going easy in the early days of the *intifada*, and predictably began blaming the messenger for its difficulties. Officials accused reporters of anti-Israel bias and in some cases of anti-semitism. It was not long before Israel's hard-pressed military began declaring wide swathes of the West Bank and Gaza closed to the press, and more particularly to television crews. For Israel's propagandists, the unpleasant story told through the unblinking eye of the television camera was almost impossible to counter, and nowhere was television making a bigger impact than in the all-important court of American opinion. 'The Israeli feeling that the world is against them is being fed by the enormity of the coverage,' Harry Wall, director of the Jerusalem office of the Anti Defamation League of B'Nai B'rith, would complain late in January.[20] The news for Israel throughout the first months of the *intifada* went from bad to worse.

Two episodes seemed particularly shocking. In one, Israeli soldiers attempted on 5 February to bury alive four Palestinian youths in the village of Salem near the large Arab West Bank town of Nablus. In the other, late in February, the American CBS network filmed four soldiers brutally beating two Arab youths in Nablus itself in a long sequence that was almost unbearable to watch, even for the most hardened observers of violence in the territories. Israel disciplined those responsible, but it was difficult to convince a highly sceptical world that these incidents were aberrations.

What surprised Israel and even Palestinians themselves was the speed with which the resistance organized itself into a mass movement, and into popular committees in almost every town and hamlet, giving the uprising the strength to weather mass arrests of thousands of activists and the deportation of some of its leaders. At the core of this activism was the pro-Fatah al-Shabibeh, or youth movement, which had become deeply entrenched in the universities. Scores of its leaders had received their political education in Israeli jails: a generation of Palestinian youth referred to prison experience as 'revolutionary school'. 'It was excellent experience. Given that we were well organized in jail, it helped us to organize ourselves outside,' declared a hardened activist and one of the founders of the youth movement in 1977.[21]

Ever so slowly, after the 1974 Palestine National Council had called for a 'national authority' in the West Bank and Gaza, the territories had come into focus as the next theatre of the Arab-Israeli conflict. The scaling down of the quixotic dream of liberating all of Palestine had obliged the PLO to examine what might be achieved underground, and later above ground in the occupied territories. All factions – Fatah, the Democratic and Popular Fronts, the Communists and, with increasing strength, Islamic groups – were engaged in institution-building, and often in conflict with one another.

But it was not until after the PLO's bloody defeat in Lebanon in 1982 that its leaders, and in particular Khalil al-Wazir, the PLO's military chief, really focused their energies on the West Bank and Gaza. 'The PLO took a long time to realize the possibilities of mass organization in the occupied territories,' observed a Palestinian activist from the territories. 'They had their own infrastructure and fighters in Lebanon; they were a power there; they were part of the game of Arab politics.'[22]

After Lebanon, Wazir moved with some speed to strengthen his hand in the territories and before long he established himself as the absentee czar of the West Bank and the Gaza Strip from his base in Amman. Wazir's word was law in the 400 towns, villages and hamlets of the territories. Although Jordan was nominally responsible, between 1983 and his expulsion from Amman in 1985, even relatively minor decisions such as the appointment of a clerk in an Arab West Bank town would be referred to Wazir. A hard core of youth activists emerged, most of whom were Arafat supporters, and it was these youth leaders who took charge of the *intifada* in its early days.

Heightened PLO activism in the territories had coincided with the opening of universities in the West Bank and the Gaza Strip. Bir Zeit College became a university in 1976; An-Najah, Bethlehem and Gaza opened in 1977. 'Ironically, the Israelis had fuelled the nationalist spirit they were trying to crush by allowing the universities to open. They thought that educating Palestinians to be professionals would cause them to forget about Palestinian nationalism. They thought we could be Americanized – that Bir Zeit would become one big disco. We had the choice between working underground or becoming an open, mass organization, and we chose the latter. The Israelis couldn't arrest 40,000 people, after all,' recalled one student leader.[23]

'In spring 1981, we had a meeting of students at Bir Zeit and founded the Palestinian Youth Organization of Social

Work. The goals were social: cleaning streets and camps, helping the mayors and their employees, instituting special days in the camps and villages such as medical day, folklore day, volunteers day; supporting poor families and martyrs' families. We decided we didn't need money at the start; we wanted to be independent.

'Our names were openly announced, and Fatah supporters came under this umbrella, although it was not openly proclaimed as a Fatah organization. But because it was not underground, this organization removed people's fears. We decided to send individuals out into the camps and villages to recruit for the organization and publicize our activities through the media. A few months later we had ninety-eight committees; all the presidents of the individual areas got together in Al-Bireh [an Arab town near Jerusalem]. Our aim was to provide an infrastructure for the Palestinian national movement on all levels.'[24]

By the time Ariel Sharon sent the tanks into Lebanon in June 1982, a political re-awakening in the West Bank and Gaza was already well under way. The Sabra and Shatila massacres, the expulsion of Fatah from Lebanon in 1983 and a realization in the territories that there was little prospect of an end to occupation unless the residents themselves took matters into their own hands fuelled the resurgence.

For Faisal al-Husseini the idea of 'non-violent demonstrations' had begun to take shape on the first anniversary of Sabra and Shatila in September 1983 when he organized a protest in Jerusalem. In his view the peaceful protest, which attracted fewer than one hundred people, was a failure: 'But the aggressive way the Israeli police attacked us gave me the feeling that if they were so afraid of such a thing, maybe this was the way. When I saw an officer hitting my daughter who was in those days nine years old, it was obvious they wanted to cut the roots of such a movement from the beginning.'[25]

Husseini continued to assert himself quietly as a figure of authority in the territories. The heir to a Palestinian dynasty, the son of Abdel Kader, was slowly emerging as a natural leader, filling a vacuum that had existed for a very long time. His links with Arafat, which went back to his childhood in Cairo, set him apart from his contemporaries. The Israelis recognized the danger signs, which is why they repeatedly detained him. Husseini's Arab Studies Society – founded with the blessing if not the direct financial support of Tunis – gave him a platform from which to operate. More to the point, he was becoming a bridge between the 'street' activists and the notables who frequented East Jerusalem's quaint American Colony Hotel, briefing diplomats, journalists and earnest fact-finding delegations from the US and Europe. He demonstrated his increasing authority in the late summer of 1986, when he successfully opposed plans by the salon Palestinians to meet George Bush. The then vice-president and presidential aspirant was making an obligatory pre-election swing through the Middle East to be photographed in the smiling company of Israel's leaders: the American Jewish vote beckoned.

Husseini appeared on Salahadin Street, Arab East Jerusalem's main thoroughfare, and appealed for a strike and a boycott of Bush to protest at the lack of American support for the Palestinians. In the end a compromise was struck and the East Jerusalem newspaper editor, Hanna Seniora, handed the US president-to-be a letter outlining Palestinian grievances. The episode would prove, in the words of one Palestinian observer, a 'last hurrah' for established spokesmen such as Seniora and Elias Freij, the Bethlehem mayor.[26] The power of the 'street' was beginning to make itself felt.

The episode did not go unnoticed in Tunis, but even the most percipient observer could hardly have judged this mini-struggle to represent the authentic voice of the Palestinians as a signpost to the *intifada*. Arafat himself believes that the reaction in the West Bank and Gaza to the long-drawn-out and bloody 1985–6 'Camps War' in Lebanon between the PLO and the Syrian-backed Amal militia was another straw in the wind, that angry demonstrations protesting over the first phase of the war in mid-1985 led to a closer identification between younger militants inside and their brothers and sisters outside.[27]

Throughout 1987, attitudes in the territories hardened. Frustration with the Americans, in particular, was building. When George Shultz, the US Secretary of State, visited the Middle East in the third week of October, pressure from the 'street' forced Palestinian notables to boycott a meeting with him: leaflets and graffiti scrawled on walls expressed their fury at continuing US attempts to exclude the PLO from the peace process. The tired old American dream of having King Hussein represent the Palestinians didn't match reality and as the lugubrious Shultz waited in vain in his room on the eighteenth floor of Jerusalem's Hilton Hotel for eight secretly invited Palestinians to attend for consultations, his advisers at last began to realize that. Richard Murphy, Shultz's senior Middle East aide, later described the mission as the 'end, not the beginning' and 'the bottom of the barrel'. 'The idea,' Murphy observes, 'was to get the parties – Jordan, Israel and Egypt – together in the shadow of the Reagan-Gorbachev summit to take place later in the year. It was a very limited idea, with limited appeal that the Israelis half nodded to, and King Hussein said, No! It marked the end of a period. We had, for the best part of five years, travelled back and forth, cabled back and forth, but there just wasn't much there any more. Six weeks later came the *intifada*.'[28]

In a Washington that had engaged for the most part in some mild and largely meaningless criticism of its Middle East ally, there was increasing alarm at the way things were going in the territories. The power of television was making itself felt and liberal American Jews were by no means the least outspoken among those demanding action. In late January George Shultz reluctantly began to make preparations for a return to the Middle East on his second mission in less than six months, but he despatched Richard Murphy to the region first, to sound out opinion before committing himself. In the event, his visit was viewed cynically by the Arabs as a limp attempt to reduce pressure on Israel.

Their shaky confidence in American intentions was hardly strengthened by the leaking late in February, as Shultz was on his way to the Middle East, of an egregious contribution to the debate from Henry Kissinger. At a breakfast meeting with American Jewish leaders early in February, the former Secretary of State had urged that the Palestinian uprising be 'brutally and rapidly' suppressed,[29] and that television cameras be banned from the territories. According to a four-page memo summarizing his remarks, Kissinger argued that the 'insurrection must be quelled immediately, and the first step should be to throw out television, *à la* South Africa. To be sure, there will be criticism . . . but it will dissipate in short order. There are no rewards for losing with moderation.'[30] An embarrassed Kissinger observed that the leaking of the memo was 'enough to drive you to drink'.[31]

Shultz arrived in Israel on the first stage of a long and fairly aimless series of peace shuttles that would continue until June, the last desultory attempt by the Reagan Administration to improve its indifferent record in the Middle East. Shamir had already despatched Ehud Olmert, one of the young 'princes' of Israel's rightist Likud bloc, to Washington to tell the administration in no uncertain terms that Israel would not be party to any plan that involved exchanging 'land for peace'. Like an overweight bloodhound who has lost the scent, Shultz visited Jerusalem, Amman, Damascus and Cairo in a fruitless search for a common denominator. Only in Egypt, dependent as it was on US largesse, did he receive any real encouragement. In Jerusalem, a familiar pattern repeated itself.

Shultz received a second snub in less than six months from Palestinian notables, some of whom were referring to themselves deprecatingly as the 'Mickey Mouse leadership'.[52]

Arafat, who was by then desperately casting around for ways to capitalize politically on the *intifada* before it ran out of steam, was at first prepared to sanction discussions between pro-PLO notables and Shultz. But he speedily changed his mind when he became aware of the furious opposition in the territories. 'The Palestinian people in revolt reject the Israeli-American conspiracy that some Arab elements are trying to help further,' said the underground leadership in a leaflet. 'They are trying to force it on our people in a hopeless attempt to abort the uprising.'[33] Tunis got the message. It quickly denied that it was planning to approve an encounter with Shultz inside the territories.

Instead, in an episode highly revealing of the evolving power relationship between the 'street' activists and Tunis, the inventive Arafat proposed a meeting involving a joint delegation of Palestinian representatives from inside and outside the territories to take place in a neighbouring country, possibly Egypt. There was never any possibility that the cautious Shultz would meet a PLO-sanctioned delegation in these circumstances, and plans for a direct dialogue between him and representative Palestinians collapsed.

The dogged Shultz turned up at the American Colony Hotel in the heart of Arab East Jerusalem on a grey, winter day in late February to read a brief statement in lieu of his meeting with Palestinian notables. In it, he talked about the need to respect Palestinian 'political and economic rights' – a slight advance on previous American positions. But there was no mention of self-determination. Among the few 'real' Palestinians who witnessed the performance were members of the hotel's largely Palestinian staff. Hanna Seniora, the East Jerusalem newspaper editor who had been on the list to meet Shultz, observed:

'Basically we are back to square one because of the reluctance of the United States to recognize the fundamental rights of the Palestinian people.'[34]

Shultz travelled next to London early in March for a meeting with King Hussein before returning to the Middle East to continue his efforts. But on 4 March when he belatedly unveiled a peace plan that called for an accelerated process of negotiations on Palestinian autonomy under the auspices of an international conference, his initiative was already dead.[35] Israeli intransigence and Arab suspicion – not least Hussein's – had seen to that.

Clearly judging Shultz's peregrinations to be irrelevant, Israeli leaders had taken a decision that amounted to nothing short of an act of war against the PLO. In early March, Israel's military and intelligence chiefs, and the so-called 'club of Prime Ministers' – Yitzhak Shamir, Shimon Peres and Yitzhak Rabin – decided in principle to assassinate Khalil al-Wazir, the 'godfather' of the uprising. Israel, they reasoned, needed a military success to balance domestic disappointment at the army's failure to curb the troubles. What would better serve their purposes, they asked themselves, than the slaying of one of the PLO's top leaders?

Wazir was the logical target. Hadn't he helped build the resistance in the territories? Wasn't he far and away the single most important figure in the PLO when it came to directing hostilities in the West Bank and the Gaza Strip? Hadn't he stepped up efforts to infiltrate guerrillas across Israel's borders to carry out terrorist actions? And to make matters worse, wasn't he audaciously communicating directly with his men inside the territories by telephone calls and fax messages routed through Europe and Cyprus? Wazir was a menace, and the quicker he was eliminated the better.

On 7 March, three Fatah guerrillas seized a bus in the southern Negev desert not far from Israel's Dimona nuclear facility. Their objective was to attack Dimona but they never got that far. They were killed in a shoot-out with security forces that also left three Israelis dead. Wazir had authorized the suicide mission and he also personally wrote the communiqué in the name of al-Asifa, Fatah's military wing, hailing their sacrifice. Israel's 'club of Prime Ministers' had found an excuse to put its assassination plan into action.

Israel took no chances, mobilizing scores of men from its various services to carry out the mission. A veritable armada of patrol boats was sent across the Mediterranean to transport élite Sayaret Matkal commandos to the shores of Tunis with a fleet of aircraft in support. Not since the killing of three top PLO leaders in Beirut almost exactly fifteen years previously, on 9 April 1973, had Israel devoted quite so many resources to the elimination of one of its sworn enemies. The meticulous preparation, under the direction of Dan Shomron, Israel's chief of staff, was a measure of the importance the Jewish state attached to removing the PLO military commander from the scene.

When Khalil al-Wazir returned in the early hours of 16 April to his villa in the picturesque Tunis suburb of Sidi Bou Said, a contingent of Israeli commandos supported by agents of Mossad was lurking in the darkness. Soon after 1.30 a.m. they made their move, breaking into the house, killing a driver and two guards in the process. They knew the layout of the house backwards. They made for the main upstairs bedroom. Wazir was at work – on a message, as chance would have it, to the underground leadership of the uprising. He would never finish it. Disturbed by the commotion downstairs, he hastily grabbed a pistol and with his wife, Intissar, following close, made for the door of their bedroom. Emerging into the corridor, he had time to fire just one round from his pistol at figures ascending the stairs before he was cut down. Trained assassins, the Israeli commandos calmly poured dozens of shots into him. So intense were the bursts of gunfire that his pistol hand was almost severed from his wrist, his body riddled with more than sixty bullets from head to toe, while his horrified wife looked on. It was all over in seconds. In a parting gesture one of the assassins entered the bedroom and fired a quick burst of machine-gun fire above the bed of Wazir's infant son, Nidal. Peering from an upstairs window Intissar al-Wazir saw some two dozen dark figures running away from the house. She had no doubt they were Israelis.[36]

Hearing the news, a distraught Arafat rushed back to Tunis from the Gulf. The loss of Wazir was a devastating blow. He and Arafat had been close friends for more than thirty years, and comrades in arms for well over twenty. He had been a pillar of the PLO and of Fatah, his dogged, calm personality complementing Arafat's volatile temperament to an uncanny degree, and he had saved Arafat from his own miscalculations on numerous occasions. The two men were so close that Arafat still says of him today: 'We were one spirit in two bodies.'[37]

In the first rush of grief, Arafat vowed vengeance. 'Those who think the assassination of Abu Jihad will smother the Palestinian uprising are deluding themselves,' he declared. 'His death will give new life to this heroic revolt. The blood of Abu Jihad will be dearly paid for.'[38] Blood did flow, but it was not Israeli. At least twelve Palestinians died in violent protests that swept the territories on the day of the assassination, the *intifada*'s worst single day of violence. Seven of those killed by Israeli bullets were from the Gaza Strip – the breeding ground for Wazir's early resistance activities some three decades before.

George Shultz and his aides recognized that the slaying of Arafat's right-hand man would hardly improve the climate for conciliation in the Middle East, but he nevertheless pursued his proposal for an international peace conference on yet another shuttle mission to the Middle East in May. He left Israel early in June after failing again to budge Israeli Premier Shamir. Exasperated, Shultz issued what was, for him, an unusually blunt statement.

'The continued occupation of the West Bank and the Gaza Strip, and the frustration of Palestinian rights, is a dead-end street,' he declared. 'The belief that this can continue is an illusion.'[39]

As Shultz shuffled off the Middle East stage, Arab leaders assembled for a summit meeting in a dowdy hotel in Algiers to debate a development that filled them all with varying degrees of unease: the six-month-old Palestinian uprising. The central player was a man whom many of the same leaders had done their best to ignore at their last meeting in Amman the previous November. The indefatigable Yasser Arafat was back at centre-stage, demanding Arab endorsement for the struggle in the occupied territories and a fresh injection of Arab money for the PLO. He had been agitating for the summit for months, but the initial answer from Arab leaders, worried lest the sight of Palestinian youths engaging in spontaneous protests should prove contagious at home, had hardly been enthusiastic. Now, they could hold out no longer and Arafat was determined to use the occasion to the full as a means of consolidating the revival of his political fortunes.

He was not disappointed. However fervently many of the assembled leaders may have wished the PLO and Arafat would melt away, they buried their misgivings in fulsome praise of the 'heroic' uprising against Israeli rule and promised (falsely, as it turned out) to increase their donations to PLO coffers, and to reinvigorate their diplomatic efforts in defence of the Palestinian cause. Even King Hussein, who had been trying over the preceding two years to preserve a role for himself as representing the Palestinians, felt obliged to defer to his old rival. In a long and melancholy speech, he complained that Jordanian intentions had all too frequently been misunderstood and promised to bow out of efforts to represent the Palestinians if the Arab states so wished. Behind his public display of magnanimity, however, lay both a profound sense of bitterness and worry lest the *intifada* spill over the Jordan river into his own kingdom. He was dismayed that the Palestinians of the occupied territories seemed to be spurning him as much as they were rejecting the Israelis, and when his fellow Arab leaders handed over sole responsibility for distributing their proposed aid money in the territories to Arafat's PLO, he was furious.

Never one to advance on only one front, Arafat was also engaged in another of his Byzantine efforts to push the Palestinian movement towards more conciliatory policies. The means chosen was an anonymous article distributed to journalists while Arafat was being insincerely fêted in the conference room. It purported to set out the PLO's view of the prospects for an Israeli-Palestinian peace settlement and represented another Arafat trial balloon, albeit one floated so discreetly that it could almost have passed unnoticed.

Those who did pick it up, however, were struck by a quite unusual tone. 'We believe that all peoples – the Jewish and the Palestinians included – have the right to run their own affairs, expecting from their neighbours not only non-belligerence but the kind of political and economic co-operation without which no state can be truly secure,' the article said. 'The Palestinians want that kind of lasting peace and security for themselves and the Israelis because no-one can build his own future on the ruins of another's.'[40]

What was more remarkable still was the article's provenance, for the author swiftly identified himself as none other than Bassam Abu Sharif, an Arafat aide and former chief spokesman for the hardline Popular Front for the Liberation of Palestine. Abu Sharif had impeccable 'revolutionary' credentials, and was well known to journalists who had followed the Palestinian movement over the years. Actively involved in PFLP terrorist activities during the 1970s, he had in 1972 been scarred, deafened in one ear and deprived of several fingers by an Israeli parcel bomb delivered in a book with a cover depicting Che Guevara. But since 1987, when he was expelled from the PFLP Central Committee for refusing to toe the party line, he had nailed his colours firmly to Arafat's mast. Now here he was putting his name to an article with language as conciliatory as any produced by the PLO in more than two decades.

Abu Sharif claims that the piece was his own handiwork. 'I started thinking about writing such an article in March 1988,' he says. 'The idea was mainly that our *intifada* should have a political programme that is realistic, achievable and accepted internationally. I thought that there should be one article, one proposal, that would clarify in a straightforward manner what we have been talking about for a long time in broad, general terms. I wanted to tell the world that the Palestinians, after years and years of struggle for one democratic state called Palestine, have realized that the only realistic solution is a two-state solution.'[41]

But behind Abu Sharif was Arafat, as always keeping his options open in public and encouraging his acolytes behind the scenes. To keep the matter deniable, he even declined an offer to read the piece before publication. 'He knew what I had in my mind, and he knew that I knew what he had in his mind. But he never read it,' says Abu Sharif.[42] It was on the basis of such nods and winks that Arafat had always operated.

On this occasion, the gesture set off major political waves, both within the PLO and in the outside world. The Abu Sharif document attracted particularly keen attention in Washington, where the US administration was already beginning to cast around for new approaches to the Arab-Israeli conflict following the failure of George Shultz's last peace mission. Says a former senior Shultz aide: 'We heard that and we thought, Jesus, they're being sensitive to Israeli security concerns. Now that's the way to make an impact. It was the tone as much as anything – the language that said: believe me, we understand your

Israeli concerns, we've got the same concerns. They just had not gotten that across as sensitively before as they did in that single document.'[43]

An influential section of the American Jewish community was also roused to something like enthusiasm. After Abu Sharif's article was reproduced in the American press, he received a letter expressing interest in it from a feisty New York lawyer with excellent political connections. Her name was Rita Hauser, and she was to play an important role in the US effort to institute a dialogue with the PLO that took place later that year.

Inside the PLO, by contrast, many people were furious. 'There were a lot of questions,' Abu Sharif recalls. 'There were different reactions from support to criticism of the language to criticism of the timing to criticism of the idea.'[44] The overwhelming verdict – even from within Fatah, whose members were piqued that someone from outside the mainstream had been used to convey Arafat's latest signal – was negative.

Recriminations were continuing when, nearly two months later, the PLO received an unanticipated jolt from Amman. King Hussein had not forgotten the snub administered to him by the Arab summit which had vested the PLO with sole authority to distribute the new allocation of funds in the territories. Ruminating over the outcome with his advisers on the plane home from Algiers, he had kept coming back to one gloomy conclusion. 'The Palestinians don't want me,' he said sadly.[45] Soon after his return to Jordan, he had headed off to his luxurious London residence in something of a sulk. A decision was taking shape in his mind that would change the ground rules of the Middle East conflict.

# 16
# *Independence*

'The State of Palestine is the state of Palestinians wherever they may be . . . It will join with all states and peoples in order to assure a permanent peace based on justice.' Yasser Arafat, proclamation of an independent Palestinian state, Algiers, 15 November 1988.

In the early evening of 31 July 1988, the citizens of Jordan saw a familiar, melancholy face peering out from their television sets. 'In the name of God, the compassionate, the merciful,' intoned King Hussein in the sepulchral voice he reserves for such occasions. Only this time there was an added hint of gloom in his demeanour. Clearly, what he was about to say was causing him pain.

Hussein had gone on television to announce the end of a dream: the idea that he could one day restore his dynasty's rule over the Palestinians of the West Bank. For twenty-one years, since the Israelis had captured the half of his kingdom that lay across the Jordan river in the Six-Day War, he had clung to the belief that he would one day get it back. Despite endless statements from the Arab world that the PLO, not Jordan, represented the Palestinians of the West Bank, he had retained close ties with the Arabs under Israeli rule. Now, seated before a large portrait of his grandfather King Abdullah, who had annexed the West Bank in 1950, he was preparing to break with his ancestor's legacy.

'Since there is a general conviction that the struggle to liberate the occupied Palestinian land could be enhanced by dismantling the legal and administrative links between the two banks, we have to fulfil our duty, and do what is required of us,' he said wearily. 'Jordan is not Palestine. And the independent Palestinian state will be established on the occupied land after its liberation, God willing.'[1]

Hussein's move was a gesture both of resignation and of bitterness. Deeply preoccupied with the surge of Palestinian nationalism that had found its voice in the *intifada*, he wanted to punish the Palestinians for rejecting him, and to show that they would make no progress towards their goal without him. In the process, he also dealt a lethal blow to American-sponsored Middle East peace moves which had, to that point, hinged on the idea that the West Bank should maintain a close association with Jordan after an eventual Israeli withdrawal. If the US administration had been gradually reaching the conclusion that its previous Middle East policy was bankrupt, Hussein's announcement delivered the *coup de grâce*.

The one person who stood to gain or lose most from Hussein's announcement was Yasser Arafat. For twenty years as PLO chairman he had claimed to represent the Palestinians of the West Bank but had been shielded by Jordan from having to exercise direct responsibility for them. Now the PLO and the Palestinians under occupation were being brought face-to-face. Sooner or later, the latter were bound to ask the former what it was doing to relieve their plight.

Arafat was in Baghdad preparing for a meeting of the PLO's Central Council when he received word via a Reuters news flash of Hussein's decision. 'This dear old king, he must have problems,' he quipped uneasily over lunch in his heavily guarded guest house. 'OK, now we'll go in tomorrow and take over the West Bank.' And with that, he sank into moody contemplation.[2]

On the face of it, the Jordanian move did not bode well. Hussein had not deigned to consult Arafat before making his announcement and it looked very much as if he was up to his old machinations against the PLO. Arafat's joke posed the problem in stark terms. Unlike King Hussein, who had developed a cosy co-operative relationship with Israel over the years, the PLO was simply in no position to assume responsibility for the occupied territories. Unless Arafat moved fast, a dangerous political vacuum might arise.

As Salah Khalaf put it: 'We knew that the king had not made his decision for the benefit of the cause. I believe personally that the king was betting that the PLO would not be capable of making an initiative. The bet was that either there would be a failure to take a decision, or a failure to implement it, and that in either case the PLO would have to go back to him again.'[3] But what if Hussein had miscalculated? What if Arafat and his colleagues were able to defy the sceptics and mount a new diplomatic initiative? This time, in the absence of Jordan from the equation, the world would have to listen. 'The main argument of the Americans and the Israelis about the Jordanian option had been eliminated,' said Khalaf. 'It confronted them with the fact that they would have to deal with the PLO.'[4] The more Arafat thought about it, the more tantalizing this prospect became.

After several days of nervous debate, the Baghdad meeting concluded that the king's decision presented an opportunity which the PLO could not afford to pass up. A special committee was set up to consider a response, and it was agreed that an emergency meeting of the organization's main decision-making body, the Palestine National Council, should be convened within weeks. There could be no mistaking the pressures on the PLO leadership. In the occupied territories, influential voices were calling openly for a unilateral declaration of independence for the West Bank and Gaza, to give form to the struggle for a state. One man who was emphatically of this view was Faisal al-Husseini. When the Israeli authorities arrested Husseini yet again at the beginning of August, they even found a draft of such a declaration in his files. Prime Minister Shamir termed it 'a crazy idea, since there is no chance whatsoever that it will be realized.'[5]

Crazy or not, the idea of declaring independence was laden with historical significance for Arafat and his colleagues. It would entail formal acceptance of something that the previous generation of Palestinian leaders had unequivocally rejected more than forty years before: the United Nations proposal to partition Palestine into two states, one Jewish, one Arab. It would involve, in effect, recognizing UN General Assembly Resolution 181, the vote that had served as a birth certificate for the state of Israel.

This was precisely the idea for which Arafat set out to muster support during August. Batteries of Palestinian experts in international law got to work on an independence formula and Arafat's favourite poet, the Palestinian 'laureate' Mahmoud Darwish, was brought in to polish the wording. Leaders of the various PLO factions huddled in Tunis and elsewhere, heatedly debating the politics of the move over cigarettes and Scotch.

Arafat himself clocked up thousands of air miles jetting between Arab and other capitals in an effort to build a consensus for an independent Palestinian state, and ferried a diverse cast of outside advisers to see him in a plane placed at his disposal by Palestinian millionaire Hassib Sabbagh. It was an unusually delicate task even for an experienced political high-wire artiste, for what Arafat was proposing was more than a simple independence declaration. He was also anxious for the PLO to adopt a new and realistic political programme that would break with the taboos of the previous twenty years. Specifically, he wanted acceptance of UN Security Council Resolution 242 of 1967, setting out Israel's right to exist in peace and security.

Such a decision, as Arafat saw it, could pave the way for increased recognition for the PLO at a time when rapid change in the international climate had raised hopes for the settlement of regional conflicts, as it had contributed to a ceasefire in the Gulf war that summer. With relations between the superpowers thawing, it might even win him a prize that had eluded his grasp for the past fifteen years: dialogue with the United States. For although Arafat's colleagues did not realize it, he was once again making overtures to Washington, and in return was receiving indications of serious American interest in talking to the PLO.

Arafat's chosen intermediary for this most tentative and clandestine of courtships was a Washington-based Palestinian, Mohammed Rabieh. In early August, Rabieh showed up in the office of William Quandt, a former US official who retained influential contacts with the State Department's Arabists. His message was simple: the PLO was ready to accept Resolution 242 in return for American agreement to open a dialogue and recognition of Palestinian 'political rights'. Together, the two men drafted a statement which Quandt then took to the State Department. What would the administration's response be if this became PLO policy? Considering the almost visceral contempt in which Secretary of State George Shultz was known to hold Arafat, the answer was surprisingly positive. Quandt was told that if the PLO would meet long-standing US conditions, a dialogue could begin within twenty-four hours.[6]

The fact was that the Americans had been seriously wrong-footed by Hussein's disengagement from the West Bank. If they were to retain any credibility as a peace-broker in the Middle East, they badly needed to come up with a fresh approach. Not that there could be any question of parlaying openly with the Palestinians at this stage, even through intermediaries. The whole idea was far too sensitive in American political terms for that. It all had to be at more than arm's length, top secret and, above all, deniable. Fortunately for Shultz and for Arafat, there were third parties on hand to provide the necessary 'cover' for their diplomatic manoeuvring.

Principal among them was a hard-headed Swedish politician, Sten Andersson. Andersson, a big, somewhat rumpled man who exuded a ready charm, was a veteran leader of Sweden's Social Democratic Party who had been a long-time confidant of the country's late premier, Olof Palme. In the post of Foreign Minister since 1986, he had inherited Palme's sense of mission as an international peace-maker and was anxious to continue his country's long tradition of mediation in the Middle East that dated back to the late 1940s, when the Swedish special UN envoy, Count Folke Bernadotte, was murdered by Jewish terrorists. Haunted by what he had seen on a visit to the region in March 1988, he had turned his attention to the Arab-Israeli conflict. Could Sweden's good offices now be turned to useful effect in breaking down the obstacles to a dialogue between Israel and the Palestinians?

On one side at least, the circumstances did not seem all that encouraging. Andersson had concluded during his Middle Eastern tour that the Israelis were in a bind of their own making: they were 'not capable of taking any peace initiative themselves'.[7] But he had been told privately by Shimon Peres, the Israeli Labour leader and Foreign Minister: 'If you get the PLO to renounce terrorism and recognize Israel, I would respect them.'[8]

Unsure what that remark might mean, Andersson resolved to test it out and did so a couple of weeks after returning from the Middle East when he discussed the issue with George Shultz during a visit to Washington. During a lunch in the State Department banqueting room, Andersson and Shultz repaired to the balcony for fifteen minutes' private chat, and Andersson put forward his idea. What if Sweden were to try to arrange a meeting between a group of prominent American Jews and the PLO as a first step towards breaking the ice? Shultz's reaction was typically Delphic. According to Andersson's aides, he 'neither supported nor opposed'[9] the suggestion, but that was enough for Andersson. In the ensuing weeks, he established regular contact with Arafat advisers and with suitable American Jews – people who would be both respectable enough to give his effort credibility and sympathetic enough to his aims not to run off and inform the Israelis. During a visit to Moscow, he informed the Soviets in 'very general terms' of his plans. The last thing he wanted was for the PLO's allies in the Kremlin to play a spoiling role.[10]

Before anything else could happen, however, the PLO had to be encouraged to move. How was Arafat to persuade the movement to adopt a conciliatory statement without provoking something that had happened on so many previous occasions: a walkout by the rejectionists, in particular by his old rival, the ailing revolutionary George Habash?

Arafat spent an inordinate amount of time that autumn wooing and soothing the Marxist leader. Outsiders Arafat had drafted in to join the debate were despatched one by one to present their views to Habash, and they were all asked to handle him with kid gloves. 'He wanted to show Habash his respect, and ensure that he was fully involved,' recalled one such, the veteran Egyptian journalist Ahmed Baha El-Dine. 'Arafat told me that he did not want Habash to feel left out. It was a question of taking precautions.'[11]

As the debate wore on, many observers not privy to the smoke-filled rooms began to wonder whether Arafat's plans for a new political initiative were in trouble. The promised meeting of the Palestine National Council was repeatedly put off and all manner of contradictory statements continued to emanate from the PLO leadership. Arafat, however, true to his oft-repeated maxim that 'politics is the art of timing', was playing a clever hand. Unbeknown to his colleagues, he had received a secret promise from Shultz that the US would respond positively to any PLO peace gestures, and that it would give its answer after the American presidential elections. Meantime Arafat was waiting for the right moment to convene the troops, and using the delay to wear his opponents down.

In November the moment arrived. With elections in Israel as well as the United States safely out of the way, the Palestinian 'parliament' was preparing to meet at a heavily guarded marble conference centre on the Algerian coast. Late one night at the beginning of the month, the PLO faction leaders gathered in a hall in a Tunis suburb for one last discussion of the agenda. It was a solemn occasion, in keeping with the importance of the issues. 'I have attended all sorts of organizational meetings and debates over the last twenty-one years,' said Salah Khalaf. 'But for the first time, the discussion did not use exaggerated, hyped language. It was the first time that there had been a responsible and serious discussion among the factions.'[12]

The meeting did not resolve differences between supporters and opponents of a conciliatory political programme but it did take a decision that was in effect just as important. Participants agreed that the factions would be free to express their opinions for and against at the forthcoming National Council session but that nobody would have a veto and nobody would walk out. The *intifada*, in whose name the session was being convened, had forced a new unity on the fractious PLO. What Khalaf called 'the etiquette of the *intifada*' had arrived.[13]

Ten days later, 380 Palestinian worthies assembled at the secluded Club des Pins conference centre 30 kilometres west of Algiers. It was a fitting venue for such a meeting: Algeria, though far from Palestine, had provided inspiration for Arafat's Fatah movement in the early 1960s and been its first and most consistent supporter. The atmosphere was tense and security tight, for the Algerian capital was still smouldering following the violent suppression of price riots the previous month. But despite these difficult circumstances Algeria was now providing facilities for what would prove one of the most important sessions of the Palestine National Council.

With anti-aircraft batteries outside guarding against aerial attack and a Soviet warship anchored offshore, the delegates assembled in the circular conference hall decked with red, green, white and black Palestinian flags. This assortment of dignitaries, activists and ageing revolutionaries was the essence of the Palestinian movement Arafat had led for almost exactly twenty years, the parliament of a people without a country. It was an extraordinary talking shop, in which Palestinian doctors rubbed shoulders with American university professors, trades unionists with terrorists, socialist revolutionaries with capitalist plutocrats, Christian intellectuals with Islamic fundamentalists. It was a travelling stage, a forum without parallel for the exercise of Arafat's histrionic talents.

Only this time, there was a difference. The change was obvious from the start. The old chants about 'revenge' and 'revolution until victory' came out with less gusto that before and intermingled with them were new slogans in support of the *intifada*. When 'the great fighter Yasser Arafat' was cheered to the podium, it was to audiences well beyond the hall, rather than to the battered strugglers in exile, that he addressed his speech: to the 'people of the glorious blessed *intifada*' and, astonishingly, to the president-elect of the United States, George Bush. 'I appeal to President Bush to adopt a new policy, not one simply aligned with Israel,' he said. 'We are not asking for the impossible.'[14]

The tone was set, and so was the target. In the face of Arafat's determination to push through a new political platform, the rejectionists were in retreat. Try as he might during three days of arduous debate to win delegates over to his side, George Habash found himself outmanoeuvred at every step by an Arafat using all the tactical skills he had assembled during twenty years of PLO infighting. Instead of distributing the text of the controversial declaration, he insisted on having it read out loud, thus handing an instant advantage to those on his side who already knew what it contained. He worked assiduously behind the scenes, intervening on points of order and ensuring that no loophole was left open for his opponents to exploit. At the climax of the debate he left it to his deputy Salah Khalaf, who had always been a much better public speaker, to clinch the argument. Khalaf received a big ovation and as he sat down, a bemused Habash could only remark: 'What's all this? You're speaking about treason, and they're clapping you?'[15]

In the small hours of 15 November 1988, the Palestinian flag was raised in the conference centre to the sound of a blustering brass band, and Yasser Arafat read out a solemn declaration in florid prose. 'The Palestine National Council, in the name of God and in the name of the Palestinian Arab people, hereby proclaims the establishment of the State of Palestine on our Palestinian territory with its capital Holy Jerusalem,' he declaimed. 'Now at last the curtain has been dropped around a whole epoch of prevarication and negation.'[16]

There was a certain unconscious irony in the latter statement, for although Arafat was referring to the changes in attitudes to the Palestinian cause that had been wrought by the 'heroic' uprising in the occupied territories, he might just as well have been talking about the PLO's own position. For years, in hope more than expectation, his movement had clung to extravagantly unrealistic visions of what it could achieve. Now, with a political statement issued alongside the independence declaration, it spelled out in clearer terms than ever before that its goal was the establishment of a state living in peace alongside Israel.

The PLO's new programme was not without flaws. As the Israelis and other critics hastened to point out, the phrasing was often obscure and circumlocutory, bearing all the hallmarks of a document written by committee. Neither it, nor the independence declaration, signalled the definitive abandonment of the PLO's dream: the replacement of Israel with a single democratic state for Arab and Jew. But the members of the Palestine National Council were in no doubt about what they had done. Four decades after the Jewish nationalist movement had accepted partition and declared independence, the Palestinians had steeled themselves to do the same, settling for a state in less than a quarter of the land called Palestine.[17]

Small wonder that the declaration was a subdued affair. All present in the conference hall knew, too, that even the modest state they had proclaimed did not exist, except on paper. Many felt that in agreeing to confine their demands for sovereignty to the West Bank and Gaza, they had signed away part of their birthright. In the Israeli-occupied territories, festivities were muffled by a strict curfew restricting all Palestinians to their homes for twenty-four hours. At its very inception, the plan for statehood was overshadowed by the grim reality of Israeli rule.

If Arafat was disturbed by such thoughts, he certainly did not show it. Armed with his movement's conciliatory programme, he was bent on using it to win new international respectability and an opportunity to address the United Nations for the first time since 1974.

On 6 December 1988, Arafat and a group of aides strode down the steps of his private jet at Stockholm airport. Without delay, they were whisked off by helicopter to the Haga Palace, the modest nineteenth-century residence of the kings of Sweden. Snow lay on the ground and Arafat and his entourage shivered in their thin cotton clothes against the cold. But if the climate caught them unawares, they were even less prepared for what they were about to hear in their discussions with the Swedish Government.

In the three weeks since the declaration of independence, things had not entirely gone Arafat's way. To be sure, many nations around the world had granted his symbolic Palestinian state formal diplomatic recognition and the countries of western Europe had warmly welcomed the PLO's new political programme. But the government he was most anxious to address, the one in Washington, had been at best luke-warm. Although the White House had murmured faint praise about 'positive elements' in the Algiers declaration, both Reagan and President-elect George Bush agreed that it was not sufficiently clear to meet America's conditions for dealing with the PLO. To add insult to injury, George Shultz had just refused Arafat a visa to visit New York for his planned address to the UN General Assembly. Arafat, Shultz had proclaimed to a chorus of indignation from around the world, was 'an accessory to terrorism', and as such represented a threat to US national security.[18] It seemed like a defiant parting shot from a Secretary of State with deeply held views about terrorism and an almost equally passionate dislike for Arafat.

But all was by no means lost. If the Americans were still unimpressed and the Israelis resolutely refused to see anything new in what the PLO was now saying, many other countries were determined not to let slip this opportunity to present Arafat the peace-maker to the widest possible public. The UN General Assembly, outraged by Shultz's move, resolved to transfer its deliberations across the Atlantic to Geneva for a day on 13 December, just in order to hear the PLO leader. A removal of this kind, costing an estimated 645,000 US dollars, was without precedent and showed conclusively that Arafat, despite all he had been through since his previous UN appearance, was back at the centre of world attention.

Against this backdrop, Arafat's visit to Stockholm, a capital that had long been friendly to the Palestinian cause, was not just a routine diplomatic stop. He was there to meet a group of influential American Jews seeking to encourage PLO 'moderation'. Although Arafat had met American Jews before, just as he had held talks with Israeli peace campaigners, this group was different from any he had encountered in the past. It included Republican lawyer Rita Hauser, a wealthy liberal called Stanley Scheinbaum, and a professor and Holocaust survivor, Menachem Rosensaft. It carried credibility and political clout and its members were anxious to facilitate an official dialogue between the PLO and the US.

Just a fortnight before, also in Stockholm and in conditions of great secrecy, Hauser and Scheinbaum had held talks with Arafat's veteran foreign policy adviser Khaled al-Hassan, and elicited from him after fierce debate a statement clarifying the PLO peace platform. Now, summoned back to Sweden with a cryptic message from its embassy in Washington saying that 'the big man' was coming, they were after an endorsement of the same words from Arafat himself. Getting it would involve pushing him beyond what was said at Algiers, to a crystal-clear recognition of Israel and a formal renunciation of terror, the two main conditions that Washington had long set. 'The problem with the Algiers declaration was that it was not a legally drafted document,' says Hauser. 'It was repetitive, inconsistent and incoherent. It was really a very confusing document.'[19]

As the two sides sat down to talk in the Haga Palace, Arafat was in convivial mood. He and Hauser, whose New York law practice was active in the Middle East, notably in Lebanon, swiftly discovered that they had friends in common. What Arafat did not realize, as the haggling got under way, was that another, ultra-serious and ultra-secret diplomatic game was about to commence. For his hosts had a surprise up their sleeve: an unexpected missive from the highest echelon of the US Administration. In his quiet, methodical way, Sten Andersson had been working on the Americans since the Algiers meeting, keeping Washington informed of the latest nuances in PLO policy. A week earlier, he had sent word to Secretary Shultz of Arafat's imminent arrival, and he had asked Shultz gently whether he might have anything to tell the PLO leader.

The result outstripped the Swedes' wildest expectations. At almost exactly the same time as Shultz was deciding to deny Arafat a visa to go to the UN, he wrote a confidential letter to the Swedish Government holding out the prospect of an American dialogue with the PLO provided the latter would clearly recognize Israel and renounce terrorism. The letter was considered so sensitive that Shultz even kept its contents from some of his own staff, and the Swedes had it carried back from Washington by hand.[20] No wonder, for it appeared to presage a breakthrough of major proportions: in effect, Shultz was writing the precise lines that Arafat would have to speak to qualify for recognition by Washington, and telling him in advance what the Americans would say in return. While one half of the Secretary of State's legalistic mind was excoriating Arafat as a terrorist, the other was admitting that the PLO could not forever be excluded from Middle East peace-making.

When Arafat was privately shown the Shultz letter, he was astonished. Here, on the American Secretary of State's personal stationery, was the clearest and most formal overture he had ever received from Washington. It was the opportunity he had been waiting for and he swiftly set about formulating a response. In his euphoria at coming within sight of such a political prize, Arafat was even inclined to cancel further meetings with the American Jewish group. If I can talk to Washington directly, he reasoned, why should I need to deal with such third parties? It was a foolish and graceless reaction which the Swedes had their work cut out persuading him to reverse.[21]

Throughout the evening of 6 December, the faxes flew across the Atlantic carrying suggested amendments to the US wording. Most of the PLO's proposals were accepted on the spot. The stage was set for what the Swedes hoped would be a dramatic declaration by Arafat in Stockholm the very next day and an even more dramatic American answer, but they were reckoning without Arafat's legendary caution. Now that he was so close to what had been his obsessive goal, he was gripped by a sudden anxiety. This was too big a decision for him to make on his own. The PLO had long regarded formal, as opposed to implicit, recognition of Israel as its last bargaining card; to play it, he had to have clearance from other members of the PLO Executive Committee. To get it, he spent the entire night phoning round the world. The Swedes, who were both paying the bill and listening in, found his conversations not without interest.

Even on the threshold of success, Arafat was hesitant. Perhaps Stockholm was not the place to do the deed after all. Perhaps the Americans were setting him up for a fall. Perhaps anything he said would be eclipsed by news from the Reagan-Gorbachev summit due to take place in New York the same day. Better, after all, to wait for a wider, safer stage before committing himself to America's arms. To the frustration of the Swedes, he told them that he would give his final answer after consulting yet again with the Executive Committee. After signing the less contentious statement proposed by the American Jews, he headed back to Tunis.[22]

For five agonizing days there was silence. Then came the answer, carried to Stockholm on 12 December by Arafat's trusted aide, the Palestinian poet Mahmoud Darwish. Yes, he said, the Executive Committee had accepted the American conditions and Arafat would incorporate statements to that effect in his address to the UN General Assembly in Geneva next day. The champagne was uncorked.

Less than twenty-four hours later, Yasser Arafat marched into a packed UN conference chamber and headed for the stage. Not since his previous UN appearance in New York fourteen years before had he been the subject of so much diplomatic fuss. As then, ministers and senior emissaries had flown in from around the world to give him a standing ovation. A battery of television cameras and reporters' notebooks were poised to record his words. The Swiss had surrounded the Palais des Nations, a monolithic art-deco edifice on the snowy banks of Lake Geneva, with security almost as tight as New Yorkers had seen in 1974. And once again, the PLO leader was putting his case in a building that had played an inglorious role in the tragedy of his people – the former headquarters of the League of Nations, the body that had given Britain a mandate to rule Palestine back in 1922.

Only this time, it was a different Arafat standing behind the lectern. What was left of his hair and his beard were grey. Instead of an ill-fitting jacket and baggy trousers, he wore a neatly pressed suit of green military fatigues together with the chequered *keffiyeh*, folded as ever in the shape of Palestine. As he donned a pair of brown-rimmed spectacles to read out the prepared text in Arabic, it was clear that he had new lines to speak and a new objective in mind.

'I come to you in the name of my people, offering my hand so that we can make true peace, peace based on justice,' he proclaimed. 'I ask the leaders of Israel to come here under the sponsorship of the United Nations . . . Come, let us make peace. Cast away fear and intimidation. Leave behind the spectre of the wars that have raged continuously for the past forty years.'[23]

The tone was reasonable, the words emollient, but there was one man in the audience who listened to Arafat's speech with a mounting sense of unease: this was supposed to be the consummation of the deal which Sten Andersson had worked so hard to broker between Arafat and the Americans. Yet where were the magic phrases that the PLO leader had promised to pronounce? Where was the explicit recognition of Israel and renunciation of terror?

Andersson's alarm was shared by at least one of Arafat's advisers, who prefers to remain anonymous.[24] Little more than forty-eight hours earlier, on a miserable rainswept day in Tunis, he had helped the PLO leader put the finishing touches to an address containing all the right words that would unlock the door to negotiations with the US. But at the last minute, the unpredictable Arafat had changed his speech.

Four thousand miles away in Washington DC, a group

of senior US officials huddled in front of a television set in a small private room on the seventh floor of the State Department. George Shultz and his top aides had no illusions about the performance they were watching live. They had seen something similar so many times before. One of those present had wagered a dollar that Arafat would fluff his lines. He won the bet. Once again, in the eyes of the American administration, Arafat had sidled towards a diplomatic breakthrough but baulked at the final hurdle. Praising the 'interesting and positive developments' in the address, the State Department swiftly affirmed that it did not meet US conditions for a dialogue with the PLO. Worse still for Arafat, President-elect Bush chipped in with a statement of his own to the same effect. Much as the PLO's Arab allies – men like President Hosni Mubarak of Egypt – sought to salvage the situation with a barrage of phone calls to President Reagan, Washington would not budge. All the painstaking negotiations of the preceding two months had come to nothing.

Arafat, resting back in his top-floor suite at the Inter-continental Hotel with its breathtaking views over Lake Geneva, heard the news in disbelief, then fury, then despondency. Surely he had done what he was asked to do, he stormed. Maybe he had not spoken the words in the exact sequence demanded by Washington, but the peaceable sentiments were all there: the call for an international peace conference on the basis of UN Security Council Resolution 242, the pursuit of a 'comprehensive settlement' including Israel. Why were the Americans letting him down again?

But he had only himself to blame. In changing the speech, he had been trying to engage in one last piece of haggling, trying to say things in his own way. The legalistic Americans were bound to think he was up to his old tricks. 'He probably thought, being the wily politician that he is, that he would be able to get away with it,' said one rueful Arafat adviser. 'Well, he didn't. He simply didn't understand the way the US system works – the fact that there were teams of State Department lawyers combing through his speech looking at every last comma.'[25]

As the implications of the blunder sank in, gloom descended on Arafat's hotel suite, and his advisers engaged in a furious debate about what to do. PLO 'foreign minister' Farouk Kaddoumi, who had been deeply unhappy about the concessions Arafat had agreed to in any case, thought the matter was at an end. 'We've done all we can, and there's no point even in holding a press conference now,' he said.[26]

'What are you saying?' shot back businessman Hassib Sabbagh, who had played a key behind-the-scenes role in steering the PLO leader to Geneva. 'That we've moved the entire UN General Assembly across the Atlantic for nothing? That this opportunity is simply to be thrown away? And what are we to tell the hundreds of journalists waiting out there?'

'Tell them to go away,' was Kaddoumi's dour reply.[27]

In this vein the conversation droned on into the small hours. Through it all, Arafat sat silent, his chin cradled in his hand, his face expressionless. Gradually, the members of his entourage drifted morosely off to bed.

There the affair might well have rested, had it not been for the determination of two of the PLO leader's associates, Sabbagh and fellow-businessman Bassel Akel, to try again. Perhaps, they reasoned, pacing up and down the lakefront promenade in the morning, Arafat could read a new text to his press conference later in the day, clearly recognizing Israel and renouncing terror in US-approved language. Perhaps, after all, the Americans might be persuaded to listen if he came out with the right words at the second attempt. Racing back to the Intercontinental, they found Arafat already awake and alert and put it to him. It was, he agreed, worth one more push.

There followed a frantic and faintly absurd day of manoeuvring. The PLO leader's press conference was postponed from midday to 7 p.m. while his aides drafted and redrafted formulations for formal recognition of Israel. At the same time, Sabbagh went into action. Though not formally linked to the PLO, he had been one of its biggest Palestinian benefactors. As a wealthy businessman, he was also very well connected in Washington, having worked with George Shultz when the latter was on the board of the Bechtel engineering concern. So, as the Washington day began, he got on the phone to his old friend Richard Murphy, the US Assistant Secretary of State and, while Arafat was sitting in the room, read over the proposed new statement. Murphy said he would consult his boss Shultz, President Reagan and President-elect Bush, and get back with Washington's response. Within a couple of hours, and after a couple of minor amendments, the statement was approved. Sten Andersson, who had himself been in touch with Washington to try to salvage the situation, confirmed that the deal was once more on. Arafat's advisers, nervous in any case about his imperfect English, set about rehearsing him in his lines. Time and again, they ran over the simple phrases. This time, of all times, he could not afford to slip up.

In such strange ways is history made. At 8.30 p.m. on 14 December 1988, Yasser Arafat again walked out under the arc-lights in the Palais des Nations to face the world's press. Donning his spectacles, he picked up a sheet of paper and began to read a prepared statement in halting English. 'Between Algiers and Geneva,' he intoned in a flat voice, 'we have made our position crystal clear.'[28] But with his aides hovering at his elbow, prompting him in an audible whisper, he went on to make it even clearer. He accepted 'the right of all parties in the Middle East conflict to exist in peace and security.'[29] With redoubled emphasis, he added: 'I repeat for the record that we totally and absolutely renounce all forms of terrorism'[30] – his stage fright was such that the word came out sounding like 'tourism'.

Finally, in a blunt aside to his unseen listeners in Washington, he warned them against expecting any more concessions.

'Enough is enough. Enough is enough. Enough is enough,' he proclaimed with a mixture of fatigue and defiance. 'What do you want? Do you want me to striptease? It would be unseemly.'

Minutes later, the message, taped and transmitted by phone across the Atlantic, was being dissected by the State Department bureaucrats in Washington DC. Following a brief discussion, George Shultz picked up the handset. 'We're agreed that he did it,' he told the White House. And within another two and a half hours, scores of Palestinians gathered around their hotel television sets in Geneva to watch the Secretary of State's impassive face as he announced that the United States was prepared to open a 'substantive dialogue with PLO representatives'.

It was a dramatic moment for the Palestinian leader. The years of equivocation and hesitation were at an end. Arafat had played the PLO's 'last card'.

But there was to be no curtain call. By the time the news filtered through to snowy, staid Geneva, the elusive Yasser Arafat was airborne again, on his way to another performance of his perpetual balancing act in what was then still the Cold War capital of East Berlin.

Strapped into his seat for the brief flight across the Iron Curtain, Arafat had reason to reflect on the latest twist in his fortunes. By cajoling his movement into accepting the idea of peaceful co-existence with Israel, and by stating that goal in unambiguous terms in Geneva, he had secured unprecedented world recognition as leader of the Palestinians. Now more than ever, he felt he had ensured that the PLO could not be ignored in any settlement of the Middle East conflict.

There was only one problem. As far as Israel was concerned, the independent Palestinian state that Arafat had proclaimed was simply a figment of everybody else's imagination. He had no guarantee that his decision to pursue the struggle principally by political means would being him any closer to turning his dream into a reality, as he had admitted in Algiers when he promised that if the diplomatic tack did not work, the Palestinians could always think again. Who was to say that within a year or two, he would not find himself doing what his opponents had predicted: admitting that since diplomacy had failed, other means of struggle – including violence – would have to be reactivated?

# 17
# *The Wrong Horse*

'When I have only two options, I cannot sleep because I want a third.' Saying frequently attributed to Yasser Arafat.

It was a brilliant morning on Israel's Mediterranean coast, and the beaches were crammed with sunbathers. At the popular beach club of Nizzanim, a resort 18 miles south of Tel Aviv, the babble of 3,000 voices in animated conversations filled the air. As they did every year at this time, Israelis were enjoying the *Shavuot*, the Jewish holiday that marks the handing down of the Ten Commandments and the beginning of high summer. The date was 30 May 1990. Suddenly, the revelry was punctured by an ominous sound. From the middle distance came the clatter of machine-gun fire and the whirr of rotor blades, and as the noise grew nearer a small speedboat roared into view, pursued closely by Israeli air force attack helicopters. The craft had eleven men aboard, and they were unmistakably carrying arms. It sliced across the bay, coming at one point within 200 yards of the beach club, then weaved off to the south in a continuing hail of bullets. As police sirens wailed, the stunned holiday-makers were herded away from the shore, and the beach was sealed off.[1]

What they had just witnessed was the abortive outcome of an attempted guerrilla raid on Israel by the Palestine Liberation Front, a faction of Yasser Arafat's PLO. As the Israeli authorities subsequently discovered, it was designed to be one of the most audacious and potentially lethal Palestinian attacks on the Jewish state for many years. Three days previously, a Libyan merchant ship had sailed from the port of Benghazi carrying six Libyan-made fibreglass speedboats powered with two 22-horsepower engines and armed with 23mm machine guns and Katyusha rockets, together with a crew of sixteen or more commandos, some of whom had been training in Libya for up to two years. The mother ship had deposited the boats – named after a string of famous Arab battles – in the Mediterranean some 120 miles off the Israeli coast, and under cover of darkness they had raced for the population centre of Tel Aviv. According to the PLF leader, Mohammed Zaidan (Abul Abbas) – who had achieved earlier notoriety for the hijacking of the cruise liner *Achille Lauro* in 1985 – 'Operation Jerusalem' was aimed at a private bathing resort for senior army officers, a 'legitimate' military target; according to the Israelis, its goal was to kill and maim indiscriminately in the hotel area of downtown Tel Aviv.[2]

Fortunately for the Israelis, not much went according to plan. Three of the Palestinian boats broke down on the way to Israel, and a fourth – a fuel supply vessel – sank. Of the two that managed the full voyage, one was intercepted by an Israeli naval patrol boat near a kibbutz to the north of the metropolis, and its crew members were captured after being ordered to jump into the sea; the other was pursued to Nizzanim, where seven of its crew surrendered and the other four were killed in a gun battle in the sand dunes. No Israelis were harmed.[3]

The raid did, however, exact serious political casualties – principal among them Yasser Arafat, who heard the news with some dismay at the conclusion of a summit meeting of Arab leaders in the Iraqi capital Baghdad. For the PLO leader, the attack could scarcely have come at a worse time. For months he had been struggling to keep alive the hopes he had invested in the dialogue his organization had secured with the United States in December 1988. For months he had been arguing with colleagues that it was worth persevering with the PLO's peace initiative, despite the barely perceptible progress it had yielded towards winning recognition for Palestinian rights. Now, with the political climate in the Middle East deteriorating with a rapidity no-one could have foreseen, his attempt to garner kudos for the PLO in the West had reached a dead end. Instinctively Arafat knew that he would not be able to escape the most searching questions from the American Government over the raid, questions for which he would find it difficult, if not impossible, to provide a satisfactory answer. The Israelis, who had been conducting a rearguard action against the US-PLO dialogue from the very first, were already holding Arafat personally responsible for the attack, saying that it proved once and for all that the PLO had not, as Arafat had pledged, abandoned terrorism.[4] The Americans were demanding that in order to demonstrate the contrary, he condemn it and punish those responsible.

The problem was that in this case, 'those responsible' included some powerful friends – allies he could not afford to alienate. They included a man with whom Arafat's fortunes had by now become inextricably and fatefully entangled: Iraq's President Saddam Hussein, principal sponsor of the Abul Abbas group. Arafat was beginning to realize that his latest marriage of convenience might carry a price.[5]

In the eighteen months since his fumbling 'breakthrough' to talks with the American superpower Arafat had been on an eventful and terribly revealing journey. It started amid extravagant Palestinian hopes that in finally agreeing to a dialogue with the PLO after more than a decade's cold shoulder, the US had at least implicitly endorsed the Palestinians' right to a state of their own. It continued through forlorn expectations that Washington would use its undoubted leverage over Israel to prod it into meaningful peace negotiations. And it ended – with the Jewish state refusing to budge and welcoming a new tide of immigrants

– in a despairing sense that the Americans were content to acquiesce in the final obliteration of the Palestinians' quest for a homeland.

Part of the problem lay in the utterly divergent assumptions with which the two sides had approached the talks. As far as Arafat was concerned, a dialogue with the US in itself promised to take him three-quarters of the way to a settlement of the Palestinian problem. He had always told himself, as he remarked back in 1974, that 'the US holds the key to Israel'.[6] As he saw it, US 'recognition' of the PLO would automatically entail pressure on Israel to do likewise – and if it failed to comply it would have to face the consequences. For the Americans, agreeing to talk to the PLO was never more than a small part of the means to an end. Then Secretary of State George Shultz was very explicit about this from the outset: opening the 'substantive dialogue' neither implied recognition of the organization nor acceptance of a Palestinian state; it was merely a step which might help oil the slow-grinding wheels of the peace process.[7] The dialogue was to be restricted in scope and confined to one diplomatic channel, involving the American ambassador in Tunis, Robert Pelletreau, and a middle-level PLO negotiating team. And in the meantime, the PLO was to be pressed to the hilt to abide by the letter and spirit of Arafat's latest commitments – especially his pledge to renounce terrorism.

At the start, Arafat seemed anxious to please his new-found negotiating partners, for example by offering to help the US Administration with its inquiries over the terrorist bombing of a Pan Am jumbo jet in the skies over Scotland on 23 December 1988, an attack widely blamed on the Damascus-based Palestinian splinter group, the PFLP-GC.[8] But as the dialogue got under way the next month in a Tunisian government guest house near the ruins of Carthage, nagging questions remained – not least concerning how terrorism was to be defined. In his first formal meeting with the three-man PLO team, Pelletreau spent much of the time urging his interlocutors to order a halt to Palestinian cross-border raids into Israel. Arafat was dismayed, for he thought it had been understood that the PLO reserved the right to persist with 'legitimate acts of resistance' against the Israeli occupation of Palestinian land; and although his own Fatah forces had quietly stopped cross-border activities some weeks before in what was tantamount to a truce, he knew it would be nigh-on impossible to persuade the more militant factions within the PLO to do likewise.

Notwithstanding the desire of the newly-installed US President, George Bush, to make progress on the Middle East conflict, the history of their arm's-length dealings with Arafat had taught the Americans to be grudging and suspicious negotiators. And if Washington still harboured doubts, the Israelis, who had been shocked when the dialogue with the PLO started, were determined to amplify them. Scarcely a week went by when the Israeli propaganda machine did not find an opportunity to cast aspersions on the image of a peace–loving PLO. In February, government sources claimed that Arafat's Fatah faction had set up an underground 'Popular Army' in the occupied territories with the aim of assassinating Israelis as well as Palestinians accused of collaborating with the Israeli authorities.[9] On numerous other occasions, PLO leaders themselves provided their detractors with ammunition by uttering bloodcurdling threats against Israel or suggesting to their constituents that the organization's 'two-state' peace plan was merely a stage on the road to the recovery of all of Palestine. Arafat was no more willing or able to rein in his loquacious colleagues than he had been in the past. Over time, the Israelis were able to use the continuation of such rhetoric to sow mounting disquiet among sympathizers in the US Congress, and the administration was persuaded to set up a team with the specific job of monitoring PLO statements. Even at this early stage, the noose was tightening.

Nevertheless, the PLO's new line was beginning to bring other sorts of dividend. A stream of prestigious visitors – including for the first time a British junior Foreign Office minister, William Waldegrave – made its way to his lair in Tunis, and European governments regularly welcomed his personal envoys. Capitalizing on the PLO's unilateral declaration of an independent state the previous November, Arafat trotted the Arab, socialist and Non-aligned parts of the glove, raising the Palestinian flag outside newly-renamed PLO 'embassies'. The organization stepped up its long-standing campaign to win full membership of United Nations agencies – focusing its efforts, much to the annoyance of the US and other Western countries, on the hitherto non-political World Health Organization and on Unesco. And Arafat himself – ever a stickler for protocol – began to demand a formal enhancement of his status.

On 2 April, PLO headquarters in Tunis announced that the movement's Central Council had unanimously elected him President of the still-putative State of Palestine. He would retain the job, said his spokesman, until democratic elections could take place there. The timing of the move baffled even Arafat's closest colleagues. The idea of 'promoting' him had been a debating point for at least six months, but those who had considered it thought they had decided it could await progress towards formation of a provisional government for the state. Was their leader now intent on giving himself more than the usual airs?[10] The explanation was that Arafat was about to embark on his first meetings with some of the most important Western leaders and wanted to be able to communicate with them on an equal footing. Even if they did not recognize his state, the governments of France, Italy and Japan would have to give him presidential treatment.

His Paris visit, in May 1989, was a high point. From his heavily guarded suite in the luxurious Hotel Crillon, he watched with relish as Jewish demonstrators protested outside in the Place de la Concorde; was received with pomp and circumstance by President Mitterrand; banqueted with a phalanx of government ministers; and gave an address (impromptu, because an aide had forgotten to bring his prepared speech) to the cream of the French intelligentsia. He was even treated – by Culture Minister Jack Lang, at his own request – to a special midnight tour of the Louvre, in which he roamed the corridors and pretended, with helpful prompting from the Minister, to recognize the paintings. 'The staff had to be hauled back from their beds and bars. The Louvre had never opened out of hours for anybody before,' an Arafat confidant who was present reported. 'Imagine the publicity: terrorist turned culture vulture!'[11]

It was an act that was going to be difficult to sustain. Arafat was still under pressure from his Western interlocutors to offer further concessions to Israel – for example, by getting the PLO formally to scrap its prized National Covenant, which calls for the liberation of all Palestine through armed struggle and declares the establishment of Israel 'fundamentally null and void'. His response, as usual, was to indulge in ingenious wordplay. When in Paris he took up a suggestion from French Foreign Minister Roland Dumas and declared the Covenant *caduc* – a French legal term whose approximate meaning can be translated as 'lapsed' or 'superseded'.[12] Arafat had certainly never heard the word before; asked by an Arab journalist why he had used a French term, he said with no conscious irony that French was 'a universal language which is a treasure of legal terms – such as "*persona non grata*" '.[13] The statement won him temporary plaudits in the West and caused a minor storm within the PLO; but everybody knew that it would take a full gathering of the Palestinian clans to annul the organization's founding charter, and that such a move was about as likely as Arafat paying a state visit to Jerusalem.

Symbolically important as they were, all Arafat's diplomatic gains could not disguise the fact that there was precious little evidence of progress towards the goal he had set himself:

the convening of an international Middle East peace conference, under UN sponsorship, to bring Israel, the PLO and Arab states together and force Israeli withdrawal from the occupied territories. Israel's coalition government, dominated by hard-line Prime Minister Yitzhak Shamir and his Likud party, had other ideas. As adamantly opposed to an international conference as they were to the idea of talking to Arafat's PLO, the Likud and Labour coalition partners were cooking up a plan designed to launch a different kind of 'peace process' and to deflect external pressure on them to concede territory. The proposal, originally devised by the Labour Defence Minister, Yitzhak Rabin, and touted by Shamir during an official visit to Washington in April, was to hold elections among the 1.7 million inhabitants of the West Bank and Gaza Strip with a view to selecting a delegation for talks with Israel. While the final status of the territories would be left indeterminate, the initial objective would be to set up a limited form of Palestinian self-rule for a transitional period lasting up to five years. The plan, in emphasizing democracy, was carefully calculated to appeal to the Bush administration. But in ruling out any role for the PLO, and indeed implying that alternatives to the organization might be found were the Palestinians of the territories to be allowed to vote free from 'intimidation', it was bound to be viewed by Arafat with intense scepticism to say the least.

This was the proposal that Bush and his Secretary of State, James Baker, picked up and set about trying to 'sell' to the PLO. It was, they reasoned, about the best opening bid that could be expected from Israel's divided government. But it might just, with suitable modification, be turned into a basis for Israeli-Palestinian talks – what one Baker adviser described as 'a journey of a thousand steps'.[14]

So began a protracted and bizarre bout of shadow-boxing between Shamir, Defence Minister Rabin and Arafat, with Washington as timid referee and amid persistent heckling from Israeli and Palestinian opponents on the sidelines. The common ground was tenuous, to put it mildly. Neither Shamir nor the PLO viewed the process with anything other than distaste, but neither wanted to be blamed for bringing it to a halt; each saw his essential task as being to lure the other into a political trap. That was certainly the argument that Palestinians in the occupied territories were putting to Arafat as a justification for not saying no to elections. By playing along, they said, you stand a chance of forcing Shamir to implement a plan in which he himself does not actually believe. If you reject elections, as Shamir fully expects, you will be 'tainted as using "terror" rather than politics'.[15]

For the first few months, Arafat seemed to be winning something of a victory on points. He was heartened by some unusually robust criticism from the Bush administration of Israel's policies on the occupied territories, and further encouraged by the evident signs of discomfort in the Israeli Government. In talks with the Americans, his representatives remained suspicious but non-committal, seeking to encourage the US to flesh out Israel's ideas. 'Who can be against elections?' he exclaimed. 'But they have to be part of a whole plan from A to Z.'[16]

After the Shamir Government reached agreement on the plan in May, the PLO demanded assurances that elections would form part of a process that might lead to the establishment of a Palestinian state; it queried whether Palestinians from east Jerusalem would be allowed to take part (a controversial issue because Israel had annexed the Arab eastern half of the city and regarded it as part of its eternal and indivisible capital); it sought to ensure that in any pre-election negotiations with the Israelis, the PLO would be properly represented through the presence of Palestinian spokesmen from outside as well as inside the Israeli-occupied territories; it repeatedly made the rather ridiculous suggestion that Israel withdraw from the territories *before* elections, as South Africa had done from

Namibia. But it did not, as some in the Israeli Government undoubtedly hoped it would, reject the idea out of hand. As he later hinted, Arafat even received what amounted to personal messages about the plan from Rabin, carried by an Arab member of the Israeli Knesset, Abdelwahab Darousha.[17]

For once, the PLO was handling its side of the argument with relative discretion and some skill. Indeed, Arafat's behaviour was sensible enough to set off serious alarm bells within the Israeli Likud. Acting out of a mixture of personal ambition and ideological concern, hawks on the right of the party – principal among them the mastermind of the 1982 Lebanon invasion, Ariel Sharon – launched a full-scale challenge to Shamir. The Prime Minister, they said, was doing the unthinkable: negotiating by proxy with Yasser Arafat. His election plan, they claimed, was the first step down a slippery slope that could lead all the way to the establishment of a Palestinian state. The process had to stop.

The stratagem settled on by Sharon and his cohorts was to attempt to tie Shamir's hands by forcing him to attach conditions to the election plan that would in effect kill it stone dead. Their campaign came to a head at a raucous Likud central committee meeting in Tel Aviv on the evening of 5 July, and Shamir comprehensively gave in to their demands. There could be no elections, he stated, until the Palestinian *intifada* had been extinguished; east Jerusalem Arabs would be excluded from the process; Jewish settlement of the occupied territories would continue; and there could be no question of a Palestinian state emerging at the end.[18]

It was a serious blow to American hopes of getting negotiations moving. But within little more than twelve hours it was eclipsed by something worse – a terrible bus accident on the Tel Aviv-Jerusalem highway, apparently caused by a Palestinian extremist. With the bus nine miles west of Jerusalem, a bearded Arab man rushed up the aisle shouting '*Allahu Akbar*' (God is great), grabbed the steering wheel, and sent the vehicle plunging into a ravine. Fourteen Israelis were killed and twenty-seven injured.[19]

There was no obvious link between the political setback and the act of violence. Yet somehow, as so often in the Middle East, they seemed like two segments of the same taut piece of piano wire; one more tug, and the whole situation could snap. Together they encapsulated both the horrendous obstacles facing any effort to bring Israelis and Palestinians together, and the forces that were conspiring to drive Yasser Arafat's attempt at a political initiative on to the rocks.

The pressures on Arafat, from within and outside the PLO, were by now considerable. With the *intifada* in its twentieth month, there was nothing to suggest that the considerable sacrifices made by the inhabitants of the occupied territories had been to any avail. Moreover, Arafat was having great difficulty persuading the Arab states to live up to their pledges of financial support. At their summit in Algiers the previous year, Arab leaders had agreed to stump up 43 million dollars a month for the *intifada*, but only one country, Iraq, was maintaining a substantial and regular flow of funds. So difficult had the financial position become that Arafat was forced to institute a sweeping austerity programme throughout the organization during 1989. It was a consideration which was to weigh heavily on Arafat's mind as he reviewed his options in the coming months.[20]

In short, their hopes having been raised excessively high the previous winter, all that the Palestinians could now see was Arafat apparently making concession after concession, Israel digging in its heels, and the US administration, along with the moderate Arab states which ostensibly supported the PLO initiative, sitting helplessly by. More than that, the Americans seemed to Arafat to be conspiring to make things more difficult for him. They were repeatedly raising problems over visas for PLO officials wanting to visit the

US to put across the Palestinian case; they had refused frequent requests to upgrade or broaden the dialogue or to allow the PLO office in Washington to reopen; they were continuing to veto resolutions in the UN Security Council that they considered hostile to Israel; and they were always raising concerns about the multiplicity of apparently threatening PLO statements. Some of these slights may seem trivial, but to Arafat, for whom the diplomatic niceties are akin to matters of substance, they were a serious rebuff. 'We kept receiving letters saying our deputy representative in Djibouti had been overheard in a bar saying aggressive things about Israel,' says Nabil Shaath. 'The whole episode was really very humiliating for us, it caused great anger within the PLO.'[21]

The steam building up within the movement was evident at a closed-door meeting of the 1,290-member Fatah congress, Arafat's main power base, in Tunis in early August 1989. This was the first gathering in nine years of the guerrilla fighters and others who formed the core of Fatah, and the message it delivered could not have been clearer. There was a chorus of complaint about Arafat's leadership: his autocratic style, the concessions he had offered the US and Israel without getting anything in return, and Fatah's apparent abandonment of the 'armed struggle' across Israel's northern border. This last was a development that the military men from their camps in far-flung Yemen found particularly hard to swallow. The final resolution called for a 'continuation and escalation of armed struggle . . . to end Israeli occupation of our occupied Palestinian land', a hint that in the absence of eventual progress in the PLO peace initiative, the pressure would continue building for a return to arms. For good measure, the meeting rejected several of Arafat's nominees for key Fatah posts. Top of the poll came PLO 'foreign minister' Farouk Kaddoumi, noted for his doctrinaire views.[22]

With lines thus hardening on both the Israeli and Palestinian sides, and Arafat warning periodically that he might consider calling for an all-out campaign of civil disobedience in the occupied territories or even the use of firearms, time was slipping away for American peace efforts. Secretary Baker struggled to keep the momentum up in the next few months, enlisting Egypt's President Hosni Mubarak in a fresh bid to set up an acceptable Israeli-Palestinian negotiating framework. But nobody's heart was in it, and all the exchanges produced was an arcane collection of procedural documents, ranging from a ten-point initiative from Mubarak to a five-point plan from Baker. The proposals involved meetings of Egyptian, Israeli and American government officials and the selection of 'acceptable' Palestinian negotiating partners. But no proposal could bridge the fundamental divide between Shamir's refusal to have anything whatsoever to do with the PLO and Arafat's insistence on preserving at least a symbolic role in the process. As the PLO leader never tired of pointing out, it was probably the first time in history that one party to a negotiation was insisting on choosing the opposing team. All Baker could do to signal his impatience with the Israelis was threaten to drop the mediation effort once and for all.

By December, Arafat's exasperation was almost complete. He was fed up with the US attempts to appease Israel by whittling away the PLO's role to invisibility. He had received no reply to a direct message he had sent President Bush the previous month demanding 'a more aggressive attitude by the United States towards Israel'.[23] Moreover, he was becoming seriously irritated by the role of Egypt, whose diplomats had all but taken the place of the US-PLO dialogue as America's principal channel of communication with the organization and were beginning to apply what he saw as crude pressure on him to accept the American plan. Arafat could not accept Egypt – financially and politically beholden as it was to the US – as an impartial intermediary. His feelings were summed up by the remark of an unidentified Arab foreign minister to Caryle Murphy of the *Washington Post*: 'The process is not sustainable any longer. First they said: "Please stop terrorism and then we'll discuss with you". Second they said: "Recognize Israel and we'll discuss with you". Now they said: "Please hide yourself and we'll discuss with you". The next stage will be: "Please kill yourself and we'll discuss with you".'[24]

It was the end of the road; events in the wider world had become too momentous and too alarming for these desultory peace efforts to have much relevance. The Soviet Union, traditional ally of the Arabs, was in a state of collapse and the Middle East was far from the centre of Moscow's concerns. The PLO's other friends in what used to be communist eastern Europe – Husak in Czechoslovakia, Honecker in East Germany and Ceausescu in Romania – were falling like dominoes to democratic revolutions. Worst of all for the Palestinians, a growing flood of Jewish emigrants was being allowed to leave the Soviet Union and thanks to a recent tightening in immigration rules in the US, first choice of destination for many of them, they were heading in their thousands to Israel. As Arafat watched this latest drama unfold, he was gripped with a deepening sense of foreboding. He was going to have to admit that the current strategy had failed and explore other options with other friends.

President Saddam Hussein marched down the steps of his plane and on to the red carpet spread out on the tarmac. It was 23 February 1990, and the Iraqi leader had arrived in Amman to take part in a summit meeting to mark the first anniversary of the Arab Co-operation Council, a grouping of four Arab states – Iraq, Jordan, Yemen and Egypt – that he had been instrumental in setting up. Welcomed warmly by his friend King Hussein, he was whisked off towards the city and the usual Arab ceremonials. For Saddam, however, this was an occasion of special importance, for he planned to deliver a speech that would send ripples of excitement and alarm through the Arab world – and beyond.

When the other leaders gathered at Amman's sports centre the next day – as King Hussein remarked, the 'glorious and dear occasion' of the Prophet Mohammed's ascension – they found the Iraqi President in a grim and pensive mood. He launched forth directly. The world, he said, was changing in dramatic and for the Arabs potentially disturbing ways. The collapse of the Soviet Union had left the US in a paramount position in international politics, and the Arabs dangerously exposed to American and Israeli might. 'Given that the influence of the Zionist lobby on US policies is as powerful as ever,' he went on, 'the Arabs must take into account that there is a real possibility that Israel might embark on new stupidities within the next five years. This might take place as a result of direct or tacit US encouragement.'[25] Saddam spoke of the challenge to Arab security posed by the continuing presence of US warships in the Gulf – conveniently forgetting that this presence had been one of the factors that had helped Iraq stave off defeat at the hands of Iran only two years before. He denounced America's encouragement for 'an unprecedented exodus of Soviet Jews to Palestinian territory', and its 'increasing support for the Zionist entity's strategic arms stockpiles'. And he issued a ringing call for the Arabs to close ranks to confront the now unchallenged superpower. 'There is no place among the ranks of good Arabs for the fainthearted who would argue that as a superpower, the United States will be the decisive factor and others have no choice but to submit,' he said.[26]

One of his listeners, Egypt's President Hosni Mubarak, sat through the speech in mounting dismay. As a close ally of Washington and recipient of more than two billion dollars a year in US aid, he could not but take Saddam's statement as a personal attack. But the speech was aimed at a wider audience than that in the conference chamber.

Transmitted live on Jordanian TV, it was watched by hundreds of thousands of Palestinians in Jordan itself and in the Israeli-occupied territories, and among them it had an electrifying effect. Saddam, possessor of the largest and most powerful army of any Arab state, hardened by eight years of war with Iran, had in effect made the first public move in a bid for Iraqi leadership of the Arab world, and he was mounting his campaign in the time-honoured way by posing as the true guardian of the Palestinian cause. It was a bid that was calculated to build a groundswell of support for him among Palestinians throughout the diaspora. It was also already having curious effects on the behaviour of King Hussein of Jordan, whose kingdom contained more Palestinians than any other Arab country and who, throwing his hitherto moderate image to the winds, had started making similarly militant speeches of his own. 'That speech caught the attention of every Palestinian,' says Arafat's adviser Nabil Shaath. 'In standing up to the US and Israel in these terms, he was uttering words that had not been heard in the Arab world for a very long time.'[27]

Arafat was likewise attracted by what he had heard. Saddam had brought the litany of Palestinian complaints into the open. More than that, he had presented the Arabs with a possible course of action to redress the situation. Saddam, he reasoned, might well have the strength to force the Americans to take the PLO seriously. So began the most dangerous dalliance of Arafat's career: an open alliance with a man who was already unwittingly on course for collision with a powerful array of Western nations and half the Arab world; a man, moreover, whose real aims only tangentially coincided with those of the PLO. Already the die was being cast for a relationship that would land the Palestinian movement on the wrong side in the most devastating conflict the Arabs had ever seen.

The PLO leader had not always been on good terms with Saddam Hussein. Indeed, they had exchanged sharp words back in 1970, when Iraqi forces stationed in Jordan had failed to come to the aid of the Palestinians in the Black September civil war. And throughout the second half of the 1970s Iraq's militant ruling Baath party had conducted a violent campaign to undermine Arafat's leadership through the agency of a Palestinian splinter group, the Fatah Revolutionary Council, led by Sabri al-Banna (Abu Nidal), the erstwhile Fatah representative in Baghdad. It was Saddam who had facilitated Banna's break with Arafat in 1974, and the Iraqis who provided him with the means to assassinate a number of PLO moderates close to the chairman in subsequent years. So deep was the enmity between the two faction chiefs that a Fatah court sentenced Banna to death in absentia in 1975.

PLO-Iraqi relations began to thaw as Iraq, under pressure in the Iran-Iraq war, sought to return to the mainstream of Arab politics in the early 1980s. Baghdad became the PLO's main military base after its evacuation from Beirut in 1982, and following the Israeli bombing of his political headquarters in Tunis in October 1985, Arafat spent weeks on end in the Iraqi capital. As his feelings of insecurity grew – notably after the murder of his deputy Khalil al-Wazir in April 1988 – he came to rely more and more on Saddam's ruthlessly efficient security forces for protection. They obligingly installed anti-aircraft fortifications around his Baghdad residence and, at a time when other Arab leaders were becoming distinctly sparing in their material assistance to the PLO, provided him with free use of a stable of Iraqi official jets. 'Arafat felt at personal risk after the assassination of Wazir; the only place he felt secure was his office in Baghdad,' said an aide. 'From 1989, the Iraqis allocated three planes and crews to be at Arafat's beck and call. The only other Arab state that offered this sort of facility was Libya. Other heads of state only used to send planes to bring him on specific visits.'[28]

The Iraqis helped in other ways, not least in supporting the *intifada*. In the very earliest days of the Palestinian uprising, the PLO was stunned to receive a lump-sum payment of 50 million dollars from Baghdad. 'It was the largest single sum the PLO had ever received from anybody,' one Arafat confidant later recalled. 'And this at a time when Iraq was virtually alone in paying. Arafat went through very difficult times in 1988–89 keeping the *intifada* going. Gadaffi, for example, would pay up one month, then get angry again with the PLO for three months. But all the while, Iraq was paying systematically, regularly, four million dollars a month to the *intifada*, right from the beginning.'[29] In 1989, Saddam went further still, by according the family of every 'martyr' of the uprising a sum of money equivalent to a martyr's pension from the Iraqi army. Just as important, he provided Arafat with much-needed political backing when he was struggling to sustain his attempt to initiate peace talks. In the face of mounting criticism of Arafat's concessions from Libya and Syria, the Iraqi leader reportedly told him at one point: 'God bless you. Go ahead with your peace initiative.'[30]

It was a seductive mix, especially when contrasted with the perceived parsimony of the other Arab states. By early 1990, Arafat had become increasingly preoccupied with the lack of financial and political support he was receiving from elsewhere in the Arab world. On the one hand, he was under public pressure from the Egyptians for failing to comply with American demands over the peace process – pressure that increased sharply in early February after a grenade attack by Palestinian extremists on an Israeli tourist bus near the Egyptian town of Ismailiya, in which ten people were killed. On the other, the traditional Arab monarchies of the Gulf – main source of his funding over the previous twenty-five years – had drastically reduced their contributions to the PLO's and Fatah's coffers.

Arafat was aware that the Kuwaitis, while still collecting money for the *intifada*, were using other conduits than the PLO to funnel it into the occupied territories. A local fund-raising committee, which raised about 30 million dollars, is said to have handed part of its contribution to a member of the Jordanian chamber of commerce for distribution in the West Bank. Other funds, from both Kuwait and Saudi Arabia, were passed directly to Hamas, the Islamic fundamentalist group that was gaining increasing support in the territories, especially in Gaza, in competition with the mainstream PLO factions. While the Gulf sheikhs were probably responding to domestic fundamentalist pressures in their redirection of funds, Arafat smelled an unholy conspiracy to build up Hamas and weaken the PLO. He took to mounting thinly-veiled attacks on the Gulf rulers, contrasting the amounts they had given the Palestinian movement with the lavish sums spent, in co-operation with the US, on supporting the Afghan resistance.

'The Arab governments spent in Afghanistan in a single year more than they have provided to the PLO in the past twenty-five years,' he claimed in a February newspaper interview. 'Is it not a shame that the Arabs should be so miserly towards the *intifada*?' In a joking aside, he suggested that Jerusalem – 'al-Quds' in Arabic – should be given the Afghan-sounding name 'Qudsabad' to persuade the Arabs to support its liberation.[31]

Against this background, it is not entirely surprising that Arafat found himself lurching towards Baghdad in the spring of 1990. The storm clouds gathering over the Middle East were large enough to warrant an urgent search for shelter. The US-sponsored peace process had died its lingering death, and the coffin was slammed shut on 13 March when the Israeli Government collapsed in disagreement over the plan for Palestinian elections; its successor seemed likely to be a coalition of the hard right, led by a Shamir still less likely to make concessions. The *intifada*, main engine of the revolution these past twenty-eight months, appeared to be losing momentum, degenerating into a violent set of intra-Palestinian feuds which had already claimed the lives of more than 200 Arabs.

Deepening the gloom beyond measure was the continuing flow of *émigrés* from the Soviet Union to Israel. In the early months of 1990, as Soviet Jews took advantage of Moscow's newly relaxed emigration rules, several planeloads of them were arriving every day at Tel Aviv's Ben Gurion airport. During 1990 alone, Israel was expecting up to 100,000 to come by way of various European centres, and as many as 500,000 by 1995. For Arafat and every other Palestinian, this new influx to the promised land was a development of near-apocalyptic proportions. It gave a fresh infusion of blood to the Jewish state and eroded the demographic arguments predicting that, thanks to their higher birth rate, Palestinians would outnumber Jews in Palestine in a few decades' time. It seemed likely to add to the already severe pressures on space and resources in the land between the Mediterranean Sea and the River Jordan, and to strengthen the arguments of those Israeli politicians who favoured expanding their country's frontiers and forcibly 'transferring' Palestinians from the West Bank and Gaza. In short, it reawakened awful folk memories of previous Palestinian disasters: the waves of exodus from the land during Israel's War of Independence in 1948 and the Six-Day War in 1967. With Israel proceeding, in defiance of American pleas, to settle some of its new citizens in the occupied territories, Arafat felt a convulsion that might foreclose for ever the possibility of a Palestinian homeland was under way. Some influential commentators in the region thought they could already hear the drums of another Middle East war, though none of them could have foreseen how soon it would arrive or what form it would take.

Arafat felt these dangerous events demanded immediate action. In an attempt to staunch the flow of Jews to Israel that was as forlorn as it was ill-judged, he despatched top PLO officials on a series of missions to Moscow and the European capitals that were being used as transit points for the *émigrés*. He himself embarked in April on yet another whistle-stop tour of the Arab world. His goal: to arrange an emergency summit meeting of heads of state that would consider a unified Arab approach, in the one capital which seemed to appreciate the need to confront the problem – Saddam Hussein's Baghdad.

Saddam had his own pressing reasons for wanting to host a summit. The mixture of paranoia and overweening ambition that had given rise to his February speech in Amman had merely intensified in the intervening weeks, fuelled by threatening noises from Israel, increasing economic hardship at home, and what he took to be signs of a Western conspiracy against him. Britain and the US, in particular, had been leading an international crackdown on Iraqi efforts to augment its military arsenal with weapons of mass destruction. In March, Saddam's regime gave ammunition to its Western detractors by hanging a British-based journalist, Farzad Bazoft, on unproven charges of spying for Israel. And on 2 April, in a speech broadcast on Baghdad radio, he gave the Israelis a blunt warning not to attempt a pre-emptive strike against Iraq, as they had done nine years before in bombing an Iraqi nuclear reactor. Anyone threatening Iraq with nuclear weapons would be met with a chemical attack, he said. 'I swear to God that we will let our fire eat half of Israel if it tries to wage anything against Iraq.'[32] A summit meeting would be a means of rallying the rest of the Arab world behind him in the developing confrontation, and thereby further enhancing his status, in much the same way as Gamal Abdel Nasser had done in the 1960s. Arafat was only too happy to play along, travelling tirelessly in an effort to persuade such intensely sceptical leaders as Egypt's Mubarak of the need to take a stand.

At this stage, the PLO leader was still trying to preserve the fiction that he could continue to straddle the rapidly deepening divide at the centre of Arab politics. An alliance with both Egypt and Iraq, he told his aides, would enable him to maintain channels to the US in pursuit of his peace initiative, while at the same time demonstrating that the PLO had other options. It was a strange and self-deluding variation on the theme of 'peace through strength', as explained later by Afif Safieh, the PLO's representative in London: 'We hoped to remain equidistant between Cairo and Baghdad, to use Iraq's military power to improve our bargaining position.'[33] Another Arafat adviser concurs: 'There was a feeling that Iraq was the one country with military might in the Arab world, that the Arab threat of a gun in a field of impotence might help to propel a negotiated settlement.'[34]

In reality, Arafat was already more deeply in cahoots with Saddam than he cared to admit. In late April, the PLO Executive Committee convened in Baghdad and issued a fawning statement of support for 'His Excellency the Knight President Saddam Hussein'.[35] A few days later, reports emerged that Arafat had ordered nearly 3,000 guerrilla fighters from Jordan and Yemen to regroup in Iraq by the middle of May. Their purpose was to train and 'to protect Iraq against a possible Israeli assault', said a PLO spokesman.[36] It was another fateful tie binding the PLO's fortunes to those of Iraq, another step in Saddam's carefully calculated strategy of winning the backing of the influential Palestinian constituency for his wider aims. As one long-standing Arafat adviser put it: 'It was a two-way road. Arafat needed Saddam and Saddam needed Arafat.'[37] By no means all of the Palestinian movement was wholeheartedly in sympathy with Arafat's shift. Other senior PLO officials regarded their enforced sojourns in Baghdad with pronounced distaste; they found the atmosphere oppressive, the communications erratic, the hotels unpleasant. People from the occupied territories likewise had mixed feelings. Suspicious of Saddam's dictatorial rule, they shied away from making the journey to the Iraqi capital themselves for fear of Israeli retribution. Many in the PLO also wondered uneasily what sort of *quid pro quo* the Iraqi leader might demand for the assistance he was giving. Arafat did not hesitate to brush aside such doubts. 'He would say we are not being asked by the Iraqis to do anything,' one PLO official later recalled. 'He could not see what this would cost or what the Iraqis would require of him.'[38]

In the early morning of 20 May 1990, about fifty Palestinian men from the Gaza towns of Rafah and Khan Younis gathered at the intersection of two main roads in Rishon Le-Zion, a suburb just south of Tel Aviv. Casual construction labourers, they were waiting to be picked up for the day's work when an Israeli dressed in army uniform appeared, brandishing a rifle. Without further ado, he ordered the Arabs to sit on the ground in three rows. Then after a pause, he started to shoot at them. Indiscriminately and repeatedly he fired at the small crowd, stopped to reload, fired again, and drove off. Seven Palestinians died and eleven were wounded.[39]

With the Arab world already working itself up into a rhetorical frenzy over Soviet immigration to Israel, this senseless incident, perpetrated by a man the Israeli authorities described as 'deranged', raised the temperature to boiling point. The occupied territories erupted into some of the worst riots since the *intifada* had begun. At a meeting of the UN Security Council, specially convened in Geneva because the US administration, as in 1988, had refused him a visa to visit UN headquarters in New York, Arafat furiously demanded measures to protect the Palestinians. Behind the scenes, the Americans indicated that they would be prepared to back a major UN fact-finding mission to the occupied territories. There was no need, therefore, for the PLO to press for a fully-fledged resolution on the issue just yet. Somewhat mollified, Arafat left again for Tunis, only to discover that the Americans were having second thoughts. Nabil Shaath would report later: 'Arafat was enraged; he felt defeated; he felt tricked; he felt ambushed. He really felt at the end of the rope with the Americans reneging on everything, even a small fact-finding party.'[40] It was to be the last gasp in Arafat's faltering diplomatic attempt to engage the attention of the West.

It was also the most ominous possible backdrop for the summit meeting of Arab leaders that was about to convene in Baghdad. What had happened on Black Sunday in Israel and thereafter at the UN added fuel to Saddam Hussein's argument that since Israel was bent on crushing the Palestinians and the US government was not to be trusted to stop it, the Arab states had better get ready to act in defence of the cause themselves. As the leaders gathered on 28 May in the glass-and-marble conference centre across the road from Baghdad's Al-Rashid Hotel for their inappropriately named 'summit of hope and necessity', they knew they were about to participate in a battle for the soul of the Arab world, a struggle between advocates of confrontation and of conciliation. It had to be said that, as had been the case before the war of 1967, events were moving rapidly in the confrontationists' direction. Arafat, having persuaded Saddam to put this particular stage at his disposal, took to it with a slide-projector and maps, seeking to illustrate the Zionists' plan to establish a 'Greater Israel from the Nile to the Euphrates'.[41] And Saddam himself (the name means 'one who confronts') emerged triumphant, confirmed in the eyes of many observers as paramount leader of the Arab world and protector of the oppressed, his standing with the PLO enhanced by another cash injection of 25 million dollars.

What outsiders did not realize as the deliberations ended was that Saddam had also privately placed his own, quite different agenda on the table, and that some of those he was confronting had been right there in the conference chamber. At a closed summit session with only the other Arab leaders present, Saddam complained bitterly about over-production of oil by the pro-American states of the Gulf, which he said was driving prices down and depriving Iraq of sorely-needed income. Looking pointedly at the

Emir of Kuwait and the President of the United Arab Emirates, he proclaimed: 'You're virtually waging an economic war against my country.'[42] It was, as the other Arab states became uncomfortably aware in the next few weeks, the first shot in Saddam's real war – a campaign to intimidate his Gulf neighbours, push oil prices up and thereby bail out his bankrupt economy, a campaign in which the support of the PLO, as representative of the 'struggling Palestinian masses', was to be a vital ingredient.

Barely was the ink dry on the summit's final communiqué when Saddam sent another unmistakable message, in the form of the 30 May speedboat raid on the beaches of Tel Aviv by guerrillas of the Palestine Liberation Front. That the Iraqi leader was behind the attack could not seriously be in doubt. PLF leader Abul Abbas had long been based in Baghdad and was frequently to be seen in Saddam's company. Moreover, the raid and its consequences dovetailed neatly with Saddam's grand strategy – to undermine pro-Western Arab leaders and create an atmosphere of violent uncertainty across the Middle East. For Arafat, it was the first telltale sign that his alignment with Iraq was going to carry a cost. One PLO insider would later recall: 'It really put him in an impossible position. Arafat felt the Abul Abbas incident had been calculated by Saddam as a grand finale for the summit – not to embarrass him as such but to show other Arab leaders that the way to liberation was through arms not conciliation. The Egyptians certainly felt it was aimed at them and their moderate line.'[43] Another Arafat confidant would take a somewhat harsher view: 'The raid was designed to bring the US-PLO dialogue to an end and create an atmosphere of despair and bitterness among the Palestinians, so that they would support him in his confrontation with the US and its allies.'[44]

Whatever the intention, that was certainly the effect. Arafat came under insistent pressure from Washington to condemn the raid and discipline Abul Abbas, failing which the US-PLO dialogue would be broken off. But his continuing fury with the US over its handling of the recent UN debate – expressed the day after the raid in an American veto of a fact-finding mission to the occupied territories – and his cosy relationship with Saddam meant that he was neither willing nor able to comply. Action against Abbas, he felt, would anger the Iraqis as well as his Palestinian constituents, at a time when he was in any case wondering whether the US dialogue was actually worth saving. The signs were that his judgement was only too correct. Just after the raid, two senior Fatah figures, Salah Khalaf and Mahmoud Abbas, suggested mounting an official inquiry into it, but Saddam instantly responded by declaring Abul Abbas an 'especially honoured guest' in Iraq and Arafat hastily quashed the idea. Instead, he spent the next three weeks in futile word games, and on 20 June an exasperated President Bush announced he was suspending talks. In effect, the US and its moderate Arab allies were giving up on Arafat, whose response was to warn that the Middle East was drifting to war, and to sink ever deeper into the embrace of Saddam Hussein. He began to talk luridly of the stones of Palestinian protesters in the West Bank becoming transformed into Iraqi missiles.[45]

The growing tensions in the Arab world were all too evident at a meeting of Arab foreign ministers in Tunis in mid-July. Moderate Egypt did not even bother to attend, and Arafat joined forces with Iraqi Foreign Minister Tariq Aziz in thinly-veiled criticism of President Mubarak. In one of those arcane historical disputes that often cause rows of baffling ferocity in the Arab world, Arafat touched raw nerves with a slighting reference to a pre-revolutionary Egyptian prime minister, Mustafa Nahhas Pasha, who he said had urged the Palestinians to hand the Wailing Wall over to the Jews.[46] Cairo responded in kind, with bitter personal attacks in the press and recrimination from Mubarak himself. Egypt, he said, had worked hard to keep the US-PLO talks alive at Arafat's request. Yet his reward had been a torrent of Palestinian abuse, and silence from those he was trying to help.[47] With the Arab players who had been most keen to co-operate with American peace moves now squabbling openly, the scene was set for Saddam the confrontationist to make his big power play.

On the morning of 17 July, Aziz arrived at the office of Arab League Secretary-General Chedli Klibi and handed him a piece of paper. It was a memorandum from Saddam Hussein, and it amounted to a virtual declaration of war on Kuwait. The letter accused Kuwait and the UAE of deliberately undermining the Iraqi economy by exceeding their OPEC oil production quotas. It charged Kuwait with violating the Iraqi border to steal Iraqi oil reserves and with committing aggression by building military installations on Iraqi territory, and it bluntly demanded that the billions of dollars the Gulf states had lent Iraq during its war with Iran should be written off.[48] In his most direct style, Saddam was demanding money with menaces. Implicitly, he was also reviving a long-standing dispute over the Iraq-Kuwait frontier and the status of two small Kuwaiti islands, Bubiyan and Warbah, and reawakening memories of attempts by Iraq in the past to swallow its tiny neighbour whole. This was the conflict for which Saddam had been preparing all these months, and the reason why he had been anxious to secure political support from the Palestinians. By imposing his will on Kuwait, Saddam calculated that he would be well on the way to a dominant position in the entire Gulf region, capable of extorting more funds from his neighbours and of dictating their policies on oil production and prices, and bolstered in his determination to lead the Arab world in standing up to the US and Israel.

Klibi immediately set off for Kuwait to try to defuse the row, followed by a procession of other would-be mediators, including Mubarak. The Egyptian President secured what he thought was a promise from Saddam not to use force and an agreement between the Iraqi leader and Sheikh Jaber al-Sabah, the Emir of Kuwait, to hold talks in the Saudi Arabian port of Jeddah. But the Iraqis were also stepping up their demand for an immediate cash payment of more than 2.4 billion dollars in compensation for oil allegedly stolen by Kuwait from the Rumailah oilfield and at the same time were massing tens of thousands of troops on the Kuwaiti frontier. The auguries, to say the least, were not exactly promising.[49]

Enter, somewhat belatedly, Yasser Arafat. The PLO leader had been feeling increasingly isolated and frustrated as the war of words between Iraq and Kuwait had intensified, flitting between his lonely Baghdad redoubt and his political headquarters in Tunis. The May Arab summit had resolved none of his problems. Apart from Iraq and Saudi Arabia, none of the Arab states was paying up in support of the *intifada*; and for once nobody was even bothering to pretend that there was any life left in the 'Middle East peace process'. Any lingering hopes that Arafat might have harboured that somebody might do something to get talks moving again had been snuffed out at a lunch in Tunis in mid-July with a 'troika' of foreign ministers from the European Community, who in a somewhat aimless conversation across the heavily laden tables had conveyed a depressing, if predictable message: unless the Americans were prepared to resume the US-PLO dialogue, there was not much anybody else could do.

Arafat sought diversion from the encircling gloom in his own mediation effort. After all, the Iraq-Kuwait dispute was one of which he had first-hand experience. He had been living in Kuwait when the Iraqis had made their first post-independence grab for the emirate in 1961. And in 1972, he had worked hard to end another bout of bullying from Baghdad over the disputed islands. According to advisers, he had sent PLO executive committee member Mahmoud Abbas (Abu Mazen) to stay for three days and nights on Bubiyan island in order to forestall an Iraqi attack.[50] On Thursday 26 July 1990, Arafat summoned his ambassador in Kuwait, Awni Battash, to an urgent meeting in the Iraqi capital. He planned to ask Saddam Hussein face to face what sort of settlement he was really after, and then to sound the Kuwaitis out for signs of flexibility. There was, admittedly, not much ground for hope. Before leaving Kuwait on the Friday, Battash asked the Kuwaiti Crown Prince and Prime Minister, Sheikh Saad al-Abdullah al-Sabah, whether there was any message he wanted to convey to Arafat. 'You know our position,' was the dour reply.[51]

Flying south to Kuwait on Saturday night in his Iraqi-provided jet, Arafat felt the pull of conflicting emotions. His three-hour conversation with Saddam that day had convinced him that the Iraqi leader meant exactly what he said, and that if Kuwait did not give him what he wanted, there was a very real danger that he would grab the disputed border area by force. On the other hand, Arafat was aware that he himself owed a certain debt to Kuwait: the place where, more than three decades before, he and his colleagues had taken the first tentative steps towards launching the Palestinian revolution; the country whose Crown Prince had literally saved his life in the Jordanian civil war of 1970. He saw it as his mission – in talks with Saad and his cousin the Emir, Sheikh Jaber – to save the Kuwaitis from themselves.

'I came when I was a young man to this country,' he told the Emir on the Sunday morning in his modest Dasman palace on the Kuwaiti shore. 'I worked here as an engineer. I love your people. I love your country. I ate bread and salt with your people. So I am sincere when I tell you: please solve your problem with Saddam Hussein.

'I am coming from Baghdad and I am frightened, so please cancel the debt,' Arafat went on. 'Pay him the price of the petrol from Rumailah, and you can lease him Bubiyan and Warbah for ninety-nine years. This is the only solution to stop a catastrophe.'

'Do you mean he will use armed forces?' asked Sheikh Jaber distractedly.

'I don't know but I am afraid,' replied the Palestinian.

Jaber persisted: 'Mr Mubarak told us that Saddam would not use force.'

'Maybe President Mubarak misunderstood Saddam.'

But the Emir was losing interest in the conversation. Arafat could hardly be regarded as an impartial mediator, and what he was proposing amounted to a comprehensive cave-in to Iraq's demands. Brushing him aside with an assurance that the issues would be discussed with the Iraqis in Jeddah, Sheikh Jaber abruptly changed the subject and asked what Arafat was doing about Soviet Jewish emigration to Israel. As Arafat was ushered out of the Emir's presence, the warning was still on his lips: 'Please solve it. I am frightened something will happen.'[52] Arafat had no better luck in a subsequent private meeting with his old friend Sheikh Saad. The Kuwaitis seemed curiously fatalistic about the gathering storm, and Arafat climbed aboard his jet that afternoon for the flight to Tunis with empty hands and a heavy heart. 'I will return to Kuwait,' he proclaimed, as if to suggest that there was still room for mediation.[53] He did not.

# 18

# *Engulfed*

'Iraq and Palestine represent a common will. We will be together side by side and after the great battle, God willing, we will pray together in Jerusalem.' Arafat to a rally in Baghdad on 7 January 1991.

It was just before dawn on 2 August when Awni Battash, the PLO's long-serving ambassador to Kuwait, was awakened by the insistent ringing of the telephone beside his bed in his comfortable villa. A friend was on the phone with startling news. Iraq had invaded its tiny neighbour at 2 a.m., two hours before, sweeping aside flimsy Kuwaiti resistance in the process. Thousands of Iraqi troops, many of them from Saddam Hussein's Republican Guard, had poured across the frontier in tanks and armoured personnel carriers and were heading for the centre of Kuwait City itself.

As Battash shook himself awake and tuned in to Kuwait Radio, he knew that his most urgent task was to make contact with Tunis. Within seconds he had a familiar voice on the line. It was 2 a.m. at the other end of the Arab world and Yasser Arafat was a little surprised to hear from his ambassador at such an early hour. He had spent the night in one of his safe houses with members of his staff, and although conversation had dwelled on the implications for Arafat's own mediation efforts of the collapse that day of the Jeddah talks between the Kuwaiti Crown Prince and Saddam's deputy, no-one at PLO headquarters had expected events to unfold quite as they did. Listening to

Battash's breathless report that Iraq had invaded Kuwait, and not only that its troops were swarming into the centre of the city, Arafat was at first sceptical. At the most, he had expected the Iraqis to occupy the frontier zone around the disputed Rumailah oilfield, and perhaps seize Bubiyan and Warbah islands. But he had certainly not anticipated that his ally in Baghdad would grab the lot. Battash had some difficulty persuading Arafat that the Iraqis had come all the way into Kuwait and were in fact in the street outside his house. At one point in their seven-minute conversation he was obliged to hold the phone to the Kuwait Radio broadcast so that Arafat could hear for himself news of the invasion. So stunned was Arafat by developments, recalls Battash, that he took refuge in an appeal to the Almighty with the words: 'Nothing can be done: only by God the powerful'.[1]

Arafat got no sleep that night. Anxiously, he conferred with his lieutenants while keeping in constant touch with Battash in Kuwait. Among those summoned from their beds in the early hours of 2 August was Salah Khalaf. Together they assessed where Iraq's audacious land-grab might leave the PLO. Khalaf the chain-smoker, his face wreathed even at that early hour in a seemingly perpetual haze of cigarette smoke, felt the dangers much more acutely than his boss. The PLO Number Two worried about the fate of the more than 400,000 Palestinians in Kuwait, the largest and most important Palestinian community in the Gulf, among them his own wife and children. He feared that the crisis, and even then he was under no illusions about its dimensions, would further deflect the Arab world's flickering attention from the Palestine issue. And perhaps most important, he sensed with his keen analytical mind that Saddam Hussein's gamble would confront the PLO with one of its most agonizing choices. In short, he felt a foreboding, for he had never shared Arafat's enthusiasm for the tilt towards Baghdad. Khalaf was an infrequent visitor to the Iraqi capital. He found the atmosphere there oppressive, and he was most certainly not persuaded that Saddam, with his ambitions to lead the Arab world towards a new dawn, was the answer to the Palestinians' dreams.[2]

Arafat, on the other hand, saw it from a rather different perspective. His first reaction was that here was an opportunity to engage in one of his favourite pastimes – mediating among members of the squabbling Arab family. As so often in the past, the Iran-Iraq conflict being just one example, he found himself fluttering, like a moth to a flame, towards the role of go-between. If he could build on his pre-invasion mediating efforts he would put the Arab world in his debt. For a leader without a country and almost totally reliant on the largesse of others it was a tantalizing prospect, never mind the risks of offending one side or the other in what was to prove one of the great Arab watersheds. In his near obsession with his self-proclaimed role as mediator Arafat was to commit an historic blunder, one that would place him seriously at odds with his erstwhile benefactors in the Gulf and with Egypt, and do his shaky reputation in the West no good at all, since in Western eyes he would come to be seen as Saddam's lackey. But in those first hours after the invasion he simply did not foresee the risks, and in any case he had, by foolishly putting himself so much in Saddam's thrall, severely limited his room for manoeuvre. As explained by his longstanding adviser, the Palestinian businessman Bassel Akel, Arafat, deeply disillusioned by his experience with the US, saw in Saddam a 'chance to shuffle the deck, to mix up all the cards again and face the Americans in a different way'.[3]

Throughout 2 August, the day of the invasion, Arafat, Khalaf and others in the Palestinian leadership obsessively monitored developments in Kuwait and in the wider Arab world. Arafat was constantly on the telephone; to Arab governments; to leading Palestinians throughout the diaspora; to members of his own Executive Committee scattered about the Arab world, most especially Farouk Kaddoumi, the PLO 'foreign minister' who was chairing an emergency session of the Arab League Council in Cairo, it being Palestine's turn to chair such gatherings. The question Arafat was asking himself and others was what sort of deal would entice Saddam into disgorging most of Kuwait except perhaps for the Rumailah oilfield and Warbah and Bubiyan islands. To the PLO leader at that very early stage the issue was not one of principle, that is the inadmissibility of the seizure of territory by force, the very issue used by the PLO to assail Israel all these years, but of what bargain could be struck in the great Arab bazaar. He was not alone in this. King Hussein of Jordan was another who, having lurched into Saddam's embrace, would have immense difficulty distancing himself from the man he would describe in an interview with American television two days after the invasion as an 'Arab patriot' – a phrase that would rebound against him as he engaged in increasingly futile mediation efforts.[4]

On that first day, as Arafat plotted his mediation moves, events were proceeding with bewildering speed. Against a background of ferocious world condemnation, including an unprecedented joint US-Soviet statement, Iraq's ruling Revolutionary Command Council announced that Iraqi forces had entered Kuwait at the request of the Kuwaiti opposition, the so-called 'Interim Government of Free Kuwait'.[5] It was a sham. In the days that followed no Kuwaiti oppositionist stepped forward to provide any cover at all for Baghdad's crude lunge against its tiny neighbour. Kuwait's Emir, Sheikh Jaber al-Ahmed al-Sabah, and his cousin, Crown Prince Saad had, meanwhile, fled to Saudi Arabia just ahead of the invading Iraqis who laid siege to the Emir's Dasman palace on the Gulf seafront. In the battle for Dasman, Sheikh Jaber's youngest brother, Sheikh Fahd, was killed. Kuwaitis were to recall bitterly, as relations with Arafat's PLO soured in the days ahead, that

Fahd had once served alongside the Palestinian *fedayeen* in south Lebanon.

As Arafat prepared to set off on his travels, continuing the mediating role he had sought to play between Iraq and Kuwait before the invasion, powerful Arab figures were entering the fray and Arafat's efforts would seem puny by comparison. Syria's President Hafez al-Assad, in telephone conversations with Saudi Arabia's King Fahd and Egypt's President Hosni Mubarak on the day of the invasion, called for an emergency summit of twenty-one Arab heads of state to condemn the Iraqi aggression. President Bush, for his part, ordered the aircraft carrier USS Independence to leave its station forthwith in the Indian Ocean for the Gulf region. 'We are not ruling anything in or out,' said an American official grimly, as the Pentagon hastily dusted off its plans for military intervention to keep oil flowing from the Gulf.[6]

In fetid midsummer Cairo, Arab foreign ministers gathered in emergency session in the conference room of the Semiramis Intercontinental Hotel on the banks of the Nile. It was an acrimonious affair. After two days of sharp exchanges, the Arab League Council voted by 14–6 (the six included the PLO and Jordan) to 'condemn' the invasion and 'call for an Arab summit'. Farouk Kaddoumi, in the chair, was hard-put to keep control and came under attack from both sides. The Egyptians accused the PLO official of trying to prevent the resolution coming to a vote, while the Iraqis in the person of a furious Saadoun Hammadi, the Deputy Prime Minister, accused him of being part of the 'conspiracy' against Iraq, to which Kaddoumi replied within earshot of other foreign ministers: 'You know how much I support Iraq, and yet you accuse me.'[8] It was not the most judicious remark in the circumstances and would be counted as one more strike against the PLO's claims to evenhandedness.

Arafat himself had set off from Tunis on the morning of 3 August at the start of an ill-fated odyssey in search of an 'Arab solution'. Travelling by one of the Iraqi jets he had on more or less permanent loan from Baghdad, he went to Libya where he cooked up the first of a number of peace plans of dubious relevance. Basically, it involved frontier concessions plus the payment of money by Kuwait in exchange for an Iraqi agreement to withdraw – much the same deal as he had outlined to the Emir at his meeting with him just days before the invasion. Arafat took his 'peace plan', which the Libyan newsagency, JANA, said was aimed at blocking foreign intervention, to Egypt on Saturday 4 August, before going on to Baghdad the next day. The PLO leader was beginning to get a taste for his 'shuttle diplomacy', and to ignore the mounting costs of coming to appear, in many Arab eyes, like Saddam's messenger. When he returned to Egypt on Monday 6 August for a meeting with Mubarak at the Egyptian leader's summer residence near Alexandria, criticism was spreading like a virus in Arab capitals of the PLO's failure to condemn the invasion and unequivocally to call for Iraq's withdrawal. The best the organization could do at that early stage was to issue a limp Executive Committee statement, urging Arab leaders to end the conflict.[9]

Throughout his post-invasion manoeuvres Arafat had kept in close touch with King Hussein who, no less than the PLO leader himself, was obsessed with the search for an 'Arab solution' – a solution that seemed increasingly to Arab states opposed to the invasion like a recipe for the appeasement of Iraq. The king claimed that he had elicited Saddam's agreement to attend a mini-summit in Jeddah on Sunday 5 August, with King Fahd and other heads of state, but this had all come unstuck after the Arab League Council in Cairo condemned Iraq. A melancholy Hussein was to complain with increasing bitterness that his mediation efforts had been torpedoed by Mubarak and Fahd who had allowed the Arab League council resolution to go forward.[10] A sign of the king's troubled state of mind was his request at a meeting with

Jordanian parliamentarians in the days after the invasion that he be referred to as 'Sharif' Hussein in memory of his great-grandfather, the Hashemite Sharif Hussein of Mecca who had led the Arab Revolt against the Ottoman Turks in the early part of this century. The Saudis were not amused since Ibn Saud, the founder of the House of Saud, had displaced the Hashemites in 1924. They regarded the king's quaint request to his subjects as an affront. It was not the least of the causes of a furious onslaught against Hussein in the Saudi press and the deep chill that developed in relations between Riyadh and Amman.

Arafat was hardly faring any better than Hussein in his efforts to promote an Arab solution. When he arrived in Jeddah on Monday 6 August to be greeted by a low-ranking member of the Saudi royal family it was already becoming clear that his manoeuvrings in the Arab arena were beginning to cause grave offence among those states most bitterly opposed to Iraq's seizure of Kuwait. Pointedly, the PLO chairman was kept waiting for six hours at the palace to see King Fahd on the Tuesday and then was received for a mere half-hour, hardly time for him to outline his peace plan. The king and his courtiers were not much impressed with the bill of goods Arafat was trying to peddle, and in any case the Saudis were even then heavily engaged in discussions with the visiting US Defence Secretary, Dick Cheney, on the deployment of foreign forces. 'We think Arafat would do much better for himself if he left us alone and devoted his efforts to solving the Palestinian question,' was a Saudi official's caustic observation.[11]

Still, like a man possessed, Arafat shuttled on, going back to Baghdad to be photographed yet again in Saddam's fond embrace – an image replayed endlessly on Western television that did more than perhaps anything else to reinforce suspicions that he was somehow colluding with the Iraqi leader. And PLO propaganda continually railed against the prospect of foreign intervention, while skating over the causes of the crisis, namely Iraq's invasion of

Kuwait. 'The objective of the United States is the continuation of its hegemony over the oil-producing countries in the Arab Gulf,' charged the Voice of Palestine, broadcasting from Algiers. 'Iraq's invasion of Kuwait . . . constitutes a challenge to the United States and its policy in the area.'[12]

Cairo in midsummer is not the most comfortable of places, but when President Mubarak on 8 August, at the very height of the hot season, pleaded with Arab heads of state to hasten to the Egyptian capital for an emergency summit, most answered his call, with the notable exception of Saddam Hussein himself. 'It must not be an Arab summit at which we trade accusations and curses or tear each other apart,' Mubarak declared in a nationwide broadcast. 'It must be a summit for resolving the problem within the Arab framework which is more dignified for the Arab nation.'[13] If Yasser Arafat heard these words, there was no sign that he heeded them. Indeed, the Cairo summit of 9–10 August was to prove something of a débâcle for the hot-headed Arafat, and one for which he was to pay dearly in the weeks and months ahead.

The portents were ominous when the PLO leader arrived at Cairo airport for the summit, in an Iraqi Airlines plane with its distinctive green markings, to be greeted curtly by an unsmiling Mubarak. Arafat's use of an Iraqi jet was hardly politic, conveying an impression, as it did, that he was a hostage to the Iraqi camp. The PLO leader tried to put the best face on things as he jauntily traversed the red carpet to the halting strains of the Palestine national anthem, but Mubarak's cool reception merely served to underline the fact that he was in deepening trouble with his Arab brethren. Worse was to come.

It was a grim-faced Arafat who arrived in the late morning of 10 August at the conference hall set aside for the emergency summit in Cairo's Nasr City, not far from the district where he had spent his youth. His mood was not improved when he spied the Egyptian newspaper editor, Mahfouz al-Ansari, in conversation with Salah Khalaf. For months Arafat had been incensed by attacks on him and the PLO in the Egyptian press as relations between Tunis and Cairo came under strain in the first half of 1990. Glaring at Ansari, he tersely asked Khalaf: 'Why are you standing here with this person who insults us?' And then seeing Mubarak nearby, Arafat – who tends to be extremely thin-skinned, especially where criticism in the Arabic press is concerned – said: 'I have been insulted in your country, Your Excellency . . . there are those who insult me in the heart of Cairo.'[14] All this was a prelude to one of Arafat's more volcanic performances.

The Cairo summit was fraught enough, marked as it was by angry exchanges between members of the Iraqi delegation, led by the first Deputy Prime Minister Taha Yassin Ramadan, and the Kuwaitis. In a closed session Iraq's cigar-smoking Foreign Minister, Tariz Aziz, levelled his cigar at his Kuwaiti counterpart, Sheikh Sabah, and said menacingly, 'We have taken all your papers from your office and we found your signature on letters plotting against Iraq.'[15] Sheikh Sabah did not take this at all well and fainted on the spot. He had to be revived by a fellow member of the Kuwaiti delegation, the Minister for Cabinet Affairs, medical practitioner Dr Abdel Rahman al-Awadi.

Watching the row from the sidelines Arafat was in no mood to see it all for what it was – low-grade farce. He was determined to have his say and, more to the point, advance his latest mediating ploy which was to recommend that a five-man delegation of Arab heads of state depart immediately for Baghdad to negotiate with Saddam. He, Yasser Arafat, was to be a member of this august group that would also include Mubarak of Egypt, Hussein of Jordan, Benjedid of Algeria and Ali Abdullah Saleh of Yemen. But unbeknown to Arafat, at the precise moment he was suggesting, improbably, that leaders like Mubarak should wait on Saddam in his Baghdad citadel, a most damaging transcript was circulating among summit delegates. The Iraqi leader had chosen that very day to launch his most intemperate attack on Arab leaders, calling on the 'Arab masses' to rise up against them. 'O Arabs, O Moslems and the faithful everywhere, this is your day to rise and defend Mecca which is captured by the spears of the Americans and the Zionists,' urged Saddam. 'Revolt against oppression, corruption, treachery and backstabbing . . . revolt against the oil emirs who accept to push the Arab women into whoredom.'[16]

Any faint possibility that Arafat's proposal might be taken at all seriously vanished on the spot, but still the PLO leader pressed on, raising points of order, gesticulating wildly and challenging Mubarak's rulings as summit chairman to the intense annoyance of the dour Egyptian President. As one of Arafat's senior advisers ruefully observed: 'While Mubarak might have understood the word "order" there was no sign that he appreciated what was meant by "point of order".'[17]

For Arafat and the PLO, the Cairo summit was a disaster and any slim chance the organization had of carving out a respectable role midway between the two Arab camps – as, say, the Algerians were able to do – went out of the window. In the words of one close Arafat aide: 'He was almost obsessed with the idea of sending a delegation. He thought it was the only solution to prevent the whole thing escalating into absurdity. He was so obsessed that he could not recognize that no-one was willing to support him; that in the final analysis he was just being an irritant to the others.'[18] Arafat's protestations continued up to the last minute and even involved challenging the legality of the summit resolution which was carried by a thin majority of just twelve votes out of the twenty states present, with the PLO together with Iraq and Libya initially being recorded as having voted against.[19] In all the confusion, it took several days for PLO headquarters in Tunis to issue a clarification of the PLO position. The organization had not voted against the summit resolution, which legitimized the commitment of foreign forces to Saudi Arabia, but, like Jordan, it had expressed reservations. Explaining the confusion over the PLO's voting position, a spokesman in Tunis observed that the vote had taken place in 'indescribable disorder'.[20] Not least of those responsible for the chaos was Arafat himself.

A reflective Arafat later told Nabil Shaath that he had erred in suggesting a delegation go to Baghdad in the light of Saddam's unrestrained attack on Mubarak, Fahd and others. 'I am a self-respecting man,' he declared, 'I would never have proposed it if I had known about the speech.' Arafat also observed that part of his frustration in Cairo had stemmed from a feeling that, in his efforts to stop foreign intervention in the crisis, he was like someone 'trying to save a child from being run over by a passing truck, and yet was being prevented from doing so'.[21] Whatever the mitigating circumstances, it was one of his most lamentable performances, and marked the beginning of 'open season' for increasingly virulent criticism of Arafat and the PLO throughout the Arab world, with the Egyptian press leading the way. A few days after the emergency summit a cartoon in Egypt's leading newspaper, *al-Ahram*, depicted the PLO chairman as a pair of identical Siamese twins facing in opposite directions – one twin was following a sign that read 'occupied Kuwait', the other a sign that said 'occupied Jerusalem'. Each of the Arafats was carrying a placard. One read 'Up with taking territory by force', and the other 'Down with taking territory by force'. *Al-Ahram*, it might be said, had gone for the jugular.[22]

Arafat withdrew in disarray from the city of his birth in a dark mood reminiscent of the high dudgeon in which he left Cairo in November 1977 after President Sadat made his surprise announcement that he was prepared to go to Jerusalem. He was belatedly beginning to understand the dimension of the problems confronting the PLO in its growing isolation. Just as in 1977 it would be some time before he would return to the Egyptian capital. Arafat had burned one of his most reliable bridges. Egypt would not quickly forgive him his transgressions. But as Arafat headed back to Tunis for a meeting of the enlarged PLO leadership – including members of the Executive Committee and the Fatah Central Committee – he was buoyed by an announcement from Baghdad. Taking his cue from the Security Council resolutions of condemnation that were raining down almost daily upon Iraq, Saddam announced on 12 August that 'all issues of occupation, or those projected as occupation, in the whole area, should be resolved on the same basis and principles as put forward by the Security Council.'[23]

Thus Saddam called for 'an immediate and unconditional Israeli pull-out from the Arab occupied territories in Palestine, Syria and Lebanon, the withdrawal of Syria from Lebanon and withdrawal between Iraq and Iran, in addition to laying down arrangements for the case of Kuwait.' An implementation of this withdrawal programme should begin with the occupation that took place first, he added, and subsequently 'a successive implementation of all (UN) resolutions . . . related to all these cases until we reach the last one (Iraq's occupation of Kuwait).'[24] And so the word 'linkage' entered the Gulf War vocabulary, the idea that the issues of Palestine and Kuwait could be resolved in tandem. PLO leaders clung forlornly to this notion in the hope that it would somehow provide a respectable escape from their growing isolation in a bitterly divided Arab world. It was an illusion, since even most Arab states themselves saw it for what it was – a cynical and belated attempt by Saddam to find a less than dishonourable way out of his predicament.

Some of Arafat's closest advisers are particularly scathing about his failure to keep the 'linkage' issue in perspective and are equally scornful of his argument that, in the stand he took in support of Iraq, he was somehow a captive of the Palestinian 'street'. 'Arafat is quite intelligent,' Bassel Akel has since said. 'But was he so naive as to link the solution of a forty–year-old problem with the solution of a one-month-old problem, an occupation resisted by the whole world? I had a couple of rows with him before the war, in November, 1990. I told him: "You can't get deeper and deeper involved with Saddam Hussein". He merely replied: "This is the will of my people".'

Akel had then observed: 'When you managed to carry the National Council in November, 1988 to accept Resolution 242, the majority of your people were not behind you. And yet you managed to convince them. So, on one occasion you did not take into account the will of your people because vital interests were at stake; on another occasion you say this is the will of my people. Why this contradiction?'[25]

When the Palestinian leadership assembled in Tunis on the night of 14 August at their customary meeting place in a large villa near the city's sports stadium, the mood was sullen and resentful. The PLO position on the Gulf crisis was being thoroughly misrepresented, the leadership believed, and there was much gloomy talk about a 'conspiracy' against the organization. Arafat, for his part, was coming to understand his predicament. According to Nabil Shaath, 'Arafat was feeling very, very lonely. He was beginning to comprehend the great risk he had taken. He was really quite worried about the Iraqi gamble. He felt it might destroy everything. He had warned Saddam Hussein in every way possible of the dangers of continuing to occupy Kuwait. Saddam seemed totally confident. He would say that withdrawal from Kuwait should be accompanied by withdrawal from Palestine. Saddam had assured him he was serious about linkage. But Arafat was very sceptical and very anxious during these days. It was not like 1982 (the Lebanon war) when he was personally at risk. In this case he was worried about the whole cause and the Arab world going to hell. He had a lot of scepticism and fear of the consequences.'[26]

Arafat also confided details at this time to close associates of a conversation he had held with Saddam in the first week of August in which the Iraqi leader, tiring of warnings of the dangers of continuing to occupy Kuwait, had accused the PLO chairman of 'trying to instil doomsday in my heart'. Saddam had added, recalling something Arafat had told him about his own preparations for martyrdom during the siege of Beirut: 'Abu Ammar, am I not to smell the fragrance of paradise as you did? Should I be denied the privilege you talked about? So let it be, I'm not afraid of the challenge.'[27]

As discussion droned on among Palestinian leaders throughout that mid-August period, often into the early hours of the morning, it was clear that the leadership itself was far from united on how to assess and respond to the latest catastrophe to befall the Arab world. There were those, like veteran PLO cadres Hail Abdul-Hamid, Sakher Abu Nizar and Abbas Zeki who, while not in favour of the Iraqi takeover of Kuwait, saw in it an intriguing challenge to the status quo in the region – in the words of one of those present 'a rippling storm in a stale pond'.[28] This group also included the PLO 'foreign minister' Farouk Kaddoumi who was so tantalized by developments, as one of his colleagues observed, that he 'was seeing the minarets of Jerusalem'.[29]

The other main trend, led by Salah Khalaf and the long-standing Executive Committee member, Mahmoud Abbas, was very sceptical about the Kuwaiti adventure and, in private, extremely critical. However, they muted their criticism in public, partly because of fevered support for Saddam among many Palestinians in the occupied territories and throughout the diaspora, most notably in Jordan, and partly because Arafat's own ill-advised closeness to Baghdad had fatally compromised the organization. Among PLO leaders in Tunis there was one especially discordant voice. As so often in the past Khaled al-Hassan, the PLO maverick and a founder of Fatah in Kuwait, where he had lived for many years, went his own way. Protesting at the organization's equivocation, its failure to condemn the invasion without qualification, he took himself off to Morocco in a sulk. Arafat had his own difficulties in discussions with his senior comrades in those mid-August days in Tunis. Under fire over the public presentation of the PLO position, he even offered to resign – a tactic he had employed so often in the past when criticized by his peers.

Out of the leadership meetings between 14–18 August came a new PLO peace plan, masterminded in part by Nabil Shaath in close consultation with Arafat. It was to prove the basis of the PLO's faltering diplomatic efforts that would continue right up to the Security Council 15 January deadline for Iraq's withdrawal from Kuwait. Its salient points included a proposal for the withdrawal of Iraqi forces in stages from Kuwait matched by a similar staged US pull-back from the Gulf to coincide with fresh attempts to arrive at an 'Arab solution' to the Kuwait crisis. While the plan was stillborn, since hardly anyone was of a mind to listen to the Palestinians as the region slid inexorably towards war, it did have the merit of being somewhat more principled than Arafat's first effort which had effectively required Kuwait to accede to Iraq's bullying demands for money and territory.

As Arafat resumed his vain attempts to sell a PLO peace plan to the few who would listen – his movements throughout the Arab world were by now severely restricted since he was *persona non grata* in the Gulf, in Egypt and in Syria – the news for his organization from the Gulf itself went from bad to worse. Incensed by Arafat's stand on the crisis, Kuwaiti leaders vowed retribution against the 400,000-strong Palestinian community in Kuwait, accusing Palestinians of collaborating with the Iraqi occupiers. Most damagingly, Gulf states terminated their financial contributions to the PLO. Arafat was in desperate trouble among Gulf rulers who had always been his organization's most consistent benefactors, pouring hundreds of millions of dollars into PLO coffers and those of Fatah. Such was the ire of the Gulf sheikhs, and the rulers of Saudi Arabia in particular, that his aircraft was even banned from crossing Saudi airspace. Just as bad from his own point of view, Arafat was the target of some of the most vicious personal attacks ever levelled against an Arab leader.

One particular broadside stood out, not just because of the extreme language used, but also because of its provenance. Ghazi al-Qosaibi, Saudi Arabia's ambassador to Bahrain, a respected former minister and sometime poet, lambasted Arafat as a 'sad clown' who had betrayed his friends and let down his people. 'This sad clown is now trying to snuff out the last candle left flickering in the long, dark tunnel – the Palestinian people's relationship with the Gulf . . . ' charged Qosaibi in response to a Palestinian statement accusing Kuwaiti officials of killing and raping Palestinians in Kuwait. 'This sad clown – when will he stop howling and check into the Home for Aged Sad Clowns?'[30] It was a deeply wounding attack and, as Arafat would have noted, it came just days after the Saudi-owned London-based newspaper *Al-Sharq al-Awsat* had published a call for a change in the Palestinian leadership from an organization called the Supreme Arab Committee for Palestine.[31] Most Palestinians had believed this organization, set up after the creation of Israel to represent the Palestinians, had lapsed in 1964 when the PLO was founded. Its shadowy reappearance at this time, with attacks against him in the Gulf at their peak, looked to Arafat like a deliberate attempt to undermine him.

For the almost one million Palestinians resident in the Gulf, one of the PLO's most important constituencies, the crisis had also become something of a nightmare. Ahmad Kalash, a Palestinian journalist in Abu Dhabi, summed up the dilemma in a commentary in the London-based

Palestinian daily *al-Quds al-Arabi* in which he wrote: 'Black clouds are gathering on the horizon promising woe to the Palestinian whomever and wherever he may be, and whatever side he takes.'[32] Nowhere was this Palestinian dilemma greater than in Kuwait itself where the large Palestinian community was literally torn apart by the crisis.

Energized, nevertheless, by the formulation of the new PLO peace plan, Arafat redoubled his peacemaking efforts, shuttling between Baghdad, Amman, Tripoli, Tunis and Rabat. But it was all to no avail. The fissures in the Arab world were simply too deep to facilitate any co-ordinated effort to end the crisis. When Chedli Klibi, the Arab League's long-serving Secretary General, resigned on 3 September, just a few days after presiding over an Arab League foreign ministers' meeting in Cairo, boycotted by the PLO among eight absentees, it merely emphasized the depth of the divisions between the anti-Iraq majority led by Egypt and the rest.[33]

In mid-September, Arafat was briefly distracted from the Gulf crisis itself by events in Lebanon where fighters of his Fatah mainstream faction expelled guerrillas of the Abu Nidal-led renegade Fatah Revolutionary Council (FRC) from the large Ain al-Hilweh refugee camp near the city of Sidon in a fierce three-day battle. The crushing victory by the Arafat forces, which consolidated Fatah's influence throughout Lebanon, gave the PLO leader one of his few causes for celebration in many months. The episode showed, if nothing else, that even in the midst of a wider Middle East crisis Lebanon continued to be a focus of tension for the fractious Palestinian movement and Arafat could not ignore threats to his Fatah powerbase there.[34] The PLO leader would also, no doubt, have derived wry amusement at this time from the spectacle of his two old sparring partners, George Habash of the Popular Front and Nayef Hawatmeh of the Democratic Front, returning to Amman twenty years after they fled King Hussein's vengeful legions in the 1970 war of 'Black September'.

The two, who had threatened to devote all their energies to removing Hussein from the face of the earth, were received by the Hashemite monarch at his hilltop palace. The Gulf Crisis was making for strange bedfellows.

Arafat did his best to repair the damage to his all-important relationships with the Saudis and with the Egyptians, but in these efforts he made no progress. He met the Saudi Foreign Minister, Prince Saud al-Faisal in Rabat in mid-October[35] and asked him to convey what amounted to a forlorn message of reconciliation to King Fahd. He also sent his trusted aide Nabil Shaath to meet Prince Saud to discuss possible ways in which tensions could be eased. Saud's response was that Arafat should 'more openly condemn the invasion and be more clearly sympathetic to the Kuwaiti and Saudi point of view'. But Shaath had explained to the Saudi official that under no circumstances could Arafat be seen to be an 'apologist' for US intervention.[36] The PLO official did not fare much better at a meeting in Cairo with Dr Osama al-Baz, President Mubarak's special adviser. Baz, according to Shaath, was very critical, and said that Arafat's position needed to be seriously reconsidered to satisfy Egypt. Shaath had replied: 'You are the war camp and we are the peace camp'. 'No,' Baz said. 'We are the camp that is threatening war to get peace.'[37]

As talk of war swirled about the Arab world and the US continued the inexorable build-up of forces in the Gulf region, one of those shocking events that are so typical of the Middle East intervened. On this occasion, and in the extremely tense circumstances that prevailed, the slaying on 8 October of eighteen Palestinians on Jerusalem's Temple Mount by Israeli border police firing indiscriminately seemed to symbolize most acutely all the unresolved problems of the region, all the hatred, all the bitterness.

According to the Palestinians the incident occurred when rumours spread that Jewish zealots were advancing on the

Haram al Sharif or the Noble Sanctuary, home of the two most important Muslim shrines outside Mecca and Medina, to press their claims for the rebuilding of the Jewish temple on the site where it had stood nearly 2,000 years ago. In the disturbances that ensued Israeli policemen had gone berserk and gunned down Palestinians at close range. According to the Israeli version, Palestinian demonstrators had begun raining rocks, sticks and pieces of masonry on thousands of Jews, including many from abroad, worshipping below at the Western 'Wailing' Wall on the Festival of the Tabernacles, one of the Jews' holiest occasions. Under extreme provocation, the police had intervened.

Whatever the truth of the matter, the episode diverted attention, momentarily, from the Gulf crisis itself and, to the acute discomfort of the US in particular, enabled Arafat and the Iraqis to press demands for 'linkage' between a settlement of the Palestine and Kuwait questions. In the hard, cruel world of Middle East politics, the Temple Mount killings could hardly have come at a more fortuitous moment for Arafat, languishing in his isolation and in danger of being consigned permanently to the sidelines. The episode was, in the callous language of a Palestinian journalist in Jerusalem, 'like manna from heaven for the PLO'.[38]

Pressing for a Security Council resolution with 'teeth' that would both condemn Israel and provide for the immediate despatch of a high-level fact-finding mission to the territories, the PLO convened an emergency session in Tunis of its 'mini parliament', the Central Council, to debate the bloodiest episode in Jerusalem since the 1967 war. In an opening address Arafat bitterly assailed the United States which he claimed was providing an umbrella for Israel 'to commit odious crimes' in the occupied territories.[39] Saddam Hussein himself had greeted the grim news from Jerusalem with a warning that Israel was coming 'closer to the abyss'. He also used the occasion to announce that Iraq had acquired a powerful new missile which would strike at Israel 'when the time of reckoning comes'.[40]

After four days of debate and much toing and froing behind the scenes, the Security Council eventually approved unanimously a resolution that condemned the 'violence' of the Israeli police, and also instructed the UN Secretary General to send a representative to the Israeli-occupied territories with a brief to report back by the end of October – a much lower level mission than the PLO had demanded.[41] It was the first time the US had actually sponsored a resolution condemning the Jewish state, but the Iraqi Foreign Minister, Tariq Aziz, denounced the measure, saying that it shamed the UN. 'It strengthens a known Arab perception that to the United States and its Western allies, Arab blood is less important than the oil they want to control,' he declared while on a visit to Amman, centre of the most fevered support for Saddam among all Arab capitals.[42] The Jerusalem slayings and their aftermath were to be the last serious diversion from events in the Gulf before the end of the war itself. As October gave way to November, the drums of war were beating ever more insistently.

Still, Arafat pressed on with his forlorn peace efforts and was briefly encouraged by a call from the King Hassan of Morocco in mid-November for a 'last ditch' Arab summit to resolve the Gulf crisis. In vain the PLO leader tried to promote the summit, shuttling between Amman for talks with King Hussein and Baghdad where he met Saddam for the umpteenth time since the crisis broke. But there was simply no support for the summit proposal in the wider Arab world. The powerful Saudi-Egyptian-Syrian axis said a meeting of Arab heads of state would be 'useless' unless Saddam agreed in advance to get out of Kuwait. Egypt's President Mubarak observed that such a gathering would simply turn into a 'shouting match'.

All the time, the US continued to pour troops, planes and warships into the Gulf region in the most massive military build-up since the Second World War, as the Security Council moved ever closer to authorizing the use of force to remove Iraq from Kuwait. A resolution to this effect came on 29 November by a vote of 12–2 with Yemen and Cuba opposing, and China abstaining. Iraq was given until 15 January to withdraw. In the meantime President Bush had authorized the despatch of an additional 100,000 troops to the Gulf in a clear sign that the US meant to go to war if all diplomatic efforts to dislodge Iraq from Kuwait failed. A day after the UN 'war resolution' was passed Bush invited Iraqi Foreign Minister Aziz to Washington for talks and offered to send the US Secretary of State, James Baker, to Baghdad. Iraq accepted Bush's offer, but insisted that it wanted to broaden the discussions to include other Middle East issues, including Palestine. In the battle of deadlines, ultimatums, brinkmanship and sheer Iraqi bloody-mindedness that ensued, the stuttering attempts to arrange the 'last gasp' Baker-Aziz meeting merely proved to be one more signpost on the road to war.

In the first week of December, Arafat was briefly buoyed by his inclusion in a 'quadripartite' meeting in Baghdad, presided over by Saddam, with King Hussein and the Yemeni Vice-President, Salim al-Bidh. The Iraqi leader used the occasion to announce the release on 6 December of all foreign hostages. Arafat was to claim some vicarious credit for the hostage release, but in truth the gesture had more to do with a realization in Baghdad that the hostages would not prove a deterrent to war, and were, in fact, fuelling foreign hostility. The selective release in preceding weeks of some of Iraq's foreign captives in a cynical attempt to cause divisions in the Western alliance had simply not worked.

As the countdown to war gathered pace, Arafat continued his fruitless peace efforts, even travelling in the third week of December to Africa for improbable meetings in the midst of the deepening Gulf crisis with Presidents Museveni of Uganda, Mwinyi of Tanzania and Mugabe of

Zimbabwe.[43] With much of the Arab world closed to him, not to mention Europe, a visit to Black Africa offered one of the few opportunities for him to be photographed in the embrace of fellow 'heads of state'. He also continued his active liaison with an increasingly beleaguered Saddam Hussein who had taken to issuing almost daily bloodcurdling threats to the rest of the world from Baghdad. In a message to Arafat on 1 January, marking the twenty-sixth anniversary of the first guerrilla attack inside Israel by Fatah, Saddam declared: 'Right is on our side. Let us persevere and fight the infidels and their agents wherever they may be.'[44]

While Arafat continued throughout the first days of the New Year to insist that war in the Gulf could be averted, alarm was growing in the PLO leadership. Nabil Shaath, for one, felt that the Iraqis and the Americans were on a 'collision course' and that war had become all but inevitable.[45] But Arafat insisted, against all the evidence, there there would be 'no war', as he kept telling reporters. Such pronouncements did nothing to dispel the sense of unreality that had settled over the Iraqi capital in the first days of January. Indeed, there are influential Arabs, such as Lakhdar Brahimi, the veteran Algerian diplomat and friend of the PLO, who blame Arafat 'to an extent for Saddam's behaviour'. 'Saddam,' he has since observed, 'lives in a world where his own propaganda is the only thing that is real. And Arafat was telling him things that gave him glimmers of hope – for example, that war was not going to happen.'[46]

Arafat's own hopes and those of his colleagues were raised by the 9 January Baker-Aziz meeting in Geneva. Here, they thought, was an opportunity for a disaster to be averted. Here was also a chance for the PLO to score points if it could be seen to help facilitate some sort of last-minute breakthrough. So Arafat sent his 'foreign minister' Farouk Kaddoumi to Geneva to liaise with Tariq Aziz. The PLO leader was still forlornly hoping against hope that 'linkage' could somehow be established between a settlement of the Palestine and Kuwait questions.

But in Geneva the Palestinians were again to be disappointed. It was becoming clearer by the day that Saddam was intent on carrying brinkmanship beyond all reasonable bounds. At Arafat's urging Kaddoumi proposed, after the failure of the Aziz-Baker talks,[47] that the Iraqi Foreign Minister, in an effort to find a way out of the impasse, meet his twelve EC counterparts, either in Tunis or in Algiers. Hopes flickered briefly at PLO headquarters in Tunis that such an encounter could be arranged, but they died almost immediately when Aziz said he was not prepared to meet the EC Foreign Ministers before the 15 January 'deadline', but rather on 17 January, two days later. Said an Arafat adviser deeply involved in those negotiations: 'We felt that would be disastrous. The attempt to flout the deadline looked disastrous. Yasser Arafat was appalled.'[48]

As the moments slipped away towards the 15 January deadline, Arafat was almost constantly in Baghdad, conferring frequently with Saddam, receiving journalists in his heavily guarded residence and dreaming up last-minute peace stratagems, in consultation with such unlikely figures as the former President of Nicaragua, Daniel Ortega. He was also on hand for the arrival in the Iraqi capital of the UN Secretary General, Javier Perez de Cuellar who, after cooling his heels for much of Sunday 13 January, eventually saw Saddam late in the day for an aimless discussion that conveyed none of the urgency that might have been expected at that late stage. Surprisingly, Perez de Cuellar did not advance any new ideas, and Saddam himself engaged for the most part in a fruitless description of the origins of Iraq's dispute with Kuwait. It seemed that he had set his face against making what he regarded as any further concessions. 'To utter the word withdrawal while there is still a chance for war means that we would be creating the psychological conditions for enemy victory over us,' Saddam told Perez de Cuellar.[49] The Secretary General left Baghdad on his UN jet, confiding to staff that what Saddam needed was not a mediator but a 'psychiatrist'.[50]

Arafat himself was briefed by Saddam on the morning of 14 January about his talks with Perez de Cuellar the evening before. The Iraqi leader claimed he had indicated a willingness to withdraw, although a transcript of his conversation with the UN official does not support such a contention. Intriguingly, Arafat has since confided to senior aides that Saddam Hussein told him at their last meeting before the war: 'Wait till 17–18 January and Baker will come to Baghdad and Bush will chicken out, and there will be no war'.[51] This, then, was the Iraqi leader's game. He was convinced that even after the 15 January deadline, the US President would go the 'extra mile' to avert war and initiate negotiations. Could it be, asks a senior PLO official privy to those last-minute discussions, that 'Saddam deliberately destroyed the Perez de Cuellar and European peace missions in the hope of bringing the Americans into the negotiations? He believed they were the only worthwhile negotiating partners.'[52] The failure of the Perez de Cuellar mission and the quick slide to war sank the last of the PLO's myriad peace stratagems. Arafat had pinned high hopes on an eleventh-hour mission to Baghdad by the French President François Mitterrand to elicit Saddam's agreement to withdraw – a mission in which Arafat himself would have been seen to play a role. The alternative, with its tantalizing prospect of Arafat cast in a role of peacemaker to the world, was for the PLO leader to appear on the steps of the Elysée Palace with Mitterrand to declare that on behalf of Saddam they had reached, in the words of an Arafat adviser, a 'great opening for peace . . . '[53]

Arafat, who had been busily telling journalists all week there would be 'no war, no war, no war'[54] left for Amman soon after his meeting with Saddam on 14 January to confer with King Hussein even as the war clouds gathered ever more ominously over the Iraqi capital. Arafat had also observed in sometimes curiously lighthearted discussions with reporters at his Baghdad residence that the only significance about the date 15 January was that it was the seventy-third anniversary of late Egyptian President Gamal Abdel Nasser's birthday. It was to be a fateful observation as events would very quickly show.

The time in Tunis was just before 11 p.m. on 14 January and Salah Khalaf had completed a simple meal in the downstairs reception room of the house in the beachside suburb of Carthage of his friend Hail Abdul-Hamid, better known in PLO circles as Abu Houl, the organization's internal security chief. Also present was Fakhri al-Omari, one of Khalaf's most trusted aides. Conversation, not surprisingly, with only hours to go before the 15 January deadline, had focused obsessively on fading prospects of peace and the increasing likelihood of war. Upstairs in Abdul-Hamid's comfortable villa, his wife Nadia and daughter had retired for the night. All seemed calm, and Khalaf took little notice when one of his host's bodyguards, a young man named Hamza Abu Zaid, wandered into the room carrying his Kalashnikov rifle. Absent-mindedly, Abdul-Hamid told his guard to help himself to some of the leftover food, but at that very moment Abu Zaid pivoted towards the small gathering and at close range let fly with a burst of automatic rifle fire. His main target was Khalaf himself who died almost instantly after four bullets ripped into his chest and another thudded into his head. The assassin then gunned down al-Omari who also died on the spot, and finally he turned his gun on Abdul-Hamid who had lunged towards him to stop the carnage. The latter bled to death in hospital.[55]

For the PLO, the slaying of the 57-year-old Salah Khalaf was a truly sickening development at a time when the organization was at a near-historic low in relations with much of the Arab world, and on the eve of what was to prove a catastrophic war. Like the death in Tunis of the PLO's military commander, Khalil al-Wazir, almost three years before at the hands of Israeli assassins, Khalaf's demise was a reminder of how vulnerable the PLO was to predators from inside and outside the organization. His loss to the PLO and more particularly to Yasser Arafat himself was almost incalculable. Their lives had been intertwined for more than thirty years, first as student politicians together in Cairo, then as founders of Fatah and comrades-in-arms through many ups and downs, and latterly as members of the PLO's dwindling band of veteran cadres. Khalaf's toughness, his keen intellect mixed with a ruthless pragmatism, his wry sense of humour, had made him virtually indispensable in an organization conspicuously short on talent. And, perhaps most important, he had provided a foil in the later years, especially since al-Wazir's death, for the mercurial Arafat – one of very few PLO officials who had the authority to curb some of their leader's excesses. Now, he was gone, and with his death Arafat was left almost alone among those who formed what had become known as the PLO's historic leadership.

When Arafat was dragged from his bed in Baghdad on the morning of 15 January, the day of the UN deadline, to be told the grim news he wasted no time returning to Tunis. As so often in the past a grief-stricken Arafat found himself rushing back to his base to pay condolences to the families of fallen comrades. As his Iraqi jet lifted off from Saddam airport en route to Tunis, nagging questions were already being asked about just who gave the order for Khalaf to be killed. It had been quickly established that Hamza Abu Zaid, the assassin, was a member of Abu Nidal's Fatah Revolutionary Council, the terrorist group that had shed so much PLO blood over the years. What was not immediately clear was on whose behalf the renegade gang was acting on this occasion. But in the minds of top PLO officials a chilling thought occurred. Hadn't Abu Nidal recently moved back into Baghdad's orbit after an absence of some years? Was it not just possible that

Saddam Hussein himself may have ordered the slaying as a warning to the PLO to stay the course with him in his looming confrontation with the Americans?

Such a possibility hardly bore thinking about, but it was well known that Salah Khalaf had been among the least enthusiastic PLO leaders about the tilt towards Baghdad; not only that, he had argued vigorously with Saddam at several meetings in an effort to persuade him to withdraw from Kuwait. On one occasion the Iraqi leader had sought to exclude Khalaf from a session he was to have with Arafat because he regarded him as an unfavourable witness. Arafat had insisted that his deputy attend and Saddam had reluctantly agreed, but Khalaf himself demurred and left Baghdad without delay. Although reluctant to speak on the record, senior Arafat advisers deeply suspect Saddam's involvement. 'There is strong reason to believe that Saddam Hussein was behind the assassination of Abu Iyad; he was being too outspoken at a time when Saddam was not allowing anyone to take exception to his views,' said one such adviser.[56]

In truth, Khalaf had frequently expressed quite daring opposition in public to the Iraqi takeover of Kuwait in contrast to Arafat's own equivocal pronouncements. Thus, on 17 August he told the London-based *Mideast Mirror* publication: 'Our view from the beginning was that there was a position of principle that must not be abandoned, which is that it is unacceptable to occupy others' territory by force or interfere in any Arab foreign state's internal affairs.'[57] Khalaf had also evinced much less enthusiasm for Saddam's 'linkage' proposal than had Arafat who has claimed that he planted the idea in the Iraqi leader's mind in the first place. In a revealing interview with a French journalist, published after his death, Khalaf had said pointedly, voicing sentiments that would not have endeared him to Baghdad, 'As a Palestinian it is difficult for me to refuse the link Saddam Hussein makes with the problems of the region, but at the same time, I do not want my cause to be associated with the destruction of the Arab region.'[58]

As Arafat set about making his condolence rounds in Tunis on the afternoon of 15 January, it was clear that the latest catastrophe to have befallen his organization had very seriously affected him. Attending a gathering for the family and friends of the deceased at the al-Quds (Jerusalem) primary school in suburban Tunis, he threw himself into the arms of a PLO comrade, crying loudly.[59] At a meeting that night of the PLO's leadership group, there was scarcely a dry eye in the house as ageing revolutionaries made speeches in memory of Khalaf and the others. The veteran Khaled al-Hassan sobbed as he argued that Salah Khalaf's remains be transported to Jordan for burial in sight of Palestine, in accordance with his family's wishes. Arafat himself was in touch with the Jordanian authorities trying to arrange the funeral. Lakhdar Brahimi recalls speaking to the PLO leader on 16 January, the day before the war, and asking why he was proposing to go to Jordan at such a dangerous moment. Arafat had replied: 'Because most of our people are in Jordan and the occupied territories'. Brahimi had reminded him that 'war is about to break out'. Arafat replied: 'Not in a million years.'[60] In the end it was decided, for security reasons, that the funeral should take place in Tunis. Khalaf was buried at the Hamman-Lif cemetery in suburban Tunis on 17 January, just hours after the US and its allies began bombing Iraq. Five hundred attended and Arafat stood silent for a long time in honour of his dead comrade. Brahimi described it thus: 'It was a cold, rainy day, a miserable occasion. There was a heavy Tunisian security force presence, since the authorities were scared of there being Palestinian demonstrations. I thought, "Abu Iyad deserves better than this".'[61]

It was well after midnight in Baghdad and the well-lit streets were deserted. The date was 17 January and the time was 2.35 a.m. (22.35 GMT, 16 January), less than nineteen hours after the deadline had expired for Iraq's withdrawal from Kuwait. There had been a certain tension in the air throughout the day, but no sign of panic in the Iraqi capital. At the Al-Rashid Hotel foreign reporters were on alert. The White House had been sending cryptic messages to the US networks, warning them that an attack against Iraq was imminent. When the aerial blitz came it was swift, brutal and quite devastating. Within hours, Iraq's air force was disabled, its Soviet-supplied electronic air defence system crippled and its military installations coming under a withering bombardment. Using the very latest technology, including Cruise missiles fired from warships in the Gulf, the allies had begun their methodical destruction of the Iraqi war machine. In an address from the White House, announcing the beginning of the 'air war', George Bush declared that the allies were 'targeting Saddam's military arsenal'.[62]

In far-off Tunis a sombre Arafat digested the war news as he prepared for Salah Khalaf's funeral. In the previous twenty-four hours he had reluctantly accepted that war was imminent, and that chances of a successful last-minute peace initiative, in which the PLO might usefully play a role, had disappeared. Khalaf's death had brought him up with a jolt, puncturing some of the illusions he had clung to with such tenacity, although he would continue throughout the next days and weeks to over-estimate to an absurd degree Iraq's ability to withstand the allied onslaught. On the eve of the battle and in the expectation that the region was about to enter a period of severely heightened tension and instability, he had advised fellow members of the leadership to disperse. In the words of one of his closest colleagues he feared that the 'Israelis might use the war to conduct another wave of assassinations'.[63]

Arafat's fears proved groundless, but in the early stages of the conflict Israel was sorely provoked when Saddam Hussein made good his threat to launch missiles into the heart of Tel Aviv, although, for the most part, these attacks did only limited damage and caused few casualties. Much more damage was rendered to the fragile process that Arafat himself had sponsored over the years towards building confidence between the PLO and liberal Israelis. Sickened by the organization's support for Iraq and appalled by the spectacle of Iraqi-flag-waving Palestinians in the territories appearing on their rooftops to cheer on the Scud missile attacks, Israeli peace campaigners vowed never again to trust the PLO. This rancour extended to the Palestinian side with complaints that the Israeli authorities had crudely discriminated against the territories in their security precautions. 'They did not even give us gas masks,' commented the Palestinian academic, Saeb Erakat, sourly. 'How can we expect them to give us a state?'[64]

As the allied air war ground mercilessly on, day by day, reducing Iraq's military assets to rubble, Arafat's was a small voice on the sidelines; alternately calling on Western leaders to 'put an end to the war which risks spreading to the entire region'[65] and at the same time issuing increasingly ludicrous forecasts about Iraq's ability to withstand the pressure. In a Radio Monte Carlo interview two weeks into the air war he described Iraq as a mountain that 'cannot be shaken by the wind', and declared: 'If we held out for three months (against the Israelis) in Beirut, then Iraq and its army and people can resist for three years.'[66] He was also warning publicly, as he had in private before the war started, of the risks that Israel would become directly involved – possibly by attacking western Iraq through Jordan.

In those late January and early February days, Arafat was having some trouble himself resisting pressure from Baghdad which was beginning to ask why the Palestinians, after all their talk about being in the 'same trench' as the Iraqis, were not doing more to put their words into action. A close Arafat aide said that tensions with Saddam grew at this time, since the PLO leader would not sanction terrorism and also steadfastly refused to move units of the Palestine Liberation Army in support of Iraq during the war.[67] An episode late in January tends to give some credence to claims Arafat was indeed resisting pressure from Baghdad, not that anything the PLO could have done militarily would have made one iota of difference to the course of events. After two days of PLO Katyusha rocket attacks from Lebanon into Israel's northern security zone, and amid Israeli charges that the organization was seeking to open a new front on behalf of Iraq, PLO headquarters in Tunis denied Arafat had sanctioned any such move and said that the officer in command of PLO forces in Lebanon, Colonel Zeid Wehbe, had been reprimanded.[68]

When Arafat returned to Baghdad in the wake of the 13 February US bombing of what Iraq claimed was a civilian bomb shelter, his first and last visit to the Iraqi capital during the war itself, renewed Soviet attempts to stave off a devastating land war were getting under way in the person of special envoy Yevgeny Primakov who had seen Saddam on 12 February. A former Middle East correspondent of the Soviet Communist Party newspaper, *Pravda*, the personable Primakov had managed to elicit an agreement from the Iraqi leader to co-operate with Soviet peace moves.[69] Three days later on the eve of a visit to Moscow by Foreign Minister Tariq Aziz, Saddam acknowledged his readiness to pull out of Kuwait under the terms of Security Council Resolution 660, provided withdrawal was linked with a settlement of other Middle East issues such as the Palestine question. President Bush immediately dismissed the offer as a 'cruel hoax' and preparations for the allied 'knock-out blow' against Iraq continued apace. It was the last time the Iraqis seriously raised the issue of 'linkage' as a precondition for withdrawal, a development that tended to confirm the suspicions of PLO sceptics that it was a cynical ploy in the first place. Lamely, Arafat said the Iraqi offer merited a 'positive response'.[70]

Undeterred, the Soviets pressed on with their peace efforts, even as the allies remorselessly continued with their bombing campaign, but Moscow's efforts would be in vain. By the time Foreign Minister Aziz announced on 23 February that Iraq had agreed to the immediate and unconditional withdrawal of its forces from Kuwait, provided Security Council resolutions passed after Resolution 660 were shelved, it was too late. An allied deadline expired that day and Bush, after consulting his main Gulf War allies, launched the long-awaited land war that, within twenty-four hours, devastated Iraq's much-vaunted defences in and around Kuwait. By 26 February, Saddam Hussein had had enough, announcing that all Iraqi troops were being withdrawn and that the emirate was no longer part of Iraq.[71] But this latest Iraqi offer was not sufficient for the allies who, intent on demolishing as much of the Iraqi military as possible before world disquiet forced an end to the carnage, continued the war for two more days. It was during this time that thousands of fleeing Iraqis perished on the road north from Kuwait to Basra in what one US pilot described, laconically, as a 'turkey shoot'.

Announcing the suspension of hostilities on 28 February, a triumphant President Bush said he was sending Secretary Baker to the Middle East forthwith to begin fashioning a durable peace. 'This war is now behind us,' Bush declared. 'Ahead of us is the difficult task of securing a potentially historic peace.'[72] Arafat, who had been rendered almost speechless by the destruction of the Iraqi military within a few hours against all his predictions, may well have taken some comfort from those words, but he also must have known that the road back for both himself and PLO would be long and difficult: not least of the problems he faced was getting back on speaking terms with leaders in the Gulf and in Egypt. He had committed in word, if not in deed, a grave mistake. There would surely be costs. But according to his close adviser, Nabil Shaath: 'Yasser Arafat's feelings are not at all remorseful. It's almost like a Greek tragedy. He was trying his best to stop a doomed situation. He failed because of the enormous forces beyond him. He would definitely put part of the blame on Saddam Hussein. He also felt there was an inexorable drive by the Americans to do what was done and nothing would have stopped that.'[73]

# Part Five

# 19

# *In the Wilderness*

'There is no forgiveness or forgetting. The crime, the sin is too big.' Abdullah Bishara, Secretary General, Gulf Co-operation Council, March 1991.

In the spring of 1991, as he surveyed the wreckage war had strewn around the Middle East, Yasser Arafat felt time and history weighing heavily on his mind. It was not only Iraq that was in ruins, having been pummelled into submission by the allied coalition. Ravaged, too, was much of what he, Arafat, had striven for in the last two decades: the PLO's carefully constructed network of support from Arab states; its fragile credibility with the West, and with at least a segment of Israeli opinion; its much-vaunted diplomatic initiative aimed at securing a Palestinian homeland alongside Israel; the flow of Arab money that had kept the organisation afloat and had enhanced his power over the years. Thanks to his alliance with Saddam Hussein during the Gulf conflict, Arafat's leadership was being called into question by some in the West, in the Arab world and even among Palestinians in the Israeli-occupied territories.

If nothing else, the war between Iraq and an allied coalition, including all Gulf states plus the Egyptians, Syrians and Moroccans, also confirmed that a much-weakened Soviet Union under the liberalising Mikhail Gorbachev no longer had either the will or the inclination to provide a counterweight to American power and influence in the Middle East. Moscow's limp last-minute diplomatic manoeuvres to get Saddam off the hook had come to naught. In any case, the Soviets had given solid support at the UN to a series of resolutions that not only provided the legal justification for the liberation of Kuwait, but also a framework for punitive post-war sanctions against Iraq.

In the immediate aftermath of a war that had been nothing short of a catastrophe for the PLO, a battered Arafat retired to his Tunis headquarters to ponder an uncertain future: bereft of friends and support among traditional allies in the Gulf; unwelcome in Egypt, the land of his birth; and ridiculed in the West where television stations endlessly had replayed film from Baghdad, taken at the height of the Gulf crisis, of his almost manic embrace of Saddam Hussein – rather like a slow-motion soccer replay. Arafat would continue in his efforts to justify his ill-starred alliance with Saddam, but his words made about as much impact as the sound of a tin whistle. How, he asked repeatedly, could the anti-imperialist revolutionary have accepted the presence of Western military forces on Arab land? 'We are writing this [history] for the generations, regardless of the results of this battle . . . The PLO cannot but be in the trenches against Israel and the champions of Israel,' he would say to those who questioned his judgement.[1]

As Arafat licked his wounds in his Tunis lair in those first days and weeks after Saddam's legions were put to humiliating flight in Desert Storm, there was one other issue which continued to bear down heavily upon him. The flow of Soviet Jews to Israel persisted in full flood. While the nationalist government of Yitzhak Shamir denied that it was channelling the new arrivals into the occupied territories, there was also no doubt that population pressures and, more to the point, pressure on housing in Israel itself, was creating a ripple effect which was spreading to East Jerusalem, where Jewish residents had come to outnumber Arabs, and to the West Bank. But with his credibility in shreds Arafat was scarcely in a position to raise his voice above a whisper, and, in any case, no one was listening.

So began one of those bleak, down periods for the PLO leader, reminiscent of other moments during his long and stormy stewardship of the fractious guerrilla movement, such as the dog days after his retreat from Lebanon in 1982. Consigned to a Middle East Coventry by his Arab brethren, most of whom were either not speaking to him or, worse, were continuing to vilify him, Arafat was left clutching at what seemed like straws and talking forlornly about his own place in history as the 'leader of one of the few liberation movements left in the world', engaged in a continuing struggle for national rights and self-determination. 'There is something here that the West seems incapable of understanding or absorbing, that the dynamism of our people is not a passing thing; the dynamism of our people is deeply rooted in history,' he told an Arab interviewer at the height of the Gulf War. 'Ours is an epic people. It has been struggling since 1917, from the Balfour declaration until today. That is 73 or 74 years, five generations . . . As chairman of this organisation and leader of this people, I do not seek wealth. If I were seeking wealth, I would go to the wealthy. I seek a place in history.'[2] He would also seek to put the best gloss on a bad situation by claiming that Iraqi defiance had 'created new facts on the strategic level that serve our cause and national struggle', as he told a meeting called to mark the 40th month of the *intifada*.[3]

Arafat's headlong rush to embrace Saddam prompted continuing dark murmurings of discontent among his lieutenants, a number of whom were convinced that Iraq had been behind the killing of Salah Khalaf who had dared to criticise. Arafat's folly, they believed, had inadvertently contributed to Khalaf's death at the hands of a renegade Palestinian assassin. Among many criticisms was one voiced by a Palestinian official in Tunis that the PLO leader had failed to 'uncouple the horses before Iraq's stagecoach went over the cliff'.[4] Another official accused him of ignoring the 'very lessons he taught us'[5] about staying out of the clutches of any one Arab power.

But in the midst of all the gloom there were glimmers of promise for Arafat, whose determined optimism, even at the bleakest moments, has always been one of his strengths. When a triumphant George Bush, at the very zenith of his power and popularity, addressed a joint session of Congress on 6 March, less than a week after the end of Gulf War hostilities, his words provided some encouragement to the leader of a movement close to the nadir of its fortunes.

'All of us know the depth of bitterness that has made the dispute between Israel and its neighbours so painful and intractable,' Bush said. 'We must do all we can to close the gap between Israel and the Arab states and between Israelis and Palestinians. The tactics of terror lead nowhere. There can be no substitute for diplomacy . . . A comprehensive peace must be grounded in United Nations Security Council Resolutions 242 and 338 and the principle of territory for peace,' he continued. 'This principle must be elaborated to provide for Israel's security and recognition, and at the same time for legitimate Palestinian political rights. Anything else would fail the twin tests of fairness and security.'[6]

The words and sentiments were hardly new, but here was an American president with enhanced credibility in the Middle East theatre, declaring unequivocally that territorial compromise was the only way forward, along with acceptance of Palestinian 'national rights' – diplomatic code language for a process that might lead to self-determination. Bush was also preparing to put words into action by despatching James Baker, the Secretary of State, back to the Middle East to start what would prove to be a protracted series of diplomatic shuttles that before the year was out would yield a remarkable diplomatic achievement.

In Tunis, a beleaguered Arafat seized on Bush's

remarks as the first good news he had heard in months. Interviewed by the Spanish daily *El Pais*, he said: 'It's the first time that a US President has spoken with total clarity in assuring that there must be peace in exchange for territory and justice in exchange for security.' Describing Bush's remarks as a 'decisive step', Arafat observed: 'He also supported the implementation of United Nations Security Council resolutions 242 and 338, and for solutions to be worked out under the auspices of the UN and in accordance with the legitimate political rights of the Palestinian people.'[7] In the same interview Arafat also repeated his defence of his alliance with Saddam, and his own position as leader of a movement that many of his critics believed was living on borrowed time. 'I have been chosen to be where I am by the Palestinian people,' he said. 'I didn't arrive here in a tank, nor by any foreign mandate. I was elected in a democratic fashion – or does the West not trust democracy when it occurs in the Third World?'[8]

These moments of promise were few and far between in those difficult post-war days, however, and Arafat had plenty of time to reflect upon the past, and to wonder whether time might not be running out for him in his ceaseless quest for what he calls Palestine; whether he would end up being lumped together with other leaders of the Palestinians who had led the early struggles against the Zionists, the Haj Amin al-Husseinis and Ahmed Shukairys who shuffled off into lonely exile, judged by their peers as failures. Edward Said, the Palestinian-American academic and sometime critic of the movement, recalls Arafat confiding these fears to him early in 1985 at a time when there was strong opposition from PLO purists to the joint peace initiative with King Hussein. 'If there's one thing, Edward, I don't want to be,' Arafat declared, 'it is Haj Amin al-Husseini. He was always right, and he ended up with nothing. I don't want to be like that.'[9]

As if his problems of loss of credibility, criticism from

within the Palestinian movement and the death of key lieutenants such as Salah Khalaf were not enough, Arafat was also obliged in early 1991 to come to terms with the severing of a financial lifeline that had helped keep his movement alive through its many ups and downs, and, more to the point, had underpinned his own domination of PLO institutions right from the moment he was elected Chairman of the Executive Committee in 1969. Early benefactors such as Saudi Arabia and Kuwait simply stopped paying, furious as they were at Arafat's alignment with Saddam in 1990. Indeed, all states of the Saudi-dominated Gulf Cooperation Council froze their donations. Iraq itself, which had become the PLO's most reliable paymaster from 1988, was in no position to maintain the flow. Arafat estimated that as a result of the crisis, the PLO had lost approximately $120 million in annual contributions from Saudi Arabia, Kuwait and Iraq alone. Loss of income and money lodged in Kuwaiti banks took the overall amount forfeited by the Palestinians as a direct result of the crisis well above $10 billion, he said.[10]

It would be several years before the Gulf states resumed contributions, albeit on a much reduced scale. Such was the continuing rage of Gulf rulers, whose anger at what they regarded as Arafat's betrayal knew almost no bounds, that Abdullah Bishara, secretary-general of the GCC, vowed at the time there could be 'no forgiveness, no forgetting . . . There is no forgiveness for this. It is not a romance where lovers quarrel. The crime is too big to forgive. Mr Arafat took a very reckless course of action and will have to bear the consequences.'[11]

Arafat – grimly aware that his predecessors Husseini and Shukairy lost their hold over the Palestinian movement in part because they ran out of money – had no choice but to order swingeing cuts in PLO expenditure. Funds were slashed for the PLO's diplomatic network, sleek PLO bureaucrats used to five-star hotel accommodation and the best whisky in the house were obliged to economise, and expenditures for the PLO's 14,000-strong military, including a tiny 'air force' and 'navy', were cut to the bone. Contributions to hospitals and social-welfare institutions across the region were much reduced, and pensions to the families of the estimated 18,000 Palestinian 'martyrs' of the Arab–Israeli conflict were pared back, or stopped altogether.[12]

Nor did the consequences stop there. During the Iraqi occupation and in its aftermath, tens of thousands of Palestinians had to leave Kuwait – one of the most important bases for the diaspora and the birthplace of Fatah – as Kuwaitis exacted their revenge for alleged Palestinian cooperation with the occupiers. More were expelled by Saudi Arabia and the other Gulf states. And Arafat himself was scarcely best-placed to plead their cause, having been declared *persona non grata* in about half the countries of the Arab world.

In running the expensive and unwieldy PLO apparatus, Arafat had always been terribly reliant on wealthy friends. The organisation had long had its own fund-raising network in the Palestinian diaspora – involving Palestinians in the Gulf, who were obliged to contribute between five and seven per cent of their gross salaries to the cause, thus raising around $40 million a year, as well as the big Palestinian business magnates to whom Arafat has always been close. Separately, Arafat had seen fit to build up a treasure chest for his own Fatah movement, including for the most part prudent investments worth more than $2 billion in equities, bonds and other securities, from which he would periodically bail out the PLO's treasury, the Palestine National Fund. But right from the start, the main source of funds was Arafat's Arab benefactors: Saudia Arabia, the most important of them, contributing about $85 million annually to the PLO and an unspecified, though almost certainly greater, amount to Fatah; the United Arab Emirates and Kuwait, which stumped up lesser amounts; Libya and Iraq, which gave sporadically.

Even when everybody was paying, as Jaweed al-Ghussein, a student friend of Arafat's and businessman who is now chairman of the Palestine National Fund, points out, the PNF was chronically in deficit to the tune of about $40 million every year.[13]

Hardly had the echoes from George Bush's imprecations before Congress concerning the need for a concerted new effort to deal with the Arab-Israel issue died down than James Baker was on his way to the Middle East on a long march that would come to be regarded as a textbook example of American diplomacy at its best and most persistent. Baker began his journey in the second week of March with impressive credentials, and, perhaps more important, with the full backing of a president who not only understood Mid-East complexities, but was prepared to risk the ire of the powerful American Jewish lobby. He would need all the backing he could get in what was to become a public test of wills with the obstinate Yitzhak Shamir who had precious little interest in seeing the peace process advance beyond the word go.

To the task of manoeuvring the various Middle East players towards a common goal, the patrician James Baker III brought the instincts of a river-boat gambler and the singlemindedness of someone unused to failure, not to mention invaluable experience gained from a previous abortive attempt that had merely sharpened his determination to succeed this time. The contrast with the flaccid efforts at Middle East peace-making of his predecessor, the plodding George Shultz, could scarcely have been more profound. Baker had given some clue to the tactics he might employ in a revealing interview with *Time* magazine early in 1989, as he was preparing to assume responsibility as Secretary of State. Musing on the relationship between turkey-shooting, one of his favourite pastimes, and the task ahead in the Middle East, he observed that the most important thing was 'getting them where you want them on your terms. Then *you* control the situation, not them. *You* have the options. Pull the trigger or don't. It doesn't matter once you've got them where you want them. The important thing is knowing that it's in your hands, that you can do whatever you determine is in your interest to do.'[14]

Stalking his prey on his return to the Middle East in March – the first of eight such visits to the region in 1991 – Baker did a good deal of listening, without revealing his hand; although Shamir and those around him could have been under few illusions that they were up against a formidable individual who had already bared his teeth in some of the most forthright criticism of the Jewish state uttered by an American official in many years. In a speech soon after becoming Secretary of State to the American Israel Public Affairs Committee (AIPAC), the principal Jewish lobby group in the US, Baker had thrown down the gauntlet, saying: 'For Israel, now is the time to lay aside, once and for all, the unrealistic vision of a greater Israel . . . Forswear annexation; stop settlement activity; allow schools to reopen; reach out to the Palestinians as neighbours who deserve political rights.'[15]

A year later, having failed to persuade the Israelis to abandon their dream of a Greater Israel, let alone sit down and talk to a 'sanitised' group of Palestinians who were prepared to disguise their PLO links, Mr Baker's patience deserted him. Testifying before Congress on lack of progress in Middle East peace-making, he laid the blame squarely at Shamir's door, and in remarks that brought squeals of anguish from Israel and its supporters, he gave the State Department telephone number as a contact if the Israelis wished to pursue discussions about peace. 'Everybody over there should know that the telephone number is 1–202–456–1414. When you're serious about peace, call us.' This observation prompted an American newspaper cartoonist to portray Baker as a Methuselahtype figure with a long white beard sitting beside the telephone awaiting a call from Israel that never came.

As Baker shuttled back and forth to the Middle East – he visited the region once in March, and then twice in April – he prompted yet again the old arguments among Palestinians about whether they should meet this harbinger of peace masquerading, in the eyes of some, as the handmaiden of Israeli designs. Baker did his best on these early visits to enlist the co-operation of Palestinians inside the territories, spending hours talking to their representatives in East Jerusalem, assuring them that he had their interests at heart.

Invariably, much of the conversation at these sessions would encompass the role of the PLO in any proposed peace conference – with the Palestinians of the territories, while appearing to enjoy more freedom of manoeuvre from Tunis in the post-Gulf War era, insisting, nevertheless, that they could not be separated from their 'national leadership' outside. Saeb Erakat, the fiery university professor and newspaper columnist, said that at one of these early sessions he had told Baker: 'I have a letter in my pocket from the PLO authorising me to be here, and without it this meeting could not take place. That is the reality everyone has to be aware of.'[16]

Watching Baker's comings and going from his Tunis isolation, Arafat was alternatively tantalised and not a little apprehensive about what the Americans might be up to. He saw in the Baker shuttles promise of progress towards an international Middle East peace conference under UN auspices, something he had been seeking for as long as he could remember; but at the same time he worried that Washington might be using the PLO's manifest weakness after the Gulf War to cut it out of the game completely. He gave voice to these concerns after a meeting in April with Algerian president Chadli Bendjedid – one of the few Arab leaders prepared to receive him at the time – when he said: 'The establishment of a new security order in the

Arab world and the normalisation of Arab-Israeli relations . . . are manoeuvres aimed at liquidating the Palestinian question and depriving the Palestinians of their legitimate rights.'[17] Later in April, however, Arafat appeared to be warming to proposals being floated by Baker for a regional conference between Israel and the so-called Arab 'front-line' states – Jordan, Syria and Lebanon – under the sponsorship of the United States and Soviet Union. After meeting Arafat in Libya, France's Foreign Minister Roland Dumas told reporters that 'Mr Arafat seemed to me to be open to the suggestion made by the US Secretary of State, but he is anxious that the core subjects not be ignored'.[18] Dumas identified among these 'core subjects' the issue of the 'authentic representation' of Palestinians in the negotiations.

From a personal standpoint, an isolated Arafat had reason to be grateful to the French. His meeting with Dumas was his first encounter with a senior Western official since the disaster of the Gulf War, and encouraged him to believe that his days of international solitude might be coming to an end. Arafat was also buoyed at that time when an apparently determined President Bush made it clear that the US was digging in its heels over an Israeli request for American loan guarantees to cover $10 billion in borrowing over five years to settle the hundreds of thousands of Jews who had arrived from the Soviet Union. Bush told the Israelis they could not expect to receive the guarantees that would enable them to borrow internationally at more favourable rates of interest while they continued their headlong rush to build settlements in territory seized in the 1967 war. Settlement building, he declared, was an 'obstacle to peace'.[19]

And so the stage was set for a bruising encounter between Israel and its guardian superpower that would drag on for months, bring relations to historic lows, and in the end serve the useful purpose of helping to educate an Israeli public that its representatives could not continue to shun international pressure, and expect to avoid penalty. Bush and Baker had begun sowing the seeds of Yitzhak Shamir's downfall at elections due in mid-1992, but in the meantime they had also entrapped him into agreeing in principle to Israel's participation at a proposed peace gathering scheduled for later in the year. By early in June when Bush despatched letters to regional leaders outlining Washington's 'ideas' for a regional peace conference, James Baker's 'turkey shoot' was beginning to assume promising dimensions.

As always, the vexed issue of Palestinian representation hovered in the background, with Shamir adamant that Israel would not sit down with Palestinians tainted by overt connection with the PLO. Nor would he countenance negotiations with Palestinians from East Jerusalem, since the Jewish state regarded the whole of Jerusalem, Arab and Jewish, as its undivided capital in perpetuity.

Thus began the circulation of 'lists' of Palestinians who might be acceptable, a process that was to continue, with Tunis's involvement, for months, and provide material for endless media speculation. Arafat himself was, by the middle of June, fully engaged in discussions on the issue of participation, and was being persuaded that his own, and the PLO's, best hope of ending their isolation was to appear to co-operate in the convening of a peace conference; although the trick was to try to ensure that the organisation would not be further marginalised by agreeing to remain out of sight.

Throughout the long, hot months of a Mediterranean summer Arafat, with his eyes firmly on Palestinian militants who were certain to oppose any concessions over PLO representation, continued to decry attempts to exclude the organisation from the conference, but all the time he plotted with trusted aides how best to secure Palestinian endorsement for a move that he knew provided the only realistic avenue forward. Typical of his public comments at the time were those to reporters in Amman in mid-July, after his first visit to Baghdad since the Gulf War, when he said: 'America's efforts are not aimed at achieving peace in the region, they are a bluff. They [US and Israel] want time for land, not land for peace.'[20]

In August he was at it again, this time in an interview with French television, in which he accused the US of yielding to Israeli 'blackmail' in setting conditions for Palestinian participation that would exclude a visible role for the PLO. 'If Israel has said yes to the conference, it's because all the conditions which it has set have been accepted by the US administration: no to the presence of the PLO, no to an independent Palestinian state, no to representatives from Jerusalem, and no to a resolution of the status of Jerusalem.' Theatrically, Arafat ended the interview by extending his hand toward the camera and saying: 'I hold my hand out to the Israelis. It's up to them now to extend theirs to truly make peace.'[21] Needless to say, there was not a flicker of response from Israel.

By now, planning was well under way for a special session of the Palestine National Council as a means of providing Arafat with the institutional cover for approving Palestinian participation in the forthcoming peace gathering. But towards the end of August an event would occur that would distract the PLO chief momentarily from his preparations for the PNC. Like much of the rest of the world the Palestinian leadership, cloistered in its sun-drenched villas in some of Tunis's classier suburbs, watched obsessively on Cable News Network the dramatic events in Moscow between 19–23 August when hardliners moved abortively against Mikhail Gorbachev, and in the process hastened the collapse of the Soviet Union. Some PLO stalwarts, who had been angered by Moscow's abandonment under Gorbachev of support for national liberation movements, applauded his apparent downfall, but for once Arafat stayed quiet. After Gorbachev re-emerged, the PLO leader congratulated him on his 'triumphant victory' and expressed the hope that he would continue to support Palestinian self-determination.[22]

Arafat's main preoccupation, however, was not international developments but preparations for the PNC to be held in Algiers in the last week of September. As always, he planned meticulously for the event to ensure that he would get exactly what he wanted: in this case the right to sanction Palestinian participation in a Middle East peace conference without direct PLO involvement.

Among the secrets of Arafat's control of his sometimes chaotic movement has been his mastery of quasi-representative institutions such as its parliament-in-exile, which has invariably bowed to his wishes while at times providing a safety valve for his opponents, such as the Popular Front of George Habash, to let off steam. Arafat likes to describe sessions of the PNC as an example of 'our Palestinian democracy', but in truth these events are more like a three-ring circus with the PLO chief acting as ringmaster.

Interestingly, in his attempts to ensure that the forthcoming PNC would prove reasonably representative of Palestinian aspirations, Arafat travelled to Khartoum in the first week of September for a meeting with Ibrahim Ghosheh, spokesman for Hamas, the Islamic resistance movement, which had its strongest roots in the Gaza Strip, and which had emerged as a powerful and militant counterweight to Fatah. For some time, Arafat had been attempting to draw Hamas into the broad PLO church on the basis that it was better to have one's opponents inside rather than outside the tent. As in the past, the discussions with Hamas went nowhere, since its conditions for engagement in the PNC were outrageous. It wanted 40 per cent of the seats to reflect what it said was its popularity in the territories. But at least after his meeting with Ghosheh Arafat could say he had tried.[23]

And so the stage was set for yet another of Arafat's *coups de théâtre*, and in this he was following a script that he had honed over many years. The Algiers PNC, the twentieth in the PLO's chequered history, and the sixteenth over which Arafat himself had presided since his election in 1969 as Chairman of the Organisation's Executive Committee, drew together the usual crew of Palestinian bureaucrats, former guerrilla fighters, and academicians – older, greyer and paunchier than on their last meeting in 1988. This time, as the more than 300 delegates gathered in the by now familiar circular conference chamber of the Club de Pins, half an hour's drive west of Algiers, their deliberations would be less momentous than their independence declaration three years previously. But their acquiesence in Arafat's careful steps towards endorsing Palestinian participation at the forthcoming US-Soviet sponsored peace conference would yield more immediate benefits.

'We renew our readiness to work with all international parties to make the peace conference succeed to fulfil what the people of the region are striving for in terms of a just peace, security and stability . . . and we renew our readiness to co-operate so that the remaining obstacles on the road to convening it can be removed,' Arafat told the opening session.[24]

But in debate on the chamber floor, in discussions in smoke-filled anterooms of the conference centre, and in talk into the early-morning hours in Arafat's luxury villa on the shores of the Mediterranean, the PLO leader was not yet ready to ask his colleagues for a clear-cut endorsement of Palestinian participation in the peace conference. Rather, he wanted something fuzzier that would give him room for manoeuvre until the last minute before the conference convened late in October. 'You are not required to say yes, but we cannot say no. You have to find a formula,' he advised delegates, using words reminiscent of an earlier PNC dubbed by its participants the 'lam' conference, a play on the Arabic words *la*, meaning 'no', and *na'am*, meaning 'yes'. Arafat also, no doubt, hoped to use continuing uncertainty over whether the Palestinians would engage as a bargaining chip to improve conditions for their involvement, and he may even have entertained a forlorn dream that at the last minute the Israelis, under pressure from the US, might have relented and allowed more overt PLO involvement.

In his careful stage-managing of the twentieth PNC, Arafat employed all his old ruses, drawing deep from his grab-bag of tricks learned over many years of manipulating and manoeuvring his Palestinian brothers and sisters towards what he considered a desirable end. Thus, he set the scene with a measured speech about the limited options available to the Palestinians, and followed that up with his familiar stratagem of offering to resign – a rhetorical ploy he had used in the past in the certain knowledge that his status as the battered symbol of the revolution made him virtually immune from challenge. 'I plead with you not to re-elect me, so that I will be relieved of my responsibility . . . This job is a catastrophe,' a sad-eyed Arafat told an early-morning session.[25]

In the end, the PNC, after a spirited debate involving Arafat loyalists on one side and the 'loyal opposition' of George Habash's Popular Front on the other, endorsed a document outlining the terms of Palestinian participation in the peace conference. The vote in favour of allowing 'non-PLO' Palestinians to negotiate directly with the Israelis was 256 to 68: a second vote on a 'declaration of principles' to guide the discussions was carried by 313 votes to 18. 'We want a peace of the brave, not capitulations. We will not make any obstacles to peace, but we reject the Israeli conditions,' Arafat told reporters at the end of the PNC.[26]

In fact, in his pragmatic decision to sanction Palestinian involvement, Arafat was falling into line with Israeli demands that excluded the PLO and representatives from East Jerusalem. An important footnote to the twentieth PNC was the appearance at a closed session late one night – journalists were ushered from the chamber – of Faisal

Husseini, Arafat's chief representative in the territories, and Hanan Ashrawi, the West Bank academic whose calm, articulate description of the Palestinian predicament was gaining widespread notice internationally. In defiance of Israeli law banning contacts with the PLO, the two mingled with conference delegates and made a persuasive case for Palestinian involvement in the forthcoming peace conference. Ashrawi, who had attended a number of meetings with James Baker, said she believed the Americans had a greater appreciation of the Palestinian viewpoint, and were indeed prepared to do something about trying to slow Israel's settlement drive in the occupied territories.[27] Back in Israel, hardliners urged that Husseini and Ashrawi be arrested on their return for fraternising with the enemy, but apart from a summons for questioning by the police the issue was not pursued. Even in Shamir's Israel taboos against the PLO were crumbling.

As the date for the opening of the Middle East peace conference at the end of October approached (no venue had yet been announced, although Lausanne was the target of much speculation), Arafat had one further hurdle to overcome: he convened a session in Tunis of the 90-member Central Council, the Palestinian 'mini-parliament', to approve the names of seven Palestinians in a joint Jordanian–Palestinian delegation. This endorsement was duly secured, and Arafat departed for consultations in Damascus and Cairo, thus ending a protracted period of diplomatic isolation following his Gulf War folly. His visit to Egypt on 21 October, his first in fourteen months, in which he held 90 minutes of talks with President Hosni Mubarak, was a low-key affair. The meeting was held in Mubarak's house, and press and television were barred.

At this time, as preparations gathered speed for the first-ever formal face-to-face meeting between Israel and its Arab foes, James Baker dispatched a letter of assurance to the Palestinians. It was more generous to Palestinian aspirations than any other official American pronouncement in the last 30 years. Importantly, it said nothing that would preclude the direct participation of the Palestinian leadership outside the territories in the process at a later date.[28]

As delegations to the Middle East peace conference began arriving at the end of October in a Madrid bathed in autumnal colours, it was clear that a diplomatic event of more than usual significance was in the offing. But few could have predicted then that within less than two years it would yield startling progress towards the beginning of a resolution of the near century-long conflict between Arab and Jew in the narrow crescent bounded by the Mediterranean and the River Jordan; or, for that matter, that by sharpening the appetite in Israel itself for progress towards peace, it would prove to be so crucial in hastening the electoral downfall of Shamir and his nationalist camp.

Vowing that never again would the Middle East dispute bring the world to the brink of war, Messrs Bush and Gorbachev opened proceedings on 30 October in the majestic Hall of Columns in Madrid's Royal Palace, before a worldwide television audience and in the presence of 4,665 journalists from 54 countries who had converged on the Spanish capital. Bush's speech was gracious and low-key, but it also left no doubt that the Americans believed that, for there to be progress towards peace, Israel would have to show much greater flexibility. 'Israel now has an opportunity to demonstrate that it is willing to enter into a new relationship with its Palestinian neighbours . . . we believe territorial compromise is essential to peace,' he declared pointedly.[29]

Proceedings over the next 36 hours of the latest, and as it turned out, most productive American effort to bring peace to the Middle East, were packed with theatrical moments, not least speeches by Haidar Abdel-Shafi, a courtly septuagenerian physician from Gaza for the Palestinians, and from Yitzhak Shamir himself. The spectacle of the Israelis sitting at a T-shaped table facing their most bitter Arab foes – the Syrians, Lebanese, and a joint Jordanian-Palestinian delegation – was something made all the more remarkable by the fact that those participating were not the doves of the centre and left, but the hardliners of the nationalist right.

By common consent, the opening round went to the Palestinians with Abdel-Shafi's speech, like Arafat's to the UN in 1974, borrowing skilfully from American political folklore. 'We, the people of Palestine, stand before you in the fullness of our pain, our pride and our anticipation. For too long the Palestinian people have gone unheeded, silenced and denied – our identity negated by political expediency, our rightful struggle against injustice maligned, and our present existence subsumed by the past tragedy of another people,' he declared before a respectful audience, while the Israelis shifted uncomfortably in their seats, aware that Abdel-Shafi had given meaning to Palestinian grievances in a way perhaps never achieved before: and this in front of a vast international television audience.[30] The Palestinian spokesman also contrived to mention Arafat by name, but he did so cunningly by quoting the PLO leader to end his speech, thus avoiding an Israeli walkout.

Watching events in Madrid obsessively from his Tunis headquarters, Arafat felt sharp pangs of disappointment, but there was much consolation in the way things turned out. Not only had the public presentation of the Palestinian position been handled skilfully by Hanan Ashrawi and others, but Arafat himself had clearly not been out of mind during the proceedings. He had also ensured that the PLO presence in Madrid, spearheaded by his trusted aide, Nabil Shaath, would be noticed, and for it to be made plain that his lieutenants were co-ordinating the efforts of the Palestinian delegation, and that he (Arafat) was in effective command from Tunis, like Tiberius with a telephone.

Indeed, Arafat representatives in Madrid made no attempt to disguise their almost constant contact with Tunis. His spokesman, Ahmed Abdel Rahman, told the Associated Press that Arafat had given final approval to the text of Haidar Abdel-Shafi's speech, which had been faxed to him in Tunis.[31] In fact, Arafat had written in his own hand in Arabic on the final draft: 'God crown your efforts with success. Abu Ammar.' Nabil Shaath, who manned round-the-clock what he described as an 'operations room', also went out of his way to emphasise the link between Tunis and the Palestinian delegation. 'We are here to make sure the Palestinian delegation is fully equipped and supported by the best Palestinian brains, expertise and the right political position. That involves doing everything except sitting at the negotiating table,' he said.[32] After labouring for years to achieve a modicum of recognition and fearing above all else the loss of control, Arafat was not going to allow a group of Palestinians from the territories to get ideas above their station.

The Madrid conference, which ended on an upbeat note with the beginning of bilateral negotiations between Israel and its neighbours, raised hopes that real advances might be made towards a resolution of outstanding problems. True, after the initial euphoria, the progress of the faltering talks in Washington, under the watchful eyes of State Department officials, would prove to be painfully slow. But there is also no doubt that Madrid provided an important launching pad for a new and more promising stage in Middle East peace-making. Old taboos had been broken and, more important as far as the Palestinians were concerned, their plight was perhaps more firmly on the international agenda than it had ever been before.

With the Madrid conference out of the way, and Middle East proceedings having entered something of a lull after the frenetic activity of previous months, Yasser Arafat sprang one of his biggest surprises. At the age of 62, and having proclaimed for as long as anyone could remember that he was betrothed to the revolution, he took a wife 34 years his junior. When it emerged, early in 1992, that he had been married secretly for several months to Suha Tawil, a 28-year-old Palestinian Christian, there was discomfort within Palestinian ranks, especially among older comrades who believed this was a frivolous act. But Arafat's decision late in life to take a young bride was revealing of his state of mind, indicating perhaps a desire to strike out in new directions.

His choice of companion was certainly an interesting one. Suha was the daughter of Raymonda Tawil, a long-standing Palestinian activist and journalist. Sorbonne-educated and fluent in English, French and Arabic, she had gone to work as Arafat's secretary in 1989, and had become a constant companion, travelling with him on his peripatetic missions across the Arab world. Her PLO connections were impeccable: two of her sisters were married to PLO officials, one of them to Ibrahim Souss, the organisation's Paris representative.

But if Arafat's close colleagues believed that marriage might mellow him, several incidents were to confound those expectations. In one, a tearful Arafat stormed out of an Islamic Summit in Dakar, the capital of Senegal, after failing to persuade his fellow summiteers to include references in the conference resolution to a *jihad*, or holy war, to recapture Israeli-occupied Arab land.[33] In another, Arafat made some extraordinarily intemperate remarks after a public outcry in France greeted the news that his old sparring partner George Habash of the Popular Front was undergoing treatment for a stroke in a Paris hospital. Jewish groups had decried a decision by the French government to permit entry to someone they regarded as an arch terrorist. According to a CNN transcript of an alleged taped conversation with Ibrahim Souss, a furious Arafat had said: 'The Jews at work! Damn their fathers!

Dogs! Filth! Dirt! All this for one sick man!' Arafat had also threatened to 'settle accounts' with 'the rotten Jews'. Israel's representative in Paris seized on this outburst and observed that the comments revealed 'a PLO double language', conciliatory in public and vitriolic in private.[34]

With peace talks in Washington meandering along without sign of progress, and with Israel becoming increasingly preoccupied with forthcoming elections, it seemed the Middle East was about to enter the doldrums as summer approached. But Arafat, who had been scarcely visible in the early part of the year, was about to remind the world of one of his more remarkable qualities, and also to underline to supporters and detractors alike within his own movement his indispensability.

On 8 April, while on a flight from Khartoum to Tunis, Arafat's plane, a Russian An–26, went down in the desert near the Libya–Sudan border after being caught in a vicious sandstorm. When news of the crash filtered out, few believed that the PLO leader had survived. In Tunis, something approaching panic gripped colleagues, who were roused from their beds to be told that the 'Old Man' was missing in the Libyan desert. Not least of their concerns was whether the secretive Arafat had entrusted anyone with details of the PLO's billions. 'Where's the notebook?' was one of the first questions anxious PLO officials asked each other, a reference to the accounting records of the organisation's investments and bank accounts.[35] Agonising hours were to pass before confirmation was received that Arafat had indeed miraculously emerged from the aircraft wreck in which three crewmen, including pilot and co-pilot, had died.

In all his years of living dangerously, Arafat had not experienced a closer call. His reputation as a survivor hardly needed burnishing, but his latest brush with death had conferred on him, in the eyes of his people at least, an almost supernatural quality. In the days after the crash, Arafat could not be accused of avoiding an opportunity to bolster the myth of invincibility, and to add some deft political touches to the story of his remarkable escape. In one interview, he revealed that he had shouted 'Abu Jihad, I am coming' as his plane hurtled towards the desert.[36] This was a reference to his old comrade-in-arms, Khalil al-Wazir, who was assassinated by the Israelis in 1988. It was not the smallest of ironies that within a fairly short time, Arafat would be doing business with the man who, as Israeli Defence Minister, had ordered his friend's execution.

# 20

# *The Reckoning*

'You don't negotiate peace with friends. You make it with very unsympathetic enemies.' Yitzhak Rabin, Israeli Prime Minister, Washington, September 1993.

For a man who had spent his life cultivating a grim, laconic style, Yitzhak Rabin spoke with unusual eloquence. Standing on the speaker's podium in Israel's austere parliament chamber, he addressed his words to the people who had just delivered him a stunning election victory and to the Arab leaders from whom he – as Israel's army chief of staff – had seized swathes of territory during the Six-Day War exactly 25 years before. It was time, he growled in his familiar gravelly voice, for Israelis to 'overcome the sense of isolation that has held us in its thrall for almost half a century' and join 'the international movement toward peace, reconciliation and co-operation'. It was time, too, for Israel's Arab neighbours: 'I invite the King of Jordan and the presidents of Syria and Lebanon to this rostrum in Israel's Knesset, here in Jerusalem, for the purpose of talking peace.' And if they were not prepared to come to him, he would go to them: 'In the service of peace, I am prepared to travel to Amman, Damascus and Beirut today, tomorrow. For there is no greater victory than the victory of peace. Wars have their victors and vanquished, but everyone is a victor in peace.'[1]

For the Palestinians of the occupied territories, Rabin – taking office as premier on 14 July 1992, for the second time in twenty years – also had a message, of a rather more ambiguous kind. He was out to negotiate a means of rapidly giving them control over their own affairs, and they should talk – if necessary, in continuous negotiations rather than the fits and starts that had characterised the peace process so far. But if they persisted in 'terror and violence', then his government would use 'every possible means' to crush them.[2]

It was a familiar theme, one that the 70-year-old Rabin had played to great effect during the election campaign in which he had just trounced Yitzhak Shamir's Likud party, mixing a hard-headed readiness to make concessions for peace with the toughest of responses to perceived security threats.

And this theme was calculated to appeal to mainstream Israeli voters tired of war but worried about the consequences of showing weakness in negotiations – people who could be persuaded to trust the former general who first captured the territories in 1967 to extricate Israel from the moral and political quagmire into which it had since been plunged.

Rabin's words found a receptive audience elsewhere. In faraway Tunis, Yasser Arafat was listening intently to every nuance. The PLO leader was still feeling a little shaky following his plane crash three months before. In early June, while on a visit to Jordan, he had complained of a chronic headache: doctors diagnosed a blood clot on the brain caused by the crash and he was swiftly carted off to the operating theatre. Now, as Rabin took office in Israel, Arafat was almost back on form – hoping that the new prime minister was planning a bold departure towards the Palestinians, fantasising that he might even be prepared to break the long-established Israeli taboo and talk direct to the enemy as Arafat himself had suggested; although the President of Palestine was conspicuous by his absence from the list of Arab leaders with whom Rabin sought to do business. Through his official spokesman, Ahmed Abdelrahman, Arafat fell back on the familiar litany of complaints and accusations. 'Mr Rabin failed to show courage and take the necessary step to react to Mr Arafat's proposal that the two men should sit down to negotiate a political solution,' he said. 'He totally forgot the Palestinians' representative. . . . What we need is a willingness to deal with issues seriously, to undo the bad taste left by Shamir.'[3]

This was all for public consumption, however. In private, Arafat harboured other ideas. His political instincts – and as important, his colleagues in the occupied territories, whom he consulted with increasing frequency concerning Israeli affairs – told him that the Israeli election of 23 June 1992 had been of potentially momentous significance, perhaps the most important in the history of the Jewish state. After fifteen years of governments dominated by a party (Likud) determined to hang on to all the occupied territories and irredeemably hostile to Palestinian political rights, Israelis had voted for a change. They had elected a government that said it favoured a rapid move towards interim Palestinian self-rule. The extent of the change this represented would become clear as the months wore on. But Shamir himself gave Palestinians and Israelis a glimpse of what might have been as he skulked off into retirement. He said after the election that he had been prepared to drag out negotiations with the Arabs for ten years while he saw to it that the occupied territories were flooded with Jewish settlers.[4]

In his more upbeat moments, the PLO leader was prepared to admit that the election had indeed broken new ground. 'They voted against Shamir: that is a vote for peace,' he told an interviewer on 1 July.[5] What is more, it was a vote he may have had a modest hand in influencing. As he rebuilt his strength after the travails of the past few months, Arafat was already exploring new ways of inserting himself back into the Middle East negotiating game – this time as direct interlocutor of the Israeli government.

His point of departure, as on so many previous occasions, was in next-door Jordan. Convalescence from surgery in the first week of June had in any case forced him to sojourn in Amman for longer than usual. But as soon as he was back on his feet, he was plotting a way to turn his presence in the Jordanian capital to political advantage by intruding on the Israeli election campaign. His chosen stratagem: a very public meeting with the Palestinian negotiating team with which the Israeli government was now regularly dealing at the Washington talks. Less than a week before the election, he invited negotiators Haidar Abdel-Shafi, Faisal al-Husseini and Hanan Ashrawi to troop across the Allenby Bridge to Amman. There, having made sure a suitable array of TV cameras and journalists were on hand, he effusively hugged and kissed the three of them as they congratulated the President of Palestine on his recovery.

This was a wheeze of some subtlety – at least in comparison with Arafat's many ham-handed and counterproductive attempts to sway past Israeli elections. Although the Palestinian negotiators had met Arafat on many previous occasions in private, it was the first time that they had done so – deliberately – in the full glare of publicity. In the act, the PLO leader blew to pieces the fiction at the heart of the serving Israeli government's Palestinian policy.

Prime Minister Shamir, true to form, had been fighting the election on a platform of implacable opposition to dealing with the PLO. The Palestinian delegates with whom he had sat at Madrid and with whom his officials had subsequently negotiated repeatedly in Washington were, he insisted, representatives of the West Bank and Gaza Arabs and had no direct link with Arafat's terror organisation. It was a convenient game of smoke and mirrors that enabled him to claim that, unlike his Labour opponents, he was preventing the dire spectre of an independent Palestinian state from impinging on the talks. But it was smoke and mirrors all the same.

Rabin's campaign was much more straightforward in this regard. He said he intended to negotiate with the West Bank and Gaza Palestinians, and he did not care with whom their representatives conferred. Charged with secretly planning to deal with the PLO, he loftily countered that this was what Shamir was doing already. 'Despite the Likud declarations and despite the fact it is sticking its head in the sand, this government has ongoing direct negotiations with the PLO,' said a Labour statement after the Amman meeting.[6] Beyond threatening to arrest the Palestinian negotiators on their return from Jordan – a move that would almost certainly have killed the peace process stone dead and led to a severe estrangement with the US – Shamir's ministers were stumped for a coherent reply. Thus was the die cast for election of a government that, on paper at least, seemed more amenable to tackling the core of the Palestinian problem than any of its predecessors.

Arafat, for his part, while clear enough concerning what Israelis had voted against, was less sure what they had voted *for*. His views about Rabin in particular were deeply ambivalent. He heard the overtures concerning a rapid push for Palestinian autonomy in the territories, but remained sceptical of the new Prime Minister's sincerity. His scepticism was fuelled by what he knew of Rabin's history. Was he not the man who, after conquering the West Bank from Jordan and Gaza from Egypt, set out to implant Jewish settlements on Arab land? Worse, was it not he who, as Defence Minister under Shamir in 1988, proclaimed a policy of 'might, force and beatings' to suppress the Palestinian *intifada* – a policy far tougher than any Likud minister had ever dared avow – and who ordered the assassination of Arafat's friend and right-hand man Khalil al-Wazir? These were themes that Arafat's left-wing rivals such as George Habash harped on in the weeks following Rabin's election – and which Arafat occasionally echoed, when he was not issuing calls on Rabin to meet him in person and strike a 'peace of the brave' or to 'join the tide of history'.[7]

'I don't see Rabin as different from Shamir,' he said in Cairo as Rabin prepared to take office. 'Unfortunately, some of our Arab brothers have slipped and welcomed him. Rabin broke the bones of our brothers. He set up the early settlements in the occupied lands.'[8]

The bitterness was predictable, and mutual. What Arafat failed fully to comprehend was that in Rabin, toughness and conciliation were two sides of the same coin. The only native-born Israeli to have served as prime minister and a man whose distinguished military record dating back to the 1948 War of Independence won him widespread public trust, Rabin often talked of a strategy of 'marching with both feet' – the military and political.[9] His coalition contained a party – Meretz, allied with the Peace Now movement – that openly favoured direct contacts with the PLO. Moreover, his Foreign Minister was another old campaigner and intelligence operative, Shimon Peres, who also privately inclined to that view. The government was already talking of curbing the growth of Jewish settlements in the territories. Before it had been in office a month, it dangled before Arafat's eyes the carrot of an end to the ban on contacts between Israeli citizens and the PLO – while still ruling out negotiating with the organisation itself.

Once more, Arafat girded himself to tone down his recriminations and do business. In Tunis, he called a top-level strategy meeting to assess the implications of the new Israeli government. And separately, in the occupied territories, his key lieutenants, Faisal al-Husseini and Saeb Erakat, began to contemplate adopting a more co-operative stance towards the occupation forces. They, of all people, were in a position to realise that the next phase was going to require extremely careful handling. They knew that Rabin intended to accompany conciliatory gestures in negotiation with an iron fist in the territories. 'He's going to be tough in the next four months,' warned Erakat. 'He will have to throw the Israelis a bone, and the bone will be his hardline stance.'[10]

The first test of the Palestinians' new, softly-softly approach was not long in coming. On 15 August, almost exactly four weeks after Rabin took office, Israeli troops moved in and surrounded Al-Najah University in the West Bank town of Nablus – in search, the Israelis said, of a group of armed Palestinian radicals who had infiltrated the campus in the midst of a fiercely contested student election. There followed a tense stand-off, in which troops kept several thousand students bottled up inside the university without food or water, demanding they surrender the gunmen. On such occasions in the past, the result had almost always been bloodshed and spreading protest. This time, a Palestinian team led by Husseini managed to secure a negotiated settlement with the Israeli administration, working under the direct control of Rabin: six radicals were deported to Jordan and the Israelis agreed to take no further action against the university. Husseini told startled reporters he did the deal to preserve the peace process and prevent further violence – and then went on to pay an unusual tribute to Rabin himself. 'He is a man who is ready to play the game,' he affirmed.[11]

It was perhaps the most striking example yet of the Palestinian leaders in the territories acting to their own script, rather than to one written in Tunis. Arafat's reaction to the university siege differed both in tone and substance from that of his men on the ground. While Husseini was locked in talks with the Israelis, he spent his time faxing out furious statements lambasting Rabin's 'authoritarian policies' and 'escalating repression' against the students, and calling on the US to intervene. Not for the first time, the Old Man seemed a little out of touch with events within what was now by far his most important constituency, the Palestinians of the West Bank and Gaza.

The 'game' to which Husseini had referred was the Washington negotiations, for which Arafat's hopes were building ahead of yet another foray into the region by US Secretary of State James Baker. He was soon to discover that his hopes were terribly premature. Rabin was in no hurry to move, and President Bush and Secretary Baker were certainly not going to exert immediate pressure on a prime minister so much more to their liking than the intransigent Shamir. Instead, in August Bush invited Rabin to his holiday retreat in Kennebunkport, Maine, welcoming him with great warmth and a promise to release the $10 billion in US loan guarantees that the US had been withholding.

To make matters worse from Arafat's point of view, the Middle East peace process was once again falling foul of the US electoral cycle. President Bush's re-election campaign was in trouble, and to attempt to save it he called Baker back from State to the White House and the hustings. Baker's departure deprived the negotiations of what little momentum they had had. To Arafat's greater, though probably unjustified dismay, his place was taken by his deputy, Lawrence Eagleburger – a man who, as the PLO leader observed, had been a 'pupil' of his old nemesis Henry Kissinger and had 'in the past shown public bias towards Israel'.[12] 'Baker's departure is bound to reflect negatively on the peace process,' said Arafat as he headed for talks in Khartoum with the Islamic fundamentalist rulers of Sudan. 'We simply have to wait and see how much.'[13]

Sure enough, as the Bush administration spent its energies in the forlorn election fight, the Washington negotiations sank into the doldrums – and the occupied territories, as was customary when peace moves had become becalmed, were gripped by a vicious upsurge in violence. This time, though, there was a twist almost as ominous for Arafat as for the Israelis and Palestinians who were being killed: the more extreme of the violent acts were being carried out by a Palestinian group that was deeply hostile to his ideas of coexistence beside Israel in a Palestinian mini-state. The organisation was called the Islamic Resistance Movement, or Hamas (Zeal), and in the Gaza Strip at least, it had grown into the biggest challenge to the PLO since Arafat had become chairman.

On the morning of 13 December 1992, a 29-year-old Israeli border policeman named Nissim Toledano was walking to work through the streets of his home town, Lod, a nondescript extension of Tel Aviv's urban sprawl. Suddenly, he was set upon by masked assailants, manhandled into a car and driven off at speed. He was not seen alive again. That night, two similarly masked Palestinians marched into a Red Cross office in the West Bank town of El-Bireh and presented an ultimatum for the release of the Hamas spiritual leader, Sheikh Ahmed Yassin, who was serving a life sentence for manslaughter. If the Israeli authorities refused to comply, Sergeant Toledano would be killed. The statement was accompanied by a police ID card in Toledano's name, and signed by Hamas's 'military wing', the Izzedine Al-Qassam Battalion.

Rabin's response was characteristically direct. Within two days of the discovery of Toledano's body pitted with stab wounds, Israel rounded up some 1600 Palestinians suspected of Hamas connections. Then, after a hurried legal wrangle in its constitutional court, it proceeded to bus a quarter of them in blindfolds across its northern border and dump them in freezing rain and fog on a Lebanese hillside. By pushing some 400 alleged activists, by far the largest group to be expelled at one time in the 25 years since Israel had conquered the West Bank and Gaza, into no-man's-land, Rabin had taken Israel's struggle with its reluctant Arab subjects to new lengths.

It thus seemed all the more puzzling that he insisted his actions were all in the cause of peace. 'Today there is before us a chance for making progress towards peace,' he told TV viewers at the height of the crisis. 'As we advance, those who oppose it will try to increase their terror. I therefore call on the public to believe in the army and in the security services, to believe in the chance for peace. You shall see, we shall achieve it.'[14]

The man who liked to deflect hecklers at political rallies by boasting of the number of Arabs he had expelled was still 'marching with both feet', and his message was addressed squarely to his Palestinian adversaries as much as to the Israelis themselves. Co-operate and negotiate, he was telling the majority of Palestinians who supported the PLO rather than the extremists of Hamas. By working together, we could combat the fundamentalist menace.

The message was certainly not lost on Yasser Arafat in Tunis. For some time he had been expressing dismay at the growing influence of Hamas, born out of the worsening economic misery in the territories. He was getting intelligence that the fundamentalists had received substantial financial aid from Iran and Saudi Arabia – according to one report, the Islamic Republic had provided the tidy sum of $30 million – for use in building their own network of schools, hospitals and other social facilities. This was galling enough for the PLO leader at a time when his own funding from former Arab benefactors had slowed to a trickle, and his ability to influence events in the territories had shrunk correspondingly. Worse, Hamas's spiralling attacks on Israeli targets and on other Palestinian groups such as his own Fatah movement were making it increasingly difficult to keep the peace process on the rails. In one revealing aside, Arafat accused the Islamists of 'fighting other Palestinians on Tehran's orders'.[15] And on the fifth anniversary of the *intifada* in early December, he issued a clarion call for 'effective national unity between all groups and forces fighting the Israeli occupation'.[16]

Arafat's first reaction to the mass deportation was in a similar vein: while urging escalation of the uprising against the 'fascist Israelis', he called on Hamas to join forces and invited its leaders to a meeting. His aim was not to hitch the PLO to some new armed struggle against the Jewish state, but to co-opt the Islamic movement into at least tacitly supporting his diplomacy. 'We have to put our differences aside,' said close aide and former left-wing firebrand, Yasser Abed Rabbo. 'We are not asking Hamas to change its policies, but we have to deal with this situation in a realistic way.'[17] Nobody was surprised when Arafat's overtures to Hamas ended without agreement: there was a world of difference between the PLO's hard-won mandate for negotiations with Israel and Hamas's demand that it pull out of the Washington talks and declare a *jihad*, or holy war.

Arafat, now in his 64th year, married and at the end of most of his nine lives, was painfully aware of the ironies of his predicament. Indeed, the dilemma had been implicit in all his maneouvrings of recent years, in all his attempts to move the Palestinian movement away from 'armed struggle' and towards the negotiating table. Now Hamas had adopted the classic guerrilla tactics with which Arafat had made his name 30 years before, and was challenging the established Palestinian leadership as Fatah's young hotheads had done in the 1960s. The danger was that, if this continued, his control over events in the territories would slip away completely – and with it the claim to lead the drive for Palestinian statehood that he had spent his life asserting. The alternatives were that stark. To align himself with the fundamentalists and other radicals would be to risk losing everything for which he had fought. Yet to rein them in, he simply did not possess the means. Not, that is, unless he contemplated the unthinkable: forging an unholy connection with the enemy, Israel itself.

Such were the calculations beginning to take shape in Arafat's restless mind as he assessed the fallout from the deportations and watched the world gearing up for one of its periodic bursts of outrage. He would have to tread delicately, seeking to secure the stiffest possible international condemnation of Israel's action but doing nothing that might seriously upset the peace talks. His nephew and UN mission chief, Nasser al-Qudwa, was detailed to rail against Israel in the ensuing Security Council debate, and Palestinian participation in the Washington Arab-Israeli negotiations was 'suspended', ostensibly until a solution could be found to the issue of the deportees. But that was a holding pattern. *Sotto voce*, the PLO chairman was sending signals that the deportees were a side issue: 'The case of the deportees is important, but we consider the basic issue to be that of Jerusalem,' he told one interviewer. 'It is not a matter of the deportees alone, it is a matter of the Palestinian cause as a whole.'[18] The peace convoy, in other words, must be made to move on, preferably with Arafat himself at the wheel.

The question was: how? The Washington negotiations would scarcely be a promising avenue even when they resumed. In the eight rounds to date, they had done little more than mark time, with Israel proposing five years of limited self-rule in the territories pending agreement on their final status, and the Palestinians constantly seeking assurances on what shape such a final settlement might take. It was a recipe for deadlock. Nor could the US be expected to lend a hand: President Bill Clinton, though committed to persevering with the process set in motion by his predecessor, was a novice and in any case had vowed to concentrate more on domestic than foreign affairs.

In Arafat's mind, the Washington talks had another serious flaw: under the negotiating format initiated at the 1991 Madrid peace conference, they did not directly involve him. True, the Palestinian delegation was careful to refer every topic back to Tunis and Arafat's adviser Nabil Shaath was omnipresent in the wings, so he was able to claim control over the process. But communications were often garbled, delayed or distorted by distance. As Arafat complained repeatedly, the 'Madrid formula' – devised to spare the embarrassment of an Israeli government not yet prepared to admit it was dealing with the PLO – had become more of a hindrance than a help. To begin to make peace, Arafat needed to cut the Gordian knot and talk more directly to his enemies – and vice versa.

So began the saga of Yasser Arafat's secret dalliance with Yitzhak Rabin. Like other illicit courtships, it started with an implausible tryst, developed in strange and shifting locations, and required careful nurturing by mutual friends to take root. Like other cases where political enemies have tentatively joined hands, it was founded in a sense of shared self-interest between two old fighters in their twilight years – an Israeli prime minister elected on a promise to deliver peace on the one hand, a PLO leader desperate to secure progress of any kind on the other.

In Israel, the genesis of the relationship was itself a complex affair, requiring unprecedented co-operation between two men – Rabin and Foreign Minister Peres – whose long rivalry for the Labour leadership had led them cordially to detest each other. But if some of the initial groundwork can be attributed to one man, it is probably an Iranian-born peace campaigner by the name of Abie Nathan. An eccentric but generally respected figure on the leftward fringe of Israeli politics, Nathan owned an offshore radio station broadcasting rock music and propaganda from the Mediterranean. He had worked tirelessly to foster negotiations between Israel and its Arab neighbours since the mid-1960s, when he had flown unannounced to Egypt to try to persuade President Nasser to make peace. In the late 1980s, it was Yasser Arafat's turn. Nathan, only two years Arafat's senior, became a regular visitor to his Tunis headquarters and in the process struck up a warm personal rapport – as well as regularly colliding with the 1986 Israeli law forbidding any contact between Israeli citizens and the PLO. Having spent four months in jail for his trouble in 1989, he was determined to keep testing the waters. In May 1991 he staged a hunger strike in protest at the law, visited Arafat again and landed back in prison.

In themselves Nathan's visits to Tunis were nothing new. Arafat had met an odd assortment of left-wing Israelis on numerous occasions since he had been under siege in Beirut in 1982, to little avail. Yet the striking fact about Nathan's continuation of this tradition was that it did nothing to dent his widespread popularity at home in Israel. Nathan had, almost literally, supped with the devil and – far from shocking ordinary Israelis – had won sympathy for the treatment he received from their government as a result. In so doing, he helped prepare the ground for a gradual 'de-demonisation' of Arafat in Israel, and for the incoming Labour government in 1992 to contemplate lifting the ban on PLO contacts.

Israeli attitudes to Arafat were in any case slowly thawing. Confronted with the alternative of Islamic extremism, Israelis were coming round to the idea that they preferred the devil they knew, but Arafat contributed to the change by becoming somewhat more successful in his efforts to reach out to Israeli public opinion – something he had often attempted but mishandled in the past. After years spent concentrating on the battle for American support, he was beginning to play to the gallery that really mattered, inviting leading Israeli journalists for interviews in his Tunis lair and endeavouring to keep his fatal tendency to say different things to different audiences in check. He was never going to be a Nelson Mandela, to be sure – but nor did he any longer provide fuel for the official Israeli propaganda machine in quite the generous way he had kept it churning for the past two decades.

Arafat saw other straws in the wind suggesting a more accommodating Israeli attitude once Rabin took office.

One was the increasing frequency of his (Arafat's) contacts with the Arab members of the Israeli Knesset, sometimes purporting to be conveying messages from the prime minister himself. Another emerged in the multilateral talks between Israel and the Arabs, on such practical issues as economic co-operation, that had been set up to complement the bilateral negotiations in Washington in 1991. For a whole year, the Israelis had adamantly refused to negotiate with any Palestinian from outside the occupied territories, for fear of encouraging discussion of issues they had no intention of addressing such as the refugee question. Then, in October 1992, Rabin and Peres quietly dropped the condition, permitting 'outsiders' – including senior figures from the PLO – to attend the talks as advisers to the Palestinian delegates.

Though largely unheralded at the time, this was an important step. It took place at a meeting of the multilateral talks in Paris in October 1992 – appropriately enough in the conference centre where US and Vietnamese officials tried to negotiate an end to the Vietnam war. Israel was coming closer to dealing directly with acknowledged representatives of the PLO. What is more the two sides were talking about basic, practical issues such as how to build confidence and improve economic conditions in the occupied territories. And to assist matters further, the negotiations were being boycotted by Syria and Lebanon, leaving ample room for the Israelis and Palestinians to make headway without 'spoiling' from other Arab states.

The leader of the PLO negotiating team – pulling the strings from a hotel near the Paris conference centre – was a balding Palestinian banker who, though little used to the limelight of international diplomacy or media attention, had worked for years in the nerve centre of Arafat's organisation. His name was Ahmed Kora'i, his *nom de guerre* Abu Ala'a, and his official title economic adviser to the chairman. In reality, he was the financial czar of 'PLO

Inc.' – controller of the investment assets that Arafat had gathered for his Fatah movement over the years. Now, assuming progress could be achieved in negotiations with Israel, Arafat had asked Kora'i to produce an investment plan aimed at effecting a rapid improvement in economic conditions in the occupied territories, and preventing further slippage in his influence there. Kora'i's presence in Paris intrigued the Israelis. A paper he had produced on economic co-operation in the Middle East in the event of peace bore striking similarities to the vision often rehearsed by Foreign Minister Peres. More to the point, he seemed to have total command over what was happening in the negotiations: that could only mean he was speaking with his master's voice. 'Everything had to be passed to Abu Ala'a in a nearby hotel for agreement,' said an Israeli negotiator. 'We had the impression that nothing could move without the PLO.'[19]

Kora'i's role was central for another reason. The PLO's need for funds, already acute after the cut-off of Arab assistance in the Gulf War, was now getting truly desperate – so much so that in January 1993, Arafat dispatched one of his key lieutenants, Mahmoud Abbas (Abu Mazen) to Saudi Arabia and the other Gulf states to make a grovelling public apology for having supported Saddam Hussein two years before. The response was cool, and in financial terms certainly not adequate to begin to meet the unfulfilled demands piling up in Tunis, not least from the occupied territories themselves. All over the West Bank and Gaza, institutions such as universities, schools, hospitals and newspapers that had previously relied on PLO funding – and generated support for Arafat – were being forced to close. Welfare payments to families of refugees and 'martyrs' had become erratic and in many cases stopped altogether.

So deep was the disenchantment coursing through the Palestinian movement that Arafat's financial as well as political management began to come under fire. Dissident voices at the highest levels of the organisation – men and women who had not taken much interest in the PLO's finances during the preceding quarter-century – demanded that he reverse the cuts. 'Where are we going to get the money?' he moaned at one stormy Central Council meeting in Tunis. 'We can barely make ends meet!'[20] Some of his rivals in the PLO's left-wing factions had an answer to Arafat's question. They called on him to extract the pot of gold he had always guarded most jealously – Fatah's own separate treasure trove, estimated at its peak to have been worth some $2 billion – and use it to bail out the PLO. Arafat was furious. Squandering Fatah's reserves on mere running expenses was something he had vowed never to do: like some latterday Croesus, he was determined to keep the gold under his and Ahmed Kora'i's direct control.

Small wonder that Arafat was so anxious to find a new political approach in that bleak midwinter of 1992/93. The PLO leader found himself contemplating the real possibility that large parts of the organisation he had spent his life constructing would simply wither and die for lack of financial sustenance. His best chance of salvaging something from the wreckage lay in the West Bank and Gaza. And as Kora'i worked on his economic development programme for the territories, an extraordinary meeting of minds with Israel began to take shape.

The catalyst was a young Norwegian social scientist, Terje Rod Larsen, whose Oslo research institute was likewise examining economic conditions in the territories. In the course of his work he had got to know a number of senior PLO officials including Kora'i, and, in Israel, a doveish Labour politician named Yossi Beilin. In the Rabin government that took power in July 1992, Beilin became deputy foreign minister, and soon afterwards Larsen came calling with a proposal from PLO headquarters. He was in a position, he said, to put the new government in contact with senior Palestinians who wanted to discuss a peace agreement with Israel. Beilin was intrigued but sceptical. The government was not yet ready to plunge into direct talks with the PLO. But he suggested that Larsen stay in touch with a history professor friend of his, Yair Hirschfeld of Haifa university, who would keep him informed. Then, on 10 September 1992, Larsen came calling again – this time in the company of a senior Norwegian diplomat, State Secretary Jan Egeland. Sitting with Beilin and Hirschfeld at the Tel Aviv Hilton, they amplified the proposal: Norway could act as a 'facilitator' for talks between Israeli and PLO representatives, in secret, away from the bright lights and rhetoric of the Washington negotiations. Beilin, still operating at arm's length, suggested that Hirschfeld give it a try.[21]

One morning the following December, just as the uproar over the violence in the territories was reaching a new pitch, Hirschfeld met for breakfast with Larsen at a hotel in London's West End. After a brief exchange of pleasantries, Larsen departed. Into his place slipped none other than Yasser Arafat's personal representative, Ahmed Kora'i. Strictly speaking, Hirschfeld was breaking the law. Israel's ban on contacts with the PLO was still in place, though the Knesset was already debating its repeal, and it was rare indeed for an Israeli citizen, operating with the government's sanction, to sit together with a man who functioned as the eyes and ears of the PLO chairman.

This was the moment at which the two sides began to do serious business, and the breaking of the logjam happened with what seemed to be preordained precision. On 19 January 1993, the Knesset finally rolled back the taboo on contacts with the PLO. The next day, Hirschfeld and Kora'i gathered with Larsen and Norwegian Foreign Minister Johan Joergen Holst – a man who had developed a cordial relationship with Arafat in the late 1970s in Lebanon – on a secluded country estate 60 miles east of Oslo. The 'Norway Channel' was formally open, and

Yasser Arafat, through his point man Kora'i, was back at the centre of events, though none but a tiny handful of his closest advisers knew it at the time. No wonder he seemed even more ebullient than usual when, on the second day of the Norwegian talks, he made an extraordinary 'live' intervention by phone on an Israeli TV programme. 'I repeat my call to Mr Rabin and his government to convene a meeting of the brave to forge a peace of the brave,' he proclaimed, sitting in his villa with Abie Nathan and praising the Israeli decision to lift the ban on talking to the PLO.

That countryside meeting was the first of fourteen Israeli–Palestinian sessions in Norway over the ensuing months. They took place in an ever-changing variety of secret locations and in unusually intimate circumstances, surrounded by the Norwegian facilitators' families and lubricated by copious food and drink. Participants used code names for their superiors: Peres and Holst were 'the fathers'; Beilin 'the son'; and Arafat and Rabin, appropriately enough, 'the grandfathers'. And completely unbeknownst to the official negotiators on both sides, they were making dramatic progress on an outline plan for Palestinian self-rule in the West Bank and Gaza. By April, they had drawn up a 'Declaration of Principles' on the subject which the Israelis deemed solid enough to be taken to Foreign Minister Peres and Prime Minister Rabin. Though the latter remained deeply sceptical about how far the process would lead, they agreed to signal their seriousness by sending a senior official, Foreign Ministry director Uri Savir, to join the talks.[22]

It was the beginning of the breakthrough Arafat had been looking for ever since he had cajoled the PLO into recognising Israel and accepting a 'two-state solution', back in 1988. For four years, he had been signalling his readiness to engage in dialogue with the Israelis, only to be repeatedly rebuffed by the Shamir government's strenuous efforts to keep him on the sidelines of the negotiating process. Now at last he had found a substantial partner to talk to, and a feasible plan to talk about: proposed arrangements for Palestinian autonomy in and Israeli withdrawal from parts of the occupied territories, starting with the Gaza Strip and a patch of land around the Jordan valley town of Jericho.

In itself this plan was nothing startlingly new. It built on several blueprints for self-rule that had been advanced in the past – ideas that Arafat had often derided as likely to create South African-style 'Bantustans', reduce Palestinian rights to those of North America's Indians, or even create a territorial map resembling a Swiss cheese. Israel's initial suggestion in the Norway talks had been that it start by withdrawing just from Gaza – an idea calculated to be of greater appeal to an Israeli public opinion tired of ruling over Gaza's violence and squalor than to the PLO. Now, however, Israel was indicating a readiness to talk about pulling out of parts of the West Bank too. Arafat and the closed circle of advisers in Tunis who knew what was afoot worked to build this into a proposal for Israeli withdrawal from West Bank population centres – known as 'the leopard spot plan'.[23] So the ideas bounced back and forth between Tunis, Jerusalem and the Norwegian woods – and finally came to rest on Gaza and Jericho.

In agreeing to this proposed 'interim arrangement' for five years, Arafat knew he was taking a huge gamble. Although he had often said over the past two decades that he would be prepared to run up the Palestinian flag on any inch of Palestine – even just the city of Jericho – he was now faced with turning rhetoric into reality. He could scarcely be sure that the Norway channel would lead either to the goal he craved – Israeli recognition of the PLO as a negotiating partner – or, ultimately, to some assurance that the Palestinians would be permitted to pursue their independent state, though he could legitimately argue that the agreement might bring statehood a giant step closer. And the outline Norway deal involved another large concession that he was going to find extremely difficult to sell to his colleagues: for the first two years at least of interim self-rule, it removed the perennially thorny issue of Jerusalem from the negotiating table. In accepting Jericho but leaving Jerusalem to one side for now, Arafat left himself vulnerable to furious charges of a sellout.

Such sensitivities were among the host of reasons for preserving such a tight shroud of secrecy around the Norway talks. For fear of leaks, Arafat – already deprived of his two most capable and long-serving lieutenants, Khalil al-Wazir and Salah Khalaf, by assassins' bullets in the past five years – kept what was going on from his negotiating team in Washington and even from the PLO's long-serving 'foreign minister', Farouk Kaddoumi. One influential figure who was in the loop and who had been with Arafat in Fatah from the early days was Mahmoud Abbas, alias Abu Mazen, head of the PLO's Arab and international affairs department. A self-effacing figure, Abbas had been a key player in Arafat's secret overtures to left-wing Israelis over the years, as well as helping to nurture Arafat's Soviet connection; in the late 1970s he completed a doctorate on Israeli affairs at Moscow University; since Khalaf's death, Arafat had come to rely increasingly on his political advice. Otherwise, though, the chairman retreated further into the company of a small band of like-minded counsellors, several of whom – men like Bassam Abu Sharif and Yasser Abed Rabbo from the Popular and Democratic Fronts – had joined his team relatively recently and at the expense of breaking with their political roots. As the tumult in the Palestinian movement at large grew louder, it was beginning to look as if the chairman, too, was cutting loose from his old moorings. Such was the price for the prize of recognition. And Arafat knew it would not be long before he would have to pay.

In the West Bank and Gaza, conditions were worsening all the time. At the end of March, the Israeli authorities

– reacting to a continuing spate of attacks on Jews – sealed off the territories, barring 120,000 Palestinian labourers indefinitely from going to work in Israel. In retrospect, this, too, was something of a psychological turning point. Once again, Rabin was resorting to drastic measures to stamp on unrest and reassure Israelis on the security front, as well as putting the economic squeeze on an Arab population already suffering considerable hardship from the curtailment of PLO funds. But in a curious way he was also laying the groundwork for the political breakthrough that was to follow. In preventing Palestinians from leaving the territories for a prolonged period, he both provided a vivid demonstration of their abject dependence on Israel and subtly reinstated the 'green line' that had separated Jews and Arabs before the 1967 war and which had been gradually eroding ever since. Rabin himself is in no doubt that his springtime clampdown was the vital precursor to reaching agreement with the PLO. 'Without it I couldn't have gone where we are going,' he said the following September.[24]

If Rabin's intention had been to send a message to Tunis, he succeeded. By May, Arafat was ready to begin the endgame. That month saw another round of negotiations in Washington between the official Palestinian and Israeli delegations and paradoxically, this round was even more fruitless than its predecessors. The Israelis realised instantly what was going on: Arafat himself had brought things grinding to a halt to force a denouement through the Norway channel. 'By the tenth round, everything was completely blocked,' said one official. 'And we knew exactly who was behind it.'[25]

The failure of that meeting finally convinced Rabin of a truth that Arafat had been energetically trying to convey to him for nearly a year: the 'Madrid formula' keeping the PLO away from the negotiating table was past its sell-by date. 'We tried negotiating with the Palestinians from the occupied territories and we found more and more that they were just messengers,' he observed later. 'They had no influence at all in what they said in the meetings.'[26] That discovery left Rabin facing a choice: 'We came to the conclusion that among the Palestinians we can either talk to the PLO and its supporters who favour an agreement, or to Hamas, which opposes one – or remain in the current situation because there is no other partner.'[27] The conclusion was beginning to seem obvious.

Days later, Arafat put his own spin on the state of play. He summoned European ambassadors to his headquarters, complained he was under pressure to discuss a US–Israeli blueprint for autonomy, and warned that the peace talks were in jeopardy because of 'Israeli intransigence and American bias'.[28] What he did not tell them was that through his secret Norwegian talks, he was doing just what the Israelis wanted.

Though few noticed at the time, something was stirring in public, too. At a session of the multilateral Middle East talks in Oslo that same month, the PLO and Israel sketched out another crucial step in their diplomatic minuet by reaching a tentative agreement on initiatives to improve the lives of the millions of Palestinian refugees in camps in the occupied territories and around the Arab world.[29] For decades, the refugee problem had been a running sore in the Middle East conflict. Now this, too, was beginning to look less intractable as Israel and the PLO moved towards an unpublished understanding that would allow hundreds of thousands of Palestinians who left the territories in the 1967 war to return. Said one Israeli official: 'In Oslo, we took a tremendous step forward. This is really where the spirit of our eventual agreement started.'[30]

Almost all the building blocks were in place. The edifice, however, was still far from secure. It was in constant danger of being toppled by premature publicity – and nearly did, when word of the Norway channel leaked to an Israeli newspaper in mid-July. Caught unawares, Arafat initially appeared to confirm its existence only to retract his statement the next day.[31] The danger could only grow as both sides broadened their contacts in order to check that what was being said in Norway corresponded to their leaders' true positions. Over the next two months, there were at least three such meetings in Cairo and Jerusalem between Israeli officials and cabinet ministers on the one hand and top Arafat advisers on the other. Then there were still sizeable problems of substance. Who, for example, would control the Allenby Bridge across the Jordan once Israeli troops had withdrawn from Jericho? And precisely how were the two Palestinian enclaves in Gaza and the West Bank to be linked? The talks nearly collapsed in July over the latter question, with Arafat demanding the establishment of what he quaintly called a 'kissing point' between the two. And finally, there lay ahead the thorny but for Arafat most vital question of all: the agreement he desired on mutual recognition between Israel and the PLO.

By the end of the month, most details of the autonomy deal had been ironed out and Arafat was ready to break cover. He did so with characteristic sleight of hand. During a visit to the region by US Secretary of State Warren Christopher in early August, the PLO leader suddenly intervened over the heads of his own negotiators. Just an hour before they were due to meet the American, he faxed them a document with instructions to hand it on. As they read it through, the negotiators were astonished to see that it bore little resemblance to the PLO position that they had steadfastly been defending for months in the Washington talks, but contained major concessions to Israel on the issue of Jerusalem and the scope of Palestinian self-rule, and suggested that the Gaza Strip and Jericho would be a useful starting point for implementation of any agreement. Had Arafat taken them into his confidence, they would not have been surprised. For what they were reading was the deal cooked up by Arafat's men and the Israelis in the Norway channel.[32]

The events that followed can only be described as an elaborate political pantomime. In the full glare of publicity, the three top Palestinian negotiators trooped off to Tunis, purportedly threatening to resign over the concessions Arafat had offered behind their backs. For days they were locked in meetings with Arafat and his colleagues, and the world's press indulged in a surfeit of speculation about alleged splits between the Palestinians in the occupied territories and the PLO outside. Such comment was wide of the mark. Arafat may have acted without their knowledge, his concessions may have been hard to stomach, but there was no question that the negotiators – chief among them Faisal al-Husseini, a loyal lieutenant since the late 1960s – would toe the line, and return to sell the deal in the territories. At the end of it all, they emerged in a new guise: as fully fledged members of the PLO leadership. Significantly, Israel raised no objection – and with that, Arafat was on the home straight to securing what he had been after in return for the autonomy deal: full Israeli recognition as a negotiating partner.

On 19 August 1993, Shimon Peres turned up in Oslo for what was billed as a routine official visit. After dinner that night, he departed from the table, headed for the back stairs and was whisked away to a government guest house. Waiting for him there were Ahmed Kora'i and a document setting out the autonomy agreement reached through the Norway channel. And in his presence, Kora'i and Israeli Foreign Ministry chief Uri Savir sat down to sign.

The deal, still ostensibly top secret, did not remain so for long. Already talk of Arafat's concessions was spreading dismay in the upper echelons of the PLO. And scarcely was the ink dry in Oslo when a succession of important figures in the organisation – from Arafat's favourite poet, Executive Committee member Mahmoud Darwish, to the veteran PLO representative in Lebanon, Shafik al-Hout – tendered their resignations, while from the Syrian capital Damascus, home of Arafat's left-wing rivals, a chorus of derision and hostility to what he was doing began to mount.

To Arafat's opponents and even for many who had supported him through the travails of the past two decades, it looked like the final capitulation. 'Ever since the negotiations started, all they have gained so far is God knows how many people killed, how many people wounded, how many homes demolished, how many new settlements established and how many people deported,' complained Shafik al-Hout from Beirut. 'The perception of the people is: "The leadership is giving concessions, so where's the reward?" '[33] Arafat, said Darwish, was 'taking uncalculated political risks. I don't want to be a witness and a collaborator in this downfall.'[34] Some of the criticism was targeted bluntly at Arafat's character and leadership style. The PLO leader, said Edward Said, the Palestinian–American professor and sometime friend, had 'sort of gone off on his own a bit. He is surrounded by sycophants, but he's also very much a loner. He has refused to delegate authority, he has been willing to sacrifice principles and values.'[35] The charge was replayed with three times the force from Damascus, where Arafat's old sparring partners George Habash and Nayef Hawatmeh forecast confidently that the deal would fail, and that Arafat and his acolytes would be consigned to the dustbin of history for forging it.[36]

The atmosphere was not improved by the state of collapse facing the PLO itself. Still starved of funds by the Gulf states and by Arafat's adamant refusal to open his Fatah coffers, it had been forced to sell off large parcels of property it owned in the Arab world to make up the deficit. Staff were being laid off in their thousands (in one celebrated example, Arafat had sent hundreds of white-collar workers off to cool their heels in a Libyan military camp); guerrilla fighters stationed in the Arab countries had not been paid their salaries for seven months; education and health services in the refugee camps faltered, and in August, four of the PLO's most important departments – those dealing with information, culture, social affairs and 'returnees' – were simply closed down.[37]

By the time the PLO Executive Committee gathered in Tunis to review the draft accord with Israel on the night of 26 August, the uproar was in full spate, with influential voices calling for a full debate in the PLO's parliament, the Palestine National Council. But Arafat was playing his cards with the usual care. He knew that the financial crisis – which may not have been quite as grave in reality as he was allowing everybody else to say – would concentrate minds wonderfully on the serious business in hand, and that the PNC could not convene for lack of a suitable Arab venue. He also knew, as even many of his critics were prepared in their hearts to concede, that there was little or no alternative to the course of action he proposed. It was this awareness, coupled with the fact that his opponents were themselves divided, that deprived the ensuing ritual demands for his resignation of much of their bite. There were dangers, to be sure: not least the threat, now looming larger than at any time he could remember following ominous mutterings from the most extreme splinter groups in Damascus, that the PLO chairman would be felled by an assassin's bullet. But in political argument, Arafat held the ace: the prediction that, whatever the Israelis might say about the deal at this stage, it could and would mark the first concrete step on the road to a Palestinian state. The critics, he declared loftily, were trying 'to belittle this historic achievement'. The PLO and Israel would reach a 'just and comprehensive peace that will take account of the Palestinian people's political rights.'[38] Before long the Palestinian flag would be fluttering from the minarets of Jerusalem.

Armed with such certainties and with the backing of his Fatah movement's Central Committee, Arafat took off on a tour of Arab capitals to enlist support for the deal.

In his wilderness years, shunned in so many parts of the Arab world, he had been prevented from indulging his penchant for whistle-stop diplomacy. Now he took to it again with gusto: he beamed his way through frosty audiences with Hafez al-Assad of Syria and Jordan's King Hussein, both fuming at the fact that Arafat had not deigned to consult them on his separate deal with Israel; he returned to Cairo and to the bear-like embrace of President Hosni Mubarak; he even inveigled his way back to the Gulf, asking Oman's Sultan Qaboos to secure forgiveness for the PLO and funding to underpin his Palestinian proto-state.

And all the while, the back channel with Israel was churning away – in Norway and in Paris, where the French government, miffed at its exclusion from the action so far, was anxious to put its seal on proceedings – to put the final touches to a mutual recognition accord. For Arafat, this was the most important barrier to surmount, and to do so, he was going to have to get his Executive Committee to meet apparently unthinkable Israeli demands: that it agree to suspend large chunks of the PLO's precious founding charter and call on Palestinians in the occupied territories to end the *intifada*.

By 5 p.m. on 8 September 1993, as Savir and Kora'i continued to haggle in a plush Parisian hotel over the wording in which Israel and the PLO were to proclaim peace, Arafat was back in Tunis and ready to leap the final hurdle. He had not slept in two nights, but was in euphoric mood as he bantered with Israeli journalists and with his wife Suha, then sped off to join bleary-eyed colleagues in the flat-roofed concrete villa where they had been awaiting his arrival. Events were moving fast. Johan Joergen Holst, the Norwegian Foreign Minister, was coming to witness Arafat's signing of a historic letter recognising Israel. And in Washington, preparations were under way for a full-dress ceremony on the White House lawn at which the Prime Minister of Israel and chairman of the PLO would meet for the first time.

All that remained for Arafat was to secure the backing of his Executive Committee, and this was not completely in the bag. Five members of the eighteen-strong Executive Committee were missing, having either resigned or decided to boycott the meeting. Five more – principal among them Kaddoumi, the 'foreign minister' – bitterly opposed the deal. But for eight hours, with a telephone line open to Kora'i in Paris, Arafat kept them at the U-shaped conference table, chipping away at the resistance of the floating voters in their midst. As debate wore through the night and into the next day, the 'No' camp was implacable. How could Arafat call for suspension of the *intifada* and revision of the charter? complained Kaddoumi. It was tantamount to abandoning the PLO's 'basic commitment' to keep up the struggle until Palestine was liberated. So what alternative did Kaddoumi propose? countered Arafat, his voice growing hoarse. The Israelis might not be offering much but if the PLO did not accept, it would get nothing at all and the offer might be gone for good.[39]

That was the clincher. The chairman got his way, though by a much finer margin than he might have wished – a vote of eight to four with one abstention was scarcely a ringing endorsement, as the critics ceaselessly pointed out in ensuing months. Satisfied nonetheless, he hurried off to meet Holst, who was waiting to carry a letter to Jerusalem and to receive a separate document pledging to urge Palestinians in the West Bank and Gaza to cease violence. And at a quarter to midnight on 9 September, an elated Arafat emerged to meet the world's press. 'I have signed. I have signed the letter,' he exclaimed.[40]

The next morning, 2,000 kilometres across the Mediterranean in Jerusalem, Holst extracted the letter from his briefcase and handed it to Yitzhak Rabin. Then, at a ceremony in his office, the Israeli Prime Minister carefully re-read the four pages, took out a plastic pen, and signed his reply. The deed was done. Arafat and Rabin were on their way to Washington. The following Monday, 13 September 1993, the two men stood alone with President Bill Clinton in the Blue Room of the White House. They looked each other in the eye, and Rabin broke the silence. 'You know, we are going to have to work very hard to make this work,' he said in a low growl. 'I know,' replied Arafat. 'And I am prepared to do my part.'[41]

# Epilogue

## *Poacher Turned Gamekeeper*

'We are in the last quarter of the hour. And next year must be the year of the dawn.' Yasser Arafat, President of the State of Palestine and Chairman of the Palestine Liberation Organisation. (Associated Press, 9 December 1992).

As all the exhilaration and excitement of the ceremony on the White House lawn subsided, as memory of an intense round of consultations and media interviews faded, as Arafat came literally down to earth after returning from Washington to Tunis, realisation dawned that the next stage in the Palestinians' long march would not be easy. Like the leaders of the Front de Libération National (FLN) in the Algerian independence struggle three decades previously, Arafat was faced with the extraordinarily delicate task of transforming his battered guerrilla movement into a functioning administration on the ground; first in the postage stamp enclaves of Gaza and Jericho, and later throughout the West Bank – if, that is, the interim self-rule agreement held together, and if internal dissension on the Palestinian side allowed local institutions to grow and stabilise. These were big 'ifs', by any standards.

It was perhaps indicative of Arafat's state of mind, and his appreciation of history, that he had taken to referring to Yitzhak Rabin as 'Israel's de Gaulle'. True, there are parallels between Rabin's gesture to the Palestinians and de Gaulle's treatment of Algerian liberationists, but there are differences, too, and they are important. For a start, the FLN was handed command of a state-in-being when the French finally agreed to withdraw, and not only that, Algerian guerrilla leaders themselves were a force on the ground. By contrast, Arafat is not being accorded control of anything like a state, and his exile leadership has little knowledge or direct experience of conditions in the dusty enclaves he will be obliged to administer, and more to the point, control from a security standpoint.

He would hardly need reminding that not only is Gaza the most densely populated strip of land in the world, it is also one of the most lawless. Apart from criminal elements, Arafat will also be obliged to contend with a restless Islamic movement embodied in Hamas and the militant Islamic Jihad which has taken deep root in Gaza's festering alleyways, and which remains bitterly opposed to his peace deal.

Not least of Arafat's challenges will involve marrying the various disparate elements of the Palestinian leadership from inside and outside the territories, and weeding out those time-servers and mediocrities who had gravitated to the movement like flies to a honey-pot. He dismisses talk of differences between the Palestinian officials of the diaspora and leaders in the West Bank and Gaza, but it would be surprising if tensions did not arise. 'The PLO is the identity of the Palestinian people: the cadres inside and outside,' he says. 'Now we are all members of the follow-up committee. But for this new stage we need to reorganise all our institutions, strengthening them to prepare for very different and difficult responsibilities.'[1]

Among his immediate concerns will be what form of governing authority might evolve – and what to do, in fact, about the Palestine Liberation Organisation itself. If, indeed, its shelf life is coming to an end, since he has forsworn the goal of liberating territory by force in favour of negotiation, what arrangements might be made to retire or transform it into something else? An enigmatic answer was provided by Nabil Shaath, the senior Arafat lieutenant, when he observed on the eve of the signing of mutual recognition between Israel and the PLO: 'Times have changed. We must move on to governing. I would say we are still a liberation movement, insofar as we believe in liberty.'[2]

Arafat himself would be mindful of the risk that rejectionist Palestinian groups bitterly opposed to his historic compromise with the Israelis – and vowing to fight on, possibly with backing from radical Middle Eastern states such as Iran and Libya – will appropriate the PLO seal for their own purposes, causing him no end of trouble in the years ahead. One logical step would be for Arafat's dominant Fatah faction to be transformed into a ruling party along the lines of the FLN in Algeria. In the meantime, and until elections can be held, authority would be vested in the Palestinian Interim Self Governing Authority (PISGA) which grew out of the Madrid process, and whose responsibilities have been fairly well defined in ongoing planning discussions involving Palestinians from inside and outside the territories.

While the Declaration of Principles (*see* Appendix II), signed in Washington on 13 September by Mahmoud Abbas and Shimon Peres, provides guidance to the way ahead, many questions remain fuzzy. Rabin and Arafat face an enormously testing time converting paper agreements into facts on the ground. A whole range of security issues, involving likely continuing acts of terror, are certain to bedevil relations between the two sides. Demarcation disputes between Israeli and Palestinian police will arise, and the issue of 'hot pursuit' – the right of one side or the other to pursue criminals or terrorists into each other's territory – is bound to bedevil relations.

There is much scope for misunderstanding, and there is little in Arafat's past to suggest that he might be equipped to deal with such problems in a magisterial way. If the behaviour of the PLO in Lebanon in the decade following Black September 1970 is any guide – the organisation created a 'state within a state' – then doubts must persist about Arafat's temperamental ability to assert effective control. In those days, the PLO leader assumed the role of a sort of sheriff of Beirut in arbitrary command of swathes of the city where the rule of the gun rather than the rule of law applied. His defenders would say that Arafat could not have handled it any other way, such was the chaos in Lebanon after 1975. This rather ignores the fact that the PLO itself played no small part in fomenting the troubles in Lebanon in those years.

Arafat's working and living habits – like a marsupial, he is most active in the middle of the night – may pose additional problems in the delicate transitional phase. Old habits are certain to die hard for someone who has tailored his life to the needs of his shadowy guerrilla movement, imposing a topsy-turvy regimen on an organisation over which he has asserted obsessive control all these years. Khaled al-Hassan, the veteran Fatah politician, once described the Arafat-led PLO as 'a revolution on a flying carpet.'[3] It is an apt description, but it also begs the question whether Arafat is capable of the huge transformation required – from guerrilla chieftain, travelling relentlessly around the Arab world and beyond, to the overseer of an embryonic state. How will he adapt as the flying carpet comes to rest?

Will he, for example, be able to loosen control, and to delegate? Given that he has never fought a conventional election campaign, how will he deal with the elections that are supposed to be held for the self-governing authority in the West Bank and Gaza in 1994? There is not much in his record that would indicate an ability to perform like a conventional political leader, beyond a fairly uncanny sense of how to manipulate the PLO's representative institutions. Indeed, he has always been miserly about sharing power, even with 'old guard' figures like Khalil al-Wazir and Salah Khalaf, and has long resisted suggestions that he might groom a successor. Were he to depart the scene, it is far from clear who could take his place and stand a chance of holding the movement together.

To his closest colleagues as much as to the outside world, Arafat remains an often maddeningly elusive figure. He has managed to control a broad and fractious PLO church by being, at times, many things to many of his followers: father figure, brother, guide and sometimes fickle friend. His colleagues express wry amusement about 'The Old Man's' endless manoeuvring, his infinite capacity for invention and his ability to juggle competing interests. Irreverent old comrades refer to him as the *gala gala* man, an Egyptian conjuror or juggler so named because he utters the words *gala gala* when performing a magic trick, as a Western magician might say *abracadabra*.

To be fair, he has also been obliged to operate under severe constraints – even more difficult, in fact, than those facing most other leaders of liberation movements who have at least been operating from within national frontiers. 'I can only deal with reality as it is, not only the Palestinian reality, but also the Arab reality with all its complications,' he said in an interview before the Gulf War. 'We are the only nationalist movement in the world which is simultaneously performing the functions of a state and a revolution – a state which has yet to be established, half of whose people live under occupation and the other half in the diaspora, with each community living in different circumstances. That is why our task is so difficult . . . Is there a revolution in the world which is required to market olive oil, oranges and vegetables? Well, we have to do it. We have to send flour to the refugee camps in Lebanon. We have to cater to all the requirements of the *intifada*.'[4]

Arafat's biggest achievement over the years is simply to have kept this chaotic show on the road, to have presided over a movement more or less united around the common aim of Palestinian statehood and preserved PLO independence from crippling interference by ruthless Arab regimes. He indelibly imprinted the Palestinian cause – more, perhaps, than that of any other stateless people in modern times – on world attention, making it difficult to imagine progress towards a durable Middle East peace settlement without at least the acquiescence of the PLO. Perhaps most remarkably, he survived. He has walked away from at least one bad car crash, several Israeli attempts on his life, sieges, wars and repeated efforts on the part of Arab states to sideline or eliminate him.

Now, as ruler of an embryonic Palestinian entity, he faces a different task but one that is no less taxing. Just how Arafat's relations will evolve in the new era with the more than one million refugees in Jordan, Lebanon and Syria is one of many imponderables, but there is also no doubt that displaced Palestinians in squalid shanty towns initially felt a sense of betrayal and bitter disappointment. For the peace deal appeared to dash the last forlorn hope of these victims of the 1948 conflict of ever returning to their homes in places like Jaffa, Haifa, Ramleh and Lydda in what is now Israel.

Their anguish was made more acute by the fact that many had made the greatest sacrifices, paid the highest price in supporting the revolution. There was scarcely a family left intact by the conflict in camps like Sabra and Shatila in the suburbs of Beirut, and elsewhere in places like the Ein el-Hilweh camp near Sidon in southern Lebanon. These were the people who had committed their sons to die for the revolution, and now they were being left out of the deal.

Within the PLO leadership, a number of whose members like Farouk Kaddoumi were 1948 refugees themselves, there was scarcely a more contentious issue. Kaddoumi's opposition to the peace package derived in part from his unhappiness over the issue of return. The veteran PLO official was not convinced by Arafat's claims of a secret agreement with the Israelis that would allow up to 400,000 refugees from the 1967 war to return to the territories over the five years of the interim agreement, with negotiations on the issue beginning after two years.[5] Kaddoumi was also apparently not much impressed by his leader's defence of the Gaza-Jericho deal, fearing that it would lead to what he regarded as a fatal embrace with the Israelis, and not yield the benefits on the ground that the PLO was seeking. Defending the agreement in an interview with the Egyptian daily *Al Ahram*, Arafat was moved to say: 'First of all it is not just Gaza-Jericho. Gaza-Jericho is just one of the points. It is something we were able to grab from the Israeli side. When we went to Madrid we went on the basis of self-rule for a transition period, but we managed to make a final deal on Gaza and Jericho which is part of a whole deal, and this is the real gain.'[6]

Kaddoumi's stand also reflected the beliefs of other prominent figures in the movement like Khaled al-Hassan, who had always had a reputation as a moderate, but who branded the agreement a sell-out. Al-Hassan gave voice to the dark fears and vain hopes of the older generation of Palestinian leaders in an interview in 1989. Then he said: 'I can understand being asked to recognise the existence of Israel. We recognise it *de facto* because we cannot kick it out. Any Palestinian who will tell it has a right to stay there is either a big liar or is stupid, because if we could defeat the Israelis, we *would* defeat the Israelis. It's our land. You cannot tell me I'm not from Haifa: this is a physical fact and you cannot change the past. You *can* change the process for the future . . .

'As for the right of return: at present, we don't have the right to return, and Jews who have not connection with this country – the Germans, the Russians, the Africans – have the right to return. International law says all refugees have the right to return. Maybe 50–60 per cent of the Palestinians will not go back. But they must feel they have decided themselves not to go. . . . We are talking about our right of return to Jaffa and Haifa as Israeli citizens under UN resolution 194. We have to be given the choice between return as Israeli citizens or compensation.

'We know it's not going to happen, but we cannot drop

this right. It is a basic natural right, much stronger than a legal right. Look, as a human being, you cannot but belong to something. You cannot live without rights, without duties, without entity, without identity. You have to be something, or you will become an animal. So to belong is a must as far as we are human beings.

'What is nationality? Why do I say Palestine is my home and why do I love Palestine more than I love, say, England? It's not because of the beauty. Switzerland and Morocco are much more beautiful than Palestine. Home means the place you practise your belonging, your values on a certain land with sovereignty and freedom . . . For us, we became stateless within a few weeks without a decision. We wanted to go back but were prevented by force. Because we cannot live without identity, entity, citizenship, rights and duties, our own values, we have to try to go back by force. Force, meaning struggle, is the way in which, philosophically, we practise our belonging. If Descartes says I think therefore I exist, the Palestinian says I struggle therefore I exist.'[7]

So it is that Arafat's generation wrestles with its memories and its dreams. Arafat's great strength over the years has been to give the appearance of transcending such bitterness, buoying his people up with the belief that Palestine was 'just a stone's throw away', that another political manoeuvre would yield real progress, even though the way ahead was unpromising, to say the least. It has been through such 'grand illusions' that he managed to prevent the revolutionary flame being extinguished all those years.

Arafat has a habit of confounding the sceptics, who have written him off time and time again. His return to a corner of the land he calls Palestine may be occasion for euphoria, but he must know that the hard part of ruling wisely, not to mention surviving, lies ahead. He is a long way from achieving his oft-stated dream of worshipping in Jerusalem's Al Aqsa at the heart of the capital of a

Palestinian state. To be sure, he has advanced further towards that goal than appeared at all possible in the bleak days after the Gulf War, but this is by no means the 'last quarter-hour of the struggle.'

# Notes

*Prologue*

1. *Washington Post*, 15 September 1993.
2. Ibid.

*Chapter 1*

1. *Fiches du Monde Arabe*, 6 August 1975, quoting UN Relief and Works Agency figures, No. 347.
2. Article in the *Observer*, 3 September 1967.
3. Abu Iyad, *My Home, My Land*, New York, 1981, p. 3.
4. Benny Morris, *The Birth of the Palestinian Refugee Problem, 1947–49*, Cambridge, 1987, pp. 113–15.
5. Menachem Begin, *Revolt: Story of the Irgun*, Jerusalem, 1951, p. 164.
6. Morris, op. cit., p. 207.
7. *Fiches du Monde Arabe*, No. 347.
8. George Habash interview, Damascus, November 1989.
9. Yasser Arafat interview, Tunis, June 1989.
10. Yasser Arafat interview, Baghdad, January 1990.
11. Yasser Arafat interview, Tunis, June 1989.
12. Interview with the authors, Jerusalem, June 1989. Name withheld on request.
13. Ibid.
14. Ibid.
15. Ibid.
16. Khaled al-Hassan interview, Kuwait, April 1989.
17. Yasser Arafat interview, Tunis, June 1989.
18. Ibid.
19. Ibid.
20. R. Mitchell, *The Society of the Muslim Brothers*, London, p. 59.
21. Walid Khalidi interview, Cambridge, Massachussetts, November 1989.
22. Zoheir al-Alami interview, Sharjah, September 1989.
23. Faisal al-Husseini interview, Jerusalem, May 1989.

24. Husam Abu Shaaban interview, Kuwait, September 1989.
25. Interview with authors, Cairo, April 1989. Name withheld on request.
26. Derek Hopwood, *Egypt: Politics and Socity, 1945–1981*, London, 1982, p. 30.
27. Hassan Doh interview, Cairo, September 1989.
28. Salah Khalaf interview, Tunis, June 1989.
29. George Habash interview, Damascus, November 1989.
30. Ibid.
31. Hopwood, op. cit., p. 32.
32. Yasser Arafat interview, Tunis, June 1989.
33. Laurie Brand, *Palestinians in the Arab World: Institution Building and the Search for State*, New York, 1988, p. 67.
34. Bashir Barghouti interview, Jerusalem, September 1989.
35. Ibid.
36. Jaweed al-Ghussein interview, Tunis, September 1989.
37. Salah Khalaf interview, Tunis, May 1989.
38. Ibid.
39. Husam Abu Shaaban interview, Kuwait, September 1989.
40. Salah Khalaf interview, Tunis, June 1989.
41. Gamal Sourani interview, Cairo, September 1989.
42. *See* Khalil al-Wazir, *Bidayat* (*Beginnings*), limited edition published by PLO Western Sector.
43. Mohammed Hamza interview, Tunis, August 1989. Hamza is Wazir's biographer.
44. Zoheir al-Alami interview, Sharjah, September 1989.
45. Yasser Arafat interview, Tunis, June 1989.
46. Ibid.
47. Zoheir al-Alami interview, Sharjah, September 1989.
48. Salah Khalaf interview, Tunis, May 1989.
49. Zoheir al-Alami interview, Sharjah, September 1989.
50. Peter Ruehmkorf, *Die Jahre die Ihr Kennt*, Hamburg, 1972, pp. 86–7.
51. Ibid.
52. Ibid.
53. Hopwood, op. cit., p. 55.
54. Yasser Arafat interview, Tunis, June 1989.
55. Ibid.
56. Ibid.
57. Ibid.

*Chapter 2*

1. Khalil al-Wazir, *Bidayat* (*Beginnings*), limited edition published by PLO Western Sector.
2. Khaled al-Hassan interview, Kuwait, April 1989.
3. Farouk Kaddoumi interview, Tunis, September 1989.
4. *See* Khalil al-Wazir, op. cit.
5. Ismail Shammout interview, Kuwait, April 1989. Shammout was the illustrator for *Filastinuna*.
6. Khalil al-Wazir, op. cit.
7. Interviews with Khaled al-Hussan, Amin al-Agha, Kuwait, April 1989.
8. Salah Khalaf interview, Tunis, June 1989.
9. Ibid.
10. Fatah internal statutes, unpublished.
11. Rafik al-Natshe interview, Tunis, August 1989; *also* Hosni Zoaroub interview, Kuwait, September 1989. Natshe was a member of the Qatar group and is now Fatah representative in Saudi Arabia.
12. Interviews with Palestinian contemporaries, Kuwait, April 1989. Names withheld on request.
13. *Playboy* magazine, August 1988, p. 62.
14. *Time* magazine, 7 November 1988, p. 34.
15. Khaled al-Hassan interview, Kuwait, April 1989.
16. Rafik al-Natshe interview, Tunis, August 1989.
17. Abu Nabil interview, Tunis, June 1989.
18. Hani al-Hassan interview, Tunis, August 1989; *also* Abdullah Franji interview, Bonn, July 1989; *also* discussion with German intelligence official, November 1989.
19. Khaled al-Hassan interview, Kuwait, April 1989.
20. Zoheir al-Alami interview, Sharjah, September 1989.
21. Yasser Arafat interview, Tunis, December 1989.
22. Mohammed Abu Mayzar interview, Paris, August 1989.
23. Mohammed Hamza interview, Tunis, August 1989; *also* Intissar al-Wazir interview, Amman, June 1989.
24. *See* Hashim Behbehani, *China's Foreign Policy in the Arab World*, London, 1981.
25. Mohammed Abu Mayzar interview, Paris, August 1989.
26. Ahmed Sidki al-Dajani interview, Cairo, November 1989.
27. Gamal al-Sourani interview, Cairo, October 1989.

28. Khaled al-Hassan interview, Kuwait, April 1989.
29. Khaled al-Fahoum interview, Damascus, May 1989. Fahoum was a founder member of the PLO executive committee and later served as speaker of the Palestine National Council; he is now an Arafat opponent in Damascus.
30. Salah Khalaf interview, Tunis, June 1989.
31. Ibid.
32. Father Ibrahim Iyad interview, Amman, November 1989.
33. Yasser Arafat interview, Tunis, December 1989.
34. Ibid.
35. Selim Zaanoun (Abul Adeeb) interview, Kuwait, April 1989. Zaanoun is now Fatah's chief representative in the Gulf.
36. Yasser Arafat interview, Tunis, June 1989.
37. Selim Zaanoun (Abul Adeeb) interview, Kuwait, April 1989.
38. Zoheir al-Alami interview, Sharjah, September 1989.
39. Farouk Kaddoumi, quoted in John Amos, *Palestinian Resistance*, New York, 1980, p. 57.
40. Rafik al-Natshe interview, Tunis, August 1989.
41. Yasser Arafat interview, Tunis, December 1989.
42. *Al-Rai al-Am*, 7 January 1965, quoted in Amos, op. cit., p. 293.
43. General Aharon Yariv interview, Tel Aviv, November 1989.
44. Interview with former Fatah official, name withheld on request.
45. Al-Anwar, Beirut, 2 January 1965.
46. Fathi al-Dib, quoted in *Al-Gumhuriah*, Cairo, August 1966. Al-Dib was head of the Arab affairs department in the Arab Socialist Union.
47. Hani al-Hassan interview, Tunis, August 1989; *also* Abdullah Franji interview, Bonn, July 1989.
48. Text of Fatah central committee report, 2 May 1966 (unpublished).
49. Yasser Arafat interview, Tunis, December 1989.
50. Ibid.
51. Zakaria Abderrahim (Abu Yahia) interview, Tunis, December 1989. Abderrahim, now director of Farouk Kaddoumi's office, was imprisoned with Arafat in 1966.
52. Farouk Kaddoumi interview, Tunis, November 1989.

53. Salah Khalaf interview, Tunis, December 1989.
54. Yasser Arafat interview, Tunis, December 1989.
55. Ibid.
56. Ahmed Shukairy, quoted in David Hirts, *The Gun and the Olive Branch*, London 1977, p. 289.

*Chapter 3*

1. Nasser's resignation broadcast, Cairo Radio, 9 June 1967, reproduced in Laqueur and Rubin (eds.), *The Israel-Arab Reader*, London 1984, pp. 189–94.
2. Salah Khalaf interview, Tunis, June 1989.
3. Nabil Shaath interview, Cairo, March, 1989.
4. Hani al-Hassan interview, Tunis, August 1989; *also* Mohammed Abu Mayzar interview, Paris, September 1989; *also* Farouk Kaddoumi interview, Tunis, September 1989.
5. Hani al-Hassan interview, Tunis, August 1989.
6. Ibid.
7. Yasser Arafat interview, Tunis, December 1989.
8. Faisal al-Husseini interview, Jerusalem, May 1989.
9. Ibid.
10. Yasser Arafat interview, Tunis, December 1989.
11. Ibid.
12. *Fiches du Monde Arabe*, No. 959.
13. Yasser Arafat, quoted in *The Middle East* magazine, March 1988, p. 22.
14. Abdullah Franji interview, Bonn, July 1989.
15. George Habash interview, Damascus, October 1989.
16. Reported in *Time* magazine, 13 December 1968, p. 35.
17. Abdulmajeed Shoman interview, Amman, September 1989.
18. Ibid.; *also* Ibrahim Bakr interview, Amman, September 1989. Bakr was the PLO's first and only deputy chairman under Arafat and has since left the movement.
19. General Aharon Yariv interview, Tel Aviv, November 1989.
20. Yasser Arafat interview, Tunis, December 1989.
21. Ibid.
22. Ibid.
23. Interviews with participants; *also* Filastin al-Thawra; *see also* Uri Milstein, *A History of the Israeli Paratroopers*, Tel Aviv, 1985, Vol. III, pp. 1276–80.
24. Yasser Arafat interview, Tunis, December 1989.

25. Mashour Haditha al-Jazy interview, Amman, June 1989.
26. General Aharon Yariv interview, Tel Aviv, November 1989.
27. Ihsan Bakr interview, Cairo, October 1989.
28. Salah Khalaf interview, Tunis, June 1989.
29. Mohammed Abu Mayzar interview, Paris, August 1989.
30. Michael Bar-Zohar and Eitan Haber, *The Quest for the Red Prince*, New York, 1983, p. 99.
31. Mohammed Hassanein Heikal interview, Cairo, May 1989.
32. Ibid.
33. Ibid.
34. Tahseen Bashir interview, Cairo, October 1989. Bashir was Nasser's spokesman.
35. Edgar O'Ballance, *Arab Guerrilla Power, 1967–72*, London, 1974, p. 59.
36. Mohammed Hassanein Heikal interview, Cairo, May 1989.
37. Yasser Arafat, quoted in *Al-Sayyad*, Beirut, 23 January 1969.
38. Abu Iyad, *My Home, My Land*, New York, 1981, p. 139.
39. Essay by Zvi Elpeleg in *Jerusalem Quarterly* No. 50, spring 1989.
40. Nabil Shaath, quoted in Alain Gresh, *The PLO: The Struggle Within*, London, 1985, p. 37.
41. Salah Khalaf interview, Tunis, June 1989.
42. Programme of February 1969 Palestine National Council, quoted in Gresh, op. cit., p. 18.
43. Nabil Shaath interview, Cairo, March 1989.
44. Mohammed Abu Mayzar interview, Paris, September 1989.
45. Khaled al-Fahoum interview, Damascus, May 1989. Al-Fahoum was a member of the PLO executive committee at the time.
46. Yehoshafat Harkabi, *The Palestinian Covenant and its Meaning*, London and New York, 1979, p. 61.
47. Abu Daoud interview, Tunis, November 1989.
48. *Al-Ahram*, Cairo, 4 February 1969.
49. Nabil Shaath interview, Cairo, December 1989.
50. Khaled al-Hassan interview, Kuwait, April 1989.

*Chapter* 4

1. Abu Iyad, *My Home, My Land*, New York, 1981, p. 75.
2. John Cooley, *Green March, Black September*, London, 1973,

pp. 103–4; *also Fiches du Monde Arabe*, 11 January 1978, No. 850; and interviews with Arafat aides.

3. Moshe Shemesh, *The Palestinian Entity, 1959–74*, London, 1988, p. 130.
4. Yasser Arafat interview, Tunis, December 1989.
5. King Hussein, quoted in *Le Monde*, 23 March 1968.
6. Khalil al-Wazir, August 1972, quoted in Shemesh, op. cit., p. 133.
7. Zeid al-Rifai interview, Amman, June 1989. Rifai was Jordanian Prime Minister in the mid-1970s and again in the late 1980s, and a friend of King Hussein from childhood.
8. Asad Abdelrahman, *History of the PLO* (in Arabic), Cyprus, 1989, p. 178.
9. Yasser Arafat, quoted in *Time* magazine, 13 December 1968, p. 32.
10. Zeid al-Rifai interview, Amman, June 1989.
11. Abu Daoud interview, Tunis, November 1989.
12. Salah Khalaf interview, Tunis, August 1989.
13. Jamal Sha'er interview, Amman, June 1989.
14. William Quandt, *Decade of Decisions*, Los Angeles and London, 1977, p. 91.
15. *Fiches du Monde Arabe*, 18 January 1978, No. 885; *also* Edgar O'Ballance, *Arab Guerrilla Power, 1969–74*, London, 1974, pp. 120ff; *also* Shemesh, op. cit., p. 138.
16. Mashour Haditha al-Jazy interview, Amman, June 1989.
17. Ibrahim Bakr interview, Amman, September 1989.
18. Yasser Arafat, quoted in *Al-Hayat*, London, 1 January 1990.
19. Yasser Abed Rabbo interview, Tunis, August 1989.
20. *See* O'Ballance, op. cit., pp. *128–9*; *also* James Lunt, *Hussein of Jordan*, London, 1989, p. 12.
21. Yasser Arafat, quoted in *Al-Hayat*, London, 1 January 1990.
22. General Aharon Yariv interview, Tel Aviv, November 1989.
23. Henry Kissinger, *White House Years*, New York and London, 1979, pp. 341, 344, 362 and 558 passim.
24. Shemesh, op. cit., p. 109.
25. Ibrahim Bakr interview, Amman, September 1989.
26. Ahmed Baha el-Dine interview, Cairo, October 1989. El-Dine was a prominent Egyptian journalist and confidant of Nasser.

27. Zoheir al-Alami interview, Sharjah, September 1989.
28. Ibrahim Bakr interview, Amman, September 1989.
29. Zeid al-Rifai interview, Amman, June 1989.
30. Yasser Arafat interview, Tunis, December 1989.
31. Abu Daoud interview, Tunis, November 1989.
32. Ibid.
33. Yasser Arafat interview, Tunis, December 1989.
34. Tahseen Bashir interview, Cairo, October 1989. Bashir was Nasser's spokesman.
35. Ibid.
36. *See* Mohammed Hassanein Heikal, *The Cairo Documents*, London, 1972, p. 17.
37. Ibid.
38. Tahseen Bashir interview, Cairo, October 1989; *also* Anwar Sadat, *In Search of Identity*, London, 1978, pp. 201–2.
39. William Quandt, Fuad Jabber and Ann Mosely Lesch, *The Politics of Palestinian Nationalism*, Los Angeles and London, 1973, p. 128.
40. Shemesh, op. cit., p. 146.
41. Ibrahim Bakr interview, Amman, September 1989.
42. Munib al-Masri interview, London, August 1989.
43. Ibid.
44. General Aharon Yariv interview, Tel Aviv, November 1989.
45. Abu Iyad, op. cit., pp. 92–3.

*Chapter 5*

1. Information from west European intelligence official. Name withheld on request.
2. US Foreign Broadcast Information Service, *Middle East Monitor*, Vol. 3, No. 8, 15 April 1973, pp. 7–8.
3. Abu Daoud interview, Tunis, November 1989.
4. Yasser Abed Rabbo interview, Tunis, August 1989.
5. Interview with Arafat adviser, Tunis, November 1989. Name withheld on request.
6. *An-Nahar Arab Report*, Beirut, 6 December 1971, quoted in John Cooley, *Green March, Black September*, London, 1973.
7. Abu Iyad, *My Home, My Land*, New York, 1981, p. 96.
8. Ibid., p. 97.
9. Yasser Arafat, quoted in *Journal of Palestine Studies*, Washington and Kuwait, winter 1973, p. 174.

10. Abu Iyad, op. cit., p. 95.
11. Ibid., p. 98.
12. BBC Summary of World Broadcasts, Amman domestic radio, 17 December 1971.
13. Lester Sobel (ed.), *Palestinian Impasse: Arab Guerrillas and International Terror*, New York, 1977.
14. Ibrahim Bakr interview, Amman, September 1989. Bakr served as PLO deputy chairman under Arafat, 1969–70.
15. Interview with West German intelligence official, Germany, July 1989. Name withheld on request.
16. General Aharon Yariv interview, Tel Aviv, November 1989.
17. Western intelligence report on planning and preparation of Olympic attack, November 1972 (unpublished).
18. Interview with a colleague of Zamir, Tel Aviv, December 1989. Name withheld on request.
19. Abu Iyad, op. cit., pp. 112–13.
20. Sobel, op. cit., p. 123.
21. Ibid, p. 121.
22. Mahmoud Darwish, 'Going to the World: A Stranger to the World', from *The Complete Works of Mahmoud Darwish*, Beirut, 1979.
23. Sobel, op. cit., p. 123.
24. General Aharon Yariv interview, Tel Aviv, November 1989.
25. Ibid.
26. Interview with Israeli official, Jerusalem, December 1989. Name withheld on request.
27. Interview with PLO intelligence official, Cairo, June 1989. Name withheld on request.
28. Abu Iyad, op. cit., p. 126.
29. Interview with PLO intelligence official, Cairo, May 1989. Name withheld on request.
30. Sobel, op. cit., p. 129.
31. Interview with Israeli intelligence official, Jerusalem, December 1989. Name withheld on request.
32. Sobel, op. cit., pp. 126–7.
33. *Washington Post*, 4 March 1973.
34. BBC Summary of World Broadcasts, Khartoum radio, 6 March 1973.
35. *Washington Post*, 13 February 1986.
36. Interview with US intelligence official, Washington,

November 1989. Name withheld on request.
37. US State Department cable 039764, 7 March 1973, released under the Freedom of Information Act.
38. Abu Iyad, op. cit., p. 102.
39. Interview with Nimeiri adviser, Cairo, December 1989. Name withheld on request.
40. Yasser Arafat, quoted in Sobel, op. cit.

*Chapter* 6

1. General Vernon Walters interview, Bonn, November 1989.
2. Ibid.
3. Nabil Shaath interview, Cairo, March 1989.
4. *See* Yehoshafat Harkabi, *Fedayeen Action and Arab Strategy*, International Institute for Strategic Studies, Adelphi Paper No. 53, London, December 1968.
5. Yasser Arafat interview, Tunis, December 1989.
6. Khaled al-Hassan interview, Kuwait, April 1989.
7. Mehdi Abdel-Hadi interview, Jerusalem, June 1989. Abdel-Hadi is director of Passia, a Palestinian study institute in the West Bank.
8. Yasser Arafat on PLO Radio, quoted in Moshe Shemesh, *The Palestinian Entity 1959–74*, London 1988, p. 161.
9. Salah Khalaf interview, Tunis, June 1989.
10. Alain Gresh, *The PLO: The Struggle Within*, London, 1985, p. 105.
11. Moshe Ma'oz, *Palestinian Leadership in the West Bank*, London, 1984.
12. *Washington Post*, 29 September 1972.
13. Gresh, op. cit., p. 112.
14. Salah Khalaf, quoted by Eric Rouleau in *Foreign Affairs*, Washington, spring 1975.
15. Gresh, op. cit., pp. 88–9.
16. Shemesh, op. cit., p. 259.
17. Yasser Arafat, quoted in *Filastin al-Thawra*, 1 January 1973, reprinted in *Journal of Palestine Studies*, Vol. II, No. 3, spring 1973.
18. Nayef Hawatmeh interview, Damascus, May 1989.
19. Ibid.
20. Salah Khalaf interview, Tunis, August 1989.
21. Yasser Abed Rabbo interview, Tunis, August 1989.

22. Ibid.
23. Salah Khalaf interview, Tunis, August 1989.
24. For accusation against Khalaf, *see* Sadat, quoted in John Amos, *Palestinian Resistance: Organisation of a Nationalist Movement*, New York, 1980, p. 414.
25. Salah Khalaf interview, Tunis, August 1989.
26. Abu Iyad, *My Home, My Land*, New York, 1981, p. 129.
27. Mohammed Abu Mayzar interview, Paris, August 1989.
28. Yasser Arafat, quoted in *Journal of Palestine Studies*, Vol. IV, No. 2, winter 1974–5.
29. William Quandt, *Decade of Decisions*, Los Angeles and London, 1977, p. 160.
30. Henry Kissinger, *Years of Upheaval*, London and New York, 1982, pp. 626–7.
31. Ibid., pp. 503, 626–7.
32. Alfred (Roy) Atherton interview, Washington, November 1989.
33. General Vernon Walters interview, Bonn, November 1989.
34. Kissinger, op. cit., pp. 628–9.
35. Interview with the authors, Washington, November 1989. Name withheld on request.
36. Nabil Shaath interview, Cairo, December 1989.
37. Abu Iyad, op. cit., pp. 135–6.
38. Ibid.
39. George Habash, quoted in *Journal of Palestine Studies*, Vol. III, No. 3, spring 1974.
40. Programme of 12th PNC, broadcast on Voice of Palestine, Cairo, 8 June 1974, quoted from BBC Summary of World Broadcasts, 11 June 1974.
41. Shlomo Avineri interview, London, October 1989.

*Chapter 7*

1. Nabil Shaath interview, Cairo, December 1989.
2. Harris Schoenberg, *A Mandate for Terror: the United Nations and the PLO*, New York, 1989, pp. 1–40.
3. Ibid.
4. Ibid.
5. Ibid.
6. *Fiches du Monde Arabe*, 15 November 1978, No. 1113.
7. Nabil Shaath interview, Cairo, December 1989.

8. Abu Iyad, *My Home, My Land*, New York, 1981, p. 144–9.
9. Ibid.
10. Ismail Fahmy, *Negotiating for Peace in the Middle East*, London, 1983, p. 98.
11. Ibid.
12. Farouk Kaddoumi interview, Tunis, September 1989.
13. Quoted in *Akhbar al-Yom*, Cairo, 2 November 1974, pp. 3–4.
14. Mahmoud Riad interview, Cairo, May 1989.
15. Walter Laqueur and Barry Rubin (eds.), *The Israel- Arab Reader*, London, 1984, p. 518.
16. Lester Sobel, (ed.), *Palestinian Impasse: Arab Guerrillas and International Terror*, New York, 1977, p. 204.
17. Yasser Arafat, quoted in *Journal of Palestine Studies*, Vol. IV, No. 2, winter 1975.
18. *Time* magazine, 11 November 1974, p. 31.
19. Ibid.
20. Zeid al-Rifai interview, Amman, June 1989.
21. Nabil Shaath interview, Cairo, December 1989.
22. Yasser Arafat, quoted in *Journal of Palestine Studies*, winter 1982. Arafat was reflecting in an interview on what he had said at the time.
23. Brian Urquhart interview, London, May 1989. Urquhart was formerly UN Under-Secretary-General for Special Political Affairs.
24. Ibid.
25. Yasser Arafat, quoted in Laqueur and Rubin, op. cit., pp. 504–18.
26. Ibid.
27. Stephen Day interview, Tunis, August 1989. Day served as press attaché in the UK mission to the UN and later as British ambassador to Tunis.
28. Nabil Shaath interview, Cairo, December 1989.
29. *New York Times*, 14 November 1974.
30. Schoenberg, op. cit., pp. 40ff.
31. Ibid.
32. Farouk Kaddoumi interview, Tunis, September 1989.
33. Yasser Arafat interview, Tunis, December 1989.
34. Fahmy, op. cit., p. 211.
35. Yasser Arafat interview, Tunis, December 1989.

36. Khaled al-Hassan interview, Kuwait, April 1989.
37. Alain Gresh, *The PLO: The Struggle Within*, London, 1985, p. 161.
38. Ilan Halevy interview, Paris, August 1989. Halevy is PLO representative to the Socialist International.
39. Ibid.
40. Ibid.
41. *The Times*, 16 November and 17 December 1973.
42. Uri Avnery interview, Tel Aviv, November 1989.
43. Ibid. *See also* Uri Avnery, *My Friend, The Enemy*, London, 1986.
44. Ilan Halevy interview, Paris, August 1989.

*Chapter* 8

1. Salah Khalaf interview, Tunis, August 1989.
2. Walid Khalidi interview, London, October 1989.
3. Suleiman Franjieh's speech to the UN, reproduced in *Journal of Palestine Studies*, Vol. IV, No. 2, winter 1975.
4. Kemal Salibi, *Crossroads to Civil War: Lebanon* 1958–76, London, 1976, p. 98.
5. Quoted in Walid Khalidi, *Conflict and Violence in Lebanon: Confrontation in the Middle East*, Cambridge, Massachusets, 1979, p. 185.
6. Mahmoud Riad interview, Cairo, May 1989. Riad was Egyptian foreign minister at the time and later Secretary-General of the Arab League.
7. Walid Khalidi interview, Cambridge, Massachusetts, November 1989.
8. Mamdouh Nofal interview, Tunis, August 1989.
9. Sakher Abu Nizar interview, Tunis, September 1989.
10. Yasser Abed Rabbo interview, Tunis, August 1989.
11. Walid Khalidi interview, London, October 1989.
12. Salah Khalaf interview, Tunis, August 1989.
13. Interview with the authors, London, November 1989. Name withheld on request.
14. Walid Khalidi interview, London, October 1989.
15. Sakher Abu Nizar interview, Tunis, September 1989.
16. A widely circulated piece of PLO folklore.
17. Abu Iyad, *My Home, My Land*, New York, 1981, p. 172.
18. Walid Khalidi interview, London, October 1989.

19. Abu Iyad, op. cit., p. 169.
20. Interview with senior Fatah intelligence official, Cairo, May 1989. Name withheld on request.
21. Ibid.
22. Adeed Dawisha, *Syria and the Lebanese Crisis*, London, 1980.
23. Khalidi, op. cit., p. 52.
24. *Fiches du Monde Arabe*, 18 October 1978, No. 1093.
25. Abu Iyad, op. cit., p. 184.
26. Ibid., p. 181.
27. *Fiches du Monde Arabe*, 21 January 1981, No. 1798.
28. Kamal Jumblatt, *This Is My Legacy*, Paris, 1978, p. 105.
29. Salah Khalaf interview, Tunis, August 1989.
30. Interview with the authors, London, July 1989. Name withheld on request.
31. Interview with aide to al-Wazir, Cairo, May 1989. Name withheld on request.
32. Abu Iyad, op. cit., p. 196.

*Chapter* 9

1. Cyrus Vance interview, New York, November 1989.
2. Ibid.
3. *New York Times*, 15 December 1976.
4. Programme of 13th PNC, quoted in Helena Cobban, *The Palestinian Liberation Organisation*, Cambridge, 1984, p. 85.
5. Yasser Arafat's UN speech, reproduced in *Journal of Palestine Studies*, Vol. IV, No. 2.
6. Yasser Arafat interview, Tunis, December 1989.
7. Talcott Seelye interview, Washington, November 1989.
8. Ibid.
9. Abu Iyad, *My Home, My Land*, New York, 1981, pp. 189–90.
10. Interview with the authors, Washington, November 1989. Name withheld on request.
11. Abdel Latif Abu Hijleh (Abu Jaafar) interview, Tunis, September 1989.
12. Ibid.
13. Salah Khalaf interview, Tunis, June 1989.
14. Abdel Latif Abu Hijleh (Abu Jaafar) interview, Tunis, September 1989.
15. Edward Said interview, New York, November 1989.

16. Uri Avnery, *My Friend, The Enemy*, London, 1986, pp. 144–5.
17. Farouk Kaddoumi interview with *Al-Ahram*, quoted in Cobban, op. cit., p. 84.
18. William Quandt, *Camp David: Peacemaking and Politics*, Washington, 1986.
19. Yasser Arafat, quoted in David Hirst and Irene Beeson, *Sadat*, London, 1981, p. 257.
20. Quandt, op. cit., pp. 40–57.
21. Cobban, op. cit., p. 89.
22. Quandt, op. cit., pp. 101–2.
23. Interviews with former State Department officials, Washington, November 1989. Names witheld on request.
24. Jimmy Carter, quoted in *New York Times*, 1 September 1979.
25. Cyrus Vance interview, New York, November 1989.
26. Yasser Arafat, quoted in *New York Times*, 9 March 1984.
27. Yasser Arafat, quoted in *Al-Hayat*, 1 January 1990.
28. Interview with the authors, London, April 1989. Name withheld on request.

*Chapter* 10

1. Quoted in David Hirst and Irene Beeson, *Sadat*, London, 1981, p. 255.
2. Mahmoud Riad, *The Struggle for Peace in the Middle East*, London, 1981.
3. Ismail Fahmy, *Negotiating for Peace in the Middle East*, London, 1983.
4. Yasser Arafat interview with *Al-Hayat*, 1 January 1990.
5. Mohammed Sobhieh interview, Cairo, November 1989. Sobhieh is Secretary-General of the Palestine National Council, and resides in Cairo.
6. Abdel Latif Abu Hijleh (Abu Jaafar) interview, Tunis, August 1989.
7. Yasser Arafat interview, Tunis, December 1989. Salah Khalaf interview, Tunis, August 1989.
8. Abu Iyad, *My Home, My Land*, New York, 1981, pp. 210–2.
9. Jimmy Carter, quoted in *New York Times*, 16 December 1977. *Fiches du Monde Arabe*, 23 January 1980, No. 1486.

10. Mamdouh Nofal interview, Tunis, August 1989. Nofal is a senior DFLP commander in Lebanon.
11. Ahmed Kora'i (Abu Ala'a) interview, Tunis, June 1989.
12. Interview with authors, London, June 1989. Name withheld on request.
13. Likud coalition platform, quoted in Walter Laqueur and Barry Rubin (eds.), *The Israel-Arab Reader*, London, 1984, pp. 591–3.
14. *Fiches du Monde Arabe*, 10 May 1978, No. 952.
15. Ibid., Nos. 945–6.
16. *Middle East Reporter*, Beirut, 12 August 1978.
17. Brian Urquhart interview, London, May 1989.
18. Mohammed Sobhieh interview, Cairo, November 1989.
19. Yasser Arafat, quoted in *New York Times*, 2 May 1978.
20. *Middle East Reporter*, Beirut, 7 October 1978.
21. *Fiches du Monde Arabe*, 15 November 1978, No. 1118.
22. *Middle East Reporter*, 27 January 1979.
23. Edward Said interview, New York, November 1989.
24. Yasser Arafat, quoted in *Al-Hayat*, 1 January 1990.
25. Interview with the authors, Tunis, June 1989. Name withheld on request.
26. Ibid.
27. Ibid.
28. Helena Cobban, *The Palestinian Liberation Organisation*, Cambridge, 1984, p. 104.
29. Aaron David Miller, 'The PLO' in *The Middle East Since Camp David*, ed. Robert Freedman, Boulder, Colorado, 1984.
30. Interview with Fatah intelligence official, Tunis, June 1989. Name withheld on request.
31. Yasser Arafat quoted in *Time* magazine, 9 April 1979.
32. Cobban, op. cit., p. 107.
33. Cyrus Vance interview, New York, November 1989; *also* Edward Said interview, New York, November 1989.
34. Interview with Fatah intelligence official, Tunis, June 1989. Name withheld on request.
35. Ibid.
36. Interview with the authors, London, July 1989. Name withheld on request.
37. Ibid.

38. Ibid.
39. Interview with Arafat opponent, Damascus, May 1989. Name withheld on request.
40. Fatah intelligence official, Tunis, June 1989. Name withheld on request.
41. *Washington Post*, 25 April 1981.
42. Interview with Arafat adviser, London, October 1989. Name withheld on request.
43. Emad Shakur interview, Tunis, June 1989. Shakur is Arafat's adviser on Israeli affairs.
44. Cobban, op. cit., pp. 111–12.
45. *Washington Post*, 27 July 1981.
46. Fahd plan quoted in Walter Laqueur and Barry Rubin (eds.), *The Israel-Arab Reader*, London, 1984, pp. 623–4.
47. John Edwin Mroz interview, New York, November 1989.
48. Ibid.; *also* Nicholas Veliotes interview, Washington, November 1989; and *New York Times*, 19 February 1984. Nicholas Veliotes is a former Assistant Secretary of State and later served as US ambassador to Egypt.
49. *Washington Post*, 20 February 1984.
50. John Edwin Mroz interview, New York, November 1989.
51. Ibid.
52. Ibid.
53. Ibid.

*Chapter* 11

1. Interview with Arafat aide, London, June 1989. Name withheld on request.
2. Nicholas Veliotes interview, Washington, November 1989.
3. Ariel Sharon, *Warrior*, New York, 1989.
4. Nicholas Veliotes interview, Washington, November 1989.
5. General Avraham Tamir interview, Tel Aviv, November 1989.
6. Interview with Arafat adviser, Tunis, September 1989. Name withheld on request.
7. Brian Urquhart interview, London, May 1989.
8. Ibid.
9. Ibid.
10. Marwan Qasem interview, Amman, November 1989.
11. Yezid Sayigh interview, Oxford, October 1989.

12. Interview with the authors, Cairo, October 1989. Name withheld on request.
13. Nicholas Veliotes interview, Washington, November 1989.
14. *Yediot Ahronoth*, 14 May 1982.
15. Interview with the authors, Cairo, October 1989. Name withheld on request.
16. General Avraham Tamir interview, Tel Aviv, December 1985.
17. Ze'ev Schiff and Ehud Ya'ari, *Israel's Lebanon War*, New York, 1984, p. 98.
18. *Fiches du Monde Arabe*, 19 February 1986, No. 2521.
19. Ibid.
20. Avraham Tamir, *A Soldier in Search of Peace*, London, 1988, p. 128.
21. Yezid Sayigh interview, Oxford, October 1989.
22. *Fiches du Monde Arabe*, 19 February 1986, No. 2521.
23. Walid Khalidi interview, Cambridge, Massachussetts, December 1989.
24. Sharon, op. cit., p. 472.
25. *Journal of Palesine Studies*, Vol. XI, No. 4, 'The War in Lebanon', summer/autumn 1982.
26. Bassel Akel interview, London, October 1989.
27. Ibid.
28. Rashid Khalidi, *Under Siege: PLO Decisionmaking during the* 1982 War, New York, 1986, p. 110.
29. Ibid., p. 113.
30. WAFA report, quoted in Khalidi, op. cit., p. 118. WAFA is the official PLO news agency.
31. Yasser Arafat interview, Tunis, December 1989.
32. Interview with the authors, London, February 1990. Name withheld on request.
33. *Guardian*, 4 July 1982.
34. Ibid., 3 July 1982.
35. *Haaretz*, 5 July 1982.
36. Sharon, op. cit., p. 486.
37. Interview with the authors, Cairo, October 1989. Name withheld on request.
38. Interview with the authors, London, July 1989. Name withheld on request.
39. Colonel Mohammed al-Natour interview, Tunis, May 1989.

40. Interview with former White House staffer, London, February 1990. Name withheld on request.
41. Ibid.
42. WAFA report, reprinted in *Journal of Palestine Studies*, Vol. XI, No. 4, summer/autumn 1982.
43. *Fiches du Monde Arabe*, 5 March 1986, No. 2540.
44. David Kimche interview, Tel Aviv, December 1989.
45. Afif Safieh interview, the Hague, July 1989. Safieh was the PLO representative in the Netherlands, and an Arafat confidant.
46. *Fiches du Monde Arabe*, 4 December 1985, No. 2537.
47. *Haaretz*, 20 September 1982.
48. *Jerusalem Post*, 24 September 1982.
49. Nabil Shaath interview, Cairo, December 1989.

*Chapter* 12

1. Yasser Arafat interview, Baghdad, January 1990.
2. *See* Yezid Sayigh, 'Struggle Within, Struggle Without: The Transformation of PLO Politics Since 1982' in *International Affairs*, London, Vol. 65, No. 2, spring 1989, p. 251, footnotes.
3. Nabil Shaath interview, Cairo, December 1989.
4. Walter Laqueur and Barry Rubin (eds.), *The Israel-Arab Reader*, London, 1984, p. 664.
5. Ibid., pp. 656–63.
6. Ibid.
7. Marwan Qasem interview, Amman, November 1989.
8. Ibid.
9. Emile Sahliyeh, *The PLO after the Lebanon War*, Boulder, Colorado, 1986.
10. Laqueur and Rubin, op. cit., p. 365.
11. Interview with the authors, Washington, November 1989. Name withheld on request.
12. Richard Viets interview, Washington, November 1989.
13. Colonel Said Musa interview, Damascus, May 1989.
14. Nabil Shaath interview, Cairo, December 1989.
15. Eric Rouleau, 'The PLO After Lebanon' in *Foreign Affairs*, Washington, autumn 1983, p. 143.
16. Ibid., p. 150.
17. *International Herald Tribune*, 11 April 1983.

18. Mamdouh Nofal interview, Tunis, November 1989.
19. Ibid.
20. Yezid Sayigh interview, Oxford, October 1989.
21. WAFA report from Damascus, 15 May 1983.
22. Mamdouh Nofal interview, Tunis, November 1989.
23. Ibid.
24. *International Herald Tribune*, 5 June 1983.
25. Ibid., 21 June 1983.
26. Intissar al-Wazir interview, Amman, June 1989.
27. Ibid.
28. *Washington Post*, 25 June 1983.
29. *New York Times*, 27 June 1983.
30. *International Herald Tribune*, 25 June 1983.
31. Ibid., quoting Syrian news agency SANA.
32. Khaled Fahoum interview, Damascus, May 1989.
33. Nabil Shaath interview, Cairo, December 1989.
34. Abdullah Hourani interview, Tunis, June 1989.
35. Sahliyeh, op. cit., p. 165.
36. Ibid., p. 148.
37. Yasser Arafat interview, Tunis, December 1989.
38. Yezid Sayigh, *Quest for a Homeland: Palestinian Military History*, 1949–88 (working title, unpublished).
39. Ibid.
40. Yasser Arafat interview, Tunis, December 1989.
41. Associated Press, 5 November 1983.
42. Ibid.
43. Kuwaiti news agency Kuna, 21 November 1983, quoted in Sahliyeh, op. cit., p. 171.
44. *New York Times* editorial in the *International Herald Tribune*, 18 November 1983.
45. Associated Press, 8 December 1983.
46. Associated Press, 15 December 1983.
47. Yasser Arafat quoted in *Washington Post*, 25 December 1983.

*Chapter* 13

1. *Middle East Reporter*, 24 December 1983.
2. Yasser Arafat interview, Tunis, December 1989.
3. Mohammed Sobhieh interview, Cairo, November 1989.
4. Widely circulated PLO joke.

5. Ahmed Abdel Rahman interview, Tunis, June 1989.
6. *New York Times*, 23 December 1983.
7. *Washington Post*, 23 December 1983.
8. Yasser Arafat interview, Tunis, December 1989.
9. *Washington Post*, 27 December 1983.
10. *New York Times*, 17 January 1984.
11. Quoted by Palestinian news agency WAFA, 1 July 1984.
12. Accords published in *Democratic Front for the Liberation of Palestine Bulletin*, No. 84/85, July 1984.
13. Ibid.
14. Mohammed Hamza interview, Tunis, August 1989. Hamza is Wazir's biographer.
15. West Bank Data Base project: A survey of Israel's Policies, American Enterprise Institute, Washington, 1984.
16. PLO radio recorded by US Foreign Broadcast Information Service, 14 November 1983.
17. *Middle East Reporter*, 1 December 1984.
18. Ibid.
19. *Guardian*, 29 November 1984.
20. Ibid.
21. *Daily Telegraph*, 29 November 1984.
22. Ibid.
23. Ibid.
24. *Washington Post*, 28 November 1984.
25. *New York Times*, 30 November 1984.
26. *Washington Post*, 28 November 1984.
27. *New York Times*, 30 November 1984.

*Chapter* 14

1. Taher al-Masri interview, Amman, December 1989.
2. Ibid.
3. *New York Times*, 24 February 1984.
4. Abdel Latif Abu Hijleh (Abu Jaafar) interview, Tunis, August 1989.
5. *Al-Sharq al-Awsat*, 26 April 1985.
6. *Al-Qabas*, 6 June 1985.
7. *Washington Post*, 13 May 1985.
8. *New York Times*, 30 May 1985.
9. Ahmed Abdel Rahman interview, Tunis, September 1989.

10. *New York Times*, 2 October 1985.
11. *Newsweek* magazine, 14 October 1985.
12. Ahmed Abdel Rahman interview, Tunis, June 1989.
13. Ibid.
14. Interviews with Egyptian officials, Cairo, October 1985.
15. *Financial Times*, 13 October 1985.
16. Taher al-Masri interview, Amman, December 1989.
17. Ibid.
18. *New York Times*, 8 November 1985.
19. Interview with the authors, Amman, September 1989. Name withheld on request.
20. Ibid.
21. Ibid.
22. *Financial Times*, 20 February 1986.
23. *Middle East Reporter*, 3 March 1986.
24. Author's note on press conference, 15 July 1986.
25. *Middle East Reporter*, 3 March 1986.
26. US Foreign Broadcast Information Service, 11 December 1984.
27. *Middle East International*, 1 May 1987.
28. William Quandt (ed.), *The Middle East Ten Years After Camp David*, Washington, 1988, appendix G, p. 475.
29. *New York Times*, 13 May 1987.
30. Interview with Jordanian journalist, Amman, September 1989. Name withheld on request.
31. Taher al-Masri interview, Amman, November 1989.
32. Author's note on press conference.

*Chapter* 15

1. Interview with Arafat adviser, Tunis, September 1989. Name withheld on request.
2. *Middle East Reporter*: Contemporary Mideast Backgrounder, No. 244, December 1987.
3. Salah Khalaf interview, Tunis, June 1989.
4. Avraham Tamir interview, Tel Aviv, December 1989.
5. Ibid.
6. *Washington Post*, 28 January 1988.
7. Meron Benvenisti, *The West Bank Data Base Project*, Jerusalem, 1987.
8. *Washington Post*, 27 November 1987.

9. *New York Times*, 27 November 1987.
10. Zachary Lockman and Joel Beinin (eds.), *Intifada*, Washington, 1989, p. 100.
11. Faisal al-Husseini interview, Jerusalem, May 1989.
12. Ibid.
13. Suleiman Najab interview, Tunis, June 1989.
14. Qais al-Samarai (Abu Leyla) interview, Damascus, June 1989.
15. *Al-Sayyad*, 8 January 1988.
16. *Washington Post*, 4 January 1988.
17. Yasser Abed Rabbo interview, Tunis, August 1989.
18. Ibid.
19. *See* William Quandt (ed.), *The Middle East Ten Years After Camp David*, Washington, 1989, p. 485.
20. *Washington Post*, 30 January 1988.
21. Interview with the authors, Jerusalem, June 1989. Name withheld on request.
22. Ibid.
23. Ibid.
24. Ibid.
25. Faisal al-Husseini interview, Jerusalem, May 1989.
26. Daoud Kuttab interview, Jerusalem, October 1989. Kuttab is a Palestinian journalist.
27. Yasser Arafat interview, Tunis, June 1989.
28. Richard Murphy interview, London, April 1989.
29. *Washington Post*, 28 February 1988.
30. Ibid.
31. *Washington Post*, 6 March 1988.
32. Interview with Palestinian insider, Jerusalem, November 1989. Name withheld on request.
33. *Washington Post*, 26 February 1988.
34. Ibid.
35. See 'The Shultz Initiative, 4 March 1988' in Quandt, op. cit., appendix K, p. 488.
36. Intissar al-Wazir interview, Amman, June 1989.
37. Yasser Arafat interview, Baghdad, January 1990.
38. *Financial Times*, 19 April 1988.
39. *Washington Post*, 6 June 1988.
40. PLO brochure distributed to press at Algiers summit, June 1988.

41. Bassam Abu Sharif interview, Tunis, August 1989.
42. Ibid.
43. Interview with authors, London, April 1989. Name withheld on request.
44. Bassam Abu Sharif interview, Tunis, August 1989.
45. Interview with Hussein aide, Amman, December 1989. Name withheld on request.

*Chapter* 16

1. Text issued by the royal palace, Amman, 31 July 1988.
2. Interview with Swedish envoy present at the lunch, Stockholm, July 1989. Name withheld on request.
3. Salah Khalaf interview, Tunis, June 1989.
4. Ibid.
5. *New York Times*, 15 August 1988.
6. William Quandt interview, Jerusalem, June 1989.
7. Interview with Swedish foreign ministry official, Stockholm, July 1989. Name withheld on request.
8. Ibid.
9. Ibid.
10. Ibid.
11. Ahmed Baha el-Dine interview, Cairo, October 1989.
12. Salah Khalaf interview, Tunis, June 1989.
13. Ibid.
14. Text of speech distributed by PLO, 15 November 1988.
15. Salah Khalaf interview, Tunis, August 1989.
16. Text of declaration distributed by PLO, 15 November 1988.
17. *See* declaration in Zachary Lockman and Joel Beinin (eds.), *Intifada*, Boston, 1989, pp. 395–9.
18. *New York Times*, 28 November 1988.
19. Rita Hauser interview, London, April 1989.
20. Interview with Swedish official, Stockholm, July 1989. Name withheld on request.
21. Ibid.
22. Interview with Arafat aide, Tunis, August 1989. Name withheld on request.
23. *New York Times*, 14 December 1988.
24. Interview with the authors, London, October 1989. Name withheld on request.

25. Ibid.
26. Ibid.
27. Ibid.
28. *New York Times*, 15 December 1988.
29. Ibid.
30. Ibid.

*Chapter* 17

1. *Washington Post*, 31 May 1990.
2. *Al-Siyassa*, Kuwait, 4 June 1990; *Mideast Mirror*, 6 June 1990.
3. *Washington Post*, 31 May 1990.
4. Ibid.
5. Interview with Arafat aide, London, February 1991. Name withheld on request.
6. *Time* magazine, 11 November 1974.
7. *New York Times*, 15 December 1988.
8. *Washington Post*, 3 January 1989.
9. *Washington Post*, 2 February 1989.
10. Interviews with PLO officials, Tunis, April 1989. Names withheld on request.
11. Leila Shaheed interview, Paris, 29 May 1989.
12. Arafat on French television, BBC Summary of World Broadcasts, 4 May 1989.
13. Radio Monte Carlo, BBC SWB, 5 May 1989.
14. Dennis Ross interview, Washington, November 1989.
15. *See* article by Daoud Kuttab, *Washington Post*, 16 April 1989.
16. *Washington Post*, 18 May 1989.
17. Interviews with PLO officials, Tunis, June 1989. Names withheld on request.
18. *Financial Times*, 7 July 1989.
19. Ibid.
20. Bassel Akel interview, London, April 1991.
21. Nabil Shaath interview, London, February 1991.
22. Accounts of Fatah meeting from Fatah officials, Tunis, August 1989.
23. *Washington Post*, 23 November 1989.
24. *Washington Post*, 4 December 1989.
25. BBC SWB, 26 February 1990.

26. Ibid.
27. Nabil Shaath interview, Cairo, April 1991.
28. Interview with Arafat adviser, London, February 1991. Name withheld on request.
29. Bassel Akel interview, London, April 1991.
30. Mohammed Milhem interview, Amman, March 1991.
31. Quoted in *Mideast Mirror*, 12 February 1990.
32. *Mideast Mirror*, 2 April 1990.
33. Afif Safieh interview, London, April 1991.
34. Interview with Arafat adviser, London, February 1991. Name withheld on request.
35. BBC SWB, 23 April 1990.
36. *Middle East Reporter*, 12 May 1990.
37. Interview with Arafat adviser, London, April 1991. Name withheld on request.
38. Interview with PLO official, Amman. March 1991. Name withheld on request.
39. *Washington Post*, 21 May 1990.
40. Nabil Shaath interview, Cairo, April 1991.
41. BBC SWB, 30 May 1990.
42. Iraqi account of summit session, quoted in Pierre Salinger, Secret Dossier, London, 1991, p. 31.
43. Interview with PLO official, Amman, March 1991. Name withheld on request.
44. Interview with Arafat adviser, London, April 1991. Name withheld on request.
45. BBC SWB, 12 June 1990.
46. *Mideast Mirror*, 23 July 1990.
47. Ibid.
48. *Financial Times*, 19 July 1990.
49. *Financial Times*, 25–26 July 1990.
50. Nabil Shaath interview, London, February 1991.
51. Awni Battash interview, Amman, March 1991.
52. Account of conversation from Gamal Sourani interview, Cairo, April 1991.
53. Awni Battash interview, Amman, March 1991.

*Chapter* 18

1. Awni Battash interview, Amman, March 1991.

2. Interview with Khalaf confidant, Amman, March 1991, Name withheld on request.
3. Bassel Akel interview, London, April 1991.
4. *Mideast Mirror*, 6 August 1990.
5. *Middle East Reporter*, 4 August 1990.
6. Ibid.
7. Ibid.
8. Interview with PLO official, Amman, March 1991. Name withheld on request.
9. Associated Press, 7 August 1990.
10. *Mideast Mirror*, 6 August 1990.
11. Associated Press, 7 August 1990.
12. BBC Summary of World Broadcasts, 5 August 1990.
13. BBC SWB, 10 August 1990.
14. *Akhbar al-Yom*, Cairo, 9 March 1991.
15. Interview with PLO official, Cairo, April 1991. Name withheld on request.
16. *Middle East Reporter*, 11 August 1990.
17. Interview with Arafat adviser, Cairo, April 1991. Name withheld on request.
18. Interview with Arafat aide, Amman, March 1991. Name withheld on request.
19. *Middle East Reporter*, 11 August 1990.
20. *Financial Times*, 21 August 1990.
21. Nabil Shaath interview, Cairo, April 1991.
22. *Financial Times*, 21 August 1990.
23. *Middle East Reporter*, 18 August 1990.
24. Ibid.
25. Bassel Akel interview, London, April 1991.
26. Nabil Shaath interview, Cairo, April 1991.
27. Interview with Arafat associate, Amman, March 1991. Name withheld on request.
28. Interview with PLO official, name withheld, Amman, March 1991.
29. Ibid.
30. *Mideast Mirror*, 21 September 1990.
31. Reuters, 13 September 1990.
32. *Mideast Mirror*, 21 September 1990.
33. *Middle East Reporter*, 6 October 1990.
34. *Mideast Mirror*, 11 September 1990.

35. BBC SWB, 18 October 1990.
36. Nabil Shaath interview, Cairo, April 1991.
37. Ibid.
38. *Financial Times*, 20 October 1990.
39. Associated Press, 11 October 1990.
40. Reuters, 9 October 1990.
41. *Middle East Reporter*, 17 October 1990.
42. Reuters, 13 October 1990.
43. Associated Press, 19 December 1990.
44. Associated Press, 1 January 1991.
45. Nabil Shaath interview, Cairo, April 1991.
46. Lakhdar Brahimi interview, London, February 1991.
47. *Middle East Reporter*, 12 January 1991.
48. Interview with Arafat adviser, London, April 1991. Name withheld on request.
49. For transcript, see the *Independent*, 14 January 1991.
50. Interview with Western official, Amman, January 1991. Name withheld on request.
51. Interview with Arafat aide, Amman, March 1991. Name withheld on request.
52. Interview with PLO official, Cairo, April 1991. Name withheld on request.
53. Interview with Arafat adviser, London, April 1991. Name withheld on request.
54. Reuters, 13 January 1991.
55. Interview with PLO official, Amman, March 1991. Name withheld on request. Also see *Vanity Fair*, April 1991.
56. Interview with Arafat adviser, London, April 1991. Name withheld on request.
57. *Mideast Mirror*, 17 August 1990.
58. *The Middle East* magazine, February 1991.
59. Associated Press, 15 January 1991.
60. Lakhdar Brahimi interview, London, February 1991.
61. Ibid.
62. *Middle East International*, 25 January 1991.
63. Interview with PLO official, Amman, March 1991. Name withheld on request.
64. *Financial Times*, 26 January 1991.
65. WAFA despatch, Algeria, 24 January 1991.
66. BBC SWB, 1 February 1991.

67. Interview with Arafat aide, Cairo, April 1991. Name withheld on request.
68. *International Herald Tribune*, 31 January 1991.
69. *Time* magazine, 4 March and 11 March 1991.
70. Associated Press, 16 February 1991.
71. *Middle East Reporter*, 2 March 1991.
72. Ibid.
73. Nabil Shaath interview, Cairo, April 1991.

*Chapter* 19

1. *Mideast Mirror*, 11 February 1991.
2. Ibid.
3. Associated Press, 9 March 1991.
4. *Washington Post*, 2 March 1991.
5. Ibid.
6. *Washington Post*, 7 March 1991.
7. *El Pais*, 11 March 1991.
8. Ibid.
9. Edward Said interview, New York, December 1989.
10. *New York Times*, 16 March 1991.
11. *Washington Post*, 1 April 1991.
12. *See* Walid Khalidi, *At a Critical Juncture: the United States and the Palestinian People*, Washington DC, 1989, pp. 23–8.
13. Telephone interview with the authors, February 1990.
14. *Time* magazine, 13 February 1989.
15. United States Information Service bulletin, 23 May 1989.
16. *Washington Post*, 13 March 1991.
17. Associated Press, 7 April 1991.
18. Associated Press, 23 April 1991.
19. *New York Times*, 24 May 1991.
20. Associated Press, 14 July 1991.
21. Associated Press, 3 August 1991.
22. WAFA report, 23 August 1991.
23. Associated Press, 8 September 1991.
24. *Washington Post*, 25 September 1991.
25. Associated Press, 26 September 1991.
26. Associated Press, 28 September 1991.
27. See *Washington Post*, 27 September 1991.
28. *See* William Quandt, *Peace Process: American Diplomacy*

*and the Arab–Israeli Conflict since 1967*, Washington, 1993, Appendix M, pp. 497–501.

29. Ibid., pp. 504–5.
30. *Independent on Sunday*, 3 November 1991.
31. Associated Press, 31 October 1991.
32. Ibid.
33. Associated Press, 12 December 1991.
34. Associated Press, 12 February 1991.
35. *Washington Post*, 5 June 1992.
36. *Guardian*, 20 April 1992.

*Chapter* 20

1. Reuters, 13 July 1992.
2. Ibid.
3. Reuters, 14 July 1992.
4. Reuters, 30 June 1992.
5. Reuters, 1 July 1992.
6. Reuters, 19 June 1992.
7. Reuters, 28 June 1992.
8. Reuters, 11 July 1992.
9. *The Age*, 3 June 1992.
10. Reuters, 26 June 1992.
11. *Washington Post*, 16 August 1992.
12. Associated Press, 16 August 1992.
13. Ibid.
14. Associated Press, 14 December 1992.
15. *Guardian*, 21 December 1991.
16. Associated Press, 8 December 1992.
17. Associated Press, 18 December 1992.
18. Associated Press, 6 March 1993.
19. Interview with Freddy Zach, Israeli co-ordinator in multilateral talks, Jerusalem, September 1993.
20. Associated Press, 6 February 1993.
21. *New York Times*, 5 September 1993.
22. Ibid.
23. *Washington Post*, 6 September 1993.
24. Interview with the authors, Jerusalem, September 1993.
25. Ibid.
26. Ibid.
27. *Washington Post*, 9 September 1993.

28. Associated Press, 26 May 1993.
29. Associated Press, 13 May 1993.
30. Interview with Freddy Zach, Jerusalem, September 1993.
31. Associated Press, 12–13 July 1993.
32. Associated Press, 8 August 1993.
33. *Middle East Reporter*, 28 August 1993.
34. Associated Press, 20 August 1993.
35. *Middle East Reporter*, 28 August 1993.
36. Reuters, 3–4 September 1992.
37. Associated Press, 22 August 1993.
38. Associated Press, 31 August 1993.
39. Debate reported by Mona Ziade of the Associated Press, 10 September 1993.
40. Associated Press, 10 September 1993.
41. Account by Clinton in interview with Israel TV reported in *Washington Post*, 14 September 1993.

*Epilogue*

1. *Time* magazine, 27 September 1993.
2. *Washington Post*, 11 September 1993.
3. *Wall Street Journal*, 19 December 1988.
4. Interview with Al-Qabas, reproduced in *Mideast Mirror*, 10 May 1990.
5. See *Jerusalem Post*, 19 September 1993.
6. *Al Ahram*, 7 September 1993.
7. Interview with the authors, Kuwait, April 1989.

# Bibliography

*Books*

Adams, J. *The Financing of Terror*, London, 1986.

Amos, John W. *Palestinian Resistance: Organisation of a Nationalist Movement*, New York, 1980.

Arian, A. *Politics in Israel: The Second Generation*, London, 1985.

Attayib, Abu, *Flash Back: Beirut* 1982, Nicosia, 1985.

Avnery, U. *My Friend, The Enemy*, London, 1986.

Bakhash, S. *The Reign of the Ayatollahs: Iran and the Islamic Revolution*, London, 1985.

Ball, George W. *Error and Betrayal in Lebanon: An analysis of Israel's invasion of Lebanon and the implications for US-Israeli relations*, Washington, 1984.

Bar Zohar, M. and Haber, E. *The Quest for the Red Prince*, New York, 1983.

Becker, J. *Hitler's Children: The Story of The Baader-Meinhof Gang*, London, 1977.

——*The PLO: The Rise and Fall of the Palestine Liberation Organisation*, London, 1984.

Begin, M. *The Revolt: Story of the Irgun*, Jerusalem, 1951.

Behbehani, H. *China's Foreign Policy in the Arab World*, 1955–75, London, 1981.

Blechman, B. and Kaplan, S. *Force without War: US Armed Forces as a Political Instrument*, The Brookings Institution, Washington.

Brand, L. *Palestinians in the Arab World: Institution Building and The Search for State*, New York, 1988.

Brzezinski, Z. *Power and Principle*, New York, 1985.

Bulloch, J. *Death of a Country: The Civil War in Lebanon*, London, 1977.

Carter J. *The Blood of Abraham: Insights into the Middle East*, Boston, 1985.

Chapman, C. *Whose Promised Land?* London, 1983.
Chomsky, N. *The Fateful Triangle: The United States, Israel and the Palestinians*, London and Sydney, 1983.
Christopher, W. and others, *American Hostages in Iran: The Conduct of a Crisis*, New Haven and London, 1985.
Cobban, H. *The Palestinian Liberation Organisation: People, Power and Politics*, Cambridge, 1984.
Collins, L. and Lapierre, D. *O Jerusalem*, London, 1972.
Cooley, J. *Green March, Black September*, London 1973.
Curtis, M. (editor) *The Palestinians: People, History, Politics*, New Brunswick, New Jersey, 1975.

Darwish, M. *The Complete Works of Mahmoud Darwish*, Beirut, 1979.
Dawisha, A. *Syria and the Lebanese Crisis*, London, 1980.
Day, A. *East Bank/West Bank: Jordan and the Prospects for Peace*, New York, 1986.
Dayan, M. *Story of My Life*, London, 1976.
Deacon, R. *The Israeli Secret Service*, London, 1977.
Dobson, C. and Payne, R. *The Never-Ending War: Terrorism in the 80s*, New York, 1987.

Eisenberg, D. *The Mossad: Inside Stories*, New York, 1978.

Fahmy, I. *Negotiating for Peace in the Middle East*, London, 1983.
Fallaci, O. *Interview with History*, Boston, 1976.
Franji, A. *The PLO and Palestine*, London, 1983.
Freedman, R. *The Middle East since Camp David*, Boulder, Colorado, 1984.
Friedman, T. *From Beirut to Jerusalem*, New York and London, 1989 and 1990.

Ghabra, S. *Palestinians in Kuwait: The Family and the Politics of Survival*, Boulder, Colorado, 1987.
Gibb, H. and Kramers, J. *Shorter Encyclopaedia of Islam*, Leiden, 1974.
Gilbert, M. *The Arab-Israeli Conflict: Its History in Maps*, London, 1988.
Gilmour, D. *Dispossessed: The Ordeal of the Palestinians* 1917–1980, London, 1980.

Goldschmidt, A. *A Concise History of the Middle East*, Boulder, Colorado, 1979.
Gordon, D. *The Republic of Lebanon: Nation in Jeopardy*, Boulder, Colorado, 1983.
Gresh, A. *The PLO: The Struggle Within*, London, 1985.

Harkabi, Y. *Israel's Fateful Decisions*, London, 1988 (first published in Hebrew in 1986).
——*The Palestinian Covenant and its Meaning*, London and New York, 1979.
Hart, A. *Arafat: Terrorist or Peacemaker?* London, 1984.
Heikal, M. *The Sphinx and the Commissar: The Rise and Fall of Soviet Influence in the Middle East*, New York, 1978.
——*Cutting The Lion's Tail: Suez Through Egyptian Eyes*, London, 1986.
——*Nasser: The Cairo Documents*, London, 1972.
——*The Road to Ramadan*, London, 1975.
——*Autumn of Fury: The Assassination of Sadat*, London, 1983.
Herzog, C. *The Arab-Israeli Wars: War and Peace in the Middle East from the War of Independence to Lebanon*, London, 1982.
Hiro, D. *Inside The Middle East*, London, 1982.
Hirst, D. *The Gun and The Olive Branch: The Roots of Violence in the Middle East*, London, 1977.
Hirst, D. and Beeson, I. *Sadat*, London, 1981.
Hopwood, D. *Egypt: Politics And Society, 1945–1981*, London, 1982.
Horne A. *A Savage War of Peace*, London 1977.

Jumblatt, K. *This is My Legacy*, Paris, 1978.

Ignatius, D. *Agents of Innocence*, New York 1987.
Israeli, R. (editor) *PLO in Lebanon: Selected Documents*, London, 1983.
Iyad, Abu (with Eric Rouleau), *My Home, My Land: A Narrative of the Palestinian Struggle*, New York, 1981.

Kamel, M. *The Camp David Accords*, London, 1986.
Kepel, G. *The Prophet and Pharaoh*, London, 1985.
Khalidi, R. *Under Siege: PLO Decisionmaking During the 1982* War, New York, 1986.

Khalidi, W. *Conflict and Violence in Lebanon: Confrontation in the Middle East*, Cambridge, Massachusetts, 1979.
Kiernan, T. *Yasir Arafat: The Man and the Myth*, New York, 1975.
Kirisci, K. *The PLO and World Politics: A Study of the Mobilisation of Support for the Palestinian Cause*, London, 1986.
Kissinger, H. *White House Years*, New York and London, 1979.
——*Years of Upheaval*, New York and London, 1982.

Laqueur, W. and Rubin, B. (editors) *The Israel-Arab Reader: A Documentary History of the Middle East Conflict*, London, 1984.
Lockman, Z. and Beinin, J. (editors) *Intifada: The Palestinian Uprising Against Israeli Occupation*, Boston, 1989.
Lunt, J. *Hussein of Jordan: Searching for Just and Lasting Peace*, London, 1989.

McDowall, D. *Palestine and Israel: The Uprising and Beyond*, London, 1989.
Ma'oz, M. *Palestinian Leadership on the West Bank*, London, 1984.
——*Asad: The Sphinx of Damascus*, New York, 1988.
Mansfield, P. *The Arabs*, London, 1982.
Martin, D. and Walcott, J. *Best Laid Plans: The Inside Story of America's War against Terrorism*, New York, 1988.
Meir, G. *My Life*, London, 1975.
Melman, Y. *The Master Terrorist: The True Story Behind Abu Nidal*, New York, 1986.
Melman, Y. and Raviv, D. *The Imperfect Spies: The History of Israeli Intelligence*, London, 1989.
Midkadi, L. *Surviving the Siege of Beirut: a personal account*, London, 1983.
Milstein, U. *A History of the Israeli Paratroopers*, Tel Aviv, 1985 (in Hebrew).
Mishal, S. *The PLO Under Arafat: Between Gun and Olive Branch*, New Haven and London, 1986.
Mitchell, R. *The Society of the Muslim Brothers*, London, 1969.
Morris, B. *The Birth of the Palestinian Refugee Problem, 1947–49*, Cambridge, 1987.

O'Ballance, E. *Arab Guerrilla Power*, 1967–72, London, 1974.
Odeh, B. *Lebanon: Dynamics of Conflict*, London, 1985.
Owen, R. (editor), *Essays on the Crisis in Lebanon*, London, 1976.

Palumbo, M. *The Palestinian Catastrophe: The 1948 Expulsion of a People from their Homeland*, London, 1987.
Perlmutter, A. *Two Minutes Over Baghdad*, London, 1982.
Plascov, A. *The Palestinian Refugees in Jordan* 1948–57, London, 1981.

Quandt, W. *Camp David: Peacemaking and Politics*, Washington, 1986.
——*Decade of Decisions: American Policy Toward the Arab-Israeli Conflict*, 1967–1976, Los Angeles and London, 1977.
——(editor), *The Middle East: Ten Years after Camp David*, Washington, 1988.
Quandt, W., Jabber, F. and Moseley Lesch, A. *The Politics of Palestinian Nationalism*, Los Angeles and London, 1973.

Randal, J. *The Tragedy of Lebanon: Christian Warlords, Israeli Adventurers and American Bunglers*, London, 1983.
Rhodes James, R. *Anthony Eden*, London, 1986.
Riad, M. *The Struggle for Peace in the Middle East*, London, 1981.
Rodinson, M. *Israel: A Colonial-Settler State?* Paris, 1973.
——*Israel and the Arabs*, London, 1968.
——*Mohammed*, London, 1983.
Rosie, G. *The Directory of International Terrorism*, Edinburgh, 1986.
Roth, S. (editor), *The Impact of the Six-Day War: A Twenty-Year Assessment*, London, 1988.
Rubenberg, C. *Israel And The American National Interest: A Critical Examination*, Chicago, 1986.
Ruehmkorf, P. *Die Jahre die Ilr Kennt*, Hamburg, 1972 (in German).

Sadat, A. *In Search of Identity*, London, 1978.
Sahliyeh, E. *The PLO After the Lebanon War*, Boulder, Colorado, 1986.

——*In Search of Leadership: West Bank Politics since 1967*, Washington, 1988.
Said, E. *The Question of Palestine*, New York, 1979.
Salibi, K. *Crossroads to Civil War: Lebanon, 1958–1976*, London, 1976.
Sayigh, R. *Palestinians: From Peasants to Revolutionaries*, London, 1979.
Sayigh, Y. *Quest for a Homeland: Palestinian military history 1949–88* (working title, unpublished).
Schiff, Z. and Rothstein, R. *Fedayeen: The Story of the Palestinian Guerrillas*, London, 1972.
Schiff, Z. and Ya'ari, E. *Israel's Lebanon War*, New York, 1984.
Schoenberg, H. *A Mandate for Terror: The United Nations and the PLO*, New York, 1989.
Seale, P. *Asad of Syria: The Struggle for the Middle East*, London, 1988.
Segal, J. *Creating the Palestinian State*, Chicago, 1989.
Sharon, A. *Warrior*, New York, 1989.
Shemesh, *The Palestinian Entity, 1959–1974: Arab Politics and the PLO*, London, 1988.
Shimoni, Y. *Political Dictionary of the Arab World*, London, 1987.
Shipler, D. *Arab and Jew: Wounded Spirits in a Promised Land*, New York, 1986.
Shoman, A. *The Indomitable Arab: The Life and Times of Abdulhameed Shoman, Founder of the Arab Bank*, London, 1984.
Silver, E. *Begin: A Biography*, London, 1984.
Sobel, L. (editor), *Palestinian Impasse: Arab Guerrillas and International Terror*, New York, 1977.
Sterling, C. *The Terror Network: The Secret War of International Terrorism*, London, 1981.
Stephens, R. *Nasser: A Political Biography*, London, 1971.
Steven, S. *The Spymasters of Israel*, New York, 1982.

Tamir, A. *A Soldier in Search of Peace*, London, 1988.
Timerman, J. *The Longest War*, London, 1982.

Urquhart, B. *A Life in Peace and War*, New York, 1987.

Vatikiotis, P. J. *The History of Egypt: From Muhammad Ali to Mubarak*, London, 1985.
Venn-Brown, J. (editor), *For a Palestinian: A memorial to Wael Zuwaiter*, London, 1984.

Woodward, R. *Veil: The Secret Wars of the CIA 1981–1987*, London, 1987.
Wright, R. *Sacred Rage: The Wrath of Militant Islam*, London, 1986.

Yodfat, Y. and Arnon-Ohanna Y. *PLO: Strategy and Tactics*, London, 1981.

*Monographs, Documents and Periodicals*

Arab Studies Society, 'Uprising in Palestine: The First Year' (Documentation on Human Rights and the Palestinian Uprising). Chicago, 1989.

Benvenisti, M. 'Demographic, economic, legal, social and political developments in the West Bank', The West Bank Data Base Project, Jerusalem, 1987.

Dodd, P. and Barakat, H. 'River Without Bridges: A Study of the Exodus of the 1967 Palestinian Arab Refugees', Institute for Palestine Studies, Beirut, 1968.

*Fiches du Monde Arabe*, Beirut.
*Financial Times*, London.
*Foreign Affairs*, Washington.
*Foreign Policy*, Washington.

*Guardian*, London.

Haddad, W. 'Lebanon: The Politics of Revolving Doors', The Washington Papers, New York, 1985.

*International Affairs*, London, spring, 1989.
'Israel in Lebanon': The Report of the International Commission to inquire into reported violations of International Law by

Israel during its invasion of the Lebanon, London, 1983.

Jaffee Centre for Strategic Studies, 'International Terrorism in 1988', Tel Aviv, 1989.

Jaffee Centre, 'The West Bank and Gaza: Israel's Options for Peace', Tel Aviv, 1989.

Jaffee Centre, 'The International Dimension of Palestinian Terrorism', Tel Aviv, 1986.

*Journal of Palestine Studies*, Washington and Kuwait.

*The Jerusalem Quarterly*, Nos. 47–49, 1988.

*The Jerusalem Journal of International Relations*, June, 1989.

Khalidi, W. 'At A Critical Juncture: The United States and the Palestinian People', Washington, March, 1989.

McDowall, D. 'The Palestinians: The Minority Rights Group Report' No. 24., London, 1987.

Miller, A. D. 'The Arab States and the Palestinian Question: Between Ideology and Self-Interest' The Washington Papers, New York, 1986.

——'The PLO and the Politics of Survival', published with the Centre for Strategic and International Studies, Georgetown University, Washington, DC, 1983.

*Middle East International*, London.

*The Middle East Journal*, autumn, 1988.

Mussalam, S. 'The PLO: The Palestine Liberation Organization', Brattleboro, Vermont, 1988.

*New York Times*, New York.

*Playboy* magazine, New York.

Roy, S. 'The Gaza Strip Survey', The West Bank Data Base Project, Jerusalem, 1986.

Safieh, A. 'One People Too Many?' Nijmegen, 1987.

*Time* magazine, New York.

The Tower Commission Report, *New York Times*, New York, 1987.

The Washington Institute's Presidential Study Group, 'Building for Peace: An American Strategy for the Middle East', Washington, 1988.

*Washington Post*, Washington.

Ziad, Abu-Amr, 'The Origins of Political Movement in the Gaza Strip (1948–67)', Bir Zeit University, West Bank.

# The PLO network

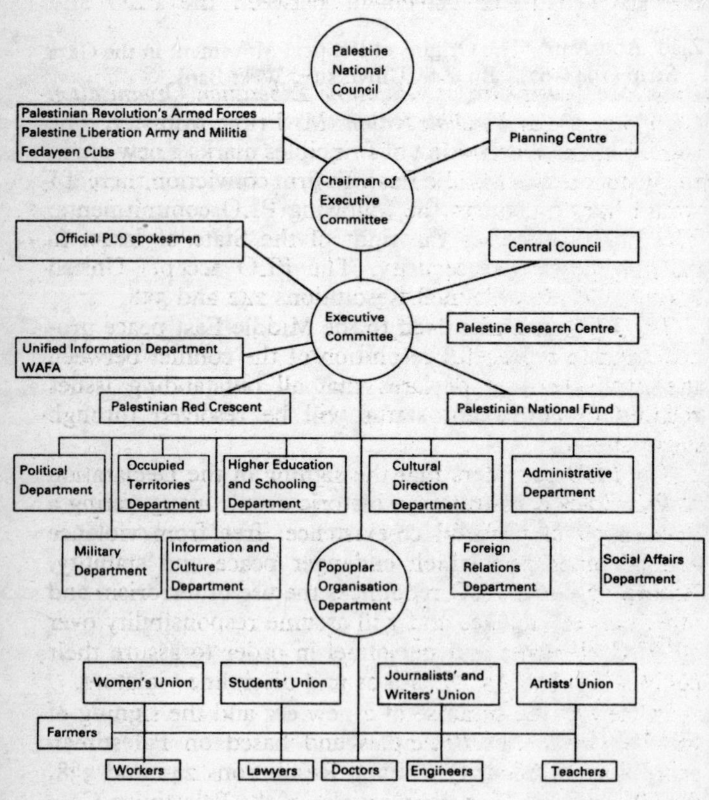

# *Appendix I*
# *Letters of recognition*

Following is the text of three letters, which form the mutual recognition agreement between the PLO and Israel.

*From Mr Yasser Arafat, Palestine Liberation Organisation Chairman, to Mr Yitzhak Rabin:* Mr Prime Minister, The signing of the Declaration of Principles marks a new era in the history of the Middle East. In firm conviction thereof I would like to confirm the following PLO commitments: The PLO recognises the right of the State of Israel to exist in peace and security. The PLO accepts United Nations Security Council Resolutions 242 and 338.

The PLO commits itself to the Middle East peace process, and to a peaceful resolution of the conflict between the two sides and declares that all outstanding issues relating to permanent status will be resolved through negotiations.

The PLO considers that the signing of the Declaration of Principles constitutes an historic event, inaugurating a new epoch of peaceful co-existence, free from violence and all other acts which endanger peace and stability. Accordingly, the PLO renounces the use of terrorism and other acts of violence and will assume responsibility over all PLO elements and personnel in order to assure their compliance, prevent violations and discipline violators.

In view of the promise of a new era and the signing of the Declaration of Principles and based on Palestinian acceptance of Security Council Resolutions 242 and 338, the PLO affirms that those articles of the Palestinian Covenant which deny Israel's right to exist and the provisions of the Covenant which are inconsistent with the commitments of this letter are now inoperative and no longer valid. Consequently, the PLO undertakes to submit to the Palestinian National Council for formal approval the necessary changes in regard to the Palestinian Covenant.

Sincerely, Yasser Arafat, Chairman, Palestine Liberation Organisation.

*From Mr Rabin to Mr Arafat:* Mr Chairman, In response to your letter of September 9th 1993 I wish to confirm to you that, in light of the PLO commitments included in your letter, the government of Israel has decided to recognise the PLO as the representative of the Palestinian people and commence negotiations with the PLO within the Middle East peace process.

Yitzhak Rabin, Prime Minister of Israel.

*From Mr Arafat to Mr Johan Joergen Holst, Norwegian Foreign Minister:* I would like to confirm to you that, upon signing of the Declaration of Principles, I will include the following positions in my public statements: In light of the new era marked by the signing of the Declaration of Principles, the PLO encourages and calls upon the Palestinian people in the West Bank and Gaza Strip to take part in the steps leading to the normalisation of life, rejecting violence and terrorism, contributing to peace and stability and participating actively in the shaping of reconstruction, economic development and co-operation.

Sincerely, Yasser Arafat, Chairman, Palestine Liberation Organisation.

# *Appendix II*
# *Declaration of Principles*

The following is an unofficial text of the agreement between Israel and the Palestine Liberation Organisation on interim self-rule for Palestinians in the Israeli-occupied territories.

Final agreed draft of 19 August 1993: DECLARATION OF PRINCIPLES ON INTERIM SELF-GOVERNMENT ARRANGEMENTS.

The Government of the State of Israel and the Palestinian team (in the Jordanian–Palestinian delegation to the Middle East Peace Conference) ('the PLO'), representing the Palestinian people, agree that it is time to put an end to the decades of confrontation and conflict, recognise their mutual legitimate and political rights, and strive to live in peaceful coexistence and mutual dignity and security and achieve a just, lasting, and comprehensive peace settlement and historic reconciliation through the agreed political process. Accordingly, the two sides agree to the following:

Article I. AIM OF THE NEGOTIATIONS
The aim of the Israeli–Palestinian negotiations with the current Middle East peace process is, among other things, to establish a Palestinian Interim Self-Government Authority, the elected Council, ('the Council') for the Palestinian people in the West Bank and the Gaza Strip, for a transitional period not exceeding five years, leading to a permanent settlement based on Security Council Resolutions 242 and 338.

It is understood that the interim arrangements are an integral part of the whole peace process and that the negotiations on the permanent status will lead to the implementation of Security Council Resolutions 242 and 338.

Article II. FRAMEWORK FOR THE INTERIM PERIOD

The agreed framework for the interim period is set forth in this declaration of Principles.

Article III. ELECTIONS

1) In order that the Palestinian people in the West Bank and Gaza Strip may govern themselves according to democratic principles, direct, free, and general political elections will be held for the Council under agreed supervision, while the Palestinian police will ensure public order. 2) An agreement will be concluded on the exact mode and conditions of the elections in accordance with the protocol attached as Annexe I, with the goal of holding the elections not later than nine months after the entry into force of this Declaration of Principles. 3) These elections will constitute a significant interim preparatory step towards the realisation of the legitimate rights of the Palestinian people and their just requirements.

Article IV. JURISDICTION

Jurisdiction of the Council will cover West Bank and Gaza Strip territory, except for issues that will be negotiated in the permanent status negotiations. The two sides view the West Bank and Gaza Strip as a single territorial unit, whose integrity will be preserved during the interim period.

Article V. TRANSITIONAL PERIOD AND PERMANENT STATUS NEGOTIATIONS

1) The five-year transitional period will begin upon the withdrawal from the Gaza Strip and Jericho area. 2) Permanent status negotiations will commence as soon as possible, but not later than the beginning of the third year of the interim period, between the Government of Israel

and the Palestinian people's representatives. 3) It is understood that these negotiations shall cover remaining issues, including: Jerusalem, refugees, settlements, security arrangements, borders, relations and cooperation with other neighbours, and other issues of common interest. 4) The two parties agree that the outcome of the permanent status negotiations should not be prejudiced or preempted by agreements reached for the interim period.

Article VI. PREPARATORY TRANSFER OF POWERS AND RESPONSIBILITIES

1) Upon the entry into force of this Declaration of Principles and the withdrawal from the Gaza Strip and the Jericho area, a transfer of authority from the Israeli military government and its Civil Administration to the authorised Palestinians for this task, as detailed herein, will commence. This transfer of authority will be of preparatory nature until the inauguration of the Council. 2) Immediately after the entry into force of this Declaration of Principles and the withdrawal from the Gaza Strip and Jericho area, with the view to promoting economic development in the West Bank and Gaza Strip, authority will be transferred to the Palestinians on the following spheres: education and culture, health, social welfare, direct taxation, and tourism. The Palestinian side will commence in building the Palestinian police force, as agreed upon. Pending the inauguration of the Council, the two parties may negotiate the transfer of additional powers and responsibilities, as agreed upon.

Article VII. INTERIM AGREEMENT

1) The Israeli and Palestinian delegations will negotiate an agreement on the interim period ('the Interim Agreement'). 2) The Interim Agreement shall specify, among other things, the structure of the council, the number of its members, and the transfer of powers and responsibilities from the Israeli military government and its Civil

Administration to the council. The Interim Agreement shall also specify the Council's executive authority, legislative authority in accordance with Article IX below, and the independent Palestinian judicial organs. 3) The Interim Agreement shall include arrangements, to be implemented upon the inauguration of the Council, for the assumption by the Council of all the powers and responsibilities transferred previously in accordance with Article VI above. 4) In order to enable the Council to promote economic growth, upon its inauguration, the Council will establish, among other things, a Palestinian Electricity Authority, a Gaza Sea Port Authority, a Palestinian Development Bank, a Palestinian Export Promotion Board, a Palestinian Environmental Authority, a Palestinian Land Authority and a Palestinian Water Administration Authority, and any other Authorities agreed upon, in accordance with the Interim Agreement that will specify their powers and responsibilities. 5) After the inauguration of the Council, the Civil Administration will be dissolved, and the Israeli military government will be withdrawn.

Article VIII. PUBLIC ORDER AND SECURITY

In order to guarantee public order and internal security for the Palestinians of the West Bank and Gaza Strip, the Council will establish a strong police force, while Israel will continue to carry the responsibility for defending against external threats, as well as the responsibility for overall security of Israelis for the purpose of safeguarding their internal security and public order.

Article IX. LAWS AND MILITARY ORDERS

1) The Council will be empowered to legislate, in accordance with the Interim Agreement, within all authorities transferred to it. 2) Both parties will review jointly laws and military orders presently in force in remaining spheres.

Article X. JOINT ISRAELI–PALESTINIAN LIAISON COMMITTEE

In order to provide for a smooth implementation of this Declaration of Principles and any subsequent agreements pertaining to the interim period, upon the entry into force of this Declaration of Principles, a Joint Israeli–Palestinian Liaison Committee will be established in order to deal with issues requiring coordination, other issues of common interest, and disputes.

Article XI. ISRAELI–PALESTINIAN COOPERATION IN ECONOMIC FIELDS

Recognising the mutual benefit of cooperation promoting the development of the West Bank, the Gaza Strip and Israel, upon entry into force of this Declaration of Principles, an Israeli–Palestinian Economic Cooperation Committee will be established in order to develop and implement in a cooperative manner the programmes identified in the protocols attached as Annexe III and Annexe IV.

Article XII. LIAISON AND COOPERATION WITH JORDAN AND EGYPT

The two parties will invite the governments of Jordan and Egypt to participate in establishing further liaison and cooperation arrangements between the Government of Israel and the Palestinian representatives, on one hand, and the Governments of Jordan and Egypt, on the other hand, to promote cooperation between them. These arrangements will include the constitution of a Continuing Committee that will decide by agreement on the modalities of admission of persons displaced from the West Bank and Gaza Strip in 1967, together with necessary measures to prevent disruption and disorder. Other matters of common concern will be dealt with by this Committee.

Article XIII. REDEPLOYMENT OF ISRAELI FORCES

1) After the entry into force of this Declaration of Principles, and not later than the eve of elections for the Council, a redeployment of Israeli military forces in the West Bank and Gaza Strip will take place, in addition to withdrawal of Israeli forces carried out in accordance with Article XIV. 2) In redeploying its military forces, Israel will be guided by the principle that its military forces should be redeployed outside populated areas. 3) Further redeployments to specified locations will be gradually implemented commensurate with the assumption of responsibility for public order and internal security by the Palestinian police force pursuant to Article VIII above.

Article XIV. ISRAELI WITHDRAWAL FROM THE GAZA STRIP AND JERICHO AREA

Israel will withdraw from the Gaza Strip and Jericho area, as detailed in the protocol attached as Annexe II.

Article XV. RESOLUTION OF DISPUTES

1) Disputes arising out of the application of interpretation of this Declaration of Principles, or any subsequent agreements pertaining to the interim period, shall be resolved by negotiations through the Joint Liaison Committee to be established pursuant to Article X above. 2) Disputes which cannot be settled by negotiations may be resolved by a mechanism of conciliation to be agreed upon by the parties. 3) The parties may agree to submit to arbitration disputes relating to the interim period, which cannot be settled through conciliation. To this end, upon the agreement of both parties, the parties will establish an Arbitration Committee.

Article XVI. ISRAELI–PALESTINIAN COOPERATION CONCERNING REGIONAL PROGRAMMES

Both parties view the multilateral working groups as an appropriate instrument for promoting a Marshall Plan, the regional programmes and other programmes, including special programmes for the West Bank and Gaza Strip, as indicated in the protocol attached as Annexe IV.

Article XVII. MISCELLANEOUS PROVISIONS
This Declaration of Principles will enter into force one month after its signing. All protocols annexed to this Declaration of Principles and Agreed Minutes pertaining thereto shall be regarded as an integral part thereof.

ANNEXE I. PROTOCOL ON THE MODE AND CONDITIONS OF ELECTIONS
1) Palestinians of Jerusalem who live there will have the right to participate in the election process, according to an agreement between the two sides. 2) In addition, the election agreement should cover, among other things, the following issues: a. the system of elections; b. the mode of the agreed supervision and international observation and their personal composition; c. rules and regulations regarding election campaign, including agreed arrangements for the organising of mass media and the possibility of licencing a broadcasting and TV station. 3) The future status of displaced Palestinians who were registered on 4 June 1967 will not be prejudiced because they are unable to participate in the election process due to practical reasons.

ANNEXE II. PROTOCOL ON WITHDRAWAL OF ISRAELI FORCES FROM THE GAZA STRIP AND JERICHO AREA
1) The two sides will conclude and sign within two months from the date of entry into force of this Declaration of Principles, an agreement on the withdrawal of Israeli military forces from the Gaza Strip and Jericho area. This agreement will include comprehensive arrangements to apply in the Gaza Strip and the Jericho area subsequent to the Israeli withdrawal. 2) Israel will implement an accelerated and scheduled withdrawal of Israeli military forces

from the Gaza Strip and Jericho area, beginning immediately with the signing of the agreement on the Gaza Strip and Jericho area and to be completed within a period not exceeding four months after the signing of this agreement. 3) The above agreement will include, among other things: a. Arrangements for a smooth and peaceful transfer of authority from the Israeli military government and its Civil Administration to the Palestinian representatives. b. Structure, powers and responsibilities of the Palestinian authority in these areas, except: external security, settlements, Israelis, foreign relations and other mutually agreed matters. c. Arrangements for the assumption of internal security and public order by the Palestinian police force consisting of police officers recruited locally and from abroad (holding Jordanian passports and Palestinian documents issued by Egypt). Those who will participate in the Palestinian police force coming from abroad should be trained as police and police officers. d. A temporary international or foreign presence, as agreed upon. e. Establishment of a joint Palestinian–Israeli Coordination and Cooperation Committee for mutual security purposes. f. An economic development and stabilization programme, including the establishment of an Emergency Fund, to encourage foreign investment, and financial and economic support. Both sides will coordinate and cooperate jointly and unilaterally with regional and international parties to support these aims. g. Arrangements for a safe passage for persons and transportation between the Gaza Strip and Jericho area. 4) The above agreement will include arrangements for coordination between both parties regarding passages: a. Gaza–Egypt; and b. Jericho–Jordan. 5) The offices responsible for carrying out the powers and responsibilities of the Palestinian authority under this Annexe II and Article VI of the Declaration of Principles will be located in the Gaza Strip and in the Jericho area pending the inauguration of the Council. 6) Other than these agreed arrangements, the status of the Gaza Strip and Jericho area will continue to be an integral part of the West Bank and Gaza Strip, and will not be changed in the intermin period.

## ANNEXE III. PROTOCOL ON ISRAELI–PALESTINIAN COOPERATION IN ECONOMIC AND DEVELOPMENT PROGRAMMES

The two sides agree to establish an Israeli–Palestinian Continuing Committee for Economic Cooperation, focusing, among other things, on the following:

1) Cooperation in the field of water, including a Water Development Programme prepared by experts from both sides, which will also specify the mode of cooperation in the management of water resources in the West Bank and Gaza Strip, and will include proposals for studies and plans on water rights of each party, as well as on the equitable utilisation of joint water resources for implementation in and beyond the interim period.

2) Cooperation in the field of electricity, including an Electricity Development Programme, which will also specify the mode of cooperation for the production, maintenance, purchase and sale of electricity resources.

3) Cooperation in the field of energy, including an Energy Development Programme, which will provide for the exploitation of oil and gas for industrial purposes, particularly in the Gaza Strip and in the Negev, and will encourage further joint exploitation of other energy resources. This Programme may also provide for the construction of a Petrochemical industrial complex in the Gaza Strip and the construction of oil and gas pipelines.

4) Cooperation in the field of finance, including a Financial Development and Action Programme for the encouragement of international investment in the West Bank and the Gaza Strip, and in Israel, as well as the establishment of a Palestinian Development Bank.

5) Cooperation in the field of transport and communications, including a Programme, which will define

guidelines for the establishment of a Gaza Sea Port Area, and will provide for the establishing of transport and communications lines to and from the West Bank and the Gaza Strip to Israel and to other countries. In addition, this programme will provide for carrying out the necessary construction of roads, railways, communications lines, etc.

6) Cooperation in the field of trade, including studies, and Trade Promotion Programmes, which will encourage local, regional and inter-regional trade, as well as feasibility study of creating free trade zones in the Gaza Strip and in Israel, mutual access to these zones, and cooperation in other areas related to trade and commerce.

7) Cooperation in the field of industry, including Industrial Development Programmes, which will provide for the establishment of joint Israeli–Palestinian Industrial Research and Development Centres, will promote Palestinian–Israeli joint ventures, and provide guidelines for cooperation in the textile, food, pharmaceutical, electronics, diamonds, computer and science-based industries.

8) A programme for cooperation in, and regulation of, labour relations and cooperation in social welfare issues.

9) A Human Resources Development and Cooperation Plan, providing for joint Israeli–Palestinian workshops and seminars, and for the establishment of joint vocational training centres, research institutes and data banks.

10) An Environmental Protection Plan, providing for joint and/or coordinated measures in this sphere.

11) A programme for developing coordination and cooperation in the field of communication and media.

12) Any other programmes of mutual interest.

## ANNEXE IV. PROTOCOL ON ISRAELI–PALESTINIAN COOPERATION CONCERNING REGIONAL DEVELOPMENT PROGRAMMES

1) The two sides will cooperate in the context of the multilateral peace efforts in promoting a Development

Programme for the region, including the West Bank and the Gaza Strip, to be initiated by the G–7. The parties will request the G–7 to seek the participation in this programme of other interested states, such as members of the Organisation for Economic Cooperation and Development, regional Arab States and institutions, as well as members of the private sector.

2) The Development Programme will consist of two elements: a) an Economic Development Programme for the West Bank and the Gaza Strip; b) a Regional Economic Development Programme.

A) The Economic Development Programme for the West Bank and Gaza Strip will consist of the following elements: 1) A Social Rehabilitation Programme, including a Housing and Construction Programme. 2) A Small and Medium Business Development Programme. 3) An Infrastructure Development Programme (water, electricity, transportation and communications, etc.). 4) A Human Resources Plan. 5) Other programmes.

B) The Regional Economic Development Programme may consist of the following elements: 1) The establishment of a Middle East Development Fund, as a first step, and a Middle East Development Bank, as a second step. 2) The development of a joint Israeli–Palestinian–Jordanian Plan for coordinated exploitation of the Dead Sea area. 3) The Mediterranean Sea (Gaza)–Dead Sea Canal. 4) Regional Desalinisation and other water development projects. 5) A regional plan for agricultural development, including a coordinated regional effort for the prevention of desertification. 6) Interconnection of electricity grids. 7) Regional cooperation for the transfer, distribution and industrial exploitation of gas, oil and other energy resources. 8) A Regional Tourism, Transportation and Telecommunications Development Plan. 9) Regional cooperation in other spheres.

3) The two sides will encourage the multilateral working groups, and will coordinate towards its success. The two

parties will encourage intersessional activities, as well as pre-feasibility and feasibility studies, within the various multilateral working groups.

## AGREED MINUTES TO THE DECLARATION OF PRINCIPLES ON INTERIM SELF-GOVERNMENT ARRANGEMENTS

### A. GENERAL UNDERSTANDINGS AND AGREEMENTS

Any powers and responsibilities transferred to the Palestinian pursuant to the Declaration of Principles prior to the inauguration of the Council will be subject to the same principles pertaining to Article IV, as set out in those Agreed Minutes below.

### B. SPECIFIC UNDERSTANDINGS AND AGREEMENTS

Article IV. It is understood that: 1) Jurisdiction of the Council will cover West Bank and Gaza Strip territory, except for issues that will be negotiated in the permanent status negotiations: Jerusalem, settlements, military locations, and Israelis. 2) The Council's jurisdiction will apply with regard to the agreed powers, responsibilities, spheres and authorities transferred to it.

Article VI (2). It is agreed that the transfer of authority will be as follows: (1) The Palestinian side will inform the Israeli side of the names of the authorised Palestinians who will assume the powers, authorities and responsibilities that will be transferred to the Palestinians according to the Declaration of Principles in the following fields: education and culture, health, social welfare, direct taxation, tourism and any other authorities agreed upon. (2) It is understood that the rights and obligations of these offices will not be affected. (3) Each of the spheres described above will continue to enjoy existing budgetary allocations in accordance with arrangements to be mutually agreed upon. These arrangements also will provide for the necessary adjustments required in order to take into account the taxes collected by the direct taxation offices. (4) Upon the execution of the Declaration of Principles, the Israeli and Palestinian delegations will immediately commence negotiations on a detailed plan for the transfer of authority on the above offices in accordance with the above understandings.

Article VII (2). The Interim Agreement will also include arrangements for coordination and cooperation.

Article VII (5). The withdrawal of the military government will not prevent Israel from exercising the powers and responsibilities not transferred to the Council.

Article VIII. It is understood that the Interim Agreement will include arrangements for cooperation and coordination between the two parties in this regard. It is also agreed that the transfer of powers and responsibilities to the Palestinian police will be accomplished in a phased manner, as agreed in the Interim Agreement.

Article X. It is agreed that, upon the entry into force of the Declaration of Principles, the Israeli and Palestinian delegations will exchange the names of the individuals designated by them as members of the Joint Israeli–Palestinian liaison committee. It is further agreed that each side will have an equal number of members in the Joint Committee. The Joint Committee will reach decisions by agreement. The Joint Committee may add other technicians and experts, as necessary. The Joint Committee will decide on the frequency and place or places of its meetings.

ANNEXE II. It is understood that, subsequent to the Israeli withdrawal, Israel will continue to be responsible for external security, and for internal security and public order of settlements and Israelis. Israeli military forces and civilians may continue to use roads freely within the Gaza Strip and the Jericho area.

# Index